AFRICA AND THE ICC

Africa and the ICC: Perceptions of Justice comprises contributions from prominent scholars of different disciplines including international law, political science, cultural anthropology, African history and media studies. This unique collection provides the reader with detailed insights into the interaction between the African Union and the International Criminal Court (ICC), but also looks further at the impact of the ICC at a societal level in African states and examines other justice mechanisms on local and regional levels. This investigation of the ICC's complicated relationship with Africa allows the reader to see that perceptions of justice are multilayered.

Kamari M. Clarke is Professor of Global and International Studies at Carleton University. Her research explores issues related to legal institutions, human rights and international law and the interface between culture, power and globalisation. Her recent publications include *International Criminal Court and the Challenge of Legal Pluralism in Sub-Saharan Africa* (Cambridge University Press, 2009) and *Mirrors of Justice: Law and Power in the Cold-War Era* (with Mark Goodale, Cambridge University Press, 2010).

Abel S. Knottnerus is currently a PhD researcher in International Law and International Relations at the University of Groningen. His research focuses on the law and politics of international courts and explores the interplay between perceptions, power and justice.

Eefje de Volder is currently a PhD researcher in International Law at Tilburg University. Her research focuses on the regionalisation of collective security, with a particular focus on the collective security of the African Union. In addition, she has researched the interconnection between conflict, migration and human trafficking.

Africa and the ICC

PERCEPTIONS OF JUSTICE

Edited by

**KAMARI M. CLARKE, ABEL S. KNOTTNERUS
AND EEFJE DE VOLDER**

CAMBRIDGE
UNIVERSITY PRESS

CAMBRIDGE
UNIVERSITY PRESS

University Printing House, Cambridge CB2 8BS, United Kingdom

One Liberty Plaza, 20th Floor, New York, NY 10006, USA

477 Williamstown Road, Port Melbourne, VIC 3207, Australia

4843/24, 2nd Floor, Ansari Road, Daryaganj, Delhi - 110002, India

79 Anson Road, #06-04/06, Singapore 079906

Cambridge University Press is part of the University of Cambridge.

It furthers the University's mission by disseminating knowledge in the pursuit of education, learning and research at the highest international levels of excellence.

www.cambridge.org
Information on this title: www.cambridge.org/9781316602119

First published 2016
First paperback edition 2017

A catalogue record for this publication is available from the British Library

Library of Congress Cataloging in Publication data
Clarke, Kamari M., 1966– editor. | Knottnerus, Abel S., editor. | Volder, Eefje de, editor.
Africa and the ICC : Perceptions of Justice / Kamari M. Clarke, Abel S. Knottnerus and Eefje de Volder (eds.).
New York, NY : Cambridge University Press, 2016. | Includes bibliographical references and index.
LCCN 2016029156 | ISBN 9781107147652 (alk. paper)
LCSH: International Criminal Court. | International criminal courts – Africa. | International crimes – Africa. | Criminal justice, Administration of – Africa. | Criminal justice, Administration of – International cooperation.
LCC KZ7312 .A347 2016 | DDC 345.01096–dc23
LC record available at https://lccn.loc.gov/2016029156

ISBN 978-1-107-14765-2 Hardback
ISBN 978-1-316-60211-9 Paperback

Contents

Notes on Contributors

Kamari M. Clarke is Professor of Global and International Studies at Carleton University. Her research explores issues related to legal institutions, human rights and international law and the interface between culture, power and globalisation. She has held numerous prestigious fellowships, grants and awards, the most recent being a large three-year National Science Foundation research grant on the relationship between the ICC and Africa. Her publications in this area include *International Criminal Court and the Challenge of Legal Pluralism in Sub-Saharan Africa* (Cambridge University Press, 2009) and *Mirrors of Justice: Law and Power in the Post-Cold War Era* (with Mark Goodale, Cambridge University Press, 2010).

Stephen Smith Cody is Director of the Atrocity Response Program at the Human Rights Center at the University of California, Berkeley School of Law. He holds a PhD in sociology from the University of California, Berkeley, a JD from Berkeley Law School and an MPhil in social anthropology from Cambridge University. A former Fulbright Fellow and Truman Scholar, he has contributed to reports at Human Rights Watch and co-authored reports and articles on various topics within international criminal law. His current research focuses on victims' participation in proceedings at the International Criminal Court. He is an active member of the California Bar.

Solomon A. Dersso serves as Commissioner at the African Commission on Human and Peoples' Rights. Adjunct Professor of Law at the College of Law and Governance at Addis Ababa University and an analyst of African affairs, among other roles, he initiated and published a new yearly publication, the *Annual Review of the AU Peace and Security Council*, for which he received the ISS's innovation award in 2014. His recent publications have covered issues such as the responsibility to protect and Africa's relationship with the International Criminal Court.

Kristin C. Doughty is Assistant Professor of Anthropology at the University of Rochester, New York. She has been conducting research on the political, legal and cultural dynamics of reconciliation in Rwanda since 2002, including undertaking twenty months of ethnographic fieldwork in Rwanda conducted in Kinyarwanda, French and English. She is currently finishing a book manuscript entitled *Remediation of Rwanda: Harmony and Punishment in Grassroots Legal Forums*, which examines the contradictory dynamics in how the Rwandan government embedded reconciliation efforts in grassroots legal forums. She has published her research for academic and practitioner audiences, and has presented this work at conferences in the United States, Canada, Rwanda and Israel.

Sammy G. Gachigua is a Kenyan researcher working towards a PhD in applied linguistics at Lancaster University, UK. His thesis focuses on the tensions between power-elite and public interests in Kenyan parliamentary debates using a discourse-historical approach. His research interests include: critical discourse analysis; argumentation theory; parliamentary, media and political discourses; cartoon research; and power and ideology.

Sara Kendall is Lecturer in International Law at the University of Kent, UK. She received her doctorate from the University of California at Berkeley, where she conducted research on the Special Court for Sierra Leone, followed by a four-year project at Leiden University investigating the socio-political effects of International Criminal Court interventions in African states. She has previously taught international law and international relations at Leiden University and at the University of Amsterdam.

Abel S. Knottnerus is a Junior Scholar in International Law, History and International Relations. His research focuses on the law and politics of international courts and explores the interplay between perceptions, power and justice. He holds a Master of Law in international and European law, as well as a Research Master in modern history and international relations from the University of Groningen, the Netherlands. Knottnerus is currently a PhD researcher at the University of Groningen.

Alexa Koenig, JD, PhD, is Executive Director of the Human Rights Center and a Lecturer in Residence at the University of California, Berkeley School of Law. Her most recent publications include *Hiding in Plain Sight: The Pursuit of War Criminals from Nuremberg to the War on Terror* (2016; co-authored with Eric Stover and Victor Peskin) and *Extreme Punishment* (2015; co-edited with Keramet Reiter). Koenig currently serves as a member of the Technology

Advisory Board of the Office of the Prosecutor at the International Criminal Court.

Patryk I. Labuda is a PhD Candidate at the Graduate Institute of International and Development Studies and a Teaching Assistant at the Geneva Academy of International Humanitarian Law and Human Rights. He previously worked in Sudan and South Sudan as a Research Fellow for the Max Planck Institute for International Law and in the Democratic Republic of Congo as a Civilian Justice Expert for the European Union Police Mission. He holds an LLM from Columbia Law School, a Certificate of Transnational Law from the University of Geneva and degrees in law (Magister iuris) and history (BA) from Adam Mickiewicz University, Poland.

Shamiso Mbizvo is Associate International Cooperation Adviser in the Jurisdiction, Complementarity and Cooperation Division in the Office of the Prosecutor (OTP) of the International Criminal Court. She provides legal and policy advice on international cooperation issues arising in the context of the OTP's engagement in Kenya. Mbizvo holds a JD from New York University School of Law, where she was a Filomen D'Agostino Scholar for Women's and Children's Rights. She received a Master of Science degree in forced migration (development studies) from Oxford University, where she was a Shell Centenary Scholar in 2003. She graduated magna cum laude in international relations from Harvard University in 2002.

Makau W. Mutua is SUNY Distinguished Professor and the Floyd H. & Hilda L. Hurst Scholar at SUNY Buffalo Law School, The State University of New York. He is the former Dean at SUNY Buffalo Law School and the author of *Human Rights Standards: Hegemony, Law, and Politics* (2016); *Kenya's Quest for Democracy: Taming Leviathan* (2008); *Human Rights NGOs in East Africa: Political and Normative Tensions* (2008); and *Human Rights: A Political and Cultural Critique* (2002).

Lee J. M. Seymour is Assistant Professor of Political Science at the University of Amsterdam. He studied political science at Northwestern University, Sciences Po Paris, Dalhousie University and the University of British Columbia. His current research on factionalism, alignment and fragmentation in civil wars is supported by a VENI grant from the Dutch Organisation for Scientific Research (NWO). His work has appeared in the *Journal of Conflict Resolution*, *Perspectives on Politics* and the *European Journal of International Relations*. His interests include the role of truth and deception in international diplomacy, the politics of international justice and civil wars.

Paul D. Schmitt is an Attorney with DLA Piper LLP (US). His practice focuses on appellate and international litigation, including foreign sovereign immunity, sovereign debt, anti-corruption issues and human rights. Dr Schmitt received his PhD in history from the University of Maryland and his JD from Georgetown University Law Center. His doctoral dissertation focused on France's diplomatic relationship with its former colonies after World War II. Dr Schmitt previously served as a legal intern with the ICTY and has taught courses at the university level on human rights, war crimes and genocide, colonialism and European history.

Clare da Silva is a Canadian lawyer and legal consultant for the United Nations and others on addressing firearms trafficking and armed violence reduction. She was the legal advisor for Amnesty International (AI) on their Arms Control, Security Trade and Human Rights programme and represented the interests of AI in lobbying states during the drafting process of the Arms Trade Treaty. In the past she was a Research Fellow at the Lauterpacht Centre for International Law at Cambridge University and acted as defence counsel at the Special Court for Sierra Leone.

Eric Stover is faculty director of the Human Rights Center and Adjunct Professor of Law and Public Health at the University of California, Berkeley School of Law. His most recent books include *The Graves: Srebrenica and Vukovar* (1998); *My Neighbor, My Enemy: Justice and Community in the Aftermath of Mass Atrocity* (2004; co-edited with Harvey Weinstein); *The Guantánamo Effect: Exposing the Consequences of U.S. Detention and Interrogation Practices* (2009, with Laurel E. Fletcher); and *The Witnesses: War Crimes and the Promise of Justice in The Hague* (2005).

Eefje de Volder is a Junior Scholar in International Law and Cultural Anthropology. She holds a Master of Science in cultural anthropology from Radboud University Nijmegen, the Netherlands, a Master of Law in international and European law from Tilburg University, the Netherlands, and a Research Master in Law from Tilburg University/University of Leuven, Belgium. Her research focuses on the regionalisation of collective security, with a particular focus on the collective security system of the African Union. Her research interests also include the interconnection between conflict, migration and human trafficking. De Volder is currently a PhD Researcher and Lecturer at the University of Tilburg and works simultaneously at the Coordination Centre on Human Trafficking.

Karin Willemse is Assistant Professor at the Erasmus School of History, Culture, and Communication, Erasmus University Rotterdam. She holds a PhD in anthropology from Leiden University (2001), and was Chair of the Netherlands Association of Feminist Anthropologist (LOVA) and a member of the Academic Advisory Board of the Islam Research Project (Ministry of Foreign Affairs and Leiden University). She has worked with scholars from South Africa, Senegal and Sudan, focusing on issues of gender, religion, violence, urban youth and migration. As a Fellow of the Royal Anthropological Institute, she currently conducts research in Nubia, Sudan, in cooperation with the British Museum.

Thomas P. Wolf is currently a Research Consultant/Analyst at Ipsos Public Affairs, Kenya. Dr Wolf first came to Kenya as a US Peace Corps secondary school teacher in 1967. He holds an MA in African studies (Ohio University) and a DPhil in comparative politics (University of Sussex). Previously he taught at the University of Nairobi, and served as Democracy/Governance Advisor for USAID/Kenya. The subject matter of his published works includes the political history of the Kenyan Coast, Kenya's constitution, East African terrorism, several Afrobarometer Working Papers, the immunity of retired President Moi and the accuracy and political impact of political opinion/voter-intention polls in Kenya.

Acknowledgements

This volume comprises a selection of essays that were presented in May 2014 during the multidisciplinary conference entitled 'Africans and Hague Justice: Realities and Perceptions of the International Criminal Court in Africa', and further includes a handful of specially commissioned chapters. The themes and issues discussed during the conference that was hosted by The Hague University of Applied Sciences has been a tremendous source of inspiration in compiling this volume. The excellent contributions and challenging questions that were raised during the conference set the ground-work for a matrix of complex and invigorating debates concerning the relevance of international law today and the roles that justice projects play around the world – and in particular in Africa.

We are grateful to The Hague Municipality, the Netherlands Association of African Studies, The Hague University of Applied Sciences, the School of Human Rights Research, the African Studies Centre and the Democracy and Media Foundation for making this conference possible. We thank the conference organising committee (Froukje Krijtenburg, Ingrid Roestenburg, Jos Walenkamp, Abel S. Knottnerus and Eefje de Volder), the conference scientific committee (Felix Ameka, Margot Leegwater and Tom Zwart) and all those who helped in making the conference a success, and in particular Mirjam Schoenmaeckers-Damen, Colette van Heck and Monique van Casteren. We would also like to express our gratitude to Voices of Africa Media Foundation and Creative Court for organising wonderful side events.

We further thank Carleton University for its institutional support and Godfrey Mwampembwa (Gado), Victor Ndula, Celestine Wamiru (Celeste) and James Kamawira (Kham) for the rights to reproduce their cartoons in this volume. We express our appreciation to our editors and to the manuscript staff for the teamwork and commitment needed to prepare the volume for publication.

Finally, we would like to give a word of thanks to our friends and colleagues who supported this project from the start to its completion and without whom the road would have been a lot more difficult to traverse, and to our families and loved ones for their ongoing support during the life of this project.

1

Africa and the ICC: An Introduction

Kamari M. Clarke, Abel S. Knottnerus, and Eefje de Volder

The International Criminal Court (ICC) is going through turbulent times. After years of almost romantic enthusiasm for international criminal justice, states and commentators have started to question whether the international prosecution of a handful of high-level perpetrators is always the most suitable way to address mass atrocity crimes. Calls for alternate forms of justice that may be delivered by local and regional justice mechanisms, rather than an international court or tribunal, have become more vocal. To be sure, the ICC still enjoys the support of large parts of the international community, but it cannot be overlooked that the Court increasingly faces criticism, even from some of its strongest allies.

At this moment, one of the most serious challenges for the ICC is its embattled relationship with Africa. Since the announcement of the prosecution of the Sudanese president, Omar al-Bashir, in 2008, many African states have expressed their concerns about the Court's track record, while some have even threatened to withdraw from the Rome Statute altogether.[1] Although this opposition has not been univocal, and clearly does not reflect the views of all African states, let alone of all Africans, it has become common to speak of the ICC's 'Africa problem'.

For quite some time, it appeared that this problem was not seen as a priority by the Court and by the majority of its States Parties. Although the ICC suffered a backlash from al-Bashir's indictment, the Court's first Prosecutor, Luis Moreno-Ocampo, refuted the criticism of African states. Time and again he repeated that his duty was 'to apply the law without bowing to political considerations'.[2] For its part, the UN Security Council (Security Council) also proved unwilling to address the concerns of African states. Despite numerous requests from the African Union (AU), the Security Council refused to defer the prosecution of al-Bashir and later to suspend the prosecution of the Libyan leader, Muammar Gaddafi.[3]

In the last few years, the Court and its supporters have started to take the objections of African states more seriously. The Court's second Prosecutor, Fatou Bensouda, and a large group of States Parties have called for 'a dialogue' with the AU and with concerned African states.[4] Even though Bensouda has continued the rhetorical strategy of her predecessor and has repeatedly stressed that she cannot take political considerations into account, she has acknowledged the concerns of African states and has used some of her diplomatic leverage to ease the ongoing tensions.[5]

In this respect, the election of ICC indictees Uhuru Kenyatta and William Ruto as president and deputy president of Kenya in March 2013 has been a real game changer. In the autumn of 2013, the scheduled start of their trials generated such a political turmoil that the Court and its States Parties had no choice but to respond. While a Security Council deferral was narrowly averted – with seven votes in favour and eight abstentions – the Assembly of States Parties (ASP) recognized the urgent need to address the situation. Amidst threats of an African mass withdrawal, the ASP's annual meeting in November 2013 witnessed the very first inter-state debate on the Court's fractious relationship with Africa, and more specifically on 'the indictment of sitting Heads of State and Government and its consequences on peace and stability and reconciliation'.[6] Eventually, the States Parties 'gave in' to one of the AU's demands by amending the Court's rules on presence at trial for those accused who fulfil extraordinary public duties at the highest national level. These amendments were effectively intended to reduce the amount of time that Kenyatta and Ruto would have to spend in The Hague.[7]

This 'sign of goodwill' did not lead, however, to a rapid improvement of the ICC's relationship with Africa. A few weeks after the ASP, the AU Assembly of Heads of State and Government (AU Assembly) welcomed the new rules on presence at trial, but also expressed its 'deep disappointment' that the Security Council had not acted on its deferral request(s) and stressed that the Council should do more 'to avoid the sense of lack of consideration of a whole continent'.[8] To prevent future deferral requests from being ignored and to ensure that no other sitting African Head of State would be indicted by the Court, the AU Assembly called for several amendments to the Rome Statute. Most importantly, the gathered African states demanded that the UN General Assembly would be authorized to defer the Court's proceedings and that Heads of State would become immune from prosecution by the Court during their time in office.

Furthermore, the African leaders decided to expedite the process of establishing the African Court of Justice and Human and Peoples' Rights (African Court).[9] This involved giving the African Court jurisdiction over a range of crimes, including the four international crimes that form the subject matter jurisdiction of the ICC: crimes against humanity, war crimes, the crime of genocide, and the crime of aggression. The result is the early formation of an 'African Criminal Court', which in the future may come to function as a regional alternative to the ICC. The Amendment Protocol of this new Court, which was adopted by the AU Assembly in June 2014, provides immunities for incumbent heads of state and remains silent on the African Court's complementarity with the ICC.[10]

In December 2014, the Prosecutor's decision to withdraw the charges against Kenyatta marked another dramatic moment in the Court's relationship with Africa. In explaining her decision, Prosecutor Bensouda accused the government of Kenya of failing to provide the Office of the Prosecutor (OTP) with 'important records', and claimed that 'hurdles' caused by Kenya's lack of cooperation had 'a severe adverse impact' on the case.[11] With the collapse of Kenyatta's trial, one of the main triggers behind the recent intensification of the AU's campaign against the ICC disappeared, but it did not take all the concerns of African states away. While the assembled African leaders welcomed the withdrawal of charges in January 2015, they also expressed their regret over 'the period it took the Office of the Prosecutor to arrive at [this] decision', and noted with concern that the case against Deputy Ruto still continues.[12]

In addition to the Kenyan cases, the indictment of the Sudanese president al-Bashir also remains an important source of tension between Africa and the ICC. While it seems that the AU has given up on its initial deferral request for al-Bashir, the AU continues to argue that the Sudanese president enjoys immunity from arrest. Despite decisions of the Court's Pre-Trial Chamber countering this claim, al-Bashir has travelled to several African States Parties, including Nigeria, the Democratic Republic of the Congo (DRC), and, most recently, South Africa.[13] All this illustrates that, for the time being, the ICC's 'Africa problem' is far from over.

A Debate on Africa and the ICC

How have scholars approached the continuing tensions between Africa and the ICC? With the risk of overgeneralizing, we find that until now the debate has followed two trajectories. First, scholars have analysed the legal arguments that have been raised and the amendments that have been suggested by the AU.[14] Based on their assessments of these arguments and amendments, this first group of scholars has formulated a range of recommendations on how 'to solve' the tensions.[15] Their approach may be described as *legalist* or *pragmatic*.

These scholars have taken the 'law' and the Court as frames of reference and have thought alongside it – that is, together with the Prosecutor, the ASP, and the Security Council – to seek solutions within the legal order that the Rome Statute constitutes.[16]

A second tenor in the existing literature has been to assess the appropriateness of the concerns that African states have voiced about the ICC. Much has been said and written about whether Africa's concerns are simply false rhetoric from self-interested leaders.[17] This question has sparked a debate on the structural selectivity of international criminal justice or, to phrase it more sharply, the alleged neo-colonial and racial politics behind the Court's investigations and prosecutions in Africa.[18] The approach underlying the relevant contributions has been to make a *normative* assessment of the concerns and criticisms of African states. Put differently, are African leaders 'right' to criticize the Court?

This volume also takes the ongoing tensions between Africa and the ICC as its starting point, but focuses on different sets of questions. Instead of pragmatic solutions or normative assessments, our aims are to explore and understand the different perceptions of the ICC in Africa. How has the ICC manifested itself in Africa and how do African audiences perceive the Court? We approach these and related questions from different angles, looking at the interactions between African states and the ICC, but also *beyond African states*, at the 'societal impact' of the ICC in different African communities, and *beyond the ICC*, at other local and regional justice mechanisms in Africa.

First, we seek to deconstruct the origins of the Court's fractious relationship with Africa. Is there something inherent to the ICC as a legal system or to the contemporary political and socio-economic state of Africa that may enhance our understanding of the current tensions? Second, we study the interactions between African states and the ICC to make sense of what has motivated African states to criticize but at times also to support the Court. In this context, we also ask how the ICC has reacted to the concerns of African states. Third, we look beyond African states at the engagements between the ICC and different audiences and individuals in Africa, including those who are directly concerned with the Court as 'victims' or witnesses. How do they perceive the ICC and how are attitudes toward its investigations and prosecutions formed? How do local media portray the ICC, how has the Court's involvement affected domestic politics, and in what ways, if at all, have its proceedings helped to shape the public narratives of local and regional conflicts? Finally, we look beyond the ICC at local and regional justice mechanisms that have been developed before, alongside, or as an alternative to the Court in Africa.

How have different African communities dealt with mass atrocity crimes since the end of the Cold War? What types of judicial and non-judicial mechanisms can be identified and how do they relate to the ICC?

These and other relevant questions about the engagement of the ICC with Africa are viewed in this volume through different disciplinary lenses. The background of the various contributors includes international law, anthropology, sociology, African history, political science, critical theory, and media studies. Moreover, some of the authors have been directly involved with the work of the ICC and with other local and regional justice mechanisms that are discussed in this volume. Their contributions add a helpful practitioner's view to the mix of interdisciplinary perspectives on the questions that this volume seeks to answer.

Of course, the questions and perspectives that we raise can and should not always be separated from the normative, legalist, and pragmatic approaches that have until now dominated the debate on Africa and the ICC. As a matter of fact, several chapters in this volume do make normative claims, analyse relevant legal provisions, and discuss practical solutions. Still, the point of departure for this volume as a whole is not to assess the concerns of African states or to solve the Africa problem of the ICC, nor is it to presume that judicial mechanisms are the only tools that are available to post-conflict states. Instead, the ultimate aim of this volume is to expose the complexity of the Court's troubled relationship with Africa and to ponder the plethora of judicial and non-judicial developments underway in Africa.

B Perceptions of the ICC in Africa

The remainder of this introductory chapter sets the stage for these explorations, and is divided into four parts. We begin with a reflection on how scholars can study the perceptions of international courts among different audiences. In this first part we also explain how these perceptions relate to the 'legitimacy' of international courts. It is often said that the criticism from African states threatens to undermine the ICC's legitimacy. Yet, as we shall see, this claim is subject to competing interpretations, depending on whose perceptions are being addressed and in what manner this is done.

In the second part, we introduce three different phases in the Court's relationship with Africa. Starting with the negotiations on the Rome Statute, we highlight some of the political structures and uneven power relations that are embedded in the ICC's legal system and which may help to explain shifts in Africa's engagement with the Court. Specifically, in its early years, there appears to have been a form of strategic cooperation between individual

African states and the ICC. However, developments after 2008, starting in particular with the indictment of al-Bashir, have prompted an ongoing phase of active opposition against the Court and, as of late, a reorientation towards other justice mechanisms, such as the early development of an African Criminal Court.

In the third part, we briefly consider some of the different local and regional justice mechanisms that were developed long before, but in some cases also as an alternative to, the ICC in Africa. While some of the responses to mass atrocity crimes in Africa and corresponding justice mechanisms have retributive components that are similar to international criminal prosecutions, others take a more restorative and relational approach. By introducing these different justice mechanisms in Africa, this part foreshadows the chapters in this volume that look beyond 'Hague Justice'.

In the final part of this introductory chapter, we provide an overview of the themes, organization, and contents of this volume.

I PERCEPTIONS OF INTERNATIONAL COURTS AND TRIBUNALS

The political battles that have defined the Court's relationship with Africa over the last few years sometimes create the image of a univocal African continent with a uniform position on the ICC. This image is wrong, or at least overly simplified. Not all African states have, for example, criticized the prosecution of al-Bashir, and not all Kenyans have opposed the trials of Kenyatta and Ruto.[19] It should be stressed that the ICC has many different audiences throughout Africa, ranging from government officials, national courts, local communities, sub-regional organizations, and civil society groups to witnesses, victims, and legal experts.[20] Among these different audiences, understandings and ideas about the Court and its practices are not uniform. Whereas some may have never heard of The Hague, even in regions that are under investigation by the Court, others will read about the latest developments at the ICC in their daily newspapers. This highlights the reality that perceptions of the Court among its different African audiences are *multilayered*.

A Why Do Perceptions Matter?

For the ICC and for international courts and tribunals more generally, the perceptions of their different audiences tell us something about the effectiveness and appropriateness of the norms that they represent and the decisions that they take. Perceptions can, in this sense, spark social behaviour, but can also function as a normative yardstick for scholars.[21]

First of all, perceptions can be an internal motivation for social actors to behave in a certain way. A positive perception of an institution like an international court can be an incentive to comply with the rules and decisions of that court, whereas a negative perception can lead to (active) opposition. In political science, but also in social psychology, anthropology, and sociology, scholars often refer in this regard to sociological, socio-cultural, or perceived legitimacy, by which they mean the perceptions or subjective beliefs of social actors that a norm or institution is 'appropriate, proper and just'.[22] These perceptions or beliefs can be studied among different audiences to unravel how they influence the thoughts, feelings, and behaviour of these audiences, and ultimately to explain the (in)effectiveness of an international court or tribunal.[23] For the ICC, effectiveness may be defined as its ability 'to engender respect for its rulings and for the rules it enforces'.[24] In this sense, studying the 'sociological legitimacy' of the ICC means deconstructing how the perceptions of different audiences about the ICC may affect their behaviour towards the Court and how this in turn influences the Court's ability to achieve the objectives of the Rome Statute.[25]

Second, the perceptions of audiences can also be a normative yardstick for scholars to assess the appropriateness of the norms and decisions of an international court or tribunal like the ICC. To give an example, if victims do not perceive prosecutions as just, then this could be a reason for scholars to question whether these prosecutions are really offering what is intended to be delivered. In other words, 'justice misperceived' may be equated with 'justice denied'. Scholars in political science, but especially in political philosophy and international legal theory, have developed different and often competing standards for the normative or moral legitimacy of international law, global governance, and institutions, including international courts and tribunals.[26] In addition to criteria like procedural correctness and fairness, it is often stressed that the relevant audiences of an international court should perceive its workings as legitimate, whatever that may require.[27] Studying the perceptions of the ICC, as this volume aims to do, thus also opens up an argumentative space in which the moral value of the Court can be defended or challenged. In other words, studies on the sociological legitimacy of the ICC can be part of the debate on its normative legitimacy as well.[28]

B *Whose Perceptions Matter and How Can These Perceptions Be Studied?*

When analysing the perceptions of international courts and tribunals, it is important to distinguish between different levels at which the effectiveness and appropriateness of their norms and decisions can be examined. Whose perceptions are we talking about and how can they be studied? In this volume, we broadly distinguish between three different 'levels' of perceptions: (1) state actors, (2) particular communities, and (3) individuals who have been directly affected by violence, such as victims and witnesses. Whereas the first level is the main field for scholars in International Law and International Relations (IL/IR), the second and third levels call for, among others, sociological, anthropological, historical, and social psychological approaches.

These three levels and associated approaches are, in many ways, interconnected. For instance, what state actors have to say about an international court or tribunal will likely affect the perceptions of domestic audiences about its proceedings, and *vice versa*. Yet, as scholars we cannot problematize everything at once. The essays in this volume share an interest in the perceptions of the ICC in Africa, but they focus on different audiences. Lee Seymour's chapter looks, for example, at the behaviour of African states and government officials (level 1); Sammy Gachigua's chapter analyses how the ICC is portrayed for and by domestic audiences in Kenya through newspaper cartoons (level 2); and Chapter 12, written by Stephen Smith Cody, Alexa Koenig, and Eric Stover, studies how ICC witnesses have perceived and experienced their participation in the Court's proceedings (level 3).

Furthermore, even when studying the same audience, one can take different paths in analysing their perceptions. The contributions in this volume work with different theoretical assumptions and methodologies, which are developed in response to dominant debates within their respective disciplinary field(s). For the purpose of this introduction, some general patterns in the theoretical assumptions and methodologies that are 'applied' throughout this volume may be identified.

First of all, on the level of state actors, the relevant contributions explore the interactions between African states and the ICC, and examine how the Court and its States Parties have responded to the concerns and accusations that African states have voiced, especially through the AU. An important theoretical question in this respect is what shapes the behaviour of states towards international courts? To what extent do perceptions and legitimacy play a role in states' decisions to support or criticize the ICC?

As IL/IR scholarship remains strongly divided between different 'isms',[29] there are many competing theories about the relations between states and international courts and tribunals.[30] Some of the relevant approaches can generally be described as 'rationalist', in the sense that they assume that states are strategic unitary actors who behave instrumentally in creating and interacting with international judicial bodies. To the extent that perceptions play a role in these approaches, it is mainly as perceptions of utility. A second set of approaches may be labelled 'constructivist', in the sense that they focus on the role that norms, discourse, and culture play in constituting the interests of states and in shaping their behaviour towards international courts and tribunals. In constructivist models, perceptions of appropriateness are seen as constitutive of state interests and are therefore an important factor in explaining the behaviour of state actors. While discussions on the sociological or socio-cultural legitimacy of international courts are 'constructivist' at heart, since they point to perceptions of appropriateness, the various chapters that examine the interactions between African states and the ICC do not apply strictly 'constructivist' or 'rationalist' assumptions and methodologies. Instead, they combine both approaches in order to explore instrumental considerations behind the behaviour of African states as well as the perceptions of African states about the appropriateness of the ICC's norms and decisions.[31]

Second, on the level of particular communities, this volume aims to study the Court's 'societal impact' in Africa. How have the Court's proceedings been perceived within different communities? How have domestic media portrayed the ICC? How has the Court's involvement affected domestic politics and national legislation? And how, if at all, have its investigations and prosecutions helped to shape the public perceptions and narratives of local and regional conflicts?

Throughout this volume, the chapters apply various methods for answering these and related questions about the perceptions of the ICC in different African communities. One method that is used is population-based surveying; perceptions can be 'measured' and analysed with the help of public polls, focus groups, and semi-structured interviews.[32] A second method is to trace the impact of the Court's involvement in domestic politics and national legislation by studying policy documents, public statements and speeches, news reports, and secondary literature, as well as through conducting one-on-one interviews with involved officials. These sources can be collected and interpreted to 'reconstruct' and explain how the Court's investigations and prosecutions have influenced political and legislative developments at the national or local level. A third method is to study how domestic media have portrayed the ICC, which likely has significant effects on public perceptions of the Court as well. There are various ways to go about this, including employing ethnography and discourse reconstruction by analysing TV or written news reports, but also by interpreting artistic objects like editorial cartoons that have appeared in national or local newspapers. In composing this volume, we have sought to include contributions that apply different methods in order to show some of the ways in which scholars have studied the impact of the ICC in particular African communities.

Finally, at the level of individuals who have been directly affected by violence, we are interested in how they perceive either the ICC's proceedings or other methods for achieving justice and how these perceptions might shape affective responses. This includes especially the witnesses and 'victims' that have participated in the Court's proceedings, but we also consider the experiences of 'victims' with different local and regional justice mechanisms, such as the *Gacaca* courts in Rwanda. The main methods for studying the perceptions of witnesses and 'victims' are ethnographic, involving participant observation, semi-structured interviews, and focus groups.

In short, the collected contributions analyse the perceptions of different audiences in Africa and apply a variety of methods for studying these perceptions. By investigating how state actors, particular communities, and individuals that are directly affected by violence perceive the ICC, we highlight that the perceptions of the Court in Africa are multilayered. Ultimately, this demonstrates that the ICC's fractious relationship with Africa is much more complex than the problematic – but powerful – image of a unified African continent with a common position on the ICC.

II DIFFERENT PHASES IN THE ICC'S RELATIONSHIP WITH AFRICA

In pondering the different perceptions of the ICC in Africa, it is important to recognize that the Court's relationship with the continent has changed significantly over time. One might characterize the shift from Africa's initial support for the ICC to the current campaign of African states against Hague Justice as a result of how the political structures and uneven power relations that are embedded in the ICC's legal framework have played out since the adoption of the Rome Statute in 1998. Inequalities are reflected in the rules and decisions of the ICC in various ways, including the nature of the crimes that are part of the jurisdiction of the Court, the nature of the mechanisms that are available to trigger the Court's jurisdiction, and its strong focus on individual culpability for crimes that are fundamentally collective.

Remarkably, these and other socio-political factors that may influence perceptions of the ICC that are often overlooked in legal analysis. The reason for this is that legal questions easily lead scholars to disregard the socio-political foundations of 'the law' itself. As a result, in studying the Court's rules and decisions, many legal scholars work on the implicit assumption that the negotiations on the Rome Statute were somehow part of a democratically driven process of consensus decision-making and that with the adoption of the Rome Statute all elements of politics were erased. A notable example of this way of thinking is the frequent heralding of the Rome Statute for revolutionizing the ways that people understand states' responsibilities to 'humanity' (para. 2 of the Preamble).

To be sure, the Statute has created a new relationship between international and national forms of justice by, on the one hand, emphasizing that the ICC 'shall be complementary to national criminal jurisdictions' (para. 10 of the Preamble and Article 1) and, on the other hand, identifying the international, rather than the national, as the principal unit for acting out of humanitarian concern (para. 4 of the Preamble and Article 1). As envisioned in the Statute, 'complementary' is thus meant both as a nod to the primacy of the nation-state and to ensure that at least certain standards of international adjudication are used as an ultimate measure of justice. In practice, however, the complementarity regime of the Court also allows for a process of negotiation in which states are able or at least try to protect their interests. It is through this process of negotiation that the complementarity regime has set in place structures of inequality, because some states are simply better equipped to protect their interests in these negotiations than others.

With respect to Africa, one of the main challenges is that many African states have remained fragile since independence, with some even weakening under the leadership of African strongmen over the past fifty years. The reduction of state-supported social services combined with a rise in paramilitary formations has frequently led to violent struggles over governance. Many African states have suffered serious consequences from civil and inter-state warfare – wars that are often also the product of various local and international entities vying for economic possibilities within particular competitive domains, along with relentless population growth and other factors.

Of course, it cannot be overlooked that many African states and NGOs actively participated in the development of the Rome Statute. However, cloaked in the universalist language of the ICC, relations of dominance have privileged particular norms of 'juridical justice' over others. The reality is that during the negotiations on the Rome Statute, politically 'weak' states were rarely in positions to overpower 'stronger' ones. Moreover, as a matter of course, the relations between different types of states and international institutions derive, at least to a certain extent, from contests over the 'the power to decide'. This power encompasses the ability to claim universal jurisdiction and to form alliances with international institutions, but also the capacity to implement amnesty laws and to defer to some notions of state sovereignty.

The path to international criminal justice in Africa has, all in all, come to mask an unequal distribution of power through a language of jurisdiction and law. This is not because the ICC is 'targeting Africans'; it is because the contemporary violence in Africa is actually symptomatic of a global problem of inequality over resource distribution and quests to control government. Thus, participation in the Rome Statute has not necessarily involved equality or the absence of state interests. Contrary to what many scholars assume, there is unevenness in the political structures of the ICC that remains central to the rule of law movement that it stands to represent.

In thinking historically about the negotiations leading up to the Rome Conference and the early practice of the ICC, there are particular moments and tensions that highlight turning points in the relationship between the ICC and Africa. These shifts can be characterized by three different phases: (1) the first phase represents the creation of the ICC's political structures and points attention to the discussions over which crimes should fall within the Court's jurisdiction; (2) the second phase underlines the triggers for ICC jurisdiction and the practice of self-referrals which initially led to a form of strategic cooperation between African states and the ICC; (3) the third phase is the 'rediscovery' of the socio-political roots of the ICC's legal process by African states in the context of the indictment of al-Bashir in 2008 and more recently the cases against Kenyatta and Ruto. This phase is connected to the contemporary state of the Court's relationship with Africa, in which the continued questioning of Hague Justice has spurred calls for a turn to other local and regional justice mechanisms in Africa.

A Phase 1 – Creating the ICC's Political Structures: the Drafting of the Rome Statute (1980–2002)

There is no question, empirically, that African states were central participants in the formation of the ICC. Senegal was, for example, the first country to ratify the Statute, and South Africa implemented the terms of the treaty into its domestic legislation within the first five years of the Court's existence.[33] Despite the suggestion that participation and ratification imply enthusiasm for all aspects of the ICC system, it is also important to realize, however, that the making of the Rome Statute was a tumultuous process that involved negotiations, protests, pushbacks, and concessions.

An examination of this process begins with the recognition that the selection of the crimes that are now part of the Rome Statute is the result of political jockeying that took place over many years. As traced by Kamari M. Clarke, the original 1954 version of the 'Code of Offences against the Peace and Security of Mankind' was based on the laws and legal principles codified in the Geneva Conventions (1864–1949) and the Nuremburg War Crimes Trials (1945–1949).[34] Later versions of the draft continued to incorporate principles based on treaties, tribunal decisions, and customary law rather than to progressively develop new practices into the Statute. In 1981, the International Law Commission (ILC) continued its work on the draft Code at the request of the UN General Assembly.[35] By 1989, representatives from Trinidad and Tobago requested that the ILC resume the process of establishing an international criminal court to deal with the major drug-trafficking issues in the region.

Over the next decade, the process of drafting the Rome Statute passed through several stages of negotiation and refinement. The ILC used government reports in the drafting process to create the comprehensive Draft Statute for an International Criminal Court. In 1994, it presented a draft for the establishment of the ICC to the UN General Assembly, which convened the Preparatory Committee to advance the process to the next level.[36] The Preparatory Committee met six times over the course of two years (1996–1998), during which it gathered feedback from national delegates, government reports, NGOs, and intergovernmental organizations.

At an early stage in this drafting process (1991), the ILC adopted a Draft Code, which identified twelve crimes that could become part of the jurisdiction of the ICC.[37] Four years later, however, just before the Preparatory Committee was set up, the ILC's Special Rapporteur omitted six of these twelve crimes in a subsequent draft.[38] The omitted crimes included colonial domination and other forms of alien domination; apartheid; recruitment, use, financing, and training of mercenaries; wilful and severe damage to the environment; international terrorism; and illicit traffic in narcotic drugs. The Special Rapporteur gave several justifications for these omissions, with the most important being that if the court were ever to gain universal acceptance among nations, it would have to avoid crimes that were too controversial or too widespread.[39]

Once the revisions were completed, the Code was presented to a diplomatic conference, which eventually led to the adoption of the Rome Statute in 1998. After decades of debate, the crimes under the jurisdiction of the Rome Statute were ultimately reduced to four: genocide, war crimes, crimes against humanity, and the crime of aggression. It is this genealogy that has placed a particular category of crimes at the heart of the Rome Statute, and has led the ICC to focus on explicit forms and specific consequences of mass violence, rather than on its origins and underlying structures.

B Phase 2 – Jurisdictional Triggers: Self-Referrals and Strategic Cooperation (2003–2008)

After the ICC became operational in 2002, 'the politics of referrals' produced much of the Court's ongoing focus on Africa. Encouraged by the OTP, Uganda and the DRC were the first two states to refer a situation for investigation to the ICC in 2003 and 2004. On first sight, these so-called self-referrals seemed to demonstrate a strong commitment of these states to the pursuit of international criminal justice. Yet, as the investigations unfolded, it turned out that their cooperation with the Court also had a 'strategic' character.

The first investigation that the ICC opened was the result of political consultations, if not negotiations, between the OTP and high-level Ugandan officials. In fact, it was together with President Yoweri Museveni that the Prosecutor announced in 2003 that his office would launch an investigation into crimes committed in the conflict in northern Uganda between the Ugandan People's Defence Force and the Lord's Resistance Army of Joseph Kony. In front of international media, the Prosecutor promised to investigate both sides of the conflict, but as the investigation proceeded, it became increasingly clear that the OTP would only focus on the LRA and would hardly consider the role of the Ugandan government.

The OTP's second investigation, which was triggered by a referral of the government of the DRC in 2004, followed a similar trajectory. This referral resulted in the indictment and arrest of several high-ranking rebel leaders and politicians, including Thomas Lubanga, who became the first accused before the Court. However, the investigation never targeted anyone close to President Kabila, creating the perception that, like the referral of Uganda, the investigation into the DRC was based on an unspoken political deal that the OTP would not target the heart of the Congolese government.[40]

Ultimately, these first investigations and prosecutions triggered perceptions of one-sided prosecutions and raised questions about 'statist justice', which prioritizes states over non-state actors that cannot refer situations to the Court. Most importantly, it was asked whether a government that may itself be involved in international crimes should be the one to refer situations for investigation to the ICC. Over time, and in cases of post-election violence, the perceived problem also became one of 'victor's justice'. In this sense, victor's justice is the idea that the leader to win a given embattled election surrounded by violence is the one to refer its opponents to the ICC, as seen in the more recent case of Ivory Coast (2011).[41] As African states engaged in strategic cooperation with the ICC, it thus became evident that these referrals could undermine the Court's legitimacy. What is more, they produced a terrain of ICC selectivity, as the self-referrals of Uganda, the DRC, and later the Central African Republic (number I, 2007) led the Court to focus, almost exclusively, on African cases.

C Phase 3 – Rediscovering the Political structures of the ICC: The Cases against al-Bashir, Kenyatta, and Ruto (2008–Present)

The third and most recent phase that can be identified in the Court's relationship with Africa is characterized by active opposition of African states against the ICC, and in particular against the prosecution of African presidents.[42] This campaign, which has been led by the AU, has to be understood in relation to various juxtapositions – first of all, the reality that the Court and its supporters have repeatedly stated that they cannot take political considerations into account, and second that it has often been argued that the ICC's involvement with international crimes in Africa is what African states signed up for when ratifying the Rome Statute.

After the Prosecutor announced in July 2008 that he would seek to indict the Sudanese president, al-Bashir, many African leaders called upon the Security Council to defer his prosecution by claiming that this step undermined the promotion of peace and stability in Darfur. Although back in 2005 several African states had supported the decision of the Security Council to refer the situation in Darfur to the Court, they now portrayed the Prosecutor's decision to indict a sitting African Head of State as a very dangerous political step.

Regardless of whether their concerns were genuine, the heart of the problem was that the Rome Statute was conceptualized as a voluntarily accepted treaty to which Sudan was not a party. While one of the central principles of international law is that without their consent, treaties do not create rights or obligations for non-involved states (*pacta tertiis nec nocent nec prosunt*), non-state Parties may still have legal obligations in relation to the ICC when a situation is referred by the Security Council. To be sure, most African states have accepted this legal logic and the responsibilities therein. Yet, the manner in which the Security Council decided to exercise its powers, by deferring and referring some cases and not others, revived concerns of African states about the political selectivity that is embedded in the Rome Statute through the Council's powerful role.

In addition to the failed deferral requests for al-Bashir, the unsuccessful attempts to refer the situation in Syria to the ICC is a tragic case in point. Over recent years, Syria has been engulfed in a violent conflict, with over 6 million internally displaced and more than 2 million refugees, and a death toll surpassing well over 100,000. Both government forces and non-government armed groups have committed widespread attacks, including murder, rape, torture, and enforced disappearances.[43] In response, sixty-five states, of which several were African, co-sponsored a draft resolution in May 2014 asking the Security Council to refer the situation to the ICC. This proposal was vetoed, however, by China and Russia, revealing the strong influence of political interests in the dynamics between the Security Council and the ICC.

We find more examples of concerns that African states have voiced about the political structures of the Rome Statute and the ICC's alleged selectivity with the cases of Uhuru Kenyatta and William Ruto. During an extraordinary AU Summit in October 2013, the AU Assembly responded to the scheduled start of Kenyatta's trial with a decision that insisted on the relevance of official capacity in the context of international investigations and prosecutions. As their decision read, 'to safeguard the constitutional order, stability and integrity of Member States, no charges shall be commenced or continued before any International Court or Tribunal against any serving AU Head of State or Government or anybody acting or entitled to act in such capacity during their term of office'.[44]

This decision was followed by a second important event, the already-mentioned special segment during the annual meeting of the ASP in November 2013 on 'the indictment of sitting Heads of State and Government and its consequences on peace and stability and reconciliation'. This special segment was organized to discuss, amongst others, an amendment that has been introduced by the AU to reinstate immunities for sitting heads of state in the Rome Statute. While this proposal has so far failed to gain any meaningful support, the special segment of the ASP and the extraordinary meeting of the AU did lead to the adoption of special rules on presence at trial for senior officials, and six months later to the inclusion of an immunity provision for sitting heads of state in the AU's protocol for a Criminal Chamber of the African Court. This shows that the 'rediscovery' of the political structures of the ICC has encouraged African states to seek a revision of these structures and to consider possible alternatives outside the legal order that the Rome Statute constitutes.

D Contemporary Status – 2015/2016

What the different phases in the ICC's relationship with Africa highlight is an increased reluctance towards Hague Justice. To be sure, various African states continue to believe that the ICC can play an important role in Africa, as exemplified by the recent self-referrals of Mali (2013) and the Central African Republic (number II, 2014). Yet, the battles over the cases against al-Bashir, Kenyatta, and Ruto, and accusations of politicization and selectivity and the perceived unequal politics of the United Nations Security Council (UNSC) have moved many within the AU to turn against the ICC, which has recently sparked serious threats of an African mass withdrawal.

Beyond African states, the turmoil surrounding the ICC's involvement in Africa has also led African scholars, NGOs, and victims of mass atrocity crimes to doubt the Court's ability to satisfy their perceptions of justice. In response to the ICC's track-record in Africa, they have raised questions about whether violence should be managed by a court outside the African continent and whether judicial action always advances the overall process of post-conflict reconstruction. All this has spurred calls for alternative local and regional justice mechanisms that may better serve 'African' perceptions of justice. The questioning of the appropriateness of international criminal proceedings has thus unfolded a new terrain for interrogating what justice is and what mechanisms are best suited to its procurement in Africa and beyond.

III BEYOND THE ICC: LOCAL AND REGIONAL JUSTICE MECHANISMS IN AFRICA

Politicians, scholars, and practitioners have long been preoccupied with the question of how mass atrocity crimes should be dealt with in the process of post-conflict reconstruction.[45] What makes this question extremely complex is not only the devastating impact that mass violence has on the functioning of societies, but also that there are strongly competing perceptions of what 'justice' requires in this context. Moreover, persons who carry responsibility for mass atrocity crimes might still hold power in a post-conflict society.

In the aftermath of mass atrocities, criminal proceedings tend to focus on punishing those who have violated existing societal norms (retribution) and on preventing future violations (deterrence). However, from the perspective of restoring and reconciling societies, different approaches to justice might be preferred.[46] While the retributive element of criminal proceedings has a liberalist focus on establishing criminal responsibility for individuals, restorative approaches are based on relational perceptions of justice. At their core, restorative approaches are not so much concerned with 'responding to wrongs but rather with the harm and effects of wrongs on relationships at all levels'.[47]

Even though they do not necessarily contradict one another, retributive and restorative approaches to justice can be at odds with each other, especially when amnesties are included in the reconciliation process. In this sense, questions about how to balance retributive and restorative approaches to justice are closely linked to the (in)famous 'peace-versus-justice' debate.[48] In post-conflict situations where societal tensions are high and the judicial system may not function properly, the need for a prompt resolution of disputes is critical. As perceptions of impunity may be a catalyst for societies to return to conflict-based solutions, many have argued that (legal) accountability is of utmost importance.[49] Yet, in response, others have argued that it is not for nothing that immunity measures like amnesties have long fulfilled a key role in post-conflict reconstruction.[50]

Since the early 1990s, international criminal justice has gained a prominent place in thinking about post-conflict reconstruction. However, in recent years, many scholars have also become more critical about the role of criminal proceedings in moving conflict-torn societies forward.[51] Carsten Stahn has characterized this shift in thinking as a transformation from faith to fact.[52] International criminal justice is now more and more perceived as one specific measure among a range of judicial and non-judicial options, which all carry the potential to assist societies in coming to terms with past atrocities. In this regard, the focus has increasingly moved from top-down and one-size-fits-all models towards calls for a variety of mechanisms and tools.[53] This more plural thinking about post-conflict reconstruction acknowledges the limits of international criminal justice and departs from the idea that there are significant advantages to justice mechanisms that are more culturally embedded and locally owned than international criminal proceedings.

The shift in thinking about post-conflict reconstruction has found much inspiration in how African states have sought to restore societies from past abuses in the course of the last two decades. Throughout the 1990s, Africa has served as 'a vast testing ground for new policies to address impunity, seek truth and justice, and enable reconciliation in fractured societies'.[54] In an attempt to harmonize these various justice and accountability initiatives, the AU has recently ventured into developing an African Policy Framework on Transitional Justice. This framework, which will likely be endorsed during the AU Summit in July 2016, details a range of measures that may help to ensure peace, justice, and reconciliation on the continent.[55] In laying down minimum standards and benchmarks, the framework is meant to serve as a guide for African countries in transitional processes and underscores that alongside formal systems of criminal justice like the ICC, other mechanisms can also help in dealing with mass atrocity crimes.

The AU's recent interest in alternative justice mechanisms is not unrelated to Africa's embattled relationship with the ICC. However, it would be a mistake to simplify the AU's focus on alternate forms of justice as a mere by-product of its campaign against the Court. Instead, the development of an

African Policy Framework on Transitional Justice, as well as the early formation of an African Criminal Court, should be seen in the context of the above-mentioned shift in thinking about the role of international criminal proceedings in post-conflict reconstruction and the existing tradition of alternative justice mechanisms in Africa.

Below, we briefly introduce some of the different approaches that have been taken in response to mass atrocity crimes in Africa in the course of the last two decades in order to foreshadow the chapters in this volume that deal with several of these different mechanisms. For this purpose, we a draw a distinction between: (a) traditional justice mechanisms, (b) truth commissions,[56] and (c) domestic and regional prosecutions.[57]

A *Traditional Justice Mechanisms*

In Africa, so-called 'traditional' justice mechanisms (though in most cases significantly altered by the colonial and post-colonial state) continued to exist alongside and at times in opposition to formal judicial structures. These mechanisms, which generally aim to settle disputes in a peaceful manner, are community-based and involve informal and ritualistic practices.[58] The importance that these proceedings place on communal interdependence is generally linked to the African philosophy of *Ubuntu*, whereby 'individual rights cannot be meaningfully exercised in isolation of broader community rights'.[59] At the heart of this philosophy is the idea that the breaking of individual social relationships can cause conflict within the community and should therefore be restored.[60]

Although most traditional justice mechanisms are designed to deal with less complex community-based disputes than mass atrocity crimes, the underlying tradition and societal values have in several cases incorporated elements of the national judicial structures and (international) legal notions in order to deal with these crimes. One can speak, in this regard, of 'tradition-based justice mechanisms'. These mechanisms focus on reconciliation and restoration in the form of truth-telling and forgiveness, as witnessed in the case of the Acholi of northern Uganda, and have been successful in ensuring the peaceful reintegration of ex-combatants in conflict-torn societies, like in the case of the *Curanderos* in Mozambique or the *Kpaa Mende* in Sierra Leone. In the case of Rwanda, the local *Gacaca* processes went a step further as it integrated formal prosecution and restorative justice to complement the International Criminal Tribunal for Rwanda (ICTR) and domestic trials.[61]

B Truth Commissions

In the past decades, several African states have also established truth commissions, which have functioned alongside or as an alternative to criminal proceedings at the domestic or international level.[62] Although the mandates of the respective truth commissions differ, they are generally state-authorized bodies with a temporary nature that investigate and document past atrocities that occurred during a specified period. What truth commissions can offer, and which criminal trials can only provide to a certain extent, is an exposure of the historical narrative.[63] Some of these truth commissions have been combined with amnesties, as witnessed in the case of South Africa, or have been used as an alternative to official trials, like in Ghana and Liberia. Other truth commissions have, however, operated alongside domestic or international prosecutions, such as in Sierra Leone (through the Special Court for Sierra Leone) and Ivory Coast (through the ICC).[64]

Many of these commissions have been praised for creating an historical account of what happened during the course of a conflict. What is important to keep in mind, however, is that whereas truth commissions may indeed promote truth telling, reconciliation, and peace building, they may also be established to further the political agenda of a new regime. To give an example, Ugandan president Museveni allegedly used the truth commission in 1986 to discredit the former government.[65] In this sense, a poorly executed truth commission may actually be worse than having no truth commission at all, at least to the extent that the interest of the 'vanquished' are concerned.[66]

C Domestic and Regional Prosecutions in Africa

A third alternative or complement of international criminal proceedings are domestic and regional prosecutions. Within Africa, a prominent example of domestic prosecutions are those held in Rwanda in the aftermath of the 1994 genocide. At least 10,000 perpetrators have faced trial in Rwanda and many cases are still ongoing or outstanding.[67] Another example, albeit on a vastly smaller scale, can be found in the DRC, where the Congolese military tribunals have expanded their jurisdiction and have held over twenty trials for war crimes and crimes against humanity since 2006.[68]

In contrast to these important examples of successful domestic trials for perpetrators of mass atrocity crimes, in many other post-conflict societies in Africa formal structures have been destroyed to the extent that domestic prosecutions have been impossible. Moreover, the criminal justice settings in many African states are not designed to deal with the scale and specific nature of mass atrocity crimes.[69] In the absence of proper national judicial structures and/or the political will to prosecute, there have hardly been any alternative possibilities in the region to prosecute perpetrators. The failure of national judicial structures has left the prosecution of mass atrocities like those committed in Uganda, Sudan, or Sierra Leone to the ICC or to specialized international tribunals. The only example of regional prosecution has been the establishment of the Extraordinary African Chambers in 2013 as a hybrid court in the Senegalese justice system, which came into being after an agreement between the AU and Senegal to try former president of Chad, Hissène Habré, and others who were allegedly responsible for mass violence in Chad between 1982 and 1990.[70]

On the sub-regional level, the East African Community (EAC) has ventured into providing the EAC Court of Justice (EACJ) with criminal jurisdiction over crimes against humanity, but this process has recently been halted by Kenya and Tanzania. These states have opposed such expansion on the grounds that four of the five EAC Member States (Kenya, Tanzania, Uganda, and Burundi, with Rwanda being an exception) are also States Parties to the Rome Statute.[71] These considerations have not, however, prevented African States Parties to the Rome Statute from accelerating the establishment of the 'African Criminal Court' as a regional alternative to the ICC. As noted, in June 2014, the AU adopted the Amendment Protocol to expand the jurisdiction of the African Court to include a broad range of economically motivated crimes seen as being root causes of Africa's violence (e.g. mercenarism, toxic dumping, plunder of natural resources, and drug trafficking), in addition to the four core crimes that form the subject matter jurisdiction of the ICC. Including both individual and corporate criminal responsibility, the Amendment Protocol represents another attempt of African states to redefine the structures of international criminal justice.

The expansion of the jurisdiction of the African Court has been criticized by some as an attempt to secure regional exceptionalism in the face of the ICC's current investigations and prosecutions in Africa.[72] However, its development is not just a result of the embattled relationship between the AU and the ICC.[73] Establishing a regional criminal justice institution is part of a broader commitment of the AU to put in place a comprehensive continental framework which includes mechanisms, instruments, and institutions that seek to resolve conflicts, ensure accountability, and promote peacebuilding, justice, and reconciliation. The so-called African Peace and Security Architecture and the African Policy Framework on Transitional Justice are driven by a desire to develop continental policies that direct the region's path to peace and justice on African terms. In providing a regional venue to prosecute mass atrocity crimes, the establishment of an African Criminal Court should be seen as a novel addition to the existing range of African-specific transitional justice measures that have recently been outlined in the Policy Framework.

What all this shows is that an African vision of justice entails much more than Hague Justice alone. Procedures before the ICC are, in this vision, not necessarily the best way to ensure that justice is perceived to be done in communities that seek to recover from mass atrocities. While the existence of many alternative justice mechanisms predates the establishment of the ICC and are part of a much broader agenda, the tension between African states and the ICC has given further momentum to the AU's efforts to promote the plurality of options for African states in dealing with mass atrocity crimes. With the simultaneous expedition of the establishment of an African Criminal Court and an African Policy Framework on Transitional Justice, the AU ultimately seeks to advance African perceptions of justice, while ensuring that the decisions on how to move forward remain 'African owned'.

IV AN OVERVIEW OF THE VOLUME

This volume seeks to explore and understand the different perceptions of the ICC in Africa. It is organized into four thematic sections that consider the origins of the Court's fractious relationship with Africa (Part I), the interactions between African states and the ICC (Part II), the impact of the ICC in different African communities (Part III), and the potential and actual role of other local and regional justice mechanisms in Africa (Part IV).

Part I emerged as a set of four keynote lectures that were given at the conference in The Hague that invigorated the themes around this book.[74] It opens with a contribution by Shamiso Mbizvo – international lawyer in the Jurisdiction, Complementarity and Cooperation Division in the Office of the Prosecutor (OTP) of the ICC – discussing the relationship between the ICC and Africa from the perspective of the Court. Without disregarding the current constraints, Mbizvo recalls Africa's support for and cooperation with the ICC, as well as the active involvement of Africans in leading the Court. She further stresses the continued demand to do more for survivors of mass atrocities in Africa and challenges the alleged African bias of the Court by highlighting what the OTP is doing for non-African constituents of the ICC.

The next three chapters in Part I respond to Mbizvo's contribution. They offer supplemental, overlapping, as well as competing perspectives on the roots of the current tensions between Africa and the ICC. Makau W. Mutua begins with a critical assessment of the AU's claims of the Court's selectivity and 'race-hunting'. His contribution supports Mbizvo's assertion of the importance of international criminal justice but is also productively critical of it. He is even more critical, however, of the AU's position. For by exposing the AU's hypocrisy and contradictions (where on the one hand it is promoting democracy and human rights, and on the other it is enabling impunity by insisting on the insertion of immunity for African heads of state in the Amendment Protocol of the African Court), he argues that our perceptions of the ICC and AU justice need to be rethought.

Solomon Dersso focuses in turn on the politics and limits of international criminal justice, which he sees as the main catalyst for the embattled position of the ICC in Africa. In contrast to Mbizvo and Mutua, Dersso traces the Court's Africa problem to the Western bias of international law and to the power structures of the international political system. He singles out a number of issues that need to be addressed to ease the relationship between the ICC and Africa. Most importantly, Dersso argues that peace and justice demands need to be balanced in a more sophisticated manner, in order that room is given to national policy in articulating transitional justice processes, and that the limits of prosecutorial justice have to be acknowledged.

In the last chapter on the origins of the Court's fractious relationship with Africa, Kamari M. Clarke explores the relationship between ICC and anti-ICC narratives and how history is often narrativized to provide perceptions of what is real. In foregrounding the way that law is often mistaken as the only route to justice, Clarke both responds to Mbizvo's contribution as well as to prominent anti-ICC narratives by highlighting how perceptions of justice are shaped by affective constructions. By detailing the manner in which members of the OTP have narrowed the meaning of justice through the presumption that justice must be driven by judicial mechanisms and by examining Uhuru Kenyatta's rhetorical strategies, Clarke insists that historical narratives are often deployed in order to conjure sentimental reactions towards the production of the 'real'. She ends by suggesting that we need to rethink the way we understand perceptions of justice through an understanding of the strategic production of emotional climates in daily life.

Part II of the volume examines the interactions of African states with the ICC. It includes three chapters that seek to expose how and why African states have criticized the Court, how this has affected the legitimacy of the ICC, and how the Court and its supporters have responded to their concerns and accusations.

First, Lee Seymour studies the repeated accusations of hypocrisy levelled by the AU and individual African leaders against the ICC, and explains how this rhetorical action undermines the Court's legitimacy. After charting the shifts in the ICC's (dis-)engagements with African states, Seymour assesses the interests that the charges of hypocrisy serve and identifies the ways in which the Court has tried to address these accusations.

Next, Paul Schmitt provides a historical case study of France's close connections with the ICC and its strong presence in many African states. In light of the criticism of African states that the Court has become a neo-colonial institution, Schmitt's contribution gives insight into how France's post-colonial practice of maintaining influence in its former African colonies has threatened the Court's legitimacy.

In the final chapter of Part II, Abel S. Knottnerus examines the concerns that the AU has voiced about the prosecution of African presidents by the ICC. After explaining that the AU's campaign is powerful in its ability to influence how the Court is perceived in Africa, Knottnerus analyses the different ways in which the ICC and its States Parties have tried to counter the arguments that the AU has advanced against the prosecution of al-Bashir, Kenyatta, and Ruto. He concludes that despite recent efforts to improve the Court's relationship with Africa, the AU will likely continue to oppose the prosecution of African presidents and will as such put further pressure on the legitimacy of the ICC.

Part III looks beyond the interactions between African states and the ICC and considers the impact of the Court in different African communities, and especially in Kenya and the DRC. It includes four chapters that reflect on the perceptions of the ICC in Africa from different angles, including studies on editorial cartoons and voting behaviour, as well as on how the ICC has shaped domestic politics, narratives of conflict, and the experiences of witnesses.

In the opening chapter, Sammy Gachigua offers an innovative take on the ICC's presence in Kenya through the analysis of editorial cartoons in national Kenyan newspapers. Gachigua illustrates how the cartoons have documented the evolving public perception of the ICC in Kenya from a highly appraised to an ambivalent institution.

This change in public perception in Kenya also comes to the fore in the contribution of Thomas Wolf. Using data from national survey research as well as material from local media and conducted interviews, Wolf argues that demands for accountability have been inseparable from the contest for political power in Kenya. This not only facilitated the electoral triumph of Kenyatta and Ruto in 2013, but has also undermined the Court's standing among many Kenyans.

How the ICC can affect domestic politics is further discussed in Patryk Labuda's contribution on the Court's involvement in the DRC. His chapter traces the impact of the ICC's proceedings on domestic political and military developments, before shifting attention to the military justice system's uses of international criminal law. Labuda further considers the challenges of enacting judicial reform, and in particular the attempts to establish a hybrid war crimes tribunal for past atrocities in the Eastern part of the DRC.

In the last chapter of Part III, Stephen Smith Cody, Eric Stover, and Alexa Koening present empirical data on the experiences of witnesses who testified in the cases against Thomas Lubanga and Germain Katanga. They demonstrate how failures to adequately protect sensitive witnesses and to prevent alleged witness intimidation and tampering can undermine criminal prosecutions. In this light, they propose new mechanisms that will have to ensure the ongoing evaluation of witness experiences.

Part IV of this volume looks beyond the ICC by focusing on local and regional justice mechanisms in Africa. The four chapters in this last thematic section highlight the limitations and possibilities of different responses to mass atrocities on the African continent, including local justice mechanisms in Darfur and Rwanda as well as the newly established 'African Criminal Court'.

This part opens with an account on local justice mechanisms in Darfur. Karin Willemse introduces the different 'tribal judicial institutions' in the context of Sudanese national politics. In addressing the question whether, by providing reparations through restorative justice, Darfur victims are better served than through retributive justice, she highlights the importance of the historical political contexts in which these African forms of justice operate. Willemse argues that the relevance of tribal judicial institutions to the Darfur population can only be properly understood when they are considered in relation to historical legal regulations regarding access to land and struggles over citizenship.

In the second chapter, Kristin C. Doughty juxtaposes the locally rooted trials in *Gacaca* courts with the proceedings of the ICTR, specifically focusing on the lens of interpretation. She uses the technical task of interpretation at the ICTR and the lack of a structural corollary before *Gacaca* courts to examine the relationship between linguistic and legal interpretation. The focus on interpretation assists in moving beyond the false dichotomy wherein international law is equated with objective neutrality while local courts are equated with a politicized bias, and allows one to trace how in all legal systems certain forms of power and expertise privilege some interpretations over others.

The chapter by Abel S. Knottnerus and Eefje de Volder analyses the early formation of an 'African Criminal Court'. This chapter seeks to counter the emerging image of the African Court as a deliberate attempt of African leaders to weaken international criminal justice. Knottnerus and De Volder explain why it is too simplistic to depict the proposed Criminal Chamber of the African Court as 'an anti-ICC Court', and why warnings for a future 'clash' with the ICC are exaggerated. Instead of a threat to international criminal justice, they argue that the adopted Amendment Protocol may actually help to articulate an African vision on international criminal justice.

In the last chapter of Part IV, Clare da Silva and Sara Kendall explain why state responsibility should be an important part of the responses to mass atrocity crimes in Africa. Their contribution highlights that one of the key material conditions of possibility of these crimes – the global trade in arms – has been largely absent in the discussions on criminal accountability and transitional justice. In this light, they explore how the recently adopted Arms Trade Treaty provides a regulatory framework that has the potential to foster greater state responsibility for ensuring that the international trade in conventional arms does not contribute to the commission of mass atrocity crimes on the African continent.

Finally, in the Epilogue, we draw out the key insights of the book and consider possibilities for future research by highlighting the importance of studying the different perceptions of international courts and other justice mechanisms. Ultimately, the volume seeks to unravel the complexity of the Court's fractious relationship with Africa by exploring the multilayered perceptions of the ICC's involvement in different African communities. We see this approach as key to other contemporary issues within the realm of international law and politics. In order to understand and possibly improve the functioning of international courts and alternative justice mechanisms, we argue that one needs to take perceptions of justice seriously, because 'justice misperceived' can eventually turn into 'justice denied'.

Notes

The authors would like to thank the anonymous reviewers of Cambridge University Press, as well as André de Hoogh, Froukje Krijtenburg, Lee J. M. Seymour, and Thomas P. Wolf, for their comments on earlier drafts of this introduction.

1. See both the June 2016 AU withdrawal directive from the Report of the Fourth Meeting of the Open Ended Committee of Ministers of Foreign Affairs on the International Criminal Court. Also see the earlier call of the Ugandan president, Yoweri Museveni, upon the African States Parties to the ICC to consider withdrawing from the Rome Statute: Gashegu Muramira, 'Uganda: Museveni Calls On African Countries to Review ICC Membership', *The New Times*, 10 October 2014. See also the proposal of South Africa's largest political party, the African National Congress, to pull the country out of the ICC: James Butty, 'ANC Wants

South Africa out of International Criminal Court', *Voice of America*, 12 October 2015.

2. Luis Moreno-Ocampo, 'The International Criminal Court: Seeking Global Justice' (2008) 40 *Case Western Reserve Journal of International Law* 224.

3. On the law and politics of the Security Council's deferral powers: Kamari M. Clarke and Sarah-Jane Koulen, 'The Legal Politics of the Article 16 Decision: The International Criminal Court, the UN Security Council and Ontologies of a Contemporary Compromise' (2014) 7 *African Journal of Legal Studies* 297–319; Abel S. Knottnerus, 'The Security Council and the International Criminal Court: The Unsolved Puzzle of Article 16' (2014) 61 *Netherlands International Law Review* 195–224.

4. See for example the statement of Prosecutor Bensouda during Africa's Legal Aid Conference in 2014: OTP, Presentation of Fatou Bensouda at Legal Aid Conference – 'Africa and the International Criminal Court (ICC): Lessons Learned and Synergies Ahead', 10 September 2014. See also the statements of Australia, Brazil, Canada, Costa Rica, Czech Republic, Denmark, Finland, France, Germany, Italy, Japan, Jordan (also on behalf of Liechtenstein), Lithuania (on behalf of the European Union), Luxemburg, New Zealand, Peru, Philippines, Portugal, Spain, Trinidad & Tobago, and the United States (as observer State) in: ASP, General Debate of the Twelfth Session, 20–26 November 2013.

5. OTP, Keynote Address Institute for Security Studies – 'The ICC: A Response to African Concerns by Fatou Bensouda', 11 October 2012.

6. ASP, Special segment as requested by the African Union: 'Indictment of sitting Heads of State and Government and its consequences on peace and stability and reconciliation' – Informal summary by the Moderator (ICC-ASP/12/61), 27 November 2013.

7. On the amended rules on presence at trial: Abel S. Knottnerus, 'Extraordinary Exceptions at the International Criminal Court: The (New) Rules and Jurisprudence on Presence at Trial' (2014) 13 *Law and Practice of International Courts and Tribunals* 261–285.

8. AU Assembly, 'Decision on the Progress Report of the Commission on the Implementation of the Decisions on the International Criminal Court', Assembly/AU/Dec.493 (XXII), 30–31 January 2014, paras. 6–8 and 10.

9. Currently the African Court on Human and Peoples' Rights only considers alleged human rights violations. In the AU Constitutive Act, the establishment of another court, the AU Court of Justice, has been provided for. For efficiency purposes, a merger protocol was adopted to expand the jurisdiction of the existing court with a General Affairs Chamber. The name of the court was supposed to change to the African Court of Justice and Human Rights. While the merger protocol has

entered into force, the expansion has not yet taken place. The discussions on adding a Criminal Chamber have led to the adoption of another protocol in June 2014, that is, the Protocol on Amendments to the Protocol on the Statute of the African Court of Justice and Human Rights (Amendment Protocol). After the adoption of the Amendment Protocol, the Court will be named African Couto s Justice and Human and Peoples' Rights (Article 1 of the Amendment Protocol).

10. Article 46A*bis* provides that: 'no charges shall be commenced or continued before the Court against any serving African Union Head of State or Government, or anybody acting or entitled to act in such capacity, or other senior state officials based on their functions, during their tenure of office'. The complementarity provision (Article 46H) only refers to competent courts of regional economic communities and national jurisdictions.

11. OTP, Statement of the Prosecutor of the International Criminal Court, Fatou Bensouda, on the Status of the Government of Kenya's Cooperation with the Prosecution's Investigations in the Kenyatta Case, 5 December 2014.

12. AU Assembly, 'Decision on the Progress Report of the Commission on the Implementation of Previous Decisions on the International Criminal Court', Assembly/AU/Dec.547 (XXIV), 30–31 January 2015, paras. 8–9.

13. For references, see Chapter 8 by Abel S. Knottnerus.

14. See for example Charles C. Jalloh, 'Regionalizing International Criminal Law?' (2009) 9 *International Criminal Law Review* 445–499; Charles C. Jalloh, Dapo Akande and Max du Plessis, 'Assessing African Union Concerns about Article 16 of the Rome Statute of the International Criminal Court' (2011) 4 *African Journal of Legal Studies* 5–50; Manisuli Ssenyonjo, 'The Rise of the African Union Opposition to the International Criminal Court's Investigations and Prosecutions of African Leaders' (2013) 12 *International Criminal Law Review* 385–428. Charles Jalloh, 'Reflections on the Indictment of Sitting Heads of State and Government and Its Consequences for Peace and Stability and Reconciliation in Africa', (2014) 7 *African Journal of Legal Studies* 43–59.

15. See for example Max du Plessis, 'The International Criminal Court that Africa Wants' (ISS Monograph 172, 2010); Makau W. Mutua, 'The International Criminal Court in Africa: Challenges and Opportunities' (Noref Working Paper, 2010); Tim Murithi, 'The African Union and the International Criminal Court: An Embattled Relationship?' (The Institute for Justice and Reconciliation Policy Brief no. 8, 2013).

16. See also the different contributions in: Gerhard Werle, Lovell Fernandez, and Moritz Vormbaum (eds.), *Africa and the International Criminal*

Court (The Hague: Asser Press, 2014). This volume seeks, among other things, 'to develop proposals for cooperation between international courts, domestic courts outside Africa and courts within Africa'.

17. See for example Charles M. Fombad and Enyinna Nwauche, 'Africa's Imperial Presidents: the Immunity, Impunity and Accountability' (2012) 5 *African Journal of Legal Studies* 91–118.

18. See for example Mahmood Mamdani, 'Darfur, ICC and the New humanitarian Order – How the ICC's "Responsibility to Protect" Is Being Turned into an Assertion of Neo-Colonial Domination', *The Nation*, 29 September 2008; Dire Tladi, 'The African Union and the International Criminal Court: The Battle for the Soul of International Law' (2009) 34 *South African Yearbook of International Law* 57–69; Kai Ambos, 'Expanding the Focus of the "African Criminal Court"', in William A. Schabas, Yvonne McDermott, and Niamh Hayes (eds.), *Ashgate Research Companion to International Criminal Law: Critical perspectives* (Aldershot: Ashgate, 2012), pp. 499–530; 'Africa Debate: Invited Experts on Africa Question – Is the ICC Targeting Africa Inappropriately?', *ICC Forum*, 2013.

19. Kurt Mils, '"Bashir Is Dividing Us": Africa and the International Criminal Court' (2012) 34 *Human Rights Quarterly* 404–447; See further Chapter 9 by Sammy G. Gachigua and Chapter 10 by Thomas P. Wolf.

20. Margaret M. deGuzman, 'Gravity and the Legitimacy of the International Criminal Court' (2009) 32 *Fordham International Law Journal* 1444–1449.

21. Note that perceptions or beliefs can have both causal and constitutive effects: Alexander Wendt, *Social Theory of International Politics* (Cambridge: Cambridge University Press, 1999), pp. 77–88.

22. Tom R. Tyler, 'Psychological Perspectives on Legitimacy and Legitimation' (2006) 57 *Annual Review of Psychology* 376. For one of the first contributions on the sociological legitimacy of the ICC: Alison M. Danner, 'Enhancing the Legitimacy and Accountability of Prosecutorial Discretion at the International Criminal Court' (2003) 97 *American Journal of International Law* 510–552.

23. A distinction needs to be drawn between the sociological legitimacy and the de facto authority of international courts; see Karen J. Alter, Laurence R. Helfer, and Mikael Rask Madsen, 'How Context Shapes the Authority of International Courts' (2016) 79 *Law & Contemporary Problems* 1–36.

24. This is a 'narrow' definition of effectiveness. The effectiveness of international courts or tribunals may be understood more broadly 'as their ability to promote the attainment of a set of policy goals assigned by the political organs that create them'. Cesare P. R. Romano, Karen J. Alter, and Yuval Shany (eds.), *Oxford Handbook of International Adjudication* (Oxford: Oxford University Press, 2014), p. 18. See generally Yuval Shany,

Assessing the Effectiveness of International Courts (Oxford: Oxford University Press, 2014).

25. A next step, which is not undertaken here, is to 'apply' knowledge about the perceptions of the ICC in an attempt to engineer its practice in such a way that the Court's work is perceived more positively and thus supported by relevant audiences. On the idea of strategically enhancing the sociological legitimacy of the ICC: Danner, 'Enhancing Legitimacy and Accountability', 550; Margaret M. deGuzman, 'Choosing to Prosecute: Expressive Selection at the International Criminal Court' (2012) 33 *Michigan Journal of International Law* 256–320; Stuart Ford, 'A Social Psychology Model of the Perceived Legitimacy of International Criminal Courts: Implications for the Success of Transitional Justice Mechanisms' (2012) V*anderBilt Journal of Transnational Law* 405–476.

26. See generally Allen Buchanan and Robert O. Keohane, 'The Legitimacy of Global Governance Institutions' (2006) 20 *Ethics and International Affairs* 405–434; Daniel Bodansky, 'Legitimacy in International Law and International Relations', in Jeffrey L. Dunoff and Mark A. Pollack (eds.), *Interdisciplinary Perspectives on International Law and International Relations* (Cambridge: Cambridge University Press, 2013), pp. 321–341.

27. Note that if normative legitimacy would be entirely reducible to sociological legitimacy, then there would be no basis for attempting to persuade social actors to change their views. See Daniel Bodansky, 'The Legitimacy of International Governance: A Coming Challenge for International Environmental Law?' (1999) 93 *American Journal of International Law* 601–603.

28. For one of the first thorough contributions on the normative legitimacy of the ICC: Aaron Fichtelberg, 'Democratic Legitimacy and the International Criminal Court – A Liberal Defence' (2006) 4 *Journal of International Criminal Justice* 765–785.

29. See generally Dunoff and Pollack, *Interdisciplinary Perspectives on International Law and International Relations*, pp. 3–32.

30. See generally Karin Alter, *The New Terrain of International Law* (Princeton: Princeton University Press, 2014), pp. 32–33. With respect to the ICC, see Steven C. Roach (ed.), *Governance, Order, and the International Criminal Court: Between Realpolitik and a Cosmopolitan Court* (Oxford: Oxford University Press 2009).

31. Note that Ian Hurd's seminal work on sociological legitimacy in international politics explicitly aims to combine the logics of rationalism and constructivism. Ian Hurd, *After Anarchy: Legitimacy & Power in the United Nations Security Council* (Princeton: Princeton University Press, 2007), pp. 73–77.

32. For one of the first population-based surveys on the ICC, see: Phuong Pham, Patrick Vinck, Eric Stover, Andrew Moss, Marieke Wierda, and

Richard Bailey, 'When the War Ends – A Population-Based Survey on Attitudes about Peace, Justice, and Social Reconstruction in Northern Uganda' (Human Rights Center Berkeley, Payson Center for International Development and International Center for Transitional Justice, 2007).

33. Note that several scholars have documented the range of other African contributions to the work of the Court, see for example Phakiso Mochochoko, 'Africa and the International Criminal Court', in Evelyn A. Ankumah and Edward K. Kwakwa (eds.), *African Perspectives on International Criminal Justice* (Accra: Africa Legal Aid, 2005), pp. 241–258.

34. Kamari M. Clarke, *Fictions of Justice: The ICC and the Challenge of Legal Pluralism in Sub-Saharan Africa* (Cambridge: Cambridge University Press, 2009). See also Kamari M. Clarke, 'The Rule of Law Through its Economies of Appearances: The Making of the African Warlord' (2011) 18 *Indiana Journal of Global Legal Studies* 7–40; Kamari M. Clarke, 'Rethinking Africa through Its Exclusions: The Politics of Naming Criminal Responsibility' (2010) 83 *Anthropological Quarterly* 634–640.

35. UN Doc. GA/Res/36/108, 10 December 1981.

36. 'Report of the International Law Commission', UNGAOR, 46th Session, Supp. No 10, UN Doc. A/49/10 (1994).

37. 'Report of the International Law Commission', UNGAOR, 43rd Session, Supp. No. 10, UN Doc. A/46/10.

38. 'Report of the International Law Commission', UNGAOR, 47th Session, UN Doc. A/50/10 (1995). Topical summary of the discussion during its fiftieth session prepared by the Secretariat (16 February 1996).

39. *Ibid*.

40. See Chapter 11 by Patryk I. Labuda.

41. See Chapter 7 by Paul D. Schmitt.

42. See Chapter 8 by Abel S. Knottnerus.

43. Kamari M. Clarke, Forthcoming Manuscript, 2017.

44. AU Assembly, 'Decision on Africa's Relationship with the International Criminal Court (ICC)', Ext/Assembly/AU/Dec.1(Oct.2013), 12 October 2013, para. 10(i).

45. Over the past fifteen years, transitional justice has consolidated as a field of study. Early pioneering studies include: Nico Kritz, *Transitional Justice* (Washington DC: United States Institute for Peace, 1995); A. James McAdams (ed.), *Transitional Justice and the Rule of Law in New Democracies* (Notre Dame: University of Notre Dame Press, 1997); Martha Minow, *Between Vengeance and Forgiveness. Facing History after Genocide and Mass Violence* (Boston: Beacon Press, 1998) and Ruti G. Teitel, 'Transitional Justice Genealogy' (2003) 16 *Harvard Human Rights Journal* 69–94.

46. Robert Cryer, Hakan Friman, Darryl Robinson and Elizabeth Wilmshurst, *An Introduction to International Criminal Law and Procedure* (Cambridge: Cambridge University Press, 2010), pp. 18–22.

47. Jennifer J. Llewellyn and Daniel Philpott, 'Restorative Justice and Reconciliation: Twin Frameworks for Peacebuilding', in Jennifer J. Llewellyn and Daniel Philpott (eds.), *Restorative Justice, Reconciliation and Peacebuilding* (Oxford: Oxford University Press, 2014), p. 16.

48. Janine N. Clark, 'Peace, Justice and the International Criminal Court: Limitations and Possibilities' (2011) 9 *Journal of International Criminal Justice* 521–545; Laurel E. Fletcher, Harvey M. Weinstein and Jamie Rowen, 'Context, Timing and the Dynamics of Transitional Justice: A Historical Perspective' (2009) 31 *Human Rights Quarterly* 163–220; Chandra L. Sriram and Suren Pillay, *Peace versus Justice? The Dilemma of Transitional Justice in Africa* (Durban: University of Kwazulu-Natal Press, 2009).

49. Mahmoud C. Bassiouni, 'Searching for Peace and Achieving Justice: The Need for Accountability' (1996) 59 *Law and Contemporary Problems* 9–28, at 9–13.

50. John Dugard, 'Dealing with Crimes of a Past Regime. Is Amnesty Still an Option?' (1999) 12 *Leiden Journal of International Law* 1001–1015, at 1002; For an historical overview of the use of amnesties, see, for example, Fania Domb, 'Treatment of War Crimes in Peace Settlements: Prosecution or Amnesty?', in Yoram Dinstein and Mala Tabory (eds.), *War Crimes in International Law* (Leiden: Martinus Nijhof Publishers, 1996).

51. Martii Koskenniemi, 'Between Impunity and Show Trials' (2002) 6 *Max Planck Yearbook of United Nations Law* 1–35; Stephanos Bibas and William W. Burke-White, 'When Idealism Meets Domestic-Criminal-Procedure Realism' (2010) 59 *Duke Law Journal* 637–704; Payam Akhavan, 'The Rise, and Fall, and Rise, of International Criminal Justice' (2013) 11 *Journal of International Criminal Justice* 527–536.

52. Carsten Stahn, 'Between "Faith" and "Facts": By What Standards Should We Assess International Criminal Justice?' (2012) 25 *Leiden Journal of International Law* 251–282.

53. Nico Kritz, 'Where We Are and How We Got Here: An Overview of Developments in the Search for Justice and Reconciliation', in Alice H. Henkin (ed.), *The Legacy of Abuse: Confronting the Past, Facing the Future* (Washington D.C.: Aspen Institute, 2002); Diane F. Orentlicher, 'Settling Accounts' Revisited: Reconciling Global Norms with Local Agency' (2007) 1 *International Journal of Transitional Justice* 10–22.

54. AU Panel of the Wise, 'Peace, Justice, and Reconciliation in Africa: Opportunities and Challenges in the Fight Against Impunity' (International Peace Institute African Union Series, February 2009), p. 39.

55. Upon recommendation by the Panel of the Wise in 2009 (see former footnote), several consultations have been held with AU Member States and experts to work out the African-Policy Framework on Transitional Justice. The latest validation workshop was held in August 2014 to finalize the document. See: African Union, 'Concept Note: Validation Workshop on the Draft African Transitional Justice Policy Framework (ATJPF)' (South Africa, 18–19 August 2014). The likely endorsement of the ATJPF during the 2015 summit was expressed by Aisha Abdullahi, AU Commissioner for Political Affairs in her address in commemoration of the African Human Rights Day. See: Aisha L. Abhulahi, 'Human Rights for All: For a Peaceful and a Secure Africa', 21 October 2014.

56. To avoid confusion, we opted for the general term truth commission to include both truth commissions and truth and reconciliation commissions. In referring to country-specific mechanisms the formal name will be used, such as in the case of the TRC in South Africa.

57. The Transitional Justice Framework underscores the importance of individual prosecutions; truth seeking; reparations (including work on memory, memorials and memorialization); local community based justice mechanisms; and institutional reform (including vetting and dismissal of staff). African Union Panel of the Wise, 'Peace, Justice, and Reconciliation in Africa', at 16.

58. Luc Huyse, 'Introduction: Tradition-based Approaches in Peacemaking, Transitional Justice and Reconciliation Policies', in Luc Huyse and Mark Salter (eds.), *Traditional Justice and Reconciliation after Violent Conflict: Learning from African Experiences* (Stockholm: International Institute for Democracy and Electoral Assistance, 2008). Not all tradition-based mechanisms are focused on peaceful settlement. The Taita in Kenya, for example, banish/drive away criminals, while others are thrown to their deaths off high cliffs, in the absence of any state-like structures, including prisons.

59. *Ubuntu* is commonly explained with the phrase: 'I am what I am because of what we are'. According to Drucilla Cornell and Karin van Marle, *Ubuntu* appears in almost every African language, either literally or as something very close to it: Drucilla Cornell and Karin van Marle 'Exploring Ubuntu: Tentative Reflections' (2005) 5 *Human Rights Law* 195–220.

60. Surely, the rapidly changing populations living in mixed-ethnic areas increasingly makes it problematic to define 'community'.

61. Martien Schotsmans, 'Justice at the Doorstep: Victims of International Crimes in Formal Versus Tradition-Based Justice Mechanisms in Sierra

Leone, Rwanda and Uganda', in Rianne Letschert, Roelof Haveman, Anne-Marie de Brouwer, and Antony Pemberton (eds.), *Victimological Approaches to International Crimes: Africa* (Antwerp: Intersentia, 2011), p. 358

62. Three of these commissions were created before 1991 and three after the opening of the ICC in 2002. According to the estimates of Llewellyn and Philpott and using a broad definition of truth commissions, forty Truth Commissions have taken place in the last forty years, of which thirteen have been established in Africa (Uganda (1974); Zimbabwe (1985); Uganda (1986–1995); Chad (1991–1992); South Africa (ANC) (1992,1993); Burundi (1995–1996); South Africa (TRC) (1995–2000); Nigeria (1999–2000); Sierra Leone (2000–2001); Ghana (2002); Morocco (2004–2006); Liberia (2005); Kenya (2009–present). See Jennifer J. Llewellyn and Daniel Philpott, 'Introduction', in Llewellyn and Philpott, *Restorative Justice*, p. 12.

63. While criminal proceedings do assist in writing the historical narrative to some extent (see Richard A. Wilson, *Writing History in International Criminal Trials* (Cambridge: Cambridge University Press, 2011)), it remains a curtailed version of what actually happened.

64. Chandra L. Sriram, 'Transitional Justice and Peacebuilding' in Sriram and Pillay, *Peace versus Justice*, p. 3.

65. See Joanna R. Quinn, 'Constraints: The Un-doing of the Ugandan Truth Commission' (2004) 26 *Human Rights Quarterly* 401 427.

66. See Priscilla Hayner, *Unspeakable Truths. Facing the Challenge of Truth Commissions* (London: Routledge, 2002).

67. UN, 'Background Information on the Justice and Reconciliation Process in Rwanda' (Outreach Programme on the Rwandan Genocide and the United Nations, 2015).

68. See Chapter 11 by Patryk I. Labuda.

69. AU Panel of the Wise, 'Peace, Justice, and Reconciliation in Africa', p. 18.

70. While the Court has requested the extradition of Saleh Younous and Mahamat Djibrine, Chad continues to refuse: 'Senegal: Chad's Inaction Won't Prevent Habré Trial Refusal to Transfer Alleged Accomplices to Senegal Special Court', *Human Rights Watch*, 22 October 2014. The Extraordinary African Chambers have been established in response to an ICJ ruling on the matter. Habré has been living in exile in Senegal since he was overthrown in 1990. The ICJ has found that Senegal is under the obligation to submit the case to a competent court, meaning that Senegal either had to prosecute him without further delay or else to extradite him to Belgium. *Questions Relating to the Obligation to Prosecute or Extradite (Belgium v. Senegal)*, Judgment, [2012] ICJ Rep 422.

71. Christabel Ligami, 'Kenya, Tanzania Opposed to Giving EACJ Powers to Hear International Cases', *The East African*, 25 October 2014.

72. See Chapter 15.
73. Max Du Plessis, 'A Case of Negative Regional Complementarity? Giving the African Court of Justice and Human Rights Jurisdiction over International Crimes', *EJIL Talk*, 27 August 2012.
74. Conference 'Africans and Hague Justice: Realities and Perceptions of the International Criminal Court in Africa' (The Hague, 23–24 May 2014).

PART I

THE ORIGINS OF A FRACTIOUS RELATIONSHIP

2

The ICC in Africa
The Fight against Impunity

Shamiso Mbizvo

I INTRODUCTION

From 15 June to 17 July 1998, representatives from 160 states and over 200 civil society organizations participated in five intense weeks of negotiations over the text of the treaty that would establish the world's first permanent international criminal court. One civil society activist who was present during those negotiations recalls waiting for the sun to rise on the final day of the Rome Conference. She stated,

> as the final hours of the Rome Diplomatic Conference approached, there were no more illusions, just an unbearable feeling of anxiety. Knowing that every outcome was possible, NGO representatives paced the halls, waiting for the release of the last and most important part of the International Criminal Court Statute. What would the final 'package' contain?[1]

That day, on 17 July 1998, 120 states adopted the Rome Statute, establishing the International Criminal Court (ICC). Why was that day so significant? The final text of the Rome Statute of the International Criminal Court is the culmination of almost a hundred years of hard work, unyielding determination and stubborn hope on the part of individuals from all over the world, from many different walks of life, who have all shared the vision of an independent, permanent International Criminal Court.[2] The ICC was established to intervene on behalf of the most vulnerable when their own governments have failed to hold their abusers accountable. The Court was set up to provide justice for victims of genocide, crimes against humanity and war crimes, when their pleas for accountability have fallen on deaf ears.

The Statute of the International Criminal Court entered into force on 1 July 2002. To date, 124 states are party to this comprehensive, global criminal justice system. By ratifying the Rome Statute, states commit themselves to using the rule of law to protect their own citizens from the most atrocious crimes – by investigating and punishing genocide, crimes against humanity or war crimes when committed in their territory.

The mandate of the Prosecutor of the International Criminal Court is to investigate and prosecute such crimes; crimes that shock the consciousness of humanity. Specifically, where the Court has jurisdiction, the Prosecutor's duty under the Rome Statute is:

(a) to investigate Rome Statute crimes, so as to unveil the facts and establish who is criminally responsible for these crimes,
(b) to apply the law independently, objectively and fairly, and in doing so,
(c) to contribute to the prevention of these crimes.[3]

The Rome Statute recognizes that there is an inextricable link between justice and sustainable peace; by combatting impunity for the most serious crimes, the Court can ultimately contribute to the prevention of those crimes. In the words of UN Secretary General, Mr Ban Ki Moon,

> ...the balance between peace and justice... [is] a false choice. In today's conflicts, civilians have become the chief victims. Women, children and the elderly are deliberately targeted. Armies or militias rape, maim, kill and devastate towns, villages, crops, cattle and water sources – all as a strategy of war. The more shocking the crime, the more effective it is as a weapon. Any victim would understandably yearn to stop such horrors, even at the cost of granting immunity to those who have wronged them. But this is a false peace. (...) [T]he time has passed when we might speak of peace versus justice, or think of them as somehow opposed to each other. ... We have no choice but to pursue them both, hand in hand. ... Now, we have the ICC. Permanent, increasingly powerful, casting a long shadow. There is no going back. In this new age of accountability, those who commit the worst of human crimes will be held responsible. Whether they are rank-and-file foot soldiers or military commanders; whether they are lowly civil servants following orders, or top political leaders, they will be held accountable.[4]

II AFRICANS AND THE ICC

The Rome Statute represents a vast international coalition that extends far beyond heads of state, and encompasses the citizens of each state that is party to the Statute. In other words, the Rome Statute of the ICC is a safety net for millions of people around the world. It serves and protects over 600 million Africans who belong within the Statute's regime. Under the Rome Statute, millions of Africans enjoy a guarantee that if their leaders use massive violence against them, they cannot do so with impunity; their leaders *can* be held accountable.

Africans, both leaders and activists, played a critical and leading role in advocating for the international criminal court, and in negotiations over the text of the Rome Statute. The paralysis of the international community during the Rwandan genocide, where over a million Africans were slaughtered, spurned many Africans to insist on and work to realize the vision of a permanent international court that could potentially deter such massive crimes.

In 1998, Abdou Diouf, then president of Senegal, facilitated key meetings in Dakar leading up to the Rome Conference. The Rome Conference was presided over by an African, Kofi Annan, then secretary-general of the United Nations (UN). During the negotiations over the Statute, Africans such as Médard Rwelamira, Phakiso Mochochoko and Sivu Maqungo played a crucial role. They shared the profound hope, expressed by South Africa's minister of justice at the Rome conference, that the establishment of the ICC 'would *ultimately* contribute to the attainment of international peace'.[5]

Fourteen African countries were among the group of 'like-minded states' that advocated the most passionately for the establishment of a strong and effective court. When the Rome Statute was finalized, forty-one African states at the Rome Conference voted for it.[6] In February 1999, Senegal became the first state to ratify the Rome Statute. Today, the largest regional constituency among ICC States Parties is Africa: thirty-four African states are States Parties to the Rome Statute.

Africans continue to play a pioneering role in implementing the Court's mandate. The current Prosecutor of the ICC, Madame Fatou Bensouda, is from The Gambia. The vice-president of the Court, Judge Joyce Aluoch, is from Kenya. The ICC's bench includes judges from Botswana, Nigeria and the Democratic Republic of the Congo (DRC). The President of the Assembly of States Parties to the Rome Statute is African. In sum, Africans have been at the forefront of advocating for, establishing and leading the Court.

Africans – activists and survivors of atrocious crimes – continue to exhort the Court to do more for the victims of mass crimes on the African continent. From the DRC, to Sudan, to the Central African Republic (CAR), to Nigeria, African citizens continue to demand *more engagement* by the ICC in Africa. For example, when the Prosecutor visited Kinshasa in March 2014, survivors of unspeakable sexual violence in the Eastern Congo appealed to her for more rather than less justice; they demanded more ICC intervention in the Democratic Republic of Congo. During her visit, 134 organizations who work in the DRC petitioned her to continue her investigations into mass crimes in the

DRC, to expand the scope of those investigations, to improve the quality of those investigations and to urgently charge *more* individuals for the horrific crimes that are being committed with impunity against Congolese civilians, particularly in the country's eastern provinces.

While the establishment of the ICC was a major milestone in our collective journey towards a more just world, that journey is by no means over. To quote from President Obama, the task now falls to this generation, our generation, and to future generations, 'to narrow the gap between the promise of our ideals and the reality of our time'.[7] While we aspire to have an International Criminal Court that has universal reach, we are still working towards fully realizing that goal.

While some African observers express discontent with the limits of the Court's jurisdictional reach, others critique how the Court decides who to prosecute, within the Court's jurisdictional realm. Inevitably, where the Court has jurisdiction to act, observers will look to the Court to dispense justice effectively, efficiently and consistently. While the Court's leadership consistently expresses its firm commitment to those ideals, notably, the Court's ability to deliver on these outcomes is contingent on effective and consistent cooperation from all States that have ratified the Rome Statute. The ICC was designed to rely on States to arrest and surrender suspects, to provide the Court's personnel with access to evidence, and to enforce the Court's judgements, *inter alia*.

Notwithstanding the challenges that arise from this structural reliance on the support of sovereign States, the Court's leadership, indeed, the Prosecutor has publicly and repeatedly underscored her commitment to continually enhancing the Office's practices and efficiency on the strength of lessons learned. In this vein, the Office of the Prosecutor (OTP) recently promulgated and distributed for comment a draft *Case Selection and Prioritization Policy Paper*. Following an extensive and open consultative process, this landmark paper articulates the Office's policy and practice on case selection and prioritization. By communicating the legal requirements, guiding principles and criteria that the OTP applies in order to determine which cases it will bring, this Policy Paper has reassured many observers that the OTPs' decision-making on case selection is governed by a clear, non-political process.

III WHAT THE COURT IS DOING OUTSIDE AFRICA

Many observers ask what the Court is doing for non-African victims of genocide, crimes against humanity and war crimes. Many sceptics have posed the question, 'Why is the ICC not investigating crimes in Syria, Burma, Nepal, Bahrain, China, Russia or Pakistan?' None of these countries are States Parties to the Rome Statute. The ICC would only have jurisdiction over international crimes in these particular countries if the UN Security Council, under Chapter VII of the UN Charter, were to refer one of these situations to the Prosecutor, or if the state concerned accepted the Court's jurisdiction.

The Prosecutor determines whether and when to initiate an investigation by conducting preliminary examinations, a process during which the Office comprehensively assesses information about alleged crimes on the basis of strict legal criteria laid out in the Rome Statute. These criteria are jurisdiction, admissibility and the interests of justice – and they apply irrespective of the manner in which the investigation is triggered.

With regard to jurisdiction, the Prosecutor assesses whether:

(a) the alleged crimes appear to constitute genocide, war crimes or crimes against humanity,
(b) the alleged crimes are committed on the territory of states that are party to the Rome Statute or by nationals of States Parties,
(c) the crimes were committed after the entry into force of the Rome Statute on 1 July 2002 (or, if the state ratified the Statute after July 2002, *after* the date of ratification).

With regard to the admissibility criterion, the Office has a duty *not* to proceed to investigate when there are genuine national investigations or prosecutions. This is the principle of complementarity.

Finally, in accordance with the Statute, the Prosecutor should not proceed with an investigation or prosecution if it is not in the 'interests of justice'.[8] It would be exceptional for the Prosecutor to decide that an investigation would not be in the interests of justice, or indeed the victims. The Prosecutor has repeatedly stressed that the 'interests of justice' is not to be confused with the interests of peace and security – the latter falls within the mandate of the UN Security Council.

So what is the Office of the Prosecutor doing for non-African constituents of the ICC? The Office is currently conducting eight preliminary examinations under the criteria described. In this context, the Office is carefully gathering and assessing information about alleged war crimes by UK nationals during the conflict in Iraq from 2003 to 2008. The OTP is gathering information to determine whether there is a reasonable basis to believe that crimes within the jurisdiction of the Court have been or are being committed in Ukraine, in the context of the 'Maidan events' and other developments in Ukraine since 20 February 2014. In Afghanistan, the Office has found that there is a reasonable basis to believe that war crimes and crimes against humanity were and continue to be committed in Afghanistan. That examination is ongoing. The OTP is conducting a preliminary examination into alleged crimes committed in the occupied Palestinian territory since 13 June 2014; the Office is analysing alleged crimes by all parties to establish whether crimes within the jurisdiction of the Court have been or are being committed.

The practice of the Office has shown that the mere initiation of such preliminary examinations can have a deterrent impact. For example, in Colombia the ICC is monitoring national prosecutions of crimes that fall within the Court's jurisdiction. There is a clear indication that the presence of the ICC is bolstering national investigations into the relevant crimes. In Columbia, prosecutors, judges, legislators and members of the Executive Branch have publicly acknowledged that the prospect of the ICC attaining jurisdiction was a key reason for them to implement the Justice and Peace Law and ensure that they will prosecute the chief perpetrators of the relevant crimes.

In Georgia, shortly after the Prosecutor confirmed that the Office had started the examination of the situation in Georgia, on 14 August 2008, the Office received information from the Georgian and the Russian governments that their respective General Prosecutor's Office had begun investigations into alleged violations committed during the armed conflict that broke out between the two countries in August 2008. Since then, the Office has requested and received a considerable volume of information about the ongoing investigations. On 27 October 2016, the ICC's Pre-Trial Chamber granted the Prosecutor's request for authorization to begin an investigation into the Situation in Georgia, regarding crimes allegedly committed in and around South Ossetia between 1 July 2008 and 10 October 2008.

IV WHAT THE ICC WILL CONTINUE TO DO IN AFRICA

In sum, the Court is busy outside of Africa; it can and will certainly continue to work outside of Africa. However, the question remains whether the ICC is somehow working against Africans. *Nothing could be further from reality*. The Court is working *with Africans* to guarantee the rights of Africans.

- The ICC investigated, prosecuted and convicted Thomas Lubanga, former president of the Union des Patriotes Congolais (UPC), for recruiting African children in the DRC.
- The ICC investigated, prosecuted and convicted Germain Katanga, former president of the *Front de Résistance Patriotique en Ituri* (FRPI), for brutal crimes that his group inflicted on African civilians in Ituri in 2003.
- When the Prosecutor visited the DRC, Congolese rights groups told the Prosecutor that seeing Bosco Ntaganda, a man who 'had become a symbol

of impunity in Congo', in hearings before the Court 'was a powerful signal' that could 'serve as a warning to other commanders of armed groups and forces in eastern Congo'.[9]

– The ICC successfully prosecuted Jean-Pierre Bemba, former presidential opposition candidate in the DRC, for his responsibility as a commander over a campaign of horrific sexual violence and unbridled pillage in the CAR.

– The ICC has indicated Joseph Kony and other leaders of the Lord's Resistance Army (LRA) for abducting and enslaving Ugandan children, and forcing them to kill.

– The Court is seeking to prosecute Omar al-Bashir for his alleged responsibility for the extermination of scores of Africans in Darfur.

– The Court is investigating attacks against Libyan civilians, ensuring that it is clear that such attacks can constitute crimes against humanity or even war crimes.

These are illustrations of what the ICC is doing in Africa. Perhaps, though, some may still be asking why the Court is in Africa? The Rome Statute says that the Court shall only step in when the domestic authorities do not pursue genuine accountability for these crimes. In all these cases, there were no such proceedings. When the legal criteria are met, the Office of the Prosecutor shall open investigations.

Notably, African leaders requested the Court to intervene in most of the Court's situations under investigation; President Museveni in Uganda referred the situation in Uganda to the Office of the Prosecutor. President Kabila referred the situation in the DRC to the Office of the Prosecutor. President Bozize referred the situation in CAR. In the Ivory Coast, both Presidents Gbagbo and Ouattara accepted the jurisdiction of the ICC. Benin and Tanzania voted in the UN Security Council to refer the Darfur situation to the Court. South Africa, Gabon and Nigeria voted in the UN Security Council to refer the Libya situation to the ICC. These decisions reflect the commitment of Africans to ensuring that these type of crimes do not go unpunished.

When discussing the role of the ICC in Africa, it is important that we not amplify critiques of the Court until they drown out the reality of what the Court *can* and is doing for the African continent. Ultimately, the Prosecutor will continue to do everything she can to bring justice to the scores of women and children who have been subjected to brutal and systematic sexual violence in the DRC. This Prosecutor will continue to demand accountability for ongoing crimes in Darfur. The Prosecutor of the ICC is working toward a more just world – where there are consequences for the most powerful individuals when they inflict atrocious crimes on the most vulnerable.

Notes

This chapter was adapted from an Office of the Prosecutor (OTP), keynote lecture given at the 'Africans and Hague Justice' conference, which took place in The Hague on 23 and 24 May 2014.

1. Jelena Pejić, 'The International Criminal Court Statute: An Appraisal of the Rome Package', *The International Lawyer* (2000) 34, 65.

2. Key markers on the road to the Rome Statue include: (1) the 8 August 1945 International Military Tribunal at Nuremberg, which prosecuted National Socialist leaders for aggression, genocide, crimes against humanity and war crimes; (2) the October 1946 Paris Congress that called for an international criminal code that would prohibit crimes against humanity; (3) the 9 December 1948 adoption of the Genocide Convention by the UN General Assembly and the request for the International Law Commission (ILC) to study the possibility of establishing an International Criminal Court; (4) the June 1989 initiative by Trinidad and Tobago that spurred the General Assembly to resurrect the proposal for the ILC to prepare a draft statute; (5) the 9 December 1994 presentation by the ILC to the General Assembly of a final draft statute on the ICC and the appointment of an ad hoc committee to work on setting up the court; (6) the 11 December 1995 resolution by the General Assembly establishing the *Preparatory Committee for the Establishment of the International Criminal Court*; (7) the 15 June–17 July 1998 Rome Diplomatic Conference, where 160 states and 250 NGOs, including the NGO Coalition for the International Criminal Court (CICC), negotiated the final text of the Rome Statute. The CICC comprised approximately 800 organizations and was led by a ten-member Steering Committee that included Amnesty International, Human Rights First, Human Rights Watch, the International Commission of Jurists and others.

3. This is articulated in the Preamble of the Rome Statute, which states that the Court is 'determined to put an end to impunity for the perpetrators of these crimes and thus to contribute to the prevention of such crimes'.

4. Secretary-General's address to ICC Review Conference, 1 June 2010, SG/SM/12930L/3158.

5. Rome Conference, Official Records, A/CONF.183/13 (Vol.2), 15 June–17 July 1998, p. 65 (emphasis added).

6. *Ibid*. Libya voted against the Rome Statute.

7. President Obama, 'A More Perfect Union', 18 March 2008 (Speech at the National Constitution Center in Philadelphia, Pennsylvania).

8. Article 53 of the Rome Statute.

9. As quoted from: '134 NGOs Call on ICC Prosecutor to Continue Investigations in Congo', *HRW*, 13 March 2014.

3

Africans and the ICC
Hypocrisy, Impunity, and Perversion

Makau W. Mutua

I INTRODUCTION

Contemporary discussions of the International Criminal Court (ICC) and
Africa are characterized by intellectual disagreement and political passion.
There is a rich diversity of perspectives, many of them open to contestation.
But the location and identity of the speaker, or author, are critical. So is the
place of history and the relationship between the post-colonial African state
and the struggle for human dignity. The subject is complicated by Africa's
tortured place in geopolitics. However, the pain of history – and its echo in
Africa – must not be used to sabotage the cry of victims for justice. There is no
doubt that a conversation about the legitimacy of the ICC in Africa in view of
the deeply emotional and historical issues raised by the African Union is
a matter that has preoccupied political elites, civil society, and intellectuals
on the continent, hence the title (and sub-title) of this chapter. Shamiso
Mbizvo of the Office of the Prosecutor engages the ICC's critics on this debate
in her speech published here (see Chapter 2). While I welcome the OTP's
response to its sceptics, I believe it should go further and acknowledge the
heavy focus on African perpetrators to the exclusion of others. In my view, the
ICC will not be able to blunt the charges of a racist agenda if it cannot produce
indictments of senior officials from continents other than Africa. It will not
suffice to promise investigations outside Africa. ICC Chief Prosecutor Fatou
Bensouda must aggressively pursue perpetrators without regard to station,
race, identity, and national origin for the ICC to be seen to do justice without
fear, favour, or prejudice.

The title of my chapter directly wades into this charged debate and recalls,
ironically, the charge that the "ICC is hunting Africans".[1] I want to make clear
that this is not hyperbole, but an actual statement made by the prime minist~

of Ethiopia – Hailemariam Desalegn – as chair of the African Union. Presumably, he was speaking for the African Union.[2] Desalegn's calculated use of the phrase "hunting Africans" is, needless to say, both evocative and deeply disturbing because it conjures up – indeed dredges up – the most unspeakable images and memories of the subordination of Africans by white Europeans and the West. How did the ICC, a court that was built to deal with those same unspeakable crimes, come to be accused of committing them? This is but one of many ironies inherent in this conversation.

That is why the subtext – perhaps the actual text – of this conversation is not possible without stipulating a few historical truths and narratives about international law and the Third World, and in this case Africa in particular. It is true that what one considers a historical truth might be contested, but those biases are unavoidable. History is clear that no other continent has suffered more trauma than Africa over the past 500 years. Much of that trauma has been inflicted on Africa by the North Atlantic communities – Europe and the United States. The Arab slave trade was equally damaging. The plunder and theft of Africa's resources for the benefit of the West cannot be gainsaid. It was thought independence from European colonialism would bring relief to a beleaguered continent. The cauldron of the Cold War and a scandalous international economic order combined to ravage the emergent African states.[3] Yet those who attack the ICC seem to suffer from historical amnesia and selective memory. Their arguments want to place all the blame for the trauma of Africa on the European West. Theirs is an apology for the sins of their fathers and a hypocritical pan-Africanism by ruling elites and their ideologues. They deliberately pervert history to hoodwink ordinary Africans and play on white guilt. I reject this false historical narrative and its sinister attempt to hijack the stories of genuine pan-Africanism and the pain of victims to maintain bankrupt African elites in power.

At a minimum, African post-independent rulers must share the blame for the failure of the continent to incubate democratic states. They could not even successfully implant the liberal constitution to achieve a credibly bare republican state. The elites chose to become kleptocrats bent on first consolidating their own personal power. They stifled dissent, sheathed themselves in corrupt ethnic cocoons, dismantled liberal constitutions, and buttressed the patrimonial state.[4] High corruption and crude patronage became a culture. The rule of law died. Judiciaries became proxies for executive repression. Legislatures were turned into executive rubber stamps. Infrastructures collapsed, societies fragmented, and religious, civil, and armed conflicts – many along ethnic lines – erupted and became intractable. A number of states either failed or collapsed completely. There is no doubt African elites had a lot of help from their Cold War allies in destroying their states. But it is revisionist history to invoke the spectre of Western domination and exploitation without taking responsibility for collaborationist African elites. Nor is the ICC an imposition on Africans by the West. There was a stampede in Africa to ratify the Rome Statute of the ICC. It was only after the Court indicted leading African kleptocrats, such as Uhuru Kenyatta of Kenya and Omar al-Bashir of Sudan, that the AU raised the bogeyman of racism to discredit the Court. This chapter takes issue with this perverted narrative of the ICC and the history of African marginalization by the West. Repressive African leaders grouped in the AU – a club of dictators – have no moral standing to attack the ICC, an institution built through a participatory global consensus to combat impunity and bring justice which elites deny victims at home.

II HISTORICAL TRUTHS ABOUT INTERNATIONAL LAW

A paradox of Africa's problems with international law is that the continent itself – by which it is meant the modern states that comprise it – is largely a creation of international law. International law treated Africa as tabula rasa,[5] a blank slate on which Europe could scribble its forms of logic, hierarchies, and forms of social organization. That is to say that Africa's identity in the era of modernity has largely been shaped by its encounter with the West, the normative home of international law.[6] In that sense, Africa is an "outsider" to international law[7] – it is, to wit, one of the originally subordinated continents in which international law was used as a means of ordering and organizing the exploitation of the globe for the benefit of the North Atlantic communities.[8] So, at the outset, scholars need to acknowledge a number of basic and unarguable historical facts.

Modern African states, themselves illegitimate creations of colonialism,[9] were frozen in place by the international legal principle of *uti possidetis*,[10] even when they were patently dysfunctional. The facts are the following: first, that modern international law was inimical to Africa's interests;[11] second, that modern international law was used to cannibalize Africa's resources and people;[12] third, that modern international law was used to justify the "management" of Africa as indeed all of the Third World for the hegemonic interests of North Atlantic states.[13] It is not an overreach to say that international law was used to stamp Africa and Africans with sub-humanity so that they and their resources could be exploited for the benefit of others.

There really is no other way to understand the three historical traumas that define modern Africa. First, the trauma of slavery, which international law recognized, and which deeply depopulated the continent while building

Europe and the Americas;[14] second, the trauma of colonialism, which international law structured, and some say invented;[15] and third, the trauma of the
Cold War, in which Africa was plundered by both the East and the West and
used as a pawn in proxy wars of supremacy.[16] Africa is now in a fourth phase,
with the legacies of the first three traumas still exerting their influence, but in
the context of a resurgent Africa that is demanding more respect and equity in
global affairs.[17] It is because of these traumas that Africa has had an ambivalent – if not at times completely hostile – relationship with international law
and international institutions, including the International Criminal Court.[18]
But African views of international law are not monolithic, as these sketches of
the typologies of African views to international law demonstrate. However,
a distinction must be made between the views of the states, and those of the
African peoples, for the two are rarely congruent.

III TYPOLOGIES OF AFRICAN VIEWS ON INTERNATIONAL LAW

One way to understand and characterize African views of international law is
not only by segmenting them by the constituency of scholars, but particularly
by historical period. First, the early African international law scholarship dealt
with the colonial moment and whether, and how, Africa could enter the
community of nations and leverage existing regimes, or transform them to
cater to its own interests. Here, at the dawn of the Independence Decade,
there was much hope and optimism in Africa and its potential.[19] Mostly newly
minted African states sought entry into the world community on an equal
footing – exemplified most poignantly by membership in the United
Nations.[20] African scholars held a dichotomous view on whether or how the
continent could leverage its status of juridical equality with other states.[21]
Many were clearly accomodationist[22] – seeking to understand the system
and effectively participating in it without necessarily questioning its basic
norms and whether they were biased against Africa. This group sought inclusion without being critical of the normative edifice of international law – many
African states adopted this view early on.

Second, another group of African scholars was highly critical of the international legal regime, and questioned its ability for fairness – scholars like
Professor Issa Shivji of Tanzania or jurists like Mohamed Bedjaoui of the
International Court of Justice come to mind.[23] But as African states experienced structural and normative barriers to entry into the global system,[24] the
tone of the continent's scholars turned increasingly critical of international
law. These problems were exacerbated by regime instability and state decay
through coups usually backed by the West or East[25] and economic stagnation

in spite of enormous natural resources. African states and elites could not cohere into nation-states because of economic inequities, ethnic divisions, and elite dissensus. In other words, the optimism of the early independence period evaporated sooner than one might have expected, in part due to the inability of the African post-colonial state, itself an artificial creature, to cohere into a nation amidst a hostile international system. These protest scholars, many of them with a leftist ideological hue, spawned a new generation of critical thinkers. That is why they – and African states – turned into dialogues focused on South–South Cooperation and the New International Economic Order.[26] But political efforts for a more equitable international order were blunted by the West and the re-assertion of the primacy of the Bretton Woods institutions in African states through structural adjustment programs and other neo-conservative and neo-liberal markets measures.

Third, in the late 1970s to the 1990s, African international legal scholars – many of them with intellectual roots on the political left – increasingly turned to the equal protection language of the human rights project. This was partly a response to the collapse of the Soviet and Socialist models as alternatives. Some, like Justice Keba Mbaye of the International Court of Justice, tried to imbue human rights with an African fingerprint.[27] Many sought to use human rights as a language to disrupt neo-colonial abusive regimes still in cahoots with international capital and their Western sponsors. Their focus was – and has been – to rewrite the internal charters of African states and African regional bodies.[28] The idea was to reconstitute the fabric of the state by deploying home-grown liberal norms and through African institutions. These scholars now focus on questions of regional economic integration, technology innovation, gender equality, international criminal law (ICC, Rwanda, Sierra Leone), and local intellectual entrepreneurship.[29] It is this school of thought that has been responsible for the democratic renaissance in Africa over the last two decades. But they have not reaped the benefits of their aspirations. These progressive elites helped overthrow the corrupt and dictatorial one-party states, only to see power captured by established political elites from the old order.[30] The bottom line is that most states in Africa have adopted the forms and processes of democratic government, but the practices of governance are either still autocratic in culture, or subject to manipulation by vested political elites. The point is that various African state actors today pursue duplicitous and hypocritical views of international law. Some speak the language of human rights and democracy when it is convenient, but use hypocritical arguments when they need to protect the interests of illegal cabals that control the states. For example, Kenyatta, whose case for crimes against humanity at the ICC was suspended in 2014 for lack of sufficient evidence amid claims of witness tampering, often attacked the ICC as a colonial court even as he shielded himself and other suspects of heinous crimes from justice.[31] In what is interpreted as a culture of impunity, Kenya refused to prosecute other suspects, claiming lack of evidence.[32] In other acts of subterfuge by African leaders, the AU have attempted to establish an African Court of Justice and Human Rights to try heinous offenders to render the ICC unnecessary.[33] These are attempts to sabotage the ICC by establishing a toothless body. One might call African leaders pragmatic – they will use international law where and when it benefits elites and even the states, but clearly oppose it where it seeks to curb the power and authority of ruling political elites.

IV THE RATIONALE OF THE ICC

The International Criminal Court was created to deal with impunity by bringing to account those who commit the most heinous crimes – war crimes, crimes against humanity, genocide,[34] and, in 2017, crimes of aggression.[35] The creation of the court culminated a decades-old struggle to create a permanent international criminal tribunal.[36] It is a court of last resort – a complementary court – which acts only when states are unable, or unwilling, to prosecute offenders.[37] To date, the Rome Statute has been ratified by 123 states, and this includes all of South America, most of Europe, most of Oceania, and thirty-four African states – or two-thirds of all African countries.[38] Three states – the United States, Israel, and Sudan – unsigned the Rome Statute without ratifying it.[39] Russia has signed, but not ratified the Rome Statute.[40] Forty-one states, including India and China, are not signatories and are openly critical of the Court.[41] The United States was deeply hostile to the ICC under George W. Bush,[42] but has reversed course and is seen as helpful to the ICC's work under President Barack Obama.[43]

V AFRICA AND THE ICC

Many African states and NGOs were early and enthusiastic supporters of the ICC.[44] In fact, contrary to the traditional script of international law in which Africa is seen as an afterthought, and a consumer of ideas, as opposed to a producer of thought, the continent was a central player in the birth of the ICC.[45] Africa's enthusiasm about the ICC was a result of two factors: first, the large and activist civil society, mostly in human rights, that has emerged since the early 1990s[46] as the wave of democratization swept the continent; second, the political inclination of most African states emerging out of dictatorship to embrace calls to end impunity.[47] These two factors combined to create a fertile ground for the legitimacy of the ICC in Africa. Emerging democracies in Africa during the wave of the so-called Second Liberation were keen to signal their repudiation of the culture of impunity cultivated by the preceding one-party states and military dictatorships. That was partly the case because many post–Cold War regimes included among their leaders prominent civil society actors and pro-democracy advocates. In fact, the African bloc of thirty-four States Parties constitutes the largest contingent at the ICC.[48]

VI THE ICC'S INVESTIGATIONS AND CASES

To date, the ICC has opened twenty-one cases in nine "situations" or countries, all of which have been in Africa (DRC, Kenya, Libya, Sudan, CAR, Mali, Cote d'Ivoire, and Uganda).[49] Of these nine, five were self-referrals by the states concerned (Uganda, DRC, CAR, Mali, and again the CAR). Two cases (Libya and Sudan) were referred to the Court by the UN Security Council. Two others (Kenya and Cote d'Ivoire) were started by the Prosecutor *proprio motu*, or on his own initiative. For its part, Kenya had agreed pursuant to a peace accord brokered by former UN Secretary-General Kofi Annan to end the 2007–2008 near-genocidal violence that Kofi Annan would hand over an envelope containing the names of suspects from a government commission of inquiry to the ICC for investigation and prosecution if Kenya failed or was unwilling to prosecute them. Kenya refused to establish a local tribunal, thereby triggering the ICC's investigation.[50] So, in a sense Kenya's case could be viewed as a quasi-self-referral. The case of Cote d'Ivoire, involving the deposed President Laurent Gbagbo and his wife, was urged on the ICC by the African Union.[51]

VII CONFLICT BETWEEN THE AFRICAN UNION AND THE ICC

The first signs of conflict between the African Union and the ICC occurred when the ICC indicted and charged President Omar al-Bashir of Sudan and several high-ranking officials for the pillage of Darfur.[52] Al-Bashir mobilized support from the African Union and some Arab states,[53] although the support he received was quite tepid – in fact, some African states including Botswana, South Africa, Malawi, and Uganda threatened to arrest him and hand him over to the ICC should he set foot on their soil.[54] Even among the AU heads of state, who jealously protect their own from justice and are defined by the impunity with which they act, al-Bashir was difficult to openly protect because of the Darfur situation.

The second instance of conflict occurred when the UN Security acted with stunning speed to refer Muamar Gaddafi and his associates to the ICC and the Court acted immediately to take up the case.[55] Africa was incensed over the Libyan situation because it was largely viewed as an act of hegemonic powers using the Court to get rid of an old enemy by disregarding the pleas of the AU to mediate the conflict.[56] Many African states felt that the ICC was being used to fight the wars of the West against an African leader. The resolution to refer Libya to the ICC was unanimously adopted with the African states sitting as Security Council (SC) members (South Africa, Nigeria, and Gabon).[57] The African states wanted the SC to send a clear message to Libya to end the carnage.

Third, it was in this climate that the Court proceeded to open the trials of Uhuru Kenyatta and William Ruto,[58] who had mobilized their supporters to elect them in March 2013 as president and deputy president knowing that they were ICC indictees.[59] Kenya is an influential regional power in Africa, a strategic partner to the West on the war against terrorism, and a gateway to stability and humanitarian missions in East Africa. It has a sophisticated political elite and large business and middle classes. Kenyatta has exploited all of these diplomatic, social, economic, and political assets in a bid to get the cases dropped altogether, or deferred by the UN Security Council (under Article 16 of the Statute).[60] The UN Security Council rightly rejected a joint AU/Kenya request for a deferral late 2013.[61] However, on 5 December 2014, ICC Prosecutor Fatou Bensouda withdrew the charges against Kenyatta, citing a lack of sufficient evidence because of the failure of the Kenyan state to cooperate with the Court by providing it with information required by the prosecution.[62] On 20 January 2015, Bensouda released the entire sixty-nine-page pre-trial brief on Kenyatta.[63] The document, which she would have used against Kenyatta had the case gone to trial, is an explosive and damning account of charges against Kenyatta and his associates. It details how Kenyatta planned and financed the Mungiki, a deadly Kikuyu tribal militia, to commit crimes against humanity. Perhaps most chillingly, the legal brief documents specific cases of the murder, bribery, and intimidation of scores of witnesses. It leaves little to the imagination. The logical conclusion from the brief is that Kenyatta had to kill the witnesses, in what the prosecution termed a "clean up" operation to avoid a conviction.

But even before his case was withdrawn, though not terminated, Kenyatta had succeeded where al-Bashir failed – he managed to unite the entire AU in endorsing a call for a deferral, or complete stoppage of the cases.[64] The AU voted in October 2013 that Kenyatta should not show up for his trial at The Hague in a "colonial white man's court"[65] that is a "tool of Western powers".[66] Mr. Kenyatta himself, in an address to the AU, said this: "The ICC has become a farcical pantomime, a travesty that adds insult to the injury of victims. It stopped being the home of justice the day it became the toy of declining imperial powers".[67] He asked the AU leaders gathered to be wary of "persistent machinations by the West".[68]

The ICC has been brought under tremendous pressure by the AU, and even some of the UN Security Council permanent members to "show flexibility"[69] – perhaps allowing the indictees to skip most Court sessions, or trying them through a video link. The provision of "trial by Skype" – as mocked by critics – showed how beleaguered the ICC was.[70] Kenya and the AU went further and pushed for amendments to the Statute to exempt sitting heads of state from the court's jurisdiction,[71] which would have stricken a blow against the object and purpose of the treaty. Fortunately, this attempt at neutering the court failed. But at the Twelfth Session of the Assembly of States Parties to the Rome Statute of the International Criminal Court (ASP), which concluded on 28 November 2013, the ASP adopted several new rules and amendments to its Rules of Procedure and Evidence.[72] The core of the amendments were the use of video technology, excusal from presence at trial, and excusal from presence at trial due to extraordinary public duties.[73] These amendments deeply politicized the ICC and left no doubt that it is responsive to political pressure and can be bent to the will of powerful leaders, even if they are indictees. It is a blow against the principle of equality before the law and a terrible indictment of the commitment of the Assembly of States to fight impunity. Even so, a deferral would have most likely posed an existential threat to the Court.

VIII CONCLUSION

It is undeniable that the ICC faces a challenge to its legitimacy if all its cases continue to be African – the appearance of selective, race-based justice will be difficult to avoid if the ICC does not vigorously pursue egregious offenders elsewhere. To her credit, Bensouda has opened preliminary investigations into several situations outside Africa – Palestine, Syria, Afghanistan, Colombia, Ukraine, Honduras, and Iraq. Time will tell whether these investigations will mature into full-fledged cases. But while the charge of selectivity is persuasive, it does not vitiate the need to pursue African heads of state who have been indicted – the failure to prosecute *all* of the suspects does not mean that *some* of the suspects should not be prosecuted. This is especially true because the AU itself seeks to do the same thing that it is accusing the ICC of doing – it does not mind selectively exempting certain African heads of state from its grip, nor does it oppose the ICC trying ordinary Africans. The AU's concern is only for heads of state. In fact, the Kenya government and the AU did not seek a deferral for the case facing the third accused Kenyan – journalist Joshua Sang.[74] Most tellingly – and underscoring the hypocrisy of the AU and some of its leaders, such as Yoweri Museveni of Uganda who has called on Africa to pull out of the ICC en masse – he and the AU agreed to and did hand over Dominic Ongwen of Uganda's Lord's Resistance Army to the ICC for trial.[75] This conduct is both duplicitous and hypocritical. The AU viciously attacks the ICC as an evil imperialist instrumentality when it targets ruling elites, such as Kenyatta, but becomes a legitimate court to which the AU hands over rebels, such as Ongwen, for trial. There is no principle at stake here except a protection racket among African rulers within the AU.

The AU is not always on the same page as ordinary Africans. To drive this point home, the leading opinion pollster in Kenya showed in 2013 that 67% of all Kenyans wanted Kenyatta and Ruto be tried at The Hague.[76] This divergence is startling and worthy of note. African states clearly feel bitter about the ICC, but the African publics hold a different view. The AU's position is hypocritical and only intended to shield from justice the wealthy and the powerful by demagoguing powerful and legitimate arguments about the inequity of international law. Africans have legitimate claims against international law, but attacking the ICC through race baiting because it seeks to hold accountable African heads of state is illegitimate. Kenyatta and his AU counterparts are the wrong Africans to charge the ICC and international law with targeting Africans. How can leaders whose hands are bloody – if we are to believe the ICC charges against Kenyatta, al-Bashir, Ruto, and other African leaders – manipulate legitimate African grievances against international law to defeat justice? These leaders know that there is no one else to whom they will answer if the ICC does not do its job. Their attacks on the ICC are nothing short of an affirmation of impunity with which they govern. It is important for the ICC to end the perception of selectivity and race-based prosecutions. But those indicted should *not* find cover and succour in race-based arguments.

Notes

1. 'African Union Accuses ICC of "Hunting" Africans', *BBC News*, 27 May 2013.
2. *Ibid.*
3. Mohammed Bedjaoui, *Towards a New International Economic Order* (New York: Holmes and Meijer Publishers, 1979).

4. See, for example, Makau W. Mutua, 'Kenya's Quest for Democracy: Taming Leviathan' in John W. Harbeson and Donald Rothchild (eds.), *Africa in World Politics: Reforming Political Order*, 4th edn (Colorado: Westview, 2008).

5. Tiyanjana Maluwa, *International Law in Post-Colonial Africa* (Leiden: Brill-Nijhoff Publishers, 1999), p. 69.

6. Antony Anghie, 'Africa, Sovereignty and International Law', *Think Africa Press*, 2 November 2012.

7. Makau W. Mutua, 'Critical Race Theory and International Law: The View of an Insider-Outsider' (2000) 45 *Villanova Law Review* 841.

8. *Ibid.*, at 846.

9. See generally Pierre Englebert, 'Pre-Colonial Institutions, Post-Colonial States, and Economic Development in Tropical Africa' (2000) 53 *Political Research Quarterly* 7, 13.

10. See Makau W. Mutua, 'Putting Humpty Dumpty Back Together Again: The Dilemmas of the Post-Colonial African State' (1995) 21 *Brooklyn Journal of International Law* 505, n.1. See generally 'Nigeria: Bakasi and the uti possidetis Principle', *Daily Trust*, 2 July 2012.

11. Walter Rodney, *How Europe Underdeveloped Africa* (Oxford: Fahamu Books, 1972).

12. Ali Mazrui, *The Africans: A Triple Heritage* (New York: Little, Brown, 1986).

13. *Ibid.*

14. Basil Davidson, *Africa in History* (New York: Simon & Schuster, 1991).

15. *Ibid.*

16. Ira W. Zartman (ed.), *Collapsed States: The Disintegration and Restoration of Legitimate Authority* (London: Lynne Rienner Publishers, 1995).

17. David Leonhardt, 'Africa's Economy Is Rising. Now What Happens to Its Food?', *New York Times*, 22 January 2015.

18. William Eye and Beth Goldberg, 'A Critique of the Evolving US-ICC Relationship', *Humanity in Action*, 2012.

19. Mutua, 'Critical Race Theory and International Law'.

20. See UN Website, 'Growth in United Nations membership, 1945-Present' and 'Africa'.

21. See e.g. Nic J. Rhoodie, *Conflict Resolution in South-Africa: The Quest for Accomadationist Policies in a Plural Society* (Pretoria: Institute for Plural Studies, University of Pretoria, 1978).

22. Taslim O. Elias, *Africa and the Development of International Law* (Leiden: Martinus Nijhoff Publishers, 1988).

23. Issa G. Shivji, *The Concept of Human Rights in Africa* (Dakar: Codesria, 1989).

24. Bedjaoui, *Towards a New International Economic Order*.
25. Elizabeth Schmidt, *Foreign Intervention in Africa: From the Cold War to the War on Terror* (Cambridge: Cambridge University Press, 2013).
26. Ralph I. Onwuka, *The Future of Africa and the New International Economic Order* (London: Palgrave Macmillan, 1986).
27. See generally President Higgins, 'Tribute to the Memory of Judge Kéba Mbaye' (International Court of Justice, 4 June 2007).
28. See generally Council on Foreign Relations, 'The Global Human Rights Regime' (Issue Brief, 19 June 2013), p. 19.
29. See generally Mutua, 'Critical Race Theory and International Law'.
30. *Ibid.*
31. Emeka Mayaka-Gekara and Dave Opiyo, 'President Kenyatta's Stinging Attack on ICC and Europe', *Daily Nation*, 12 October 2013.
32. Ouma Wanzala, 'State Frustrated by PEV Cases', *Daily Nation*, 12 February 2014.
33. Jane Goin, 'Pan African Movement Roots for African Court of Justice', *Capital News*, 10 August 2015.
34. The Registry, 'Understanding the International Criminal Court', ICC-PIDS-BK-05-003/13.
35. *Ibid.*
36. Council on Foreign Relations, 'The Global Human Rights Regime'.
37. *Ibid.*
38. Coalition for the International Criminal Court, 'Africa (Sub-Saharan)', *ICC Now*.
39. Andrew Morgan, 'Non-Signatory Countries', *Jurist*, 20 July 2013.
40. Eye and Goldberg, 'A Critique of the Evolving US-ICC Relationship'.
41. *Ibid.*
42. *Ibid.*
43. *Ibid.*
44. Arlette Afagbegee, 'The International Criminal Court's Relationship with Africa: An Unfair Bias?', *Pambazuka News*, 4 June 2014.
45. *Ibid.*
46. Paul Gready (ed.), *Fighting for Human Rights* (London: Routledge, 2004), p. 1.
47. Coalition for the ICC, 'Africa (Sub-Saharan)'.
48. *Ibid.*
49. See the ICC website, 'Situations and Cases', www.icc-cpi.int/pages/situations.aspx#. Stephen A. Lamony, 'Is the International Criminal Court really picking on Africa?', *African Arguments*, 16 April 2013.
50. *Ibid.*
51. *Ibid.*

52. Coalition for the ICC, 'Africa (Sub-Saharan)'.

53. *Ibid.*

54. 'ICC Not for Africans – Say New Prosecutor', *Face of Malawi*, 25 May 2012.

55. UN, 'In Swift, Decisive Action, Security Council Imposes Tough Measures on Libyan Regime, Adopting Resolution 1970 in Wake of Crackdown on Protesters', SC/10187/Rev.1, 26 February 2011.

56. Afagbegee, 'The International Criminal Court's Relationship with Africa'.

57. United Nations, 'In Swift, Decisive Action, Security Council Imposes Tough Measures'.

58. Bernard Momanyi and Simon Jennings, 'Kenya Seeks Delay to ICC Trials', Institute for War & Peace Reporting, 17 October 2013.

59. *Ibid.*

60. *Ibid.*

61. *Ibid.*

62. OTP, 'Statement of the Prosecutor of the International Criminal Court, Fatou Bensouda, on the Withdrawal of Charges against Mr. Uhuru Muigai Kenyatta', 5 December 2014.

63. OTP, 'Public Redacted Version of "Second Updated Prosecution Pre-Trial Brief"', 26 August 2013, ICC-01/09-02/11-796-Conf-AnxA.

64. Javier Blas, 'AU to Call for Suspension of ICC Cases while Leaders Are in Power', *Financial Times*, 12 October 2013.

65. Makau W. Mutua, 'Why Matsanga Is a Liability to Uhuru and Ruto at the ICC', *Standard Digital*, 17 November 2013.

66. Pascal Fletcher and Edmund Blair, 'Insight: Kenya Cases Stir African Backlash against ICC', *Reuters*, 16 September 2013; Mark Doyle, 'African Union Urges ICC to Defer Uhuru Kenyatta Case', *BBC News Africa*, 12 October 2013.

67. Walter Menya, 'International Criminal Court Critique Haunts Uhuru', *Daily Nation*, 5 April 2014.

68. *Ibid.*

69. 'International Court Chiefs Brief UN Assembly on Progress, Challenges', *UN News Centre*, 31 October 2013.

70. 'Uhuru Kenyatta Insists He Can Run Government from The Hague', *Kenya Today*, 24 January 2013; James Mbaka, 'Kenya -ICC: Ruto Seeks Exemption from Attendance', *Africa: News and Analysis*, 13 January 2014.

71. Coalition for the ICC, 'Africa (Sub-Saharan)'.

72. ASP, Resolution ICC-ASP/12/Res.7, 27 November 2013.

73. *Ibid.*

74. Coalition for the ICC, 'Africa (Sub-Saharan)'.

75. OTP, 'Statement of the Prosecutor of the International Criminal Court, Fatou Bensouda, following the Surrender and Transfer of Top LRA Commander Dominic Ongwen', 21 January 2015.

76. '67 per cent Want Uhuru to Attend ICC Trials – Poll', *Star*, 14 November 2013; Musa Haron, 'Kenyans Want Kenyatta to Attend ICC Trial', *Safari Africa*, 14 November 2013.

4

The ICC's Africa Problem
A *Spotlight on the Politics and Limits of International Criminal Justice*

Solomon A. Dersso

I INTRODUCTION

While the ICC has been operational for a relatively short period of time, the issues it has faced in its relationship with Africa have brought the Court to an important crossroad. Despite attracting its largest regional membership from Africa, the ICC's current role in Africa is fiercely contested. If this is to be reversed and the ICC is made to be a significant part of the fight against impunity and for Africa's quest for justice and sustainable peace, it is imperative to engage these issues directly. Despite the apparent polarization on the subject, the need for robust debate and dialogue has to be recognized. The challenges facing the ICC are not limited to the struggle to make it achieve universal reach in its membership, as highlighted by Shamiso Mbizvo's chapter in this book. As it will be shown below, the narrow and legalistic prism that animates Mbizvo's chapter for defending ICC's record is utterly inadequate.

The central contention here is that in societies facing major peace and security challenges, for international criminal justice processes to be effective and successful, they should be designed as part of a comprehensive framework. This framework should address the structural issues that produced mass atrocities in the first place. It is only such formulation of the work of the ICC as part of a comprehensive process that best engages both the peace-versus-justice tension and the limits of prosecutorial justice, a form of justice that occupies a central place under the ICC system. Equally important is the need for sensitivity to the history of Africa's troubled relationship with international law and how the impact of the power structure of the international system on the ICC shapes how the ICC is perceived in Africa.

Such a framing of the ICC's Africa problem emphasizes the need to transcend 'the misbegotten duel between supposed imperialists and alleged impunity apologists' and engage the various issues (creating the conditions or the excuses) souring the relationship between the ICC and Africa.[1] Convinced that this is a question that merits our serious consideration in the effort for overcoming what has become the ICC's troubled engagement in Africa, I draw attention to the major conditions shaping the current state of Africa's relationship to the ICC. Before outlining these major issues, however, it is necessary to highlight the significance of the ICC's relationship with Africa, and therefore it is this point that we immediately turn our attention to.

II ICC'S AFRICA PROBLEM

Africa played a key role in the years preceding the Rome conference where the Rome Statute of the ICC was adopted. It is well documented that African states were active during the negotiations of the Rome Statute and lent critical support for its adoption and eventual entry into force. Not only individual states but also regional organizations including the Organization of African Unity (OAU), predecessor of the African Union (AU) and the African Commission on Human and Peoples' Rights, supported the establishment of the ICC. One of the manifestations of this support is the sheer number of African States Parties to the Rome Statute. African states account for about one-third of the membership of the ICC: of the 122 States Parties to the Rome Statute, thirty-four are African states. With this number representing about two-thirds of the number of countries on the continent, African States Parties represent the single largest regional bloc in the membership of the ICC.

This enthusiastic African embrace of the ICC was in no insignificant part premised on the belief that the ICC would reinforce the efforts of the continent to deal with both violent conflicts and the occurrence of mass atrocities. At the time of the Rome Statute negotiations, Tyanjana Maluwa, the legal counsel of the OAU, stated that Africa had a special interest in the establishment of the ICC because its people had for centuries endured human rights atrocities.[2]

In the years after the ICC became operational in 2003, Africa's enthusiastic support for and embrace of the ICC started to dissipate. Since 2008, African states have expressed increasing displeasure and even outright opposition to certain elements of the ICC processes on the continent. In late 2013, the tension between Africa and the ICC reached a new height when, frustrated by what they called ICC's disregard of Africa's views and concerns, AU Member

States convened an extraordinary summit focusing on Africa's relationship with the ICC and entertained withdrawal from the ICC.[3]

All of the situations and cases that the ICC is currently investigating or prosecuting are from the African continent. To date, the ICC's Prosecutor has opened cases in eight situations. These are Uganda, the Democratic Republic of Congo (DRC), Sudan, the Central African Republic (CAR), Kenya, Libya, Cote d'Ivoire and Mali.[4] While four situations, namely Uganda, DRC, CAR and Mali, were opened on the basis of the 'self-referral' procedure, two situations (Sudan and Libya) were a result of a UNSC referral and the remaining two (Kenya and Cote d'Ivoire) were a product of the Prosecutor's own initiative. The thirty-six people indicted by the Court to date have all been African. Of the eight situations, twenty-one cases have now been brought before the Court for prosecution. As Charles Jalloh noted, regrettably enough 'African states are likely to be the frequent users, or "repeat customers", for the Court because of a relatively higher prevalence of conflicts and serious human rights violations and a general lack of credible legal systems to address them'.[5]

Despite the ICC's particular association with Africa and perhaps partly because of that, the ICC today faces its fiercest opposition from Africa. Yet, given that African States Parties represent the single largest regional bloc in the ASP, opposition from African states serves to undermine the ICC's efforts to nurture its global legitimacy and standing. In a context where major national state powers have opted to stay outside of the ICC,[6] the rising discontent that African states have been expressing since 2008 presents a serious challenge to the ICC.

Apart from the trouble that the opposition from African states poses to the legitimacy of the ICC, it can also undermine its current work and future. As I argued elsewhere, the 'lack of confidence African member states are expressing may lead to strong reluctance on the part African member states to cooperate with the ICC.'[7] Indeed, this view was borne out by events when, following AU's July 2009 decision on non-cooperation with ICC, a number of countries including Malawi, Djibouti, Chad and Kenya refused to enforce the arrest warrant of the ICC against Sudanese President Omar al-Bashir. Most recently, South Africa became the latest ICC member state that hosted President al-Bashir without executing the arrest warrant. Unable to proceed with the case, ICC Chief Prosecutor Fatou Bensouda announced on 12 December 2014 that she has decided to discontinue investigations concerning the cases from the Darfur situation.[8]

The deepening opposition from Africa in the context of the ICC's African focus also threatens its future. Although it did not eventually materialize, the call in late 2013 by African states for mass withdrawal from the Rome Statute illustrated that this threat was not hypothetical.[9] Notably, for the very first time in the history of the international relations, countries outside of the traditional power centre of the international legal order threatened the very survival of an international institution embodying a significant component of international law, namely international criminal law.

Should Africa's displeasure with the ICC worsen and any number of African states decide to withdraw from the Rome Statute, 'the Court faces a bleak prospect of having no cases to adjudicate'.[10] In the light of the self-exclusion of other parts of the world where similar problems of conflicts and violence take place, any retreat by African states from the ICC may precipitate it to close shop altogether. African states expressing concerns about the ICC not only undermines the role that the ICC stands to play in Africa, but it also negatively affects the prospects of expanding its member-ship and reach to states in other parts of the world – states that are not yet parties to the Rome Statute. In this context, the announcement by the government of South Africa in June 2015 that it will consider its participa-tion in the ICC[11] in the context of the legal and political debacle over its decision to give precedence to its commitments to the AU over the execution of the ICC's arrest warrant against al-Bashir should be a cause for serious concern for the ICC.

III CONDITIONS SHAPING THE CURRENT STATE OF AFRICA'S RELATIONSHIP WITH THE ICC

Since the ICC has become operational, it has operated in isolation from national contexts and other important efforts necessary for peace, justice and reconciliation. The resultant challenges of integration and synergy thus pre-sent a major issue to the ICC's operations in Africa. These challenges relate to three sets of issues. The first is the dilemma of working out the relationship between the demands of peace and of justice. This concerns both the timing of the launching of prosecution proceedings against alleged perpetrators and whether such a process is initiated with due regard to and as part of the overall effort to achieve a new dispensation. The second and related issue is a concern about national policy space for articulating transitional justice processes. The last item pertains to the limits of prosecutorial justice.

A *Peace versus Justice*

The constraints on justice, reconciliation and healing, in the midst of a war and a political stand-off between the Government and the Armed Movements, is self-evident. The importance of restoring peace and order was therefore reiterated time and again in the Panel's hearings throughout Darfur.[12]

One of the major issues at the centre of Africa's opposition to some of the ICC's decisions is the pursuit for prosecutorial justice within a framework that might jeopardize efforts for the achievement of sustainable peace. This was the major factor when the AU first expressed its opposition to the ICC's arrest warrant against Sudanese president al-Bashir. In the communiqué that the Peace and Security Council adopted soon after the ICC Prosecutor's application for an arrest warrant, it expressed 'its strong conviction that the search for justice should be pursued in a way that does not impede or jeopardize efforts aimed at promoting lasting peace'.[13] In a number of similarly formulated decisions adopted subsequently, while reiterating its commitment to the fight against impunity, the AU strongly contended that in the light of the 'delicate nature' of the processes underway for making peace in Darfur, prosecution could result in further destabilization and hence may not be in the interest of justice or the victims.

At the heart of this strong view is whether in the context of an ongoing war in Sudan (or anywhere else) the issue of justice (by prosecuting the country's president) can be pursued simultaneously with the efforts for ending the war and achieving peace and reconciliation. The AU seems to hold the view that in a situation of an ongoing war, at the very least peace and justice must be sequenced in such a way that priority is accorded to ending war and achieving peace. In 2009, the then chairperson of the AU Assembly, Tanzania's president Jakaya Kikwete, thus argued 'what is critical, what is the priority is peace. That is number one.'[14]

While the motivation of the AU and its implications for the fight against impunity are legitimate concerns, the AU's point that initiating a prosecution while efforts for making peace are underway can have a disastrous outcome cannot be written off as undeserving of serious consideration. It is on this account that Comfort Ero noted at the time that 'one cannot dismiss the AU's concern that the execution of an arrest warrant without a carefully managed transition could lead to further instability in Sudan and its nine neighbouring countries'.[15] The widely hailed AU High Level Panel on Darfur Report as quoted at the beginning of this sub-section established that for affected communities the most urgent need was restoration of peace and security. Indeed, this issue is not limited to the Darfur case. It applies equally in all situations where there is an ongoing civil war or violent conflict. In the event, after a review of various case studies, a study by the Brookings Institute concluded that '[a]ll of the cases suggest an inherent tension between the exigencies of peace and those of justice'.[16]

From the foregoing, two major conclusions can be made. The first is that in politically charged and complex crisis situations, peace and justice, involving the apportioning of blame and prosecution, cannot be mutually reinforcing if they are pursued simultaneously. As the Brookings Institute study pointed out, 'there is an inherent tension in simultaneously pursuing a strategy that assigns criminal scrutiny and/or blame to a party in the midst of peace negotiations that depends on the full cooperation of those accused'.[17] Where the most pressing need is to achieve a peaceful settlement of violent conflicts, the pursuit of prosecutorial justice entails the risk of rendering peace-making efforts very difficult, if not altogether untenable. In a widely debated recent opinion piece, Thabo Mbeki and Mahmood Mamdani contended that in a context of a civil war, '[t]o call simply for victims' justice, as the ICC does, is to risk a continuation of civil war'.[18]

Second, the debate on peace versus justice is in significant measure centred on the timing of the opening of criminal proceedings. As Mbeki and Mamdani counselled, 'there is a time and a place for courts, as in Germany after Nazi, but it is not in the midst of conflict or a nonfunctioning political system'.[19] With respect to the ICC, this obviously implicates, among others, the Prosecutor's discretionary authority to determine when and against whom to open investigations and proceedings. The idea here is that a non-arbitrary and well-considered exercise of this discretion demands that the Prosecutor be considerate of the timing and implications of the opening of investigations and proceedings to avoid a scenario where societies and victims are forced to choose between peace and justice. This suggests that in countries coming out of politically sensitive and highly complex conflicts, the opening of criminal proceedings should be designed as part of or in complementarity to a comprehensive political settlement leading to a new political dispensation, or should be suspended until such a political settlement has been crafted.

The experience of Kenya, perhaps more than any other, illustrates this point. This is best summed up in an opinion piece that former Secretary-General Kofi Annan wrote for the *New York Times*:

> I was appointed chairman of the African Union Panel of Eminent African Personalities and mediated an agreement to end the (2007/2008 post-electoral) crisis in Kenya. I arrived in Nairobi as the violence was intensifying, prompting fears that the country could ignite into civil war. *The first aim of the mediation was to stop the violence, which it did.* Recognizing the complex roots of the conflict, the agreement also called for establishing responsibility for the crimes committed and for constitutional, electoral and security-sector reforms, so that the cycle of violence would not be repeated.

One concrete outcome was the Waki commission, a national inquiry into the postelection violence ... the commission recommended that Kenya form a special tribunal to bring to account those most responsible. But the commission also foresaw that Kenya's entrenched political interests might undermine justice, so in the event of inaction, the matter was to be turned over to the International Criminal Court. Kenya's president, prime minister and parliament agreed to these terms. The commission also gave me a sealed envelope with the names of high-level people allegedly responsible for the violence.[20]

B National Policy Space for Choosing Transitional Justice Processes

Although, as Mbizvo noted in the second chapter of this volume, the principle of complementarity is the basis on which ICC exercises its jurisdiction, this principle has only de jure and abstract – as opposed to de facto and actual – application to countries with weak or dysfunctional national systems. The result is that for cases relating to such countries, ICC ends up becoming the first port of call. Together with the ICC's focus on prosecution, this tendency of using ICC as first resort forestalls discussions within affected societies on the methods and means of overcoming the injustices and divisions of the past and 'crowds out' alternative ways of dealing with political violence.[21] This is particularly the case where ICC proceedings are launched before society had the opportunity to debate and articulate the mechanisms of dealing with all the challenges arising from the violent conflicts or major political upheavals which occasioned the violations and from which they are trying to move forward.

This concern for national policy space is premised on the view that the political, security, socio-economic and governance challenges facing various countries that are going through or coming out of violent conflicts are unique to each country. And in order that such countries progress towards a sustainable path of peace, stability and justice, each country should be given the policy space to design a transitional political process tailored to meet its particular needs.[22] As Mbeki and Mamdani argued with respect to many of the countries in transition, 'what we need is a political process driven by a firm conviction that there can be no winners and no losers, only survivors'.[23] This does not mean that an interest in justice for past crimes should be abandoned. As noted above from Kofi Annan's experience in Kenya, it rather demands a comprehensive process that offers satisfaction, within an agreed programmatic framework, to the interests of achieving lasting peace, the imperative of mending the divisions that violence sowed, the demands of preventing continued violence and the need for redressing past violations. In other words, justice is best served if the society, together with the international community, designs appropriate mechanisms for holding perpetrators of serious violations accountable, providing redress to victims and facilitating the emergence of a just and democratic political dispensation.

The issues that this concern for national policy space touches on are twofold. The first is that such a focus on ICC processes carries the risk of ignoring national actors, including victims, while giving significant and undeserved leverage to international actors. The other concern is that the emphasis on prosecutorial justice marginalizes other, perhaps more, important concerns of the society in which alleged ICC crimes occurred in the course of a civil war or violent conflict. This issue of prosecutorial justice is the area of concern to which we now turn.

C The Inadequacy of Criminal Prosecution

One of the assumptions on which the ICC process is premised is that establishing individual accountability delivers justice to victims and affected communities. Speaking for the Office of the Prosecutor of the ICC, Mbizvo, in Chapter 2 of this volume, asserts that the focus for the ICC Prosecutor is the pursuit of justice for victims, be it in Darfur or the DRC. There is no doubt that individual criminal responsibility is important and necessary. It is not, however, clear whether it is the only and main concern for these communities. This is not only for the simple reason that individual criminal responsibility alone is inadequate, but also that it integrates victims only tangentially. This is inadequate in the sense that the aim of criminal processes is 'to portion blame and punish the guilty', and hence represents a very narrow conception of justice, as it is done in an individualized way. As Justice Albei Sachs of the South African Constitutional Court explains, '[c]ourts are concerned with accountability in a narrow individualised sense. They deal essentially with punishment'.[24] Contrary to Mbizvo's claim, by placing its emphasis on punishment, the focus of the ICC is more on the perpetrator than the victim. As Makau W. Mutua aptly pointed out,

> Such [legal] sanctions are not at the core victim-centred. Criminal sanctions ... are the revenge that society takes against the wrongdoer. Thus, such sanctions mollify society at large, but may do nothing for the victim.[25]

There is also a more substantive issue of whether criminal justice is the justice that victims are seeking. The AU High Level Panel on Darfur (AUHPD), in its report entitled *Darfur: The Quest for Peace, Justice and Reconciliation*,[26] clearly shows that for victims and Darfuris, while they are supportive of the ICC process, the prosecution of a few individuals is not their only and immediate concern. According to the AUHPD report, '[t]heir most immediate demand was for protection and security guarantees, followed by a political settlement that can lead to an equitable distribution of wealth, development, the rule of law and a political system that gives them a significant say over their own affairs within Darfur'.[27] They are also concerned with broad issues of justice, reconciliation and wider socio-economic, cultural and political reforms.

The other and perhaps more problematic assumption concerns identifying the source of our problem. In imposing individual criminal responsibility on those bearing the greatest responsibility and putting a near-exclusive premium on individual accountability, it suggests, albeit implicitly, that mass atrocity crimes are a result of an aberration in political leadership. If this is the correct assessment, then we have another reductionism about the centrality of individual criminal responsibility and retribution in international justice. This sentiment places too much focus on individuals as the source of the problem and not the much deeper sources of mass atrocity crimes. However, in most instances, mass atrocity crimes are rooted in the political, socio-economic and cultural power structures of the state and the use and distribution of such power among various sections of society. The problem with the focus on individual criminal responsibility is therefore that the question that it addresses is a very limited one.

As Justice Sachs observed, the result of such a judicial process is that '[t]he social processes and cultural and institutional systems responsible for the violations remain uninvestigated'.[28] Justice is not and should not be reduced to imprisoning a handful of perpetrators. Rather, we need approaches that will attend to the concerns of victims and the wider society, such as reparations, rehabilitation and truth telling. We also need approaches that address the broader national questions that foster inter-ethnic rancour and impede peaceful coexistence and national reconciliation. In other words, the judicial approach alone would be utterly inadequate.

Another major drawback of criminal prosecution is that it is more about the past than the present and the future. Certainly, victims of violence wish to see that justice is done and those responsible for serious violations are not left unpunished. For societies that experienced armed violence and the devastations of mass atrocity crimes, there is additionally the much broader interest of charting out an inclusive, just and democratic order that guarantees stability and peace, promotes national reconciliation and cohesion and secures the interests of all members of society.

IV THE CONSTRAINTS OF THE POWER STRUCTURE
OF THE INTERNATIONAL SYSTEM

The ICC was born into and operates within a skewed global political and socio-economic power structure. The nature of this feature of the power structure of the global order and the pre-eminence of geo-strategic interests in it presents major constraints for the pursuit of international criminal justice. Applying global power relationships and the propensity of major powers to use international institutions for advancing their own geo-strategic interests, there are those who view ICC's engagement in Africa as being susceptible to manipulation. This fear is a manifestation of the burden of history in Africa's relationship with the international system.

One of the direct ways by which the ICC is affected by the constraints of the skewed power structure of the international system concerns the role of the UN Security Council. Article 13 (b) of the Rome Statute invests the UNSC with the power to refer to the Prosecutor of the ICC any crimes falling under the Court's jurisdiction. The referral power of the UNSC applies to situations in any country, regardless of its status as a party to the Rome Statute. The UNSC shall exercise its Article 13 authority by passing a resolution under Chapter VII of the UN Charter. The UNSC has exercised its Article 13 power twice, and on both occasions it was with respect to African situations. The UNSC exercised this authority for the first time when it referred the situation in Darfur, Sudan, to the ICC Prosecutor with in its resolution 1593 (2005) of 31 March 2005. It did the same with respect to the situation in Libya in its resolution 1970 (2011).

With respect to the role of the UNSC, part of the discontent arises from the fact that while not being States Parties to the Rome Statute, members of the UNSC enjoy under Article 13 the power to refer cases to the ICC even with respect to states that are not parties to the Rome Statute. This means that the three veto-holding powers (China, Russia and the United States) not party to the Rome Statute can have the ICC take action against states not party to the Rome Statute while they will never submit themselves or their allies not party to the Rome Statute to the ICC process.

The ICC president insists that the 'ICC operates strictly within the mandate and legal framework created by the Rome Statute ... cannot take political factors into account'.[29] Despite being a judicial body, the ICC may not be able to intricate itself from the influences of a global order in which the pursuit of geo-strategic interests by big powers often hugely affects the workings of international actors.

The ICC's first decade in existence has revealed how the interests of the P5 and other major powers (members and non-members) has significantly influenced the Court's work. The ICC is ultimately dependent on the world's leading powers providing the clout and muscle (whether diplomatic, military or financial) necessary for it to function and arrest suspects, yet through direct and indirect means they have routinely marginalised the Court when its work threatened to negatively impact their interests. In practical terms, this has resulted in ICC investigations *not* being pursued in places like Afghanistan, Georgia or Palestine, even though jurisdictionally strong arguments could be made that they should.[30]

In the light of the foregoing, not only should the ICC aspire to exert but it also should be seen to be exerting all the necessary efforts within the limits of its authority to insulate itself from the constraints of global power politics. In this regard, lessons need to be taken from the nature of the ICC's engagements such as in Uganda and Libya (one involving 'self-referral' and another a result of a UNSC referral). Most notably, these cases show that ICC can be made prone to instrumentalization and politicization as national actors call on it to settle scores against opponents or international actors use it selectively.

A The Burden of History

As Makau W. Matua argues in Chapter 3 of this volume, we need to pay attention to the burden of history as central to shaping Africa's perceptions of the ICC. I end with some reflections on the influence of international law's historical role in Africa's traumatic experiences of slavery and colonialism on ICC's engagement in Africa.

B Focus on Africa

As already noted, all of the cases so far launched by the ICC concern African situations and were against Africans only. This 'Africanization' of the ICC is one of the major sources of the ICC's troubles in the continent. Indeed, Africa's opposition to the ICC in part draws on this exclusive focus of the ICC on Africa and the resultant perceptions of selective application of ICC justice in the world.

As acknowledged within the ICC itself, there is fear that the ICC's current list of cases puts into question the international character of the ICC,[31] giving credence to descriptions of the court as being the 'International Criminal Court for Africa'. Echoing this sentiment, Mamdani wrote that '[i]ts name notwithstanding, the ICC is rapidly turning into a Western court to try African crimes against humanity'.[32] Certainly, serious violations have occurred in the situations in which the ICC is involved. As long as ICC's involvement in these cases is undertaken even-handedly, its engagement alone is not to be condemned. What makes the ICC's apparent focus on Africa particularly troubling, though, is that it remains blind to similar situations in other parts of the world. Accordingly, the question is, as William Schabas observed: 'Why prosecute post-election violence in Kenya or recruitment of child soldiers in the Democratic Republic of the Congo, but not murder and torture of prisoners in Iraq or illegal settlements in the West Bank?'[33]

A recent report by the Brenthurst Foundation observed that 'the absence of ICC cases from elsewhere has reinforced the (erroneous) impression that atrocities happen only in Africa'.[34] This is of particular importance when considered against the background of Africa's history and stereotypical image. Seen in this light, the concern is, as I pointed out previously, that the ICC's 'focus only on Africa ... unwittingly perpetuates the old and tired Conardian caricature of Africa as the embodiment of the Hobbesian state of nature: brutal barbaric, monstrous, and the theatre of ICC crimes'.[35]

C Disregard of African Views and Concerns about the Conduct of the ICC's Processes in Africa

[O]ur goal is not and should not be a crusade against the ICC, but a solemn call for the organisation to take Africa's concerns seriously.

AU Assembly Chairperson, Ethiopian prime minister Hailemariam Desalegn[36]

There is a widely held view, as the quote above suggests, that the concerns that African states raise with regard to ICC processes are not given a serious hearing. Undoubtedly, this accounts in significant measure for the recent spate of threats of mass withdrawal and the unprecedented convening of an extraordinary summit. During the meeting of the General Assembly in New York held at the end of September 2013, a number of African leaders, including the then AU chairperson and Ethiopian prime minister as well as the presidents of Uganda, Tanzania and Rwanda, expressed their disappointment over 'the failure' of ICC to have regard to their repeated appeals on the handling of cases perceived to be very sensitive. Tanzanian president Jakaya Kikwete said 'The ICC continues to ignore repeated requests and appeals by the African Union', and this 'attitude has become a major handicap that fails to reconcile the court's secondary and complementary role in fighting impunity'.[37]

There are at least two issues that the view of African states over the lack of regard to their views and concerns touch on. One such issue concerns the perceived inflexibility of the ICC to accommodate and entertain the requests made by the AU. As President Kikwete observed, 'the court's rigidity has proven counterproductive and stands to undermine the support it enjoys in Africa'.[38] The other is the perception that there is a tendency to dismiss views of African states in platforms where the most influential opinions on the ICC's works and the policies of powerful states on the subject are formulated. More often than not, African states' views (as articulated within the AU framework) were not substantively engaged with and appropriately responded to, or they are dismissed as apologies for impunity.

There were two requests from the AU whose disregard resulted in major disappointment on the part of African states. The first request was on AU's repeated call on the UNSC to exercise its Article 16 power to defer the arrest of the Sudanese president. The second concerns the request made with respect to the president of Kenya and his deputy to be afforded flexibility in terms of their presence during their trial at The Hague. Apart from the letter that the AU sent to the ICC intervening on behalf of Mr Ruto, Burundi, Eritrea, Rwanda, Tanzania and Uganda also filed an application requesting the Court to apply a flexible interpretation of the requirements of Article 63 of the Rome Statute on the presence of the accused during proceedings. They contended that 'flexibility [would] ensure [that] a balance is struck between those subject to the court's jurisdiction but who also occupy high profile office positions'.[39]

From an international law perspective, these requests cannot be dismissed as having no legal significance. As ICC Judge Chile Eboe-Osuji argued in a separate opinion, holding otherwise 'ignores the legal phenomenon that the views of leaders of States often comprise state practice that are, in turn, an ingredient in the formation of customary international law.'[40]

The prevalent perception among African states that their voice is not taken seriously and given a proper hearing challenges the suggestion in Mbizvo's chapter that the statistics of the representation of Africans in the ICC system in the OTP and as judges reflects evidence of Africa's leverage on the ICC process. One thus agrees with Tiyanjana Maluwa that what matters is not the statistics but the quality and nature of Africa's participation.[41]

IV CONCLUSION: THE FUTURE OF HAGUE JUSTICE IN AFRICA

The ICC's engagement in Africa has been the most defining aspect of the operationalization of the international criminal justice system anchored on the Rome Statute. Although the ICC was received in Africa with a great deal of enthusiasm at the point of its founding, the way the ICC has gone about implementing its mandate triggered serious opposition from Africa. In the light of the challenge that this poses to the pursuit of international criminal justice in Africa, it is worthwhile, as I outlined in the foregoing, to go beyond the polarizing politically charged debate and address the major conditions shaping the current state of Africa's relationship to the ICC.

The pursuit of international criminal justice in isolation from reforms and similar processes at the national level is doomed to fail. So long as it promises too much (delivering justice to victims), it can only deliver too little. As outlined above, without adequate integration and synergy between the pursuit of international criminal justice and national transitional justice processes, ICC prosecutions that target a few individuals will certainly be ineffective. Apart from leaving large numbers of actors involved in the perpetration of violence untouched and thereby creating a major impunity gap, it also fails to address the underlying conditions that precipitated serious violations of human rights and humanitarian law. Despite ongoing prosecutions against alleged perpetrators of ICC crimes from DRC, eastern DRC has continued to witness serious violations of human rights and humanitarian law, including rape and other forms of sexual violence.

Apart from addressing the challenges of integration and synergy, there is also a need to have particular sensitivity to two major factors that define the political context in the ICC–Africa controversy. The first is the impact of the skewed character of the power structure of the international system on the ICC and how this informs African views on the ICC's engagement in Africa. In this context, how the role of the UNSC is implemented and how the ICC engages in international politics (of significance here is how the Prosecutor determines the opening of investigations or prosecutions) are key factors.

The other is the legacy of the burden of history with respect to Africa's historical interaction with international law. Although Africa has been and remains one of the participants of the founding and operations of the ICC system, there is a feeling that not enough consideration is given to the views of African states. This is further compounded by the fact that the content of the current docket of the ICC remains exclusively African. In this regard, the ICC's disposition to giving due hearing to the views of African states, along the lines suggested by Judge Eboe-Osuji, and to take on cases from other parts of the world are set to shape the future of Hague Justice in Africa.

The cause for which ICC stands, justice, is most noble, even if it is somewhat narrow. Africa not only supports but also stands to be the beneficiary of the pursuit of this noble cause, particularly where it is pursued as part of a comprehensive process for peace, justice and reconciliation. As this chapter has argued and demonstrated, major issues surrounding how the ICC has until now pursued its mandate have come to cast serious questions on its legitimacy in Africa, its largest regional constituency. Whether and how these issues are adequately addressed would determine both the ICC's future role in Africa and, by extension, its global legitimacy and standing.

Notes

1. Solomon A. Dersso, 'The Controversy over ICC beyond the Polarizing Political Context', *ISS Today*, 31 August 2009.
2. T. Maluwa, Legal Adviser OAU Secretariat, Statement at 6th Plenary Session, 17 June 1998. See United Nations Diplomatic Conference of Plenipotentiaries on the Establishment of an International Criminal Court, Official Records, UN doc. A/CONF.183/13 (Vol. II) 104, 115–118 at para. 116.
3. See Solomon A. Dersso, 'Unplanned Obsolescence: The ICC and the African Union', *Al Jazeera*, 11 October 2013.
4. See ICC Website, 'Situations and Cases', www.icc-cpi.int/pages/situations.aspx#.
5. Charles C. Jalloh, 'Regionalizing International Criminal Law?' (2009) 9 *International Criminal Law Review* (2009) 445, 447.
6. China (the leading emerging global power and the most populous country), India (the world's largest democracy), Russia and the United States (the most powerful states in the world) are among the countries of the world that opted not to be part of the ICC.
7. Dersso, 'Unplanned Obsolescence'.
8. 'ICC Suspends Darfur Crime Investigations over "Lack of Action"', DW, 12 December 2014.
9. Solomon A. Dersso, 'The AU's Extra-ordinary Summit Decision on Africa-ICC Relationship', *EJIL Talk*, 28 October 2013.
10. Dersso, 'Unplanned Obsolescence'.
11. 'SA May as a Last Resort Withdraw from ICC – says Radebe', *Business Day Live*, 25 June 2015.
12. AU High Level Panel on Darfur, 'Darfur: The Quest for Peace, Justice and Reconciliation', African Union communiqué, Peace and Security Council, PSC/AHG/2(CCVII), 29 October 2009.
13. AU Peace and Security Council, Communiqué, PSC/MIN/Comm(CXLII), 21 July 2008, para. 3.
14. Andrew Heavens, 'AU Chairman Backs Sudan's Bashir over Court', *Reuters*, 8 September 2008.

15. Comfort Ero, 'Understanding Africa's Position on the International Criminal Court', in Par Engstrom, R. Beaton, J. Paulson _Debating International Justice in Africa: Oxford Transitional Justice Research Collected Essays (2008–2010)_ (Oxford: Oxford University Press, 2015), p. 12.
16. Jacqueline Geis and Alex Mundt, 'When to Indict? The Impact of Timing of International Criminal Indictments on Peace Processes and Humanitarian Action' (Conference Paper, World Humanitarian Studies Conference Groningen, Netherlands, February 2009), p. 13.
17. _Ibid._
18. Thabo Mbeki and Mahmood Mamdani, 'Courts Can't End Civil Wars', _New York Times_, 5 February 2014.
19. _Ibid._
20. Kofi Annan, 'Justice for Kenya', _New York Times_, 9 September 2013 (emphasis added).
21. Jalloh, 'Regionalizing International Criminal Law', 489.
22. It was thus contended that '[c]ountries should retain the right to pursue justice ... using restorative justice in addition to punitive ones, if they believe that is more conducive to peace'. Martin Kimany, 'Kenya Can Heal Itself', _New York Times_, 4 December 2013.
23. Mbeki and Mamdani, 'Courts Can't End Civil Wars'.
24. Albie Sachs, _The Strange Alchemy of Life and Law_ (Oxford: Oxford University Press, 2009), p. 84.
25. Makau W. Mutua, 'A Critique of Rights in Transitional Justice: The African Experience', in Gaby Ore Aguilar and Felipe Gomez Isa (eds.), _Rethinking Transitions: Equality and Social Justice in Societies Emerging from Conflict_ (Mortsel: Intersentia, 2011) 38.
26. AU High Level Panel on Darfur, 'Darfur', para. 204.
27. _Ibid._, para. 203.
28. Sachs, _The Strange Alchemy_, p. 84.
29. Presidency of the ICC, 'ICC Underlines Impartiality, Reiterates Commitment to Cooperation with the African Union', 29 May 2013.
30. Terence McNamee, 'The ICC and Africa, Between Aspiration and Reality: Making International Justice Work Better for Africa' (The Brenthust Foundation Discussion paper 2, 2014).
31. _Kenyatta_ (ICC-01/09-02/11), 'Decision on the Prosecution's Motion for Reconsideration of the Decision Excusing Mr Kenyatta from Continuous Presence at Trial – Separate Further Opinion of Judge Eboe-Osuji', 23 October 2013.
32. Mahmood Mamdani, 'Darfur, ICC and the New Humanitarian Order', _Pambazuka News_, 17 September 2008.
33. 'Global Insider: Ten Years in, ICC's Acquittal Rate Is Extraordinarily High', _World Politics Review_, 19 March 2013.

34. McNamee, 'The ICC and Africa, Between Aspiration and Reality'.
35. Solomon A. Dersso, 'The International Criminal Court's Africa Problem', *Al Jazeera*, 11 June 2013.
36. Benard Namunane, 'Why Africa Leaders Failed to Strike Deal on ICC in Ethiopia', *Daily Nation*, 13 October 2013.
37. Kevin J. Kelley, 'ICC Rigidity Undermines Its Support in Africa – Kikwete', *Daily Nation*, 28 September 2013.
38. *Ibid.*
39. *Ruto* (ICC-01/09-01/11), 'Decision on Mr. Ruto's Request for Excusal from Continuous Presence at Trial', 25 October 2013, paras. 40 and 41.
40. *Kenyatta*, 'Separate Further Opinion of Judge Eboe-Osuji'.
41. Tiyanjana Maluwa, 'Is Africa a Participant or Target of International Justice?' Speech delivered at the review conference of the International Criminal Court, 31 May–11 June 2010 (on file with author).

5

International Justice and the Politics of Sentimentality

Kamari M. Clarke

I INTRODUCTION

How do leaders, lawyers, judges, bureaucrats, and members of various publics tap into prevailing emotional regimes and deploy sentiments that become institutionalized? How do they become entrenched within institutions like the ICC, NGOs, and regional courts like the African court, and how are they transferred within constituent publics – from person to person, leader to constituency? How are they reattributed to make new historical lineages feasible? This chapter explores the way that perceptions are shaped through feelings of alliance and compassion. The goal is to demonstrate how various Pan-Africanist, anti-colonial justice narratives as well as ICC discourses involving post-Nuremberg triumphs are institutionalized. By highlighting the way that individuals make sense of what justice is, I demonstrate how this happens through what Arlie Hoshschild[1] refers to as feeling rules. Through feeling rules, the terms for the appropriateness of discourses are regulated and institutionalized, producing what Joseph de Rivera[2] referred to as an emotional climate.

Though not traditionally addressed in legal studies, some of the psychological literature on emotions has explored these questions in relation to emotional climates. They have examined how collective feelings of fear or excitement, for example, are used to ensure order as well as to explain how feelings of anger are expressed as a result of things like corruption. As social constructions, these collective feelings reflect individual perceptions but are actually reflections of group transference. As a product of collective emotions generated through social interactions,[3] emotional climates shape social norms that establish 'how people feel or ought to feel' (Ibid) and set the affective terrain within which public emotions operate.[4] The foregoing explores

emotional climates through histories of anti-colonial struggle and their relationships to ICC indictments. It also demonstrates how rhetorical strategies
are deployed through which feelings of stigma and hierarchies of value are
reinscribed through stigma.[5]

In legal circles, these affects are often silenced as unsayable and outside of
the realm of accusation. Popularized by Judith Butler (Butler, 2009: XVII), the
concept of the unsayable has been discussed through the designation of the
contemporary public sphere as a domain in which particular things cannot be
said. Through the allocation of stigma, particular discourses, such as 'ending
impunity', are precluded from criticism and, as such, they eventually have the
effect of producing norms of acceptability and popular determinations of
which lives are worthy of saving. In pro-accountability, post-mass-violence
movements, the emergence of the victim to be saved and the perpetrator to be
held accountable have complicated the way many in this movement understand the value of lives worth protecting. As we shall see, such values are what
shape perceptions deemed appropriate or what mobilizes counter sentiments
towards the production of counter movements.

***

In 1952, Jomo Kenyatta, the father of independent Keya and of Uhuru
Kenyatta, was arrested by the British colonial army following a state of emergency declared by the British administrators of colonial Kenya. Kenyatta had
been indicted the year before, together with five others known as the
Kapenguria Six – Achieng' Oneko, Bildad Kaggia, Fred Kubai, Kung'u
Karumba, and Paul Ngei. By April 1953, all six were incarcerated for their
membership in and organization of the Mau Mau freedom fighters. Kenyatta
denied the charges but was convicted by what many believe were trumped up
charges. He served six years as a political prisoner, until 1960 when the
demands for his release grew with native Kenyans gathering daily in the
town square to protest the injustice. This mobilization succeeded and
Kenyatta was released. Once released, the story told is that Kenyatta led his
people in the petitioning for Kenya's independence from the British. When
the first Kenyan elections were finally held in May 1963, Jomo Kenyatta was
elected as the prime minister of the Kenyan African National Union (KANU)
and it was in that context that he negotiated the terms for Kenya's independence on 12 December 1963.

Approximately fifty years later, Jomo Kenyatta's son, Uhuru Kenyatta,
became the president of the Republic of Kenya and with his deputy-
presidential partner, William Ruto, established a landmark consolidation of
two previously antagonistic political groups aligned along competing ethnic

cleavages. However, this consolidation is related to another landmark event –
the 2012 indictment of Uhuru Kenyatta by a European-based court, the
International Criminal Court (ICC). Though there are distinct differences
between the conditions and contexts of both cases, Kenyan politicians have
presented the embattled prosecution of Uhuru Kenyatta as a historical continuity of Jomo Kenyatta's political struggle for independence against imperial
rule. Kenyatta's popularly hailed speech is a case in point.

On 20 October 2013, Uhuru Kenyatta presided over his first Heroes' Day
(known as *mashujaa* day in Swahili), a national public holiday to collectively honour all those who contributed to the struggle for Kenya's
independence.[6] That day Kenyatta's speech began with a unifying call to
the characteristically ethnic divided nation, 'Fellow Kenyans'. He opened
his message to the nation by highlighting the importance of celebrating
the past. Upon establishing a sense of a shared political community that
has long struggled for independence, he went on to reinforce the after-
effects of colonialism and its impact on social and economic inequality.
In an attempt to celebrate their independence journey, he highlighted the
material and psychological consequences of the colonial project and its
impact on their Kenyan forefathers:

> We are here to commemorate the sacrifice and heroism of many Kenyans
> whose vision and conviction won us freedom and sovereignty. Colonialism
> had stripped all Kenyans of their fundamental rights. They had no land, and
> were considered inferior in their own home. There was neither dignity nor
> freedom for Kenyans then. Our forefathers waged a struggle of conviction and
> principle, supported with no resources except the burning fire of humiliation
> and the indefeasible yearning for independence and respect.
>
> They were brave and noble.
>
> Many took up armed struggle in the forests, as others formed and led
> movements for the civil agitation for independence. The colonial reaction
> was repressive and brutal. Heroes were killed and imprisoned, while the rest
> were stigmatised and hunted down like animals. The cost of the struggle was
> painful, because the settlers did not consider Africans equal human beings
> worthy of rights.[7]

As we see by this narrative, Kenyatta's story is one about the humiliation of
Africans at the hands of colonial administrators and settlers and the subsequent freedom struggles for respect and dignity that ultimately led to Kenyan
independence. This backdrop is what set the terms for the contemporary
predicament that he then discusses. He went on to articulate how Africans
suffered at the hands of imperial colonizers and emerged victorious in their
fight against those forces:

This day marks the official beginning of the worst phase of colonialism, and the most harrowing period of our struggle for independence. The brutality our independence heroes underwent from 20th October 1952 until the attainment of self-government ten years later defies imagination. It is the reason that we have reverently emblazoned our national flag with the red of their sacred blood. That is why our constitution states that, We the People honour those who heroically struggled to bring freedom and justice to our land. In history, Mashujaa Day is a day written in blood by the hand of our heroes.[8]

After discussing the 'brutality' that their 'independence heroes' endured, Kenyatta likened his judicial indictment by the ICC to his father's indictment by the British colonial administration in Kenya, thereby connecting the brutality of the colonial past to contemporary international law. What is interesting is that the attempt to make this symbolic connection involved the creation of a gap between what was said and what remained to be deduced. The audience – seasoned and acutely aware of Africa's history of colonial domination – was invited to share sentiments of horror from colonial injustice and accept the connection to the other injustice – that of Kenyatta's subsequent indictment. As he emphasized:

Our forefathers rejected colonialism and imperial domination in their time. We must honour their legacy, and stay true to our heritage, by rejecting all forms of domination and manipulation in our time. Let us confront without flinching those external forces seeking to thwart our collective aspirations. They may be powerful and rich, but so were the colonialists. They may disrespect and even hate us; we have defeated their ilk before.[9]

Kenyatta's and the audience's sense of continued external domination reflect postcolonial emotional regimes of perceived colonial defiance at work. It reflects the way that popular feelings about Kenyan postcolonial futures are bound up by a particular sentimental defiance against colonial degradation. These affective sentiments are made real through *a priori* events that shape what the present and future becomes. The structures of sentimentality involved in new judicial movements represent what Russian philosopher Michael Bahkin called dialogic.[10] It is dialogic because of the way in which contemporary imaginaries are continually informed by past conceptions. Such an approach to the social retelling of relevant events in daily life provides a space for making sense of the way that emotions guide reality and a domain for understanding the senses of injustice that motivate them. This approach to understanding emotions through their rhetorical strategies can help us make sense of the way that affective regimes shape emotional climates expressed through narratives of stigma, empathy, and sympathy. The study of emotion presumes that such feelings are grounded in particular socio-moral orders expressed through responses that are deemed ordinary. For example, where stigma makes possible the terms for regulating what is acceptable in relation to what is abhorrent, narratives of empathy produce the terms for shared collective sentiments.

Kenyatta's reference to the ordinary aspirations of Kenyan dreams of freedom from 'imperial domination' was juxtaposed by his suggestion that there were 'external forces seeking to thwart our collective aspirations'. The political reality of colonial trials often seen as sham trials and their parallel with the son, Kenyatta's, indictment by the ICC was conjured to produce a key moment of linkage. As he affirmed, '[t]hey may be powerful and rich, but so were the colonialists'. Here Kenyatta attributed to the ICC the same colonial armature of subjugation[11]. This did not involve an explicit reference to the ICC. There was no need to name it. It was unsayable; it was almost unnecessary. Rather the point was pinpointed with the profound declaration, '[w]e have defeated their ilk before'.[12] The use of the words 'this ilk' refers to judicial external bodies such as the ICC in which *the colonial* is tied to *the international* (read: European). Kenyatta called out the ICC as an 'ilk' of domination – and equated symbolically the known facts that, to date, the ICC has only indicted Africans with African judicial struggles against imperial domination. His conclusion: Kenya's Mau Mau revolutionaries used constitutionalism to defeat their oppressors and so will Kenya's contemporary democratic vanguard.

By comparing his indictment before the ICC to the arrest and political conviction of his father, Jomo Kenyatta, some fifty years earlier, Uhuru Kenyatta attempted to construct personal meaning from historical and contemporary realities through a cultural template of subordination and an emotional process known in psychoanalysis as 'transference'.[13] Transference represents the circulation of emotion from one object to another, from one person to another. For Sigmund Freud, it was connected to the process of projecting unresolved issues in one's primary kinship relationships onto others. I use transference to link both these internalities of emotion with intersubjective cultural fields to show how it is used in meta-contexts such as crowds and large audiences.

Affective transference, as an intersubjective process, fuelled by emotional regimes is not only manifest among those protesting the presence of the ICC in Africa. We also see transference in the rhetorical practices of those engaged in the rule-of-law movement, such as the members of the ICC's Office of the Prosecutor (OTP). Key to this analysis is the understanding that once those narratives are aligned with their own respective forms of legitimacy they have the power to mobilize sentiments that can ultimately shape new social actions.

In the ICC's early days, the court gained popular traction as a symbol of protection for victims and as a means for 'ending impunity'. The reality is that the domain of state authority, which had (since the Peace of Westphalia in 1648) long dominated approaches to sovereignty, began to topple. Theories of state responsibility to its citizens transformed with the emergence of a new moral order, which took shape with the emergence of the Responsibility to Protect doctrine (R2P). This conception led to the terms for the expansion of global executive action that obligated states or international institutions to protect victims of mass atrocities if the state that bore that responsibility failed to do so.[14] R2P established core principles which became institutionalized as shared moral principles which national citizens were expected to embody. Notions of the 'international community' emerged as an outgrowth of such formations and became a critical component of the ICC's moral architecture.

Members of the OTP, such as Shamiso Mbizvo, remind us that the court was set up on behalf of the 'international community to intervene when the nation state fails'. As she suggested in her keynote at the ICC and Africa conference in The Hague in May 2014 and also included in this volume:

> The final text of the Rome Statute of the International Criminal Court is the culmination of almost a hundred years of hard work, unyielding determination, and stubborn hope on the part of people all over the world, from many walks of life, who have all shared the vision of an independent, permanent International Criminal Court. The ICC exists to hear the voices of victims of the most atrocious crimes, when their cries fall on deaf ears. It is a Court that was set up to intervene on behalf of the most vulnerable, when their own governments fail to hold their abusers accountable.[15]

Mbizvo's discussion of the existence of the ICC as a culmination of 'almost a hundred years of hard work' in order to establish a mechanism to intervene on behalf of the 'most vulnerable' suggests a historical continuity over a longer period of time than the mid-1990s, when international law was instrumentalized morally and politically. Like Kenyatta's symbolic linkages, she describes the contemporary ICC's formation metaphorically as a one-hundred year Road to Rome, culminating in the formation of the Rome Statute for the ICC.

This chapter is about the imbrication of law, justice and the place of sentimentality in the contemporary rule-of-law movement. It is about linguistic expressions of affective states and the rhetorical practices that, through *affective transference*, produces sentimentality in situations of otherwise unrelated causality. The sentimentalism that inspires the connection between one distinctive national or military trial to another criminal tribunal, or the attempt to connect colonial indictments with the ICC's charges of co-perpetration that contributed to Kenya's post-election violence, provide examples of the constructed architecture in which these rhetorical practices take place. For while the anti-ICC sentiments expressed by some in African countries have to do with a widespread objection to Western dominance or a selective application of the law, the reality is that what they are responding to is the perception that with its preponderance of African cases, the ICC is being seen as being instrumentalized for political purposes. Kenyatta's linguistic strategies are reflective of that and highlight the affective politics of social protest as aestheticized through injustice imaginaries. Such imaginaries highlight how various rhetorical strategies like fetishizing the unsayable conjure sentiments that respond to domination through the production of alternative narratives.

Like Kenyatta, Shamiso Mbizvo's articulation of the histories that led to the formation of ICC justice is, thus, an example of affective transference as it highlights the way that historical relatedness is constructed through some of the most powerful forms of sentimentalisms. Studying the micro-politics of sentiments, a key in shaping perceptions of the past and the present, allows us to consider the embodiment of injustice through public oration and its publics. As we will see, feelings of anger, resentment, pain, and victory are made real not through their exacting equivalences, but through the production of 'the real' as dialogically constituted through new formulations of the social. I argue that speech acts that include facts that are evidently disjunctural and unrelated can produce new social truths not because its audiences are uninformed, but because of the power of the intersubjective in tapping into particular emotional histories, thereby shaping meaning. What is important is how these meanings index events, people, and power relations that enable emotional sharing of seemingly disconnected events. The success of affective transference in such rule-of-law language, therefore, is possible because of the ongoing gaps in historical consciousness. In order for affective transference to happen, the roads of causality must be assembled in ways that are presented as old and part of a dialogic continuum.

In the foregoing, I have explored the rhetorical uses of sentimentality and the way affective transference enables speakers to produce continuities by establishing the horrors of past events and tying them to contemporary developments. These speech acts, as a form of dialogism, produce the opportunity for otherwise structural differences to be erased and new connections to be established. By showing how such sentimental tools fill gaps in historical relationalities, we see how modes of sentimental linkage can happen not only in these examples but also throughout widespread forms of public oratory in locations in which ICC-rule-of-law and anti-rule-of-law discourses are prevalent.

Today, the popular contemporary story of the birth of the Rome Statute and its judicial legitimacy is understood as being based on a particular history of the ICC that characterizes the 'Road to Rome' as beginning in the early nineteenth century. That story, as told by various representatives of the ICC, often begins with the 1872 founding of the International Committee of the Red Cross (ICRC) in which a permanent court was proposed to respond to the crimes of the Franco-Prussian War. And if those narrative origins are not emphasized, the attempt of the 1919 Treaty of Versailles to try German war criminals of World War I (WWI) or the 1948 Convention on the Prevention and Punishment of the Crime of Genocide (used to set up the Nuremberg and Tokyo tribunals to try various war criminals) are seen as key to the founding history of the Court.

In this story, WWI is described as having contributed to the launching of the first global effort to use international and domestic criminal jurisdiction to address international crimes. Following the war, the Allied and Associated Powers (i.e. Great Britain, France, Russia, and the United States) convened a Commission on the Responsibility of the Authors of the War and on the Enforcement of Penalties to inquire into culpable conduct by the Central Powers (i.e. Germany, Austria, Hungary, Bulgaria, and the Ottoman Empire). The Commission was charged with considering the feasibility of asserting criminal jurisdiction over particular individuals, 'however highly placed', accused of committing breaches.[16] Objectors of this approach, led by a predominantly American delegation, objected on the grounds that, by holding heads of state and other state actors liable for collective actions, state sovereignty would be diminished.[17] They also took issue with the reality that no precedent existed in law for such an approach.[18]

In 1919, the Commission presented to the Paris Peace Conference its final report of which crimes should be prosecuted before an international 'high tribunal' composed of representatives of the Allied Powers, or before national tribunals.[19] The United States advanced four fundamental objections to this approach, among them that to prosecute a Head of State outside of his national jurisdiction would violate the basic precepts and privileges of sovereignty.[20] From here, the potential liability for German and Ottoman defendants proceeded down separate paths.

The Treaty of Versailles ended the war with Germany in 1919 and required it to accept full responsibility for causing the war, make territorial concession, and pay reparations.[21] It was Article 227 that proposed the establishment of an international tribunal composed of representatives from the United States, Great Britain, France, Italy, and Japan to try former the German emperor, Kaiser Wilhelm II.[22] By the time the Versailles Treaty had entered into force, the Kaiser had fled to the Netherlands, which refused to extradite him for trial.[23] Article 227 never came to fruition and the Allies never enforced any other penal provisions of the Treaty.[24] In the end, only a few prosecutions took place in domestic courts in Germany, and those who were prosecuted received disproportionately low sentences or were acquitted.[25]

Following WWI, a number of policy makers and lawyers, often described as constituting the international community, took action to build institutions to settle international disputes. The League of Nations announced a commitment to safeguard the peace of nations without resorting to war and in 1920, recommended the creation of a permanent international criminal court.[26] The proposal was rejected as premature, and instead the Permanent Court of International Justice (PCIJ), the precursor to the International Court of Justice (ICJ), was established with civil jurisdiction over states.[27] Following that narrative trajectory, the most critical period in the development of modern international criminal law (ICL) occurred in the period following WWII. Two international tribunals were established for adjudicating international crimes which took place during the war: the International Military Tribunal for the Trial of German Major War Criminals (the IMT or Nuremberg Tribunal) and the International Military Tribunal for the Far East (the IMTFE or Tokyo Tribunal).

The Nuremberg Tribunal was established through the London Agreement of 8 August 1945 between the four victorious Allied Powers: France, the Soviet Union, the UK, and the United States.[28] The Tribunal convened from 20 November 1945 to 1 October 1946 during which time it heard the matters of twenty-one Nazi defendants.[29] The Tokyo Tribunal was, by contrast, established by a special proclamation issued by the Supreme Allied Commander of the Far East, US General Douglas MacArthur, with the agreement of the Allied Powers.[30] The Tokyo Tribunal convened from 3 May 1946 to 12 November 1948, and was heavily influenced by the United States, with the prosecutions led by a single American Chief of Counsel chosen by MacArthur (with Associate Counsel from the Allied Powers).[31] In addition to these two tribunals, hundreds of trials occurred before military and civilian tribunals in various locales in the zones of occupation of the victorious powers.[32]

Van Schaack and Slye argue that it is difficult to overstate the significance of the post– WWII period to the field of international criminal law. They insist that 'these legal proceedings established many core principles of the field'.[33] Indeed, the establishment of a spectacle in which high-ranking state officials could be held individually criminally responsible for international crimes created a set of discourses that were profoundly powerful.[34] Many show that the Nuremberg and Tokyo tribunals made explicit the commitment to holding various officials responsible for their orders to lower ranking officers to facilitate or directly perpetrate violence. The argument that is often made is that by rejecting the basis for both state sovereignty and discarding principles of immunity through a movement that insists on the irrelevance of official capacity, this post–WWII movement certainly produced a few examples where those culpable for mass crimes were held criminally accountable.[35] However, the reality is that for every instance in which sovereign heads of state were held responsible for violent mass crimes in Europe and South America, there were a plethora of other cases where this was not the case. While the Nuremberg example provides a mechanism for understanding particular instances of criminal liability of commanders, British imperial forces engaged in gross violations with impunity. Significant populations involved in self-determination/independence struggles in the Caribbean, Latin America, Africa, and Indigenous and first Nations peoples were arrested, indicted, and subjected to violence. Yet, if we presume that the word 'international' refers to a wide range of countries and populations, then the absence of the criminal prosecution of former colonial leaders in places like England or even France during twentieth-century independence struggles calls into question the often told narratives about the trend towards criminal prosecutions.

The story that is told by the Office of the Prosecutor (OTP) and many others within the field of international criminal justice as the Road to Rome is one in which the immediate post–WWII period witnessed the United Nations (UN) emerging from its predecessor, the League of Nations. This was followed by the emergence of an international human rights regime that led to the drafting of the Universal Declaration of Human Rights, the International Covenant on Civil and Political Rights, and the International Covenant on Economic, Social and Cultural Rights. The codification of ICL continued with the development of the 1948 Convention on the Prevention and Punishment of the Crime of Genocide and the four Geneva Conventions of 1949.[36] And in 1947, the General Assembly requested that the International Law Commission (ILC) study the possibility of establishing an international judicial body for crimes such as genocide, war crimes, and crimes against humanity.[37] As the story is told, in the early 1950s, the ICL was invited to assess the interest, thus possibilities, for establishing a permanent international judicial institution. It was to codify the Nuremberg and Tokyo principles into a Draft Code of Offenses Against the Peace and Security of Mankind that would provide the subject matter jurisdiction for the proposed tribunal.[38] But it did this with numerous stops and starts – dealing with pressure to abandon it during the Cold War and over various ideological and political disagreements of the type of crimes that would be under the subject matter jurisdiction of such an institution.

As the story is told, in the early 1990s the General Assembly once again prompted the ILC to draft a statute for a permanent international criminal court. On 6 October 1992, Resolution 780 was adopted by the United Nations Security Council (UNSC) to establish a Commission of Experts to document violations of international law.[39] In response to the Commission's recommendation, as well as calls from a wide spectrum of international actors, on 25 May 1993 the UNSC unanimously adopted Resolution 827 to create the International Tribunal for Yugoslavia (ICTY), an international tribunal to prosecute those responsible for crimes committed in the former Yugoslavia since 1991.[40] The following year, the genocide in Rwanda led to the establishment of the ICTR.[41]

Additional ad hoc tribunals were later established (through the UNSC) to respond to crimes committed in Sierra Leone, East Timor, Lebanon, and Cambodia. The ILC completed a draft statute in 1994 that formed the basis for consideration by the Ad Hoc Committee on the Establishment of an International Criminal Court and then a Preparatory Committee on the Establishment of an International Criminal Court (PrepCom).[42] And while this popular trajectory was seen by many in the growing rule-of-law movement as a positive development, the ILC's project and the subsequent General Assembly deliberations led to the consolidation of the UN's ICL assemblages, resulting in the formation of the ICC.

On 17 July 1998, 120 of the world's states came together and signed the Rome Treaty for the establishment of the ICC. By 2002, the Rome Statute came into force, thereby consolidating genocide, war crimes, the crime of aggression, and crimes against humanity as 'the most serious crimes of concern to the international community'. After this period, international criminal law was heralded by a discourse driven by the Rome Statute's preambular conviction that all peoples are united by common bonds that could be shattered at any time by violence, and that millions of children, women, and men have been 'victims of unimaginable atrocities that deeply shock the conscience of humanity'. This message represents a popular moral imaginary that is persuasive in such rule-of-law movements. Its moral fortitude gains currency both through its reference to various legislative and legal precedents as well as through the telling of a history of its founding. But what is left out of the retelling are the real differences in places like Nuremberg and Tokyo that established the conditions for state compliance with prosecutorial designs.

In Nuremberg and Tokyo, the status of those defeated in the war led to victor's justice and set the conditions for prosecutorial justice. As Mahmood Mamdani has recently helped to clarify,[43] the hidden pre-requisites for trial in all these cases were (i) a war, that was (ii) won decisively by one side, and to which one might add (iii) the historical institution of 'unconditional surrender', which includes the concession of sovereign power.[44] By contrast, in the African situations that the ICC has taken up, different conditions led to the possibility of the court's reach. These conditions of possibility were not unrelated to the inability of African states to use decolonization towards new frontiers that disrupted spheres of inequality, ethnic patronage, and poverty that prevailed in the post-1960 independence periods.

III AFFECTIVE RE-ATTRIBUTIONS: THE ROAD FROM RWANDA, NOT NUREMBERG

Violence in the former Yugoslavia and then Rwanda, Liberia, and Sierra Leone led to the formation of new judicial institutions that also contributed to a new set of discourses about the ICC. These discourses further reinforced the affective contours of international law. From Kenya to South Africa, Namibia to Mozambique, Zimbabwe to Algeria, independence negotiations from the late 1950s to the mid-1990s were brokered without attention to criminal prosecutions of the former colonial power. Even as various African leaders were strategically optimistic about the potential of using international justice in their newly independent states, they also knew that unless the roots of inequality were also addressed, violence would remain a mode for managing law's failures. This is what happened during the Cold War.

The postwar momentum to develop permanent ICL institutions resulted in a panoply of rights that were articulated, but there were no judicial institutions available that stakeholders could use to act on them. The absence of international institutions to intervene in wide-scale violence in places like South Africa, for example, was reflective of the same architecture that produced the Rome treaty. From 1948 to 1990, apartheid in South Africa existed as an international crime without an international criminal court to prosecute it. However, when, in 1966, the UN General Assembly classified it as a crime against humanity,[45] the OAU attempted to lobby for the establishment of an international penal court in the 1970s to prosecute the crime.[46] Initially, its stakeholders had hoped that they could establish a criminal chamber through the African Charter of Human Rights, but they abandoned this when the UN Security Council affirmed in 1984 that apartheid was a crime. This opened up the possibility of establishing in the late 1980s a UN international penal court in order to prosecute various apartheid crimes on the basis of universal jurisdiction. But the reality was that in order to pursue apartheid as a crime, national states had to enact legislation to prosecute individuals through universal jurisdiction.[47]

When the Rome Statute crimes were negotiated, apartheid offences were eventually dropped as a core crime. Instead, apartheid was collapsed into crimes against humanity and subject to a post-2002 temporal jurisdiction. This meant that the period of brutal domination of South African or Kenyan natives was beyond the temporal jurisdiction of the court. Rather, the international rule-of-law movement took hold of post-civil rights judicial agendas propelled by various agents of change in the United States, Europe, and Australia. And, as the story is often told, the late 1980s and early 1990s led to the establishment of new judicial institutions that deal with a range of crimes in which criminal responsibility was narrowly tailored to the 'now', namely to the 'present', and the 'future' goals of ending impunity. The irony is that when African states needed prosecutorial justice against colonial domination, international law could not be mobilized to provide viable solutions. During the Rome treaty negotiations, African state brokers participated at varying degrees of involvement. Yet, even as the law was deployed to establish African independence and membership in the newly changing world order, they were well aware that were limits to its use as tools for justice.[48] For states that were actively engaged in the ICC's success, such as England, France, the Netherlands, Spain, and Portugal, involved unaddressed histories in which law was used both as an instrument of historical subjugation as well as a tool for social change. Kenya's history of native subjugation provides a vivid example of this relationship. It shows that even as African states engaged in ICC membership as a response to the demands of new democratic forms of constitutionalism, the reality is that for a range of leaders and their publics in the Global South, the institutionalization of post–Cold War democracies carry with them an internal tension by which various sentimental responses are not only logical but are in keeping with the affective histories of law's ambiguities. It is this form of structural violence that is unsayable, with stigma, because it falls outside of the law's orbit. Instead, the ICC emerged as a mechanism for protecting other types of victims – of African postcolonial violence – while the prosecution of Northern perpetrators, such as those states that were war in Iraq and Afghanistan, are unthinkable because their violence is protected by legality.

IV KENYAN SUBJUGATION AND THE LIMITS OF THE LAW

Historically, British colonialism in Kenya (which lasted from 1895 to 1963) involved varying degrees of profoundly overt violence perpetrated by the colonial state. Problems caused by the imposition of taxes, unliveable wages, and the threat of new settlers claiming previously indigenous land led to social movements such as the Mau Mau resistance. During the twentieth century, over 30,000 British settlers forcibly displaced over a million members of the Kikuyu tribe from their land. In the absence of British-owned land titles, they lived as itinerant farmers without rights. Known as a radical mobilization force to reclaim the land taken from Kenyans, the Mau Mau began a violent campaign in the 1950s against white settlers and the colonial government. They were then outlawed by British colonial authorities for their violent tactics and a range of political leaders were arrested, including Jomo Kenyatta, who was classified as a Mau Mau terrorist.

According to the documented history, Kenyatta and the Kapluna Five were tried and convicted. While in prison the Mau Mau escalated its tactics to a guerrilla war. British troops fought them and created strict measures against civilians in which large numbers of people were detained in concentration camps or moved to 'protected' villages.[49] With the escalation of the British military strategy using a native Home Guard and new 'special forces' (often from competing ethnic groups), Mau Mau guerrilla tactics, which eventually led to the Mau Mau's military defeat. Among those arrested were independence revolutionary figures such as Dedan Kimanthi – a feared member of the Mau Mau Kikuyu guerrilla. The capture of the movement's political icons and revolutionary figures further fractured the relationship between various ethnic groups and created deep-rooted resentments that remain today. What is often explained is that once he was captured by the Special Forces, the colonial government organized a trial, seen by locals as a 'sham trial', where Kimanthi was quickly convicted and immediately executed. With the capture of Kenyatta and the death of Kimanthi, the Mau Mau mechanism floundered and a social movement grew to advocate for the freedom of those imprisoned.

The Kenyan post-independence period led to new realignments. During and after the Cold War, underlying tensions further accentuated by colonial land appropriation collided in Kenya. The over one million Kenyans who were moved from native villages and relocated to squatter zones remained dispossessed. Therefore, the story that is now told by Uhuru Kenyatta and others is that the violence that emerged during Kenya's successive elections in the 1980s, 1990s, and most recently in 2007–2008 emerged out of latent and unsettled distributional politics that was buttressed by the continuing crimes of white settlers and colonial warfare. This story of the historical plunder of land and of the injustice of relocation by the British formed the basis for long-standing resentments of external (read: colonial) interference.

The most related contemporary development, therefore, has involved the proposal to expand the criminal jurisdiction of the African Court. This has been adumbrated by the reality that in the first twelve years of its existence, the ICC had only pursued cases in Africa. As a result, it has come to be seen by various constituencies in Africa as an extension of the histories of colonial inequalities. As of August 2015, the ICC had pursued twenty-two cases in nine situations across several African states: the Central African Republic (CAR), the Democratic Republic of the Congo (DRC), the Ivory Coast, Sudan, Uganda, Kenya, the Republic of Mali, and Libya. It issued indictments for thirty-six individuals, including twenty-seven warrants of arrest and nine summonses to appear before the court.[50] Four individuals were on trial and proceedings were concluded in twelve cases: two individuals had been convicted, one had been acquitted, four had the charges dismissed, two had had the charges withdrawn, one had been held inadmissible, and three individuals have died prior to trial.[51] From the cases of alleged African warlords to the indictments of African leaders – ranging from Uhuru Kenyatta and William Ruto, Omar al-Bashir, and Laurent Gbagbo – the predominance of African subjects of international criminal justice has created amongst a range of Africans a suspicion about prosecutorial justice. Though the criticism of the selectivity of African cases is a popular rebuttal to contemporary ICL, it is also the case that the lure of the rule of law's apocalyptic potential has also opened spaces beyond the state for addressing violence in a range of postcolonial contexts. These alternate spaces highlight the deep-seated recognition by agents of the African state that violence is a by-product of unresolved political inequalities that undergird the postcolonial state. And until those inequalities are addressed in African contemporary democracies, criminal prosecutions will only provide a spectacle by which histories of subjugation are hidden and criminal prosecutions are celebrated as the norm.

The persistence of such ironies make it all the more important to examine the sentimental foundations of Kenyatta and others' anti-ICC protest speech or the seductions of the OTP's celebration of the place of judicial possibility. These domains are key to making sense of the affective life of the law and call on us to ask hard questions that explain why significant numbers of leaders, academics, members of civil society, and policy makers who may have formerly supported the ICC's potential have since advocated the withdrawal from its jurisdiction. They are key to understanding the promotion of recent popular rethinking about the law's ability to hide histories of inequality. These developments propel us to reflect on how sentimental reactions to the law's inequality or promise shapes one's ability to engage in value of international rule-of-law projects. I am arguing that these seductions do not work through pre-given formulations that tip and cascade in particular directions to establish particular pro-accountability or post-colonial freedom fighter discourse. Rather, it is through a subjective politics of perception fuelled through affective transference that people deploy affects and consolidate narratives of power. I close by showing that these pre-existing histories are not pre-given formulations for the expression of some sentimental forms. They are not sites for the arbitrary invention of the past. Histories of law and the making of its perceived legitimacy or illegitimacy are actively created and, therefore, require work to sustain their seductions as rational.[52] Understanding how these sentimental seductions work through historical narrative is critical for rethinking the place of criminal prosecutions as characteristic of new norms. I end with the workings of affective transference as seen in the speeches delivered by Mbizvo and Kenyatta to their respective audiences. For a deeper reflection on the speeches delivered by Mbizvo and Kenyatta to their respective audiences can shed light on how people's relationship to the law is tied to the emergence of a new contemporary socio-moral order. They do this by rendering particular types of violence unsayable and instead communicating the appropriateness of justice norms and their emotional climates through the fetish of "the victim to be saved" by international adjudication.

V AFFECTIVE TRANSFERENCE AND THE REMAKING OF HISTORY

Shamiso Mbizvo's audience involved a room full of seventy-five to one hundred scholars of international law, human rights law, literature, and anthropology of law as well as a range of historians of Africa and the West who were committed to various ways of studying international law's impact on and relationship to Africa. Immediately following her speech she received a standing ovation from scholars who remain sceptical about the court's work. Uhuru Kenyatta's speech was delivered to an outdoor assembly of thousands committed to new justice possibilities of the coalition parties. In both cases their narratives about international law were framed in relation to different historical formations. The past was interwoven with the present to make the contemporary period meaningful.

Like Kenyatta's narrative, Mbizvo's retelling of the ICC's past reflected morally coherent explanations concerning the making of the Rome Statute. The moral mission that led to the establishment of the contemporary rule-of-law movement was tied to its judicial inheritance. In both speeches, messages about inter-relationships between the past and the present responded to various past events and make the present meaningful. As we will see, the viability of those attempts at linkage is more about the seeming success of affective transference through the speaker's ability to communicate sentiments that are meaningful to others than they are about real modalities of interconnection.

To critique international criminal institutions, Kenyatta identified an ongoing violation in order to foreground a stigma that demarcates what is or is not acceptable. He then forced a 'community of survivors' discourse by using language that invoked Kenyan citizens as beneficiaries of yesterday's victim/freedom fighters. From the opening, in which he asserts that the 'sacrifice and heroism of many Kenyans ... won us freedom and sovereignty', to his later invocations of 'our forefather' in order to index kinship, we see attempts to constitute a community.

Once 'senses of community' were constructed, Kenyatta reconciled the substantively disjunctural historical narratives. He decentred the violence of the colonial project and brought it into relevance with the ICC's African trials. By grounding his intervention in Kenya's history of colonial violence and the popular perception of colonial sham trials, Kenyatta engaged in the transmission of feelings of resentment – from one person to another, from a leader to his constituency. Here transmission is possible through a colloquial knowledge about the colonial past and its related subjugation that is embodied in pre-existing responses to loss, sham trials, and experiences of poverty. Suggestions about Africa's place in a unequal past conjure sentiments that produce parallels with the contemporary world order, where feelings of anger from past inequality prevail. Affective transference is possible with the invocation to celebrate the survivors of that inequality. The reference to 'their' ilk highlights the assignment of stigma. But the violence of colonial institutions whose continuities seem to be reflections of contemporary inequality contributes to the feelings of anger at play.

Transference was possible and effective because the histories of colonial violence and its related dispositions were 'decontextualized' from their earlier historical logic and 'recontextualized' into contemporary realities. It was this decontextualization and recontextualization that characterized the magnetism of such forms of postcolonial transference and that oriented the way Kenyatta's message was received. However, the message was contingent on knowledge about colonialism, the relegation of colonial trials to sham trials, and African subordination, which were critical to the connections that audience members had to make. The achievement of transference allowed the sympathetic listener to create mutually linked freedom fighters and revolutionaries out of both Jomo Kenyatta and Uhuru Kenyatta. As such, it affected the perception that Kenyans had of the functioning of the ICC. However, as I show, the message was contingent on an unconscious inventory in which knowledge about colonialism, the relegation of colonial trials to sham trials, and African subordination are critically central to the connections that audience members are left to be made. Such forms of transference allow the sympathetic listener to create mutually linked freedom fighters and revolutionaries out of both Jomo Kenyatta and Uhuru Kenyatta. Mbizvo's uses of transference also allow us to establish ICL and the ICC and its actors, the OTP, as heroes and heroines of victims around the world.

What normally operates in the unconscious is formulated through a specified inventory of popular references that are more socially held and known than they are individually experienced. Themes of long historical connections establish particular affective resonances and connect socially or institutionally moments to emotive templates. In this light, the subordination of the past becomes a mechanism for articulating contemporary inequalities but the past is always signalled dialogically. That is, it is seen as building on the present, thereby constituting a reflection of itself in the present. Through protest speech or celebratory rhetoric, all that is necessary is to demonstrate this dialogism. As a partial practice it is a powerful modality as it makes possible emotional transference in contexts that may be otherwise argued to be substantively different.

Throughout Kenyatta's speech, the audience applauded and shouted for more. When he finished, they roared uncontrollably. Transference happened as a momentary affect that filled a space in the subconscious and produced the terms by which emotional expressions are performed. Such a moment of rhetorical frenzy offers a productive way of understanding how the affect passes from person to person and group to group, creating what Margaret Wetherell refers to as pulses of energetic relations.[53] By accepting the rhetorical link (this 'ilk') between Kenyatta's fight against the ICC and the larger anti-imperial struggles that characterized Kenya's colonial relationships with imperialism over the past century, what they confirmed was the effectiveness of the conjuncture. What interests me here has been how meaning-making is remade as joint projects of historical memory and embodied affects by which

new constructs constantly shape the way the past and present meanings are not
only understood but also regulated in particular ways. For what we see are the
uses of rhetorical strategies that involve popular metaphors used to refer to
deeply traumatic phenomena. And once articulated, those discourses are
sustained through expressive phrases deemed acceptable and networks of
socialization, affective practices, and expressions.

   Through the use of partial knowledge, through partial invocations, Kenyatta
succeeds in getting his audience to connect contemporary justice to selective
histories of colonial sham trials. The logic is that the political histories of
subordination that created Kenya as a colony were the same histories that led
Uhuru Kenyatta to a subordinate place in the realm of international justice
and politics. These historical logics highlighted the way that morally coherent
causalities can be mobilized to produce moral sentiments whose celebrations
are fetishized as the victim-survivor.

   For her part, Mbizvo's use of transference allows her to establish the ICL,
the ICC, and its actors – the OTP – as the heroes and heroines of 'victims'
around the world in which utterances such as 'The ICC exists to hear the
voices of victims of the most atrocious crimes, when their cries fall on deaf
ears' can be used to suggest that the judicialization of political issues can offer
tangible solutions. As such, discourses that might normally operate in the
unconscious through words such as 'victims' or 'ending impunity' can be
formulated through a specified inventory of popular references that are
more socially familiar than they are individually experienced. Themes of
long historical connections establish particular affective resonances and connect socially or institutionally to emotive templates. In this light, past subordination becomes a mechanism for articulating contemporary inequalities,
but the past is always signalled dialogically. That is, it is seen as building on the
present, thereby constituting a reflection of itself in the present. Protest speech
or celebratory rhetoric needs to demonstrate this dialogism. As a partial practice, protest speech is a powerful modality because it makes emotional transference possible in contexts that may be substantively different otherwise. This
connection between particular types of violence and historical facts that are
evidently disjunctural can produce new social truths by dialogically constituting 'the real' through new realignments of the social. This happens not
because the audiences are uninformed, but because of the power of the
intersubjective in tapping into particular existing emotional histories, thereby
shaping meaning.

   The success of affective transference in such rule of law publics is possible
precisely because of the gaps in the violence that the law recognizes. In order
for affective transference to happen, the roads of causality must be presented as

part of a dialogic continuum that renders violence unsayable and unrelated. That the adjudication of colonial violence is not even thinkable connects it to the unsayability of that violence. What is important is how the gaps enable the flow of connections between those prosecutions that are made visible in international legal histories. The related events, people, and the power relations that enable emotional sharing contribute to the establishment of the ordinary logic of law's work. Like Mbizo's description of the ICL's one hundred years of development, what we see is the profound imagery of the grand march to establishing the permanent court as the ultimate evolutionary form of justice for all. A plethora of key international criminal law scholars – from Beth Van Shaack and Ronald Slye, to Kathryn Sikkink and Antonio Cassese – have popularized these narratives about international criminal prosecutions shaping new senses of justice for victims.[54] This use of sentimentality is emotionally pervasive in the literature. *Who wouldn't want to protect victims?*

While only a handful of international relations or international criminal law scholars[55] have explored the construction of the victim as the central fetish of justice, most of those interested in the vicissitudes of social change have focused on changing norms and the linear legal imperatives that shape them. But what I have shown in this chapter is that substantively unrelated histories are often made real, not through actual equivalences but through the symbolic construction of the victim fetish. This production of the real involves the deployment of sentiments of compassion and responsibility around the protection of victims who are seen as being connected to the culmination of a one-hundred-year history of judicial strategies that are ultimately sustained through subsequent networks of socialization. It is also shown through the re-signification of the victim/survivor of colonialism narrative through which particular tropes of imperial justice are narrativized.

VI SENTIMENTALIZED NARRATIVES AND THEIR INSTITUTIONALIZATION

Beth Van Schaack and Ronald Slye, as well as Kathryn Sikkink, have popularized the way that contemporary norms around international criminal prosecutions are shaping new senses of justice for victims as the victorious march to prosecutorial justice.[56] Mbizvo's description of one hundred years of the development of ICL as a historical cascading of justice, a grand march to establish the permanent court as the ultimate evolutionary form of development, supports this imagery. Coining the term *justice cascades*, Sikkink explored how international trials are shaping new norms through the establishment of new expectations of criminal prosecutions throughout the world. But in presuming transformations in the United States, Latin America, the Balkans, and Europe, what she and others have missed is how contemporary notions of ICC justice, that once enjoyed wider popularity, continue to be supplanted by other analyses of what justice looks like. Instead, many of these objectors are insisting on the need for innovative solutions to political problems that are historically continuous and that are meant to address those forms of violence that even ICC-Prosecutorial justice is seen as being unable to address.

For Kenyatta and many other African state and non-state actors, the disavowal of the ICC cannot be said to have led to a public disillusionment with international law. Nor can it be said that it has led to a cascading effect in which judicial mechanisms are being foregrounded as a key modality for addressing violence. Rather, international law is being decontextualized and recontextualized in ways that address African concerns. Amongst those resisting ICC trials as the solution to African violence, what we are seeing is an affective shift to repatriating justice spatially and politically.

Justice cascades, represented as new prosecutorial norms for some, are actually, for others, a metaphor for law's inequalities in which gaps in prosecutorial justice are what characterize the contemporary moment. This identification of the rule of law as constitutive of inequality highlights the competing realities of justice as well as the differences in how its formations are perceived.

VII CONCLUSION

What I have shown in this chapter is that substantively unrelated histories are often made real not through actual equivalences, but through the symbolic 'production of the real'. The production of the real involves the deployment of sentiments around the protection of victims who are seen as connected to the culmination of a 100-year history of judicial strategies. Yet, despite the profundity of the production of the genesis of the Rome Statute as a result of a century old history, even some of international criminal law's juridical architects, such as Antonio Cassese and Cherif Bassiouni, never accepted – empirically, legally, and normatively – the dominant Road to Rome narrative, because they understood that up until 1993 such an institution was not enough to destabilize the modern legal concept of sovereignty. The story that is often left out of the 'Road to Rome' trajectory is the reality that it was the production of the moral responsibility to protect victims of violence that led to the viability of the ad hoc tribunals and eventually the ICC. This is very different from the linear story above. The old Grotian organizing principles of law and sovereignty only changed after a newer Kantian paradigm was said to be superimposed onto it. This development highlights the transformation of legal systems in which old and new legal orders co-existing alongside each other. Such was the case advocated by Cassese in which he clarified that the contemporary legal order characterized by the formation of the ICC was extrapolated from modern statist criminal law. For Cassese, the new sovereignty is a single unitary, top down, and subjecting institution with three sets of international law logics based on: (1) reciprocal relationships; (2) international 'community rights' agreed to by sovereign states through sovereign institutions like treaties, and, after 1994, with the creation of the ICTY, it became shaped by the (3) logic of the notion of the common global good.[57] While for some, the continuity of the pre–WWII period with the post–WWII period is an important trajectory through which to narrativize the rise and success of the rule of the law, what I am highlighting here is that while such discourses can procure powerful means through which to establish law's global ascendance, the reality is that the various selective stops and starts that constitute the history of international criminal law is better seen as a product of affective imaginaries by which social location and embodied logic shape the making of judicial meanings. Through sentimental transference of particular meanings we see how structurally dissimilar phenomena can be decontextualized and recontextualized to produce otherwise contested linkages. For the ICC's OTP, this involves the encounter with new 1990s moral sentiments in which the promise of the ICC's one-hundred-year historical trajectory demonstrates the construction of international law's moral legitimacy as a crucible for social change. The movement's mantra that 'no one is beyond the law' informs the OTP's invocations of their work as being centrally about protecting victims. When understood in relation to affective transference, we see how hope for judicial legitimacy[58] can be breathed into new justice experiments.

For the ICC's OTP, this involves the encounter with new 1990s-based moral sentiments in which the promise of the ICC's one-hundred-year historical trajectory demonstrates the construction of international law's moral legitimacy as a crucible for social change. The movement's mantra that 'no one is beyond the law' informs the OTP's invocations of the new justice as victim's justice. When understood in relation to affective transference, we see how hope for judicial legitimacy can be breathed into new justice experiments.

For various African leaders and their publics, notions of judicial justice involve the articulation of a new vocabulary for analysing the historical underpinnings of violence. In the end, determining which justice mechanisms are appropriate and, by extension, how to respond to them is central to the shifts by which new moral orders are being mobilized to inspire sentimental responses to injustice. Notions of justice are made real through the crafting of postcolonial entitlements in which the law is seen as being unable to deliver. Through spheres of re-signification, perceptions of 'Hague Justice' as injustice are made to undo themselves and new histories are mobilized to produce fetish-like linkages that are difficult to contest but that are also reflective of postcolonial narrative constructions. The sentimentalisms that are both part of postcolonial narratives of colonial violence and the expansion of the rise of the ICC treaty domain are reflective of histories of passion alongside histories of protest and conviction. As an assemblage of social justice imaginaries, affective circuits of meaning-making constitute the way that ordinary knowledge, histories of violence, and geographies of justice produce structures of feeling that are palpable. Yet, as we have seen, these senses of the past do not need to be recuperated through linear and exacting histories in order to create social experiences that make the past meaningful. The reality is that the past is embodied in the present, in senses of being and belonging, and emanates in social encounters that are lived and embodied in public speeches, silences, selective memories, and referential musings. It is manifest in sentimental attachments that accent the cadence of daily life. In the end, such pro-accountability forms of justice, alongside post-colonial formulations, come into being through affects that are normalized, regulated, and institutionalized in particular ways. Through these processes various justice epistemologies are formed and shape the way that senses of justice are narrativized in the contemporary period.

Notes

1. Arlie Russell Hochschild, 'Emotion Work, Feeling Rules, and Social Structure' (1979) 85(3) *American Journal of Sociology* 551–575.
2. Joseph De Rivera, 'Emotional Climate: Social Structure and Emotional Dynamics', in K. T. Strongman (ed.), *International Review of Studies on Emotions* (New York: John Wiley & Sons, 1992).
3. De Rivera, J. and Páez, D., 'Emotional Climate, Human Security, and Cultures of Peace' (2007) 63 *Journal of Social Issues* 233–253. DOI: 10.1111/j.1540-4560.2007.00506.x
4. J. Valsiner, 'Process Structure of Semiotic Mediation in Human Development' (2001) 44 *Human Development* 84–97. DOI:10.1159/000047048.
5. Judith Butler, *Frames of War: When Is Life Grievable?* (New York: Verso, 2009).

6. Previously known as Kenyatta Day, celebrated to commemorate the detention of the Kapenguria Six. However, following the establishment of the new Kenyan constitution in August 2010, Kenyatta Day was renamed 'Mashujaa Day'.
7. See 'Mashujaa Day Speech by Uhuru Kenyatta', *Capital FM*, 20 December 2013.
8. *Ibid.*
9. *Ibid.*
10. Michael Holquist (ed.), *The Dialogic Imagination: Four Essays. By M. M. Bakhtin* (Austin: University of Texas Press, 1981), especially 'Forms of Time and the Chronope in the Novel. Notes toward a Historical Poetics'.
11. Interestingly, despite Kenyatta's attempt to highlight the wealth and power of the West, Kenyatta's own family's wealth and power is ironic as it was seen by the ICC's Office of the Prosecutor (OTP) as an impediment to its investigations as Kenyatta was seen as using his financial and political resources to influence witnesses and the political and legal process.
12. *Ibid.*
13. See Sigmund Freud, 'The Ego and the ID', in Sigmund Freud, *The Standard Edition of the Complete Psychological Works of Sigmund Freud, Vol XIX: 'The Ego and the ID' and Other Works* (London: Vintage Books, 2001) pp. 19–28.
14. Anne Orford, 'On International Legal Method' (2013) 1 *London Review of International Law* 166–197. Anne Orford, 'Locating the International: Military and Monetary Interventions after the Cold War' (1997) 38 *Harvard International Law Journal* 443–486.
15. See Chapter 2 by Shamiso Mbizvo in this volume.
16. Beth Van Schaack and Ronald C. Slye, 'A Concise History of International Criminal Law: Chapter 1 of Understanding International Criminal Law' (Legal Studies Research Paper Series Working Paper No. 07–42, 2007), p. 21.
17. *Ibid.*
18. *Ibid.*
19. *Ibid.*
20. *Ibid.*, p. 23.
21. William A. Schabas, *An Introduction to the International Criminal Court* 4th edn (Cambridge: Cambridge University Press, 2011), p. 3.
22. Treaty of Peace between the Allied and Associated Powers and Germany ('Treaty of Versailles'), (1919) TS 4, Art. 227.
23. Schabas, *An Introduction to the ICC.*
24. Van Schaack and Slye, 'A Concise History of International Criminal Law', p. 24.

25. Schabas, *An Introduction to the ICC*, p. 4.
26. Antonio Cassese, 'From Nuremberg to Rome: International Military Tribunals to the International Criminal Court', in Antonio Cassese, Paola Gaeta and John R.W.D. Jones (eds.), *The Rome Statute of the International Criminal Court: A Commentary*, Vol. 1 (Oxford: Oxford University Press, 2002), pp. 3–19, at 4–5.
27. *Ibid.*
28. Schabas, *An Introduction to the ICC*, pp. 5–6.
29. Van Schaack and Slye, 'A Concise History of International Criminal Law', pp. 30–31.
30. Cassese, 'From Nuremberg to Rome', 7.
31. Van Schaack and Slye, 'A Concise History of International Criminal Law', pp. 30, 32.
32. *Ibid.*, at 32; Schabas, *An Introduction to the ICC*, p. 7.
33. Van Schaack and Slye, 'A Concise History of International Criminal Law', p. 34.
34. *Ibid.*, p. 37.
35. *Ibid.* Cassese, 'From Nuremberg to Rome', p. 8.
36. Van Schaack and Slye, 'A Concise History of International Criminal Law', p. 38.
37. Schabas, *Introduction to the ICC*, pp. 8–9; Cassese, 'From Nuremberg to Rome', 9–10.
38. Schabas, *Introduction to the ICC*, p. 9.
39. UN Doc. SC Res. 780, 6 October 1992.
40. UN Doc.SC Res. 827, 25 May 1993.
41. Schabas, *Introduction to the ICC*, p. 12; Cassese, 'From Nuremberg to Rome', 14.
42. See 'Report of the Ad Hoc Committee on the Establishment of an International Criminal Court', G.A., 50th Sess., Supp. No. 22, A/50/22, 1995; 'Report of the Preparatory Committee on the Establishment of an International Criminal Court, Volume I' (Proceedings of the Preparatory Committee During March, April and August 1996), G.A., 51st Sess., Supp. No. 22, A/51/22, 1996, p. 193; 'Report of the Preparatory Committee on the Establishment of an International Criminal Court, Volume II', G.A., 51st Sess., Supp. No. 22, A/51/22, 1996.
43. The clearest location of Mahmood Mamdani's argument that it was necessary to produce Nuremberg and the model it created for transitional justice is in his 'The Logic of Nuremberg' (2013) 35(21) *London Review of Books* 33–34.
44. This point about the Nuremberg model is clarified more substantively in Mahmood Mamdani's 'Beyond Nuremberg: The Historical Significance of the Post-Apartheid Transition in South Africa' (2015) 43(1) *Politics & Society* 61–88.

45. See Ademola Abass, 'Prosecuting International Crimes in Africa: Rationale Prospects and Challenges' (2013) 24(3) *European Journal of International Law* 933–946, at. 937, citing UN Doc GA Res 2202 A (XXI), 16 December 1966.

46. International Convention on the Suppression and Punishment of the Crime of Apartheid, New York, 30 November 1973, in force 18 July 1976, 1015 UNTS 243., Art. V.

47. See Ademola Abass, 'Prosecuting International Crimes in Africa', at 937, citing J. Dugard, 'International Convention on the Suppression and Punishment of the Crime of Apartheid' (Audio visual Library of International Law, 2008). Also see Art. V of the Apartheid Convention.

48. Siba N. Grovogui, *Beyond Eurocentricism and Anarchy: Memories of International Order and Institutions* (London: Palgrave Macmillan, 2006); Kamari M. Clarke, Forthcoming Manuscript, 2017.

49. Mark Curtis, 'The Mau Mau War in Kenya, 1952–60', *Blog*, 12 February 2007. Edited extract from: Mark Curtis, *Web of Deceit: Britain's Real Role in the World* (London: Vintage, Random House, 2003).

50. Arrest warrants were issued for the following individuals: Joseph Kony, Raska Lukiya, Okot Ohiambo, Dominic Ongwen, Vincent Otti, Thomas Lubanga Dyilo, Bosco Ntaganda, Ahmed Haroun, Ali Kushayb, Germain Katanga, Mathieu Ngudjolo Chui, Jean-Pierre Bemba Gombo, Omar al-Bashir, Callixte Mbarushimana, Muammar Gaddafi, Saif al-Islam Gaddafi, Abdullan al-Senussi, Laurent Gbagbo, Charles Blé Goudé, Simone Gbagbo, Abdel Rahim Hussein, Sylvestre Mudacumura, Walter Barasa, Narcisse Arido, Jean-Jacques Kagongo, Aimé Kilolo Musamba, and Fidèle Wandu. Summons to appear were issued for Bahr Idriss Abu Garda, Abdallah Banda, Saleh Jerbo, Mohammed Ali, Uhuru Kenyatta, Henry Kosgey, Francis Muthaura, William Samoei Ruto, and Joshua Sang.

51. Jean-Pierre Bemba Gombo, William Samoei Ruto, Joshua Sang, and Bosco Ntaganda are currently on trial; Thomas Lubanga Dyilo and Germain Katanga were convicted and serving sentences of fourteen and twelve years respectively; Mathieu Ngudjolo Chui was acquitted; charges were dismissed against Bahr Abu Garda, Callixte Mbarushimana, Mohammed Ali, and Henry Kosgey; charges were withdrawn against Uhuru Kenyatta and Francis Muthaura; the case against Abdullah al-Senussi was declared inadmissible; and proceedings against Raska Lukiya, Saleh Jerbo, and Muammar Gaddafi were terminated due to the death of the individuals.

52. Margaret Wetherell, *Affect and Emotion: A New Social Science Understanding* (London: Sage Publications, 2012), p. 142.

53. Wetherell, *Affect and Emotion*.

54. Van Schaack and Slye, 'A Concise History of International Criminal Law', p. 7; Kathryn Sikkink. *The Justice Cascade: How Human Rights Prosecutions Are Changing World Politics* (New York: W. W. Norton & Company Inc., 2011).

55. See Gerry Simpson, 'The Sentimental Life of International Law' (2015) *London Review of International Law*. Also see Andrew Ross, *Mixed Emotions: Beyond Fear and Hatred in International Conflict* (Chicago: University of Chicago Press, 2014).

56. Van Schaack and Slye, 'A Concise History of International Criminal Law', p. 7; Kathryn Sikkink. *The Justice Cascade: How Human Rights Prosecutions Are Changing World Politics* (New York: W.W. Norton & Company Inc., 2011).

57. Ronald C. Jennings, 'Cosmopolitan Subjects: Critical Reflections on Dualism, International Criminal Law and Sovereignty. Lessons for the African Union from the Yugoslavia Tribunal' (2014) *African Journal of Legal Studies* 321–350, at 327.

58. Here judicial legitimacy refers to the instantiation of legal processes as viable and with the potential to achieve law's goals – that of fairness, certainty, and predictability.

PART II

AFRICAN STATES AND THE ICC

6

The ICC and Africa
Rhetoric, Hypocrisy Management, and Legitimacy

Lee J. M. Seymour

I INTRODUCTION

The International Criminal Court (ICC) was established to prosecute individuals for the most serious crimes of international concern – genocide, war crimes, crimes against humanity, and the crime of aggression. The creation of a permanent, independent court represented a remarkable innovation. The ICC intrudes into both the sovereignty of individual states to administer justice in their territories and the diplomatic administration of justice through *ad hoc* tribunals controlled by states. African states were generally supportive of the ICC through its formation and first years of operation. The institution held the promise of rule-of-law solutions to abuses and a potential defence against the aggression of more powerful states. Perhaps most importantly, the ICC seemed to offer African Member States a more prominent standing in international society.

Initially, the strongest opposition to the ICC came from states outside the institution, both from repressive regimes likely to be targeted for crimes and powerful states sceptical of devolving authority to an institution outside their control. In recent years, however, opposition to the ICC has shifted to a number of important African states and the African Union (AU). Using the collective legitimation functions of the AU, these states have pressured fellow Member States not to cooperate with the ICC, proposed a rival African court with overlapping jurisdiction, refused efforts to open an ICC liaison office in Addis Ababa, and repeatedly lobbied at the UN Security Council for Article 16 deferrals of cases against African heads of state. An extraordinary session of the African Union in October 2013 was accompanied by rumours of a diplomatic push by key African states, including Sudan, Kenya, Rwanda, and Ethiopia, for a mass withdrawal of African states from the ICC. In late 2014, Uganda's president, Yoweri Museveni, renewed his call for African states to withdraw from the court.[1] The South African government's willingness to ignore its own High Court's ruling to prevent Omar al-Bashir's departure from an African Union meeting in June 2015 was yet another public slight to the Court's authority.[2]

It is important not to overstate African opposition to the ICC, however. Indeed, after claiming to be 'done with a court' he described as a 'vessel for oppressing Africa', President Museveni cooperated with the ICC in handing over Dominic Ongwen, an LRA commander, for trial in the Hague.[3] As representatives of the Court note: 'African states received more than 50 percent of the Office of the Prosecutor's requests for cooperation, and some 80 per cent of these requests are met with a positive response'.[4] Backing among African civil society organizations also remains relatively strong. In October 2013, 130 civil society organizations urged African States Parties to the ICC to affirm their support for the Court at the extraordinary AU session on the ICC. Yet the African campaign against the Court arguably represents the most serious threat to its moral authority yet, with important repercussions for the diplomacy of international justice.

The recent backlash against the ICC from African states and the AU has been especially dramatic in light of the initially enthusiastic support for the Court across much of the continent. African states, regional organizations, civil societies, and wider publics played a key role in the creation of the Court. Groups of African lawyers and human rights campaigners made visible contributions to the Campaign for an International Criminal Court (CICC).[5] Senegal was the first state to ratify the Rome Statute creating the Court on 2 February 1999, and a number of conflict-affected states initially considered unlikely to sign up – such as Liberia, the Democratic Republic of Congo (DRC), Burundi, and the Central African Republic (CAR) – soon followed. Africans have been well represented in the Court, not least by the current Chief Prosecutor, Fatou Bensouda from Gambia, but also among the Court's judges and permanent staff. Thirty-four African countries are currently represented among the States Parties to the Rome Statute, comprising over two-thirds of AU Member States. This makes Africa the largest regional bloc in the Assembly of States Parties and underscores the stakes in the present crisis of Africa–ICC relations.

Charges of hypocrisy have been prominent in the campaign against the ICC waged by African statesmen, diplomats, and the AU. The notion of double standards is central to their case. In its almost fourteen-year history, the Court has only indicted Africans, namely in the DRC, Uganda, the CAR, Sudan (Darfur), Kenya, Libya, Cote d'Ivoire, and Mali, with investigations ongoing in Georgia.[6] Yet Africans hardly exercise a monopoly on the commission of serious crimes. For critics of the Court, this record of failing to prosecute serious crimes elsewhere demonstrates the political influence of powerful states in administering international justice. The institution, critics argue, sidelines Africans as it favours Western intervention in the guise of universal justice. What explains this shift in Africa's relations with the Court and why are charges of hypocrisy so prominent? Does hypocrisy matter and how might it be managed? Some observers dismiss concerns over hypocrisy. If anything, they argue, a degree of hypocritical dissembling should be encouraged. Michael Struett, for instance, counsels the ICC to continue 'pretending' to ignore politics. 'To acknowledge the role of non-legal factors would be to open the Court up to accusations of bias, and would serve to undermine the entire project'.[7] The ICC Office of the Prosecutor (OTP) effectively adopts the same strategy in publicly discounting the role of politics. Benjamin Schiff echoes this view in dismissing charges that the ICC is inherently discriminatory. 'This charge is substantial, but does not differentiate the ICC from other international organizations, including the United Nations'.[8] Yet this overlooks the fact that not all international organizations are equally vulnerable to accusations of discrimination from their members. The United Nations (UN) draws on a universal membership, a deep reservoir of institutional legitimacy, and support of the most powerful states in the international system, and would arguably survive the withdrawal of its African Member States. The same cannot be said of the ICC.

I argue that hypocrisy, defined as deeds inconsistent with proclamations of moral value and virtue, is inevitable for an institution such as the ICC.[9] But when it moves from background rumbling to the foreground of rhetoric and diplomacy around the Court, hypocrisy erodes the ICC's legitimacy, defined broadly as the normative belief that an institution ought to be obeyed.[10] Indeed, I contend that the diplomacy around Africa's relationship to the ICC reveals much about the social structure of international diplomacy and Africa's social positioning in the wider international system. The ICC's legitimacy is bolstered through recourse to the norms and values of an idealized vision of justice beyond politics and draws heavily on the legitimating force of law. This renders the Court vulnerable to accusations of hypocrisy that expose obvious contradictions between this vision and the manifestly political world in which legal justice is pursued. Accusations of hypocrisy by the ICC's African critics are highly strategic, frequently made by actors with agendas as self-interested as those they claim to expose. Yet they have found sympathetic audiences by identifying morally problematic contradictions in the Court's record. The African-led campaign against the ICC has imposed real costs and dented its legitimacy, particularly among the African officials on whose cooperation it depends. This has generated significant dilemmas over how to respond to these charges for the ICC and its supporters.

I begin by demonstrating how the normative foundations of the Court's legitimacy in a universal vision of law autonomous from politics render it vulnerable to accusations of hypocrisy. Reviewing the origins of the African campaign against the ICC, I locate its origins in a divergence of interests between key African states and the Court beginning with the al-Bashir indictment and continuing with the Kenyan and Libyan situations. This transformed key African elites from sympathetic observers of ICC hypocrisy with a stake in the institution's legitimacy into actors seeking to use this hypocrisy to undermine a Court that increasingly and repeatedly infringed upon their interests. By implication, the way for the ICC to manage hypocrisy is to put an end to the mutually destructive anti-hypocrisy campaigns waged by both sides and return to the shared social purposes that initially brought Western and African states together around the ICC.

II LEGITIMACY AND INTERNATIONAL JUSTICE

Legitimacy in contemporary international society derives much of its force from international law and the norms and values associated with it.[11] The Rome Statute's backers relied explicitly on the legitimating force of international law to establish the Court. The ICC continues to derive its moral authority from its claim to pursue international criminal law on legal rather than political grounds. Given the absence of coercive powers and reliance on state cooperation in pursuing its mandate, the ICC is highly dependent on its continual legitimation.

In legitimating its actions, however, the ICC has to navigate the political interests of multiple constituencies whose visions seldom overlap. Satisfying them is a complex political task, not least in reconciling legal principles and political realities. On one side, we find deeply socialized core supporters who believe in the institution and support it more or less unconditionally in its pursuit to end impunity, support rule of law, and deter atrocity crimes. Their support hinges, in part, on publicly preserving the illusion of law's autonomy from politics at the core of human rights liberalism. On the other side, however, there is arguably a far higher number of weakly socialized actors whose support for the Court is far more conditional, and perhaps even cynical, including many African elites subsequently disillusioned with the ICC. For these actors, the ICC serves potentially useful political functions and its legitimacy hinges on its ability to further their self-interests. To the extent that the Court's usefulness for these actors is enhanced by this same illusion of the Court's autonomy from politics, elites with little belief in the liberal and cosmopolitan ideals underpinning the Court were willing to cooperate in pretending that the ICC stood above politics. When the Court began to pose a danger to their interests, however, they were no longer willing to play along. Instead, they began to expose this notion of political neutrality as a hypocritical sham.

The notion of emancipating law from politics was central to the ICC's institutional design, which masked inequalities of power behind rules that applied, at least potentially, to everybody, hence the Rome Statute's language of the determination 'to put an end to impunity for the perpetrators of the most serious crimes of concern to the International Community as a whole'. In order for the ICC to be seen as legitimate, States Parties took the legal power they sought to wield through the Court and institutionalized it at a distance. As with any institution autonomous from state control, this created opportunities to act counter to state interests, which for many actors was precisely the point. For Western countries with highly capable legal systems and only distant memories of violent conflict, the ICC's complementarity provisions made it unlikely that crimes committed on their territory or by their nationals would ever be brought before the Court. Powerful states hostile to the Court were also largely beyond its remit, owing to their non-signatory status, ability to veto Security Council referrals, and the informal pressure they could bring to bear, even as they sought to use the Court for their own ends. The United States, most notably, has used the ICC instrumentally in ways that has subjected it to accusations of hypocrisy. African states, however, were in a far more vulnerable position, both legally and politically, owing to the greater proportion of crimes committed in their jurisdictions and their limited power in international diplomacy.

The vulnerability of African states was initially offset by the promise of a substantial voice within an institution where the most powerful states were absent. In the ICC's first years, there was little talk among Africans of double standards in the situations investigated by the ICC. Eager to establish the ICC's credentials, the Prosecutor investigated a number of African situations and prosecuted several politically marginal African defendants. In the first three situations investigated by the ICC, the governments of the DRC, CAR, and Uganda had all referred their own conflicts to the ICC. This seemed to demonstrate how the ICC could work in ways compatible with the interests of African states, complementing state sovereignty rather than infringing upon it. At the time, those Africans with concerns about ICC justice in these cases largely hailed from the excluded communities jointly targeted by military and judicial interventions – most notably in northern Uganda – with little voice in international diplomacy.[12]

Hypocrisy is particularly endemic in the politics of liberalism, Judith Shklar reminds us, which generates an 'ample fund of hypocrisy'.[13] Having to persuade others through idealism and make compromises to realpolitik, as supporters of the ICC have sought to do in building the Court, leaves the institution vulnerable to critics pointing to the inconsistencies that follow. In part because hypocrisy is so pervasive, it is often overlooked, particularly when those acting hypocritically do so in ways that elicit sympathy among others for the conflicting values at hand.[14] ICC supporters, for instance, did not much mind when unsavoury leaders such as Joseph Kabila and Yoweri Museveni worked with the Court in referring situations in their countries to the ICC. Supporters of the Court likewise welcomed the US votes in favour of Security Council resolutions referring situations in Libya and Syria (the former successfully and the latter defeated by Russian and Chinese vetoes), despite Washington's refusal to ratify the Rome Statute, and a history of limitations on engagement with the ICC and bilateral agreements that seek to prevent states from handing over US citizens to the Court. In all of these instances, justice is politically instrumentalized in ways at odds with the legal and ethical vision of the ICC. But owing to sympathy with the underlying values pursued, most observers politely ignored these inconsistencies. For friends of the Court, such political compromises were a price worth paying, allowing at least some serious crimes to be prosecuted while preserving good relations with governments and avoiding a diplomatic backlash against a vulnerable Court.

It is therefore worth recalling that the trigger for initial African opposition to the ICC was not a record of biased prosecutions targeting Africans by what several African leaders have since referred to as a racially biased, neo-colonial institution. Rather, it was the way the diplomacy around the ICC sidelined key African leaders and diplomats around a series of crises in Africa. In many African capitals, this transformed the ICC from an instrument extending African influence in international diplomacy into another instrument for western intervention on the continent. It was the al-Bashir indictment – notably foreshadowed by a diplomatic dispute over Western efforts to exercise 'universal jurisdiction' against African leaders – that brought what might be termed the institution's 'era of easy hypocrisy' to a close.[15] Tensions were further aggravated by the subsequent Kenyan and Libyan situations, which also proceeded against the expressed opposition of a number of key African states and the AU. A brief history of these three episodes sheds light on what motivates charges of hypocrisy and double standards from African critics of the ICC. The diplomacy around the ICC's involvement in Darfur, Kenya, and Libya exemplify the marginalization of African states and the AU in conflict management and international justice.

A *The Turning Point: The al-Bashir Indictment*

Investigations in Darfur leading to the prosecution of Sudan's president, Omar al-Bashir, exposed the limits to African influence in the ICC. In this and subsequent indictments targeting African heads of state, the interests of a number of Western and African states conflicted. The episode engendered scepticism about the way the ICC afforded new opportunities to use international law and morality to the detriment of African interests.

The situation in Sudan was referred to the ICC through a UN Security Council resolution (1593), confirming to many the political nature of the investigations. Sudan's government noted the double standards inherent in the application of international criminal law to enemies of the West, overlooking crimes committed by Western states and their allies.[16] Far more consequential than the objections of an isolated government, however, was AU and Arab League opposition as the ICC's Darfur investigations proceeded. The AU did not protest when the situation was referred to the ICC, or when the ICC issued its first arrest warrants for government minister Ahmed Harun and rebel leader Ali Kushayb in April 2007. When investigations led to Sudan's president, however, the AU strongly objected. The Prosecutor ignored African requests not to proceed in its case against al-Bashir, including an AU decision warning against the exercise of 'universal jurisdiction' in Africa just two weeks before the Prosecutor applied to the Pre-Trial Chamber (PTC) for an arrest warrant for al-Bashir on 14 July 2008.[17]

The AU's role in Darfur compounded the impact of these diplomatic slights. The AU had taken on the thankless task of peacekeeping and peace-making interventions in Darfur, owing largely to the reluctance of Western states to play a political role on the ground commensurate with their expressions of moral indignation.[18] In early July 2008, as the diplomatic crisis over the impending application for al-Bashir's arrest warrant unfolded, seven African peacekeepers were killed in Darfur. The AU's Peace and Security Council, in a resolution subsequently extending the mandate of the joint AU–UN force in Darfur, requested the UN Security Council to defer the process initiated by the ICC. The request argued that the indictment jeopardized ongoing peace efforts, reiterated African opposition to the exercise of 'universal jurisdiction' against African leaders, and stressed 'the need for international justice to be conducted in a transparent and fair manner, in order to avoid any perception of double standard'.[19]

Both the UN Security Council and the ICC refused to heed this request for an Article 16 deferral. The PTC issued an arrest warrant for al-Bashir in March 2009. The next day, the AU's Peace and Security Council again called upon the UN Security Council to defer the case. The request was repeated at a meeting of African States Parties to the Rome Statute in June 2009, and again at the AU Assembly a month later, where the AU expressed its deep regrets that its prior request for a deferral had 'neither been heard nor acted upon'. It also decided that 'AU Member States shall not cooperate pursuant to the provisions of Article 98 of the Rome Statute of the ICC relating to immunities, for the arrest and surrender of President Omar El Bashir of The Sudan'.[20] This marked a new low in Africa–ICC relations.[21]

B Opposition Deepens: The Kenyan Situation

Subsequent investigations in Africa, especially in Kenya, further escalated tensions.[22] The Kenyan government reacted to the violence that followed the 2007–2008 elections by setting up an inquiry, the Waki Commission. But when efforts to prosecute those responsible for election violence through a national mechanism stalled in the Kenyan parliament, mediator Kofi Annan handed the ICC a list of individuals that the Waki Commission thought should be investigated. The Kenyan government repeatedly stalled on its promises to initiate proceedings and breached an agreement to self-refer the case to the ICC. In response, Chief Prosecutor Luis Moreno-Ocampo requested the PTC to open an investigation in November 2009. The judges agreed in March 2010. In December, the Prosecutor named six high-level individuals as suspects, evenly distributed between rival factions.

The Kenyan government responded by mobilizing against the ICC, relying heavily on charges of hypocrisy in its rhetoric. Kenya's parliament followed the announcement of the 'Ocampo Six' by voting to withdraw from the ICC. One minister argued that 'it is only Africans from former colonies who are being tried at the ICC. No American or British will be tried at the ICC and we should not willingly allow ourselves to return to colonialism.'[23] In February 2011, the Kenyan government unsuccessfully pushed the Security Council to defer the cases. Uhuru Kenyatta and William Ruto – former rivals in the 2007–2008 violence – were among the six accused and subsequently formed an alliance to contest the March 2013 elections. Building on the Kibaki government's opposition to the ICC, they campaigned for elections by denouncing the Court and claiming the vote to be a referendum on the ICC. When they prevailed with 50.7% of the vote, the African campaign against the ICC gained new prominence.

The Kenyatta government has proved adept at undermining the ICC cases, both internationally and domestically.[24] The Kenyan government gained the AU's backing to defer investigations in January 2011 and pushed the East African Legislative Assembly to request that the cases be transferred to the East African Court of Justice (EACJ). Kenya escalated the situation with a request to the UN Security Council for 'immediate termination' of the cases in May 2013 to no avail, then pushed unsuccessfully for a mass withdrawal at an AU special summit in October 2013. The AU then again pushed for an Article 16 deferral at the UN Security Council in November 2013 in a resolution that failed to pass, garnering seven votes and eight abstentions.[25] Throughout this diplomatic offensive, Kenya's campaign has attracted the support of a number of key African states opposed to the ICC, including Rwanda, Ethiopia, Sudan, and Uganda. At home, the Kenyan government blocked investigators and intimidated and bribed witnesses. This led the court to suspend its case against President Kenyatta before the trail had even begun and suspend its case against Deputy President William Ruto.

C Libya

As popular protests in Libya degenerated into a stalemated civil war in 2011, AU leaders sought to negotiate a transfer of power. The French, British, and US-led NATO intervention authorized by UN Security Council resolution 1973, adopted on 17 March, quickly overtook the efforts of an ad hoc committee of African leaders to mediate. Though African states were divided on whether President Gaddafi should step down, they shared an interest ending a conflict that threatened to destabilize large parts of the Sahel. With NATO stretching the interpretation of 'civilian protection' in its Security Council mandate into the pursuit of regime change, and marginalizing AU mediation attempts, African leaders questioned the 'legality and legitimacy' of NATO's intervention.[26] When the ICC issued an arrest warrant for Gaddafi on June 27, thus complicating the AU initiatives to end the conflict by pushing the dictator into exile, the African Union resolved not to cooperate with the arrest warrants. South Africa, whose President Zuma had led efforts to broker a settlement, remarked that 'it's quite unfortunate that the ICC could take such a decision whilst the African Union [AU] through its ad hoc committee has done so much'.

III HYPOCRISY, RHETORICAL ACTION, AND INTERNATIONAL JUSTICE

The diplomatic campaign waged by African states against the ICC can be understood as a form of rhetorical action premised on the exposure of hypocrisy. Though the campaign is not exclusively discursive, there has been much talk and little action. In rhetorical action, strategically motivated actors use a logic of appropriateness to their advantage, manipulating norms-based arguments to change behaviour through social shaming that underscores hypocrisy. The sort of allegations made by African states have been especially pernicious ones, touching on institutional and legal hypocrisy, more specifically. Institutional hypocrisy stems from 'a disparity between the publicly avowed purposes of an institution and its actual performance or function'.[27] Similarly, legal hypocrisy involves actions 'that betray the avowed values of the legal system' in order to 'gain some sort of benefit'.[28]

The back-and-forth arguments over the ICC's role in Africa play out a familiar politics of anti-hypocrisy, with each side seeking to delegitimize the other. As Judith Shklar argues, the fact that hypocrisy is systematic public life, and in liberal politics in particular, helps sustain this system of hypocrisy and counter-hypocrisy. Thus, the Court's African opponents underscore contradictions between the ICC's lofty moral proclamations and the track record of an institution forced to reconcile itself to power politics. Proponents of the ICC counter by pointing out the self-serving nature of the African opposition to the Court. The Court's chief Prosecutor argues that 'the greatest affront to victims of these brutal and unimaginable crimes ... is to see those powerful individuals responsible for their sufferings trying to portray themselves as the victims of a pro-western, anti-African court'.[29] Kenyan President and former ICC defendant Uhuru Kenyatta proclaims that the Court 'stopped being the home of justice the day it became the toy of declining imperial powers. Africa is not a third-rate territory of second-class peoples.'[30]

Arguments that are more truthful tend to carry a greater rhetorical punch, but even false arguments can be effective when the speaker is credible and can devise a compelling frame for the audience that exposes prior normative commitments to the test of hypocrisy.[31] The audience for rhetorical action includes both opponents accused of hypocrisy, who are susceptible to shaming because they care about the underlying norms and values at stake, as well as influential audiences who can bring pressure to bear on the target. One thus sees African opposition to the ICC strategically targeting the Court and its supporters, as well as influential states and domestic publics sympathetic to the case being made. The charge of bias against Africa, for instance, finds empirical support in the ICC's record of investigations and prosecutions. This bias is not necessarily racially motivated, but the accusation of institutionalized racism taps into compelling frames of imperial governance systems that used legal systems built on racial categories to reinforce Western hegemony. Certain African opponents of the Court have more credibility than others; to foreign audiences at least, indictees and defendants of the Court are the least credible owing to their self-interest. But even actors directly implicated in the outcome of the campaign against the ICC have been joined by a wider array of states whose interests are less obvious.

It is possible to identify three basic variations in the arguments advanced by the Court's African opponents, namely bias against the weak, political motivations, and racist and neo-colonial interference. These are the most important substantive critiques in anti-ICC rhetoric from Africa, all focusing on the institutional and legal hypocrisy at stake. I examine these rhetorical themes using Martha Finnemore's operationalization of hypocrisy: 'First, the actor's actions are at odds with its proclaimed values. Second, alternative actions are available. Third, the actor is likely trying to deceive others about the mismatch between its actions and values.'[32] Here, I concentrate on the hypocrisies of the ICC and its supporters. The dissembling of the ICC's Africa's opponents is relevant, particularly for the credibility with which their claims are met by outside audiences. But the legitimacy of the Court is ultimately shaped by perception of hypocrisy from the ICC itself.

A Bias against the Weak

Perhaps the most frequent claim is that the ICC is a tool for powerful states. The hypocrisies here are the pretensions to universality and claim to 'speak law to power' when the Court is hemmed in by powerful states and used for their purposes to discipline political enemies in weak states.

The ICC's self-representation opens it up to allegations of kowtowing to powerful states and their allies. The current ICC Chief Prosecutor, reflecting the view of many ICC supporters, argues that '[i]nternational justice gives power of leadership to small and medium countries, to principled states, those who are determined to use the power of the law, not the power of arms, to protect their citizens and their territories'.[33] As the Prosecutor has argued elsewhere, 'I believe in law as power for all; it is the ultimate weapon that the weak have against the strong. Indeed, when implemented equally and fairly, the law sets one standard for everyone; it empowers all peoples and provides justice for all.'

Conversely, African leaders frequently point to power politics and power asymmetries at odds with the notion of small state leadership in the ICC. For many, recent revelations portray the institution in its early years as eager to work with powerful states in establishing the Court's credibility.[34] The subsequent record of investigations has done little to alter this impression. As Mahmood Mamdani observes, '[i]ts name notwithstanding, the ICC is rapidly turning into a Western Court to try African crimes against humanity. Even then, its approach is selective: it targets governments which are adversaries of the US and ignores US allies, effectively conferring impunity on them.'[35] Opposing the arrest warrant of Libyan leader Muammar Gaddafi, AU chairman Jean Ping argued that the exclusive focus on Africa was 'discriminatory', since it ignored crimes committed by Western powers, including in Afghanistan, Iraq, and Pakistan. The Court's relationship to the Security Council is especially suggestive of the sinews of power behind the Court's ability to flex its judicial muscle. After the failed attempt to pass a UN Security Council resolution to defer the cases against Kenyatta and Ruto, which had the support of all three African states on the Council, the Rwandan ambassador to the UN noted that 'today's vote undermined the principle of sovereign equality and confirmed the long-held view that international mechanisms were manipulated to serve select interests'.[36] Article 16, he added, was only for powerful states to 'protect their own'.

What makes this hypocritical on the ICC's part, African critics imply, is that the Court could have pursued the alternative course of taking on politically powerful opponents. Any number of situations outside Africa should have seen more sustained scrutiny from the Court. Moreover, instead of repeating the same staid defences of the Court's independence, the ICC might be more forthright about the political constraints under which it operates. While rhetorically powerful in attempting to forge a coalition of weaker states in the South, this critique arguably says less about the grievances precipitating the current crisis than the other two themes prominent in African criticism.

B Political Justice

Another key theme is the notion that the ICC is politically motivated. The hypocrisy here concerns the claim that legal criteria guide prosecutions, when in fact they provide a convenient cover for the pursuit of political interests by those exercising control over the Court.

Under Luis Moreno-Ocampo, the Office of the Prosecutor (OTP) consistently refused to accept either political considerations or the responsibility for peace. In a 2007 position paper, the OTP stated that 'there is a difference between the concepts of the interests of justice and the interests of peace and that the latter falls within the mandate of institutions other than the Office of the Prosecutor'.[37] The OTP strategy continues this insistence on adhering to legal criteria in selecting situations to investigate and individuals to prosecute:

> The Rome Statue provides the [OTP] with a precise framework made up of legal criteria used to select situations to investigate; these are jurisdiction, admissibility, and the interests of justice ... The Prosecutor determines independently whether these criteria are met and bases his decision to open an investigation on this analysis without taking political considerations into account.[38]

As Chief Prosecutor Bensouda argues: 'We are a new tool, a judicial tool, not a tool in the hands of politicians who think they can decide when to plug or unplug us'.[39] Yet the ICC is at the whim of the Security Council's ability to issue Article 16 deferrals. In the Darfur case, for instance, we know that the American, British, and French governments coordinated a referral of the situation in Darfur with diplomacy in Sudan, and then debated the political logic of deferring the al-Bashir indictment in the context of negotiations over Darfur.[40] Effectively, they treated the Court as a tool to be 'plugged or unplugged'.

Indeed, African opponents of the Court see politics as inextricably caught up in ICC justice. Rwandan foreign minister Louise Mushikiwabo, for instance, points to diplomatic manoeuvring behind the ICC to dismiss it as 'political court'. These criticisms build on the many moments when politics intrude into the Court's functioning, not least the ICC's problematic relationship to the Security Council and efforts to mollify powerful states. The political foundations of international justice are obvious to many audiences. In fact, alongside charges of political motivation by African leaders there tend to be calls for the ICC to be more political. In the push back against the al-Bashir, Kenyatta, and Ruto indictments, for instance, one observes calls for more and not less emphasis on political considerations. Whether in ceding to African demands that prosecutions not proceed, be better sequenced with mediation efforts, or not legitimate regime change, African critiques demand that the ICC operate politically in ways congruent with African interests.

What is at stake, then, is not the discrepancy between an idealized vision of law distinct from politics, but clear disagreements on the kind of politics that the ICC should play. The alternative actions ICC critics see as underscoring hypocrisy thus run not towards purging politics from the ICC but giving due consideration to African political interests in dispensing justice. It is the divergent purposes that Western and African states see for the Court in situations such as Darfur and Kenya, and the sense that the Court persistently favours the ICC's Western backers, that motivate African efforts to unmask the political foundations of ICC justice.

C Racism and Neo-colonialism

The final theme in African criticism of the ICC, the charge of institutionalized racism with neo-colonial resonances, is perhaps the most loaded. Racial hierarchies receive little acknowledgement in international diplomacy. Their existence is an affront to pretensions to universalism in international law. The response of the ICC and its supporters is thus to dismiss the notion. Makau W. Mutua, defending the Court, considers the 'preposterous accusation' of racist hypocrisy as 'the homage that vice pays to virtue'.[41] For the Court's supporters, whether from Africa, the West, or elsewhere, the ICC does represent a universal will to justice that is as much Western as African.

Yet African leaders frequently express opposition to the ICC in racial overtones. In his capacity as AU chair, Ethiopian prime minister Hailemariam Desalegn recently noted that: 'African leaders have come to a consensus that the (ICC) process that has been conducted in Africa has a flaw. The intention was to avoid any kind of impunity ... but now the process has degenerated to some kind of race hunting'.[42] Addressing the AU, Uhuru Kenyatta complained that 'we would love nothing more than to have an international forum for justice and accountability, but what choice do we have when we get only bias and race-hunting at the ICC?'[43]

The self-serving agendas behind such statements and their targeting of domestic African audiences for whom the neo-colonial frame resonates invite quick dismissals from supporters of the Court. However, these fail to engage with the essence of the critique, which is less the personal hypocrisy of racists than the colonial origins of the sort of historical institutional and legal hypocrisy the ICC regime reflects. As Siba Grovogui writes:

> The practice of sovereignty has been characterized by concurrent but parallel coordinates that prescribe and legitimize specific patterns of actions in each region of the world. The resulting institutional arrangements or international regimes gave form to international governance through different but complementary rules, norms and standards of behavior for agents and actors situated in different regions of the world and held together by historic power relations.[44]

Behind the charge of racism are the divergent political interests and uneven power relations that lead the ICC to focus on Africa. These have deeper historical resonances in forms of rule that privileged Western states over African ones and, in the perception of many African states, continue to do so. Correspondingly, the alternative course of action that renders the roster of exclusively African defendants hypocritical to the institution's critics goes beyond prosecuting non-Africans. It is about remedying the perceived exclusion of African states in the construction of international criminal law and morality through the ICC and other instruments of global governance – an exclusion based in contemporary practices of marginalizing African states and the AU in the diplomacy around contemporary conflicts.

IV HYPOCRISY MANAGEMENT

This analysis has implications for how the Court and its backers should respond. Hypocrisy management denotes 'strategies that involve some combination of social strength (i.e., deep legitimacy) and sympathy among potential accusers with the values conflict that prompts' hypocrisy in the first place.[45] In multiple ways, the Court has sought to engage its critics, but seldom addresses the underlying causes of the current crisis. Continuing to engage their arguments concerning institutional and legal hypocrisies, even when they appear venal and self-serving, is a necessary task. But effective hypocrisy management ultimately involves restoring the Court's legitimacy with key African states and regaining their understanding for the sorts of hypocrisy endemic to the functions of an institution such as the ICC.

Some observers, building on the African critique of the Court's excessive deference to the powerful, argue that the ICC needs to reinvigorate itself with a prosecution that directly confronts the powers dominating the Court. As William Schabas diagnoses the problem, the Court needs to stray 'beyond the comfort zone of the [UN Security Council] permanent members' to recover the enthusiasm in global civil society, Africa and the South more broadly.[46] What is remarkable, however, is how sustained support for the Court has been outside Africa's ruling elite. Despite propaganda denouncing the Court in key African states, public opinion generally remains supportive. In 2009, for instance, 77% of Kenyans and 71% of Nigerians approved of the ICC indictment of al-Bashir. In Kenya, where anti-ICC propaganda has been most intense, opinion has wavered but was largely split between those favouring terminating the ICC cases against Kenyans or proceeding.[47] Over 800 African civil society organizations are represented in the CICC. These audiences, it would appear, do not see the hypocrisy of only targeting the weak as a problem. In fact, many expressions of support from these audiences applaud the Court's attention to Africa. Moreover, the call to prosecute the powerful misdiagnoses the fundamental nature of the ICC's legitimacy crisis among African leaders and the AU. Precipitating a crisis with a powerful state, inviting American or British opposition when the Court is already fending off a legitimacy crisis in Africa, appears unwise.

The history of the conflict between Africa and the ICC and the specific charges levelled against the institution suggest that the disaffection of particular African states stems more from a sense of dislocation from the diplomacy around the Court. Accordingly, the Court needs to realign with the shared social purposes that brought African states so enthusiastically on board the project the ICC represents. For the ICC and its supporters, this involves as a first step abjuring prosecutions of African heads of state that have proven so contentious and expanding the ICC's caseload beyond Africa. Rather than going after situations implicating powerful states, as some suggest, more modest steps of deferring to African leaders in the situations investigated and prosecutions pursued would return to the era of easy hypocrisy that characterized the Court in its initial years. For those impatient to realize a more perfect international criminal law regime, this is likely unsatisfactory. However, as Martha Finnemore reminds us: 'judicious use of hypocrisy can, like good manners, provide crucial strategies for melding ideals and interests. Indeed, honouring social ideals or principles in the breach can have long lasting political effects.'[48]

V CONCLUSION

The ICC potentially represents an important transformation of the social structure of the international system. The institution plays an important role in the contemporary politics of peace and justice – one unimaginable just two decades ago. But stable legal orders require legitimacy.[49] And legal hypocrisy, as Ekow Yankah argues, can 'drain the legitimacy – that is to say the lifeblood – out of a legal system'.[50] As Judith Shklar observed of anti-hypocrisy campaigns: 'in the unending game of mutual unmasking, the general level of sham rises. As each side tries to destroy the credibility of its rivals, politics becomes a treadmill of dissimulation and unmasking.'[51] In marginalizing key African states and the AU from management of the politics of justice and conflict in Africa, the Court and its state backers put the institution in a difficult position. Charges of hypocrisy are morally loaded, and when they stick, they have effects beyond the particular behaviour in question, recasting the identities of the institution and its supporters.

There is much misunderstanding of the roots of this crisis. As Human Rights Watch Director Kenneth Roth observes, 'the court's future now rests to a large extent on the battle being waged between African leaders with little interest in justice and those Africans, including many activists and victims, who see an end to impunity for mass atrocities as essential for Africa's future'.[52] While this observation is accurate, it also misses the real problem. By focusing on the hypocrisy of African leaders, whose narrow self-interest pushes them to under-mine the ICC for personal benefit, we overlook the ability of these leaders to persuade a wider set of African states and publics to mobilize against the Court and reduce the costs of non-compliance with the institution. To end the mutually destructive anti-hypocrisy battle being waged, the Court and its supporters would do well to heed broader African concerns over the ways the ICC is implicated in the continent's marginalization in international diplomacy.

Notes

1. 'Uganda's Museveni Calls on African Nations to Quit the ICC', *Reuters*, 12 December 2014.
2. Norimitsu Onishi, 'Omar al-Bashir, Leaving South Africa, Eludes Arrest Again', *New York Times*, 15 June 2015.
3. Jeffrey Gettleman, 'Senior Rebel from Uganda to Be Moved to The Hague', *New York Times*, 13 January 2015.
4. Olivia Swaak-Goldman, 'Remarks by Olivia Swaak-Goldman' (2012) 106 *ASIL Annual Meeting Proceedings* 313–316.
5. Marlies Glasius, *The International Criminal Court: A Global Civil Society Achievement* (London: Routledge, 2006).
6. The Office of the Prosecutor is undertaking ongoing preliminary investigations in Afghanistan, Colombia, Georgia, Guinea, Honduras, Iraq, Nigeria, Palestine, and Ukraine, in addition to closed investigations where the prosecutor decided not to proceed in Comoros, Republic of Korea, and Venezuela. See OTP, Report on Preliminary Examination Activities 2014, 2 December 2014.
7. Michael Struett, 'Why the International Criminal Court Must Pretend to Ignore Politics' (2012) 26(1) *Ethics and International Affairs* 90.
8. Benjamin Schiff, 'The ICC's Potential for Doing Bad When Pursuing Good' (2012) 26(1) *Ethics and International Affairs* 75.
9. For an expanded definition, see Martha Finnemore, 'Legitimacy, Hypocrisy and the Social Structure of Unipolarity' (2009) 61(1) *World Politics* 58–85.
10. See Ian Hurd, *After Anarchy: Legitimacy and Power in the United Nations Security Council* (Princeton: Princeton University Press, 2008), p. 7.

11. Ian Hurd, 'Legitimacy and Authority in International Politics' (1999) 53(2) *International Organization* 379–408; Allen Buchanan, *Justice, Legitimacy, and Self-Determination: Moral Foundations of International Law* (Oxford: Oxford University Press, 2005). See the Introduction to this volume for an extended conceptual discussion of legitimacy and why it matters in the Court's relationship with Africa.

12. See Erin Baines, 'The Haunting of Alice: Local Approaches to Justice and Reconciliation in Northern Uganda' (2007) 1 *International Journal of Transitional Justice* 91–114.

13. Judith Shklar, *Ordinary Vices* (Cambridge: Harvard University Press, 1985).

14. See Finnemore, 'Legitimacy, Hypocrisy and the Social Structure of Unipolarity'.

15. I borrow this term from Martha Finnemore and Henry Farrell, 'The End of Hypocrisy: American Foreign Policy in the Age of Leaks' (2013) 92 *Foreign Affairs* 22–28.

16. Sarah Nouwen and Wouter Werner, 'Doing Justice to the Political: The International Criminal Court in Uganda and Sudan' (2012) 21(4) *European Journal of International Law* 941–965.

17. See AU Assembly, 'Decision on the Report of the Commission on the Abuse of the Principle of Universal Jurisdiction', Assembly/AU/Dec.199 (XI), 1 July 2008.

18. Lee J.M. Seymour, 'Let's Bullshit! Arguing, Bargaining and Dissembling over Darfur' (2014) 20(3) *European Journal of International Relations* 571–595; Lee J. M. Seymour, 'The Regional Politics of the Darfur Crisis', in David Black and Paul Williams (eds.), *The International Politics of Mass Atrocities: The Case of Darfur* (London: Routledge, 2010), pp. 49–67.

19. See AU Peace and Security Council, 'Communiqué', PSC/MIN/Comm(CXLII), 21 July 2008.

20. See AU, 'Decisions and Declarations,' Assembly/AU/13(XIII), 3 July 2009.

21. ICC States Parties Chad, Kenya, Djibouti, Malawi, Nigeria, and the DRC have all subsequently played host to President al-Bashir.

22. Though overshadowed by the crisis sparked by events in Kenya, the brief dispute over the arrest warrant for Muammar Gaddafi, pre-empted by his killing, also merits further attention. See Alex de Waal, 'African Roles in the Libyan Conflict of 2011' (2012) 89(2) *International Affairs* 365–379.

23. Eunice Rugene, 'Kenya Lawmakers Vote to Pullout of International Criminal Court', *Daily Monitor*, 24 December 2010.

24. Susanne Mueller, 'Kenya and the International Criminal Court (ICC): Politics, the Election and Law' (2014) 8(1) *Journal of Eastern African Studies* 25–42.

25. Azerbaijan, China, Morocco, Pakistan, the Russian Federation, Rwanda, and Togo voted in favour; Argentina, Australia, France, Guatemala, Luxembourg, the Republic of Korea, the United Kingdom, and the United States abstained.

26. De Waal, 'African Roles in the Libyan Conflict of 2011'. See, e.g., AU Commission, 'Report of the Chairperson to the Executive Council, 19th ordinary session', Malabo, 23–28 June 2011.

27. Dennis Thompson quoted in David Runciman, 'Institutional Hypocrisy' (2005) 27(8) *London Review of Books* 3.

28. Ekow Yankah, 'Legal Hypocrisy', Unpublished Paper, University of Pennsylvania, p. 3.

29. David Smith, 'New Chief Prosecutor Defends International Criminal Court', *The Guardian*, 23 May 2012. See Chapter 3 of this volume.

30. Damien McElroy, 'Kenyan President Kenyatta's ICC Trial Set to Be Suspended', *The Telegraph*, 13 October 2013.

31. See Frank Schimmelfennig, 'The Community Trap: Liberal Norms, Rhetorical Action, and the Eastern Enlargement of the European Union' (2001) 55(1) *International Organization* 47–80.

32. Finnemore, 'Legitimacy, Hypocrisy and the Social Structure of Unipolarity', 76.

33. In Smith, 'New Chief Prosecutor'.

34. See, e.g., a WikiLeaks cable suggesting Ocampo was keen to 'dispose of Iraq issues [i.e. not investigate them]' and 'put the USG at ease and assure us that the court will proceed carefully and not launch controversial investigations'. Wikileaks, The Hague Cable, 'ICC: A Cautious Beginning with Mixed Signals from the Prosecutor', 15 July 2003.

35. Mahmood Mamdani, 'Responsibility to Protect or Right to Punish?' (2010) 4(1) *Journal of Intervention and Statebuilding* 62.

36. See UN Press Release, 'Security Council Resolution Seeking Deferral of Kenyan Leaders' Trial Fails to Win Adoption, with 7 Voting in Favour, 8 Abstaining', UN Doc SC/11176, 15 November 2013.

37. OTP, 'The Interest of Justice', September 2007.

38. Olivia Swaak-Goldman, 'Remarks', 315.

39. In Smith, 'New Chief Prosecutor'.

40. See the Wikileaks cable covering these discussions, Wikileaks Sudan Cables, 'Sudan-P3 Discussions on Sudan-ICC Issues', 27 August 2008.

41. Makau W. Mutua, 'Kenya Tests International Justice', *New York Times*, 5 November 2013.

42. Aislinn Laing, 'International Criminal Court is "Hunting" Africans', *Telegraph*, 27 May 2013.

43. Geoffrey York, 'African Union Demands ICC Exempt Leaders from Prosecution', *Globe and Mail*, 12 October 2013.

44. Siba Grovogui, 'Regimes of Sovereignty: International Morality and the African Condition' (2002) 8(3) *European Journal of International Relations* 315–338.
45. Finnemore, 'Legitimacy, Hypocrisy and the Social Structure of Unipolarity', 83.
46. William Schabas, 'The Banality of International Justice' (2013) 11 *Journal of International Criminal Justice* 545–551.
47. See Chapter 10 by Thomas P. Wolf in Part III of this volume.
48. Finnemore, 'Legitimacy, Hypocrisy and the Social Structure of Unipolarity'.
49. Thomas Franck, *The Power of Legitimacy Among Nations* (Oxford: Oxford University Press, 1990).
50. Ekow Yankah, 'Legal Hypocrisy'.
51. Judith Shklar, *Ordinary Vices*, p. 67.
52. Kenneth Roth, 'Africa Attacks the International Criminal Court', *New York Review of Books*, 6 February 2014.

7

France, Africa, and the ICC
The Neocolonialist Critique and the Crisis of Institutional Legitimacy

Paul D. Schmitt

I INTRODUCTION

This chapter examines how the legacy of colonialism continues to exacerbate the growing rift between African states and the International Criminal Court, thus weakening the Court's institutional legitimacy in Africa. Specifically, the Court's almost-exclusive focus to date on crimes committed in Africa has led to criticisms that the Court is a 'neocolonialist' institution, purportedly dispensing justice at the whims of Western powers.[1] The resulting legitimacy crisis comes at a crucial point in the Court's history and development, and threatens to undermine the Court's mission to prosecute grave violations of human rights throughout the world. In this sense, the crisis faced by the Court is similar to Christian Reus-Smit's definition of an 'international crisis of legitimacy', whereby an international institution has arrived at a 'critical turning point when decline in an actor's or institution's legitimacy forces adaptation (through re-legitimation or material inducement) or disempowerment'.[2]

The genesis of the Court's legitimacy crisis in Africa can be traced to the indictment of Sudanese president Omar al-Bashir for war crimes and crimes against humanity in March 2009, and later for genocide.[3] Although reaction against the indictment by African states was relatively muted at the time, the successive indictment of two additional African leaders – Côte d'Ivoire's Laurent Gbagbo (for actions taken during and after his presidency) and Kenya's Uhuru Kenyatta (for actions taken prior to his presidency)[4] – lent momentum to a growing campaign of critics seeking to curtail, or end altogether, the Court's jurisdiction over international crimes in Africa.[5] These views have been supported by various academics, notably Mahmood Mamdani, who has argued that the ICC's almost exclusive focus on situations in Africa suggests that it is 'rapidly turning into a Western court to try African crimes against humanity'.[6]

This chapter presents the case study of France in order to examine the longer historical roots of discontent with the ICC. Although Western nations such as the United Kingdom (UK), Belgium, and the United States (US) have supported the Court in varying degrees,[7] France is particularly vulnerable to the 'neocolonialist' critique given its historical and ongoing role in Africa. Once an imperial power, France maintained a significant presence in Africa both before and after decolonization, and has often intervened militarily to preserve favoured regimes (a dynamic known as *Françafrique*).[8] Further, France has long been one of the Court's major supporters, as it was one of the first signatories of the Rome Statute and has taken an active role in encouraging the prosecution of crimes carried out during civil wars in Libya, Côte d'Ivoire, and Mali. France's unique standing as both former colonial power and present military intervener in Africa can serve to under-mine France's endorsement of the Court as a proper instrument of post-conflict justice. To that end, this chapter examines recent conflicts in former French colonies Côte d'Ivoire and Mali – the former referred to the ICC by the Prosecutor, and the latter self-referred by Mali. I explore the intersection of the historical roots of French intervention and the current political atmo-sphere. Understanding this convergence is a necessary component of engaging with the 'neocolonialist' critique – and resulting legitimacy crisis – faced by the Court.[9]

II FRANCE'S HISTORICAL ROLE IN AFRICA

Systematic French involvement in Africa can be traced to the nineteenth century, starting with the invasion of Algeria in 1830.[10] During the mid-nineteenth century, Louis Faidherbe, the governor of France's settler com-munity in Senegal, conducted a series of expeditions into the interior of West Africa. This territory, eventually known as Afrique Occidentale Française, or AOF, would eventually encompass the colonies of Senegal, Niger, Mauritania, Côte d'Ivoire, Haute Volta (now Burkina Faso), Dahomey (now Benin), Guinée, and Soudan Française (now Mali).[11] France also acquired colonial territory in central Africa, known as Afrique Equatoriale Française (AEF), through the efforts of Pierre Savorgnan de Brazza. In 1880, he founded Brazzaville (in modern-day Republic of the Congo), the eventual capital of AEF. By 1910, France had consolidated the territories of Moyen Congo (now the Republic of the Congo), Gabon, Oubangui-Shari (now the Central African Republic), and Chad into AEF.[12] At its height, the French Empire held approximately one-third of Africa, including AOF, AEF, and French possessions in North Africa and Madagascar.

During the first half of the twentieth century, French made efforts to 'civilize' France's subjects in AOF by providing Western-style education, limited voting rights, and access to the colonial bureaucracy.[13] Of course, the magnanimity of such efforts was belied by the use of *corvée* slave labour by French colonial governments (despite the fact that France had abandoned slavery in the late eighteenth century), as well as political disenfranchisement and other repressive policies.[14] World War II marked a turning point for the colonial system, and especially in the French empire. After the invasion of France by Nazi Germany, the collaborationist Vichy regime struggled to maintain control over the empire against Free French forces led by Charles de Gaulle. Free France's victories in Africa, as well as significant military contributions by France's African subjects in the fight against Vichy and Germany, led to an effort to grant more autonomy to France's African territories after the war. This was, however, a limited policy; at the January 1944 Brazzaville Conference, Free France sought to preserve France's presence in Africa by promising only modest reforms.[15] However, after violent and failed attempts to suppress armed rebellions in Vietnam and Algeria in the 1950s, the proverbial writing was on the wall for the French colonial system.[16] With the return of Charles de Gaulle to power in 1958, France embarked upon a course of returning virtually all control over its African territories to local governments, with these new entities free to choose independence or remain loosely affiliated with France. Most of the former colonies chose continued affiliation, but regional African rivalries and France's inability to manage the larger relationship led to a movement for greater autonomy, culminating in full independence for most of France's African colonies in 1960.

Despite the loss of the empire, France maintained its strong influence on the continent. Notably, De Gaulle organized a special division of African affairs led by Jacques Foccart, who reported directly to the president. For decades, this 'Africa cell' was primarily responsible for French foreign relations in Africa, at times taking precedence even over the Ministry of Foreign Affairs. The legacy of the Africa cell's policies is extremely mixed. On one hand, it provided invaluable funds for stability and development.[17] However, it also inspired countless controversial policies in Africa, including support for Nigerian rebels in Biafra in the 1960s,[18] the propping up of dictators like the Central African Republic's Jean Bedel Bokassa and Zaire's Mobutu Sese Seko,[19] corruption scandals, including one involving the government-owned oil company Elf, and arms deals.[20]

Events in Rwanda brought increased international scepticism regarding France's role in Africa. In the aftermath of the Rwandan genocide, increased attention focused on France's relationship with the genocidal Hutu regime. Although Rwanda had not been a French colony, its status as a French-speaking country led France to consider it as part of France's sphere of influence in Africa. Consequently, France provided significant economic aid and military to Hutu president Juvenal Habyarimana against Paul Kagame's Tutsi-led Rwandan Patriotic Front, the military arm of the Tutsi expatriate community in neighbouring Uganda.[21] As Andrew Wallis has documented, France was likely involved in facilitating the flow of weapons and military equipment to the Hutus,[22] enabling the escape of Hutu *genocidaires* into neighbouring Zaire,[23] and possibly even providing support for Hutu militias.[24] To be certain, France simply followed practices employed by other major powers during the Cold War, when both the United States and the Soviet Union took turns propping up autocratic regimes throughout the world. Nevertheless, growing awareness of France's actions before and during the Rwandan genocide lifted the veil in international perception of French military involvement in Africa.[25]

More recently, both Presidents Nicolas Sarkozy and François Hollande have attempted to steer France away from its past cynical efforts to maintain power and influence in Africa. Under Sarkozy, France de-emphasized unilateral military interventions on the continent.[26] In addition, Sarkozy visited the Rwandan capital of Kigali on 25 February 2010 (albeit only for three hours) and alluded to France's involvement with the Hutu regime, admitting that France had to 'reflect on its errors which interfered with the prevention and arrest of this terrible crime'.[27] Essentially, both Sarkozy and Hollande have emphasized a more humanitarian-based policy that seeks to foster democracy and rule of law in Africa.[28] As Hollande recently explained:

> France has a special relationship with Africa. That relationship is linked to history, and that history has sometimes been tragic ... But times have changed. Relationships can no longer be what they have been in the past. I have on several occasions, wherever I have been in Africa, said that a new era is dawning, that Africa needed full control of its destiny and that to achieve that, it needed to ensure its security itself – yes, itself.[29]

Nevertheless, given France's history in Africa, scepticism remains among African leaders, as well as scholars and observers within the international community, concerning France's motives in its continued engagement with the continent.[30]

III FRENCH SUPPORT FOR INTERNATIONALISM, INTERNATIONAL LAW, AND THE ICC

The view of France's long-term strategic interests in Africa must be contextualized by France's traditionally strong defence of international institutions and international law.[31] As the nation that authored the Declaration of the Rights of Man and the Citizen of 1789, France has always considered itself – with considerable justification – the 'home' of universal human rights, and a champion of those rights in the international community. This defence of human rights and international law is justified by what French scholar Emmanuelle Jouannet refers to as the 'formalist/positivist' mode of French legal culture, by which law – and consequently, international law – is viewed 'exclusively as a body of rules and principles' which seek to avoid consideration of purely pragmatic concerns.[32] Consequently, 'the French regard the formal international rule as the preeminent final product and essential to resolving, constraining, or limiting violence within the context of international law itself'.[33] Of course, this view towards international law, and the United Nations, as being *'a priori* in the service of the common good',[34] underlay France's opposition to the Bush administration's much-maligned pre-emptive war policy in Iraq.[35] This view of the objectivity of international law is highly compatible with the 'legalist' ethos advocated by supporters of the Court, which, as explained by American scholar David Bosco, makes geopolitical considerations secondary to the pursuit of a neutral and objective form of justice.[36]

The French commitment to internationalism is also reflected in the French legal system's reliance on the principal of universal jurisdiction to investigate, and in some cases prosecute, international crimes. Notably, in August 2010, France amended its *code de procédure pénale* to provide for universal jurisdiction over genocide, war crimes, and crimes against humanity (torture and forced disappearances had already been covered by French law), subject to certain jurisdictional requirements.[37] Among the prosecutions that France has undertaken over the years was that of Mauritanian army officer Ely Ould Dah in 2005, for acts of torture carried out during the course of an aborted rebellion in Mauritania in 1990–1991.[38] France has also prosecuted Tunisian police chief Khaled Ben Sa'id *in absentia* for acts of torture carried out in Tunisia.[39] More controversially, in 2006, French investigating magistrate Jean-Louis Bruguière indicted and requested international arrest warrants for nine Rwandan officials (all supporters of President Paul Kagame) for their alleged role in the assassination of former president Juvenal Habyarimana – the event that sparked the Rwandan genocide.[40] Notably, the AU refused to recognize the warrants and accused France of violations of international law in connection with the case.[41] Also a target of criticism was the investigation by a French magistrate judge of the Republic of Congo's president, Denis Sassou Nguesso, along with his military and political supporters, for alleged disappearances, crimes against humanity, and torture carried out against hundreds of Congolese nationals.[42] Regardless of the substantive merit of any of these efforts, they reveal a French commitment to prevent impunity within the international legal regime, even when crimes were not committed within France.

France's general commitment to internationalism has also been reflected in its support for international tribunals. As a member of the Security Council, it supported both the creation of the ICTY and the ICTR.[43] With regard to the ICC, despite initial concerns, particularly from the French military, about potential criminal liability for French peacekeeping and humanitarian intervention forces,[44] France was one of the first states to sign the Rome Statute on 18 July 1998.[45] In addition, after the French Conseil Constitutionnel held in January 1999 that portions of the ICC statute conflicted with the French constitution, France made a further commitment to the Court by amending Article 53 of its constitution to allow ratification of the Rome Statute.[46] In the ICC's early years, France was a significant source of communications received by the Office of the Prosecution (OTP) as to situations around the world meriting further investigation.[47] French support for the ICC was powerfully manifested by the escort of Thomas Lubanga, the first defendant tried by the ICC, to The Hague by the French military in March 2006 after his arrest by DRC authorities.[48] French police also cooperated with the ICC during the 2010 arrest in Paris of Callixte Mbarushimana, a DRC rebel army leader from Rwanda.[49]

France has also recently been a powerful advocate for the Court's investigation and prosecution of international crimes. As David Bosco has recounted, French diplomacy played a vital role in garnering support for the Security Council's referral of the situation in Sudan to the Court in March 2005.[50] In particular, the French ambassador to the UN, Jean Marc de la Sablière, was instrumental in persuading the American delegation not to veto the referral.[51] During the 2011 conflict in Libya – in which France intervened militarily with the United States and the United Kingdom in an attempt to end attacks on civilian populations by dictator Muammar Gaddafi – French authorities prominently advocated for Gaddafi to be tried before the ICC.[52] French diplomats were also instrumental in drafting the referral of the situation in Libya to the Court, and persuading the Security Council to approve it.[53] Finally, French officials have been outspoken about the need for the Court to address war crimes committed in Syria.[54]

However, France's strong support for the Court is tempered by the reality of the Court's almost exclusive focus on Africa conflicts, as well as the legacy of France's colonial history on the continent. France's penchant for military interventions – regardless of the humanitarian merits of France's current and recent involvement in Côte d'Ivoire, Libya, Mali, and the Central African Republic – undermine the notion of France as a disinterested observer. This dynamic is particularly evident in the recent events in Côte d'Ivoire and Mali – both former French colonies – during which France has both intervened militarily and advocated for the Court's involvement in prosecuting international crimes.

IV CÔTE D'IVOIRE

With regard to Côte d'Ivoire, France is a supporter of the International Criminal Court's current proceedings against former president Laurent Gbagbo, as well as Gbagbo's close ally Charles Blé Goudé. This support, as well as Gbagbo's criticism of that support,[55] can only be understood against the backdrop of France's long-term relationship with the country, as well as tensions between France and the Gbagbo regime after France's military intervention in 2004 during the Ivorian civil war.

A *France's History in Côte d'Ivoire*

Starting with independence from France in 1960, and continuing until 1993, Côte d'Ivoire was governed by Felix Houphouët-Boigny, a French-educated doctor, farmer, and union leader who maintained a strong relationship with all of France's presidents, and was commonly seen within French diplomatic circles as the linchpin in France's policy in Africa.[56] However, Houphouët-Boigny's death in 1993 ushered in an era of political instability in Côte d'Ivoire, leading to the military overthrow of his successor, Henri Konan Bédié, in 1999 and the imposition of martial law. Elections were scheduled for 2000, but the Supreme Court ruled that neither Bédié nor northerner Alassane Ouattara could run, the latter on the basis he did not meet the requirement that both parents be born in Côte d'Ivoire.[57] The exclusion of Ouattara, who served as prime minister under Houphouët-Boigny, only exacerbated an already existing perception that Côte d'Ivoire's northern, largely Muslim population was being disenfranchised. Without Bédié or Ouattara participating, Laurent Gbagbo, a rival of Houphouët-Boigny's, defeated the military's hand-picked candidate, General Robert Guéi. This led to an attempted military coup by Guéi and his followers in September 2002. While forces loyal to Gbagbo were successful in preventing the coup from taking control of the country, they could not prevent the outbreak of a civil war. Quite naturally, France took a strong interest in the deterioration of the country. In 2003, France brokered a cease-fire agreement between the two sides, and the UN established the United Nations Mission in Ivory Coast (MINUCI) to oversee a political agreement in the country.[58] MINUCI was replaced in February 2004 by a peacekeeping force of 6,000 troops, known as the United Nations Operation in Côte d'Ivoire (UNOCI).[59] At the same time, under the UN-authorized "Operation Licorne" (Unicorn), France sent an additional 4,000 troops to the country, justified in part by a mutual defence treaty signed with Côte d'Ivoire just after decolonization.[60] In July 2004, the two sides signed a ceasefire, which implemented plans for disarmament and eventual elections.

However, the relative stability resulting from these efforts subsided in October 2004 when the rebel Force Nouvelles (FN) in the northern part of the country and loyalist army units again clashed. By November 4, the army had begun a bombing campaign against the FN, focusing on strongholds in Bouaké and Korhogo[61] and culminating in the November 6 incident that ultimately led to French military intervention.[62] The impetus for the events of that day remains disputed, but what is clear is that the Ivorian air force opened fire on a French military camp in Bouaké, killing several French soldiers, and wounding over thirty others. The government of Côte d'Ivoire claimed the attack was an accident, and that national forces had mistaken French soldiers for rebel forces.[63]

These claims did not matter to French president Jacques Chirac, who ordered an immediate and overwhelming retaliation against Côte d'Ivoire. French planes carried out an airstrike the following day against a military installation in Abidjan, killing seven people and destroying several planes.[64] Additional engagements near Abidjan resulted in the shooting down of two more planes from the Ivorian air force. French forces also took control of the airport, shutting out Côte d'Ivoire personnel and preparing it as a staging ground for additional French forces to arrive. French forces also engaged in significant crowd control measures, opening fire on anti-French protesters and deploying concussion grenades and tear gas to turn back demonstrations.[65] At the same time, French officials attempted to deflect any criticism about France's direct military engagement with Ivorian military and civilians; Prime Minister Jean-Pierre Raffarin emphasized that France had only 'the sole aim of ending the civil war and encouraging all actors to fulfil their responsibilities'.[66]

The French counter-attack against the Ivorian military enraged President Gbagbo and his followers. Côte d'Ivoire immediately filed a protest at the UN through its ambassador Philippe Djangone-Bi, who labelled French actions 'a flagrant violation of Ivorian sovereignty' and requested that an independent commission be formed to review the propriety of the attack.[67] He also condemned the action as a violation of international law, claiming that it was taken both unilaterally and out of any sense of proportion.[68] According to the NGO Fédération Internationale des Ligues des Droits de l'Homme, French attacks against anti-French demonstrations throughout Côte d'Ivoire took at least sixty lives and wounded over a thousand in November alone.[69] Mamadou Koulibaly, president of the country's legislature, complained that 'Côte d'Ivoire has become an overseas territory in Jacques Chirac's head'.[70] For his part, President Gbagbo later stated that 'France's attitude [was] scandalous' and compared French military action to the Soviet Union's invasion of Prague in 1968.[71] 'If a state does not march on the path that [France] wants it to march, then it sends in the tanks. I cannot accept this', he noted. 'Africa cannot accept this much longer.'[72]

Despite this sentiment within the Ivorian government, the international community largely backed France. Notably, while the African Union sent Thabo Mbeki to mediate the conflict, it also pressured the Ivorian government to pull back its military forces to calm tensions within the country.[73] Further, the UN Security Council's unanimous resolution of 15 November 2004 condemned the attacks against French forces by Côte d'Ivoire and approved of France's retaliation, noting its 'full support for the action undertaken by UNOCI and French forces in accordance with their mandate under resolution 1528 (2004)'.[74] Indeed, the resolution specifically exempted France from additional measures taken by the Security Council to keep the peace, including the transfer of arms by other countries to the conflict – thus effectively ending any debate regarding French compliance with international law.

B *The 2010–2011 Electoral Crisis*

After the 2004 settlement, the country remained effectively split between the remainder of the original rebel forces in the north and those areas still loyal to Gbagbo in the south. This split was the catalyst for the 2010–2011 electoral crisis, which pitted Gbagbo against his longtime adversary, northerner Alassane Ouattara. Ouattara had hoped to run for the presidency in an election scheduled for 2005, but that election was cancelled.[75]

The Ougadougou Peace Agreement, signed in March 2007 by Gbagbo and Guillaume Soro (leader of the rebel Forces Nouvelles), again established that an election would be held, but it would be delayed until late 2010. This delay, combined with the north–south tensions, was particularly problematic for the prospects of electoral legitimacy. As one scholar has explained, this was a recipe for disaster; Gbagbo had spent much of his tenure as president fostering a policy of 'ressentiment' of northerners, while northerners and Ouattara supporters resented 'being second-class citizens in their country'.[76]

The first round of the election was held on 31 October 2010, with Gbagbo earning a plurality of the vote (38%), Ouattara 32%, and Bédié 25%. Because no candidate had reached a majority, a run-off was held, with Ouattara prevailing with 54% of the vote to Gbagbo's 46%. However, when the electoral commission attempted to announce the votes, Gbagbo supporters refused to recognize them, and the Gbagbo-controlled Constitutional Council threw out the results of the elections a week later, declaring Gbagbo the winner.[77] Both Gbagbo and Ouattara eventually took an oath of office. The Security Council recognized Ouattara as the winner of the election on 20 December[78] and later urged Gbagbo to surrender power.[79] On 6 January 2011, Ouattara petitioned ECOWAS to intervene militarily to force Gbagbo out of the country.[80] Just two weeks later, the UN Security Council authorized the deployment of an additional 2,000 military personnel to UNOCI.[81] For its part, the African Union was divided, with some member states opposing Gbagbo and others opposing foreign intervention.[82] Without the existence of a strong consensus within its Member States, the AU attempted to mediate the conflict between the two sides and did not recognize Ouattara's victory until March 2011.[83]

The electoral crisis set off a wave of violence throughout the country that lasted four months. The Pre-Trial Chamber of the ICC has since held that there was a reasonable basis to believe that pro-Gbagbo forces carried out war crimes and crimes against humanity (including murder, rape, arbitrary arrest and detention, and enforced disappearance), through widespread and systematic attacks against civilian Ouattara supporters in Abidjan and western Côte d'Ivoire from December 2010 through May 2011, and that Gbagbo was in charge of the state apparatus for these attacks.[84] The Pre-Trial chamber also found that there was a reasonable basis to believe that pro-Ouattara forces carried out war crimes and crimes against humanity, including attacks against civilian supporters of Gbagbo in western Côte d'Ivoire in March 2011, and that these attacks were pursued according to an organizational policy and were widespread and systematic.[85] The crisis ended in April 2011, when Gbagbo was arrested, very likely with the help of French forces.[86]

C *The ICC and France*

In line with Sarkozy's policy of de-emphasizing French involvement in Africa, French officials made clear that, at the very least, France would not oppose, and would consider supporting, potential ICC involvement.[87] In December 2010, then French president Nicolas Sarkozy made clear France's position in favour of possible ICC involvement:

> C'est à lui [Laurent Gbagbo] de choisir quelle est l'image qu'il veut laisser dans l'Histoire. S'il veut laisser l'image d'un homme de paix, il est encore temps mais le temps presse et il doit partir ... Ou est-ce qu'il veut laisser l'image de quelqu'un qui a tiré sur des civils parfaitement innocents? Et, dans ce cas-là, il y a des juridictions internationales et une cour pénale [internationale]. Le procureur [de la CPI] a lui-même indiqué qu'il regardait de très près la situation et que ceux qui avaient fait tirer auraient à en rendre compte.[88]

For its part, the AU took no firm stance during the crisis regarding the possibility of Gbagbo being sent to the ICC. However, numerous diplomatic efforts were made, including a high-level mediation led by Nigeria's Goodluck Jonathan and Kenya's Raila Odinga, to attempt to persuade Gbagbo to leave the country in exchange for not being prosecuted for his actions.[89] These entreaties were rejected by Gbagbo.[90] As it became clear that Gbagbo would not go peacefully, French officials continued to raise the possibility of ICC involvement. In April 2011, at the height of the crisis, Foreign Minister Alain Juppé noted that '[a]s for Gbagbo's fate, it's neither for me nor the French government to decide. There will be judicial proceedings: Ivorian, if that's what the Ivorian government decides, or international if the International Criminal Court continues the investigation into Gbagbo.'[91]

The ICC issued an arrest warrant for Gbagbo on 23 November 2011, on the grounds that he was allegedly responsible, as an indirect perpetrator, for four counts of crimes against humanity for post-electoral violence, including murder, rape and sexual violence, persecution, and other inhumane acts.[92] He was transferred to The Hague a week later.[93] On 5 December 2011, Gbagbo made his first appearance before the Court – the first time that a former Head of State had done so. At his hearing, Gbagbo relied on the neocolonialist critique of France and the Court, stating that 'I was arrested under French bombs. It was the French army that did the job.'[94] Gbagbo's lawyers labelled the Court as 'neocolonialist',[95] and Gbagbo's advisor Alain Toussaint remarked that '[t]he International Criminal Court has become a pathetic tool, which France uses to advance its dark political designs, orchestrate Africa's political affairs, put its own friends in power'.[96]

This stance was consistent with the resentment Gbagbo maintained against France for the 2004 crisis. As Mike McGovern has explained, 'many of those surrounding Gbagbo ... believe that one of the primary dynamics in the Ivorian conflict is France's attempt to retain neocolonial control of its former "showcase colony".'[97] Many Ivorians harbour similar sentiments regarding French involvement. As one expatriate Ivorian journalist and professor noted at the time of Gbagbo's arrest, '[w]hen it comes to the relationship between France and Côte d'Ivoire, Gbagbo symbolizes the resistance against neocolonial interference ... France is a neocolonial power, and does everything it can in order to break every leader it doesn't control.'[98] Gbagbo's first appearance in The Hague also drew a large gathering of pro-Gbagbo supporters outside the Court, protesting French neocolonial policies.[99]

To be sure, there is little concrete evidence that France pressured Côte d'Ivoire to refer Gbagbo to the ICC. Côte d'Ivoire had accepted the ICC's jurisdiction since 2003, and Ouattara himself had signalled the country's willingness to cooperate with the Court as early as December 2010.[100] Nevertheless, Gbagbo's comments, as well as support for Gbagbo *vis-à-vis* the ICC in certain circles, serve as a powerful reminder that the neocolonialist critique of the Court and its supporters can, with some success, draw on colonial and post-colonial history in a rhetorical attempt to undermine the legitimacy of the Court.

IV MALI

As it did in Côte d'Ivoire, France has intervened militarily in the crisis in Mali, which arose from a rebellion in the country's northern region in January 2012. As of July 2015, the Office of the Prosecutor's investigation of the Mali conflict was still in its preliminary stages and no warrants had yet been issued. France has been a strong advocate of the Court's investigation of crimes committed during the course of the conflict, and has been subject to criticism for its military involvement and its advocacy for the Court's involvement.

A *France in Mali*

As already noted, Mali had been part of France's significant in West African empire (AOF). French involvement there originated in the nineteenth century; these initial forays led to conflict with Toucouleur leader El Hadj Umar Tall, who harassed French forces throughout the region. France would eventually subdue the territory that is now modern-day Mali, adding it to its empire in AOF in 1880 and calling it French Sudan. However, as Alex Thurston has noted, French attempts to secularize its colonies heavily conflicted with a strong Muslim tradition in Mali, and therefore colonial rule 'intensified Islamization in Mali'.[101] Accordingly, the French colonial presence in Mali was a turbulent one; it was marked by uprisings against French administration, especially in the 1920s and 1930s. After World War II, Mali hosted the 1946 Bamako Congress, during which the Rassamblement Démocratique Africain (RDA) formed as a cross-border political party that sought to represent all West African interests. The cross-border relationships established at the Bamako Congress would plant the seed for the short-lived Mali Federation, under which Mali and Senegal united in 1959. However, like many other African nations, Mali became independent from France in 1960, thus ending the short-lived Federation.

After decolonization in 1960, France sought to maintain its influence in Mali through relationships with Malian leaders whom French leaders believed could preserve French interests. This initially manifested in strong ties with the country's first elected president, Modibo Keita. However, when Keita's promised economic reforms largely failed and it became clear that he could not maintain popular legitimacy, he was deposed in 1968 in a coup d'état by eventual autocrat Moussa Traoré. French officials quickly supported Traoré after his rise to power.[102] Traoré would himself be deposed in March 1991 by the military, leading to the election of Alpha Oumar Konaré as president of Mali in 1992 and 1997.

B The 2012 Crisis

The present-day crisis in Mali has its roots in a series of rebellions by the Tuareg peoples, inhabitants of large parts of North Africa, including Mali.[103] During the 1960s and again during the 1990s, the Tuaregs had attempted to overthrow Malian forces in parts of northern Mali and establish their own state.[104] These rebellions, and the separatist mentality in general in Mali, are partially enabled by Mali's unique geography: its southern half is connected by a relatively thin area of land (found in the region of Mopti) to the significantly more arid desert area of the north. Ethnic divisions have also contributed to the north–south divide, and these tensions flared significantly from 2006 through 2009, when the Malian army engaged in several clashes with Tuareg rebels.[105] As Lecoq *et al.* note, this situation was further exacerbated by the destabilization of nearby Libya; when the Gaddafi regime fell in 2011, 'Libyan rebels forced open Gaddafi's arsenals, which fell under the control of various militant groups' – including militants from Al-Qa'ida in the Lands of the Islamic Maghreb (AQIM), who would later enter the conflict in Mali.[106]

The flashpoint for the crisis occurred on 17 January 2012, when the Mouvement National de Libération de l'Azawad (MNLA), composed of Tuareg forces, attacked a military base in the northern region of Gao.[107] Over the next three months, a number of groups – including the MNLA, AQIM, AQIM splinter group Mouvement pour l'unicité et le jihad en Afrique de l'Ouest (MUJAO), and Ansar Dine – flourished in the north; by April 2012, large portions of the regions of Gao, Kidal, and Timbuktu had fallen to these forces, leading to the withdrawal of Mali's army from the north.[108] The crisis exacerbated already existing discontent in Bamako and other southern areas with President Amadou Toumani Touré, who had long been accused of being corrupt and unable to maintain firm control over the country. As a result, forces loyal to General Amadou Haya Sanogo carried out a coup in March 2012, seizing key government installations and deposing Touré. The end of the Touré regime and the crisis in Bamako further galvanized the rebels in the north, as the already weak and overstretched Malian military was required to maintain its focus primarily on the capital and surrounding regions, thus enabling rebel groups to commandeer the remainder of the north. By mid-2012, the Tuaregs and AQIM were effectively in control of most of northern Mali. At the same time, ideological fissures began to develop between the rebel groups.[109]

The rapid advance of the northern rebel forces, as well as reports of violence against civilians in the north, alarmed international observers. Notably, the Office of the Prosecutor issued a statement on 24 April 2012, reminding the international community that Mali is a state party to the Rome Statute, and that the ICC would have jurisdiction over any war crimes or crimes against humanity committed during the conflict.[110] Also concerning was the fact that rebel positions had now drawn dangerously close to striking distance from Bamako, and that terrorist groups – notably AQIM and MUJAO – were legitimate threats to take control over all of Mali. Accordingly, the Security Council passed Resolution 2085 on 20 December 2012, demanding that 'Malian rebel groups cut off all ties to terrorist organizations' – notably AQIM and MUJAO. The resolution further authorized the establishment of an African-led International Support Mission in Mali (AFISMA) to assist the Malian defence forces, and called upon member states to support it.[111]

Although French president François Hollande had initially sought to keep France out of the Mali crisis, the threat to the regime in Bamako, as well as growing international reaction, provided France with the justification it needed to intervene militarily on behalf of the beleaguered state. Under the aegis of Resolution 2085, in January 2013, France commenced Operation Serval, which sought to reinforce Malian control over the south and to begin to weaken rebel control over northern areas. To this end, François Hollande ordered approximately one thousand French troops to be sent to Mali, and the French military began a series of air strikes against rebel positions – first concentrating on the areas towards the middle of the country, and then extending northwards into Gao and Timbuktu. The attack on the In Amenas gas facility in Algeria on 16 January 2013 by followers of AQIM member Mokhtar Belmokhtar further hardened French determination to repel rebel forces in Mali, as it underscored the continuing threat of terrorism in the Maghreb and West Africa. By summer of 2013, French forces had restored a semblance of order to the country. The United Nations opened its UN Mission in Mali in July 2013. The situation had settled sufficiently to allow elections to be held in September 2013, with former prime minister Ibrahim Boubacar Keita elected as president. As of December 2014, over three thousand French soldiers remained in Mali as part of an ongoing regional counter-terrorism and counter-insurgency operation against Islamic militants.[112] While French forces were joined in their efforts by the Malian army and some additional forces from Chad, as a whole, France's intervention undermined efforts by the AU – for example, through the African Peace and Security Architecture (APSA) – to implement African solutions for conflicts on the continent.

C The ICC's Investigation in Mali and France's Support

As already noted, the Office of the Prosecutor signalled in April 2012 that it was monitoring the crisis in Mali. On 18 July 2012, after encouragement by ECOWAS, Mali's Minister of Justice Malick Coulibaly wrote to ICC Prosecutor Fatou Bensouda and officially requested an investigation into crimes committed in Mali starting in January of that year.[113] Among the crimes that Mali requested the ICC to investigate were summary executions, rape, massacres of the civilian population, the conscription of child soldiers, torture, pillage, disappearances, and the destruction of state and religious property.[114] After a preliminary examination, the OTP officially opened an investigation on 16 January 2013.[115] In its Article 53(1) report, the OTP indicated its concern that armed groups (both in the north and supporting the Sanogo junta) had committed crimes during the crisis, including summary executions, mutilations, looting, destruction of religious and cultural sites, rape, torture, and disappearances.[116] That same day, the Court noted that it was not 'only targeting African countries', as it was also investigating situations on four other continents. It emphasized that '[t]he International Criminal Court is an independent judicial institution that is not subject to political control'.[117]

As of the date of this chapter, no indictments or arrest warrants have been issued.

From the beginning of its military involvement in Mali, France's official position has been support for the Malian government's referral of the situation to the ICC.[118] In particular, French president François Hollande has been outspoken about the need for the ICC to try war crimes committed during the Mali conflict.[119] In a speech discussing the French interventions in Mali and the CAR, Hollande made clear that France favours prosecution of 'serious crimes committed in Africa' and that '[t]his is the role of the International Criminal Court – to rule on such crimes when national legal systems are unable to do so'.[120]

However, the dynamics of the crisis in Mali also lend some credence to the neocolonialist critique. As the former colonial power and a present military intervener, France is rhetorically handicapped in attempting to advocate that the Court is best placed to provide a neutral forum for crimes committed during the crisis. To be sure, the Malian government invited the initial ICC investigation, as well as the French military intervention. Further, Mali's neighbours, the AU, and much of the larger international community supported the intervention.[121] However, French involvement nevertheless was the subject of scepticism. Perhaps most prominently, Senegalese novelist and journalist Boubacar Boris Diop commented that '[e]verything suggests that the French will defeat the jihadists, but this victory will cost the Malians their government and their honour', and questioned 'how is it that the French troops who occupied Mali for centuries as barbaric colonisers have come back fifty years later to be greeted as liberators?'[122] Further, in the immediate aftermath of the arrival of French troops in Bamako, the press in neighbouring Algeria criticized France for its 'colonial' mentality in intervening in Mali.[123] Then-president of Egypt Muhammed Morsi also opposed French action, suggesting that it could only further destabilize North and West Africa.[124] There has also been scepticism of France within the academic community; African expert Baz Lecocq recently stated that '[u]ndoubtedly, the French Ministry of Defence and French Military HQ État-Major des Armées had a plan ready despite President Hollande's public assurances that France would not pursue a neocolonial intervention in a sovereign state', and linked France's decision to intervene to France's desire to resuscitate its declining influence in Mali.[125]

While these criticisms have been relatively muted, they are nonetheless representative of the larger neocolonialist critique, and illustrate the importance of understanding France's larger history in the region when addressing criticisms of the Court and its neutrality. To date, it is not apparent as to where the Prosecutor's investigation of the Mali conflict will lead. However, if the ongoing critique of France regarding the Gbagbo prosecution is any indication, France's long history in Mali, and its motives in intervening in favour of the regime in Bamako, will be critical components of the neocolonialist critique of the Court's involvement in Mali going forward.

V CONCLUSION

The purpose of this chapter is not to support the proliferating belief that the mission of the ICC is hopelessly tainted by the history and policies of its Western supporters. This line of thought overstates the role of political considerations in the Court's decisions, and risks overlooking the suffering of countless victims of international crimes. Nor do I seek to portray France as the lone Western power with a history of dubious involvement – clearly, the United Kingdom and Belgium have equally problematic colonial histories in Africa, and the United States' actions on the continent demonstrate that it is hardly above reproach. Nevertheless, there are reasons why the neocolonialist critique of the Court has found fertile ground, and why French interventions in Africa and support for the Court are particularly vulnerable to such criticisms. As one historian recently noted, '[a]rguably, if France wants genuinely to establish itself as a leader in purely humanitarian interventions, it should do so anywhere but Africa, where the past weighs so heavily'.[126]

In his essay on international crises of legitimacy, Christian Reus-Smit explains that an institution can remedy the decline that accompanies such crises by 'reconstitut[ing] the social bases of its legitimacy'.[127] In the case of the ICC, part of that effort must come from its Western supporters. Only through engagement with the West's history in Africa, as well as with the sentiments of Africans who increasingly view the Court with scepticism, can this growing threat to the institutional legitimacy of the Court (which, after all, seeks to protect and uphold rights and values accepted by virtually all of the actors in this ongoing debate) be properly addressed.

Notes

1. This is not the first time that international courts have faced such criticisms; the Nuremberg Trials were labelled by some as 'victors' justice', while more recently, during his trial before the International Criminal Tribunal for the Former Yugoslavia (ICTY), the late Slobodan Milosevic famously referred to the ICTY as 'the giant machine of the NATO court, a political machine'. See Danilo Zolo, *Victors' Justice:*

From Nuremberg to Baghdad (New York: Verso, 2009); 'Milosevic Vows to Defeat the '"NATO Machine"', *Breaking News*, 23 August 2001.

2. Christian Reus-Smit, 'Institutional Crises of Legitimacy' (2007) 44 *International Politics* 167. For an exemplary study of institutional legitimacy in the international courts context, see Sanja K. Ivkovich and John Hagan, *Reclaiming Justice: The International Tribunal for the Former Yugoslavia and Local Courts* (Oxford: Oxford University Press, 2011), which draws on interviews and polling data to assess acceptance and legitimacy of the ICTY.

3. Xan Rice, 'Sudanese President Bashir Charged with Darfur War Crimes', *The Guardian*, 4 March 2009.

4. After being directed by Trial Chamber V to either withdraw the charges or file notice with the Court that the evidentiary basis had improved to a degree which would justify proceeding to trial, Prosecutor Fatou Bensouda withdrew the charges against Kenyatta on 5 December 2014. OTP, 'Statement of the Prosecutor of the International Criminal Court, Fatou Bensouda, on the Withdrawal of Charges against Mr. Uhuru Muigai Kenyatta', 5 December 2014.

5. For example, Rwandan president Paul Kagame stated that the Court: 'has been put in place only for African countries, only for poor countries ... Rwanda cannot be part of colonialism, slavery and imperialism'. Mari Kimani, 'Pursuit of Justice or Western Plot?', *Africa Renewal*, October 2009. In May 2013, Ethiopian prime minister Haïlé Mariam Desalegn criticized the ICC for engaging in a 'sort of a racial hunt'. 'L'Union africaine dénonce la « chasse raciale » de la CPI', *Le Monde*, 29 May 2013.

6. Quoted in Charles C. Jalloh, 'Africa and the International Criminal Court: Collision Course or Cooperation?' (2011–2012) 34 *North Carolina Central Law Review* 203, 210. Professor Jalloh's article also contains an insightful response to the criticism raised by Mamdani and others.

7. Despite having 'un-signed' the Rome Statute during the Bush presidency, the United States has nevertheless since advocated for the Court to investigate and prosecute crimes in Africa – as seen by its support for the referrals of the situation in Sudan and Libya, and its unsuccessful attempt to refer the situation in Syria. Somini Sengupta, 'Politics Seen Undercutting Credibility of a Court', *New York Times*, 2 June 201.

8. See François-Xavier Verschave, *La Françafrique: Le plus long scandale de la République* (Paris: Stock, 1998).

9. This chapter does not address the conflict in the Central African Republic (CAR) between Christian and Muslim groups, which as of mid-2015 was still ongoing. France sent a limited intervention force to the country in December 2013 to protect civilians. On 10 April 2014, the

Security Council passed a resolution, drafted by the French delegation, authorizing the deployment of over 10,000 troops to maintain peace in the CAR. UN Doc. S/RES/2149, 10 April 2014. On 30 May 2014, the Central African Republic referred the situation to the ICC. See OTP, 'Letter of Referral to the ICC, Government of the Central African Republic', 30 May 2014.

10. See generally Benjamin Stora, *Algeria 1830–2000: A Short History* (Ithaca: Cornell University Press, 2004).

11. A survey of the French colonial mission in Africa can be found in Patrick Manning, *Francophone Sub-Saharan Africa: 1880–1995* (Cambridge: Cambridge University Press, 1999).

12. De Brazza's mission in Africa has been chronicled in Edward Berenson, *Heroes of Empire: Five Charismatic Men and the Conquest of Africa* (Berkeley: University of California Press, 2010), pp. 49–82 and 197–227.

13. See generally Alice Conklin, *A Mission to Civilize: The Republican Idea of Empire in France and West Africa, 1895–1930* (Stanford University Press, 1997).

14. See generally Frederick Cooper, *Decolonization and African Society: The Labor Question in French and British Africa* (Cambridge: Cambridge University Press, 1996).

15. See Tony Chafer, *The End of Empire in French West Africa: France's Successful Decolonization?* (Oxford: Berg, 2002).

16. See generally Alistair Horne, *A Savage War of Peace: Algeria 1954–1962* (New York: NYRB Classics, 2006); Martin Shipway, *The Road to War: France and Vietnam, 1944–1947* (Oxford: Berghahn Books, 1996).

17. See generally Jacques Foccart, *Foccart Parle: Entretiens avec Philippe Gaillard* (Paris: Jeune Afrique, 1997).

18. Schmidt, *Foreign Intervention in Africa*, p. 184; Chinua Achebe, *There Was a Country: A Personal History of Biafra* (New York: Penguin Press, 2012), pp. 101–102.

19. Martin Meredith, *The Fate of Africa: From the Hopes of Freedom to the Heart of Despair, A History of 50 Years of Independence* (New York: Public Affairs, 2005), pp. 224–231; Schmidt, *Foreign Intervention in Africa*, pp. 187–188.

20. Henri Astier, 'Elf Was Secret Arm of French Policy', *BBC News*, 19 March 2003; Lizzy Davies, 'French Elite on Trial in $791 Million Angola Arms Case', *The Guardian*, 7 October 2008.

21. Gerard Prunier, *The Rwanda Crisis: History of a Genocide* (New York: Columbia Press, 1997), pp. 108–114.

22. Andrew Wallis, *Silent Accomplice: The Untold Story of France's Role in the Rwandan Genocide* (London: I.B. Tauris, 2007), pp. 113–122.

23. *Ibid.*, pp. 164–175.

24. I have discussed France's actions during the Rwandan genocide in Paul D. Schmitt, 'The Future of Genocide Suits at the ICJ: France's Role in Rwanda and Implications of the Bosnia v. Serbia Decision' (2009) 40 *Georgetown Journal of International Law* 585.

25. See Shiva Eftekhari, 'International Criminal Justice: Rwanda and French Human Rights Activism' (2001) 23 *Human Rights Quarterly* 1032.

26. See Hélène Gandois's discussion of France's 'disengagement' from Africa in 'France's Policy towards Africa within the Security Council from 2007 to 2010: A Real Multilateral Turn?' (2011) 4 *Dynamique Internationales* 1.

27. 'Sarkozy au Rwanda: 'la France doit réfléchir à ses erreurs', *Le Monde*, 25 February 2010; Anjan Sundaram, 'On Visit to Rwanda, Sarkozy Admits "Grave Errors" in 1994 Genocide', *New York Times*, 25 February 2010. Despite these efforts at reconciliation, the French ambassador was later asked by Rwanda not to participate in events commemorating the twentieth anniversary of the genocide. 'Rwanda Bans French Envoy From Genocide Memorial', *The Telegraph*, 7 April 2014.

28. See David A. Bell, 'Double Entendre: The Paradox of France's Humanitarian Interventions', *Foreign Affairs*, 14 January 2014.

29. François Hollande, 'Address by François Hollande for the Opening of the Elysée Summit for Peace and Security in Africa', 7 December 2013.

30. See Baz Lecocq, 'Mali: This Is Only the Beginning' (2013) 14 *Georgetown Journal of International Affairs* 59.

31. As one commentator has noted, '[f]or the past several decades, the French government and political establishment have been strong supporters of supranational law and institutions'. Martin A. Rogoff, 'Application of Treaties and the Decisions of International Tribunals in the United States and France: Reflections on Recent Practice' (2006) 58 *Maine Law Review* 406, 470.

32. Emmanuelle Jouannet, 'French and American Perspectives on International Law: Legal Cultures and International Law' (2006) 58 *Maine Law Review* 292, 309.

33. *Ibid.*, p. 314.

34. *Ibid.*, p. 317.

35. See Sophie Clavier, 'Contrasting Perspectives on Preemptive Strike: The United States, France, and the War on Terror' (2006) 58 *Maine Law Review* 566, 567.

36. David Bosco, *Rough Justice: The International Criminal Court in a World of Power Politics* (Oxford: Oxford University Press, 2014), pp. 3–4.

37. For an excellent summary and discussion of the 2010 amendments, see Human Rights Watch, 'The Legal Framework for Universal Jurisdiction in France' (2014).

38. See Jean Paul Pierini, 'Prosecuting Acts of Torture Committed Abroad despite Foreign Amnesty: The ECtHR Decision in Ely Ould Dah v. France' (2009) 48 *Military Law and the Law of War Review* 211.

39. Maximo Langer, 'The Diplomacy of Universal Jurisdiction: The Political Branches and the Transnational Prosecution of International Crimes' (2011) 105 *American Journal of International Law* 1, 22.

40. The indictment was based largely on testimony collected from former members of the Tutsi-led Rwandan Patriotic Front (RPF), who later became opponents of Kagame during his presidency. Fergal Keane, 'Rwanda Leader Defiant on Killing Claim', *BBC News*, 30 January 1997. For a summary of the controversy, see Vanessa Thalmann, 'French Justice's Endeavours to Substitute for the ICTR' (2008) 6 *Journal of International Criminal Justice* 995–1002.

41. 'Senior Rwandan Official Arrested', *BBC News*, 10 November 2008.

42. The Nguesso case would eventually lead to proceedings at the International Court of Justice, *Case Concerning Criminal Proceedings in France (Republic of the Congo v. France)* Summary of the Order 1 of 17 June 2003.

43. See UN Doc. S/RES/827, 25 May 1993 (establishing the ICTY); UN Doc. S/RES/955, 8 November 1994 (establishing the ICTR). France has faced criticism by Rwanda for favouring limitation of the ICTR's jurisdiction to crimes committed in 1994. Felly Kimenyi, 'Rwanda: ICTR – Rwanda Was Justified to Shun Resolution 955', *All Africa*, 8 April 2014.

44. To partially address these issues, France declared upon signing the Rome Statute that the Statute 'does not preclude France from directing attacks against objectives considered as military objectives under international humanitarian law'. William A. Schabas, *An Introduction to the International Criminal Court*, 4th edn (Cambridge: Cambridge University Press, 2011), p. 499.

45. Bosco, *Rough Justice*, pp. 40–41.

46. See generally Beate Rudolf, 'Statute of the International Criminal Court, Decision No. 98–408 DC, 1999 J.O. 1317' (2000) 94 *American Journal of International Law* 391.

47. Schabas, *Introduction to the International Criminal Court*, p. 180.

48. Bosco, *Rough Justice*, p. 125; Schabas, *Introduction to the International Criminal Court*, p. 47.

49. Patricia M. Wald, 'Apprehending War Criminals: Does International Cooperation Work?' (2012) 27 *American University International Law Review* 229, 233. Mbarushmena was later freed by the ICC.

50. Bosco, *Rough Justice*, pp. 108–112, 167–168.

51. *Ibid.*, pp. 109–110.

52. 'Gaddafi Must Face Justice – France', *Reuters*, 6 September 2011.

53. Bosco, *Rough Justice*, pp. 167–168.
54. Natalie Nougayrède and Thomas Wieder, 'Laurent Fabius: sur la Syrie, "la France est favorable à ce que la CPI soit saisie"', *Le Monde*, 29 May 2012.
55. David Smith, 'Laurent Gbagbo Appears before International Criminal Court', *The Guardian*, 5 December 2011.
56. See Pierre Nandjui, *Houphouet-Boigny: L'homme de la France en Afrique* (Paris: L'Harmattan, 1995); Mike McGovern, *Making War in Cote d'Ivoire* (Chicago: University of Chicago Press, 2011), pp. 148–151.
57. McGovern, *Making War*, p. 18.
58. Ana Peyro Lopis, 'Collective Security and the International Enforcement of International Law: French and American Perspectives' (2006) 58 *Maine Law Review* 544, 555; McGovern, *Making War*, p. 20.
59. UN Doc. S/RES/1528, 27 February 2004.
60. UN Doc. S/RES/1464, 4 February 2003; 'Press Worry over Ivoirian Violence', *BBC News*, 8 November 2004.
61. 'La Côte d'Ivoire depuis le début de la rébellion en septembre 2002', *Le Monde*, 7 November 2004.
62. UN Doc. S/RES/1572, 5 November 2004, para. 1.
63. 'La FIDH accuse la France d'avoir outrepassé son mandat en Côte d'Ivoire', *Le Monde*, 30 November 2004.
64. 'Huit soldats français tués et 23 blessés lors d'un raid aérien de l'armée ivoirienne', *Le Monde*, 6 November 2004; McGovern, *Making War*, p. 133.
65. 'France Rolls out Ivory Coast Force', *Associated Press*, 8 November 2004.
66. 'La situation est de plus en tendue à Abidjan où au moins sept personnes sont mortes lors de heurts avec l'armée française', *Le Monde*, 9 November 2004.
67. *Ibid.*
68. *Ibid.*
69. 'La FIDH accuse la France d'avoir outrepassé son mandat en Côte d'Ivoire', *Le Monde*, 30 November 2004.
70. Ann Talbot, 'Ivory Coast: Protests Erupt vs. French Military Strikes', *World Socialist Website*, 9 November 2004.
71. ''L'attitude de la France est scandaleuse', estime le président Gbagbo', *Le Monde*, 16 December 2004.
72. *Ibid.*
73. Robyn Dixon, 'Violence Ebbs, Tension Persists in Ivory Coast', *Los Angeles Times*, 8 November 2004.
74. UN Doc. S/RES/1572, 5 November 2004, para. 1. Notably, all three African states then seated in the Security Council – Algeria, Angola, and Benin – voted for the resolution, UN Doc. S/PV.5078, 15 November 2004.

75. McGovern, *Making War*, p. 23.

76. *Ibid.*, pp. 90–91.

77. *Ibid.*, p. 211.

78. UN Doc. S/RES/1962, 20 December 2010, para. 1.

79. UN Doc. S/RES/1975, 30 March 2011, paras. 3–5.

80. Julie Dubé Gagnon, 'ECOWAS's Right to Intervene in Côte d'Ivoire to Install Alassane Ouattara as President-Elect' (2013) 3 *Notre Dame Journal of International and Comparative Law* 51–72, at 51.

81. UN Doc. S/RES/1967, 19 January 2011.

82. Scott Baldauf, 'African Union Leaders Divided about Ivory Coast Intervention', *Christian Science Monitor*, 26 January 2011.

83. 'Ivory Coast's Ouattara Rejects African Union Mediator', *BBC News*, 27 March 2011.

84. OTP, Letter Reconfirming the Acceptance of the ICC Jurisdiction, 14 December 2010.

85. *Ibid.*

86. Wald, 'Apprehending War Criminals', 261–262.

87. Although Côte d'Ivoire was not a State Party to the Rome Statute, Gbagbo accepted the Court's jurisdiction during the Ivorian civil war in 2003. 'Is Africa on Trial?', *BBC News*, 27 March 2012. Ouattara later re-affirmed the country's acceptance of ICC jurisdiction in 2010. OTP, 'Letter Reconfirming the Acceptance of the ICC Jurisdiction', 14 December 2010.

88. 'It is up to him [Gbagbo] to choose what image he wants to leave to history. If he wants to leave the image of a man of peace, there is still time but time is running out, and he has to go . . . Or, does he want to leave the image of someone who shot at completely innocent civilians? And in this case, there are international courts and the ICC. The [ICC] prosecutor himself has said that he has closely watched the situation and that those who have caused the shooting will be brought to account.' 'La pression internationale contre Laurent Gbagbo s'accentue', *Le Monde*, 17 December 2010.

89. 'U.N. Focuses on Human Rights Abuses in Ivory Coast', *USA Today*, 2 January 2011.

90. 'Ivory Coast Struggles to Regain Stability under New Leader', *CNN*, 12 April 2011.

91. Interview with Alain Juppé, 'France/UN/Côte d'Ívoire – Libya/French Role/NATO Role', *France Info*, 12 April 2011.

92. *Situation in the Republic of Côte d'Ivoire* (ICC-02/11), Warrant of Arrest for Laurent Koudou Gbagbo, 23 November 2011.

93. On 12 June 2014, Pre-Trial Chamber I confirmed the charges against Gbagbo and committed the former president to trial. *Situation in the Republic of Côte D'Ivoire* (ICC-02/11-01/11), 'Decision on the

Confirmation of Charges Against Laurent Gbagbo, In the Case of the Prosecutor v. Laurent Gbagbo', 12 June 2014, para. 266.

94. David Smith, 'Laurent Gbagbo Appears before International Criminal Court', *The Guardian*, 5 December 2011. Gbagbo has expounded on his rivalry with France in Laurent Gbagbo and François Mattei, *Pour la Vérité et la Justice: Côte d'Ivoire – Révélations sur une Scandale Français* (Du Moment: Paris, 2014).

95. 'Laurent Gbagbo, Ivory Coast Former President, Makes First Appearance Before International Criminal Court', *The Huffington Post*, 5 December 2011.

96. Laura Lynch, 'Laurent Gbagbo Faces International Criminal Court', *Public Radio International*, 5 December 2011.

97. McGovern, *Making War*, p. 88.

98. Larry Luxner, 'Côte d'Ivoire Pulls Back from War, But Now Must Pick Up the Pieces', *The Washington Diplomat*, May 2011.

99. 'Pro-Gbagbo Rally outside of the International Criminal Court', *Niger Delta Politics*, 4 November 2012.

100. Correspondence from Alassane Ouattara to OTP, 'Letter Reconfirming the Acceptance of the ICC Jurisdiction', 14 December 2010.

101. Alex Thurston, *Towards an Islamic Republic of Mali?* (2013) 37(2) *Fletcher Forum of World Affairs* 45, 48.

102. M. Schaffhauser, Chargé d'Affaires de France A.I. à Dakar, à M. Debré, Ministre des Affaires Étrangères, Nov. 20, 1968, *Documents Diplomatiques Français 1968 Tome II* (Paris: Imprimerie Nationale, 2010), pp. 858–859.

103. There is very little scholarship on the history of Mali. I am indebted to a recent collaborative article – Baz Lecocq, Gregory Mann, Bruce Whitehouse, Dida Badi, Lotte Pelckmans, Nadia Belalimat, Bruca Hall and Wolfram Lacher, 'One Hippopotamus and Eight Blind Analysts: A Multivocal Analysis of the 2012 Political Crisis in the Divided Republic of Mali' (2013) 137 *Review of African Political Economy* 343–357. See also Thurston, *'Towards an Islamic Republic of Mali?'*.

104. Lecocq and Mann (et al.), 'One Hippopoamus and Eight Blind Analysts', 2.

105. *Ibid.*

106. *Ibid.*, p. 3.

107. OTP, Situation in Mali – Article 53(1) Report, 16 January 2013, p. 4.

108. *Ibid.*, pp. 9–10.

109. Lecocq and Mann, 'One Hippopoamus and Eight Blind Analysts', 7.

110. OTP, Situation in Mali – Article 53(1) Report, p. 6.

111. UN Doc. S/RES/2085, 20 December 2012.

112. John Irish, 'French Forces in Mali Kill Islamist on U.S. Wanted List', *Reuters*, 11 December 2014.

113. Letter from Malick Coulibaly to Fatou Bensouda: OTP, Referral Letter by the Government of Mali, 13 July 2012. See also Gino Naldi and Konstantinos Magliveras, 'The Ever Difficult Symbiosis of Africa with the International Criminal Court' (2013) 66 *Hellenic Review of International Law* 59, 125.

114. OTP, Referral Letter by the Government of Mali, 13 July 2012.

115. OTP, ICC Prosecutor opens investigations into war crimes in Mali: 'The Legal requirements has been met. We will investigate', 16 January 2013.

116. OTP, Situation in Mali – Article 53(1) Report, pp. 13–14.

117. ICC, Questions and Answers: Opening of an ICC Investigation in Mali, 16 January 2013.

118. 'Mali (Q&A – Excerpt from the Daily Press Briefing', *France Diplomatie*, 16 January 2013.

119. David Lewis and Richard Valdmanis, 'Mali Hails "Savior" Hollande, He Says Fight Not Over', *Reuters*, 2 February 2013.

120. Francois Hollande, 'Address for the Opening of the Elysée Summit for Peace and Security in Africa'.

121. See the recent comments of Senegalese president Macky Sall supporting French actions in Mali in 'Africa's Turn – A Conversation with Macky Sall' (2013) 92(5) *Foreign Affairs* 2–9. See also 'African Union Head Congratulates France for Sending Troops to Mali', *The Canadian Press*, 11 January 2013.

122. Souleymane Ndiayeis, 'French Intervention 'Will Cost Mali Its Independence'', *The Guardian*, 8 February 2013.

123. Hélène Sallon, 'La presse algérienne critique l'attitude "coloniale "de la France au Mali', *Le Monde*, 14 January 2013.

124. 'Egypt's Morsi Opposes French Intervention in Mali', *France24*, 22 January 2013.

125. Lecocq, 'Mali: This Is Only the Beginning', 59–60.

126. Bell, 'Double Entendre'.

127. Reus-Smit, *International Crises of Legitimacy*, p. 167.

8

The AU, the ICC, and the Prosecution
of African Presidents

Abel S. Knottnerus

I INTRODUCTION

In recent years, the African Union (AU) has initiated a powerful campaign against the International Criminal Court (ICC), and especially against the prosecution of African presidents. In response to the indictment of Omar al-Bashir and the cases against Uhuru Kenyatta and William Ruto, the AU has argued that by prosecuting African leaders the ICC jeopardizes the promotion of peace and stability in Africa. In addition, the AU has claimed that al-Bashir enjoys immunity from arrest under customary international law and has warned that the Court's trial proceedings distract Kenyatta and Ruto in the exercise of their official responsibilities. On these and related grounds, the AU has asked the UN Security Council to suspend their prosecution and has even called for an amendment to the Rome Statute so that sitting heads of state and their deputies can be exempted from prosecution by the ICC.[1]

For many commentators, especially within international law, this opposition against the prosecution of African presidents raises traditional questions of substantive law and normative decision-making. In discussing the ICC's immunity regime or the deferral powers of the Security Council, they assess whether there is a legal basis for the concerns that the AU has voiced about the ICC. The questions that they address are important, in particular for the Court's supporters, who are trying to resolve the ongoing tensions between the AU and the ICC. Yet, when looking at the impact of their political battles it does not necessarily matter whether African states are 'right' to criticize the Court. A much more relevant question is how the AU's campaign has shaped perceptions of the ICC in Africa.

Clearly, the concerns that the AU has expressed about the Court do not reflect the views of all African states, and certainly not of all Africans.[2]

By constantly criticizing the ICC, however, the AU and like-minded voices do encourage their different audiences in Africa to question whether the Court deserves support. To the extent that the AU is successful in shaping the perceptions of these audiences, it puts the Court's legitimacy under pressure.[3] This, in and of itself, makes the AU's declarations about the ICC powerful.[4] Whatever the motivations of the actors involved may be, the AU is able to influence how the Court is perceived in Africa and may as such convince state actors, local communities, and even victims and witnesses not to cooperate with the ICC. Since the Court is largely dependent on their cooperation, it is fair to say that the AU's opposition against the ICC poses great difficulties for the Court.

Until now, questions about the perceptions and legitimacy of the ICC have not received much attention in the debate on the Court's fractious relationship with Africa. Instead, the predominant focus has been on legal and other normative questions, with scholars taking various positions on the arguments that the AU has advanced against the ICC.[5] Without denying the relevance of these questions, this chapter underscores the importance that this volume places on studying the societal, political, and institutional implications of the Court's contested presence in Africa. Key questions in this context are how the ICC has been portrayed and perceived in different African communities, but also how actors within and outside the Court have reacted to the ongoing tensions.

In exploring the interactions between the AU, the ICC, and its States Parties, I concentrate in this chapter on the concerns that the AU has expressed about the prosecution of African presidents. Apart from accusations about the selectivity and the politicization of the Court's proceedings, the opposition of the AU has mainly been directed at the indictment and trial of sitting African heads of state and at the repercussions that the ICC's prosecutions would have on the states concerned and on their official representatives. Through its decisions and communiqués, the AU has portrayed the prosecution of African presidents as a threat to the stability and sovereignty of African states. It has done so, first and foremost, by arguing that these prosecutions jeopardize the interests of peace, but also by placing the obligation to arrest al-Bashir against the immunity that he would normally enjoy under customary international law and by claiming that the Court's trial proceedings adversely affect the ability of sitting heads of state to exercise their demanding responsibilities. In short, the AU has built its campaign against the prosecution of African presidents around three juxtapositions: (1) prosecution versus peace, (2) arrest versus immunity, and (3) trial versus presidential responsibilities.

In the following, I analyse these three juxtapositions and examine the different ways in which the prosecutor, the Court's judges, and the ICC's States Parties have tried to respond to each of them. With this examination I seek to explain what it is that makes the AU's campaign against the ICC powerful and why the Court and its supporters have been struggling to address the AU's concerns. More generally, this chapter offers insights into how the AU has portrayed the ICC, how its actions have shaped perceptions of the Court in Africa, and how different actors within and outside the ICC have attempted to resolve the ongoing tensions. It concludes that despite recent efforts of the Court's States Parties to improve the ICC's relationship with Africa, the AU will likely continue to oppose the prosecution of African presidents and will as such put further pressure on the perceived legitimacy of the Court.

II PROSECUTION VERSUS PEACE

The first and most general concern that the AU has voiced about the prosecution of African presidents is that the ICC jeopardizes the promotion of peace and stability. Since 2008, the AU has warned that the indictment of President al-Bashir undermines 'the ongoing efforts aimed at facilitating the early resolution of the conflict in Darfur'.[6] Furthermore, in the wake of the election of Kenyatta and Ruto as president and deputy president of Kenya in early 2013, the AU has cautioned that the continuation of their cases poses a threat to the 'stability and peace' of Kenya and the wider region.[7] Based on this alleged tension between the interests of peace and prosecution, the AU has repeatedly asked the UN Security Council to defer the prosecution of al-Bashir and to suspend the cases against Kenyatta and Ruto in accordance with Article 16 of the Statute. Under this provision, the Council has the discretionary power to suspend an investigation or prosecution of the Court for a renewable period of twelve months when the Council determines that there exist a threat to the peace under Chapter VII of the UN Charter.[8]

A *The Deferral Request for al-Bashir*

The first time that the AU introduced a proposal of this kind to the Security Council was within weeks after the prosecutor's application for an arrest warrant against al-Bashir in July 2008. In the build-up to a previously scheduled meeting on the joint peacekeeping mission of the UN and the AU in Darfur (UNAMID), the AU actively lobbied for a deferral and received support for this request from Russia, China, the League of Arab States, the

Organization of the Islamic Conference, and the Non-Aligned Movement.[9] During the Council's actual meeting, it became clear, however, that the United States and the Court's States Parties in the Council (the UK, France, Belgium, Croatia, Italy, Costa Rica, and Panama) were not willing to suspend the prosecution of al-Bashir. The United States argued that even suggesting the possibility of a deferral 'would send the wrong signal' to the Sudanese president and would 'undermine efforts to bring him and others to justice'.[10]

In the months thereafter, the Council addressed the AU's 'peace concerns' during several informal consultations. While there are hardly any reports of these meetings, different sources note that in late 2008, 'exploratory, low level discussions' took place 'between South African, French and British diplomats on what, hypothetically, could be contained in an Article 16 deferral resolution for Bashir'.[11] What is more, the UK and France hinted at several occasions that they would be willing to consider a deferral in exchange for Sudan's full cooperation with UNAMID and with the ICC's outstanding warrants for Ahmed Harun, Sudan's minister of state for humanitarian affairs, and for Ali-Kushayb, a senior commander of one of the militias that played a key role in the conflict in Darfur.[12]

These informal discussions over a 'peace-for-deferral deal' did not, however, change the position of the United States and most of the Court's States Parties in the Council.[13] Especially after the window between the moment that the prosecutor filed an application for an arrest warrant (July 2008) and the Pre-Trial Chamber's (PTC) formal indictment of al-Bashir (March 2009) had passed, it proved difficult for the Council to agree on a formal response to the AU's request. The Council did not convene a public debate and did not adopt a resolution or even a presidential statement on the matter. Instead, commentators reported in March 2011 that the Council's rotating membership had 'little appetite' to continue debating the issue. Shortly thereafter the proposed deferral disappeared from the Council's agenda completely.[14]

B The Deferral Request for Kenyatta and Ruto

Upon the Kenyan presidential elections in March 2013, Kenya and the AU submitted another deferral bid to the Council. As part of a range of efforts to terminate or at least postpone the Kenyan cases, the AU called for a twelve-month suspension of the prosecution of Kenyatta and Ruto. In first instance, the Council set this request aside. The proposal gained renewed momentum, however, after an extraordinary summit of the AU Assembly, which took place on 11 and 12 October 2013. During this meeting, the gathered African leaders agreed that the cases against Kenyatta and Ruto would have to be 'suspended until they [would] complete their terms of office'.[15] In order to give effect to this decision, the Assembly installed a Contact Group of five states that would have to obtain feedback from the Council on the AU's deferral request before the scheduled start of Kenyatta's trial, which was scheduled to begin in November 2013.[16]

In response to the AU's decision, the Council invited the foreign minister of Kenya and the members of the AU's Contact Group for an interactive dialogue on 31 October. Already during this first meeting the Council proved divided, more or less, along the same lines as with the proposed deferral for al-Bashir.[17] Whereas the three African members of the Council and most non-States Parties, including China and Russia, supported a deferral, the other members of the Council, and in particular the United States and the Court's States Parties from Europe and Latin America, opposed the AU's request. When brought to a vote by the African states, this stand-off resulted in a rejection of the proposed deferral with seven votes in favour and eight abstentions.[18]

From the statements that the members of the Council made after casting their votes, it appears that the debate in the Council focused especially on the applicability of Article 16 and on the necessity of the requested deferral.[19] For the states supporting the deferral, the 'functionality of the offices of the elected President and Deputy President of Kenya' was the most important argument.[20] Article 16 would have to be invoked, because these trials could otherwise 'create serious obstacles to the normal functioning of State institutions in Kenya and thereby pose a threat to the ongoing efforts to ensure and promote peace and stability in the region'.[21] Some of the opponents of the deferrals questioned, however, whether this justified a deferral under Article 16.[22] They recognized that the two Kenyan leaders faced 'a serious challenge in trying to meet their trial obligations at the same time as devoting their attention to tackling threats in their country and the region', but stressed that Article 16 should only be invoked 'in exceptional circumstances when the proceedings themselves threaten international peace and security'.[23] In their view, the security situation in Kenya and East Africa was 'volatile and precarious', but the prosecution of Kenyatta and Ruto did not constitute 'in itself a threat to international peace and security'.[24]

In addition, several States Parties to the Court argued that a deferral would not be necessary at this point in time. They noted that the ICC's Trial Chamber had shown flexibility by relieving Ruto of his duty to be present during several trial sessions after the Westgate Attacks in Nairobi and by postponing the start of Kenyatta's trial until February 2014 (which had been announced two weeks earlier).[25] All this would ensure that 'at any time either the President or the Vice-President [would] be fully available to manage the affairs of Kenya'.[26] Any remaining concerns about the proceedings against Kenyatta and Ruto could be addressed by the Assembly of States Parties (ASP).[27]

Finally, aside from questions about the applicability of Article 16 and the necessity of a deferral, some of the Court's States Parties criticized the AU's proposal because it would set a 'dangerous precedent'.[28] By suspending the cases against Kenyatta and Ruto, the Council would only 'promote the law of the jungle' and encourage other sitting heads of state to demand a deferral for their prosecution.[29] In other words, the respective states suggested that Article 16 should never be invoked, because the Council should not create a political precedent by interfering in the Court's proceedings.

For the AU, the Council's response to the deferral request for Kenyatta and Ruto was a major disappointment. In their first reaction, the African members of the Council proclaimed that Article 16 was apparently 'never meant to be used by an African State'.[30] A few days later, in a statement on behalf of the AU to the ASP, Uganda said that the Council's rejection made Article 16 'redundant' and that 'the irresistible conclusion' had to be that the ICC 'is no longer a Court for all, but only to deal with Africans in the most rigid way'.[31] These and other statements reflected the frustration of the AU and many of its Member States with the response of the Council. Essentially, the AU felt that the Council should have reserved a more 'timely and appropriate response' to its deferral requests in order to avoid 'the sense of lack of consideration of a whole continent'.[32]

C Alternative Deferral Mechanisms

The response of the Council to the AU's deferral requests for al-Bashir, Kenyatta, and Ruto raised the question whether other actors should become involved with the Court's 'deferral politics'. In this context, two alternative deferral mechanisms have been proposed that could complement (or replace) the Council's deferral powers under Article 16. First of all, several commentators have advocated that the Prosecutor should play an active role in balancing the interests of peace and prosecution through her wide discretion under Article 53 of the Statute to no longer pursue the initiation or continuation of the Court's proceedings when this would not be in the 'interests of justice'.[33] Secondly, in reaction to the Council's inaction on the deferral request for al-Bashir, the AU has asked the ASP to amend Article 16. This amendment would give the UN General Assembly the power to defer an investigation or prosecution when the Council would fail to decide on a deferral request.[34]

The Court's current Prosecutor has so far rejected the first proposal. Through her decisions and statements, Fatou Bensouda has proven reluctant to change the parameters of the ICC's deferral politics and has argued that the Council is the appropriate forum to address peace concerns. Like her predecessor,[35] she has taken the position that the OTP 'cannot take into consideration the interests of peace, which is the mandate of other institutions, such as the UN Security Council'.[36] For this reason, the OTP would not be able to use its discretion under Article 53 to balance the interests of peace and prosecution.

The proposed amendment to Article 16 has not received much support either. Upon the introduction of this amendment to the ASP by South Africa in December 2009, thirteen non-African states spoke out against a revision of Article 16. Among other reasons, these states argued that the proposed amendment would broaden 'the scope for political interference with the activity of the Court' and that it might not be compatible with the UN Charter.[37] Furthermore, it was recalled that Article 16 was 'a unique solution designed to reflect the special role of the UN Security Council' and that an 'expansion of that … carefully crafted negotiation … would not serve the interests of the Court'.[38] Eventually, the ASP decided that the AU's proposal would be discussed further during informal consultations in the next meeting(s) of the newly established working group on amendments, but it was already clear that most non-African states were reluctant to consider, let alone support, any amendment to Article 16.

From the available reports of the ASP's working group, it appears that the scheduled consultations did not take place.[39] What is more, there is no indication that the ASP discussed the AU's peace concerns in any other way during its subsequent meetings between 2010 and 2012. Only in November 2013, after threats of an African mass withdrawal became stronger in reaction to the Council's rejection of the deferral request for Kenyatta and Ruto, the ASP decided to organize an interactive dialogue on the AU's peace concerns under the title 'Indictment of sitting Heads of State and Government and its consequences on peace and stability and reconciliation'.[40] During this event, African states reintroduced the amendment to Article 16. Since then there have been some low-level discussions in the ASP's working group on amendments about a possible revision of Article 16.[41] Yet nothing concrete has emerged from these discussions. This has led the AU to express its frustration about 'the failure by the ASP to consider the concerns and proposal for amendments by the [AU]'.[42]

D The ICC's Deferral Regime

What all this shows is that both the Court's States Parties and the Prosecutor have taken the position that the Security Council is responsible for addressing the AU's peace concerns. The ASP – by remaining more or less silent on the matter – and the Prosecutor – by explicitly saying so – have tried to outsource these concerns to the Council. From a strategic point of view, this reluctance of the Prosecutor and the ASP to become involved with balancing the interests of peace and prosecution makes sense. For her part, Fatou Bensouda seeks to legitimize her Office by depoliticizing its decision-making as much as possible. As such, she sees any explicit consideration of the interests of peace under Article 53 as a threat to the perceived impartiality of the OTP.[43] With similar pragmatism, most members of the ASP consider formal changes to the ICC's deferral regime as inexpedient. After all, an amendment to Article 16 means a revision of the Court's relationship with the Council, which is one of the most fundamental political structures that is embedded in the ICC's legal framework and therefore one of the most sensitive issues to bring up for amendment.

Presumably, the AU is not completely insensitive to these considerations either. Yet what really frustrates African states is that Article 16 has proven inaccessible to them.[44] The AU and its Member States have stated many times that the Council should take their peace concerns more seriously and should reserve a more fitting response to their deferral requests.[45] To the extent that the debate in the Council on the proposed deferrals for al-Bashir, Kenyatta, and Ruto gives any indication, it is that the views among the rotating members of the Council on how to balance the interests of peace and prosecution are too far apart to agree on *any* deferral request under Article 16, unless perhaps they are pressured to do so by a powerful state like the United States. Contrary to the AU's deferral bids, some of the Court's States Parties have set a very high threshold for the use of this provision by saying that it should only be invoked when prosecution by the ICC poses 'by itself' a threat to the peace in the sense of Article 39 of the UN Charter, and other states have even hinted that the Council should never use its deferral powers. It is these kind of responses that have led the AU to question the usefulness of Article 16, as they foreshadow that any of its deferral requests will fail in front of the Council, no matter what the circumstances are.

Ultimately, the AU's repeated deferral requests under Article 16 exemplify how the AU has, at least rhetorically, sought to reconcile the claimed interests of African states ('peace') with the legal obligations of its Member States under the Rome Statute and the UN Charter (to cooperate with the Court's 'prosecution'). The responses to these deferral requests have disappointed the AU in several ways, not just because its requests have been rejected, but also because the responses of the Court and its States Parties expose how unequal power relations influence the ICC's deferral regime. In this sense, the AU's proposal to revise Article 16 may be understood as an attempt to open up the debate about the political structures of the Court and especially about ways to circumvent the continuing dependence on the Security Council.[46] For the time being, however, the Court's States Parties are reluctant to engage in a debate of this magnitude, leaving the AU's powerful juxtaposition between peace and prosecution unresolved.

III ARREST VERSUS IMMUNITY

A second objection that the AU has advanced against the prosecution of African presidents, and especially against the indictment of al-Bashir, is that sitting heads of state normally enjoy immunity from arrest under customary international law. In reaction to the warrant that the Court's judges issued for al-Bashir in March 2009, the Assembly of the AU decided that its Member States will not cooperate with his surrender to the Court because the Security Council 'never acted upon' its deferral request.[47] Furthermore, in an attempt to justify its decision under the Rome Statute, the Assembly referred to Article 98(1), which provides that the Court may not proceed with a request for surrender or assistance when this would require a state 'to act inconsistently with its obligations under international law with respect to the State or diplomatic immunity of a person or property of a third State'.[48] While the assembled African leaders did not further explain this reference in the decision itself, they seemingly agreed that Article 98(1) offered a legal basis for the African States Parties to the ICC to circumvent their obligation under the Rome Statute to enforce the warrant for al-Bashir.[49] In other words, the obligation to arrest the Sudanese president would be trumped by his alleged immunity from arrest under customary international law.

A The Initial Response of the Pre-Trial Chamber

Following the AU's decision, the question concerning whether a State Party can invoke Article 98(1) for not arresting the Sudanese president gained urgency when al-Bashir travelled to several African States Parties in the course of 2010 and 2011.[50] In first instance, the PTC responded to these visits by informing the Security Council and the ASP about al-Bashir's presence on the territory of States Parties in order for these bodies to take 'any measure they may deem appropriate'.[51] The Council and the ASP proved, however, more or less irresponsive to the Chamber's rulings, and eventually the Court's judges decided to take the matter in their own hands.

In reaction to al-Bashir's next visits to Chad and Malawi in 2011, the Chamber initiated formal proceedings against these states for failing to cooperate with the Court.[52] In the resulting decisions, the Court's judges emphasized the vertical nature of the ICC's cooperation regime.[53] According to the Chamber, it is for the Court and not for a State Party or a regional body like the AU to decide whether a provision such as Article 98(1) offers a valid ground to refuse cooperation with the Court. In reference to Article 119(1) of the Statute, which provides that 'any dispute concerning the judicial functions of the Court shall be settled by the decision of the Court', the Chamber stressed that if Chad and Malawi had actually believed that they could not arrest al-Bashir they should have immediately brought this problem to the attention of the Court's judges.

In the second part of its rulings, the Chamber considered whether a State Party can rely on Article 98(1) for refusing to arrest al-Bashir.[54] Instead of examining the scope of this provision, however, the Chamber turned to customary international law. In taking what some have described as a 'modern positivist approach' to the ascertainment of custom, the Chamber found that 'the principle in international law' is that the immunities of heads of state cannot be invoked 'to oppose a prosecution by an international court'.[55] In the opinion of the Chamber, the rationale underlying the existence of these immunities in relation to foreign domestic courts does not apply with respect to international courts like the ICC, which are 'totally independent of states and subject to strict rules of impartiality'.[56] In support, the Chamber referred, most notably, to the prosecution of Slobodan Milosevic and Charles Taylor. These precedents show, according to the Chamber, that the international prosecution of sitting heads of state had 'gained widespread recognition as accepted practice'.[57] Furthermore, the Chamber reasoned that if Article 98(1) would relieve a State Party from its obligation to arrest al-Bashir, as claimed by the AU, then this would 'disable the Court and international criminal justice in ways completely contrary to the purpose of the Statute'.[58] All this would confirm that there exists 'an exception' under customary international law which stipulates that sitting heads of state do not enjoy immunity 'in respect of proceedings before international courts'.[59] Consequently, a State Party, and 'by extension' the AU, cannot rely on Article 98(1) to justify not arresting al-Bashir.[60]

This rejection of the AU's position on the immunity of al-Bashir sparked powerful criticism from different directions, and not least from the AU itself.

In a press statement, the AU Commission expressed its 'deep regret' that the Chamber had purported to 'change customary international law' and emphasized that the decisions rendered Article 98(1) 'redundant, non-operational and meaningless'.[61] In its view, this provision was included in the Statute 'out of recognition that the Statute is not capable of removing an immunity which international law grants to the officials of States that are not parties to the Rome Statute ... because immunities of State officials are rights of the State concerned and a treaty only binds parties to the treaty'.[62] By ruling that immunities are irrelevant in relation to the ICC, the Chamber would have deprived Sudan and all other non-States Parties of these rights.

Alongside the AU, the Chamber's decisions also received strong criticism from various commentators. Apart from questioning the dubious precedents and traces of state practice that the Chamber had invoked for the asserted exception under customary international law, the most often-heard critique was that the Chamber had failed to explain the rationale of Article 98(1) in relation to Article 27(2).[63] Most commentators agreed that Article 27(2), which provides that immunities that are attached 'to the official capacity of a person ... shall not bar the Court from exercising its jurisdiction over such a person', implies that the personal immunities of the officials of *States Parties* cannot be invoked to refuse cooperation with the Court.[64] This provision offers, in other words a waiver of immunities for the purpose of Article 98(1) when the Court asks a State Party to arrest the sitting Head of State of another Member State. Yet, it was widely questioned why Article 98(1) is there at all, if the personal immunities of the officials of *non-States Parties* would be irrelevant in relation to the ICC as well.

B *The Revised Response of the Pre-Trial Chamber*

Following the rulings on the non-cooperation of Chad and Malawi, the Court's judges did not address the question of al-Bashir's immunity in reaction to his next visits to Chad and Nigeria in 2013. In response to his return to Chad, the Chamber limited itself to saying that Chad had again failed to respect its obligation under the Statute to cooperate with the Court.[65] Later that year, after the Sudanese president had briefly attended a special summit of the AU in Abuja, the Chamber was satisfied with Nigeria's explanation that al-Bashir had left the country in a rush at a time that the Nigerian authorities 'were considering the necessary steps to be taken ... in line with Nigeria's obligations'.[66] While Nigeria did not confirm that it was actually under an obligation to arrest al-Bashir and also failed to explain why it had not contacted the Court upon his (unexpected) arrival, the Court's judges decided, without giving further reasons, 'that it [was] not warrant in the present circumstances' to refer the matter to the Council and the ASP.[67]

In contrast, al-Bashir's trip to the Democratic Republic of the Congo (DRC) in February 2014 triggered an outspoken reaction from the Chamber, including on the question of his alleged immunity. As in its decisions on the non-cooperation of Chad and Malawi, the Chamber first stressed that it is for the Court and not for a State Party itself to decide whether there is a valid reason not to enforce a cooperation request.[68] The Court's judges then continued to discuss whether a State Party can possibly rely on Article 98(1) for refusing to arrest al-Bashir. Unlike its earlier decisions, however, the Chamber did not answer this question on the basis of customary international law. Instead, it turned attention to the rationale of Article 98(1) in relation to Article 27(2).

In line with what many commentators had said in response to its earlier rulings, the Chamber reasoned that Article 27(2) provides an 'exception' for lifting personal immunities under customary international law and that this exception 'should, in principle, be confined to those States Parties who have accepted it', because under Article 34 of the Vienna Convention of the Law of Treaties (VCLT), a treaty cannot impose obligations on third States without their consent.[69] As argued by the AU, the Chamber found that Article 98(1) was included in the Statute to ensure that a State Party is not forced to act 'inconsistently with its international obligations towards [a] non-State Party with respect to the immunities of the latter's Head of State'.[70]

According to the Chamber, this does not mean, however, that the Court's States Parties were relieved from their obligation to arrest al-Bashir. Article 98(1) would not apply in the present case, because the Security Council, by referring the situation in Darfur to the ICC, would have 'implicitly waived' the immunity that al-Bashir would normally have enjoyed under customary international law.[71] This waiver would follow from the obligation that the Council had placed in resolution 1593 upon Sudan to cooperate fully with the Court.[72] In its view, the cooperation requirement 'was meant to eliminate any impediment to the proceedings before the Court, including the lifting of immunities'.[73] The reference of the DRC and the AU to Article 98(1) for refusing to arrest al-Bashir could therefore not be accepted.

C The ICC's Immunity Regime

These separate decisions show that the Court's judges have struggled to formulate a consistent response to the AU's claim that al-Bashir enjoys immunity from arrest. What has made this issue particularly complex for the Court's judges is that the Rome Statute encompasses two competing visions on the relevance of personal immunities before the ICC. The first vision, ingrained in Article 27(2), is that immunities attached to the official capacity of a person should not affect the prosecution of international crimes in any way. The second view, as embedded in Article 98(1), is that officials of non-States Parties may still possess personal immunities under customary international law and that the Court should not force its States Parties to violate these immunities.

As discussed, the Chamber has advanced two different approaches to resolve the tension between these two visions and thereby to counter the juxtaposition that the AU has highlighted between the obligation to arrest and the duty to respect the immunity of sitting heads of state under customary international law.[74] In first instance, the Chamber turned to customary international law and argued that immunities simply do not pose an obstacle to the prosecution of sitting heads of state by any international court or tribunal. The AU's juxtaposition would be an outdated one. Second, in its decision on the non-cooperation of the DRC, the Court's judges tried to resolve the tension by arguing that Article 98(1) does not apply because the Security Council implicitly waived al-Bashir's immunity.

For some commentators, the second approach is preferable over the first one, because it makes more sense of Article 98(1).[75] Other scholars have argued, however, that the Chamber's decision on the non-cooperation of the DRC raises unresolved questions about the interpretation of Security Council resolution 1593 and about the legal powers of the Council in relation to the ICC.[76] Most importantly, they have questioned if the Council can (implicitly) remove immunities on behalf of a state for the purpose of the Court's proceedings, and whether the Council has actually done this with respect to Sudan.[77] In this regard, it can be noted that the AU Commission stated back in 2012 that 'the Security Council has not lifted President Bashir's immunity' and claimed that 'any such lifting should have been explicit, [the] mere referral of a "situation" . . . to the ICC or requesting a state to cooperate with the ICC [could not] be interpreted as lifting immunities granted under international law'.[78] This position has also been adopted by China and in particular by Russia, which has stated in front of the ASP that 'in the absence of any clear language in the [Council's] resolutions about the possibility of lifting . . . immunities, those resolutions should not be interpreted as undermining the effect of the norms of general international law, which grant immunities to the heads of states'.[79]

In June 2015, the question of al-Bashir's immunity again received a lot of attention in the context of his visit to South Africa for a summit of the AU.

A few days prior to his scheduled arrival, South Africa consulted the Court and argued in front of Single Judge Tarfusser that there was still a 'lack of clarity in the law' and that South Africa 'was subject to competing obligations'.[80] In response, Judge Tarfusser recalled the Chamber's earlier decision on the DRC and stated that 'there exists no ambiguity or uncertainty' with respect to al-Bashir's alleged immunity.[81] This response stands in stark contrast to the dissenting views that both states and commentators have expressed upon South Africa's decision to welcome al-Bashir.[82] In light of these different reactions, it can hardly be denied that the scope of the ICC's immunity regime remains contested.

Back in 2012, the AU Assembly considered approaching the UN General Assembly to request an advisory opinion from the International Court of Justice (ICJ) on this matter.[83] For some reason, this proposal never gained much momentum within the General Assembly. This means that for the time being, the judges of the Pre-Trial Chamber have the 'final' say in the disagreement between the AU and the ICC on the alleged immunity of al-Bashir. Yet, by tapping into the ambiguity and uncertainty that the responses of the PTC have left, the AU's juxtaposition between arrest and immunity continues to be powerful in its ability to shape perceptions of the Court and provides a discourse for states who seek to justify their non-cooperation with the ICC.

IV TRIAL VERSUS PRESIDENTIAL RESPONSIBILITIES

A third concern that the AU has advanced against the ICC, especially in the context of the cases against Kenyatta and Ruto, is that the Court's trial proceedings have a negative effect on the demanding responsibilities of African presidents. After 'UhuRuto' won the Kenyan presidential elections in March 2013, the AU and the newly installed Kenyan government took several steps aimed at terminating or at least postponing their cases before the ICC.[84] Apart from a deferral request to the Security Council and an unsubstantiated proposal to refer the Kenyan cases back to the Kenyan Judiciary,[85] the AU decided to put its weight behind requests of Kenyatta and Ruto to be excused from continuous presence during the course of their trials (which were scheduled to start within a matter of months). In a letter to the Presidency of the Court in September 2013, the AU argued that 'the Head of State of Kenya and his Deputy [should be able] to choose the sessions they wish to attend in accordance with their constitutional obligations'.[86] Much like its deferral bid, this proposal called for a short-term solution that would have to ensure that the Court's proceedings would not adversely affect the ability of the two Kenyan leaders to discharge their presidential responsibilities.

A *The Trial Chamber(s) versus the Appeals Chamber*[87]

The most important provision of the Rome Statute with regard to these unprecedented excusal requests is Article 63(1), which states that 'the accused shall be present during trial'. According to the Prosecutor's initial reply to the excusal requests of Kenyatta and Ruto, the 'plain language' of this provision shows that the presence of the accused is a 'statutory requirement' of the Court's trial proceedings. Consequently, the judges would have no discretion to excuse an accused who wants to waive his or her right to be present. They would simply have to reject the requests of Kenyatta and Ruto.[88]

Trial Chamber V.A. (with Judge Carbuccia dissenting) and Trial Chamber V.B. (with Judge Ozaki dissenting) decided, however, to grant first Ruto and later Kenyatta a conditional excusal from continuous presence at trial for the purposes of accommodating their presidential responsibilities.[89] The majority of the two Trials Chambers found that Article 63 envisages continuous presence as a general rule, but that in 'exceptional circumstances', the Court's judges would have the discretion to 'excuse an accused, on a case-by-case basis', and thus to allow the accused to be represented by counsel only.[90] In the opinion of Judge Eboe-Osuji and Judge Fremr, who sat in both Chambers, the fact that Kenyatta and Ruto had to perform 'important functions of an extraordinary dimension', justified such an exceptional excusal.[91] For this reason, they allowed the two Kenyan leaders to be absent from all trial hearings, except for the opening statements, closing statements, and the delivery of the judgment.

A few months later, the Appeals Chamber decided to reverse the Trial Chamber's earlier ruling on Ruto's excusal request, because it would amount 'to a blanket excusal before the trial had even commenced, effectively making his absence the general rule and his presence an exception'.[92] The judges of the Appeals Chamber agreed with the Trial Chamber that this provision is not an 'absolute bar in all circumstances to the continuation of trial proceedings in the absence of the accused' and noted that the Chamber has 'discretion to excuse an accused person, on a case-by-case basis'.[93] Yet, in their view, the Trial Chamber had not exercised this discretion 'properly'.[94] They explained that the absence of the accused would only be permitted 'in exceptional circumstances and must not become the rule'.[95] The Trial Chamber should have considered 'reasonable alternative measures', including 'changes to the trial schedule or a short adjournment of the trial'.[96] An excusal would only be allowed if such alternative measures would be inadequate, and even then, these absences would have to be limited to 'what is strictly necessary' and any decision 'must be taken on a case-by-case basis, with due regard to the subject matter of the specific hearings that the accused would not attend'.[97] In short, the Appeals Chamber foreshadowed that Ruto as well as Kenyatta would not have to attend all, but certainly most of their trial hearings in The Hague.[98]

B The Intervention by the ASP

A few weeks after the Appeals Chamber's ruling, and only five days after the Security Council had rejected the proposed deferral under Article 16, Kenya and the AU turned to the ASP to come up with a solution for the competing responsibilities of the two Kenyan leaders. Despite the insistence of the Appeals Chamber that the accused would have to be present during most trial hearings, the African States Parties argued that the ASP would have to develop an automatic excusal regime for sitting heads of state or at least a more flexible approach towards presence at trial. Guided by the AU and under the threat of a mass withdrawal, they called upon the ASP to amend the relevant provisions of the Rome Statute (Articles 27 and 63) as well as the more specific Rules of Procedure and Evidence (RPE) on presence at trial.[99]

As a result of the AU's campaign against the prosecution of Kenyatta and Ruto, the Court's embattled relationship with Africa became the main item on the agenda of the ASP's meeting in November 2013. Already in their opening statements, many States Parties stressed that the 'most critical job' for the ASP would be to engage in a 'constructive and transparent dialogue' with the AU, because there would be 'a very real possibility that a significant number of parties to the Rome Statute ... [would] leave the Court if their concerns [were] not addressed'.[100] The special segment that was requested by the AU on the indictment of sitting Heads of State showed, according to the informal summary of the moderator, that there was 'broad agreement' among the Court's States Parties that 'practical solutions' needed to be found.[101] For the first time since the indictment of al-Bashir, the Court's States Parties proved ready to address the 'concerns expressed by the African Union' about the prosecution of African presidents.[102]

Seeing that most States Parties opposed any substantive change to the Rome Statute and also because such amendments could take years to enter into force, the negotiations in the ASP soon focused on possible changes to the RPE.[103] After a week of intense negotiations, the ASP approved – by consensus – three amendments to the RPE on presence at trial (Rules 134 *bis, ter,* and *quater*), which entered into force immediately.[104] The first of these amendments allows defendants to be virtually present through video technology and the second provides that the Trial Chamber may excuse an accused under the exact same conditions that were set by the Appeals Chamber. Yet the real attempt to address the concerns of the AU, and thus to move beyond the juxtaposition between trial and presidential responsibilities, was the adoption of Rule 134 *quater*. With this last and most controversial amendment, the ASP created a special excusal regime for those who are 'mandated to fulfil extraordinary public duties at the highest national level'. Under this new Rule, the Trial Chamber has to 'expeditiously' consider a request from an accused that fulfils such extraordinary public duties and 'shall' grant this request under a number of conditions, including that an excusal is in the 'interests of justice'.

The reason why this last amendment was considered to be the most controversial, and precisely why the AU pushed for it, is that this rule deviates from the conditions of the Appeals Chamber. Rule 134 *quater* allows the absence of the accused to be the rule rather than the exception and suggests that excusal decisions do not have to be taken on a case-by-case basis or that the period of the excusal has to be limited to what is strictly necessary. Because of these differences with the Appeals Chamber's interpretation of Article 63(1), but also the distinction that the new Rule seems to draw on the basis of official capacity, several commentators questioned the consistency of Rule 134 *quater* with the Statute.[105]

Yet, despite these and similar objections of the Prosecutor about Rule 134 *quater*, the Trial Chamber soon confirmed the validity of the new Rule and used it to excuse Ruto from significant parts of his trial. According to the judges of the Trial Chamber, the new Rule has to be understood as a subsequent agreement in the meaning of Article 31(3)(A) of the VCLT, providing 'greater clarity' on the scope and application of Article 63(1) to 'a specific type of situations' that was not 'explicitly addressed when the Statute was being drafted'.[106] Despite the Appeals Chamber's conflicting judgment, the judges of the Trial Chamber thus decided to follow the 'intervention' of the ASP.[107]

C Continued Opposition against the Prosecution of African Presidents

For its part, Kenya saw the adoption and enforcement of the new excusal regime as a 'major victory'.[108] According to the Kenyan foreign minister, Amina Mohamed, Rule 134 *quater* implied that the Court's judges could no longer pretend that Kenyatta and Ruto are 'merely accused persons before the ICC'.[109] Among the other delegations of the ASP, the general feeling was one of relief. Many of its members were convinced that the new excusal regime would help to address the 'Kenyan and African Union's concerns around trial procedures, while upholding the principle of justice and accountability'.[110] The tension between presence at trial and presidential responsibilities would have been dispelled without undermining 'the principle that no one is above the law within the Rome Statute'.[111]

Following the eventful meeting of the ASP, it soon became clear, however, that the new excusal regime did *not* mean the end of the AU's campaign against the prosecution of African presidents. In addition to its unresolved concerns about the Court's deferral and immunity regime, the AU continued to argue that the Court had to suspend the cases against Kenyatta and Ruto until they completed their terms of office, and called upon the ASP to amend the Statute in such a way that sitting heads of state and their deputies can be exempted from ICC prosecution.[112] Along the lines that it had set out in October 2013, the AU's official position is that 'to safeguard the constitutional order, stability and, integrity of Member States, no charges shall be commenced or continued before any International Court or Tribunal against any serving AU Head of State or Government or anybody acting or entitled to act in such capacity during their term of office'.[113]

A powerful symbol of this ongoing opposition is Kenyatta's decision to temporarily step down from office in October 2014 in order to attend a status conference on his adjourned trial.[114] After the Trial Chamber had rejected his request to be excused from presence during the status conference,[115] Kenyatta announced in front of a special joint session of the Kenyan Parliament that he would travel to The Hague in his personal capacity and that he would appoint Deputy President Ruto as acting president during his absence.[116] Kenyatta explained his decision by saying that he did not want to compromise the sovereignty of Kenya or set a 'precedent for the attendance of presidents before the Court'.[117] In this way, Kenyatta sought to keep his election promise that he would cooperate with the Court to prove his innocence, while at the same time epitomizing the protest of the AU against the prosecution of sitting heads of state.[118]

Shortly after Kenyatta's brief appearance at the ICC, the Prosecutor announced that she had to withdraw the charges against him. In a dramatic statement, speaking of 'a dark day for international criminal justice', Bensouda argued that 'the Government of Kenya had failed to adequately cooperate' with her investigation.[119] According to the Prosecutor, Kenya's refusal to provide 'important records' to the OTP and the consistent intimidation of witnesses in Kenya had made the continuation of the case impossible.[120] Rather than dropping the case because the investigation had shown

Kenyatta to be innocent, Bensouda portrayed his prosecution as an impossible struggle for the OTP due to the ongoing efforts of the Kenyan government to obstruct the proceedings. With this 'political' manoeuvring, Bensouda turned the discontinued case against Kenyatta into a debate about Kenya's alleged non-cooperation.[121]

Like Kenyatta's decision to temporarily step down from office to attend his 'last day' in The Hague, this unfinished battle over the status of Kenya's cooperation with the ICC is all about perception.[122] The question at play is who is responsible for the collapse of Kenyatta's trial. For her part, the Prosecutor seeks to blame Kenya for this by portraying Kenyatta's government as a 'false' friend of the Court. As such, she seeks to protect her office from accusations of politicization and incompetence. On the other side of the fence, supporters of Kenyatta claim that their president has proven his inno-cence and that even though the Prosecutor tried to fabricate a case against him, there was simply no evidence to be found. In doing so, they seek to characterize the Court as a continuing threat to the stability and sovereignty of African states, which is powerful in the sense that it can undermine the Court's legitimacy among its different audiences inside and outside of Kenya.

Amidst the tug of war between the Prosecutor and the Kenyan government, the AU has welcomed the withdrawal of charges against Kenyatta, but not without expressing its regret over 'the period it took the Office of the Prosecutor to arrive at [this] decision'.[123] What is more, in its resolutions of January and June 2015, the AU Assembly has recalled its proposed amend-ment to Article 27 of the Statute and has reiterated its request 'to terminate or suspend' the proceedings against Ruto and al-Bashir 'until the African con-cerns and proposals for amendments are considered'.[124] All this illustrates that neither the new excusal regime nor the collapse of Kenyatta's trial has silenced the AU in its campaign against 'the wisdom of the continued prosecution against African Leaders'.[125] On the contrary, it seems that since the explicit consideration of the AU's concerns in the ASP in late 2013, its position has become more outspoken and consistent in juxtaposing the indictment and especially the trials of African presidents against the sovereignty of African states and the demanding responsibilities that their highest official represen-tatives have to fulfil.

V CONCLUDING REMARKS

Apart from accusations about the selectivity and the politicization of the ICC, the AU's opposition against the Court has focused on the prosecution of African presidents and on the repercussions that these prosecutions would have on African states and their officials. Through its public deliberations, the AU has argued that the prosecution of African leaders undermines the promotion of peace and stability in the region. Furthermore, the AU has claimed that President al-Bashir enjoys immunity from arrest under customary international law and that the Court's proceedings have adversely affected the ability of Kenyatta and Ruto to discharge their responsibilities as president and deputy president of Kenya. In advancing these and related concerns, the AU has placed (1) the importance of prosecution against the interests of peace, (2) the obligation to arrest under the Rome Statute against the immunity from arrest under customary international law, and (3) the Court's trial proceedings against the demanding responsibilities of sitting heads of state.

Regardless of whether the AU is somehow justified in its criticism of the ICC, it is these three juxtapositions that have made the AU's campaign against the prosecution of African presidents powerful, in the sense that it has put the Court's legitimacy under pressure. Its public message that the sovereignty and stability of African states are at threat is what can shape perceptions about the Court in Africa. In this way, the AU may lead state officials, local communities, and other relevant audiences of the ICC to refuse cooperation with the Court's investigations and prosecutions in Africa. Moreover, these alleged threats provide a discourse for those who want to delegitimize the ICC and the principles that it stands to represent.[126]

Of course, the actors and forces behind the decisions of 'the' AU have to be unpacked. It cannot be overlooked that the AU's initial opposition against the indictment of al-Bashir was spearheaded by Colonel Gaddafi, and that the recent campaign against the prosecution of Kenyatta and Ruto has been spurred by Yoweri Museveni (president of Uganda since 1986) and Robert Mugabe (leader of Zimbabwe since 1980 and president since 1987), with Namibia and Ethiopia doing much of the diplomatic work. Many state officials who operate at the sub-ministerial level within the AU have taken a more nuanced position on the ICC, and it has often been a handful of involved African leaders that convinced the AU Assembly to take a hard line on the matter. It is important that scholars continue to identify these and other political dynamics underlying the AU's public deliberations. At the same time however, it should be recognized that the AU's message is powerful, in and of itself, as it has the ability to undermine the Court's legitimacy.

In exploring the interactions between the AU, the ICC, and its States Parties, this chapter has shown that the Court and its supporters have so far not managed to move beyond the three juxtapositions that the AU has advanced against the prosecution of African presidents. For its part, the AU has, at least rhetorically, tried to reconcile the claimed interests of African states with the legal obligations of its Member States under the Rome Statute. Apart from proposals to amend the Statute, it has called for deferrals on the basis of Article 16, for a recognition of al-Bashir's immunity from arrest under Article 98(1), and for an excusal from presence at trial under Article 63(1) of the Statute. However, with the important exception of the amended rules on presence at trial, the Court and its States Parties have proven reluctant to endorse these and related 'solutions'.

To be sure, the ICC and its States Parties have taken several other steps to counter the AU's campaign against the Court. The ICC's States Parties have, for example, appointed an African woman as Prosecutor (Fatou Bensouda from the Gambia), elected an African as president of the ASP (Sidiki Kaba from Senegal),[127] and have organized several seminars and diplomatic trips aimed at improving the Court's relationship with Africa.[128] Moreover, there is the still pending proposal for an ICC liaison office at the AU's headquarters in Addis Ababa.[129] These and other initiatives can certainly help to ease the tensions. However, they will probably not resolve the most powerful concerns that the AU has expressed about the prosecution of African presidents and can as such only be partially successful as a counter-strategy that seeks to protect the Court's legitimacy.

As things stand, the AU and many of its Member States will not likely change their position on the prosecution of sitting African heads of state, especially when the case against al-Bashir, and the battle over Kenya's alleged non-cooperation with the Court remain ongoing. What is more, the recent proposal of the African National Congress to pull South Africa out of the ICC foreshadows that, at some point, the ongoing tensions surrounding these cases may culminate in a mass withdrawal of African states from the Rome Statute.[130] Yet, even if African states remain part of the ICC, the AU's campaign against the prosecution of African presidents will probably continue. This will put further pressure on the perceived legitimacy of the Court, and as such on the ability of the ICC to obtain the necessary support for its investigations and prosecutions in Africa.

Notes

1. UN Treaties Collection (C.N.1026.2013.TREATIES-XVIII.10), Kenya: Proposal of Amendments, 14 March 2014.
2. Indeed, several African states (in particular Botswana), prominent Africans (such as Kofi Annan), and civil society organizations have publically distanced themselves from the position of the AU.

3. As explained in the Introduction to this volume, legitimacy, in the sociological understanding of the word, refers to the perceptions that the different audiences of an institution have about the appropriateness of its norms and decisions. In this sense, an international court like the ICC possesses sociological legitimacy to the extent that its rulings and broader normative framework are perceived by its audiences as 'appropriate, proper, and just'. This conception of sociological legitimacy builds on: Tom Tyler, 'Psychological Perspectives of Legitimacy and Legitimation' (2006) 57 *Annual Review of Psychology* 375–400; Ian Hurd, *After Anarchy – Legitimacy & Power in the United Nations Security Council* (Princeton: Princeton University Press, 2007), pp. 7–12, 30–45.

4. On the relation between power and perceived legitimacy: Chris Reus-Smit, 'International Crises of Legitimacy' (2007) 44 *International Politics* 160–165. More generally, on different conceptions of power: Michael Barnett and Raymond Duvall, 'Power in International Politics' (2005) 59 *International Organization* 39–75.

5. For an overview of the existing debate, see the Introduction to this volume.

6. AU Peace and Security Council, Communiqué, PSC/MIN/Comm (CXLII, 21 July 2008), para. 9.

7. AU Assembly, Decision on Africa's Relationship with the ICC, Ext/ Assembly/AU/Dec.1(Oct.2013), 11–12 October 2013, paras. 5 and 10(i).

8. There is some debate among states and commentators on the conditions under which the Security Council may issue a deferral. Elsewhere, I have taken the position that there are four conditions under Article 16: (1) the deferral has to be limited to a period of twelve months; (2) the Council has to make an 'explicit' request to the Court not to commence or proceed with an investigation; (3) the Council has to issue a deferral through 'a resolution adopted under Chapter VII' and therefore has to determine that there exists, at a minimum, a threat to the peace in the sense of Article 39 of the Chapter (although this threat does not have to be caused by the Court's involvement, as some states have argued); and finally (4) the Council has to exercise its deferral powers on a case-by-case basis, meaning that the Council can only defer (the initiation of) an investigation into existing and specific events, and when suspending prosecutions, the Court has to specify which prosecutions it wants to defer. See Abel S. Knottnerus, 'The Security Council and the International Criminal Court: The Unsolved Puzzle of Article 16' (2014) 61 *Netherlands International Law Review* 195–224.

9. See the statements of China, Indonesia, Russia, and Vietnam in UNSC, S/PV.5947, 31 July 2008.

10. *Ibid.*, statement of the United States. A few weeks later, US ambassador Richard Williamson even stated that 'if forced to vote today – the United States, if it was 191 countries against one, would veto an Article 16 [resolution]'. Daniel van Oudenaren, 'US Will Veto Attempts to Defer ICC Move against Sudan President', *Sudan Tribune*, 24 September 2008.

11. Dire Tladi, 'When Elephants Collide It Is the Grass That Suffers: Cooperation and the Security Council in the Context of the AU/ICC Dynamic' (2014) 7 *African Journal of Legal Studies* 396. See also 'Sudan/ICC: UK Strategy with Potential Bashir ICC Indictment', *Daily Telegraph*, 15 July 2011.

12. Statement of the UK in UNSC, S/PV.5947, 31 July 2008. See also the statement of France in UN General Assembly, 'Press Conference following the statement of H.E. Mr. Nicolas Sarkozy, President of France', UN Doc GA/10749, 23 September 2008. For further discussion: David Bosco, *Rough Justice: The International Criminal Court in a World of Power Politics* (Oxford: Oxford University Press, 2014), pp. 144–148.

13. This can be concluded from the official statements that were made in response to the Prosecutor's updates to the Council in December 2008 and December 2009: UNSC, S/PV.6028, 3 December 2008; UNSC, S/PV. 6230, 4 December 2009.

14. Security Council Report, 'Sudan – March 2011 Monthly Forecast', 28 February 2011.

15. AU Assembly, Decision on Africa's Relationship with the ICC (Ext/Assembly/AU/Dec.1(Oct.2013)), 11–12 October 2013, para. 10.

16. *Ibid.* Note that the decision also spoke about a deferral for al-Bashir, but that the AU did not take any further action in this regard.

17. Security Council Report, 'AU Request for ICC Deferral of Kenyan Situation', 13 November 2013. For an unofficial report on what happened during the interactive dialogue: AU's Contact Group of the Executive Council, 'Draft Report of the Mission of the African Union Contact Group on the International Criminal Court', 12 November 2013.

18. UNSC, S/PV.7060, 15 November 2013.

19. *Ibid.*

20. *Ibid.*, statement of Pakistan. See also the statements of Azerbaijan, China, Ethiopia, and Rwanda.

21. *Ibid.*, statement of Russia.

22. *Ibid.*, statements of Argentina, Australia, Luxembourg, and the UK.

23. *Ibid.*, statement of Australia.

24. *Ibid.*, statements of Australia and the UK.

25. *Ruto and Sang* (ICC-01/09/-01/11-T-37-Red-ENG), Trial Hearing – Proceedings, 23 September 2013, p.8; *Kenyatta* (ICC-01/09-02/11-847), Decision adjourning the commencement of trial, 31 October 2013.
26. Statement of Luxembourg in: UNSC, S/PV.7060, 15 November 2013. See also the statement of Australia.
27. *Ibid.*, statements of Argentina, France, Luxembourg, the UK, and the USA.
28. These are the words of Richard Dicker, Director of the International Justice Program of Human Rights Watch, as quoted in: Margaret Besheer, 'AU Presses Kenyatta ICC Deferral Request', *Voice of America*, 31 October 2013. See also the statements of Argentina, Guatemala, and South Korea in: UNSC, S/PV.7060, 15 November 2013.
29. *Ibid.*, statement of Argentina.
30. *Ibid.*, statement of Rwanda. See also the statements of Ethiopia (as representative of the chairperson of the AU), Kenya, Morocco, and Togo.
31. Statement of Uganda (on behalf of the AU), as well as the statements of Namibia, Nigeria, South Africa, and Tanzania in: ASP, General Debate of the Twelfth Session, 20–26 November 2013.
32. AU Assembly Decision on the Progress Report of the Commission on the Implementation of the Decisions on the International Criminal Court (Assembly/AU/Dec.493 (XXII)), 30–31 January 2014, para. 8.
33. For example, in his address to the ASP in 2013, Charles Jalloh stated that 'if [he] were a Court official like the Prosecutor, [he] would prefer to act using [his] statutorily conferred power over transferring the discretionary decision to a quintessentially body such as the UNSC'. Charles Jalloh, 'Reflections on the Indictment of Sitting Heads of State and Government and Its Consequences for Peace and Stability and Reconciliation in Africa' (2014) 7 *African Journal of Legal Studies* 54–55. On at least one occasion, AU Member States have also argued that the Prosecutor should 'include factors of promoting peace' in her decision-making under Article 53: AU Executive Council, Report on the Ministerial Meeting on the Rome Statute of the International Criminal Court, EX.CL/568 (XVI), 25–29 January 2010, p. 11.
34. UN Treaties Collection (C.N.851.2009.TREATIES-10), *South Africa: Proposal of Amendment*, 30 November 2009. For a detailed policy paper on the proposed amendment: Charles Jalloh, Dapo Akande and Max du Plessis, 'Assessing the African Union Concerns about Article 16 of the Rome Statute of the International Criminal Court' (2011) 4 *African Journal of Legal Studies* 5–50.
35. OTP, Policy Paper on the Interests of Justice, September 2007, p. 1.
36. OTP, Key note address Mrs. Fatou Bensouda – International justice and diplomacy: partnering for peace and international security,

20 March 2013, p. 3. It is along these lines that Fatou Bensouda has also responded to the AU's peace concerns. See for example OTP, Key note address Mrs. Fatou Bensouda – New power balances: actors for the future and challenges ahead, 23 May 2013, p. 6.

37. AU Executive Council, Report on the Rome Statute of the ICC, paras. 10–11.

38. *Ibid.*

39. ASP, Report on the Working Group of Amendments, 9 December 2011, ICC-ASP/10/32; ASP, Report of the Working Group on Amendments, 13 November 2012, ICC-ASP/11/36; ASP, Report of the Working Group on Amendments, 24 October 2013, ICC-ASP/12/44.

40. ASP, Special segment as requested by the African Union: 'Indictment of sitting Heads of State and Government and its consequences on peace and stability and reconciliation' – Informal summary by the Moderator, 27 November 2013, ICC-ASP/12/61.

41. ASP, Report of the Working Group on Amendments, 7 December 2014, ICC-ASP/13/31, para. 9.

42. AU Assembly Decision on the Progress Report of the Commission on the Implementation of Previous Decisions on the International Criminal Court, Assembly/AU/Dec.547(XXIV), 30–31 January 2015, para. 11.

43. On the Prosecutor's strategy to portray her decisions as 'a-political', see, for example: Michael Struett, 'Why the International Criminal Court Must Pretend to Ignore Politics' (2012) 26 *Ethics & International Affairs* 83–92; James Goldston, 'More Candour about Criteria – The Exercise of Discretion by the Prosecutor of the International Criminal Court' (2010) 8 *Journal of International Criminal Justice* 383–406.

44. An important consideration in this regard is that the Council has tried to employ Article 16 under the pressure of the United States to exclude nationals of non-states parties who live, work and fight on the territories of ICC States Parties from the Court's jurisdiction. UNSC, S/RES/1422, 12 July 2002; UNSC, S/RES/1487, 12 June 2003. These resolutions claimed to be 'consistent with the Provisions of Article 16' but as I explained elsewhere, they went beyond the Council's deferral powers under the Statute, see: Knottnerus, 'Security Council and the ICC', 203–207.

45. AU Assembly, Implementation of Decisions on the ICC 2014, para. 8. See also the statements of Lesotho (on behalf of the African States Parties), Namibia, Tanzania, and Uganda in ASP, General Debate of the Thirteenth Session, 8–17 December 2014.

46. Note that during the negotiations on the Rome Statute most African states accepted the authority of the Council to refer situations to the Court, but argued that the Council should 'not be able to exercise any

veto or unilaterally cause indeterminate delays to the Court's proceedings'. See the statements of Angola (p. 117), Benin (p. 128), Botswana (p. 118), Burkina Faso (p. 84), DRC (p.112), Gabon (p. 102), Ivory Coast (p. 74), Kenya (p. 77), Madagascar (p. 108), Morocco (p. 103), Namibia (p. 87), Niger (p. 110), Nigeria (p. 111), Senegal (p. 83), Sierra Leone (as quoted above – p. 86), Swaziland (p. 108), Sudan (p. 126), Tanzania (p. 74), Uganda (p. 118), and Zambia (p. 93) in Rome Conference, Official Records, A/CONF.183/13 (Vol.2), 15 June–17 July 1998.

47. AU Assembly, Decision on the Meeting of African States Parties to the Rome Statute of the International Criminal Court, Assembly/AU/Dec.245(XIII), 1–3 July 2009, para. 10.

48. *Ibid.* Note that the Assembly in the first instance referred to Article 98 and only at a later stage specified the legal basis of its decision by pointing to Article 98(1).

49. This obligation follows from Article 87 and Article 89(1) of the Statute.

50. Note that the initial decision on the (first) arrest warrant for al-Bashir did not address this question and only briefly touched upon the implications of his position as sitting Head of State. Al-Bashir (ICC-02/05-01/09-3), Decision on the Prosecution's Application for a Warrant of Arrest against Omar Hassan Ahmad Al Bashir, 3 March 2009, paras. 41–45.

51. See, for example, *Al-Bashir* (ICC-02/05-01/09-109), Decision informing the United Nations Security Council and the Assembly of the States Parties to the Rome Statute about Omar Al-Bashir's recent visit to the Republic of Chad, First Decision on the Cooperation of Chad, 27 August 2010.

52. The non-cooperation procedure is stipulated in Article 87 of the Rome Statute.

53. *Al-Bashir* (ICC-02/05-01/09-139), Decision Pursuant to Article 87(7) of the Rome Statute on the Failure by the Republic of Malawi to Comply with the Cooperation Requests Issued by the Court with Respect to the Arrest and Surrender of Omar Hassan Ahmad Al Bashir, 12 December 2011, paras. 10–11; *Al-Bashir* (ICC-02/05-01/09-140), Decision Pursuant to Article 87(7) of the Rome Statute on the Failure by the Republic of Chad to Comply with the Cooperation Requests Issued by the Court with Respect to the Arrest and Surrender of Omar Hassan Ahmad Al Bashir, 13 December 2011, para. 10. Since the PTC restated the relevant elements of the Malawi Decision in para. 13 of the Chad Decision, I will hereafter only cite the Malawi Decision.

54. ICC Malawi Decision, para. 13.

55. *Ibid.*, para. 34. Claus Kreβ, 'The International Criminal Court and Immunities under International Law for States Not Party to the

Court's Statute', in Morten Bergsmo and Ling Yan (eds.), *State Sovereignty and International Law* (Beijing: Torkel Opsahl Academic EPublisher, 2012), p. 254. This approach assumes that general principles can point to the development of 'modern custom', which may come into existence rapidly and without a voluminous body of state practice and *opinio juris*.

56. ICC Malawi Decision, para. 34.
57. *Ibid.*, para. 39.
58. *Ibid.*, para. 41.
59. *Ibid.*, paras. 43 and 22.
60. *Ibid.*, para. 37.
61. AU Commission, Press Release on the Decisions of Pre-Trial Chamber I of the International Criminal Court, N° 002/2012, 9 January 2012.
62. Ibid.
63. See, for example, Dapo Akande, 'ICC issues detailed decision on Bashir's immunity (. . . at long last . . .) but gets the law wrong', *EJIL Talk*, 15 December 2011; Dire Tladi, 'The ICC Decisions on Chad and Malawi – On Cooperation, Immunities, and Article 98' (2013) 11 *Journal of International Criminal Justice* 207; Asad Kiyani, 'Al-Bashir & the ICC: The Problem of Head of State Immunity' (2013) 12 *Chinese Journal of International Law* 490; Dov Jacobs, 'The Frog that Wanted to Be an Ox – The ICC's Approach to Immunities and Cooperation', in Carsten Stahn (ed.), *The Law and Practice of the International Criminal Court* (Oxford: Oxford University Press, 2015), pp. 293–294.
64. Dapo Akande, 'International Law Immunities and the International Criminal Court' (2004) 98 *American Journal of International Law* 422–424; Paola Gaeta, 'Does President al Bashir Enjoy Immunity from Arrest?' (2009) 7 *Journal of International Criminal Justice* 328; Dapo Akande, 'The Legal Nature of Security Council Referrals to the ICC and Its Impact on al Bashir's Immunities' (2009) 7 *Journal of International Criminal Justice* 337–339.
65. *Al-Bashir* (ICC-02/05-01/09-151), Decision on the Non-compliance of the Republic of Chad with the Cooperation Requests Issued by the Court Regarding the Arrest and Surrender of Omar Hassan Ahmad Al-Bashir, 27 March 2013. By this time the Chamber consisted of Presiding Judge Trendafilova and Judges Kaul and Tarfusser. Of these three judges, only Judge Tarfusser was part of the Chamber that issued the decisions on the non-cooperation of Chad and Malawi.
66. *Al-Bashir* (ICC-02/05-01/09-158-Anx4), Report of the Registry on Al-Bashir's visit to Nigeria – Public Annex 4, 14 August 2013.
67. *Al-Bashir* (ICC-02/05-01/09-159), Decision on the Cooperation of the Federal Republic of Nigeria Regarding Omar Al-Bashir's Arrest and Surrender to the Court, 5 September 2013, para. 13.

68. *Al-Bashir* (ICC-02/05-01/09-195), Decision on the Cooperation of the Democratic Republic of the Congo Regarding Omar Al Bashir's Arrest and Surrender to the Court, 9 April 2014, paras. 15–22.

69. *Ibid.* para. 26. Note that the Chamber speaks of 'an exception'. This implies that the Chamber assumed that personal immunities of heads of state are still the prevailing rule under customary international law even with respect to international courts.

70. *Ibid.*, para. 27.

71. *Ibid.*, para. 29.

72. This obligation derives from Article 25 of the UN Charter.

73. *Ibid.*

74. A related juxtaposition which I do not consider in this chapter is between obligations under the Rome Statute and obligations under the AU's Constitutive Act. In response to this alleged conflict of obligations, the Chamber refers in its decision on the non-cooperation of the DRC to Article 103 of the UN Charter, which states that 'in the event of a conflict between the obligations of the Members of the United Nations under the present Charter and their obligations under any other international agreement, their obligations under the … Charter shall prevail'. The Chamber concludes that because the Security Council 'has implicitly lifted the immunities' of Al-Bashir, 'the DRC cannot invoke any other decision, including that of the African Union, providing for any obligation to the contrary'. *Al-Bashir*, ICC-02/05-01/09-195, para. 31.

75. In a recent paper, Nerina Boschiero argues that the Chamber took 'the most convincing approach on the issue'. Nerina Boschiero, 'The ICC Judicial Finding on Non-cooperation Against the DRC and No Immunity for Al-Bashir Based on UNSC Resolution 1593' (2015) 13 *Journal of International Criminal Justice* 639.

76. André de Hoogh and Abel S. Knottnerus, 'ICC issues new decision on Al-Bashir's immunities – but gets the law wrong … again', *EJIL Talk*, 18 April 2014; Paula Gaeta, 'The ICC Changes Its Mind on the Immunity from Arrest of President Al Bashir, but It Is Wrong Again', *Opinio Juris*, 23 April 2014. See also the response of Boschiero to these questions, 'No Immunity for Al-Bashir', 639–651.

77. Note, for example, that the Special Rapporteur concluded in its rapport to the International Law Commission (ILC) that 'the waiver of immunity of a serving Head of State, Head of Government or minister for foreign affairs must be express'. ILC, Third report on immunity of State officials from foreign criminal jurisdiction, A/CN.4/646, 24 May 2011, para. 61(1).

78. AU Commission, Press Release on the decisions of ICC Pre-Trial Chamber.

79. Statement of Russia in: ASP, General Debate Thirteenth Session. See also the statement of China during the same debate and the earlier statements of Russia in ASP, General Debate Twelfth Session; ASP, General Debate of the Eleventh Session, 15 November 2012.

80. *Al-Bashir* (ICC-02/05-01/09-242), Decision following the Prosecutor's request for an order further clarifying that the Republic of South Africa is under the obligation to immediately arrest and surrender Omar Al Bashir, 13 June 2015, para. 4.

81. *Ibid.*, para. 5.

82. See, for example, the statements of Angola, Chad, China, Nigeria, Russia, Sudan, and Venezuela in UNSC, S/PV.7478, 29 June 2015. For different opinions on the alleged immunity of al-Bashir in relation to his visit to South Africa: Dov Jacobs, 'Does South Africa Have an Obligation to Arrest and Surrender Bashir to the ICC? No', *Spreading the Jam*, 14 June 2015; Jens Ohlin, 'More thoughts on al-Bashir, Sudan, and South Africa, *Opinio Juris*, 17 June 2015; Asad Kiyani, 'Exploring Legal Rationales for South Africa's Failure to Arrest al-Bashir', *Opinio Juris*, 18 June 2015.

83. AU Assembly, Decision on the implementation of the Decisions on the International Criminal Court, Assembly/AU/Dec.419(XIX), 15–16 July 2012, para. 3.

84. For a more extensive discussion of these efforts and the role of the ICC in the Kenyan presidential elections, Sara Kendall, '"UhuRuto" and Other Leviathans: The International Criminal Court and the Kenyan Political Order' (2014) 7 *African Journal of Legal Studies* 399–427.

85. AU Assembly, Decision on International Jurisdiction, Justice and the International Criminal Court, Assembly/AU/Dec.482(XXI), 27–28 May 2013, para. 7; AU Cabinet Letter to the Presidency of the International Criminal Court, BC/U/1657.09.13, 10 September 2013.

86. *Ibid.*

87. For a more detailed legal analysis of the relevant decisions: Abel S. Knottnerus, 'Extraordinary Exceptions at the International Criminal Court: The (New) Rules and Jurisprudence on Presence at Trial' (2014) 13 *The Law and Practice of International Courts and Tribunals* 261–285.

88. See also the other arguments for this reading of Article 63(1) in *Ruto and Sang* (ICC-01/09-01/11-713), Prosecution's Observations on 'Defence Request pursuant to Article 63 (1) of the Rome Statute', 1 May 2013, para. 7.

89. *Ruto and Sang* (ICC-01/09-01/11-777), Decision on Mr Ruto's Request for Excusal from Continuous Presence at Trial, 18 June 2013; *Kenyatta* (ICC-01/09-02/11-830), Decision on Defence Request for Conditional Excusal from Continuous Presence at Trial, 18 October 2013 (in para. 124

of this decision the Chamber stated that it 'fully adopted' the reasoning of Trial Chamber V.A. on Ruto's excusal request).

90. *Ruto and Sang* (ICC-01/09-01/11-777), para. 49.
91. *Ibid.*
92. *Ruto and Sang* (ICC-01/09-01/11-1066), Judgement on the appeal of the Prosecutor against the decision of Trial Chamber V(a) of 18 June 2013 entitled 'Decision on Mr Ruto's Request for Excusal from Continuous Presence at Trial', 25 October 2013, para. 63.
93. *Ibid.* paras. 55–56. Note, however, that Judges Kourula and Usacka took a different stand in their joined separate opinion.
94. *Ibid.*, para. 61.
95. *Ibid.*, para. 62.
96. *Ibid.*
97. *Ibid.*
98. Note that several African states intervened in the proceedings: *Ruto and Sang* (ICC-01/09-01/11-948), Joint Amicus curiae Observations of the United Republic of Tanzania, Republic of Rwanda, Republic of Burundi, State of Eritrea and Republic of Uganda on the Prosecution's appeal against the Decision on Mr. Ruto's Request for Excusal from Continuous Presence at Trial, 17 September 2013. Para. 2 of these observations states that 'Article 63 should be interpreted in a broad and flexible manner that encourages States cooperation in the widest possible set of circumstances and without endangering the constitutional obligations of the highest office holders'.
99. See the statements of Botswana, Congo, the DRC, Gambia, Ghana, Kenya, Ivory Coast, Namibia, Nigeria, Seychelles, South Africa, Tanzania, Tunisia, and Uganda (on behalf of the AU) in: ASP, General Debate Twelfth Session.
100. *Ibid.*, statement of Australia, Brazil, and New Zealand. See also the statements of Canada, Costa Rica, Czech Republic, Denmark, Finland, France, Germany, Italy, Japan, Jordan (also on behalf of Liechtenstein), Lithuania (on behalf of the European Union), Luxembourg, Peru, Philippines, Portugal, Spain, Trinidad & Tobago, and the United States.
101. ASP, special segment as requested by the African Union.
102. *Ibid.*
103. Any amendment to Articles 27 or 63 would only enter into force 'one year after instruments of ratification or acceptance have been deposited with the secretary-general of the United Nations by seven-eighths' of the Court's States Parties (Article 121(4)). In contrast, amendments to the RPE enter into force immediately upon adoption by two-thirds of the members of the ASP (Article 51(2)).

104. ASP, Resolution ICC-ASP/12/Res.7, 27 November 2013.
105. See Kevin John Heller, 'Will the New RPE 134 Provisions Survive Judicial Review? (probably not)', *Opinio Juris*, 28 November 2013; Knottnerus, 'Extraordinary Exceptions', 275–277; 279–280.
106. *Ruto and Sang* (ICC-01/09-01/11-1186), Reasons for the Decision on Excusal from Presence at Trial under Rule 134 *quater*, 18 February 2014, paras. 55–56. Note that 'this argument mistakenly conflates an amendment to the RPE, which is regulated *within* the Statute and is adopted by an organ of the ICC, with a subsequent agreement, which is an agreement of *all* States Parties to a treaty *outside* the legal framework of that treaty'. Knottnerus, 'Extraordinary Exceptions', 276.
107. See the quite remarkable and very long (twenty-three pages) Separate Further Opinion of Judge Eboe-Osuji (ICC-01/09-01/11-1186-Anx), which states in this regard (p. 12) that 'to deny the ASP the facility of using the Rules to indicate legislative intent underlying given provisions of the Statute ... is to deny them flexibility to resolve with relative speed impasses in the application of the Statute'. Note that the judges of the Trial Chamber eventually also decided to block the Prosecutor's request for leave to appeal: *Ruto and Sang* (ICC-01/09-01/11-1246), Decision on 'Prosecution's application for leave to appeal the decision on excusal from presence at trial under Rule 134 *quater*', 2 April 2014 (with Judge Carbuccia dissenting).
108. As quoted in Robert Nyasato, 'Kenya lauds AU support in reviewing ICC rules', *Standard Media*, 29 November 2013.
109. *Ibid.*
110. Mark Simmonds (Foreign Office Minister UK), 'FCO Minister Welcomes New ICC Rules on Attendance in Person', *Foreign & Commonwealth Office*, 28 November 2013.
111. Closing remarks, the President of the Assembly of States Parties, Ambassador Tiina Intelmann, Twelfth Session of the ASP, 28 November 2013.
112. AU Assembly, Decision January 2014, paras. 6 and 12.
113. AU Assembly, Decision on Africa's Relationship with the ICC (Ext/Assembly/AU/Dec.1(Oct.2013)), 11–12 October 2013, para. 10(i).
114. In early 2014, the Trial Chamber had adjourned the commencement of Kenyatta's trial until 7 October 'for the specific purpose of providing an opportunity for compliance by the Kenyan Government with outstanding cooperation requests'. In September, however, the prosecution submitted that the start of Kenyatta's trial should again be adjourned, because the Kenyan government would still not have fulfilled its cooperation requests. In response, the Chamber decided to

hold two status conferences to discuss the status of cooperation between the prosecution and the Kenyan government.

115. *Kenyatta* (ICC-01/09-02/11-960), Decision on Defence request for excusal from attendance at, or for adjournment of, the status conference scheduled for 8 October 2014, 30 September 2014. For a legal analysis of this decision: Abel S. Knottnerus, 'Kenyatta (finally) Has to Go Back to The Hague', *Opinio Juris*, 1 October 2014.

116. 'Kenyan president Uhuru Kenyatta to step down from office to attend ICC', *The Guardian*, 6 October 2014. Note that the AU Assembly expressed its 'deep concern' over the Chamber's decision, because it would not have taken 'cognizance whatsoever' of the new rules on presence at trial. AU Assembly Decision January 2015, para. 4(a).

117. Kenyatta's statement can be found at: 'Kenyatta to step down during ICC hearing', *Al Jazeera*, 7 October 2014.

118. Note that the AU Assembly commended Kenyatta for his 'leadership' and for 'the unprecedented act of appointing the Acting President so as to respect the Court Summons and protect the Sovereignty of Kenya'. AU Assembly Decision January 2015, para. 5.

119. OTP, Statement of the Prosecutor of the International Criminal Court, Fatou Bensouda, on the status of the Government of Kenya's cooperation with the Prosecution's investigations in the Kenyatta case, 5 December 2014.

120. *Ibid.*

121. Bensouda's statements are political in the sense that she has portrayed the Kenyan government and by implication Kenyatta as a 'false' friend of the Court, one that says it wants to support its investigations, but at the same time actively tries to undermine its proceedings. On the inherent political nature of the ICC and the manner in which the Prosecutor has distinguished between friends and enemies: Sarah Nouwen and Wouter Werner, 'Doing Justice to the Political: The International Criminal Court in Uganda and Sudan' (2011) 21 *European Journal of International Law* 941–965.

122. Most recently, the Appeals Chamber decided that the Trial Chamber would have to reconsider its earlier decision not to refer Kenya's non-cooperation to the ASP. See *Kenyatta* (ICC-01/09-02/11-1032), Judgment on the Prosecutor's appeal against Trial Chamber V(B)'s 'Decision on Prosecution's application for a finding of non-compliance under Article 87(7) of the Statute', 19 August 2015.

123. AU Assembly, Decision January 2015, para. 8.

124. *Ibid.* paras. 10, 17(d) and 17(e). AU Assembly, Decision on the update of the Commission on the Implementation of Previous Decisions on the International Criminal Court (Assembly/AU/Dec.586 (XXV)), 14–15 June 2015, para. 2.

125. AU Assembly Decision January 2015, para. 4(b).
126. See Chapter 5 by Kamari M. Clarke in this volume.
127. ASP, Press Release – Minister of Justice of Senegal, H.E. Mr. Sidiki Kaba, endorsed for the position of President of the Assembly, visit The Hague, ICC-ASP-20141120-PR1066, 20 November 2014.
128. Note for example the recent visits of the president of the ASP, and seminars on issues that are central to the AU's opposition against the ICC: ASP, Press Release – The President of the Assembly of States Parties meets with the Chairperson of the African Union Commission and with the Bureau of the Committee of Representatives, ICC-ASP -20150814-PR1138, 14 August 2015; ASP, Press Release – The President of the Assembly of States Parties visits Kenya, ICC-ASP-20150812-PR1137, 12 August 2015; ASP, Press Release – To commemorate the Day of International Criminal Justice, the President of the Assembly convenes a regional discussion in Dakar on state sovereignty and international criminal justice, ICC-ASP-20150722-PR1134, 22 July 2015; ASP, Press Release – Seminar on cooperation with the ICC concludes in Benin, ICC-CPI-20141105-PR1060, 5 November 2014.
129. ASP, Resolution ICC-ASP/13/Res.5, 17 December 2014, p. 36 (recalling the ASP's earlier decision to establish a representation at the AU and 'reiterating that such presence would promote dialogue with the Court and the understanding of its mission within the African Union and among African States, individually and collectively').
130. James Butty, 'ANC Wants South Africa Out of International Criminal Court', Voice of America, 12 October 2015. See also AU Assembly, 'Decision on the International Criminal Court', Assembly/AU/Dec.590 (XXVI), 30–31 January 2016, para. 10(iv).

PART III

BEYOND AFRICAN STATES
The ICC's Impact in African Communities

9

Discursive Reconstruction of the ICC–Kenyan Engagement through Kenyan Newspapers' Editorial Cartoons

Sammy G. Gachigua

I INTRODUCTION

This study offers an alternative reading of the ICC–Kenyan engagement from an alternate space, related to but distinct from the mainstream politico-legal academic literature that has dominated this topic. The study does so through the use of editorial cartoons from four national newspapers in Kenya. In this regard, the study seeks to reconstruct the complex discourses, perspectives, and debates that inform the evolution of the ICC's involvement in Kenya in order to highlight the different perceptions of the ICC in the country. The focus on editorial cartoons is informed by the understanding that editorial cartoons are artistic objects drawing from everyday occurrences, which 'can be political chronicles, editorials satire, creative cultural productions and moral statements all rolled into one'.[1] Consequently, editorial cartoons derive their social impact by being able to simultaneously appeal to one's intellect, conscience, and emotions.[2] From this understanding, editorial cartoons can provide valuable critical insights that can shed light on the everyday public discourses, debates, perceptions, and impact of the ICC's involvement in Kenya.

The ICC became part of everyday public discourse and imagination in Kenya in 2009, and has since been at the centre of complex and profound political events and fierce debates, for instance, about the perceived role of the ICC in Africa and the political impact of the Court's intervention in Kenya. The ICC's direct involvement in Kenya was set off by the adoption of the recommendation of the Commission of Inquiry on Post-Election Violence also known as the Waki commission, which was established as part of the reconciliation process after the volatile 2007–2008 post-election violence (PEV).[3] The Waki report highlighted impunity as the cause of the PEV and provided for a self-triggering mechanism that would allow the ICC to take up the Kenyan cases if the government failed to form a special tribunal of national and international judges to investigate and prosecute the perpetrators of the violence.[4]

Kenya failed to establish the tribunal even after the extension of the January 2009 deadline, prompting Kofi Annan – the mediator to the Kenyan conflict and the custodian of Waki Commission evidence – to hand the envelope containing the names of the suspected masterminds of the PEV and the evidence collected by the Waki Commission to ICC Prosecutor Luis Moreno-Ocampo on 9 July 2009. On 15 December 2010, Moreno-Ocampo named and issued summonses for six suspects bearing the greatest responsibility for the PEV. The cases against the then cabinet ministers William Ruto, Henry Kosgey, and Kass FM Radio presenter Joshua Arap Sang comprised the first case, and were each accused of three counts of crimes against humanity related to murder, forcible population transfers, and persecution. The second case comprised of the then finance minister Uhuru Kenyatta, Cabinet Secretary Francis Muthaura, and former Police Commissioner Hussein Ali who were each accused of five counts of crimes against humanity related to murder, forcible population transfers, rape, persecution, and other inhumane acts.

The suspects in the first case were associated with Prime Minister Raila Odinga, while those in the second case were associated with President Mwai Kibaki – the two co-principles of the coalition government that was negotiated to end the 2007–2008 PEV. Uhuru Kenyatta and William Ruto, the two most prominent politicians among the accused, used the platform afforded by the ICC's indictment to form a political merger that saw them mount a highly choreographed anti-ICC campaign leading to their election as Kenya's president and deputy president in March 2013. The election of the indicted politicians caused both consternation and celebration in Kenya, Africa, and across the globe as questions emerged about the fate of the fight against impunity, justice for violence victims, and how and why the two suspects triumphed despite their indictment at ICC. Other questions included how the ICC would treat the two – both as suspects and state leaders – how the two indicted leaders would simultaneously manage state affairs and attend trial, and how the trials of the two leaders would impact on Kenya's relations with international actors.

II THE DATA

The data for this study is drawn from cartoons focusing on the ICC's involvement in Kenya as published between January 2009 and February 2014 in the daily newspapers in Kenya, namely the *Daily Nation, The Standard,* the *People Daily,* and *The Star.* This study used both the online cartoon database, where such was available – mainly those by Gado of the *Daily Nation* – and hard-copy cartoons from the bulk of the other newspapers. In total, 341 cartoons were collected – 50 from the *Daily Nation,* 89 from *The Standard,* 87 from the *People Daily,* and 115 from *The Star.* Table 1 below summarizes the data and its distribution. The data is categorized both chronologically and per newspaper that published the cartoons. Each cartoon was examined and coded thematically. The identity of the actors depicted and how they were depicted were also noted for each cartoon. The key actors included the ICC and the Prosecutor(s), the six suspects, victims, the Kenyan government, ICC witnesses, the Kenyan media, the African Union (AU), the general Kenyan public, and Western states. The themes and depiction of actors was then correlated in the cartoons as published in the four newspapers within each year so as to observe any patterns in the themes and depiction of the actors for that year. Finally, an analysis was made of the composite themes and actors' depiction as coded in the cartoons published in the four newspapers as a whole within the entire period of study. From the composite analysis, dominant patterns and the actors' depictions were observed in totality.

III   EDITORIAL CARTOONS

A cartoon is a representational or symbolic drawing that makes a satirical, witty or humorous point. There are various types of cartoons, including, amongst others, single panel cartoons, narrative art cartoons, or comic strip and animated cartoons.[5] Editorial cartoons are found in the editorial page of the newspaper, which itself occupies an important space in the newspaper because it carries the weight of the media house policy, a halo that the editorial cartoon basks in.[6]

Editorial cartoons most commonly depict 'a current political issue or event, a social trend, or a famous personality, in a way that takes a stand or presents a particular point of view'.[7] Because they are mainly concerned with current political issues, editorial cartoons are also referred to as political cartoons. By virtue of addressing contemporary and newsworthy events, editorial or political cartoons are 'prized as artistic objects and historical records of contemporary attitudes'.[8]

Cartoons simultaneously operate at two distinct levels: the fictional and the real world. The real world level anchors the cartoon to the specific socio-political, cultural, and historical context the cartoon is about. The fictional level – which is achieved through artistic tools such as parody, exaggeration,

TABLE 1. *Distribution of cartoons in the newspapers*

	2009				2010				2011				2012				2013				2014			
	N	St	P	S	N	St	P	S	N	St	P	S	N	St	P	S	N	St	P	S	N	St	P	S
Jan			1	2	5		1	3	5			1		8	5	2				1		1		
Feb	2		4	1	1				1	4	2		2	2	2			1		1	5	1	3	2
Mar	2		1	2	5	3	2				5	13		1	1		2			1				
Apr		1		1		2	2	5			3	8		1		2		2	2					
May	1	1			1	1		1	1			1	1						2					
June			4	2			1	1	1		1	1	4	4		1		1		1				
July	7		9	8				1						4		1		1						
Aug	2		2								1	2		1										
Sept	1	1	4	4			2			2	5	8						7	3	9				
Oct	1		5	1		5			1		1		2	1	1	2		6	5	6				
Nov	2		4	4			2	1	1			1	1	1						6				
Dec	1		3	3			8	10	1	1			1	1				1						
Total	16	18	30	28	12	20	16	18	5	7	19	34	5	25	9	8	5	19	10	25	5	2	3	2
Grand total 341 Cartoons																								

Key: N – *Daily Nation*; St. – *The Standard*; S – *The Star*; P – *People Daily* juxtaposition, incongruity, grotesquery, pun, and allusion, among others – exposes a certain kind of 'essential truth' that prompts the audience to see things from a new angle.[9] Through the linking of the two levels metaphorically, the cartoonist is able to achieve satire, humour, irony, and criticism, or a combination of these effects.

The technical tools that allow the cartoonist to link the two levels is the deployment of a hybrid of codes – language, picture, lines, colour, and movement – that are combined in a shorthand manner to create the various effects.[10] In this regard, cartoons are best seen as multimodal, that is, they draw on various modes of communication, with each mode having its own meaning, collectively representing potential resources that are combined in creative ways to simultaneously form a composite meaning.[11]

As meaning-making potentials, editorial cartoons should be seen as discursive constructions of particular social realities. In this regard, editorial cartoons, as a multimodal meaning-making resource, are a form of social practice. As a social practice, political cartoons operate in a dialectical relation, where they are simultaneously a product of the social context in which they are anchored and also influence how the social contexts that they represent come to be perceived.[12]

As such, editorial cartoons are a site in which certain values are produced, reproduced, contested and transformed. Viewed in this way, the editorial cartoon is not a marginal genre unworthy of serious scholarly attention, as they were regarded by scholarship until recently.[13] Nor are they forms of popular culture, considered either as 'low' art form or innocent forms of entertainment not to be taken seriously.[14] Scholarly focus on this genre has demonstrated that cartoons are not only a sophisticated medium 'capable of communicating subtle multilayered messages ... difficult or impossible to express verbally',[15] but also that they can be and are used for various purposes and can have a varied social impact.

For instance, the power and impact of cartoons was aptly demonstrated by the backlash that followed from the publishing of cartoons of Prophet Muhammad by the Danish newspaper *Jyllands-Posten* that the Muslim world deemed inappropriate. Cartoons have also been used in times of war to both mobilize supporters and demoralize enemies.[16] They can also be used to dehumanize perceived enemies.[17] Furthermore, they have been used as forms of political resistance and criticism,[18] as well as in expanding the frontiers of freedom of expression by discussing what would otherwise be taboo topics, where cartoonists use the poetic licence afforded by the cartoon genre to put across views and possibilities that are difficult for genres of factual communication.[19]

Cartoons have also been used for social transformation as forms that combine entertainment-education strategies.[20]

IV CARTOONING IN KENYA

The earliest forms of cartoons in Kenya are traced to World War I, when the humorous magazine *Karonga Kronikal* was created to help boost the morale of the British troops fighting against the Germans in East Africa, as well as to denigrate the enemy.[21] The first published cartoon by an African was *Juha Kalulu*, created by E. G. Gitau around 1950. The comic series were published in various newspapers before settling in *Taifa Leo*, the Kiswahili weekly that later became a daily from 1960 and is still running.

The first political cartoon in the country was *Joe* by Terry Hirst, which was published in *Joe* magazine in the early 1970s.[22] Other political cartoonists that came after Hirst were Frank Odoi, a Ghanaian resident in Kenya, and the Kenyan Paul Kalemba 'Madd', both of whom were instrumental in pushing the frontiers of political cartooning in a politically suffocating environment under President Daniel arapMoi. The most revolutionary breakthrough that Madd made was to become the first cartoonist to caricature President Moi, something unthinkable at the time, which thereby considerably opened up the thriving of political cartooning in Kenya.[23]

Godfrey Mwapembwa (Gado) of the Nation Media Group, one of the cartoonists featured in the present study, is among the next set of political cartoonists who later came onto the scene and further pushed the limits of the politically possible in cartooning.[24] From the 1990s to the present, cartooning has matured and has become an institutionalized space in Kenyan newspapers. Most newspapers today employ a pool of editorial cartoonists who are reputed to both enjoy relative freedom and have a readership that is appreciative of cartoonists as critics who boldly thrust pressing socio-political issues into the limelight.[25] Cartoonists are also seen as important forces in pioneering freedom of expression as they use humour and satire to push the limits of religious, racial, and political taboos.[26] However, under the Jubilee government, there are concerns that the freedom cartoonists in Kenya have previously enjoyed has somewhat shrunk.

V THE NEWSPAPERS' PROFILES AND THE CARTOONISTS

It is difficult to get reliable data on newspaper readership in Kenya. Various estimates indicate that 200,000–300,000 copies of all national newspapers are sold, but even then, a survey by Ipso-Synovate found that one newspaper is

read by several members of a household or an office.[27] Furthermore, proprie-
tors of food kiosks, barbershops, shoeshine stands, and even cybercafés buy at
least one newspaper for their customers as a strategy of attracting and retaining
customers. Besides this, it is common to find newspaper vendors buying one or
several newspapers that they 'lease' out to readers for a fee that is both
affordable and considerably less than the price of the newspaper – a venture
that is potentially profitable for the vendors. Given these dynamics, newspaper
readership in Kenya is much higher than what is captured in statistics of actual
sales. Perhaps in recognition of these dynamics of newspaper consumption,
Cheeseman estimates that newspaper readership in Kenya today stands at
about 12 million readers daily in a population of 40 million.[28] The print
media is reputed to routinely set the news agenda in the country, given that
it targets the middle-class audience that has influence in the country's
politics.[29]

A notable aspect of the media ownership in Kenya is that it is marked by
cross-media ownership and is also closely associated with political players,
but the precise details of the linkages are not easy to authenticate because
the politicians' shareholding is through companies the politicians are
associated to, but whose details are again not easily verifiable.[30] Even
then, the media in Kenya is generally considered to be 'critically engaged
and balanced'.[31] However, there are concerns that the Jubilee administration has been keen on reining in the more critical elements of the media
by denying them advertisement from government (which is a substantial
source of newspaper revenue), using informal channels to warn editors
about specific content and passing legislation that is hostile to media
freedom.[32] In the recent past, both President Kenyatta and his deputy,
Ruto, have made disparaging remarks about newspapers, claiming that
newspapers are only fit for wrapping meat. These remarks have been
interpreted as a subtle way of warning the more critical newspapers that
they are not indispensable. However, for most of the period that the data
for this study is drawn from, the media enjoyed relative freedom, though
one cannot rule out that even in this period there would be instances of
the government or other powerful individuals seeking to exert control over
newspaper content. Below is a brief profile of the newspapers and the
cartoonists who published within the period of this study.

A The Star

The Star, alongside eight FM radio stations, is owned by Radio Group
Africa and associated with Patrick Quarcoo and William Pike.[33] It was

launched in July 2007 as the *Nairobi Star* as a tabloid-style newspaper publishing human interest stories. In 2008, it began to incorporate political news. In 2009, it rebranded as *The Star* and started focusing on national news in addition to incorporating op-ed pages providing a forum for political debate, as well as regional news. It adopts the slogan 'Fresh, Independent, Different' and targets a younger readership than the *Daily Nation* and *The Standard*. The cartoonist associated with *The Star* in the period of study is Victor Ndula. His work is published daily in *The Star* under the caption 'Victor's View'. Drawing cartoons for roughly a decade, Victor is member of the global organization Cartoon Movement. He has attended and exhibited his work at cartoon festivals in Switzerland, France, and Germany. His work has also been exhibited in Peru, Qatar, and the Netherlands and at the London School of Economics (LSE). Victor has won many local and international awards, key among them being the first prize winner of the United Nations/Ranan Lurie Political Cartoon Award. Victor closely follows in the tradition of cartoonists in Kenya who use cartoons for social commentary. His style seems to be hard-hitting satire, at least from the corpus in the study; he readily uses blood and skulls to put across his message. His insightful cartoons constitute the largest pool in the data for this study.

B People Daily

The *People* was established as an outspoken opposition weekly newspaper in 1992 by Kenneth Matiba, a prominent opposition politician. It became a daily in December 1998 as the *People Daily*. However, the newspaper paid dearly for being a thorn in the flesh of the then KANU government as its journalists became a target of harassment by the police, while the paper had to fight numerous law suits from the KANU regime. These actions negatively impacted the *People Daily*'s financial standing. In order to remain afloat, the paper toned down its criticism of government.[34] However, its fortunes continued to decline considerably until September 2009, when it was reported that the Matiba family had sold its stakes in the newspaper to Media Max – a company associated with the Kenyatta family. The *People Daily* is presently being published as a free newspaper. Media Max also owns or has share-holding in a TV station – K24 – and at least two local language FM stations and a Kiswahili language FM station. The company continues to acquire stakes in other media houses.

The newspaper has had three cartoonists in the period under study: Tum and Mwalimu, who published their cartoons in 2009–2010, and Celestine

Wamiru, alias Celeste. Celeste, the only female editorial cartoonist in Kenya, started drawing for the *People Daily* in February 2011. She previously worked as a children's book illustrator and as a character designer for animation. Her cartoons in this study seem to be perceptive but restrained, particularly in their critique of the Kenyan political elite. However, it was not possible to establish conclusively during this study whether Celeste's restrained style had anything to do with the newspaper ownership, her gender, or her personal approach to cartooning.

C The Standard

The Standard is the oldest Kenyan newspaper. A. M. Jeevanjee established the then *African Standard* in Mombasa in 1902. In the mid-1990s, former president Moi's family and his close associate Joshua Kulei are understood to have acquired a significant stake in the paper, then called *East African Standard*.[35] The paper's pro-Moi-government stance in the mid-1990s negatively impacted its circulation, forcing it to briefly experiment with a tabloid format in a bid to attract readership.[36] It is now generally thought to be trying to position itself as a newspaper critical to the present Jubilee government. The Standard Group also owns KTN TV and Radio Maisha.

   In the period under study, the main cartoonists for *The Standard* were James Kamawira (Kham) and Eric Ngammau (GaMMZ). GaMMZ's editorial cartoons have featured in various exhibitions in Kenya, Tanzania, Uganda, the United Kingdom (London), and Switzerland. He has also won several local and international awards. James Kamawira (Kham) has been a professional cartoonist since 1988 and has a varied experience as a cartoonist. Musila categorizes Kham's cartoons as more light-hearted than Gado's.[37] Overall, both GaMMZ and Kham's cartoons, though critical, seem to present the ironical reading of situations and would not in general be considered as hard-hitting as *The Star*'s Victor.

D Daily Nation

The *Daily Nation* is published by the Nation Media Group, which also owns two TV stations, two radio stations, and three other national newspapers and an East African regional one. The newspaper was established by the Ismaili spiritual leader the Aga Khan in 1960.[38] The newspaper is considered to have by far the highest number of readers. The chief editorial cartoonist for the *Daily Nation* since 1992 is Godfrey Mwampembwa (Gado). Gado also publishes in *The East African* – Nation Media Group's regional newspaper. Gado

is also the most syndicated cartoonist in East and Central Africa and his works
have been published in *Le Monde* (France), *The Guardian* of London, and the
Japan Times, among others.

Gado has won various awards, including the 2007 Prince Claus Laureate,
the Kenya National Human Rights Commission Award in Journalism in 2005
and 2007, and the Kenya Cartoonist of the Year for 1999. Of all the cartoonists
in Kenya, Gado's cartoons have received the most scholarly attention.[39]
Gado's work has been categorized by Musila as employing humour that
'tends to "highbrow" laughter', which is marshalled for social criticism with
the intention of creating a positive change in society.[40] In the corpus for this
study, a number of Gado's cartoons raise some profound interpretation and
critique of issues surrounding the ICC–Kenyan engagement.

VI DATA ANALYSIS

A *Cartoons in 2009*

The events that would lead to the ICC involvement in Kenya in 2009 occurred
in the backdrop of the release of the Waki report, as discussed in the introduction. In the same year, three attempts to adopt laws to establish the special
tribunal recommended by the Waki report were unsuccessful. The first one
was a bill presented to parliament by then Justice Minister Martha Karua.
Ninety-three MPs voted against the bill, some on the basis that it did not
provide sufficient independence for the tribunal, and others on the basis of the
calculation that it was politically expedient to refer the cases to the ICC.
The latter argument was based on the assumption that the ICC process would
be slow and thus by the time the cases started the political scene would have
radically changed in favour of the accused persons.[41]

The second attempt to establish a local tribunal was made by Mutula
Kilonzo, who had by then replaced Martha Karua as minister of justice.
His attempt was rejected by the cabinet on 30 July. The third attempt was
through Gitobu Imanyara's private member motion on 11 November, which
was deliberately thwarted by MPs who engineered a lack of quorum in
parliament. Consequently, the ICC Prosecutor filed a request seeking
authorization from the Pre-Trial Chamber II to open an investigation into
the crimes committed during the 2007–2008 post-election violence on
26 November.

The cartoons published in 2009 mainly depicted the political elite engaged
in calculations about which options, between the setting up of a special
tribunal and letting the ICC to take up the Kenyan case, would best secure

their interests. In weighing the two options, the political elite were depicted as scheming on how to ensure that both the judicial processes would not work. The political elite were also presented as extremely desperate and anxious about the possibility that they would be held liable for the PEV. The Kenyan government, for its part, was portrayed as obsessed with ensuring that the prosecution of the cases was thwarted.

The dead victims of the violence – regularly represented as skulls – cried for their case to be heard, but the government and the political elite were least concerned about the victims' fate, towards whom they maintained a callous indifference or whose story they wanted buried. The surviving victims, perso-nified by the internally displaced persons (IDPs), were treated callously by the politicians as they sought to close IDP camps – which were considered as an eyesore by the government – without offering an alternative settlement to the IDPs. One cartoon in this period capturing the plight of the IDPs (Figure 1) uses the biblical allusion of Moses (here represented by Kibaki and Odinga) leading the Israelites to the Promised Land, but in this case the politicians lead the IDPs to a 'Promised Fraud' that would plunge the IDPs over a cliff and into oblivion.

In many cartoons in this period, the ICC, as personified by Moreno-Ocampo, was depicted as looming large in Kenya and a source of extreme

FIGURE 1 Victor 4/12/09

FIGURE 2 Kham 12/8/2009

anxiety and irritation to the political elite and a hero and hope to the victims of the violence. The local tribunal was regularly represented as likely to be largely defective and prone to manipulation by the politicians, while the ICC was presented as very dependable. In the only cartoon that the public is explicitly depicted, they are shown as divided and confused about which options to support at the closure to PEV – the ICC, a local tribunal, or the Truth Justice and Reconciliation Commission. The perpetrators of the violence celebrate the confusion among the public, hoping that the public would remain in that state (Figure 2).

One cartoon that stands out in its profundity is by Gado (Figure 3). The cartoon captures the principals of the coalition government put in place in negotiations after the PEV – President Mwai Kibaki and Prime Minister Raila Odinga – walking a tight rope as they tried to maintain a delicate balance in relation to the intricate and bizarre interconnection between the key political actors who would possibly be complicit in the PEV.

The cartoon succinctly depicts the behind-the-scene calculations that were making it difficult to initiate the investigation and prosecution of PEV suspects. To begin with, if the principals handed over any of the suspects, they

FIGURE 3 Gado 15/11/2009

would likely go down together with those that they handed over, possibly when the suspects would expose the principals' complicity in the PEV. Secondly, it would have amounted to a betrayal of the principals' key allies. Thirdly, it would seem that the principals in the depiction sought to justify their reluctance to subject key suspects to investigation and prosecution, ostensibly because by doing so they would jeopardize the delicate peace that they had maintained through the status quo. This cartoon is therefore an early hint of the peace-versus-justice debate that would later inform the discussion of the trade-off between stability and accountability, and whether the two are compatible, irreconcilable, or are played against each other by perpetrators of crimes against humanity in order to evade accountability.[42]

The cartoon depiction also captures a fundamental aspect of the Kenyan politics in which there is an intricate interconnection between political actors in Kenya who are adept at forming confounding political alliances informed by the culture of 'amoral pragmatism'.[43] Amoral pragmatism encapsulates a political system defined by opportunism and a lack of a strong set of values that would constrain elite actions. This principle can be traced, firstly, to the establishment and practice of colonial rule in Africa.[44] Secondly, it has roots in the late colonial period as it was used by the departing British colonialists to incorporate key elites in top economic and political positions who became influential in independent Kenya. Amoral pragmatism was entrenched in Kenya's politics by the first independent regime and has since defined politics in Kenya.[45] It seems the ICC did not attend keenly to the possibility of amoral pragmatism being played out to the extent in which it was in Kenya, as the political elite and clergy build a formidable alliance based on anti-ICC rhetoric that later confounded the ICC. How the elite in Kenya played politics around the ICC's involvement in Kenya offers a germane case study of the interplay between law and politics that, Mueller contends, 'lawyers, judges and many scholars often mistakenly ignore or downplay, to their detriment'.[46] In a number of ways that will become clearer throughout the chapter, the political behaviour of Kenyan politicians with regard to PEV and the ICC stayed true to the system of values encapsulated in amoral pragmatism.

B Cartoons in 2010

The important highlights of the ICC's involvement in Kenya in 2010 included the 31 March Pre-Trial Chamber II that granted authority to the ICC Prosecutor to investigate the situation in Kenya in relation to crimes against humanity committed in the period between 1 June 2005 and 26 November 2009. Kenya also passed a new constitution on 4 August 2010, which was promulgated amid the controversy ignited by the invitation to the event of Omar al Bashir, the Sudan president to whom the ICC had issued a warrant of arrest for genocide, crimes against humanity, and war crimes. Al-Bashir's presence at the occasion was seen by critics as an affront to the auspicious occasion and as rekindling the memories of impunity that many hoped the new constitution had banished.

On 3–4 November, William Ruto, whom the Waki report had recommended for further investigation for his role in the PEV, travelled to The Hague for a meeting with Ocampo, which sparked speculations about what the two discussed. On 15 December, the ICC Prosecutor named and issued summons for six suspects bearing the greatest responsibility for the PEV (see the introduction). In reaction to the naming of what were now labelled the Ocampo Six, on 22 December, Kenyan MPs passed a motion in parliament urging the government to withdraw from the Rome Statute that established the ICC.

One important set of cartoon depictions in 2010 included two that were published early in the year before Ocampo was granted authority to investigate the Kenyan cases that eerily warned that accepting or being an ICC witness was tantamount to committing suicide (Figures 4 and 5). The cartoons also

FIGURE 4 Victor 8/01/2010

questioned the efficacy of the witness protection mechanism put in place by the ICC, and that of the government which was supposed to complement that of the ICC. In Figure 4, the possibility of taking the witness stand at the ICC is equated to standing in one's own coffin. The cartoon in Figure 5 was published against the backdrop of the enactment of the Witness Protection (Amendment) bill 2010, which amended the Witness Protection Act No. 16 of 2006 to, among other things, enhance the independence of the witness protection agency from government control and also empower the agency to complement the work of other international justice agencies such as the ICC. However, the Act provided that the police commissioner would be one of the members of the advisory board of the witness protection agency. Given that the police had been implicated as having committed grave crimes in the PEV by the Waki commission,[47] it appeared inconceivable to expect the agency would accord potential ICC witnesses protection. Gado enacted this through

FIGURE 5 Gado 23/05/2010

the incredulous act of police officers offering an ICC witness a protective vest with shooter's mark printed on it (Figure 5).

Interestingly, no further depictions of witnesses were published for the rest of the period the study covers, other than in late 2013 and early 2014 cartoons, as will be discussed below, where witnesses were shown deserting the Prosecutor's case. Unlike the cartoons in Figures 5 and 6, the later cartoons seemed restrained in broaching why the witnesses deserted the Prosecutor's case. Overall, the 'silences' in the depictions stand in contrast to various reports about witnesses in the ICC case in Kenya as reported by Mueller,[48] who documents cases of direct intimidation that might have been used to silence witnesses. A yet to be explored angle that would be worthy of media scholarship would be to examine how those opposed to the ICC intervention have sought to create a dominant anti-ICC grand narrative that seems to have created a spiral of silence,[49] thus making further publication of ICC witnesses cartoons seemingly a taboo topic. It might also be interesting to investigate if this spiral of silence applied among the general public, and if it did, how it was achieved – either passively or aggressively – and finally, how it impacted on the Kenyan

FIGURE 6 Gado 5/3/2010

cases at the ICC. However, this issue is beyond the scope of the present study, and will therefore not be addressed further.

Another set of cartoons that stood out in 2010 were those that depicted Ocampo and the ICC – who were then represented in a number of cartoons as possessing sufficient evidence to prosecute the PEV perpetrators – looming large in the country, a situation that set great panic and anxiety among the political elite (Figure 6). The anxiety became unbearable as the date set by Ocampo for naming the key PEV suspects approached, which the cartoon in Figure 7 branded as 'Hague O'clock.'

In this period as well, the political elite were depicted as continuing to scheme about how to evade prosecution, particularly with the initiation of the shuttle diplomacy waged by the Kenyan government seeking the support of African and world leaders for the deferral of the prosecution of the Kenyan cases by the ICC. The values that informed these initiatives were portrayed in cartoons as callous opportunism at two levels: the elite against the victims and the elite positioning itself for the possible political benefits that would accrue in standing by the ICC suspects or at the departure of the suspects from the political scene.

After the inauguration of the new constitution in August 2010, the document is shown by cartoonists (such as in Figure 8) as the new plank that the

FIGURE 7 Victor 15/12/2010

FIGURE 8 Gado 1/9/2010

FIGURE 9 Victor 21/12/2010

political elite used in their attempt to convince the country that Kenya did not need the ICC intervention. Other cartoons depicting a similar theme were quick to note the irony that Omar al-Bashir was conspicuously present at the inauguration of the new constitution, thus putting to question the elite suggestion that the new constitution would render the ICC intervention in Kenya irrelevant. One interesting cartoon by Victor of *The Star* intertextually drew attention to this irony by showing the African Union celebrating al-Bashir as the key to peace in Sudan, with the claim that attempts to prosecute al-Bashir by the ICC would undermine peace in Sudan. Ironically, al-Bashir's military fatigues were caricatured as 'colourfully' decorated in the skulls of his citizens.

The other striking cartoon that was published towards the end of 2010 was one by Victor (Figure 9), which in a hard-hitting depiction uses the skulls of the PEV victims to underline the clear and heartless message that the political elite were more keen to protect the suspected perpetrators of the PEV than to seek justice for the victims. Similar thematic representations by cartoonists would later regularly feature at different periods of this study.

C Cartoons in 2011

The cartoons in this year appeared against the backdrop of the government mounting an expensive, but at the time seemingly doomed, shuttle diplomacy, seeking African countries' support for the ICC to defer the Kenyan cases. The shuttle diplomacy was carried out amidst several other attempts by the government showing that the country was capable and indeed willing to try the PEV suspects locally.[50] In the same period, the government filed an application challenging the ICC's jurisdiction over the Kenyan cases. Another significant event was that the Court's Pre-Trial Chamber issued summonses for the six named suspects to appear before the court on 8 March. Later, the first three defendants (Ruto, Sang, and Kosgey) appeared before the ICC on 7 April, while the second three defendants appeared on 8 April. Also of significance was the Court's dismissal of the case questioning the ICC's jurisdiction over the Kenyan cases on August 30. The first three defendants consequently appeared at the ICC for confirmation hearings on 1–8 September, while the second three appeared on 21 September–5 October.

The cartoons in early 2011 continued representing the government's obsession with saving the Ocampo Six and its continued indifference to the PEV victims' plight. The expensive shuttle diplomacy that the government was engaged in to woo African states into compelling the ICC to defer the Kenyan cases was caricatured by Victor of *The Star* as 'mission impossible'. However, such missions persisted in the entire period of study, indicating – as has been observed by Mueller – that there was an underlying 'mega-strategy' that informed them.[51] As before, cartoons depicted politicians callously attempting to enlist PEV victims' support for the government's deferral efforts in complete disregard for the victims' pain and plight.

The government was so obsessed with saving the Ocampo Six that some cartoons caricatured a complete shutdown of other government operations. The cartoons in this period seem to feature more of political elite opportunism and the hypocrisy and double-speak of the Kenyan government and Africa with regard to the ICC intervention in the Kenyan cases. Ocampo and the ICC do not feature in cartoons as much as previously, though the ICC still looms large. In the few instances that the ICC is explicitly featured, it is projected as professional, beyond reproach, and devoid of the defects of the Kenyan courts (Figures 10 and 11).

However, after the ICC Prosecutor issued an arrest warrant for Libya's Muammar Gaddafi and his son, a cartoon by Victor (Figure 12) caricatured the nagging perception – felt even among the most ardent supporters of the ICC – that the institution seemed only to focus its attention on atrocities in Africa. This nagging perception would later be dramatically caricatured by Gado when atrocities in Syria did not seem to register as strongly with the ICC Prosecutor as the cases in Africa (Figure 13).

In this period, there are two notable cartoons by Celeste of the *People Daily*, which seem to suggest that Ocampo's evidence was defective or contrived and that the evidence of the first defendants would bear this out (Figures 14 and 15).

FIGURE 10 Celeste 9–10/04/2011

FIGURE 11 Gado 13/05/2011

FIGURE 12 Victor 29/6/2011

FIGURE 13 Gado 11/2/2014

FIGURE 14 Celeste 7/9/2011

FIGURE 15 Celeste 26/9/2011

This seems curious because at this point, apart from the political elite who were opposed to the ICC process and who held the view that the ICC Prosecutor's evidence was contrived, the trial of the suspects had not commenced, therefore this depiction seems premature. However, it is difficult to

FIGURE 16   Gado 15/04/2011

attach any significant meaning solely on the basis of these two depictions since such portrayals do not seem persistent in the cartoon data in the newspaper. But given the ownership of the *People Daily* and an assertion by the Crisis Group Africa Briefing that Uhuru Kenyatta and William Ruto used their media connections to cast themselves as victims of the ICC, it may be worth investigating other genres in the daily which reported the ICC–Kenyan engagement in order to prove or disprove whether the assertion holds true for the paper.[52]

Noteworthy too are cartoons that started to explore the wider moral implications of the politics as played out by the ICC suspects, who were returning from the court appearances at The Hague to be received heroically by throngs of supporters who met them at the airport and escorted them through the streets of Nairobi. The cartoon in Figure 16 suggests that the euphoric reception given to the PEV suspects was giving a warped sense of heroism to the younger generation who now dreamt of becoming PEV suspects in future.

FIGURE 17 Victor 2/9/2011

FIGURE 18 Celeste 24–25/9/2011

Cartoons also started questioning the media's complicity in lionizing the Ocampo Six by focusing too much attention on them at the expense of the victims and other cases deserving public attention (Figures 17 and 18). This theme continued to be the subject of cartoonists in 2012 and 2013. The cartoonists seemed to question the underlying media news structure that gave prominence to elite activities at the expense of what would otherwise be truly newsworthy. The cartoons in these depictions also suggest that the media's obsession with the Ocampo Six may have contributed to a fatigue among the public with regard to the Kenyan cases in the ICC. This fatigue likely made the call for the country to put behind the PEV that brought about the ICC intervention in Kenya and 'move on' after the election of UhuRuto in 2013 appealing to many.

D Cartoons in 2012

The salient events in 2012 were the 26 January confirmation of the charges against Uhuru Kenyatta, William Ruto, Joshua arap Sang, and Francis Muthaura, while those of Henry Kosgey and Hussein Ali were dropped. Kenya also made unsuccessful attempts to have the case against the four brought to Kenya or East Africa. Salient too was the 31 August ICC Appeals Chamber's rejection of Kenya's admissibility challenge of 31 March 2011. A prominent event also was the culmination on 4 December 2012 of a formal alliance between Uhuru Kenyatta and William Ruto to run jointly as president and deputy president respectively in the March 2013 elections.

Cartoons in this period depicted both the suspects and the country anxious before the ruling on the confirmation hearing of the Kenyan cases. Cartoons that stand out in this period are those that explored the shame and moral depravity in the Kenyan society regarding the ICC intervention. Kham (Figure 19) lamented the shame that Kenya faced for not effectively dealing with impunity, such that the ICC had to step in. Victor (Figure 20) decried the media obsession with the news about the Ocampo Four, which was depicted as ranking higher than the truly heroic stories, such as Kenyan athletes' triumph at the then London marathon. Gado (Figure 21) in dour humour re-enacted the ICC court session in which the presiding judge declares Charles Taylor of Liberia guilty of crimes against humanity but in the same verdict the judge offers Mr Taylor the brighter prospect that he could consider running for presidency in Kenya and have a real possibility of winning.

Other themes that continued from previous periods included the continuing attempts of the Kenyan government to have the ICC cases deferred. Cartoons also depicted more determined scheming by UhuRuto to scuttle the ICC process. After the ICC set the date for the start of trial for March 2013 – after the general elections in Kenya – a cartoon by Victor (Figure 22) seemed unhappy with the decision, questioning the ICC's commitment to the justice for the victims given the excruciatingly slow pace that the ICC had chosen for

FIGURE 19 Kham 25/01/2012

FIGURE 20 Victor 24/4/2012

the beginning of the trial of the accused persons, in which the cartoon depicts justice as riding on a snail, which is in turn riding on a tortoise.

Looked at in retrospect now, and together with other concessions made to the political suspects in Kenya by the ICC, an impression might be built that the ICC was not immune to 'caressing the big fish',[53] just as it might have been

FIGURE 21 Gado 27/4/2012

FIGURE 22 Victor June 12, 2012

the case in the local courts that were thought not to be immune from the influence of the powerful as seen in Figure 23, which depicts the ICC pandering to William Ruto's request not to be physically present during all of the sessions of his trial.

FIGURE 23 Victor 20/6/2013

The transition in the ICC Prosecutor's Office from Ocampo to Fatou Bensouda was also of interest to most of the cartoonists under study. In all of the cartoons at this point, Bensouda was depicted as confident and professional. Cartoon representations also showed Bensouda, like Ocampo before, looming large in Kenya – probably indicating that the transition that had taken place in the Office of the ICC Prosecutor presented a continuation of Ocampo's sustained spotlight on the Kenyan cases. Consequently, and as the 2013 elections approach, cartoons show Kenyatta and Ruto engaged in renewed efforts to work out a political arrangement that would shield them from the ICC predicament.

The victims of the PEV were largely unrepresented in the cartoons in this year but where they were, their heartless treatment by the elite continued. For example, Kham in Figure 24 caricatures a clergyman callously calling upon the victims who are living in squalor in a camp to bow down in prayer for the Ocampo Four. Prayers for the ICC suspects had become a major ritual that was used widely by the UhuRuto campaign. Ironically, these prayers were rarely extended to the victims of the PEV.

One question that dominated this period was how Kenyatta and Ruto would run the government, if they were elected to do so, while attending the ICC trials at The Hague, or indeed what Kenya's fate would be if one

FIGURE 24 Kham 30/01/2012

(or both)of them was (were) convicted while in office. A standard response
regularly proffered by their campaign was to extol the possibilities that new
technologies offered – referred to as being 'digital' – such that it would not
be necessary for one to be physically present in Kenya to be able to govern.

The possibilities of new technology became a huge political plank in
the campaign, which was not only used to deflect questions about how the
duo would govern and attend the ICC trials at the same time, but also as
a catch-all metaphor that was used to represent UhuRuto campaign as
presenting 'youthful vigour', 'new ideas', 'change', 'new possibilities', and
other progressive ideas associated with the digital era. The competitors –
Raila Odinga and Kalonzo Musyoka – were presented as 'analogue' –
denoting the 'old', 'outdated', 'tired', and 'unimaginative'. The digital-
analogue discourses seemed to latch on the ideology that acquaintance
with the 'new media technology [was] deterministic of social progress'.[54]
To cement their 'digital' image, the UhuRuto announced that they would
ensure that every child joining the first grade in public schools in Kenya
would be issued with a free laptop uploaded with the relevant curriculum.
The expediency of this announcement has since become clear now that
three years after coming to power this promise has remained hampered by

the daunting logistics of implementing such a project that were not broached in the heat of the campaigns.

The 'digital-analogue' metaphor in Kenya gained public prominence following the government's decision in late 2009 to implement early the International Communication Union's decision – made at the Regional Radio Conference of 2006 in Geneva, Switzerland – for member countries to migrate terrestrial TV broadcasting signal technologies from analogue to digital by 17 June 2015. The government's decision received wide publicity through advertisements extolling the benefits of the digital switch. This publicity was essential because the switch affected the vast majority of TV owners in Kenya – whose TVs were set to receive the analogue signal, and also because it had a cost implication since it meant that the TV owners would buy converter boxes for the analogue TVs. Further publicity to this decision came through the highly publicized court cases that the main media houses in Kenya mounted against the government decision that challenged the limited time given for the analogue-digital switch, as well as the constitutionality of some aspects of how the switch was to be implemented, which the media houses argued would undermine both citizens' and the media's rights.

How the digital-analogue politics played out in this campaign and its impact is a germane topic that needs further exploration. A further overlapping interest in this topic is borne out of the observation that most of the campaign strategies adopted by Jubilee are said to have been crafted by UK-based BTP Advisers.[55] It would therefore be interesting to investigate how the increasing reliance on international campaign consultants and spin doctors by politicians in Kenya, as was also particularly noted in the 2007 elections,[56] impacted on the perceptions of the ICC in Kenya, the 2013 elections, and the long-term effects of this phenomenon on democracy and electoral politics in Kenya.

Interestingly, similar 'digital possibilities' were to be put forward for the ICC to consider using video conference as an alternative to having the duo physically attend court sessions. Victor, the only cartoonist who took up this topic, caricatures this theme by enacting the duo's thinking about digital possibilities in running the government – branded as 'e-governance', which is made to seem as easy as just clicking away on computer keys (Figure 25) or playing a computer game (Figure 26).

E Cartoons in 2013 to February 2014

One of the most important highlights in 2013 were the general elections in Kenya held on 4 March 2013, in which Uhuru Kenyatta and William Ruto ran

FIGURE 25 Victor 26/10/2012

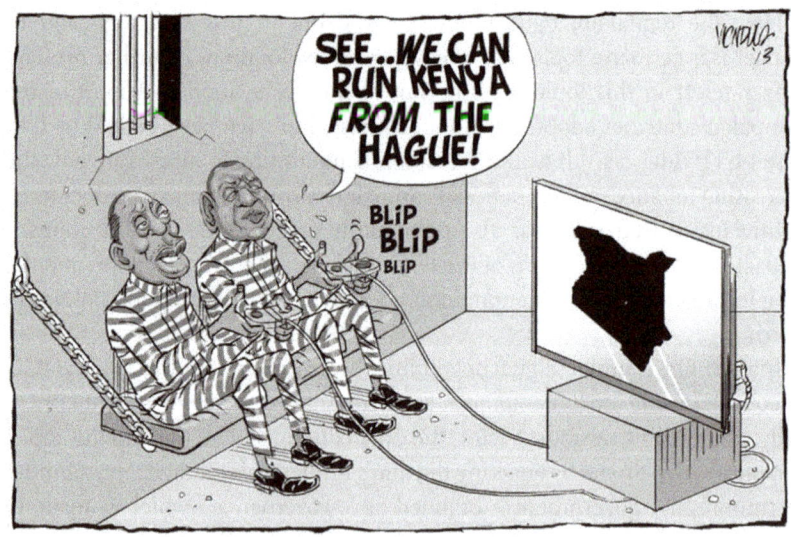

FIGURE 26 Victor 15/02/13

on a joint ticket, and were declared the winners on 9 March. On 11 March, charges against Francis Muthaura were dropped after a key witness recanted his statement. On 30 March, the Supreme Court of Kenya upheld the election of Kenyatta and Ruto, which had been challenged by the competitors the

Coalition for Reform and Democracy (CORD) and some civil societies. On 9 April, Uhuru Kenyatta and William Ruto were sworn into office.

In May, another round of shuttle diplomacy in the UN and AU was mounted by the new government as it sought either the dismissal or deferral of the cases against the two politicians. On 18 June, the ICC ruled that Ruto did not have to continuously attend court sessions because of the exceptional nature of his position as deputy president of Kenya. Later, on 18 September, the trial of Ruto and Joshua Arap Sang began after having been postponed twice on 10 April and 28 May. On 18 October, the ICC ruled that Kenyatta did not have to be continuously present at his trial either due to the exceptional duties he held as president of Kenya. On 19 December, the Prosecutor requested a three-month postponement in the case against Uhuru Kenyatta after key witnesses refused to testify. The prosecutor later withdrew Kenyatta's case.

Before the 2013 general elections, the impact of the ICC's cases upon the political direction of the country, particularly the possibility of an UhuRuto win, was a major subject of editorial cartooning. Eventually, as the duo won the elections and assumed office, a cartoon by Gado captured the hypocrisy of the Western nations,[57] particularly the USA, the UK, and EU, who were shown as cosying up to the new government when previously they had warned sternly about unnamed consequences the country would face if the two indictees were elected (Figure 27). The cartoon also depicts Kenyatta and Ruto as having gleefully outwitted the West and the ICC.

At the same time, the triumph of Kenyatta and Ruto in the Kenyan elections and the subsequent threats by the AU that its members would withdraw from the ICC if the Kenyan cases were not stopped or deferred is portrayed as having set a precedent that would embolden suspected perpetrators of grave crimes, such as Kony of Uganda, to seek high political office in order to protect themselves from being held to account (Figure 28). Locally, the triumph of Kenyatta and Ruto was depicted by Gado (Figure 29) as presenting the country with a moral dilemma where even when the new constitution demanded that prospective senior public servants with integrity issues be prevented from taking up public office, the prospective officers could easily retort that a precedent had been set where facing criminal trial would not be an impediment to taking up high office. The cartoon here enacts a parliamentary committee interview session in which Mr John Mututho, who then had a pending criminal and civil case in court, had been nominated by President Uhuru Kenyatta as chairman of the National Authority for the Campaign Against Drug Abuse (NACADA). The last six months referred to in the cartoon is when

FIGURE 27 Gado 7/5/ 2013

UhuRuto came into power, reinforced by the portraits of the two in the interview room.

An important and continual depiction carried by the cartoons in all the newspapers under review, which started around September 2013 and by February 2014 became the dominant image, is the haemorrhage of ICC witnesses (Figure 30), the waning credibility and/or collapse of the Prosecutor's evidence (Figures 31 and 32), and the depiction of the culpability of Ocampo – and perhaps by extension the ICC – in bungling the investigation and prosecution of the PEV suspects (Figures 30 and 33). A noteworthy depiction of the witnesses is that, unlike the bold depictions of the dangers to potential witnesses testifying in the Prosecutor's case in Figures 4 and 5, which from the cartoon depictions was likely to come from those that the ICC suspected of complicity in the PEV, the attribution of the cause of desertion of witnesses is mostly left vague or attributed to the incompetence, naivety, or helplessness (or maybe a combination of these) of the person of Ocampo, the Prosecutors' office, or the ICC. However, in Figures 32 and 33 there is perhaps a subtle inference of the triumph of the anti-ICC rhetoric that Ocampo and the ICC had vendetta against the accused.

FIGURE 28 Gado 21/10/2013

FIGURE 29 Gado 21/11/2013

FIGURE 30 Victor 15/2/2014

FIGURE 31 Gado 6/2/2014 27

FIGURE 32 Celeste 8/2/2014

FIGURE 33 Gado 22/2/2014

VII CONCLUSION

In light of the examination of the cartoons in Kenya's major newspapers depicting the ICC's intervention in Kenya between January 2009 and February 2014, a few observations emerge. Firstly, the study has demonstrated that the editorial cartoon is a genre capable of chronicling complex socio-political issues. Cartoons do this by drawing their content from everyday occurrences and combining graphic and written media. However, unlike the politico-legal literature, they go beyond merely recording and debating events and issues factually. Through the use of the poetic licence, they recreate the events and issues in an imaginative and artistic way in order to communicate an essential truth mainly by criticizing present realities. In the hands of a creative and socially conscious artist, cartoons can appeal to one's intellect, conscience, and emotions. As has been shown in this study, one fundamental way in which cartoons demonstrate their profundity is through moral appeal (this can be seen most conspicuously in Figures 1, 3, 9, 16, 21, 24, and 29), an element that the politico-legal literature may not frequently appeal to without seeming preachy. The other element that cartoons thrive on is criticism, which is achieved through various tropes such as allusion, juxtaposition, and the like. In Kenya today, editorial cartoons remain one of the most consistently critical and popular spaces, perhaps more so given that other mainstream media genres are regularly seen to waver in reporting elite actions. However, there is information suggesting that in the recent past cartooning as a critical space is under siege. For instance, Gado's contract as a cartoonist with the Nation Media is said to have terminated at the behest of the Jubilee administration, ostensibly because of his continued caricaturing the President in shackles during the ICC trial.[58]

Secondly, with regard to the perceptions of the ICC in Kenya, the early image of the ICC that the cartoons projected was that of an institution that was highly regarded, professional, and beyond reproach. This image seems to have created a lot of expectations among those who were keen to see the victims of the PEV in Kenya receive justice and for those who bore the greatest responsibility for the violence to be held to account. In many ways, the looming presence of the ICC in Kenya created anxiety and desperation among those that had the most to fear for their role in the PEV. On the other hand, the cartoons also show that the ICC galvanized those that had the most to fear into a frenzy of scheming to see the investigation and prosecution of suspected perpetrators of PEV crimes and the aims of the ICC's defeated. The bewildered and hopeless, but by no means celebratory, image that the cartoons unanimously project of the ICC Prosecutor in late 2013 and early 2014 suggests that the ICC naively underestimated the political intrigue and persistence of the political elite in Kenya.

Informed by amoral pragmatism that makes it possible to form confounding opportunistic alliances to secure self-interests or repulse threats to the same, as the cartoon by Gado perceptively caricatured in 2009 (Figure 3), the political elites are caricatured as cold, calculating, and opportunistic. By enmeshing their individual tribulations with those of the government, they are depicted as having outwitted the aims of the ICC in the Kenyan situation. However, the triumph is depicted as having been achieved with a concomitant heavy moral toll. The moral deficit that the UhuRuto government came into power with is bound to be one of the biggest handicaps that the duo will have to confront throughout their time in office. This handicap is likely to be most acutely felt when the Jubilee administration is confronted by corruption and other excesses among its ranks. This handicap is also likely to drive the administration to be instinctively less tolerant of dissenting opinions in the country.

The political players at the international level, as depicted by the caricatures of the African leadership and African Union on the one hand and the EU, the UK, and the USA on the other, are also seen as largely amoral and self-serving, and therefore having been readily sucked into the scheming of the political players in Kenya at the expense of the victims of PEV in Kenya. On its part, the ICC's image has suffered from the lingering perception that it is too keen in focusing on atrocities from Africa, while turning a blind eye to comparable or worse situations such as in Syria. Likewise, there is also a perception that the ICC is not immune to 'caressing the big fish'. These perceptions have dented the image of the ICC as an impartial court of last resort. Finally, it seems that the pace at which the ICC prosecutions take place seem to be so painfully slow (see Fig. 22) to match the dynamic pace of political developments in a country like Kenya. Such fast-paced dynamics easily wore out the faith of those who believed that the ICC system would deliver justice.

The victims of the PEV in Kenya in the cartoons were always depicted as a helpless group at the mercy of the elite political players in the country. Whereas they were a regular portrayal in the formative years of this study, by 2014 they had almost completely disappeared from editorial cartoons in Kenyan newspapers, yet their predicament has not found a fitting closure. It would seem that the victims of PEV in the cartoons, just like in real life, have been largely left to suffer their own fate silently as the scheming political elite take the limelight with the help of the media, whose obsessive and elitist depiction of the ICC suspects at the expense of the victims and other newsworthy activities may have created fatigue among the public in the ICC cases in Kenya. The cartoonists castigate this media folly.

The depiction of witnesses in the cartoons under study as discussed above is notable. Whereas in early 2010 two cartoonists – Victor and Gado – boldly depicted both the terrifying vulnerability of potential witnesses and the folly of witnesses in believing the witness protection mechanism provided by the government and the ICC, there seems to have been a shunning of this topic by other cartoonists, and subsequently by all the cartoonists for a long period thereafter. This spiral of silence and how it came to pre-eminence seems a topic worthy of further investigation. When witnesses are again caricatured in 2013 and 2014, which takes place through cartoons in all the newspapers, the depictions are restrained and seem to subtly blame Ocampo's sloppy investigations for the witnesses deserting the Prosecutor's case. The evolving cartoon depictions of the witnesses' calls for a re-examination of the efficacy of the witness protection mechanism as provided in the Rome Statute.

One other important issue that has emerged in the study is the place of the digital-analogue discourse in the run-up to the 2013 general elections. Firstly, digital possibilities emerged as an important discourse that was used to deflect questions about how UhuRuto would govern and at the same time attend ICC cases. Secondly, the purported lack of digital skills was used to paint political opponents as 'analogue' and unsuited to run the state in the present age. Thirdly, digital possibilities were also put forward for the ICC to consider, such as using video conference as an alternative to having the duo physically attend court sessions. The digital discourses in the campaign, which are thought to have been crafted by the UK-based BTP Advisers, presents a prospective research perspective to investigate how the twin aspects of the digital politics and international consultancy and spin-doctoring impacted on both the perceptions of the ICC in the country and the outcome of the 2013 elections in the country, and indeed what long-term impact the increasing presence of international spin doctors are having on politics in countries like Kenya.

A recent development in the ICC intervention in Kenya, which is not within the timeframe of this analysis, is the withdrawal of Kenyatta's, and later Ruto's cases by the Prosecutor because witnesses in the cases recanted their evidence. The reactions from this development are myriad. Firstly, Jubilee supporters have hailed the withdrawal of the cases as 'acquittals.' This perspective has taken the withdrawal as lending credence to the notion that Ocampo and the ICC had vendetta against the accused. There is also a second perspective that takes the view that actually Ocampo did not carry out credible and sustainable investigations, and that his claims about having prosecutable cases was based more on bravado than on competent investigations. Thirdly, there are others who register disappointment that the case did not go full circle so that the truth about what actually happened during the PEV could be determined and those most culpable held to account. This group recognizes that indeed atrocities were committed during the PEV but find themselves helpless and cynical of the politics and power games between and among the local elite (politicians, media, clergy, etc.) and states and parties in the international arena that have not helped the cause of justice. Fourthly, there are those who would wish to move on, and view the withdrawals as an opportunity for Kenyatta and Ruto to fully concentrate on the job of governing the country, now without the encumbrances of the ICC cases. However, there are those who cautiously watch to see if the duo may turn vindictive against those they perceive as behind their troubles at the ICC.

Overall, however, the ICC's intervention in Kenya has so far prevented violence occurring in the short term, but the reaction it elicited from the elite has not significantly transformed the practice of politics in the country for the better.

Notes

1. Lyombe Eko, 'It's a Political Jungle Out There: How Four African Newspaper Cartoons Dehumanized and "Deterritorialized" African Political Leaders in the Post-Cold War Era' (2007) 69 *International Communication Gazette* 219–238, at 222.
2. Fatma M. Göçek, 'Political Cartoons as a Site of Representation and Resistance in the Middle East', in Fatma M. Göçek (ed.), *Political Cartoons in the Middle East* (Princeton: Markus Wiener, 1998), p. 2.
3. Phillip Waki, 'Report of the Findings of the Commission of Inquiry into the Post-Election Violence' (Republic of Kenya, Nairobi, Government Printer 2008), p. 342 (Waki Report).
4. *Ibid.*, pp. 472–476.
5. Randall Harrison, *The Cartoon: Communication to the Quick* (Beverly Hills: Sage, 1981).
6. Grace A. Musila, 'Democrazy: Laughter in Gado's Editorial Cartoons (1992–1999)', in James Ogude and Joyce Nyairo (eds.), *Urban Legends, Colonial Myths: Popular Culture and Literature in East Africa* (Trenton, NJ & Asmara: Africa World Press, 2007), p. 119.
7. Elisabeth El Refaie, 'Multiliteracies: How Readers Interpret Political Cartoons' (2009) 8 *Visual Communication* 181–205, at 184–5.
8. Elizabeth Swain, 'Analysing Evaluation in Political Cartoons' (2012) 1 *Discourse, Context & Media* 82–94 at 82.
9. El Refaie, 'Multilitracies', 186.

10. Ben M. Mazid, 'Cowboy and Misanthrope: A Critical (Discourse) Analysis of Bush and Bin Laden Cartoons' (2008) 2 *Discourse & Communication* 433–457, at 437.

11. Jeff Bezemer and Carey Jewitt 'Multimodal Analysis: Key Issues', in Lia Litositi (ed.), *Research Methods in Linguistics* (London: Continuum International Publishing, 2010), pp. 183–185.

12. Norman Fairclough and Ruth Wodak, 'Critical Discourse Analysis', in Teun A. van Dijk (ed.), *Discourse Studies: A Multidisciplinary Introduction* Vol 2 (London: Sage, 1997), pp. 258–284; Ruth Wodak and Michael Meyer, 'Critical Discourse Analysis: History, Agenda, Theory and Methodology', in Ruth Wodak and Michael Meyer (eds.), *Methods of Critical Discourse Analysis*, 2nd edn (London: Sage, 2009).

13. See El Refaie, 'Mutiliteracies'.

14. Mazid, 'Cowboy and Misanthrope'; Erin Steuter and Deborah Wills, *At War with Metaphor: Media, Propaganda, and Racism in the War on Terror* (Lenham: Lexington Books, 2008).

15. Mazid, 'Cowboy and Misanthrope', 437.

16. See Göçek, *Political Cartoons*; Steuter and Wills, *At War with Metaphor*.

17. Erin Steuter and Deborah Wills, 'Discourses of Dehumanization: Enemy Construction and Canadian Media Complicity in the Framing of the War on Terror' (2009) 2 *Global Media Journal – Canadian Edition* 7–24.

18. See Lyombe Eko, 'The Art of Criticism: How African Cartoons Discursively Constructed African Media Realities in the Post-cold War Era' (2010) 4 *Critical African Studies* 1–27; Göçek, *Political Cartoons*; Daniel Hammett, 'Political Cartoons, Post-colonialism and Critical African Studies' (2010) 4 *Critical African Studies* 1–26; Andrew J. Mason, 'The Cannibal Ogre and the Rape of Justice: A Contrapuntal View' (2010) 4 *Critical African Studies* 32–64.

19. See Musila, 'Democrazy', 114–115.

20. See Patrick Gathara and Mary K. Wanjau, 'Bringing Change through Laughter: Cartooning in Kenya', in Kimani Njogu and John Middleton (eds.), *Media and Identity in Africa* (Edinburgh: Edinburgh University Press, 2009), pp. 275–286; Patrick Gathara, 'Drawing the Line: The History and Impact of Political Cartooning in Kenya' (Friedrich Ebert Stiftung and Association of East African Cartoonists, 2004).

21. Gathara, 'Drawing the Line'.

22. Gathara, 'Drawing the Line'. Gathaara and Wanjau, 'Bringing Change'.

23. Gathara, 'Drawing the Line'.

24. Musila, 'Democrazy', 115–116.

25. Gathara, 'Drawing the Line'.

26. Musila, 'Democrazy'.

27. Ipso-Synovate, 'Kenyans Media Consumption Habits', 2011.

28. Nicholas Cheeseman, 'Are Newspapers on Their Way Out?', *Daily Nation*, 30 March 2014, p. 26.

29. George Ogola, 'The Political Economy of the Media in Kenya: From Kenyatta's Nation-Building Press to Kibaki's Local-Language FM Radio' (2011) 57 *Africa Today* 77–95.

30. Othieno Nyanjom, 'Factually True, Legally Untrue: Political Media Ownership in Kenya' (Internews in Kenya, 2012).

31. Nicholas Cheeseman, 'Walk in Journalists,' Shoes and You Will Understand They Try to Deliver', *Daily Nation* 15 June 2014, 28.

32. See Cheeseman, 'Walk in Journalists' Shoes,' 28.

33. Nyanjom, 'Factually True', 49.

34. Ogola, 'The Political Economy', 85.

35. Nyanjom, 'Factually True', 42.

36. Ogola 'The Political Economy', 85.

37. Musila, 'Democrazy', 123.

38. See Gerard Loughran, *Birth of a Nation: The Story of a Newspaper in Kenya* (London/New York: I.B. Tauris, 2010).

39. See Eko, 'It's a Political Jungle'; Sammy G. Gachigua, 'Kenya's War on Al-Shabaab Terror Militia: A Multimodal Discourse Analysis of Gado's Cartoons as Popular Culture Security Artifacts' (paper presented at CODESRIA Democratic Governance Institute, Dakar, Senegal, 5–23 August 2013); Musila, 'Democrazy'.

40. Musila, 'Democrazy', 118.

41. See Stephen Brown and Chandra L. Sriram, 'The Big Fish Won't Fry Themselves: Criminal Accountability for Post-election Violence in Kenya' (2012) 111 *African Affairs* 244–260.

42. See Brown and Sriram, 'The Big Fish'; Maurice Dunaiski, 'Accountability vs Stability? Assessing the ICC's Intervention in Kenya', *E-International Relations*, 9 January 2014; Charles C. Jalloh, 'Lecture: Africa and the International Criminal Court: Collision Course or Cooperation?' (2012) 34 *North Carolina Central Law Review* 203; Mahmood Mamdani, 'How the ICC's "Responsibility to Protect" Is Being Turned into an Assertion of Neocolonialism Domination', *Pambazuka News*, 17 September 2008; Mahmood Mamdani, 'ICC: International Community Distorted Internal Political Process in Kenya', *The East African*, 22 February 2014; Thabo Mbeki and Mahmood Mamdani, 'Courts Can't End Civil Wars,' *The New York Times*, 5 February 2014; Chandra L. Sriram and Stephen Brown, 'Kenya in the Shadow of the ICC: Complementarity, Gravity and Impact' (2012) 12 *International Criminal Law Review* 219–244.

43. Charles Hornsby, *Kenya: A History since Independence* (London/New York: I. B. Tauris, 2012), p. 168; See also Sammy G. Gachigua 'The ICC and Kenya's 2013 Elections: A Perspective from Kenyan

Newspaper editorial Cartoons', in Kimani Njogu and Peter W. Wekesa (eds.), *Kenya's 2013 Elections: Stakes, Practices and Outcomes* (Twaweza Communications & Heinrich Böll Foundation, 2015), pp. 198–219.

44. Peter Eke, 'Colonialism and the Two Publics in Africa: A Theoretical Statement' (1975) 17 *Comparative Studies in Society and History* 91–112.

45. Daniel Branch and Nicholas Cheeseman, 'The Politics of Control in Kenya: Understanding the Bureaucratic-Executive State, 1952–78' (2006) 33 *Review of African Political Economy* 11–31; Naomi Chazan, Robert Mortimer, John Ravenhill and Donald Rothchild, *Politics and Society in Contemporary Africa*, 2nd edn (Boulder, Colorado: Lynne Rienner Publishers, 1992), pp. 137–140.

46. Susanne D. Mueller, 'Kenya and the International Criminal Court (ICC): Politics, the Election and the Law' (2004) 2 (8) *Journal of Eastern African Studies* (2014) 25–42.

47. Waki Report, Chapter 11.

48. Mueller, 'Kenya and the ICC', 9–11.

49. Elisabeth Noelle-Neumann and Thomas Petersen, 'The Spiral of Silence and the Social Nature of Man', in Lynda L. Kaid (ed.), *Handbook of Political Communication Research* (Mahwah, New Jersey: Lawrence Erlbaum associates, 2004), pp. 339–357.

50. See Kenyans for Peace with Justice and Truth (KPJT), 'Securing justice: Establishing a Domestic Mechanism for the 2007/8 Post-Election Violence in Kenya' (KPTJ, 2013), pp. 4–8; Mueller, 'Kenya and the ICC'.

51. Mueller, 'Kenya and the ICC', 11–13.

52. International Crisis Group, 'Kenya: Impact of the ICC Proceedings' (Africa Briefing no. 84, 9 January 2012), p. 11.

53. Thomas O. Hansen, 'Caressing the Big Fish? A Critique of ICC Trial Chamber V(a)'s Decision to Grant Ruto's Request for Excusal from Continuous Presence at Trial' (2013) 22 *Cardozo Journal of International and Comparative Law* 101–119.

54. Fackson Banda, Okoth F. Mudhai, and Wisdom J. Tettey, 'Introduction: New Media and Democracy in Africa – A Critical Interjection', in Okoth F. Mudhai, Wisdom J. Tettey and Fackson Banda (eds.), *African Media and the Digital Public Sphere* (New York: Palgrave/Macmillan, 2009), pp. 1, 3–4.

55. Stephen Brown and Rosalind Raddatz, 'Dire Consequences or Empty Threats? Western Pressure for Peace, Justice and Democracy in Kenya' (2014) 8 *Journal of Eastern African Studies* 52.

56. Sammy G. Gachigua, 'Fuelling the Violence: the Print Media in Kenya's Volatile 2007 Post-Election Violence', in Godwin Murunga, Duncan Okello and Anders Sjögren, *Kenya: the Struggle for a New*

Constitutional Order (London: African Nordic Institute/Zed Books, 2014), pp. 51–52.

57. See Brown and Raddatz, 'Dire Consequences'.
58. See: www.independent.co.uk/news/world/africa/daily-nation-aga-khan-accused-over-squeezing-kenya-press-freedom-after-newspaper-sacks-cartoonist-a6943171.html

10

A 'Criminal Investigation', Not a 'Political Analysis'? Justice Contradictions and the Electoral Consequences of Kenya's ICC Cases

Thomas P. Wolf

I INTRODUCTION

I am following the evidence. I present criminal investigations, not political analysis . . .
My only job is to end impunity for past crimes and prevent future crimes.

ICC Chief Prosecutor Luis Moreno-Ocampo[1]

The pursuit of those 'most responsible' for the large-scale violence that followed Kenya's disputed 2007 election by the International Criminal Court (ICC) can be viewed from various perspectives. Internationally, the earlier adoption of the Rome Statute by the Kenyan government (along with thirty-three other African states) – as well as the creation of the Court itself – can be considered part of the 'Third Wave' of global democratic expansion that followed the fall of the Berlin Wall in 1989.[2] At the same time, African ICC membership has been characterized as primarily a pragmatic tool for incumbent regimes to deal with their (violently criminal) domestic opponents, since it was never imagined that the Court's mandate would include senior incumbent officials of Member States,[3] let alone leaders of major powers which had eschewed membership from the outset.[4]

More broadly, as explored in the Introduction to this volume, this welcomed 'imposition' of 'global justice' has been interpreted as part of the evolving contest between quite divergent norms. These may be summarized as that of individual criminal responsibility, largely aimed at punishment and deterrence, as opposed to that of consensual-collective responsibility and compromise, aimed at the restoration of social harmony.

With specific reference to the ICC, Kamari M. Clarke has sought to demonstrate the irreconcilable nature of these two norms:

[T]he problem is that the reassignment of the guilt of thousands of people to a single chief commander and a few of his top aides neither ends violence nor captures adequately the complicity of multiple agents involved in the making of war. In most of the Africa-based cases, the basis for justice in war-torn regions is founded in the grassroots call for brokering peace first and then setting in place post-violence structures for rebuilding.[5]

For his part, Goran Hyden, in more explicitly comparative terms, has contrasted a less formal, consensual-collective 'African' justice model that puts a premium on 'mutual advantage' with the Western liberal-bureaucratic one, with its emphasis on individual criminal-legal responsibility:

The African sense of justice . . . operates outside the formal justice system put in place by the colonial authorities and inherited by Africans after independence . . . In situations of conflict or injustice people tend to perceive communal institutions such as families or whole ethnic groups rather than individuals to be on trial . . .

[In the liberal model institutions] . . . are scripts or schemas that human actors must learn to adopt in order to avoid sanctions . . .

Governance in Africa tends to diverge from the liberal model because the structural conditions foster political settlements that reflect competition among entities based on identity rather than interest.[6]

However stark the contrast between these two competing justice models may be, this chapter argues that settlements of violent conflict need not be exclusively of one type or the other. On the contrary, it shall be shown that it was because of the hybrid nature of the settlement of Kenya's 2007–2008 post-election crisis that the two main figures indicted by the ICC for serious international crimes – and who had been on opposite sides when these crimes were committed – could form a political alliance and then emerge as the winners in the March 2013 election.

In pursuing this argument, the chapter first summarizes the factors that had been assumed to make an electoral alliance – let alone success – for Uhuru Kenyatta and William Ruto so unlikely, and then uses national survey findings to track their increasing, and widely unexpected, popularity over the pre-election period, also seen in the eventual voting patterns.

Next, using data from these surveys, it explores attitudes across the political divide regarding both the causes of the 2008 post-election violence (PEV) and accountability 'options' (including the ICC) arising from it, showing how a 'moral reversal' over this issue was accompanied by increasing ethnic polarization.

The origin of this moral reversal is then explored with reference to certain aspects of the post-election crisis settlement. Doing so reveals how the contradictory nature of the twin goals pursued by national and international actors – peace and stability on the one hand, and accountability for the PEV on the other – created a contradiction that Kenyatta and Ruto were able to deftly exploit in their ultimately successful election campaign.

The chapter concludes by revisiting several of the comparative themes considered at the outset in the context of Kenya's 2013 election and by noting the evolving impact that these cases have had on Kenya's and Africa's relationship with the ICC. Finally, it acknowledges their continuing influence on the country's political environment, including the now-approaching 2017 election. This is so even if many key questions regarding the effort to truncate the limits of impunity in Kenya, Africa and beyond as a result of the collapse of these Kenyan cases remain unanswered.

II THE ICC AND THE ELECTION: HOW HIGH THE HURDLE?

Q: How in the world could Kenyans elect crimes-against-humanity indictees?
A: How could they not?![7]

That Kenyatta and Ruto, who jointly contested Kenya's 2013 election as candidates for president and deputy president under the 'Jubilee Alliance', could have mounted anything close to a viable campaign – let alone come out as winners, against the 'CORD Alliance' of Raila Odinga and Kalonzo Musyoka, left many incredulous. Such incredulity was not without cause.

First, their criminal-defendant status stemmed from the traumatic violence that followed the contentious 2007 presidential election, in which Kenyatta had supported the official winner, the incumbent (and fellow-Kikuyu) Mwai Kibaki, and Ruto had supported Odinga (an ethnic Luo), the official loser, with their ethnic communities (the Kikuyu and Kalenjin, respectively) likewise on opposite sides of it. Thus, their "alliance of the accused" was, at least at the outset, highly implausible, and eventually had to overcome significant resistance within their respective communities.[8]

Second, their crimes-against-humanity indictments had been issued in January 2012, suggesting that by election time the defendants would be fully occupied with their trial preparations, if not their in-court defenses.

Third, the stringent leadership-integrity provisions of Kenya's new constitution, ratified and promulgated in August 2010, implied that anyone so indicted would be barred from running for or occupying public office.[9]

Fourth, since holding to account those who were 'most responsible' for the PEV was an integral part of the reform agenda that accompanied the formation of the power-sharing government that ended the crisis, it was widely assumed that the top leaders of that government would fully support the Court's efforts in successfully prosecuting these cases, thus leaving no room for the candidacy of either Kenyatta or Ruto.

Fifth, after a decade under 'Kikuyu' rule (in addition to the country's first fifteen years under Kenyatta's father), there was a widely acknowledged sense of 'Kikuyu fatigue', presumably an insurmountable obstacle for Kenyatta.[10]

Finally, even after all other hurdles had been surmounted, supposedly influential figures, including Kofi Annan who had brokered the African Union (AU) mediation efforts that produced the power-sharing government and reform agenda, and representatives of several governments with which Kenya traditionally enjoyed deep economic and political-security relations (especially the United States and the United Kingdom), cautioned Kenyan voters against electing individuals encumbered with ICC indictments because of detrimental (if unspecified) 'consequences' that this could have for their country.

Yet however counterintuitive, this chapter argues that it was the very threat from the ICC that determined the election's outcome: first by creating an overwhelming incentive for these two 'targets-of-justice' to come together in an otherwise inconceivable alliance, and ultimately by providing them with a major share of support from the electorate.[11] At the same time, it does not depend upon the fact that, according to the Independent Electoral and Boundaries Commission (IEBC), the Jubilee Alliance pair achieved an out-right-majority win on the first round (so as to avoid a second round, run-off contest),[12] however critical it was that they did so.[13] The same applies to the fact that this result was affirmed in several highly controversial Supreme Court judgments.[14]

A Ethnic Consolidation in Kenya's 2013 Presidential Election

If the International Criminal Court is right, the two funded death squads to kill, maim, and loot each other's folks. Mr Ruto only subordinated himself to Mr Kenyatta because he couldn't win on his own. Nor did he have good options after falling out with ODM's Raila Odinga. Only a victorious partnership with Mr Kenyatta – a fellow ICC indictee – could possibly save the pair from The Hague. It was a strategic alliance.[15]

Survey results conducted over several years prior to the election demonstrate how unexpected its eventual outcome initially was. At the same time, they

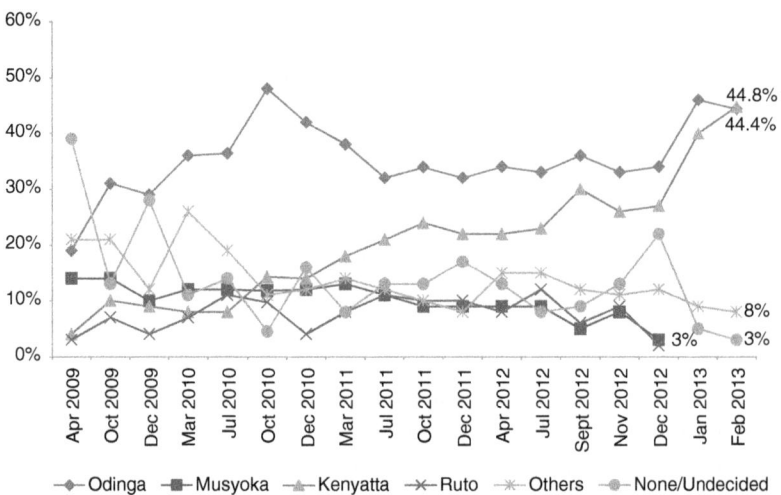

FIGURE 1* Support for Potential/Actual (Main) Presidential Candidates, 2009–2013[17]

reflect two key facts noted above: (1) that the indictments of Kenyatta and Ruto significantly boosted their respective levels of support, and (2) that their formal alliance from late 2012 gave their joint effort a much greater boost than did the similar combination of Odinga and Musyoka that materialized at about the same time, as suggested by Figure 1:

> *For reasons of visual clarity, percentages are shown for only the top two candidates, their (eventual) deputy president running-mates, all others combined, and those who preferred no one/were still undecided.[16]

At one level, some attributed Jubilee's success to a simple 'tyranny of numbers', since the combined Mt. Kenya and Kalenjin groupings constitute over 40% of the population (and an even higher proportion among registered voters).[18] As such, obtaining the most votes – if not an outright first round win – was said to be a foregone conclusion for the now-conjoined principal ICC defendants, assuming near-unanimous electoral support from their respective ethnic communities.[19]

Correlating final poll vote-choice with the country's main ethnic groups lends credence to this argument. According to survey data obtained two weeks before the actual vote, 90% of registered voters from the Mt. Kenya groups stated their intention to vote for Jubilee, as did 86% of Kalenjin voters. On the other side, 94% of registered Luo voters were prepared to vote for CORD, though Musyoka's Kamba were somewhat less unified, with only 81% lining up behind this coalition.[20] Further, both exit poll data and the official results underscore this reality.[21]

Altogether, and whatever was the precise motivational mix of particular groups of voters beyond the ICC issue in terms of such factors as policy performance expectations and individual or collective patronage debts and promises, ethnic mobilization, as in the past, was clearly the starting point on both sides of the political divide in this election.

B Accountability for the Post-Election Violence? The Ethno-Political Imperative

The principal dynamic, if nothing changes dramatically before the next elections, will be the effort to stop the pro-ICC Prime Minister from ascending to the presidency . . .

The PM will be able to call upon the support of civil society and the media, which have been fairly consistent in this support for ICC action.

Mr Odinga will also seek to win the support of the two thirds of Kenyans that opinion polls say back trials at The Hague, as he seeks to build a cross-ethnic alliance that might help him ascent [sic] to the presidency.[22]

On 30 December 2007, following an extremely competitive and divisive, if largely violence-free, campaign and a largely tranquil voting day, the Chair of the Electoral Commission of Kenya (ECK), Samuel Kivuitu, declared incumbent President Kibaki the winner over Odinga by about 230,000 votes out of some ten million votes cast.[23] With tensions having risen as the agonizingly slow (and confusing) vote count progressed, widespread violence erupted following this announcement. As doubts were raised by several election-observer groups, the Odinga side claimed massive fraud, while refusing to go to court on the grounds that the judiciary was a mere appendage of the (Kibaki-led) executive.[24] It only subsided a month later, when negotiations, mediated by a team of AU 'Eminent Persons' led by former UN Secretary-General Kofi Annan, commenced. These negotiations led to a power-sharing arrangement that was signed on 28 February.[25] By this time, beyond uncountable other human rights abuses and property loss, more than 1,100 people had died and over half a million had been displaced.

Critical to the origin of the ICC cases, as well as to the shifting positions regarding the ICC's subsequent involvement, are the four main categories of this violence.[26] While their actual boundaries were somewhat overlapping, they may be distinguished as follows:

(1) largely spontaneous attacks by Odinga supporters in Nairobi, Kisumu and a number of other mainly urban centers, especially on property but also

on perceived Kibaki supporters, that broke out immediately after the election outcome was announced;
(2) police shootings, mainly of these protestors;[27]
(3) a combination of spontaneous but also more organized (and to some extent, it is alleged, pre-planned) attacks mainly by pro-ODM (i.e., Orange Democratic Movement) Kalenjin 'militias' on Kikuyu and other 'foreigners' in the Rift Valley; and later,
(4) 'retaliation attacks' at the end of January (just before the AU-led mediation talks began) in Naivasha and Nakuru (two south-central Rift Valley towns) by Kikuyu ('Mungiki') militia, most of whom were transported from Nairobi and southern Central Province, aimed at Odinga supporters, especially Luo and Luhya, as well as several of the few Kalenjin residing in those locations.[28]

Of these, it was mainly the third category of violence, along Kenya's main transportation route to Uganda and beyond, that led key external actors to apply pressure on both sides to begin negotiations.[29]

In terms of the subsequent politicization of the ICC's involvement, the starting point is that Ruto was among Odinga's key supporters in the 2007 election, bringing almost all Kalenjin fellow ethnics with him.[30] Their electoral alliance is evident in the results obtained in the first post-election survey (March 2008), which confirmed how close the Luo and Kalenjin were over this issue, and how distant both were from members of the Mt. Kenya communities.

For example, whereas 72% of respondents from the Mt. Kenya grouping believed that the PEV was planned, only 27% of the Luo and just 11% of Kalenjin held this view.[31] Moreover, in partisan terms, more than twice as many PNU supporters took this position as did those aligned with ODM (48% vs. 20%).[32] Conversely, 77% of ODM supporters identified the 'announcement of Kibaki as the winner' as the main cause of the PEV, compared to only 46% of PNU supporters.[33] In other words, whether consciously or otherwise, it was in the 'moral interest' of most of Kibaki's supporters to perceive this violence as pre-meditated, based on such factors as land and other forms of economic conflict and competition, as well as on ODM's refusal to admit electoral defeat.[34] For their part, Odinga's supporters understood it as a largely spontaneous reaction to the crime of election theft, so that the PEV victims were only proximate surrogates of the real target: those who committed it on Kibaki's behalf.[35] Whatever the precise mix and intensity of these positions, the Kalenjin and Kikuyu/Mt. Kenya groups were at opposite ends of this violence-motivation spectrum at the time.

Such contrasting perceptions about the causes of and thus the responsibility for the PEV are mirrored in views about accountability for its associated crimes, which ultimately shaped attitudes toward the ICC and the 2013 presidential contest.

Of particular significance in this respect is that however acrimonious the disagreements were across the country's political divide about how the National Accord was being implemented, for the first two years after the 2007 election there was equal, if not greater, public support for PEV accountability among PNU supporters than among those associated with ODM. For example, in June 2008, more than twice as many residents of Central Province (i.e., the Mt. Kenya area, PNU's stronghold) supported the survey question option that 'everyone involved in it should be held accountable' as did those of Nyanza (i.e., Luo-land, ODM's stronghold; 89% vs. 40%) – with five times more ODM than PNU supporters favoring amnesty for the perpetrators (60% vs. 12%).[36] By July 2009, however, this contrast had vanished, with a substantial – indeed, an equal – proportion of both PNU and ODM supporters (68%) favoring the ICC (over a special tribunal or the regular judiciary) as the agency to pursue the 'main perpetrators' of the PEV,[37] with only 3% more of the latter opting for the 'forgiveness-with-amnesty' option (16% vs. 13%).[38] Moreover, within two years (by July 2011) a major gap had emerged between ODM and PNU supporters over the ICC's involvement, with almost twice as many of the former as the latter favoring it (72% vs. 40%).[39]

Shifting perceptions of political advantage help to explain such figures. First, in the immediate aftermath of the election, most Kenyans could support accountability for several reasons. On the ODM side, since its leaders never took responsibility for the PEV, most of their supporters could assume that any accountability measures would be directed elsewhere. Contributing to such confidence was their overwhelming perception that most of the violence caused by their adherents was a spontaneous reaction against election theft. So, too, did the fact that at the time none of their leaders had been charged with such involvement. Indeed, many assumed initially that the main focus of any accountability efforts would be the police killings of protestors, as seen in the (first) call for the ICC's intervention that was made by the ODM leadership just before the AU negotiations began.[40]

On the PNU side, support for such accountability appears to reflect the fact that it was their followers (especially Kikuyu and Gusii in the Rift Valley) who had been the most numerous PEV victims, encouraging the assumption that prosecutions would be directed mainly at their Kalenjin youth assailants.[41] The brief if ferocious retaliation attacks in Naivasha were probably much further from most of their minds, and which, in any

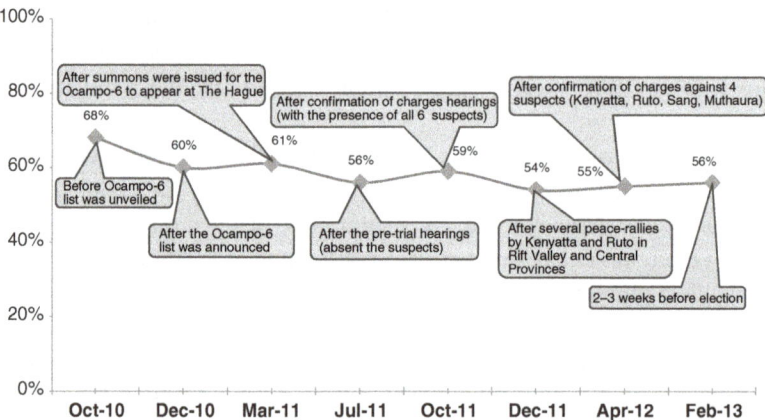

FIGURE 2 Support for ICC Trials (Showing Key Events), Oct. 2010–Feb. 2013
Source: Compiled from Ipsos' SPEC Barometer surveys (October 2010–February 2013)

case, were seen by those on this side of the political divide as defensive and thus morally justified.

In other words, strong majorities across the political divide supported the ICC's engagement among several accountability options as long as this agenda remained largely an abstract one. Even after the ICC Prosecutor named the 'Ocampo Six'[42] in mid-December 2010, total support for this option fell only slightly (from 68% to 60%).[43] As also shown in Figure 2, subsequent levels of support varied only marginally right up to the 2013 election (taking into account normal statistical error-margins), even when examining them in terms of particular ICC-related events.[44]

Beneath the surface of these composite ratings, however, significant movement was occurring in ethnic, and thus political, terms.[45]

Specifically, as shown in Figure 3, while attitudes among members of these larger communities diverged only modestly at the beginning of this period – aside from the Kalenjin, whose level of support for the ICC process was 28% lower than the next least-supportive group, the Mt. Kenya cluster, at 57% – the gaps between the indictees' and other communities widened immediately thereafter (from April 2011, following the naming of the Ocampo Six), though this had narrowed somewhat by late October 2011. This gap then (as from December 2011) widened again, and continued to do so as the election approached.

Yet, whatever these ethnic contrasts, it may appear puzzling that there was any support at all for this (now ICC-driven) accountability agenda on the election's eve among Jubilee's main ethnic base communities, even if such

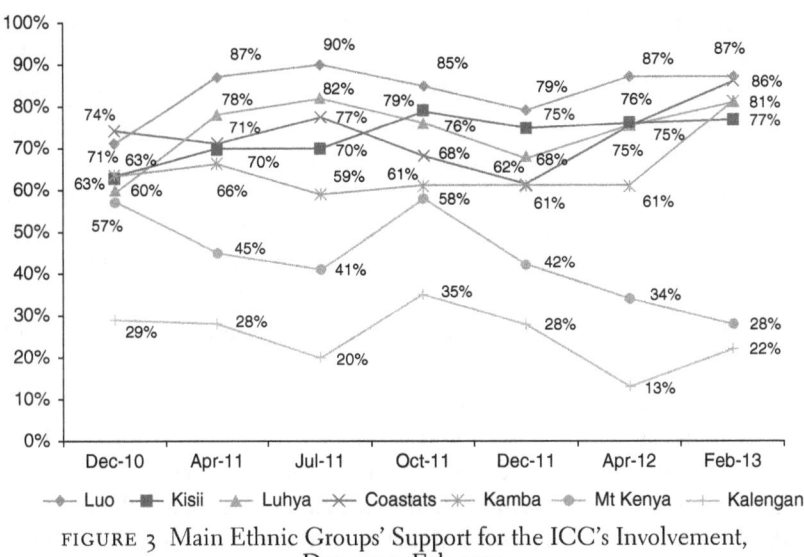

FIGURE 3 Main Ethnic Groups' Support for the ICC's Involvement,
Dec. 2010–Feb. 2013

support evidently failed to deter the vast majority of these Mt. Kenya and Kalenjin 'dissenters' from voting for Jubilee. Several factors may explain these modest, if significant, levels of support.

First, not all backing for the ICC should be equated with antipathy to the defendants, since some of their supporters, convinced of their innocence, were apparently confident not just of their eventual vindication, but that going through the justice process would actually enhance their immediate and longer-term political stature (assuming they would not be disqualified as candidates). Such an hypothesis is suggested by findings in the last pre-election survey (in mid-February, 2013), showing that a substantial proportion of Jubilee supporters (26%) supported these trials, even if more than three times as many of CORD's potential voters (84%) did likewise.[46] Conversely, this same survey found that five times as many of Jubilee's declared voters preferred 'forgiveness with amnesty' than did those of CORD (68% vs. 12%). As for the pro-ICC 'dissenters' among the Kalenjin, this 'accountability vs. vote' gap may be explained partly by the fact that the PEV directly involved only (sections of) the Nandi and Kipsigis, so that support for accountability as recorded in the survey figures likely varied across this community's sub-groups.[47]

The gap between the Mt. Kenya and Kalenjin groups is also notable. Beyond the fact of greater sub-ethnic heterogeneity among the latter,[48] until the Ocampo Six were named, most of the former apparently assumed that (as noted above) 'accountability' would be directed primarily, if not exclusively, at those who attacked their co-ethnics in the Rift Valley. The 'balance' among those indicted thus clearly came as a shock to many of them. Nevertheless, by election eve, this gap had narrowed to just 6%, suggesting that the prospect of the ICC defendants clasping state power had overridden most of the differentiating factors between these two communities.

The salience of perceived 'political opportunity,' as opposed to any 'accountability principle,' is likewise evident among the Kamba, after fellow-ethnic Kalonzo Musyoka became Odinga's deputy president running-mate in January 2013, even if a clear, if modest, majority of them had backed the Court's involvement up to this time. Dutifully serving Kibaki as vice president from the first week of the post-election crisis, he had undertaken numerous 'shuttle diplomacy' missions in this capacity, attempting to rally other African governments, as well as UN Security Council members, to the anti-ICC cause.[49] On this basis, for several years many had assumed that he would inherit much of the Mt. Kenya vote if Kenyatta did not contest the election. Indeed, in August 2012 he declared that he and Ruto had agreed on a joint ticket (presumably with himself the presidential candidate).[50] With his late-hour electoral 'marriage' to Odinga, however, support for the ICC among the Kamba jumped by 20% (from 61% to 81%), putting them at about the same level of the other main ethnic communities who had expressed approval of the Court's involvement during the previous two years.

The following synopsis by Human Rights Watch, issued shortly before the confirmation of charges, captures the political dynamics that are reflected in the survey results presented above:

> Positions on accountability for election violence have never been uniform across the coalition government. Early on the PNU took a strong pro-prosecution stance, while the ODM favored amnesty, likely because most of those arrested in the immediate aftermath of the violence were affiliated with the ODM. Later, after the ICC Prosecutor named the six suspects against whom he was seeking summons – which included key officials on the PNU side, whereas those on the ODM side were of a dissident wing that had already effectively split with Raila Odinga – the positions of leaders in both parties reversed. This is an indication of the extent to which politicians' commitment to justice has varied based on shifting personal and political interests.[51]

Also striking in this respect is that once again the focus is exclusively on 'justice' as related to the PEV; the contradictory interpretations of events that triggered this violence in the first place are completely ignored. Nevertheless, such developments illustrate the public-relations challenges that the ICC Prosecutors faced in repeatedly asserting that their task was 'a criminal investigation and not a political analysis',[52] and that the 'account-ability targets' were 'individuals rather than communities'.[53] On the contrary, the survey evidence presented above demonstrates that the Court's involve-ment was perceived by many Kenyans throughout this period in highly com-munal, and thus largely partisan, terms, just as the PEV itself was. In the words of a local media commentator:

> [O]ur definition of justice is not always what lawyers describe on the basis of fact and evidence. That is also why often we shift the goalposts, to realign with our tribal radar.[54]

As has been suggested, just how this shifting mix of personal and political interests could come to the fore can be understood only by revisiting the political origins of this accountability agenda, in which the ICC eventually came to hold center stage.

III CONTRADICTIONS IN THE DOUBLE-ACCOUNTABILITY AGENDA

Initially, America, which sees Kenya as a front-line ally in a war against Islamist militias in neighbouring Somalia, made the mistake of endorsing the President's re-election. Now Britain, America and the African Union are urging Mr. Odinga and Mr. Kibaki to talk in an effort to stop the bloodletting. That lets Mr. Kibaki off the hook far too easily. All the violence should certainly be condemned, but most of the diplomatic pressure should be exerted on Mr. Kibaki's supposed new government to annul the results and organise a recount – or a new vote.[55]

Two factors help to explain the chasm that emerged between the quite narrow confines of the ICC's criminal remit on the one hand, and the shifting set of moral positions and political interests on the other. The first, which had two main components, was the overwhelming priority placed on protecting the fragile stability of the painstakingly crafted Grand Coalition Government, given the concerns of the lingering potential for violence if it collapsed.[56] Its first compo-nent was the exclusion of the two principals (Kibaki and Odinga) from the accountability agenda, on whose behalf both the election fraud and (much of) the PEV, respectively, were perpetrated. That omission triggered considerable grievance from the outset, and which carried through to the election, as was expressed to the author by one Jubilee supporter shortly after voting in 2013:

> The ICC should have gone for Raila and Kibaki because that's where the violence started. They were the numbers 1 and 2, so why go just for numbers 3 and 4, or for numbers 5 and 6?[57]

Its second component was ensuring a political balance (between ODM and PNU) in the identities of the Ocampo Six (noted above).[58] Taken together, however, these aspects of the ICC's intervention served only to invite accusations of a distinct political (as opposed to a criminal-justice) agenda. As was noted in an analysis of these unfolding events:

> From the start, the selection of six individuals, three from each side of the conflict, suggested that the ICC was not blind to the need for careful political balancing ... The approach appeared to ensure that President Mwai Kibaki and Prime Minister Raila Odinga ... now sharing power in the Grand Coalition Government, must also equally share the bitter fruits of the post-election crisis ... However, the ICC stopped short of indicting the two top leaders themselves as the bearers of the ultimate responsibility, instead going for key lieutenants in their respective camps. The appearance of political calculation and balancing created room for propaganda about possible manipulation ... [that] Kenyatta and Ruto turned ... to their advantage during the campaigns.[59]

The second, and equally important, factor was that this attempted PNU-ODM 'balance' was quickly overtaken by events. In particular, by the time the Ocampo Six were named, Ruto, the key ODM figure among the six, had already broken with Odinga, increasingly aligning himself with the PNU side of the political divide. In addition to their quite divergent political 'origins',[60] this falling-out followed a number of personal and policy differences, among them Odinga's perceived abandonment of the Kalenjin youth who had fought for him once he was sworn in as prime minister.[61] And, as was pointed out by one commentator shortly after the Waki Commission report was released at the end of 2008, the prospect of high-level accountability for the PEV only made matters worse:

> When KANU lost power in 2002, Ruto and other orphans of the Moi regime found themselves in the cold and isolated from the corridors of power ... [since] President Kibaki's State House was closed to them ... Rallying support for Raila in 2007 was only a convenient way of hitting back at Kibaki and his GEMA [i.e., Kikuyu, Embu, and Meru, or 'Mt. Kenya'] people. But now Ruto and his friends find themselves in unfamiliar territory where leaders are being called to account for their overt and covert actions. With the threat that the Waki report might take an international dimension, they find themselves in an awkward position and they naturally expect the Prime Minister to come to their rescue.[62]

Subsequent events, including Odinga's attempted removal of Ruto from the cabinet, heightened the animosity between the two leaders.[63] Well before the

2013 election, therefore, the remaining ICC cases were portrayed by 'UhuRuto' as part and parcel of Odinga's/CORD's campaign strategy, eventually allowing Jubilee to market the Western-conspiracy slogan of 'the three Os' (i.e., Ocampo, Obama, and Odinga).[64] This is seen, for example, in the introduction to proceedings of the National Assembly documents (later determined to be fake) purporting to reveal a plot by the British government to have Kibaki arrested and taken to The Hague as well.[65] The warnings (if not threats) by Annan and various Western diplomats of dire 'consequences' for Kenya should Jubilee triumph at the polls only added fuel to this fire, its campaign teams eagerly painting Odinga's presidential aspirations with a neocolonial (if not explicitly racist) brush.[66] As a senior Jubilee operative admitted shortly after the election:

> It was a Godsend! I mean, here were foreign powers dictating to Kenyans on how to vote ... It also made Raila look like a project of Western powers and we loved it. Jubilee went into overdrive.[67]

As important as these two factors – excluding the two principals, and attempting a partisan balance – were in shaping Kenya's 2013 election at the ICC's expense, they emerged out of a more fundamental reality: the bifurcation in addressing the election crisis itself, was comprised of the flawed election on the one hand, and the resulting violence on the other.[68]

As emphasized above, the AU-led mediation effort was aimed primarily at ending the PEV through the formation of a power-sharing government. In doing so, two crucial and interrelated questions were put aside: first, who really won the election,[69] or if that was impossible to establish, who was responsible for that very impossibility?; second, to what extent was the concession of a share of power to the official loser (i.e., Odinga) a "reward" for the violence?

In a telling, if unstated, refusal to confront such questions, the National Accord assigned each of these questions to a different commission established for the purpose: the Kriegler Commission (or Independent Review Commission – IREC) and the Waki Commission (or Commission to Investigate the Post-Election Violence – CIPEV).[70] The former, however, was itself the result of a compromise alternative to either an immediate re-run of the election (since a vote recount was deemed unfeasible), or having the power-sharing arrangement assume the status of a transitional government to be followed by a new election after a limited period, which ODM considered a major concession, considering their conviction that the election had been stolen.[71]

In the event, the IREC report only suggested future electoral reforms, leading eventually to the disbanding of the ECK, whose commissioners were sent off into retirement, free of any accountability encumbrances apparently reflecting a conviction that imposing any individual responsibility would open a Pandora's Box, whose contents would threaten the uneasy peace embodied in the Grand Coalition Government.[72]

By contrast, the Waki Commission not only documented the causes and course of the PEV in detail but also recommended the prosecution of those deemed most responsible for it, by either a special local tribunal, or, failing its establishment through an act of parliament, the ICC, of which Kenya had recently become a willing member.[73] Such determination reflected not only most Kenyans' abhorrence of the PEV, but also a conviction among key external actors – including especially the AU's mediation team of Eminent Persons and Kenya's key (mainly Western) 'development partners'[74] – that the pursuit of such an uncompromising accountability agenda was essential to prevent any such recurrence, while making an historic 'dent' in Kenya's entrenched culture of impunity for both economic and human rights crimes.[75]

The head of Human Rights Watch's African Division, writing in mid-2008, was one of many who lent support to such a one-sided approach:

> Both ODM and PNU negotiators already pledged to Kofi Annan to 'identify, investigate and prosecute perpetrators' of post-election violence. So what is there to argue about? If Mr. Odinga and ODM believe the police and the justice system to be partisan, as part of the coalition government and with their new-found executive powers, it is their duty to make the system work fairly. And if Mr. Kibaki and PNU are really committed to the rule of law and rejecting amnesty then they should ensure that the leaders and inciters of violence (including those among the police and their own ranks), and not just the foot-soldiers, face justice too.[76]

For his part, Ruto, speaking at about the same time prior to his falling-out with Odinga, called attention to this schism over these twin-accountability issues (i.e., the election's wanting integrity and the PEV):[77]

> Where are the politicians who stubbornly blocked the reconstitution of the ECK last year? Where is the leadership of the security forces that failed to do its work? What about the ECK commissioners who participated in the election fraud? . . .
>
> If we are not ready to charge the politicians and the so called planners and financiers [of election theft], then what moral authority do we have to charge mere pawns in a huge political game? . . .
>
> The test the country is facing is not whether the youth should be granted amnesty. The test is whether we are prepared to continue promoting the

culture of having two sets of law for [sic] the big boys and the defenceless small fry.[78]

By the middle of the following year, after several unsuccessful efforts to establish a local tribunal as an alternative to the ICC's looming involvement,[79] those most heavily invested in the AU-brokered election crisis settlement – clearly frustrated over such failures – remained no less committed to such a 'lop-sided' accountability agenda. The principal mediator in that settlement, Kofi Annan, put it thus:

> Justice delayed is justice denied. The people of Kenya want to see concrete progress on the fight against impunity. Without such progress, the reconcilia-tion between ethnic groups and the long-term stability of Kenya is in jeopardy.[80]

For his part, a few months later, speaking at a Law Society of Kenya function, outspoken US Ambassador Michael Rannerberger had this to say:

> The window is fast closing for the meaningful reforms Kenya must undertake in order to avoid a repeat of the 2008 violence – or worse – and to ensure a stable and prosperous democratic future ... The Waki and Kriegler Commissions delivered credible, detailed reports laying out a roadmap for key reforms ... While acknowledging some progress, the most important reforms ... [that] are needed to end the culture of impunity and to ensure future democratic stability and prosperity have either not been implemented or are moving at an alarmingly slow pace ... No steps have been taken to hold accountable the principal perpetrators of post-election violence ... We continue to urge that a credible independent Special Tribunal be established in Kenya and that Kenya fully cooperate with the International Criminal Court to investigate and prosecute those suspected of orchestrating and supporting post-election violence.[81]

In the meantime, however, the two main 'accountability targets' were working tirelessly to frustrate all accountability efforts, while largely succeeding in appropriating the peace-and-reconciliation narrative for their own purposes. Here, the determination of the Kibaki side of the Grand Coalition Government (which controlled the relevant ministries of security and justice) to thwart any accountability agenda played directly into the now-joined hands (by virtue of their separate indictments) of Kenyatta and Ruto. Led initially by religious leaders,[82] an entire civil society 'industry' arose – ironically, with generous (Western) donor funding[83] – to foster reconciliation among the affected communities. Most commonly, this took the form of 'peace rallies', especially in the Rift Valley, over which they often presided.[84]

One such event, held in Eldoret, the epicenter of the PEV, shortly after the naming of the Ocampo Six, was described by the head of the Kenyan chapter of the International Commission of Jurists in these terms:

> The rally's purpose was ostensibly to promote peace between the two men's respective ethnic groups, the Kalenjin and Kikuyu, whose members were regarded as key actors during the violence. However, Ruto and Kenyatta had other reasons for this show of unity, since the accused on both sides of the ICC cases had been lobbying for a united front against the Court. The attendance by President Kibaki at the rally came as a great surprise to the public. In appearing alongside persons facing ICC cases, the president openly declared his support for their push to combine forces against the common threat of prosecution by the ICC.[85]

Moreover, the almost total failure of the Grand Coalition Government to undertake any serious investigation/prosecution of the PEV cases[86] served to magnify the perceived value of such personalized involvement in these efforts, especially for Kikuyu in the Rift Valley, thousands of whom remained in IDP camps.[87]

At the same time, some campaign operatives were not averse to employing coercive sanctions on selected 'errant' community members, such as Imenti-Central MP (and ICC-supporter) Gitobu Imanyara. Carjacked on his way home from parliament almost a year before the election, he was reportedly made to kneel on the pavement facing Mt. Kenya and pledge loyalty to Kenyatta's cause, with a *panga* (machete) pressed against the back of his head.[88]

In sum, just how effectively those subjected to this PEV-accountability agenda were able to exploit the failure to interrogate the fraudulent election that had triggered it in the first place was summarized by a Kenyan political scientist two years after the power-sharing agreement was reached:

> Kenyan society was polarised prior to 2007 ... The polarisation follows the broad contours of the two top contending political parties, ODM and PNU. Those supporting the former tend to accept the view that [the] PEV was due to election rigging ... Those favouring PNU perceive only murderous ethnic hatred in the actions of their opponent ... One would assume from these polar positions that PNU would support efforts to punish perpetrators of violence while ODM would be on the defensive, seeking to protect its luminaries from such punishment.
>
> The post-election situation in Kenya has been a lot more complicated than the PNU/ODM outline assumes. While the PNU side was content to insist that ODM was guilty of ethnic cleansing and even genocide, they have not fully supported the desire of Kenyans to have the instigators of violence punished. On the ODM side, there has been a split in their ranks that

threatens to fragment the party. Some members support punishment of the instigators of violence, coupled with their insistence that the original trigger of violence was election rigging, which in itself renders those who rigged the elections culpable.

The back and forth arguments on culpability have hardly helped the search for truth and justice.[89]

The survey and other data presented above related to both the contested election and the ICC's involvement underscore just how accurate this assessment was.

IV UNDERSTANDING THE ICC AND THE KENYA ELECTION: WHOSE JUSTICE, WHOSE VOTES?

If Uhuru wins, the ICC will just disappear, but if Raila wins he'll be sure to arrest both Uhuru and Ruto. The ICC is a tool of the West, used just to oppress Africa. Why not charge President Bush and those other Western leaders instead of only targeting Africans?[90]

The I.C.C. was definitely a factor in this election, but not necessarily the factor you would expect ... It got people out. People were saying, 'They're our boys, they're our sons, we need to protect them.'[91]

The two ICC cases that largely defined Kenya's March 2013 election are unique in several ways. First, they reached the Court through the initiative of the Prosecutor, rather than through referrals either from a Rome Statute signatory government or from the UN Security Council. Second, the cases involved defendants who, having been on opposite sides of the violence that engendered the crimes for which they were accused, subsequently became political allies. Third, these defendants then used their indicted status to successfully assume control of the very government whose cooperation was deemed essential for the Court to complete its task.

In explaining this apparently counterintuitive course of events, it was argued that the Kenyan crisis involved a number of complex and somewhat contradictory objectives, including especially: halting the PEV, establishing a stable government, reaching agreement on future institutional reforms so as to prevent any similar recurrence, and deciding whether – and if so how – those responsible for the crisis should be held accountable.

In this context, it was also argued that the overwhelming 'peace imperative' in the aftermath of the 2007–2008 crisis had the unintended (and largely unrecognized) consequence of creating a gaping moral-political opportunity that eventually allowed the 'sinners' to portray themselves as 'saints' – or, at least, as 'victims' – thereby shunting to the (political) periphery questions of individual criminal responsibility, at least within their most immediate constituencies.[92]

Indeed, once the threat of accountability became a realistic possibility, it was clearly antithetical to Ruto's or his supporters' interests for him to claim any 'credit' for the slice of power that ODM achieved through the National Accord. But Odinga's former advisor on Coalition Affairs, writing in 2012 (after his acrimonious departure from this position), had no such reluctance, and could therefore decry Odinga's lack of 'gratitude' on this very issue:

> We reminded Raila [after his falling-out with Ruto by 2009] that of all the communities that had supported him in 2007, none had acted more gallantly than the Kalenjin, especially their brave youth. Many believe, with merit, that had the Kalenjin youth not fought in defence of Raila's 'stolen vote', Kibaki wouldn't have agreed to share power with him.[93] And it was universally acknowledged that if there was one person who deserved praise for mobilizing the Kalenjin youth during that period, it wasn't the ODM chairman Henry Kosgey, it was William Ruto.[94]

As for Kenyatta, the 'retaliatory' violence with which he was allegedly associated was considered necessary both to protect the thousands of fugitives who had gathered in Naivasha, as well as to 'show ODM' that their 'victims' could 'fight back.' As one local conflict analyst noted a few months before the Ocampo Six were named in December 2010:

> I have heard some people saying openly that the violence would not have stopped, had some leaders not organised, armed and sponsored their youth to attack members of other ethnic groups in Naivasha, in order to avenge the violence that was targeting [sic] their own group in the Rift Valley and elsewhere.
>
> So deep [sic] entrenched is the problem of negative ethnicity that people, including some MPs and top politicians, whose names are likely contained in Justice Waki's envelope for prosecution either in Kenya or at The Hague, are considered as heroes by a considerable number of members of their ethnic groups, mostly for participating in these horrendous acts. After all, that is why they still hold leadership positions.[95]

That such an heroic aura was enhanced by the added ingredient of ICC 'victim status' is evident in this comment to the author by a (Kikuyu) resident of Limuru outside Nairobi (shortly after having voted for 'UhuRuto'):

> In 2007–2008 Kibaki couldn't protect Kikuyus in the Rift Valley. That's because the security forces [after many years under President Moi] had so many Luo and Kalenjin. Even now, we have them here, such as the OCS [i.e., Officer-in-Charge-of-Station] just at our local police station. So we don't blame him for not being able to protect our people then.

> Uhuru went to the Rift Valley [in late January 2008] as a peace-maker, but if it was with Mungiki [who attacked ODM supporters], then it was to save his people [from the Kalenjin who were killing them], so we support that.[96]

At the same time, a striking aspect of this moral 'disconnect' was that so many failed to recognize its political implications, even among those most intently tracking unfolding events.[97] Among them was the US ambassador, who shared this confidential appraisal with his State Department colleagues at the end of 2008 (shortly after the release of the Waki Commission report in mid-October),[98] and which, as has been shown, in the event was grossly inaccurate:

> Those calling for a go-slow approach in both ODM and PNU accuse those seeking full implementation of the report as attempting to settle political scores against rivals who are potentially implicated in post-election violence. There may be some element of truth in these charges – certainly Martha Karua's 2012 presidential bid would be helped if Uhuru Kenyatta were to face trial. Likewise, Odinga (and Mudavadi) would benefit from a potential trial of William Ruto – a potential rival whose future would be severely diminished.[99]

More than two years later, in 2011, with the ICC now squarely in the picture (though prior to the confirmation of charges in January 2012) an international criminal-legal scholar similarly misread its impact on the evolving electoral scenario:

> [S]hould the Court decide to charge Ruto and Kenyatta, both will face an uphill battle in gaining the presidency. First, many commentators argue the new Constitution should be understood to prohibit anyone charged with a serious crime from running for president ... Second, should Ruto and Kenyatta nonetheless run for president, Odinga and the other presidential candidates are likely to benefit, both because charges of crimes against humanity can hardly be seen as an asset in an election campaign and because the two suspects will be busy preparing their defenses for trials in The Hague.[100]

For his part, a Kenyan commentator (writing at about the same time) reached largely the same conclusion:

> Mr Kenyatta and William Ruto, the higher education minister who has also been summoned to The Hague, have been saying they will be candidates in the 2012 presidential election when Mr Kibaki's tenure comes to an end ... An indictment by the ICC would almost certainly end these ambitions ... The foremost beneficiary would be Mr Odinga, already being prejudged by opinion polls as the 2012 presidential frontrunner.[101]

Yet some observers had been able to sense the strength of the political-communal sentiments aroused by the ICC's looming presence that this chapter has documented. These included the authors of an International Crisis Group report released shortly before the confirmation-of-charges against Kenyatta and Ruto (as well as Muthaura and Sang) were announced in January 2012:

> The ICC's decisions will continue to play a pivotal role in Kenya's political process, especially in the crucial 2012 election. The court appears cognizant that these will not be viewed by many Kenyans simply as legal decisions and that the timing and framing of proceedings and rulings will inevitably have an impact in heightening or damping down tensions.[102]

In retrospect, however, whether any such 'cognizance' could have enabled the Court to prevent an electoral outcome that was the antithesis of its purposes in Kenya is another matter.

V CONCLUSION: GLOBAL (IN)JUSTICE VS. LOCAL REALITIES

The Hague is a classic contrast between our approach to issues and how people from elsewhere treat the [sic] cases of similar magnitude.

To us, the Waki Report is something that is supposed to be resting in peace beside the Akiwumi, Ouko, among [sic] many other reports.

Our reaction to the relentlessness of the ICC probe is one of bewilderment. How could somebody be still fixated on something that happened in 2008?[103]

This chapter has explored the impact of Kenya's ICC cases on the contours and outcome of the 2013 election. In presenting both qualitative and quantitative material, it documented how divergent, contested, and shifting were the definitions of justice among both the political class and the wider Kenyan public with regard to the crisis that followed the 2007 election. As such, it has argued that, in stark contrast to the repeated claims of the two successive ICC Prosecutors, from the outset it was impossible to separate issues of criminal responsibility from those of communal-ethnic loyalty and individual political advantage.

In doing so, it has suggested that the global-individual (Western) vs. indigenous-communal (African) dichotomy presented at the outset of this chapter is inappropriate when applied to Kenya's 2008 crisis settlement. This is reflected in the fact that it constituted a 'hybrid' of both, seeking to impose individual accountability for crimes relevant to the ICC's mandate, while largely eschewing such accountability for those responsible for what triggered that violence: the failure to hold a credible election in an extremely polarized political environment.

Moreover, this chapter has illustrated that the crafting of any such trade-offs in post-conflict situations become far more complicated when those involved are powerful figures pursuing political ambitions, and whose followers harbor a deep desire not only for 'societal healing,' but also for the material benefits assumed to depend upon the ascent to high public office of these same individuals. As the African Union's Nairobi mediation team itself (naively) admitted in assessing their achievement in the wake of the 2013 election:

> Dialogue worked. It resolved differences which had been so bitter that almost destroyed the country ... However, when the dialogue ceased, baser political habits re-emerged. Kenya is the poorer for this.[104]

It has also been suggested that the ICC's entrance into Kenyan public space in the wake of the PEV was a consequence of two 'endogamous' factors. One was Kenya's increasingly competitive politics, leading to the intense polarization that triggered the PEV. Thus, even if the Kenyan state itself is a foreign 'import,' such competition was largely the product of Kenyans' own struggles, rather than any imposed agenda.[105] The other, in the aftermath of the PEV whose scale left the nation seriously shaken, is the combination of insufficient confidence in its own judiciary and a morally impaired political elite that opened the doors to external 'fire fighters.' The fact that this same elite had (almost unanimously) supported Kenya's ICC membership without imagining any Kenyan would ever 'visit' The Hague is yet another irony of this drama.[106]

In this context, it has been shown that UhuRuto successfully transformed a justice-accountability agenda into a political-electoral opportunity because of the contradictory and contested moral understandings of the crimes it sought to address. That is, each side of the PEV 'criminal' divide sought to exploit particular grievances which – however irrelevant they might be in a courtroom – became highly salient in the context of the 2013 election. These included, on Ruto's side: the historical "loss" of Kalenjin land to 'outsiders'; the perception of a stolen election; and the fact that the main beneficiary of the PEV was Odinga, in that the latter accessed at least a share of executive power, while subsequently side-lining Ruto. As for Kenyatta's side, most important was the gratitude he earned for his alleged association with (criminal) efforts to compensate for the state's security lapses that had resulted in the death and displacement of (especially) a multitude of innocent Kikuyu. Moreover, the subsequent perception that his political opponents were more than willing to exploit such 'heroism' in order to prematurely terminate his budding public career only heightened his moral stature.

As a consequence, both leaders could exploit the very cause that the 'war against impunity' had trumpeted as its own: communal/national peace, especially in the volatile Rift Valley, arguing that this could be guaranteed only by their electoral victory, but which the ICC's involvement – certain to be enhanced in the event of an Odinga presidency – would inevitably undermine.[107]

In such a context, it seems clear that the main legitimacy criterion for the ICC – that of legal and political impartiality – was inherently unachievable.[108] As the ICC's former Prosecutor himself admitted following their 2013 electoral triumph:

> [B]asically what I see in Kenya is Kenyatta and Ruto were allegedly killing each other [sic], their groups, and then they were smart. They made an alliance and they presented themselves as the reconciliation process. And Odinga, who was the other candidate said no word about post-election violence or about ICC. So the only candidate [sic] who addressed really important issues before Kenyans were Kenyatta and Ruto. And that's why people voted for them, in addition to the tribal affiliations. So I think it's a good example of how you can help although you cannot transform Kenya into Sweden.[109]

In other words, Moreno-Ocampo finally (if unconsciously) accepted what he had so vehemently denied: that the Court's efforts to pursue its remit of individual criminal responsibility was invariably enmeshed in the politics of the post-election crisis that had engendered the relevant crimes in the first place. As a local commentator had put it several years earlier, 'A conspiracy to rig [a] presidential election is not a crime against humanity.'[110] The fact that those of greatest 'interest' to the Court had viable 2013 election ambitions even absent their ICC cases only magnified such 'irrelevant' politics.

Also apparent from the foregoing is another key factor that shackled the PEV accountability agenda to politics: regime continuity, that is, in contrast to various other situations in which international 'justice' in one form or another gained entry into African post-conflict situations (e.g., Rwanda, Chad, Cote d'Ivoire), the incumbent (Kibaki) government remained in place (even if it had to cede some space to the opposition as part of the power-sharing settlement arrangement). For as Bjork and Goebertus pointed out (several years before the election), the 'window of opportunity' that such post-conflict transitional states require in order to 'come to terms with their past' never materialized in Kenya.[111] On the contrary, 'the political and economic elite that financed much of the post-election violence is still operating and has significant influence over the justice system',[112] and – they might have added – over electoral politics as well. As such, such individuals were prepared to, and successfully did, make muscular use of the state machinery to frustrate the prosecution's efforts.[113]

Meanwhile, even with the charges in the Ruto-Sang case having been vacated (in a 2-1 decision) on 5 April 2016, the ultimate outcome – and thus impact – of the ICC's involvement in Kenya continues to unfold, with considerable uncertainty. This uncertainty relates to several issues.

The first relates to national politics. Termination of the immediate ICC threat has blown a stiff breeze of relief over the Jubilee coalition, removing the 'imbalance' between its Kenyatta- and Ruto-led constituencies.[114] This, in turn, is seen as having eliminated any possibility of Ruto being replaced as Kenyatta's running-mate, while significantly enhancing their prospects for re-election. But this outcome has likewise bolstered expectations – if not demands – among Ruto's Kalenjin that, having benefited from the mobilization of his community's support for Kenyatta in two (presumably) successful contests, the latter will do the same for him come 2022 (by which time the latter will have served his constitutional maximum of two terms). It will thus take much longer to gauge the extent to which such expectations are realized, and how they are shaped by their shared-ICC experience.

The second concerns the outstanding warrants of arrest of three individuals for alleged witness interference/intimidation.[115] In unsealing the two most recent ones the Prosecutor noted that her office's efforts in Kenya '...have been methodically undermined by a relentless campaign that has targeted individuals who are perceived to be Prosecution witnesses, with threats or offers of bribes, to dissuade them from testifying or persuade witnesses to recant their prior testimony'.[116] Indeed, the charges in the Ruto-Sang case were vacated on this basis, leaving open the possibility of its re-opening, should the OTP obtain such evidence.[117]

A related issue here is the President's announcement, at a massive 'thanksgiving' rally in Nakuru following the withdrawal of the Ruto-Sang case, that 'Kenya will longer allow any other Kenyan to follow that (Hague) road'.[118] This was followed shortly by Attorney-General Githu Muigai's declaration that the government was demanding that all evidence against these individuals should be sent to him so that these cases could be heard and determined in Kenya.[119] For his part, in an apparent attempt to rebut the Government's position, CORD leader Odinga, speaking at the Requiem Mass for a recently assassinated pro-Opposition businessman Jacob Juma, identified 10 ICC witnesses he claimed had been killed in order to prevent them from testifying at

The Hague.[120] For his part, at the about the same time, Karim Khan, head of Ruto's legal team, filed a claim at the ICC against both 'prosecution intermediaries' whom he want investigated for 'witness tampering, bribery and lying' to the detriment of his client, and certain staff working in the Office of the Prosecutor for 'witness tampering, bribery and engaging in illicit sexual relations with witnesses'.[121]

Whatever the outcome of this multilayered stand-off, it suggests just how concerned both the President and his Deputy are should these individuals face prosecution at The Hague.[122]

More broadly, and even with the suspension of these last remaining Kenyan cases, the ruling coalition's top leaders – backed by its substantial parliamentary numbers – has continued to threaten withdrawal from the Rome Statute (though with somewhat less venom), largely in line with the recent position taken by the African Union (with Kenya's energetic backing).[123]

At the same time, more generally, various punitive actions have continued against those civic groups identified as most active in support of the accountability agenda deriving from the 2008 PEV.[124] Such pressure has extended to the media as well, where the country's leading media house ejected a number of its more critical journalists, including the *Nation*'s award-winning cartoonist, Godfrey Mwampembwa ('Gado'), whose ICC-based cartoons over the years had clearly rubbed the Kenyan defendants the wrong way.[125]

As for the Court itself, even prior to its arrival in Kenya, Ginsburg argued that as a young, and thus still weak, institution, it could not afford 'a spectacular failure' that its inability to bring indicted Sudanese president Omar al-Bashir to justice would represent.[126] Yet the collapse of all the Kenyan cases may be even more damaging to the evolving international justice regime, especially considering that it was on the Prosecution's own initiative that 'Kenya' was taken to The Hague in the first place (even if this was at the behest of Kenya's own Waki Commission). As Kersten noted after the fact:

> The cases against Kenyatta and Ruto have embroiled the ICC in political and legal controversy and the writing on the proverbial wall has been etched for months... They came, they saw, they tried – and they ended up empty handed, pointing accusatory fingers at Nairobi but with no one left in the dock.

He was thus left to conclude:

> Make no mistake about it – the Kenya cases at the ICC stopped being about justice a long time ago. The ICC-Kenya debacle is a story about a state and government against an international court and institution. It has been narrative about a whole bunch of things: politics, colonialism, power, diplomacy, money, reputation, messaging, etc. But it is genuinely difficult to remember

a time when it was about achieving justice for the post-election violence. If it had been that, the government of Kenya could have simply demonstrated that it was prepared to take accountability – any accountability – for the post-election violence seriously. It hasn't and it likely won't.[127]

Based on the above, some observers (including former fierce advocates of 'international justice') have concluded that even beyond the Court's future, Kenya and the region are better off without this 'sword of Damocles' hanging over the country.[128]

On the other hand, some have argued that Kenya's 'culture of impunity' has been only more deeply entrenched, which more recent revelations of extra-judicial killings appear to suggest.[129]

As such, the final 'jury' on the ultimate impact of the ICC's foray into Kenya is still very much 'out', whatever its impact was on the 2013 election.

Notes

The analysis/views contained in this chapter are those of the author.

1. Statement taken from an interview with then ICC Chief Prosecutor Luis Moreno-Ocampo; David Clarke and Matthew Tostevin, 'Interview: ICC Prosecutor Targets up to Six Kenyans', *Reuters*, 12 March 2010.
2. In retrospect, however, this expansion has been more fleeting than permanent, in both global and African terms; regarding the former context, see, Marc F. Plattner, 'Is Democracy in Decline?' (2015) 26(1) *Journal of Democracy* 5–10, and Freedom House, 'Freedom in the World 2015: Discarding Democracy – Return to the Iron Fist' (Freedom House Annual Report, 2015); for Africa, see, E. Gyimah-Boadi, 'Africa's Waning Democratic Commitment' (2015) 26(1) *Journal of Democracy* 101–113.
3. Tom Ginsburg, 'The Clash of Commitments at the International Criminal Court' (2009) 9(2) *Chicago Journal of International Law* 506.
4. According to a former (Kenyan) aide to UN Secretary-General Kofi Annan, however, during the efforts to establish the Court, a recognition of this reality 'did not mean that we should give up the effort to find a deterrence for ruthless leaders of smaller countries'; Salim Lone, 'ICC Crisis: A United Kenyan Leadership Could Win UN Security Council Deferral', *Sunday Nation*, 18 October 2015.
5. Kamari M. Clarke, *Fictions of Justice: The ICC and the Challenge of Legal Pluralism in Sub-Saharan Africa* (Cambridge: Cambridge University Press, 2009), p. 19.
6. Goran Hyden, 'Beyond Liberal Peace and Democracy: Political Settlements in Identity-Driven Polities' (Indianapolis: African Studies Annual Meetings, 2014) (revised), pp. 11–13.

7. An exchange between a Kenyan researcher (A) and a Western ambassador (Q) shortly after the election (Personal Interview, Nairobi, 13 February 2014).

8. Gabrielle Lynch, 'Electing the "Alliance of the Accused": The Success of the Jubilee Alliance in Kenya's Rift Valley' (2014) 8(1) *Journal of Eastern African Studies* 93–144. In the wake of its formation, one (Kikuyu) commentator offered that their 'Jubilee Alliance' is best described as 'a strange beast, consisting of two such different parts that had been thought to exist only in fantasy'; David Waweru, 'Kenya: The Rise of the "Uhuruto"', *African Arguments*, 5 December 2012. Indeed, according to a Jubilee campaign 'insider', the 'UhuRuto' partnership would not have been possible had two influential Kikuyu politician-businessmen (Njenga Karume and John Michuki) not both died early in 2012, given their unrelenting antipathy to Ruto for his alleged role in the PEV (Personal Interview, Nairobi, 22 April 2014).

9. In the event, once the High Court declined to bar UhuRuto two weeks before the election, they 'framed the elections as a referendum on the ICC and intimated that, if Kenyans elected them to office, they would be voting against the ICC – a view their supporters had advanced since charges had been confirmed against them in January 2012': Graca Machel and Benjanmin Mkapa, *Back from the Brink: The 2008 Mediation Process and Reforms in Kenya* (African Union Commission, 2014) 119.

10. This – in addition to the trepidation among certain elements of the Kikuyu business class regarding possible sanctions triggered by electing the ICC defendants (see below) – was the main motivation behind the effort to have him stand aside in favor of Musalia Mudavadi, but which collapsed within days of its formulation ('"Dark forces" Arm-twisted Me – Uhuru', *Capital-FM*, 18 December 2012). 'Mudavadi: How Uhuru and Ruto tricked me', *The Star*, 9–10 July 2016.

11. While certainly not the only factor that energized the Jubilee campaign (generational leadership change for a largely youthful electorate being another important one), this 'ICC factor' has been widely acknowledged. In addition to the several works already cited, see; Mahmood Mamdani, 'Why Raila Lost', *Daily Monitor*, 10 March 2013; Dayo Olopade, 'Who's Afraid of the International Criminal Court? In Kenya, the Answer Is No One at All', *The New Republic*, 9 March 2013; Aoife Kavanagh, 'The Coalition of the Accused: Whether the International Criminal Court Helped Elect Kenya's President and Deputy President', M.A. Thesis, University College, Dublin, 2014. This argument therefore challenges the interpretation of an election day exit poll finding that only 3.3% of Jubilee voters mentioned the ICC cases as a reason for their choice; James Long, Karuti Kanyinga, Karen E. Ferree, and Clark Gibson, 'Kenya's 2013

Election: Choosing Peace Over Democracy' (2013) 24(3) *Journal of Democracy* 147.

12. Assessments of the IEBC's performance that raise questions about the official presidential results include, 'The Long, Long Vote Count', *Africa Confidential,* 21 June 2013; The Carter Center, 'Observing Kenya's March 2013 National Elections: Final Report' (Atlanta, November 2013); Mars Group Kenya, 'Kenya Audit Report on 2013 Kenyan Presidential Election Results' (Nairobi, September 2013). Since the election several major IEBC officials have been forced from office while others (including the Chairman) remain under investigation for corruption; see, 'IEBC: Secrets of Poll 2013', *Nairobi Law Monthly,* December 2014.

13. Avoiding such a second round contest was essential for two main reasons. First, by all accounts most of the 4% of the vote won by Mudavadi (who contested the presidency on a third 'alliance' ticket) would have gone to Odinga in a run-off, giving the latter a considerable advantage; second, it would have been held thirty days later, on 9 April, the very day that Ruto's case was set to begin at The Hague, and the day before Kenyatta's, 10 April. As such, the psychological impact of these imminent appearances on their section of the electorate was too uncertain to countenance.

14. Several initial critiques of the Supreme Court's judgments include Wachira Maina, 'Five Key Reasons Kenya's Supreme Court Failed Crucial Election Petition Test', *The East African,* 20–26 April 2013; and Elisha Ongoya, 'Supreme Court Too Casual in "Raila Vs IEBC & Others"', *Standard Media,* 24 April 2013. For a detailed analysis, see, John Harrington and Ambreena Manji, 'Restoring Leviathan? The Kenyan Supreme Court, Constitutional Transformation and the Presidential Election of 2013' (2015) 9(2) *Journal of Eastern African Studies* 175–192.

15. Makau W. Mutua, 'Is There Too Much Ruto at President Kenyatta's Side?', *Sunday Nation,* 14 April 2013.

16. Results are taken from Ipsos SPEC (Social, Political, Economic and Cultural) Barometer (February) 2013. Figures cited from surveys prior to October 2012 are from, first, the Steadman Group and then from Synovate, which was acquired by Ipsos at that time. To avoid confusion, 'Ipsos' is used throughout this chapter. The verbatim question, through the end of 2012, was: 'If the next election were held now, aside from President Kibaki, who would you vote for, if that person is a candidate?' For the last two (2013) polls, the question was: 'Which pair of presidential and deputy-presidential candidates do you intend to vote for?' The last two surveys entail a margin-of-error of just +/–; 1.76% based on 6,000 respondents; for all others, it is +/–2.2% (based on

samples of about 2,000). For a detailed analysis of these polls, see Thomas P. Wolf, 'Getting It "Wrong" (Again)?: Wahojiwa vs. Wapiga Kura ("Respondents vs. Voters") in the 2013 Kenyan Election', in Marie-Aude Fouere, Susan Mwangi, Mildred Ndeda and Christian Thibon (eds.), *Kenya's Past As Prologue: Voters, Violence and the 2013 Kenya Election* (Nairobi: Twaweza Communications, 2014), pp. 56–76.

17. Removing the 3% of 'undecided' increases the final figures of both pairs of candidates: Kenyatta-Ruto to 46.4%, and Odinga-Musyoka to 45.4%, thus putting Jubilee's total within a range of 45.1%–47.7% (based on an error-margin of about +/– 1.3%).

18. The former include especially the Kikuyu, Embu, Meru, and Tharaka, while the main groups within the latter 'community' are the Nandi, Kipsigis, Marakwet, Keiyo, Tugen, Pokot, and Sabaot.

19. For details of this analysis, see 'Tyranny of Numbers versus Opinion Polls', *The Star*, 16 February 2013. For more detailed considerations of their joint campaigns, see Lynch, 'Electing the "Alliance of the Accused"; Thomas P. Wolf, 'International Justice vs Public Opinion? The ICC and Ethnic Polarisation in the 2013 Kenya Election' (2013) 12(1) *Journal of African Elections* 143–177. Significantly, however, a year before the election – and just after the confirmation of charges by the ICC – Kenyatta enjoyed only 60% of such expressed support from Mt. Kenya respondents (with 8% of them backing Odinga, 7% Karua, and another 16% undecided. At this time, about the same modest level of Kalenjin expressed support for Ruto: 57%, with 8% for Odinga and 15% undecided. Such figures compare with 87% backing for Odinga among his Luo; Ipsos, SPEC Barometer (CATI) Survey', 20 February 2012.

20. Ipsos, 'Political Barometer Survey', 22 February 2013.

21. Karen E. Ferree, Clark Gibson, and James D. Long, 'Voting Behavior and Electoral Irregularities in Kenya's 2013 Election' (2014) 8(1) *Journal of Eastern African Studies* 153–172. Removing from the exit poll sample respondents who refused to reveal their vote choice, the corresponding figures are: Mt. Kenya – 90% for Jubilee, Kalenjin – 84% for Jubilee, Luo – 96% for CORD, and Kamba – 77% for CORD (author's calculations). Note here that the exit poll's results matched almost exactly those of Ipsos' final survey (to which the authors make specific reference; 165).

22. Eric Kimani and Mike Owuor, '2012: The ICC Elections' (2011) 8(4) *The Nairobi Law Monthly* 50–51.

23. Under the previous constitution, only a simple plurality was required, together with at least 25% of the votes cast in five of the country's (former) eight provinces.

24. Results were reportedly manipulated at both the constituency level and at the national tallying center in Nairobi; International Crisis Group,

'Kenya in Crisis' (Africa Report no. 137, 2008), p. 8; see also Kenyans for Peace with Truth and Justice (KPTJ), 'Election Investigation: Unwelcome Evidence' (2008) 3(8) *Truth and Justice Digest* 1–12. For general background to the violence, among other reports, see Kenya National Commission of Human Rights, 'On the Brink of the Precipice: A Human Rights Account of Kenya's Post-2007 Election Violence' (Nairobi, August 2008). In his analysis of the crisis, Ajulu asserts that 'Kibaki's theft of the election came at a point when a majority of ethnic groups increasingly resented the consolidation of economic and political power by the hegemonic Kikuyu ruling elite'; Rok Ajulu, 'Kenya's 2007 Elections: Derailing Democracy Through Ethno-Regional Violence' (2008) 1(2) *Journal of African Elections* 49, an argument that Zeleza extends to a broader range of such historical and contemporary factors; Paul T. Zeleza, 'The 2007 Kenyan Elections: Holding a Nation Hostage to a Bankrupt Political Class' (2008). A somewhat contrasting analysis rests upon the perceived collapse of an 'elite consensus'; Daniel Branch and Nic Cheeseman, 'Democratization, Sequencing, and State Failure in Africa: Lessons from Kenya' (2009) 108(430) *African Affairs* 1–26.

25. The resultant 'Grand Coalition Government' gave a modicum of executive power to the official losers: ODM, led by Odinga, who took up the specially created constitutional position of prime minister; *see* 'National Accord and Reconciliation Act (2008)' (Republic of Kenya, Nairobi, Government Printer, 2008).

26. A distinction has also been made here in terms of levels of involvement-responsibility associated with the non-spontaneous categories of the PEV: the planners/organizers/financiers, the logistic coordinators, and the actual perpetrators; see Kenya National Commission of Human Rights, 'On the Brink of the Precipice', p. 18.

27. This category accounted for nearly 40% of all fatalities; 'Report of the Findings of the Commission of Inquiry Into the Post-Election Violence' (Republic of Kenya, Nairobi, Government Printer 2008) 342.

28. According to testimony adduced by the Waki Commission, this 'retaliatory' violence was considered the only way the several thousands of (mainly Kikuyu) IDPs who had sought refuge in Naivasha could be protected, and to demonstrate to the ODM side that 'their' (innocent) people, too, could suffer. According to a (Kikuyu) resident of the area: '[T]he Naivasha violence started as revenge to show other people that we could also fight and defend our own'; Kimani Njogu (ed.), *Healing the Wound: Personal Narratives About the 2007 Post-Election Violence in Kenya* (Nairobi: Twaweza Communications, 2009), p. 311. Dozens, if not hundreds, of those involved in these attacks were reportedly killed, especially from 2009, to prevent them from becoming witnesses in any criminal investigation that might ensue; Susanne D. Mueller, 'Kenya

and the International Criminal Court (ICC): Politics, the Election and the Law' (2014) 8(1) *Journal of Eastern African Studies* 33–35.

29. This was so notwithstanding Kibaki's initial refusal to engage; see Stephen Brown, 'Donor Responses to the 2008 Kenyan Crisis: Finally Getting It Right?' (2009) 27(3) *Journal of Contemporary African Studies* 394–398.

30. Given the level of alienation of most Kalenjin from the Kibaki-led government, it could be said that it was Ruto who followed his people into ODM, rather than the other way around; Gabrielle Lynch, *I Say to You: Ethnic Politics and the Kalenjin in Kenya* (Chicago: University of Chicago Press, 2011), pp. 193–201. It is also significant that in the period leading up to the ODM presidential nominations, he had supported Musyoka, not Odinga (Personal Interview, Nairobi, 12 December 2014).

31. The converse was true for the related question as to whether the PEV would have occurred 'regardless of who was announced as the winner', with 57% of those from the Mt. Kenya community in agreement, as compared with only 16% of the Luo and 11% of the Kalenjin.

32. Such correlations are based on responses to the general survey question, 'Which political party, if any, do you feel closest to?'

33. Note that this finding ignores whether respondents believed the official results were 'true.' The other most frequent (spontaneous) responses to the question were: historical land grievances, general ethnic hostility, and local political rivalries.

34. Such factors are almost universally mentioned by the dozens of victims (as well as several assailants), whose accounts may be found in, Njogu, *Healing the Wound*.

35. As was documented (by the Waki Commission and others), various localized grievances also fed into elements of this violence, especially on the opposition side after it became clear the initial goal of overturning the election was unobtainable (Musambayi Katumanga, 'Militarized Spaces and the Post-2007 Electoral Violence', in Karuti Kanyinga and Duncan Okello (eds.), *Tensions and Reversals in Democratic Transitions: The Kenya 2007 General Elections* (Nairobi: Society for International Development/Institute for Development Studies, University of Nairobi, 2010), pp. 533–561.

36. Ipsos, 'SPEC Barometer Results', 11 February 2008. Significantly, initially it was the PNU side of the Grand Coalition Government (personified best by Justice and Constitutional Affairs Minister Martha Karua, a member of the Kibaki's team in the AU mediation talks) that argued most vehemently for accountability, while the ODM side promoted amnesty (after their leaders' initial call for ICC/UN intervention; see below), as did Odinga when he insisted that 'thousands of youth who were arrested and detained … were

exercising their democratic right to demonstrate against a stolen election and therefore committed no offence'; George Wachira, Prisca Kamungi and Kalie Sillah, *Stretching the Truth: The Uncertain Promise of TRC's in Africa's Transitional Justice* (Nairobi: Nairobi Peace Initiative, 2014), p. 122; also see the Waki Report for a summary-consideration of these contrasting positions; 'Report of the Findings of the Commission of Inquiry into the Post-Election Violence in Kenya', p. 463.

37. In all surveys reported in this chapter, questions about the ICC were asked only to those respondents who could name at least one of the two main suspects (i.e., Kenyatta and Ruto). The proportion increased from just over 80% in December 2010 to around 90% in February 2013.

38. Ipsos, 'Political Barometer Results', 21 July 2009.

39. Ipsos, 'SPEC Barometer Survey Findings', 19 August 2011.

40. 'ODM sues Kibaki in The Hague', *The Standard*, 23 January 2008. According to a journalist who covered the event (a mass funeral service in Kisumu for a number of these victims), leaders simultaneously called for the deployment of UN peace-keepers to contain such violence by state agents (Personal Interview, 7 June 2015).

41. Even a year after the 2013 election, the gap between Mt. Kenya and Kalenjin survey respondents who identified 'Kikuyu in the Rift Valley' as those who 'had suffered most in the 2008 PEV' was more than 20%.

42. In addition to Kenyatta and Ruto, they included Head of Civil Service and Secretary to the Cabinet Francis Muthaura, Police Commissioner Hussein Ali (both associated with the violence in Naivasha and Nakuru in late January, as was Kenyatta), and ODM Secretary-General and Cabinet minister Henry Kosgey, along with (pro-ODM) radio journalist Joshua arap Sang. (The latter two, like Ruto, are Kalenjin.) By the time the identities of these 'main suspects' were revealed, it had become known that the envelope contained twenty names, though the remaining fourteen remained the subject of speculation; see, 'Who Is on the Waki List?', *Standard-on-Line*, 5 March 2010.

43. This same survey found that 41% were 'very confident' that those named would be convicted, while only 17% considered this eventuality 'very unlikely'; additionally, 73% supported the proposition that those named should resign from public office. At the same time, another survey determined that barely half of all Kenyans (51%) were 'satisfied' with the Ocampo list, even if 67% stated their unwillingness to vote for Kenyatta, now that he had become a criminal suspect. More worrying for him in the short term, 82% wanted all those named holding public office 'to resign or be relieved of their duties' until and unless they were found innocent; Dave Opiyo, 'Kenyans Not Ready to Re-Elect Hague Suspects: Poll', *Saturday Nation*, 18 December 2010.

44. As noted above, the final two survey samples were limited to registered voters. In five of these surveys, the question was a preference choice between the ICC, a local tribunal, or forgiveness/amnesty (December 2010, April 2011, July 2011, October 2011, and February 2013), while in the other two it was simply one of being 'happy' or 'unhappy' with the ICC's involvement (December 2011, April 2012). With the exception of the December 2010 survey, based on computer-assisted telephonic interviews (CATI), all were based on household-level , face-to-face interviews.

45. While there is no legal restriction against doing so, survey firms invariably excluded such ethnic-based correlations in their media releases. In addition to the Mt. Kenya, Kalenjin and Luhya, the other 'composite' groups used here are 'Coastals' (including the MijiKenda, the Taita and Taveta, the Pokomo, and various Swahili sub-groups), and 'Pastoralists' (including mainly the Maasai, Samburu, Borana, and Turkana).

46. Ipsos, 'Political Barometer Survey', 22 February 2013. This also appears to be the only conclusion to be drawn from the fact that (based on data from an early 2014 survey) 25% of those who expressed support for the continuation of Ruto's trial were 'certain' of his eventual acquittal (Ipsos, Unreleased Survey Data, February 2014).

47. It was reported that Nandi youth had prepared to attack Kipsigis in some areas just as the mediation talks began at the end of January 2008 (Personal Interview, Nairobi, 20 March 2015). Tensions over land, among other issues, have existed for some time, especially between the former on one side, and the latter along with the Keiyo and Tugen, on the other, these groups considered to have been unduly privileged during the years of (Tugen) President Moi's rule; Jacqueline Klopp. 'Can Moral Ethnicity Trump Political Tribalism? The Struggle for Land and Nation in Kenya' (2002) 61(2) *African Studies* 69–94. Moi's resentment of Ruto for pre-empting one of his own son's national political ambitions may also be a factor here. Statistical parameters of the relevant survey data do not allow for such (Kalenjin) sub-group analysis.

48. Insufficient trust among at least some of Ruto's backers that the state's instruments would be employed to protect him under a Kikuyu (i.e., Kenyatta) presidency appear also to have been a factor. Such concerns are evident in Ruto's reported use of local-vernacular radio stations in several Kalenjin constituencies, where incumbent ODM (i.e. pro-Odinga) MPs were especially popular, to plead with Kalenjin voters to elect his fellow-URP (United Republican Party) contestants on the grounds that 'I need to have a big team in parliament in order to convince the other side (i.e. Kenyatta's) to give me their full support

against the ICC once we are in power' (Personal Interview, Nairobi, 12 December 2014).

49. He was also among those who argued the ICC cases should be returned for domestic adjudication by Kenya's reformed/independent judiciary following the ratification the country's new constitution; 'Kalonzo Says Kenya Can Handle Suspects', *Sunday Standard*, 3 April 2010.

50. Peter Mutai and Edwin Makiche, 'Kalonzo, Ruto to Form Coalition for Easy Win', *The Standard*, 19 August 2012. After joining the Odinga campaign, he, too, expressed support for the ICC process, though primarily in terms of Kenya's need to preserve positive relations with its main (Western) development partners, avoiding any reference to 'justice' or the need to 'end impunity.'

51. Human Rights Watch, 'Turning Pebbles', 16.

52. Among several similar statements, see, David Clarke and Matthew Tostevin, 'Interview-ICC: "Prosecutor Targets Up to Six Kenyans"', *Reuters*, 12 May 2010.

53. Karanja Njoroge and Peter Opiyo, 'Bensouda Comes Face to Face with IDPs' Misery', *The Standard*, 26 October 2012.

54. Kipkoech Tanui, 'In ICC Prayers, Be Careful What You Wish For', *The Standard*, 4 August 2011.

55. 'Kenya: A Very African coup', *The Economist*, 3 January 2008. The U.S. State Department quickly acknowledged Kibaki's 'victory', but with the violence mounting, hardly a week later the United States threatened direct international intervention if the two sides did not begin negotiations immediately; Gilbert Khadiagala, 'Forty Days and Nights of Peacemaking in Kenya' (2008) 7(2) *Journal of African Elections* 11. It remains unclear whether the initial announcement reflected a preference for Kibaki, or rather, for 'stability', though the fact that even prior to the election, Ambassador Ranneberger was lobbying his colleagues in Washington to accept whatever result the ECK would announce, among other evidence, suggests that he was (at least personally) committed to a Kibaki win; Ken Flottman, '"The War for History" Part Twelve: Why Did Rannenberger and Lambsdorf React so Differently to the Election Fraud They Witnessed Together?', *Africommons Blog*, 2 February 2015.

56. Such concerns were expressed, for example, in a letter sent by US President Barack Obama to Kibaki and Odinga in April 2008, 'warning that political feuds were a risk to Kenya's stability'; Raila Odinga with Sarah Elderkin, *The Flame of Freedom* (Nairobi: Mountain Top Publishers, 2013), p. 936.

57. Personal Interview, Limuru, 4 March 2013. Interviewed on Al-Jazeera in January 2013, Kenyatta made the same argument; Daivd Opiyo,

'Kibaki, Raila Should Be on the ICC List, Says Uhuru', *Daily Nation*, 24 January 2013.

58. The fact that all three of those indicted on the ODM side of the 'ledger' were (as noted) Kalenjin – loudly leaving Odinga's 'own' Luo 'untouched' – only exacerbated this imbalance. Moreover, the eventual dropping of the case against Kosgey (following the confirmation-of-charges proceedings in January 2012), one of the few senior political figures from this community who did not part ways with Odinga, had a similar effect.

59. Wachira, Kamungi and Sillah, *Stretching the Truth*, p. 248. By contrast – and in apparent agreement with key diplomats as well the ICC Prosecutor himself – a legal scholar who has examined these cases in detail misses this basic point in asserting that: 'the only way that the ICC could demonstrate its independence and impartiality was for there to be an even number of prosecutions of both sides of the conflict'; Lionel Nichols, *The International Criminal Court and the End of Impunity in Kenya* (London: Springer, 2015), p. 113.

60. Especially relevant here was Odinga's 'pedigree' as the son of Kenya's first vice-president and opposition party leader who was eventually detained by the (first) Kenyatta government, as well as his own lengthy periods in detention under Moi. Such a history stands in contrast to Ruto's, who entered politics as a ruling party (KANU) 'youth-winger' enlisted in 1992 to ensure Moi's continuation in power after the 'flood-gates' of multi-party competition had been opened.

61. 'Refugee Leader Tortured in Nakuru', *The Nairobi Chronicle*, 25 June 2008. Other key factors were Odinga's choice of Mudavadi rather than Ruto for the position of deputy prime minister on the ODM side of the Grand Coalition Government, and Odinga's 'leading role' in overseeing the eviction of (mainly Kalenjin) 'invaders' of the Mau Forest water-tower; Barack Muluka, 'Our Nation's Dignity Will Be in the Dock Next Week with Ocampo Six', *The Standard*, 2 April 2011. Competition between Ruto and several officials associated with Odinga regarding illegal maize imports also reportedly contributed to this break; Miguna Miguna, *Peeling Back the Mask: A Quest for Justice in Kenya* (London: Gilgamesh Africa, 2012), pp. 414–418.

62. Collins W. Munyiri, 'The Raila-Ruto Conflict: The Split of ODM Is Inevitable', *The Kenyan Column*, 2 December 2008.

63. This event, in February 2010, was described as the 'point of no return.' Ruto was sacked from the cabinet in October, officially by Kibaki, but clearly with Odinga's consent. According to one observer, 'The relationship between Odinga and Ruto is now beyond salvation'; 'Cabinet Shake-Up in Kenya as William Ruto Is Sacked', *Newstime Africa*, 22 October 2010. Ruto was subsequently appointed minister for

higher education by Kibaki, but was suspended in October 2010 due to corruption charges related to a 2004 land case; 'Ruto Out of Cabinet to Face Fraud Charges', *Daily Nation*, 19 October 2010. He was acquitted on these charges in April 2011, but was formally sacked from the cabinet by Odinga on 24 August 2011 after he and colleagues had effectively moved out of ODM; 'Raila Not Different from Moi – Ruto', *Daily Motion*, 25 August 2011; Kenyatta, while resigning as finance minister after the confirmation of charges, refused to step down as deputy prime minister on the grounds that this position, like those of prime minister and president, were protected by the constitution as part of the National Accord; Oliver Musembi, 'Uhuru: I Will Not Quit as Deputy PM', *Saturday Nation*, 28 January 2012.

64. Lynch, 'Electing the "Alliance of the Accused"', 106. In addition to the US government's support for 'an end to impunity,' as articulated by its ambassador, Obama was seen by many of Odinga's opponents more as a 'fellow Luo' than as an 'American,' given his father's (Luo) origins.

65. This claim was swiftly refuted by both its High Commission in Kenya and the Foreign and Commonwealth Office in London (David Ochami, 'UK Disowns Document, Cites Grammatical Errors', *The Standard*, 9 March 2012). Even more bizarre, a British MP (Ian Paisley) joined the anti-ICC crusade by claiming the Kenya cases were instigated by the West so as to 'help Prime Minister Raila Odinga ascend to power'; Emeka-Mayaka Gekara, 'British MP Says ICC's Kenya Case Could Benefit Raila', *Daily Nation*, 17 March 2012; David Goldman, 'Raila Odinga ICC Hague Game and French Connections Cornered', *Intelligence News*, 5 April 2011.

66. Kavanagh, 'The Coalition of the Accused', 20; Wolf, 'International Justice vs Public Opinion?', 167–169.

67. Machua Koinange, 'When ICC Land Cases Became a Major Headache for Uhuru and Ruto', *Sunday Standard*, 26 May 2013. The story was quoting an unnamed Jubilee campaign official. The fact that various Western/international officials had been lecturing Kenya on the need to support the ICC process since the cases began made this 'nationalist' stance all the more potent; see Alex Ndegwa, 'UN Chief Asks Kenya to Respect the ICC Processes', *Sunday Standard*, 3 April 2011.

68. This inconsistency has also been noted by Branch, though without linking it to the subsequent ICC cases; Daniel Branch, *Kenya: Between Hope and Despair, 1963–2012* (New Haven: Yale University Press, 2011), pp. 280–281.

69. Although Kibaki had obtained about 45% of the vote, by June 2008, only 25% of all Kenyans thought he had won the election as compared with 57% for Odinga (Gallup Africa, 'The Grand Coalition Government', Public Presentation at Nairobi Serena Hotel, 8 September 2008). This

suggests that a substantial proportion of those who had voted for the former six months earlier had come to believe he had lost.

70. Johann Kriegler, a retired South African judge, and Philip Waki, a serving Kenyan judge, chaired each, respectively. Among the IREC's Terms of Reference was to examine the processes of 'Vote-tallying and -counting to assess the integrity of the results of the entire election with special attention to the presidential contest'; 'Report of the Independent Review Commission' (Republic of Kenya, Nairobi, Government Printer, 2008), p. 3. A critical contrast between these two commissions was that unlike the latter, the former included four members directly appointed by the rival political parties (two each). As such, according to a lawyer who followed the matter closely, 'the most radical thing 'Kriegler' could have done was to recommend that the ECK be disbanded; imposing any individual responsibility for "election-theft" was never going to be a realistic option' (Personal Interview, Nairobi, 1 July 2015). Such limitations are also implied in a detailed evaluation of its work; Transparency International-Kenya, 'The Kriegler Commission: An Audit of Its Implementation' (Nairobi, 2012), pp. 10–11.

71. Miguna, *Peeling Back the Mask*, pp. 215–221. In February 2008, the US embassy in Nairobi identified three ECK commissioners against whom it recommended visa bans for complicity in election theft; Wikileaks Nairobi Cable, 'Kenya: More Visa Warning Letters Sent', 2 March 2011

72. As one local governance group concluded in its review of the Kriegler Commission report after its release: '[It] is an inadequate job that attempts to cover up offenses committed by people who deserve no such protection'; see Kenyans for Peace with Truth and Justice (KPTJ), 'Unfinished Business' (2008) 4(8) *Truth & Justice Digest* 1–8. The International Republican Institute exit poll conducted under the supervision of a team of American academics gave Odinga a definitive 6% win (Clark C. Gibson and James Long, 'The Presidential and Parliamentary Elections in Kenya, December 2007' (2009) 28(3) *Electoral Studies* 497–502). The results were embargoed for six months, however, reportedly at the behest of US government officials, starting with its ambassador in Nairobi; Ken Flottman, 'Ocampo, the Donors and "The Presumption of Arrogance"; A Story of Babes in the Woods of Mt. Kenya?', *Africommons*, 10 December 2014. The Kriegler Commission did receive testimony from the two academics involved, but drew no firm conclusions from it; 'Report of the Independent Review Commission', p. 137.

73. Kenya had ratified the Rome Statute in 2005, and made it part of the nation's judiciary through passage of the International Crimes Act of 2008.

74. As was the case with regard to the election's integrity, these external actors were not in agreement at all subsequent stages of the crisis. For example, prior to the start of the negotiations, the Europeans were more sympathetic to Odinga's insistence on revisiting the election results than were the Americans, with British prime minister Gordon Brown particularly supportive on this: Miguna, *Peeling Back the Mask*, p. 216.

75. Particular aspects of Kenya's impunity history are found in: Nichols, *The International Criminal Court and the End of Impunity in Kenya*, pp. 47–67; Susanne D. Mueller, 'The Political Economy of Kenya's Crisis' (2008) 2(2) *Journal of Eastern African Studies* 185–210; UN Human Rights Council, Mission to Kenya: 'Report of the Special Rapporteur on Extrajudicial, Summary or Arbitrary Executions', UN Doc. A/HRC/14/24/Add.6, 26 May 2009.

76. Ben Rawlence, 'Amnesty Is a Red Herring', *The Standard*, 16 June 2008. Whether Rawlence actually believed that 'the rule of law' could ever trump politics on this issue is unclear.

77. Note, however, his failure to acknowledge the overtly criminal aspects of PEV, let alone any involvement of 'politicians' in it.

78. 'ODM Says No Reconciliation without Amnesty First, Raila Answers Kibaki', *The Standard*, 3 June 2008.

79. It was subsequently noted (with considerable irony) that it was primarily the mobilization of MPs allied to Kenyatta and Ruto who ensured that the 'Hague' option won the day, based on the slogan 'Don't be vague, let's go to The Hague'; Stephen Brown and Chandra. L. Sriram, 'The Big Fish Won't Fry Themselves: Criminal Accountability for Post-Election Violence in Kenya' (2012) 111(443) *African Affairs* 253; see also, Elderkin, *The Flame of Freedom*, pp. 891–894. This is a position that Ruto defended openly at the time; 'Ruto: Why I Prefer The Hague Route', *Sunday Nation*, 22 February 2009.

80. Kofi Annan, quoted in Ben Agina, 'Ocampo to Open Waki Envelope', *The Standard*, 11 July 2009.

81. Michael Ranneberger (US ambassador) 'The Reform Agenda and Kenya's Historic Opportunity' (Speech to the Law Society of Kenya, Nairobi, 30 October 2009).

82. Well after the election, Ruto credited Eldoret (Kalenjin) Catholic Bishop Cornelius Korir for having made it possible for him and Kenyatta 'to work together' prior to the 2013 election; Dennis Lubanga, 'Moi and DP Meet at Bishop Korir's Silver Jubilee Celebrations', *Sunday Nation*, 7 June 2015.

83. For example, USAID's Office of Transition Initiative's (OTI) program allocated some US$3.5m in 110 grants during 2008–2013 to various religious and other non-governmental organizations such 'peace-building' efforts in the Rift Valley, the average grant being about

US$32,000 (Personal Communication, Senior Official, USAID/OTI Office, Nairobi, 8 September 2013). More broadly, the US Congress approved half of the Obama administration's request of US$38m for 'democracy and reconciliation programs' in Kenya, see Friends Committee of National Legislation, 'Kenya: Temporary Ceasefire or Lasting Peace?' (Policy Brief, September 2009).

84. Maupeu has termed such developments as the 'Pentecostalization' of the ICC issue; Herve Maupeu, 'The ICC, God, and the 2013 Kenyan General Elections', in Marie-Aude Fouere, Susan Mwangi, Mildred Ndeda and Christian Thibon (eds.), *Kenya's Past as Prologue: Voters, Violence and the 2013 Kenya Election* (Nairobi: Twaweza Communications, 2014), pp. 27–41.

85. George Kegoro, *On the Brink: Kenya and the International Criminal Court's Fractious Relationship: Africa and the International Criminal Court* (Nairobi: Heinrich Boll Foundation, 2011), p. 19. Various earlier highly symbolic indications of resistance to the ICC's version of accountability could be cited, including especially the invitation to/ appearance of ICC-indictee President Omar al-Bashir of Sudan at the promulgation ceremony of Kenya's new constitution in August 2010 – in blatant violation of Kenya's Treaty of Rome commitments – which only became public upon al-Bashir's arrival on the day; Xan Rice, 'Omar al-Bashir Tarnishes Kenya's Landmark Day', *The Guardian*, 27 August 2010. Earlier that year, Vice-President Musyoka had attended al-Bashir's inauguration ceremony in Khartoum. In this regard, it came as no surprise that Kibaki, following the confirmation of charges against four of the original six suspects, refused to remove his two appointees (Kenyatta and Muthaura) from their positions of deputy prime minister and secretary to the cabinet/head of civil service. Such support was perceived by some as not just an affirmation of personal loyalty, but also a tell-tale rejection of the ICC-led accountability process. Closer to the election, such signals continued in abundance, among them Annan's failure to secure a meeting with Kibaki during a three-day visit to assess the reform process in mid-October 2012; Bernard Namunane, 'Annan Warns over ICC Suspects' Bids', *Daily Nation*, 11 October 2012.

86. By the end of 2011, only two minor cases had been successfully prosecuted; Human Rights Watch, 'Turning Pebbles', p. 25. As of January 2012, according to Nichols, fewer than 3% of the 9,000 original PEV files had led to convictions, most of these for minor offenses, and with most the offenders having been discharged; Nichols, *The International Criminal Court and the End of Impunity in Kenya*, p. 28. A year later, a local NGO that had tracked this issue issued concluded that: 'Despite numerous claims made by various government officials ... there has been almost no accountability for PEV crimes ... [and] at present there appears to be

no feasible and credible plan on dealing with the files and cases relating to the PEV'; KPTJ and Kenya Human Rights Commission, 'Securing Justice: Establishing a Domestic Mechanism for the 2007/8 Post-Election Violence in Kenya' (Nairobi, 2013), p. 8. Post-election, in February 2014 the Director of Public Prosecutions disclosed that he had closed some 4,000 files of PEV suspects due to insufficient evidence; 'Most PEV Cases Cannot Be Prosecuted – Tobiko', *The Star*, 6 February 2014.

87. According to one humanitarian agency, four years later only about half of the 660,000 who were initially displaced had either been able to return to their homes or had been resettled; Peter Kahare, 'Kenya: Four Years on, IDPs Remain in Camps', *IPS News*, 24 January 2012.

88. Ibrahim Oruko and Dominic Wabala, 'Imanyara Forced to Say Uhuru Slogan', *The Star*, 19 April 2012.

89. Godwin Murunga, 'Spontaneous or Premeditated? Post-Election Violence in Kenya' (Nordiska Afrikainstitutet Discussion Paper 57, 2011), p. 48.

90. Personal Interview, Limuru, 4 March 2013. Moreno-Ocampo later (in January 2014) revealed that he had resisted "pressure from certain diplomats" to ensure that Kenyatta and Ruto were excluded from the election, insisting that the Kenyan judiciary, not he, would make that decision since 'that was not my job'; Walter Menya, 'Ocampo: Envoys Wanted Uhuru and Ruto Out of Polls', *Daily Nation*, 7 February 2014.

91. Maina Kiai as quoted in: Jeffrey Gettleman, 'Leader of Vote Count in Kenya Faces U.S. with Tough Choices', *New York Times*, 7 March 2013.

92. Several years after the election, KANU Secretary-General Nick Salat described his Kalenjin community's support for Ruto in the 2013 election as 'protective,' adding that: it 'was about uniting the two leaders who were before the ICC. It was like saying we are giving you this weapon [of state power] to go and wriggle yourself out'; Julius Sigei and Justus Wanga, 'Ruto's Hague Case Fueling Campaigns in Rift, Say Analysts', *Saturday Nation*, 28 March 2015.

93. In a recent survey, 76% expressed this view, with a significantly higher figure for Nairobi (89%), where people have the greatest access to information and thus can most closely follow such national issues (Ipsos, 'National Issues Survey', September 2013).

94. Miguna, *Peeling Back the Mask*, p. 300. Two years after becoming deputy president, Ruto himself came close to this position, asserting at a public rally (in Odinga's Nyanza region) that 'I was nearly locked up because of my support for Raila in 2007' (thus appealing for the latter's support for his own presumed presidential bid in 2022); Nelcon Odhiambo, 'Ruto: My Support for Raila Sent Me to ICC', *Daily Nation*, 29 June 2015.

95. Mwandawiro Mghanga, 'Usipoziba Ufa Utajenga Ukuta: Land, Elections and Conflicts in Kenya's Coast Province' (Nairobi: Heinrich Boll Foundation, 2010), p. 87. Given that Kenyatta had struggled to

become his 'own man' ever since Moi had imposed him as the ruling
party's (unsuccessful) presidential candidate to succeed him in the 2002
election, the accrual of such 'heroic' status clearly did him no
reputational harm.

96. Personal Interview, Limuru, 4 March 2013.

97. Significantly, with one partial exception (Brown, 'Donor Responses') not
one of the many laudatory analyses of the crisis-settlement negotiations
facilitated by Annan and his team of Eminent African Persons notes
this failure to impose any accountability on those responsible for the
election (among them, beyond the accounts already cited: Monica
K. Juma, 'African Mediation of the Post-2007 Kenya Election Crisis'
(2009) 27(3) *Journal of Contemporary African Studies* 407–430; Elisabeth
Lindenmayer and Josie L. Kaye, 'A Choice for Peace? The Story of Forty
One Days of Mediation in Kenya' (New York: International Peace
Institute, 2009); Roger Cohen, 'How Kofi Annan Rescued Kenya',
The New York Review of Books, 14 August 2008; Makumi Mwagiru,
'The Water's Edge: Mediation of Violent Electoral Conflict in Kenya'
(Nairobi: Institute of Diplomacy and International Studies, 2008);
Khaled M. Aman, 'Mediation: A Viable Mechanism in Africa's
Political Crisis – A Case Study of Kenya's Post-Election Crisis 2008'
(Asia Pacific Mediation Forum, 2008); Khadiagala, 'Forty Days and
Nights of Peacemaking in Kenya', 4–32; Human Rights Watch, 'Ballots
to Bullets: Organized Political Violence and Kenya's Crisis of
Governance' (New York, 2008).

98. It was presented to the two principals on 15 October, and submitted to
parliament on 4 December.

99. Wikileaks Cables Nairobi 0551: 'Post-Election Violence Commission
Report: Politicians Divided Over Implementation', 4 November 2008.

100. Thomas Obel Hansen, 'Transitional Justice in Kenya? An Assessment of
the Accountability Process in Light of Domestic Politics and Security
Concerns' (2011) 42(1) *California Western International Law
Journal* 1–35.

101. Gitau Warigi, 'Who Gains from Kenya's ICC Cases?', *BBC World Africa*,
7 April 2011. Presciently, however, Warigi went on to suggest that 'the ICC
matter is hurting the ODM leader almost as much … Those who are
backing Mr Ruto have been driven into a marriage of convenience with
the PNU, and specifically Mr Kenyatta, with the sole intention of stopping
the prime minister's political ambitions dead in their tracks.' Even more
forthright was another commentator's prediction that the ICC was likely
to produce a 'surprise' election result (Charles Onyango-Obbo, 'Why
Kenya Election 2012 Could Surprise Us All', *The East African*, 3 March
2012), though not as specific as the Ipsos public opinion researcher who
noted at about the same time how deftly the main ICC suspects had been

'manipulating' their core constituencies, in party by claiming 'collusion between our rivals and the ICC to have us prosecuted so that they can have the presidency in 2012'; 'Ruling on "Kenya 6" May Affect Upcoming Election', *VOA News*, 16 January 2012.

102. International Crisis Group, 'Kenya: Impact of the ICC Proceedings' (Policy Briefing No. 84, 9 January 2012).

103. Willy K. Rotich, 'Kenyans Suffer from an Ambivalence that May Soon Stymie the New Order', *Daily Nation*, 14 December 2010. The Akiwumi and Ouko reports, both the product of official investigations, examined the 'ethnic clashes' associated with the 1992 and 1997 elections, and the assassination of Foreign Affairs Minister Robert Ouko in 1990, respectively. Neither led to prosecutions, let alone convictions, for either the initial crimes or their subsequent cover-ups.

104. Machel and Mkapa, *Back from the Brink*, p. 244.

105. Two key structural factors contributing to such intensely competitive politics are the country's first-past-the-post electoral system, and the immense powers of the executive in a presidential system, only modestly diluted by the new constitution promulgated in 2010.

106. As one Kenyan MP in the previous parliament admitted, 'The last thing we ever imagined when we enacted that bill [to domesticate the Rome Statute] was that one day it would be used against any of our own leaders!' (Personal Interview, Nairobi, 12 April 2013).

107. Such is evident from the finding of a 2013 post-election survey that the vast majority would prefer 'the preservation of peace' as opposed to 'the rightful winner' being declared (85% vs. 13%) if it was necessary to choose between these two presumably universal public goods. See James Long, Karuti Kanyinga, Karen E. Ferree, and Clark Gibson, 'Kenya's 2013 Election: Choosing Peace over Democracy' (2013) 24(3) *Journal of Democracy* 151.

108. Abraham Korir Sing'Oei, 'The ICC as Arbiter in Kenya's Postelectoral Violence' (2010) 19(15) *Minnesota Journal of International Law Online*. Sing'Oei, a Kenyan, currently serves as a political-constitutional adviser to Deputy President Ruto.

109. Walter Menya, 'Ocampo: Envoys Wanted Uhuru and Ruto Out of Polls', *Daily Nation*, 7 February 2014.

110. Okech Kendo, 'It's Time to End Impunity', *The Standard*, 16 December 2010. Ruto initially took the same position, arguing that 'those who allegedly rigged elections by paying and using the disbanded Electoral Commission should be the first to be taken to The Hague'; 'Who Is in the ICC List?', *The Standard*, 5 March 2010.

111. The same analysis has been applied to the immunity that former President Daniel arap Moi has enjoyed in retirement, see, Thomas P. Wolf, 'Immunity or Accountability?: Daniel Toroitich arap Moi,

Kenya's First Retired President', in Roger Southall and Henning Melber (eds.), *Legacies of Power: Leadership Change and Former Presidents in African Politics* (HSRC Press/Nordic Africa Institute, Cape Town/ Uppsala, 2006), pp. 197–232.

112. Christine Bjork and Juanita Goebertus, 'Complementarity in Action: The Role of Civil Society and the ICC in Rule of Law Strengthening in Kenya' (2011) 14(1) *Yale Human Rights and Development Journal* 222.

113. As documented by Nichols, the Kenya government engaged in various 'foreign affairs facades,' 'promising to cooperate with the Prosecution's investigations while simultaneously obstructing them,' of which he identified four distinct types, in addition to the use of targeted bribery, intimidation, and mass disappearances that soon created a 'climate of fear' on both sides of the PEV divide among those who were prepared to cooperate with the Court; Nichols, *The International Criminal Court and the End of Impunity in Kenya*, pp. 165–168. In this connection, he notes that 'senior leaders with blood on their hands were simply not prepared to commit political suicide by supporting the prosecution of themselves or their allies' (p. 156).

114. As one national newspaper had suggested prior to this development, 'The political union between [Kenyatta and Ruto] built on the common bond of [the] ICC cases was all rosy until the President's case was dropped. Since then, a silent war has erupted...'; Mwaniki Munuhe, 'Fresh Cracks Jolt Uhuru, Ruto Union', *The Standard*, 20 September 2015. The prospect of such a fall-out (from which the Opposition hoped to reap, especially if Ruto was convicted, helps explain why 50 Opposition MPs were among the 190 (out of 349, and including ODM's party Chairman and Chief Whip) who signed the Kenya government's request to the UN Security Council for a deferral 'to allow for an independent investigation into the credibility of prosecution witnesses'; Kamau Muthoni and Fred Makana, 'Jubilee and Cord MPs Petition UN to stop DP Ruto Trial at The Hague', *The Standard*, 3 November 2015.

115. The first of which, for former journalist Walter Barasa, was issued in 2013, and the case has reached the Court of Appeal; the other two were unsealed in 2015.

116. OTP, Statement of the Prosecutor of the International Criminal Court, Fatou Bensouda, regarding the unsealing of Arrest Warrants in the Kenya situation, 10 September 2015. Moreover, after the vacation of charges, it was revealed that the OTP was investigating seven additional Kenyans, including a Cabinet Secretary, for possible indictments of a similar nature; 'ICC Probes Seven Kenyans, CS for Witness Tampering', *The Star*, 10 May 2016.

117. One of the two judges felt there was enough evidence to require continuation of the case, thus requiring the Defense to cross-examine witnesses. While the opinions of other two judges prevailed, both declared that the lack of sufficient evidence was in part a consequence of interference with witnesses and state non-cooperation; indeed, Presiding Judge Presiding Judge Chile Eboe-Osuji declared a mistrial on that basis, leaving open the possibility of a re-opening of the case should sufficient evidence become available. See, Tom Maliti, 'Why ICC Judges Did Not Acquit Ruto and Sang', *International Justice Monitor*, 6 April 2016. To some, however, this reasoning was brimming with irony, since the very alleged interference with the case by those clearing acting on the defendants' behalf was responsible for 'setting them free'; see, Mark Kersten, 'A missed trial in The Hague or a mistrial? The end of the ICC cases against Ruto and Sang', 6 April 2016.

118. 'Uhuru Cuts Off Kenya from Hague Court', *Sunday Nation*, 17 April 2016. This came despite a threat issued immediately by the ICC's spokesman should Kenya cease cooperation with the Court; 'ICC Spells Out Consequences of Cutting Ties after Uhuru Threat', *Daily Nation*, 19 April 2016. Such 'consequences' were identified as (unspecified) 'punishment' by the Assembly of States Parties.

119. 'ICC "Witness Fixers" Should Be Tried in Kenya, AG Githu Muigai Says', *Daily Nation*, 21 April 2016.

120. 'Raila Names 10 Killed ICC Witnesses', *Nairobi News*, 12 May 2016. Another political figure, Cyrus Jirongo, claimed Juma had been killed by 'the same people' who killed Meshack Yebei, one of ten on Odinga's list.

121. Walter Menya, 'DP Ruto's Lawyers Go after ICC Staff, Witnesses', *Daily Nation*, 4 May 2016. The ICC subsequently rejected Khan's demand for an independent prosecutor to be appointed to investigate his claims; 'Judges reject Ruto attack on Bensouda's witnesses', Journalists for Justice, 4 July 2016.

122. Indeed, it was subsequently reported that the ICC was investigating seven other individuals – including a Cabinet Secretary – for similar witness interference; 'ICC Probes Seven Kenyans, CS, for Witness Tampering', *The Star*, 10 May 2016.

123. Jemima Kariri and Thobeka Mayekiso, 'International Criminal Justice in Africa: It's Not All about the ICC', *ISS Today*, 21 February 2014; Kwendo Opanga, 'How Nairobi Gears to Lead Africa Out of ICC', *The Nation*, 7 February 2015. As the former writers put it, 'The AU's anti-ICC stance has resulted in further disillusionment for victims of these crimes and has reinforced perceptions of a culture of impunity on the continent.' At the AU Heads of State summit in late January 2015, Kenyatta went even further, declaring that the ICC 'poses a grave risk to peace and security not only in Africa, but to the whole world';

Sophiah Muthoni, '11 Countries Have Backed African International Crimes Court, Says Amina Mohammed', *The Standard*, 3 February 2015.

124. Freedom House, 'When Civil Society Is Attacked, Kenya's Democracy Is Imperiled', 8 January 2016; Human Rights Watch, 'Kenya: Rights Defenders Under Attack', *Human Rights Watch News*, 4 October 2015. To a large degree, this has been the backlash-consequence of the optimism and energy with which many of these groups promoted the ICC's entrance and efforts in Kenya, having long since given up on the national justice system to confront impunity; see, Bjork and Goebertus, 'Complementarity in Action: The Role of Civil Society and the ICC in Rule of Law Strengthening in Kenya' (2011) 14 *Yale Human Rights and Development Law Journal* 205–229.

125. See, Catrina Stewart, 'Aga Khan Accused of Squeezing Kenya Press Freedom after Newspaper Sacks Cartoonist and Journalists', *The Independent*, 20 March 2016.

126. Ginsburg, 'The Clash of Commitments at the International Criminal Court', p. 514.

127. Kersten, 'A Missed Trial in The Hague or a Mistrial? The End of the ICC Cases against Ruto and Sang', 6 April 2016.

128. Lone, 'ICC Crisis: A United Kenyan Leadership Could Win UN Security Council Deferral'.

129. P. Anyang'-Nyong'o, 'Extrajudicial murders and our institutionalised impunity', *The Star*, 9–10 July 2016.

11

The ICC in the Democratic Republic of Congo
A Decade of Partnership and Antagonism

Patryk I. Labuda

I INTRODUCTION

This chapter analyses the International Criminal Court's (ICC) first decade in the Democratic Republic of Congo (DRC). Against the backdrop of rising tensions between Africa and the ICC, it focuses on the pursuit of accountability for international crimes at the national level and how international criminal justice has influenced domestic law and politics. Although the Congolese state has been one of the most active ICC States Parties, ending impunity in the DRC remains an elusive goal. Despite years of international support, the political establishment struggles to reform the national judicial system and the prospect of accountability for past crimes continues to generate controversy.[1]

These developments are examined through the lens of the ICC's jurisdictional regime, which allocates judicial powers between the Court and national jurisdictions.[2] In accordance with complementarity, as the system is conventionally known, states have priority to prosecute international crimes, while the ICC intervenes as a court of last resort. Premised on the expectation that the domestic legal systems of ICC States Parties will adjust to international standards, complementarity produces a range of interactions between the ICC and domestic judicial authorities in states emerging from conflict. By examining the ICC's involvement in the DRC, this chapter situates these interactions within the broader debate about the efficacy of international criminal law and the universality of its principles and mechanisms.[3]

The ICC's impact in the DRC is studied from three angles. The chapter begins with the Office of the Prosecutor's (OTP) prosecutorial strategy and the ICC's influence on Congolese politics, most notably the relationship

between the Bosco Ntaganda indictment and peace-making as well as the
Congolese government's refusal to enforce an ICC arrest warrant against
Omar al-Bashir, the Sudanese president. The chapter then explores the
benefits and drawbacks of national trials in domesticating international justice, before turning to the political stakes of enacting domestic judicial reform
through Rome Statute implementing legislation and a hybrid tribunal for
past atrocities. The chapter argues that the ICC's intervention in the DRC is
best understood as a continuing struggle between the institutional interests
of international actors and the state-building imperatives of the Congolese
government. The outcome has been a decade of shifting alliances and recurring contestation between the Congolese state, the ICC, and local and regional actors.

II BACKGROUND

Although the DRC has experienced recurring episodes of violence in the last
fifty years, the downfall of Joseph-Desiré Mobutu in 1997 inaugurated an
especially brutal period in the country's history.[4] Estimates suggest millions
of people may have died during the first and second 'Congo Wars'
(1997–2003).[5] Despite a succession of peace agreements and elections held
in 2006 and 2011 respectively, conflict persists in the volatile east where an
estimated three dozen rebel groups operate across five provinces.[6]

Present in the DRC for the quasi-entirety of its short institutional history,
the ICC's investigations have led to: (1) the trials of Thomas Lubanga (convicted for enlisting and conscripting child soldiers, sentenced to fourteen years
imprisonment), Mathieu Ngudjolo (acquitted), and Germain Katanga (convicted on one count of crimes against humanity and four counts of war
crimes); (2) the on-going trial of Bosco Ntaganda (on thirteen counts of war
crimes and five counts of crimes against humanity); (3) the indictment of
Callixte Mbarushimana (no charges were upheld at the pre-trial stage); and (4)
an arrest warrant for Sylvestre Mudacumura on nine counts of war crimes (the
suspect has not been apprehended).[7] At the time of writing, the ICC continues
to operate in the country, with no indication that it will withdraw in the near
future.[8]

The ICC's involvement in the DRC, as in any other 'situation' country, is
defined and circumscribed by the Court's jurisdictional powers.[9] Codified in
the Rome Statute, complementarity is the rule that allocates jurisdiction
between the ICC and national legal systems.[10] In accordance with the
Statute, domestic courts have priority to enforce international criminal law,
while the ICC exercises 'complementary' jurisdiction.[11] Put differently, only if

national authorities fail to conduct genuine domestic proceedings may the ICC step in and investigate cases on the territory of a State Party.[12]

Although it forms part of the ICC's admissibility criteria for determining jurisdiction in individual *cases*, complementarity is frequently viewed as a *systemic* relationship between the ICC and domestic judicial systems.[13] In this broader sense, complementarity does not refer to a dispute over who – the ICC or a national court – should conduct a specific trial. Rather, it describes a system where the ICC monitors, assesses, and intervenes if and when a national judicial system fails to discharge its duties.[14] Depending on the relations between the international and national levels, this arrangement can range from antagonistic (when the two levels disagree about their respective powers) to accommodating (when the two levels agree and share their respective powers) and even cooperative (when the two levels choose to assist each other).[15]

This chapter argues that the ICC's investigations in the DRC have exposed conflicting imperatives between the international community's drive for retributive justice and the Congolese government's desire to prevent a relapse into conflict. During the ICC's first decade in the country, the two sides have sought to carve out a sphere of influence, without unduly undermining their counterpart. Although their relationship has produced antagonism at various times, the ICC and the Congolese authorities have, on the whole, managed to seek out accommodation, if not always cooperation.[16]

III DEFINING AND REDEFINING COMPLEMENTARITY: PARTNERSHIP OR CONFLICT?

Three snapshots of the ICC's work in the DRC illustrate the fluctuating relationship between the Court and the Congolese authorities. Firstly, the OTP's prosecutorial strategy reveals the broader institutional and political stakes of the ICC's intervention in the country. Secondly, the case against Ntaganda underscores the difficulty of reconciling accountability for past international crimes with domestic peace for the future. Thirdly, the Congolese government's refusal to arrest the Sudanese president, Omar al-Bashir, exposes the regional implications of the ICC's investigations on the African continent.

The ICC's initial intervention in the DRC resulted from a convergence of interests. On the one hand, the newly established Court needed cases to justify its existence, on the other the Congolese transitional government (established in 2003, after several years of negotiations) had little appetite for politically sensitive trials.[17] Elected only months after President Kabila ratified the Rome

Statute, the ICC's first Prosecutor actively encouraged the Congolese authorities to let him intervene in the DRC.[18] In justifying his referral to the ICC in
2004, Kabila argued that 'the competent authorities are unfortunately not
capable of investigating [international] crimes or undertaking the required
inquiries without the participation of the International Criminal Court'.[19]

This political marriage of convenience was later translated into a concrete
legal plan of action. Based on 'a consensual division of labour', the OTP
'would contribute by prosecuting the leaders who bear the greatest responsibility [while] national authorities, with the assistance of the international
community, could implement appropriate mechanisms to address other
responsible individuals'.[20] Reflecting the first Prosecutor's vision of complementarity as a system in which the OTP 'encourages' rather than 'competes'
with states for cases,[21] the agreement suggested that the international community would support the Congolese legal system in exchange for cooperation.

Although compelling in the abstract, this division of labour produced mixed
results. To date, the OTP has restricted its investigations to individuals
opposed to the government of President Kabila, who has remained in power
since 2001. Though credible reports link the Congolese military to atrocities,
none of the cases before the ICC involves officials from the state security
apparatus.[22] The OTP's focus on rebels and militias to the exclusion of state-
sponsored criminality has given rise to accusations of partiality and politicisa-
tion, exposing the ICC's dependence on the support of states in whose territory
it conducts investigations.[23]

The OTP's narrow prosecutorial strategy has also proved problematic.
Assuming that carefully tailored charges relating to 'lesser' human rights
violations would produce easy convictions and thereby establish the ICC's
credentials in the DRC, the first Prosecutor declined to charge suspects with
serious but hard-to-substantiate crimes.[24] For instance, Thomas Lubanga was
charged with enlisting and conscripting child soldiers, even though the
Congolese authorities had previously brought charges of genocide and crimes
against humanity within the domestic judicial system.[25] The Prosecutor's
strategy backfired when, contrary to expectations, the Lubanga and Katanga/
Ngudjolo trials took many years to bring to fruition and produced results that
many victims considered underwhelming.[26]

The geographic spread of the ICC's intervention in the DRC has generated
controversy as well. To date, the OTP's investigations revolve around Ituri
province, a small area in the northeast of the country, where most of the ICC's
cases – Lubanga, Ngudjolo, Chui, and Ntaganda – originate. Until recently,
the Prosecutor was reluctant to intervene in North and South Kivu, though
fighting has concentrated in those two regions in the past decade. Some have

suggested that the Prosecutor's focus on Ituri, where Kabila's supporters are less implicated in the commission of crimes, was convenient for both the ICC and the Congolese government.[27] Paradoxically, however, focusing on Ituri meant that the OTP was intervening in an area with better judicial institutions than other parts of the country and, therefore, less in need of the ICC's support.[28]

The OTP's prosecutorial strategy in the DRC, especially during the tenure of the first Prosecutor, Luis Moreno Ocampo, has received much criticism in recent years.[29] Phil Clark argues that Ocampo 'chased cases' out of self-interest, favouring state appeasement over the ICC's legitimacy among local actors.[30] Embracing a victim-oriented perspective, Pascal Kambale deplores the premature abandonment of the OTP's consensual division of labour.[31] Both Clark and Kambale suggest that the Prosecutor reneged on his obligations to local actors so that the ICC's parallel investigations in Uganda would not be jeopardised.[32] Marlies Glasius takes a slightly different view, highlighting the inherent contradiction between the lofty aims of complementarity and the reality of ICC interventions, which require the OTP to operate where judicial systems are, by definition, ill-suited to adjudicating complex international crimes.[33]

Whatever the merits of these arguments, it is important to differentiate between the OTP's *accommodation* of Congolese state interests and genuine international–national *cooperation* in prosecuting international crimes. The ICC has undoubtedly served the interests of the Kabila government and, by the same token, the Congolese authorities have facilitated the OTP's limited investigations in the country. However, a mix of political and logistical obstacles has prevented a deeper, cooperative pursuit of accountability at the national level. Contrary to the first Prosecutor's own assurances, charges against high-ranking figures and foreigners suspected of fomenting violence from abroad never materialised.[34] Instead, the OTP's investigations have focused on a handful of low- and mid-level perpetrators, such as Lubanga or Ngudjolo. There are also reports that cooperation between the ICC and the Congolese authorities has been a 'one-way street', with information flowing in one direction, from the DRC to The Hague.[35]

The case of Bosco Ntaganda, a militia leader of several Rwandan-backed groups in eastern Congo, brings many of these tensions into sharp focus. The ICC's arrest warrant against Ntaganda remained sealed until April 2008, by which time he had left Ituri and become a prominent player in the Congres National pour la Defense du Peuple (CNDP), a rebel movement operating in North Kivu. After a period of intense hostilities in 2009, Ntaganda and his soldiers were reintegrated into the regular Congolese army (FARDC) as part of a peace agreement that led to the dissolution of the CNDP. The Congolese government had made a Faustian pact: suppressing the rebellion would come at the price of making Ntaganda a general in its armed forces.[36]

Shortly thereafter, the Ntaganda arrest warrant became the object of diplomatic wrangling between the Congolese authorities and various international actors, including the ICC, the United Nations, and civil society groups.[37] Despite the Congolese government's twin policies of 'la lutte contre l'impunité' ('fight against impunity') and 'tolerance zéro pour l'impunité' ('zero tolerance for impunity'), Ntaganda's integration into the state security structure effectively shielded him from prosecution by the military judicial system.[38] The international community's calls for his arrest clashed with Kabila's plans to secure peace in North Kivu. Between 2009 and 2012, the Ministry of Justice and Human Rights (MoJ) engaged in a game of 'legal gymnastics' to justify its de facto protection of a suspected war criminal while simultaneously advocating legislation aimed at strengthening international justice, as will be discussed below.[39]

In 2012 the conflicting aims of the ICC and the Congolese state unravelled. Under intense pressure over the rigged elections that returned him to power in late 2011, President Kabila moved to enforce the arrest warrant to deflect international criticism. But his decision promptly backfired. Supported by the Rwandan government, a new rebellion began amidst cries of foul play and broken promises of security sector reform.[40] With Ntaganda in a leadership role, the M23 rebels sacked Goma in November 2012. Though the UN's robust intervention in early 2013 ultimately led to the M23's demise and Ntaganda's voluntary surrender, a year of fighting left thousands of people internally displaced amidst reports of atrocities perpetrated by both government and rebel forces.[41]

A slightly different challenge emerged for the Congolese authorities when the Sudanese Head of State came to Kinshasa to attend a regional summit of the Common Market for Eastern and Southern Africa. Wanted by the ICC on charges of genocide, crimes against humanity and war crimes, Omar al-Bashir has been at the centre of an acrimonious standoff between the African Union (AU) and various international actors.[42] Citing head-of-state immunities and the detrimental impact of al-Bashir's arrest on the peace process in Darfur, the AU has repeatedly urged African states to not comply with the ICC's arrest warrants.[43] By contrast, international actors have advocated al-Bashir's arrest, condemning the AU's position as a regressive endorsement of impunity.[44]

Despite the appeals of local civil society groups as well as an official ICC reminder of its 'obligation to cooperate',[45] the Congolese government refused to arrest al-Bashir during his visit in February 2014. Citing 'time constraints' and 'a series of legal constraints', the Congolese authorities argued that, due to their membership of the AU 'whose regulations are legally binding', the ICC's request was 'inconsistent with their obligations to respect the immunities [of heads of state].'[46] Though the ICC's judges rejected these arguments and found the Congolese government in breach of its obligations under the Rome Statute, the fact remains that on this occasion the DRC chose its regional interests over the accountability demands of international actors.[47]

The controversies over the arrest of Omar al-Bashir and Bosco Ntaganda illustrate the antagonism and ambivalence surrounding the ICC's intervention in the DRC. Meanwhile, the OTP's case selection and its dependence on government cooperation reveal deep structural problems with the practice of complementarity. And yet, despite the challenges of aligning domestic policy with international expectations, the OTP's proposed 'consensual' division of labour also underscores the potential of closer cooperation between national governments and international actors. As the ICC's intervention enters its second decade, the DRC will likely remain a country where domestic interests, regional priorities, and internationally driven accountability are negotiated and contested.

IV DOMESTIC TRIALS: THE POSITIVE EFFECT OF COMPLEMENTARITY?

Although complementarity is a technical admissibility rule that determines whether the ICC can proceed with a specific case, the concept is often understood more broadly as a systemic relationship between the ICC and domestic judicial authorities.[48] In line with this perspective, the prospect of ICC intervention ('the shadow of the ICC') can act as a 'catalyst' for domestic enforcement of international criminal law.[49] It assumes that national authorities, eager to avoid ICC investigations on their territory, will initiate domestic prosecutions of international crimes and, in so doing, remove the need for the ICC's involvement. Under the ICC's policy of 'positive complementarity', the Prosecutor and ICC States Parties may and – in some instances – should encourage such national prosecutions.[50]

The DRC is an important case study of complementarity and the ICC's catalysing effect. Unlike most other ICC situation countries, Congolese tribunals have held a significant number of trials for war crimes and crimes against humanity.[51] Commentators have heralded this as a positive effect of the ICC's intervention in the country, emphasising the role of military tribunals and mobile courts in bringing perpetrators to justice.[52] Against the backdrop of complementarity, this section explores why and how the Congolese authorities have adjudicated international crimes and whether enthusiasm for domestic enforcement of international criminal law is warranted.[53]

It is important to note that no international criminal trials took place in the DRC before the end of the Second Congo War, even though Congolese law allowed for this possibility.[54] Only after the ICC opened investigations in the DRC (late 2004) did military prosecutors initiate investigations under the Military Criminal Code (MCC).[55] To date, approximately thirty trials for war crimes and crimes against humanity have been conducted before Congolese military tribunals.[56] The use of international norms, in particular the Rome Statute, has been a recurrent theme in these cases.[57]

Confronted with various inconsistencies in the national criminal law, the Congolese authorities have resorted to international standards in domestic proceedings.[58] Citing the MCC's definitional flaws, various tribunals have applied the Rome Statute in lieu of the Code. For instance, in the *Bongi* trial, the judges argued that 'this internal legislation ... has, however, a glaring loophole and doesn't criminalize war crimes, which are left with no sanction ... in this situation, a remedy to these loopholes must be found by invoking the Rome Statute.'[59] Other tribunals have suggested that international law is a more convenient source of norms. For instance, in *Songo Mboyo*, the tribunal argued that 'the Rome Statute of the ICC is very favourable to the suspects eliminating capital punishment and providing efficient protection mechanisms for victims [meriting] its application in the on-going proceedings'.[60]

Whatever the Rome Statute's strengths and weaknesses, Congolese military judges have struggled to develop a coherent legal argument for why an international treaty can or should displace binding Congolese law.[61] Some tribunals have referred to the 2006 constitution, in particular articles 153 ('courts may also apply international treaties') and 215 ('international treaties have superior authority [*autorité supérieure*] over regular laws'), but these provisions are usually viewed as self-explanatory. Most judgments make only passing – and usually incorrect or incomplete – references to the DRC's ratification of the Rome Statute or its self-executing character in Congolese domestic law.[62] The theory of monism, arguably the strongest argument in favour of the Rome Statute's direct application, is mentioned only in the *Bongi* decision.[63]

A closer look at the case law underscores why the tribunals' (lack of) legal argumentation is problematic. No tribunal has assessed the legal status of other international legal instruments, in particular the Rome Statute's Elements of Crimes (EoC) and the ICC's Rules of Procedure and Evidence (RPE).[64] As a result, there is no legal analysis of when and how these international norms can displace binding domestic criminal law and procedure. For instance, although the *Bavi* and *Kahwa* decisions determine culpability on the basis of the EoC, they did not mention it as a source of law.[65] In *Bongi*, the judges analysed the constitutive elements of pillage and homicide as war crimes by applying the EoC's five-pronged test (art. 8, 2, c.i), but failed to acknowledge the EoC as the source of this new legal standard.[66]

Some tribunals have gone further and made direct use of the RPE to supplement domestic norms.[67] For instance, in *Kibibi*, the judges applied the RPE's provisions relating to victim protection and testimony, filling a significant gap in the Congolese criminal procedure.[68] However, they provided no legal authority for this choice of the applicable law. Lost in the enthusiasm surrounding this and other cases is the question of how an international tribunal's internal set of regulations, designed for an entirely different institutional context, can displace binding Congolese criminal law. Likewise, the fact that the *Kibibi* trial, hailed by civil society as a victory for justice, lasted barely two weeks raises questions about the military tribunal's adherence to due process standards, and especially defendants' rights.[69]

Despite these shortcomings, Congolese military tribunals have used international criminal law in progressive ways. In *Bavi*, the tribunal used the EoC and the case law of international tribunals to establish the defendant's command responsibility for ordering soldiers to commit rape.[70] In *Songo Mboyo*, the Rome Statute was used to criminalise all forms of rape, including against men. As argued by the judges: 'In fact, the interpretation provided by the Elements of Crimes . . . considerably extends the notion of rape to also include any other inhuman act with gender-specific connotations.'[71] In *Songo Mboyo* and the *Mutins de Mbandaka* (another case involving rape charges), the Rome Statute's rules allowed rape victims to testify beyond what is normally permitted in Congolese law, and helped secure convictions against the accused.[72] These and other trials have featured creative instances of judicial decision-making, with international criminal law serving as an invaluable source of inspiration.[73]

Assessing the ICC's impact on Congolese domestic judicial practice reveals a complex picture. While the Rome Statute's influence in the above trials is immediately obvious, the catalysing effect of the ICC's intervention in the DRC remains more tenuous. Given that the Congolese government has not attempted to invoke complementarity to challenge the Hague-based trials of Congolese nationals, no domestic trial has actually materialised due to the

ICC's presence in the country.[74] In other words, the Congolese authorities have yet to prosecute a suspect domestically in order to avoid the ICC prosecuting the same person in The Hague. There is also little evidence of the ICC's prosecutorial strategy encouraging similar prosecutions at the national level. For instance, although Lubanga's trial in The Hague concerned the crime of conscripting and enlisting child soldiers, only two cases – to date – before Congolese military tribunals have featured this charge. In *Biyoyo*, the Rome Statute's definition of the crime was not applied, so the defendant ended up being convicted for ordinary crimes ('illegal detention of a person' and 'kidnapping'). In *Gedeon Kungu*, though prosecutors requested an indictment for the war crime of 'enlisting . . . about 300 children below the age of 15', the military tribunal eventually issued a conviction for ordinary military crimes, terrorism, and crimes against humanity.[75]

That said, the ICC's overall impact on Congolese judicial practice appears to be considerable. Despite just a handful of trials in The Hague, a much larger number of trials has already taken place domestically. Military judges have used international norms and case law to compensate for deficiencies in the domestic legal framework.[76] It is also noteworthy that DRC's military tribunals, unlike the ICC, have prosecuted members of the Congolese armed forces, not just rebels. Yet challenges remain for domestic judges and lawyers, especially with respect to fair trial and evidentiary standards.[77] The tribunals' inconsistent use of the Rome Statute underscores how international law can be used – and abused – to enhance domestic justice. In the end, the biggest obstacle to justice in the DRC remains the fact that international crimes are prosecuted in a selective manner, with many perpetrators, especially high-ranking military commanders, firmly beyond the reach of both the ICC and the domestic judicial system.[78]

V DOMESTIC REFORM: THE FAILURE OF COMPLEMENTARITY?

Unfolding in the context of growing tensions between African states and the ICC, domestic judicial reform reveals the conflicting imperatives at the heart of the Congolese authorities' state-building project and the international community's commitment to reform under the banner of 'positive complementarity'.[79] Despite the ICC's intervention in the country and the government's official policy of *'la lutte contre l'impunité'*, it proved impossible to adopt Rome Statute–implementing legislation in the DRC for well over a decade.[80] Likewise, the idea of establishing a special jurisdiction for past atrocities has gained limited traction in spite of years of dialogue between the United Nations and the government.[81]

Domesticating the Rome Statute would align the Congolese legal framework with international standards and enable domestic judicial institutions to adjudicate international crimes more effectively. A number of legislative proposals to that effect emerged after Kabila's ratification of the Rome Statute in 2002. Two draft bills discussed between 2001 and 2002 never received the government's approval.[82] Likewise, a 2005 government-backed *projet de loi* was never put to a formal vote.[83] Despite progress on a 2008 draft bill (*une proposition de loi*), it was ultimately not adopted during parliament's five year term (2006–2011).[84] Honorable Balamage sought to revive the same implementing bill in the current legislature (2012–2016), but – at the time of writing – it had yet to be voted on in either chamber of parliament.[85]

A series of reforms aimed at harmonising the relationship between the ICC and the Congolese legal system,[86] implementing legislation has four objectives. Firstly, it would incorporate the Rome Statute's classification and definitions of international crimes into domestic criminal law.[87] Congolese courts would no longer have to choose the applicable law in each trial, so the Rome Statute would not have to be applied in lieu of domestic law, as discussed above. Secondly, a number of fair trial guarantees, especially relating to defendant rights, victim participation, and witness protection, would be guaranteed at the domestic level. Thirdly, a coherent framework regulating collaboration between the ICC's field units and the Congolese judicial authorities would be established.[88] Lastly, implementing legislation would complete the task of shifting jurisdiction over international crimes from military tribunals to civilian courts. Though a separate piece of legislation modified the jurisdictional framework in 2013, it appears that the military has exploited legal loopholes in this law to maintain its judicial powers, especially with respect to members of the military and the police.[89]

Enacting these legal reforms has generated considerable political resistance over the past decade. For reasons that remain unclear, it proved difficult to get Rome Statute–implementing legislation on the parliamentary agenda.[90] When parliamentary debates did take place, they revealed significant levels of opposition to international criminal justice among rank and file lawmakers. A variety of political and ideological objections surfaced during a November 2010 debate in the National Assembly, the lower chamber of parliament, with many parliamentarians arguing (incorrectly) that domesticating the Rome Statute would force the DRC to abolish the death penalty.[91] Others objected to the involvement of outside actors in advocating the bill's passage, which was described as a form of colonialism and a threat to national sovereignty.[92] This and subsequent parliamentary debates (see below) have made it clear that aligning the domestic legal framework with international standards cannot be taken for granted, even if the DRC remains one of the most active ICC States Parties.

Similar challenges have beset the Congolese government's efforts to prosecute past atrocities (the Rome Statute's entry into force in July 2002 means the ICC cannot investigate crimes that occurred before that date). In October 2010, the UN's 'Mapping Report' publicised several hundred instances of unresolved human rights violations committed prior to 2003.[93] Responding to international pressure, the Congolese Ministry of Justice (MoJ) proposed the establishment of a specialised jurisdiction within the Congolese judicial system to address the existing impunity gap.[94] However, these efforts have encountered political and institutional resistance from various domestic actors. In August 2011, the Congolese Senate rejected legislation that would create a 'Special Court', and in May 2014 the National Assembly declared an analogous proposal 'inadmissible'.[95]

Echoing some of the disagreements between the ICC and the AU, the debate about accountability for past crimes has unfolded in the context of shifting institutional rivalries in Congolese politics. In 2011, the legislature refused to endorse the government's Special Court proposal, while the executive obstructed the legislature's analogous efforts to domesticate the Rome Statute. During a Senate debate in August 2011, parliamentarians from across the political spectrum criticised the Special Court, though it had support from the Congolese minister of justice and the US ambassador at large for war crimes.[96] Realising that their patrons could be at risk of prosecution, some parliamentarians denounced the project, while others argued that the Court's dependence on external aid cast the entire Congolese judicial system in a negative light. During internal committee deliberations, senior Congolese senators expressly mentioned the ICC's neocolonial policies in Africa and warned against potential violations of the DRC's sovereignty.[97] In the end, neither the Special Court nor Rome Statute–implementing legislation was adopted during the 2006–2011 parliamentary term.[98]

The current government (2012–2016) tried to resurrect the idea of a hybrid jurisdiction within the Congolese court system. A revised version of the MoJ bill clarified a number of legal issues that proved controversial during earlier discussions, especially regarding the legal basis for prosecuting crimes committed before the entry into force of the Rome Statute.[99] Although civil society groups endorsed the project and in October 2013 President Kabila recommended the establishment of a 'specialised chamber' in his speech to the nation, political disagreement and serious legal problems remain.[100] Funding is expected to come primarily from international donors, but concerns persist as to the institutional set up of the hybrid jurisdiction.[101] It appears that Congolese magistrates would be able to outvote their international counterparts, which raises the spectre of politicised prosecutions against opponents of the government and the military.[102] Despite the May 2014 inadmissibility vote in the National Assembly, international actors continue to push for legislation that would provide accountability for past crimes.[103]

The fraught legislative histories of these two initiatives illustrate the political and institutional challenges of integrating international norms into domestic law. Despite the international community's support for 'positive complementarity', including financial, logistical, and technical assistance to judicial reform, the ICC's intervention in the DRC has done little to change the Congolese establishment's political calculus in this area. Failure to domesticate the Rome Statute can only be understood in the wider context of competition between rival repositories of power.[104] The MoJ represents the interests of the president and the executive, which in turn has close ties to the military. In the legislature, the political landscape is equally complex. Some political parties balk at legislative proposals that could strengthen the position of the executive, while others have little incentive to support initiatives that would implicate their party colleagues. The political establishment is well aware that adjusting the legal framework puts some high-ranking politicians and military commanders at direct risk of prosecution.[105]

It must also be remembered that efforts to reform the judicial system in the DRC are unfolding in the shadow of the standoff between the ICC and the AU. In a country scarred by colonialism, some Congolese lawmakers have expressed reservations about efforts to graft international standards onto domestic criminal law. Concerns have also been raised about the retributive nature of international justice and its lack of flexibility regarding the DRC's broader peace- and state-building agenda. Taken together, these tensions reveal a hidden dimension of ensuring accountability for international crimes in the DRC and illustrate the antagonism between the political interests of a key ICC State Party and the universalistic aspirations of international criminal justice.

VI CONCLUSION

A continuing dialogue, but also a recurring struggle between stability and accountability, the ICC's intervention in the DRC has exposed the Congolese authorities' shifting priorities with respect to international justice. Invited by Kabila in 2003, the ICC's investigations have produced the Court's first trials and, at the time of writing, only convictions in The Hague. At the domestic level, Congolese military tribunals have used international norms, especially the Rome Statute, to enhance domestic trials of international crimes. However, these instances of accommodation and cooperation, where the interests of the ICC and the Congolese have aligned, tell only half the story. The ICC's involvement in the DRC has also produced antagonism and conflict. Despite its stated commitment to the 'fight against impunity', the Congolese authorities have offered up only inconvenient rivals for international prosecution. Key actors in the state security apparatus, such as Bosco Ntaganda before his defection, are usually beyond the reach of the ICC and domestic courts. Meanwhile, reforming the domestic judicial system remains hostage to the entrenched interests of the political and military establishment. Emblematic of developments in other African states, this chapter argues that these uneven interactions are best characterised as a continuing search for a *modus vivendi* between the ICC and the DRC. Their evolving relationship should be understood as part of a broader struggle between the universalistic aspirations of international justice and the domestic constraints of peace- and state-building.

Notes

1. See generally Sigall Horovitz, 'DR Congo: Interaction between International and National Judicial Responses to the Mass Atrocities' (DOMAC Project Report/14, February 2012).
2. Rome Statute of the International Criminal Court, The Hague, 17 July 1998, in force 1 July 2002, UNTS 2187, Articles 17–19.
3. See Kirsten Fisher, *Moral Accountability and International Criminal Law: Holding Agents of Atrocity Accountable to the World* (London: Routledge, 2013), pp. 144–167. Yuval Shany, *Assessing the Effectiveness of International Courts* (Oxford: Oxford University Press, 2014), pp. 223–252.
4. See Gerard Prunier, *Africa's World War, Congo, the Rwandan Genocide, and the Making of a Continental Catastrophe* (Oxford: Oxford University Press, 2009), pp. 257–283.
5. A 2007 study calculated five million conflict-related deaths, which included non-combat-induced casualties. See 'Mortality in the Democratic Republic of Congo. An Ongoing Crisis' (International Rescue Committee, 2007). This figure, widely reported in the media, has been contested by many observers. See also Human Security Report Project, *Human Security Report 2009/2010: The Causes of Peace and the Shrinking Costs of War* (New York: Oxford University Press, 2011), pp. 123–131.

6. Jason Stearns, Judith Verweijen and Maria Eriksson Baaz, 'The National Army and Armed Groups in the Eastern Congo. Untangling the Gordian Knot of Insecurity' (Rift Valley Institute Usalama Project 11, 2013).

7. Details of these cases can be found at the ICC's webpage for the DRC, see www.icc-cpi.int.

8. The Rome Statute does not regulate when and how the ICC should close investigations and leave a situation country. See Rebecca Hamilton, 'The ICC's Exit Problem' (2014) 47 *New York University Journal of International Law and Policy* 1.

9. A term of art under the Rome Statute, the word 'situation' refers to countries in which the ICC has opened investigations. *See* Rod Rastan, 'What Is a "Case" for the Purpose of the Rome Statute?' (2008) 19 *Criminal Law Forum* 435.

10. Articles 17–19 of the Rome Statute.

11. *Ibid.* The word 'complementarity' does not appear in the Rome Statute. The Preamble and Article 1 refer only to 'complementary' jurisdiction.

12. On the legal test of complementarity and the erroneous belief that it refers to 'unable and unwilling' states, see Darryl Robinson, 'The Mysterious Mysteriousness of Complementarity' (2010) 21 *Criminal Law Forum* 67.

13. See generally Sarah M.H. Nouwen, *Complementarity in the Line of Fire The Catalysing Effect of the International Criminal Court in Uganda and Sudan* (Cambridge: Cambridge University Press, 2013), pp. 34–110.

14. See William W. Burke-White, 'A Community of Courts: Toward a System of International Criminal Law Enforcement' (2002) 24 *Michigan Journal of International Law* 1–101. William W. Burke-White, 'The Domestic Influence of International Criminal Tribunals: The International Criminal Tribunal for the Former Yugoslavia and the Creation of the State Court of Bosnia & Herzegovina' (2008) 46 *Columbia Journal of Transnational Law* 279–350.

15. For an analogous conceptual framework, see David L. Bosco, *Rough Justice: The International Criminal Court in a World of Power Politics* (Oxford: Oxford University Press 2014), pp. 11–22.

16. This stands in marked contrast to other ICC situations, in particular Sudan and Libya, where opposition to the Court has undermined, and at times completely blocked, its activities. It should be remembered that Sudan and Libya were referred – against their will – to the ICC by the Security Council, whereas the Congolese government invited the Court to intervene. See below.

17. See Thijs Bouwknegt, 'How Did the DRC Become the ICC's Pandora's Box?', *African Arguments*, 5 March 2014.

18. On Kabila's referral, see William W. Burke-White, 'Complementarity in Practice: The International Criminal Court as Part of a System of

Multi-Level Global Governance in the Democratic Republic of Congo'
(2005) 18 *Leiden Journal of International Law* 567–568. The background
to the ICC's intervention is explored in Horovitz, 'DR Congo:
Interaction', pp. 36–37.

19. Kabila's letter is available in Godfrey Musila, 'Between Rhetoric and
Action. The Politics, Processes and Practice of the ICC's Work in the
DRC' (ISS Monograph 164, 2009), Annex II.

20. Remarks by ICC Prosecutor Luis Moreno-Ocampo, 27th Committee of
Legal Advisors on Public International Law, Strasbourg, 18 March 2004,
quoted in Mahnoush H. Arsanjani and Michael W. Reisman,
'The International Criminal Court and the Congo: From Theory to
Reality', in Nadia Leila Sadat and Michael Scharf (eds.), *The Theory and
Practice of International Criminal Law. Essays in Honor of M. Cherif
Bassiouni* (Leiden: Brill 2008), p. 339.

21. The OTP issued a set of guidelines on complementarity in 2003, see
OTP, Informal expert paper, 'The Principle of Complementarity in
Practice', 2003, p. 3. On the meanings of complementarity, see also
below fn 80.

22. It should be noted that Lubanga, Katanga, and Nugdjolo were all rebels
subsequently integrated into the army as part of a policy of
demobilisation and security sector reform. Arrested after their
integration, the ICC has only pursued crimes they committed as rebels.

23. See Phil Clark, 'Chasing Cases: The ICC and the Politics of State
Referral in the Democratic Republic of Congo and Uganda', in
Carsten Stahn and Mohamed El Zeidy (eds.), *The International
Criminal Court and Complementarity: From Theory to Practice*, vol. 2
(Cambridge: Cambridge University Press 2011), pp. 1189–1197.

24. *Ibid.*, pp. 38–41.

25. See William Schabas, *An Introduction to the International Criminal
Court*, 4th edn (Cambridge: Cambridge University Press 2011),
pp. 196–197.

26. The limited gravity of the charges brought against Lubanga produced
a relatively short fourteen-year sentence, undermining Congolese
victims' support for the ICC. See Bouwknegt, 'How Did the DRC
Become the ICC's Pandora's Box?'. See also Christian M. De Vos,
'Case Note. Prosecutor v. Lubanga. Someone Who Comes Between
One Person and Another. Lubanga, Local Cooperation and the Right
to a Fair Trial' (2011) 12 *Melbourne Journal of International Law* 217–236.

27. Phil Clark, 'Law, Politics and Pragmatism: The ICC and Case
Selection in the Democratic Republic of Congo and Uganda', in
Nicholas Waddell and Phil Clark (eds.), *Courting Conflict? Justice,
Peace and the ICC in Africa* (Royal African Society, 2008), pp. 38–40.

28. *Ibid.*, pp. 37–45.

29. These critical voices stand in marked contrast to earlier commentary on the ICC's intervention in the DRC: See Arsanjani and Reisman, 'The ICC and the Congo'.

30. Clark, 'Law, Politics and Pragmatism', pp. 40–42. Clark, 'Chasing Cases', 1202–1203. Clark also highlights the ICC's failure to reconcile its legal and moral obligations under the Rome Statute with the wider political fallout of its interventions, in particular victim expectations. See Phil Clark, 'Grappling in the Great Lakes: The Challenges of International Justice in Rwanda, the Democratic Republic of Congo and Uganda', in Brett Bowden, Hilary Charlesworth and Jeremy Farrall (eds.), *The Role of International Law in Restructuring Societies after Conflict: Great Expectations* (Cambridge: Cambridge University Press, 2012), pp. 244–269.

31. Pascal Kambale, 'A Story of Missed Opportunities: The Role of the International Criminal Court in the Democratic Republic of Congo', in Christian De Vos, Sara Kendall and Carsten Stahn (eds.), *Contested Justice: The Politics and Practice of International Criminal Court Interventions* (Cambridge: Cambridge University Press, 2015), pp. 171–197.

32. *Ibid.* Clark, 'Chasing Cases', pp. 1189–1197.

33. Marlies Glasius, 'A Problem, Not a Solution: Complementarity in Central African Republic and the Democratic Republic of Congo', in Carsten Stahn and Mohammed El Zeidy (eds.), *The International Criminal Court and Complementarity: From Theory to Practice* (Cambridge: Cambridge University Press, 2011), pp. 1204–1221.

34. Pascal Kambale, 'Justice Denied? The ICC's Record in the DRC', *Open Global Rights*, 3 December 2014.

35. Horovitz, 'DR Congo: Interaction', pp. 41–42.

36. Jason K. Stearns, 'Strongman of the Eastern DRC. A Profile of General Bosco Ntaganda' (Rift Valley Institute Usalama Project Briefing, March 2013).

37. 'DR Congo: Arrest Bosco Ntaganda for ICC Trial', *Human Rights Watch*, 13 April 2012.

38. See Ministry of Justice, 'Plan d'Action pour la Reforme de la Justice', (Kinshasa, 2007); Ministry of Justice, 'Feuille de Route du Ministere de la Justice pour l'année 2009' (Kinshasa, 2009); Ministry of Justice and Human Rights, 'Projet de Loi Relative aux Chambres Spécialisées pour la Repression des Violations Graves du Droit International Humanitaire: Création, Organisation, Fonctionnement, Droit Applicable, Compétence et Procedure' (Kinshasa, 2011).

39. See below, section 4 'Domestic Reform: The Failure of Complementarity?'.

40. Maria Eriksson Baaz, 'The M23 Rebellion and the Dead End Street of Military Integration in Eastern DRC', *Congo Siasa*, 1 August 2012.

41. 'Report of the UN High Commissioner for Human Rights on the Situation of Human Rights and the Activities of Her Office in the DRC', UN Doc. A/HRC/24/33, 12 July 2013; 'Final Report of the Group of Experts on the DRC', UN Doc. S/2014/42, 23 January 2014.

42. Charles C. Jalloh, 'Reflections on the Indictment of Sitting Heads of State and Government and Its Consequences for Peace' (2014) 7 *African Journal of Legal Studies* 43–59.

43. AU Assembly, 'Decision on Africa's Relationship with the International Criminal Court', Ext/Assembly/AU/Dec. 1, 12 October 2013, pp. 1–3.

44. 'We Say No: Bashir Travels to Democratic Republic of Congo', *Bashir Watch*, 26 February 2014; 'DRC Must Arrest Omar Al-Bashir', *Federation Internationale des Droits de l'Homme*, 26 February 2014.

45. *The Prosecutor v. Omar Hassan Ahmad al Bashir* (ICC-02/05-01/09), Pre-Trial Chamber II Decision Regarding Omar Al-Bashir's Visit to the Democratic Republic of Congo, 26 February 2014.

46. *Ibid.*

47. *The Prosecutor v. Omar Hassan Ahmad al Bashir* (ICC-02/05-01/09) 'Pre Trial Chamber II Decision on the Cooperation of the Democratic Republic of Congo Regarding Omar Al Bashir's Arrest and Surrender to the Court', 9 April 2014.

48. Articles 17–19 of the Rome Statute. See above, section 2 'Background'. See also Schabas, *International Criminal Court*, pp. 190–196.

49. On complementarity and the ICC's catalytic effect on domestic prosecutions, see Nouwen, *Complementarity in the Line of Fire*, pp. 34–110, 337–410.

50. On 'positive complementarity', see above fn 22 and below fn 80.

51. See Benson Olugbuo, 'Positive Complementarity and the Fight Against Impunity in Africa', in Chacha Murungu and Japhet Biegon (eds), *Prosecuting International Crimes in Africa* (Pretoria: Pretoria University Law Press, 2011), p. 261.

52. See Geraldine Mattioli and Anneke van Woudenberg, 'Global Catalyst for Prosecutions? The ICC in the Democratic Republic of Congo', in Phil Clark and Nicholas Waddell (eds.), *Courting Conflict? Justice, Peace and the ICC in Africa* (Royal African Society, 2008), pp. 55–62; Mobile courts are used to reach remote areas without courtrooms or other judicial infrastructure, see Tessa Khan and Jim Wormington, 'Mobile Courts in the DRC: Lessons from Development for International Criminal Justice' (Oxford Transitional Justice Research Working Paper, 2011). Kelly Askin, 'Fizi Diary: Finally, Justice for All?', *Open Society Foundation Blog*, 18 February 2011; Chuck Sudetic, 'Congo Justice: The First Verdicts', *Open Society Foundation Blog*, 19 April 2011.

53. This section is based on a more extended treatment of these issues in: Patryk I. Labuda, 'Applying and "Misapplying" the Rome Statute in the

Democratic Republic of Congo', in Christian de Vos, Sara Kendall and Carsten Stahn (eds.), *Contested Justice: The Politics and Practice of International Criminal Court Interventions* (Cambridge: Cambridge University Press, 2015), pp. 409–431.

54. See Ordonnance-loi n° 72/060 du 25 Septembre 1972 Portant Institution d'un Code de Justice Militaire, art. 502, 505, 530. See also OHCHR, 'Democratic Republic of the Congo: Report of the Mapping Exercise Documenting the Most Serious Violations of Human Rights and International Humanitarian Law Committed within the Territory of the Democratic Republic of the Congo between March 1993 and June 2003' (UN, August 2010), pp. 408–409, 425 (hereafter: UN Mapping Report).

55. Code pénal militaire, Loi N°024/2002 du 18 novembre 2002, and subsequent amendments, art. 164–169, 173–175. The domestic military justice system retained exclusive jurisdiction over international crimes until April 2013.

56. There is no institutionalised case reporting in the DRC, and hence no exhaustive list of such cases. The International Center for Transitional Justice compiled some transcripts and data in International Center for Transitional Justice, 'Recommandations Atelier d'Evaluation. La Justice Militaire comme mécanisme de repression des crimes internationaux. Decisions Judiciaires', Centre Catholique Nganda Kinshasa, 8–10 June 2009) and International Center for Transitional Justice, 'The Accountability Landscape in Eastern DRC. Analysis of the National Legislative and Judicial Response to International Crimes (2009–2014), 2015.

57. For a detailed discussion of the case law, see Avocats Sans Frontieres (ASF), 'Etude de Jurisprudence. L'Application du Statut de Rome de la Cour Pénale Internationale par les Juridictions de la République Démocratique du Congo' (Brussels, March 2009). The main trials are also described by province in the Mapping Report. See UN Mapping Report, pp. 410–421.

58. The Military Tribunal in Equatorial Province was the first to invoke the Rome Statute in a domestic trial, followed by tribunals in four other provinces: Katanga, Oriental Province, South Kivu, and North Kivu. *Tribunal Militaire de Garnison*, Mutins de Mbandaka, TMG Mbandaka, jugement avant dire droit, 12 January 2006, RP 086/05.

59. TMG de l'Ituri, *Blaise Bongi*, 24 March 2006, RP 018/2006, par. 66 and 71. Other judgments that also mention the MCC's conflicting definitions include: TMG de l'Ituri, *Bavi*, 19 February 2006, p. 37; TMG de l'Ituri, *Kahwa*, 2 August 2006, RP 039/2006, p. 24. TMG de Mbandaka, *Songo Mboyo*, 12 April 2006, RP 084/2005, p. 12. TMG de Mbandaka, *Mutins de Mbandaka*, 20 June 2006, RP 101/06, p. 16. All translations by the author.

60. TMG de Mbandaka, *Songo Mboyo*, 12 April 2006, p. 12. See also CM du Sud Kivu, *Daniel Kibibi et autres*, 21 February 2011, RP 043/2011, p. 16.

61. See Antonietta Trapani, 'Bringing National Courts in Line with International Norms: A Comparative Look at the Court of Bosnia and Herzegovina and the Military Courts of the Democratic Republic of Congo' (2013) 46 *Israel Law Review* 239–242.

62. See generally Joseph Kazadi Mpiana, 'La Cour Pénale Internationale et La République Démocratique Du Congo: 10 Ans Après. Etude de L'impact Du Statut de Rome Dans Le Droit Interne Congolais' (2012) 25 *Revue Québécoise de Droit International* 58–90. See also Marcel Wetsh'Okonda Koso, 'Le Malaise Soulevé par l'Application Directe su Statut de Rome par le Jugement n RP 084/2005 du 12 Avril 2006 du Tribunal Militaire de Garnison de Mbandaka' (2006) 2 *Revue Horizons* 154–157.

63. CM de la Province Orientale, *Bongi*, 4 November 2006, RPA 030/2006, p. 11, par. 74.

64. The direct application of international law in a domestic court is a threshold legal question, which gives rise to divergent solutions depending on the type of national legal system. See Ward Ferdinandusse, *Direct Application of International Criminal Law in National Courts* (The Hague: TMC Asser Press, 2006), pp. 36–86.

65. *Ibid.*, p. 25–34. TMG de l'Ituri, *Bavi*, 19 February 2006, p. 37–43, CM de la Province Orientale, *Bavi*, 28 July 2007, RPA 003/07, p. 30.

66. *Ibid.*, p. 15, para. 95.

67. ICC Rules of Evidence and Procedure, rule 70 in particular, and rule 66.4. See ASF, 'Etude de Jurisprudence', pp. 42–48.

68. Articles 68.2 and 87.3 RPE. See 'Le Lieutenant-Colonel Daniel Kibibi Mutware condamné à 20 ans de prison pour crimes contre l'humanité', *Avocats Sans Frontières Blog*, 21 February 2011.

69. *Ibid.* ASF's press release glosses over the fact that the entire trial lasted just two weeks, despite the complexity of the charges.

70. TMG de l'Ituri, *Bavi*, 19 February 2006, p. 42–43.

71. TMG de Mbandaka, *Songo Mboyo*, 12 April 2006, pp. 27–32.

72. *Ibd.*, pp. 27–34. *See also* Jean-Pierre F. D.ofia Malewa, 'Commentaire du Jugement Songo Mboyo: Une Illustration de l'Eclairage de la Justice Nationale par les Textes et la Jurisprudence Penaux Internationaux' (2006) 2 *Revue Horizons* 119–140. TMG de Mbandaka, *Mutins de Mbandaka*, 20 June 2006 – and on appeal – CM de l'Equateur, *Mutins de Mbandaka*, 15 June 2007, pp. 12–15.

73. In August 2006, a law on sexual violence was enacted, aligning Congolese criminal law with international standards in this area (Loi no. 06/18 du 20 juillet 2006).

74. Article 17 Rome Statute. This is complementarity in the narrow legal sense. By contrast, as discussed above, the Congolese authorities have used the ICC to outsource inconvenient cases to The Hague. For a discussion of how complementarity may catalyse effects, see Nouwen, *Complementarity in the Line of Fire*, pp. 34–110, 337–410.

75. Military judges have proved more willing to sustain charges of crimes against humanity than war crimes. Although the Rome Statute has been applied without distinction to both crimes, indictments for war crimes have been thrown out in most cases, with only alternative charges concerning ordinary crimes or crimes against humanity sustained. CM du Katanga, *Ankoro*, 20 December 2004, RP 02/2004. See also, TMG de l'Ituri, *Kahwa*, 2 August 2006, RP 039/2006; TMG de l'Ituri, *Mutins de Bunia*, 18 June 2007, RP 008/2007, TMG du Haut Katanga, *Gédéon Kyungu*, 5 March 2009, RP 0134/2007; CM du Katanga, *Kilwa*, 28 June 2007, RP 00/2006.

76. Though it is beyond the scope of this chapter, military tribunals have invoked the case law of the ICC and the International Criminal Tribunals for Rwanda and Yugoslavia. See Trapani, 'Bringing National Courts in Line with International Norms', 243–246.

77. *Ibid.*, 244–248. Trapani's conclusions about the ICC's impact on the DRC are less sanguine. See also Dunia P. Zongwe, 'Taking Leaves Out of the International Criminal Court Statute: The Direct Application of International Criminal Law by Military Courts in the Democratic Republic of Congo' (2013) 46 *Israel Law Review* 249.

78. *Ibid.* See also ASF, 'Etude de Jurisprudence', pp. 42, 68, 106–109.

79. Though widely used in the literature, the term 'positive complementarity' is vague. It can refer to either (a) the OTP's policy of encouraging domestic prosecutions or b) State Party support to domestic prosecutions and judicial reform. In line with the second meaning, the most common tools in the positive complementarity 'toolbox' include: (a) legislative assistance to states, in particular drafting and passing legislation on international criminal justice, (b) technical assistance and capacity building programs focused on training of judicial personnel, and (c) the development of physical infrastructure. See ASP, 'Report of the Bureau on Stocktaking: Complementarity' (ICC-ASP/8/51), 18 March 2010. See also Carsten Stahn, 'Complementarity: A Tale of Two Notions' (2008) 19 *Criminal Law Forum* 87.

80. After this article was completed, Parliament adopted the Rome Statute implementing law in late 2015. Portions of the law were promulgated on 29 February 2016.

81. See Ministry of Justice, 'Plan d'Action pour la Reforme de la Justice'; Ministry of Justice, 'Feuille de Route du Ministere de la Justice pour l'année 2009'; Ministry of Justice and Human Rights, 'Projet de Loi

Relative aux Chambres Spécialisées pour la Représsion des Violations Graves du Droit International Humanitaire'.

82. It is worth remembering that the political situation was extremely volatile during this time, with Kabila's Kinshasa-based government controlling only parts of the country. Musila, 'Between Rhetoric and Action', pp. 16–17, especially footnotes and Annex II.

83. The distinction between a *projet de loi* and a *proposition de loi* is significant. The former is a legislative bill endorsed by the executive, usually drafted and sponsored by the Ministry of Justice. The latter is a legislative bill submitted by either an individual MP or a group of MPs, but normally without the executive's approval.

84. See International Center for Transitional Justice, 'Plaidoyer pour l'Adoption de la Loi de Mise en Oeuvre' (2008).

85. Parliamentarians for Global Action, 'Annual Report' (December 2013– September 2014). But see above, fn 80. The ICC implementing law was adopted by both houses of Parliament in late 2015.

86. See *La Proposition de loi modifiant et complétant le Code Pénal, le Code de procedure pénale, le code de l'organisation et de la competence judiciaires, le code judiciaire militaire et le code penal militaire en vue de la mise en oeuvre du Statut de Rome de la Cour Pénale Internationale.* The 2012 version of the draft bill will be referenced in this chapter, unless otherwise stated.

87. Article 9 Loi de mise en oeuvre. Implementing legislation does not have to incorporate *verbatim* the Rome Statute into domestic law. Changes and adjustments are frequently made, see Jann Kleffner, 'The Impact of Complementarity on National Implementation of Substantive International Criminal Law' (2003) 1 *Journal of International Criminal Justice* 86.

88. On the challenge of cooperation between the national institutions and the ICC, see Pascal Kambale, 'A Story of Missed Opportunities' (on file with author).

89. A longstanding demand of Congolese civil society, implementing legislation was expected to shift jurisdiction over international crimes to civilian courts (away from military tribunals). Due to political resistance, a separate piece of legislation effectuated this jurisdictional realignment. Promulgated on 4 May 2013, the organic law on 'the organization, functioning and competence of courts of the Judicial Order' gave (civilian) Appeals Courts jurisdiction over genocide, war crimes and crimes against humanity. However, it remains unclear whether these courts can try soldiers and police officers, see Human Rights Watch, 'Justice pour les Atrocités Perpetrées en République Démocratique du Congo. Soutenir la Proposition du Gouvernement de Mettre en Place des Chambres Specialisées Mixtes et Autres

Réformes Judiciaires Connexes' (1 April 2014). Articles 10–12 Loi de mise en oeuvre.

90. It is not clear when and why debate on draft legislation is allowed. The most plausible explanation is that the Congolese legislature, especially its leaders, answers to the executive.

91. Art. 80 of the Rome Statute provides that 'Nothing ... affects the application by States of penalties prescribes by their national law'. Several MPs made this point during the parliamentary debate.

92. This debate concerned the 2008 version of the Rome Statute implementing bill. Most of that bill's provisions have been incorporated into the current draft bill.

93. One of its recommendations was the establishment of hybrid chambers in the Congolese courts. See UN Mapping Report, p. 480. The possibility of an international or hybrid court had already been mooted after the 2002 peace accords.

94. The 2011 draft legislation initially referred to 'specialised chambers in the Congolese courts'. Owing to constitutional objections, a later version elevated the proposed mechanism to the status of a 'Special Court' within the Congolese judicial system. The 2014 draft legislation refers to a 'specialised chamber' within the Congolese judicial system. See also Sharanjeet Parmar, 'How to Tackle the DRC's Complex Anti-Impunity Agenda?', *African Arguments*, 23 April 2014.

95. Parliamentarians for Global Action, 'Annual Report'.

96. Projet de loi portant création, organisation et fonctionnement de la Cour spécialisée de la repression des crimes de genocide, crimes de guerre et crimes contre l'humanité, approved by the Conseil des Ministres, 2 August 2011, articles 16–26.

97. Senate PAJ Committee, August 2011. (Author's notes.)

98. The Senate rejected the revised Special Court after months of wrangling. The implementing bill was never put to a vote in parliament. See Patryk I. Labuda, 'The Democratic Republic of Congo's Failure to Address Impunity for International Crimes. A View from Inside the Legislative Process 2010–2011', *International Justice Monitor*, 8 November 2011.

99. Legislation proposed in 2011 had raised complex legal questions about the relationship between the Special Court, the ICC, and domestic courts (complementarity under the Rome Statute does not foresee a third level of jurisdiction between the ICC and domestic courts). Two issues proved difficult to resolve: (1) the temporal jurisdiction of the Special Court and (2) its substantive jurisdiction. See Human Rights Watch, 'RD Congo: Commentaires sur l'Avant-Projet de Loi Portant Création de Chambres Specialisées' (14 March 2011).

100. Discours de Joseph Kabila devant le Congrès, 23 October 2013. Open Society Justice Initiative, 'Statement to the 12th Assembly of States Parties to the Rome Statute' (The Hague, 21 November 2013).

101. The EU and the UN peacekeeping mission in the DRC did not officially endorse the project in its 2014 version.

102. The enabling law has to resolve a number of logistical and legal issues, in particular the Court's organisational and administrative structure, the participation of international and national staff, victim and witness protection mechanisms, and funding issues. See Human Rights Watch, 'Justice pour les atrocités perpetrées en République démocratique du Congo'.

103. See Amnesty International, 'L'impunité Continue d'Alimenter les Atteintes aux Droits Humains en République Démocratique du Congo' (AFR62/001/2014, 18 September 2014).

104. I have previously argued this in, Labuda, 'Applying and Misapplying the Rome Statute', pp. 418–419.

105. See Parmar, 'How to Tackle'.

12

Witness Testimony, Support, and Protection at the ICC

Stephen Smith Cody, Alexa Koenig, and Eric Stover

I INTRODUCTION

In the months before ICC Chief Prosecutor Fatou Bensouda's decision to drop the case against the president of Kenya, Uhuru Kenyatta, a growing number of witnesses recanted their stories or refused to testify.[1] Many cited fears about their personal safety and the safety of their families.[2] So great were witnesses' concerns that assurances of added protection from Bensouda reportedly could not convince witnesses to stay the course and appear at trial. One witness, identified as *Witness 5* in redacted court documents, described the personal risks as "insurmountable."[3] Allegations of witness intimidation, state-sponsored death squads, and bribery plagued the Kenyan cases and thrust the issue of witness protection out from the shadows of international justice. "Prosecution witnesses in this case have been under siege," Bensouda announced in January 2015.[4] The Kenyan cases have drawn widespread attention to the ways that allies of accused perpetrators and their political operatives can target the social ties and economic welfare of witnesses and their families and communities. ICC cases are supposed to end impunity, but it seems impunity can also end ICC cases.

Witnesses are the lifeblood of trials involving serious international crimes, such as genocide, crimes against humanity, and war crimes. Effective prosecutions depend on witness testimonies, both for the facts they provide and for their moral authority. Yet, for many witnesses, testifying in an international trial requires an act of great courage, especially when perpetrators still walk the streets of their villages and towns. Most have survived or witnessed mass killings, sexual violence, and the destruction of their homes and villages. Fearing reprisals, witnesses may even hide their participation in a trial from close friends, neighbors, and family members. The decision to testify often means confronting past ghosts and present demons.

In this chapter, we present findings from the first empirical study to evaluate the experiences of ICC witnesses. Our study design included a three-part interview structure, with semi-structured interviews conducted with witnesses at three time points: (1) prior to testimony, (2) immediately after testifying, and (3) six to twelve months post-testimony. By gathering information from witnesses at different stages of the judicial proceedings, we aimed to capture witnesses' evolving experiences and the meanings they attributed to those experiences over time.

All of the witnesses who participated in this study testified in one of the first two trials – *Prosecutor v. Thomas Lubanga Dyilo* and *Prosecutor v. Germain Katanga* – at the International Criminal Court. Both the *Lubanga* and *Katanga* trials dealt with atrocity crimes that occurred in the Democratic Republic of Congo (DRC) during 2002 and 2003.

In March 2012, Trial Chamber I found Thomas Lubanga guilty of abducting boys and girls under the age of fifteen and forcing them to fight in the Ituri region of the Democratic Republic of the Congo.[5] During the conflict, Lubanga and the forces he commanded abducted and recruited children from schools and villages, requiring them to kill on his behalf. Although Lubanga was not convicted of any crimes of sexual violence, witness testimony presented at trial revealed that many girls were forced to serve as sex slaves for ranked military members. The case stands as the court's first guilty verdict. Lubanga is currently detained at the Detention Centre in The Hague, where he is serving a fourteen-year sentence.

In March 2014, a Majority of Trial Chamber II convicted Germain Katanga as an accessory to the war crimes of directing an attack against a civilian population, pillaging, and destruction of property, as well as murder as a war crime and as a crime against humanity. In June 2014, Katanga dropped his appeal, accepting the judgment of the court. Katanga is also currently detained at the Detention Centre in The Hague, where he is serving a twelve-year sentence.[6]

Given the limited geographic focus of these cases, we caution that our study provides only a glimpse into the worlds of ICC witnesses. We have much more to learn about witness experiences in the ICC and other international criminal tribunals, and it is our hope that international courts that prosecute grave crimes will continue to monitor and evaluate their witness programs with the aim of making the process of testifying as safe, respectful, and dignified an experience as possible. Witness support and protection programs that are adequately funded and attentive to the needs of witnesses influence how they view their interaction with courts and, in turn, how they speak about those experiences in their communities. Previous research has shown that people's perceptions of the fairness of court proceedings can condition their views of judicial institutions and outcomes.[7]

The remainder of this chapter proceeds in five sections. First, we briefly describe the history of witness engagement in contemporary international trials, underscoring the significance of witness testimonies for securing convictions. Next, we discuss the specific process of testifying as an ICC witness. Third, we explain our research methodology. Fourth, drawing on our survey results, we discuss our findings regarding witnesses' experiences in the *Lubanga* and *Katanga* cases. We conclude with recommendations for improving witness handling and protection through long-term monitoring, greater attention to gender, and more targeted funding for witness protection and support services.

II WITNESSES TO GRAVE CRIMES

In the aftermath of mass atrocities, when memories are contested and social wounds fester, the act of telling one's story in a public forum can be fraught with unanticipated consequences. Psychologists have long recognized that wartime violence can negatively impact an individual's memory and conditioning; since testifying in a criminal court often means confronting an alleged perpetrator and reliving one or more crimes, there is always the danger that disturbing memories can surface and overwhelm a witness. Survivors can "react physically as well as psychologically when confronted with reminders of the trauma. That is, while feeling fear, they may sweat, tremble, and experience their heart pounding."[8]

Yet, as difficult as testifying may be, it does not mean that witnesses are necessarily traumatized by the event or consider it a negative experience. A review of the extant empirical literature suggests there is little evidence that truth-telling mechanisms, including war crimes tribunals in post-war settings, either "dramatically harm individuals ... [or] ease their emotional and psychological suffering."[9] The effects may be quite individual and varied. We simply do not know.

What we do know is that many witnesses, when asked to testify about the crimes they suffered, express trepidation about their safety and the safety of their families, as well as their ability to withstand the rigors of recalling painful memories in a public setting.[10] Such concerns, however, are not uniform and vary depending on individual factors as well as local cultural and political dynamics.

Eric Stover has documented a wide array of experiences among eighty-seven witnesses who testified at the International Criminal Tribunal for the former Yugoslavia (ICTY), ranging from empowerment to disappointment to outrage.[11] Even when witnesses have an overall positive experience of testifying, they may experience moments of distress or negative feelings about some aspects of the proceedings. Witnesses' evaluations of trials are complex and may change at different stages of the proceedings and afterwards. In addition to the dynamics of personal factors, Eric Stover found that a witness's long-term feelings about testifying "will largely be dependent upon his or her perception of the trial's outcome and the extent to which it validated his or her participation in it."[12] Thus, the actual impact of participation may not be known until after proceedings have concluded and witnesses have had an opportunity to come to terms with the results.

An internal review of the Witnesses and Victims Section of the Special Court for Sierra Leone (SCSL) also found a diversity of experiences among witnesses.[13] In general, witnesses reported high levels of satisfaction with court services during trial.[14] Yet support in the courtroom did not seem to impact how witnesses evaluated their overall experience testifying in trials.[15] Witnesses' satisfaction also varied considerably after trials, in part due to the frequency and quality of contact with court personnel after witnesses returned home and witnesses' expectations of court responsiveness following trial.[16] Ongoing communication shaped witnesses' evaluations of their participation over time, and decreased witnesses' anxiety during the course of proceedings.[17] Other scholars have shown that witnesses who receive no post-trial follow-up report feeling "abandoned."[18]

Reflecting these dynamics, the Rome Statute – the constitutive document of the International Criminal Court – requires that the court's Registry maintain a Victims and Witnesses Unit (VWU) to "provide, in consultation with the Office of the Prosecutor, protective measures and security arrangements, counselling and other appropriate assistance for witnesses, victims who appear before the court, and others who are at risk on account of testimony given by such witnesses."[19] The Statute also provides that the VWU "include staff with expertise in trauma, including trauma related to crimes of sexual violence."[20] In a sense, the VWU is the "engine room" of the Registry, unseen but providing essential support – handling requests for witnesses from prosecutors and defense attorneys, preparing orientation materials, arranging travel and security, housing witnesses, providing protection measures and psychosocial support, and following up with witnesses once they return home.

III WITNESS MANAGEMENT AT THE ICC

ICC witnesses pass through six stages as part of their interaction with the Victims and Witnesses Unit. First, they meet with VWU staff, usually in their home country. Second, before they begin their journey to The Hague, VWU staff familiarize witnesses with the judicial process and what to expect as witnesses, some of which is provided in the form of a brochure and video. In the third stage, witnesses travel to The Hague. After arriving, in the fourth stage, they spend time waiting to appear at trial. During this stage, they learn about courtroom procedures and may have an opportunity to review any prior statements. Vulnerable witnesses also undergo psychological assessments and continue to be monitored by a VWU psychologist. In the fifth stage, witnesses testify. In the sixth and final stage, they spend time in The Hague "cooling down" before returning home or to a third country.

A Contact

The VWU's engagement with a witness starts after the witness has been selected by the calling party, has agreed to testify, and has been accepted by the relevant Chamber, but prior to his or her testimony. After the Chamber approves a witness list for either the prosecution or defense, the list is sent to the VWU. Witness information must arrive at the VWU a minimum of thirty-five days before testimony is scheduled to begin.

The party calling the witness completes a Witness Information Form, which is submitted to the VWU. In addition to protection information, the form provides operational and support information, such as travel documentation and personal information. The form captures, for example, information about psychological and medical needs, children, dependent care, and whether there is a need for escorts or accompanying staff. Based on this information, a six-member support team, which consists of support officers and support assistants, tailors its efforts to meet the needs of particular witnesses during their time in The Hague. One staff person is deemed the "case manager." He or she serves as the witness's primary contact once the witness is in The Hague and closely monitors the witness's well-being from that point forward. The others provide additional support and help with coordination and logistics.

If a witness comes to The Hague, VWU staff plan the travel, working with other ICC units as appropriate. A variety of issues arise when arranging to bring a witness from his or her home country. For example, if the witness needs to take time off work, VWU staff will meet to decide what to tell the witness's employer – creating a cover story or providing the witness with a letter from the ICC that confirms the need for a leave of absence. Frequently, a support officer will shop for clothes with a witness in his or her home country to prepare for the relatively cold weather in the Netherlands.

B Pre-Trial Familiarization

After initial contact is made, the process of explaining the court and its actors, as well as providing information about The Hague, begins in the field. Many witnesses, especially those from rural areas, have limited or no prior experience with formal legal systems. To help set expectations, each witness is given a brochure and shown a video that explains what to anticipate at the court and in The Hague. These materials describe everything from the city and its weather to the trial process. Since many witnesses have never flown before, the video and brochure provide an overview of what to anticipate on their flight.

Before traveling, each witness undergoes a "fit-to-travel" check, or medical check-up, to ensure that flying to The Hague will not pose a health risk. Potentially vulnerable witnesses also undergo a preliminary psychological assessment. If the assessment indicates witness vulnerability, a VWU psychologist schedules a full vulnerability assessment. Observations and conclusions from this secondary assessment, including recommendations for special measures, are submitted to the Chamber. Based on the report, the Chamber then decides on the capacity of the witness to testify as well as the need to use any special measures.

C Travel

Meeting the needs of witnesses while protecting their safety – as well as that of ICC staff – is a balancing act. Ideally, ICC staff travel with a witness from his or her home community to the international departure point. However, in some cases, ICC staff members are not permitted to travel to the witness's home village because of security restrictions. In other cases, it may be considered dangerous for a witness to be seen with ICC staff, or a witness may prefer to keep his or her cooperation with the court confidential. When such situations arise, a witness will travel alone to the departure city or an intermediate point to meet an ICC staff member, who then accompanies him or her to a secure location.

Witnesses typically leave their home country or third country on a commercial flight. Even when multiple witnesses come from the same town at the same time, they travel independently. This procedure helps to avoid the unwanted attention a group may attract, as well as unnecessary contact between witnesses. It also helps to maintain confidentiality and protect witnesses' identities. In addition, the VWU may follow orders from Chambers or requests of the calling parties to keep witnesses separate from each other.

In general, witnesses travel to The Hague without family or friends. Only in exceptional cases have witnesses been allowed to travel with companions.[21] For example, some witnesses have dependents who need care. In such cases, the dependents may be permitted to accompany the witness.[22] Having children present can be challenging for both witnesses and their children. Yet, for witnesses with small children and nursing infants, the ability to stay together can be crucial to enable the witness to testify. On occasion, a witness will request to bring a non-dependent to accompany him or her on the trip. In such cases, the VWU will analyze whether the request is reasonable, and who is the best person to accompany him or her. Staff at the court then arrange for passports and visas for the witness and his or her companions. In the case of witnesses traveling with family members, a second escort is typically assigned to assist the additional travelers.

Travel logistics can take time. For example, the DRC now uses biometric passports, which can take more than a month to acquire and require the witness to remain in Kinshasa for several days. In addition, travel itineraries can change on short notice, creating psychological and security challenges. For example, changes can compromise witness cover stories and create additional anxieties about being identified as trial participants. Witnesses also face the everyday hassles of travel. Court rules indicate that travel should be provided at the lowest cost available on public transit, which means that service and comfort may be less than ideal, especially on long international flights. Luggage has sometimes been lost or delayed, and witnesses have complained about the food. While not extraordinary, these everyday aggravations can add to witnesses' overall discomfort and anxiety.

Once a witness lands in The Hague, a driver from the ICC, and sometimes a member of the VWU support staff, meets him or her at the airport. The witness is then taken to a secure place to rest after the trip. If the witness is not already accompanied by someone from the witness unit, a VWU escort will meet the witness at his or her lodging.

D Waiting for Trial

On their first day in The Hague, witnesses have a day of rest. A VWU support staff member greets them and provides a welcome briefing, which includes an explanation of entitlements and the schedule for their stay. VWU staff also check on their well-being, inquire if they need anything, and provide a means to call in case of an emergency.

The VWU provides welcome packages to help ease witnesses' acclimation to the social and physical environment of The Hague. When needed, the packages include a toiletries kit analogous to those provided to travelers by airlines. Items may also include a fleece jacket, closed-toe shoes, a blanket, and shawls to ease the temperature shock upon arrival in The Hague. Witnesses often encounter low early morning temperatures after disembarking from chilly overnight flights. An unexpected challenge arose when some witnesses took the kits home, inadvertently identifying their participation with the court, since many of the items were not available locally.

After witnesses recuperate from their travel to The Hague, they are brought to the ICC for "court familiarization." The goal of the familiarization process is to introduce witnesses to the courtroom and attorneys before they testify, to lessen the likelihood that they will be overwhelmed when they come to trial. For at least forty-five minutes, and sometimes more than an hour, handlers explain the process of testifying, and take witnesses to see the physical layout of the courtroom, including where they will sit during the trial and testimony. Questions are encouraged, and second visits are arranged to demonstrate any special measures ordered in the case. In collaboration with Chambers, the VWU staff continually fine-tune the protocol, which is also used for witnesses who testify via video link, to respond to the unique needs of witnesses.

E Testifying

The focal point of witnesses' journey to The Hague is the act of testifying. Testimony can range from hours to days. Motivations for testifying vary, but most witnesses initially say they want their stories to be known and to help achieve justice.

The overwhelming majority of witnesses use some form of identity protection in the courtroom, a practice that has been criticized as counter to the goals of providing a fair trial and establishing an historical record.[23] Yet even when witnesses do use pseudonyms in place of their names and have their voice and visual image distorted, some witnesses still express trepidation about testifying in court, often fearing retribution back home. In addition, witnesses frequently worry that they might not perform well in court, and will consequently let down members of their community who are depending on them to establish the truth of what has occurred.

To assuage witnesses' security and other personal concerns, a case manager accompanies a witness throughout his or her time in The Hague. Case managers have many roles, serving as a resource and assisting with bills, shopping, and processing allowances. On occasion, the VWU also recommends an in-court assistant, based on a vulnerability assessment or the recommendation of a psychologist. Chambers must approve the use of an in-court assistant, who works under the guidance of a psychologist. This option is most common with sexual violence survivors and child soldiers. These assistants offer support during a witness's testimony, and, if needed, will sit beside the witness during his or her testimony to provide a reassuring or calming presence.

During the trial, all witnesses have access to a waiting room, which offers a private space for witnesses to sit in peace and/or vent their emotions. On some occasions, children or other dependents may pass time in the waiting room as well, though the VWU tries to keep them occupied in less dull places.

Shortly after testifying, the ICC support staff and the calling attorney meets with the witness to thank him or her, and act as a sounding board for the witness to reflect on his or her experience. Vulnerable witnesses also debrief with a VWU psychologist. Unlike other international tribunals, the ICC does not provide witnesses with an official letter thanking them for participating because of the risk of witnesses being identified and targeted at home.

At night, witnesses and their companions return to their lodgings. In most cases, the staff person who has accompanied the witness throughout the process stays at that same location and is available to talk through any concerns.

F Cooling Down

Once testimony is complete, a witness enters a cooling-off period, which may last days. VWU staff reassess the witness's security to determine whether it is safe for him or her to return home. They also create a handover report, which is given to members of the field office and, where applicable and as appropriate, to defense or prosecution teams. The report addresses any issues that require follow up after a witness is back in his or her country of origin.

Once travel is deemed safe, the witness returns home. From that point forward, direct contact with ICC staff is minimized to avoid creating a security risk. However, the VWU can assist with ongoing security measures, and provides witnesses with contact information for emergencies. Staff report that witnesses have used these security services, although they declined to discuss the frequency or details of specific instances out of concern for witness confidentiality.

The final contact with the VWU occurs – if at all – post-sentencing. After testifying, each witness is asked whether he or she would like to be notified of the final judgment and how he or she would like to be contacted. Most young witnesses request information via email; others request phone contact. Contact information is kept on file at the ICC for use at the conclusion of the trial.

IV METHODOLOGY

Building on an interview survey instrument that was created for a study of victim-witnesses at the International Criminal Tribunal for the former Yugoslavia (ICTY), Human Rights Center staff developed three questionnaires to be administered to ICC witnesses at three time points: (1) prior to testifying (N=104), (2) in the first few days after testifying (N=109), and (3) six to twelve months after testifying (N=32). The Human Rights Center also helped the VWU create a database for storing and analyzing the interview data. For analysis, the VWU provided the Human Rights Center with de-identified survey data from all participating witnesses. Researchers, therefore, did not have information about the specific identities – names, addresses, or other personal information – of ICC witnesses.

A *Pre-Testimony Survey*

The pre-testimony survey records witnesses' first impressions of interactions with the court and establishes a baseline for understanding how each witness feels about the court before testifying at trial.

The pre-testimony survey was offered to nearly all ICC witnesses in the *Lubanga* and *Katanga* cases. In rare instances, the survey was administered in the witness's home country (for example, when testimony was provided from the witness's home country via video link); more often, however, it was administered shortly after his or her arrival in The Hague. VWU support staff administered surveys on a voluntary basis, with most witnesses willing to take part. Of the 123 total witnesses, 104 participated in the pre-testimony survey.

B *Immediate Post-Testimony Survey*

Soon after testifying, all witnesses appearing before the court were asked to answer a second questionnaire. Of 123 witnesses who were approached, 109 agreed to take part in this second survey. VWU staff reported that the primary reason some witnesses declined to participate was because they felt too tired after appearing in court or there was little or no time before their departure for home.

VWU support staff generally conducted this survey in the witness waiting room. However, in exceptional cases, mostly due to a lack of time or a lack of available support assistance, escorts from the VWU conducted post-testimony interviews while the witness was heading home.

C Long-Term Post-Testimony Survey

VWU staff conducted the final survey six to twelve months after witnesses left the court. At the time of this analysis, this survey had been offered to a subset of witnesses in the *Lubanga* case. However, due to security concerns and a lack of resources, not all of the witnesses who were eligible were approached to take part in the follow-up survey. Some witnesses live in areas to which ICC staff were not allowed to travel due to security concerns. Staff also did not attempt to reach witnesses who lived more than 100 kilometers from a field office. In other cases, witnesses moved without providing new addresses, lacked phones, or lived in places inaccessible by road. In one case, a witness died before the survey could be administered.

Of those witnesses who were approached to take part in the long-term post-testimony survey, staff said that "very few" declined. In fact, witnesses were reportedly more willing to participate in this survey than in the survey administered shortly after testimony, perhaps because they were no longer as fatigued or had more time to process their experiences. Despite witnesses' apparent willingness, the number of respondents decreased significantly for the long-term post-testimony survey. Ultimately, only a fraction of the total number of witnesses who appeared at trial completed the final survey – thirty-two in total. Only two were women.

V LIMITATIONS

A number of factors limit the generalizability of this study's findings. First, the data reflect the impressions of witnesses involved in only two cases, both of which address crimes in the DRC. Witnesses from other situations and countries may have different experiences with and/or views of court proceedings. Second, it was not always possible to identify whether a witness was called by the prosecution or defense, which might impact impressions of testifying. Third, a limited number of ICC witnesses participated in the long-term survey. We also have no long-term data from sexual violence survivors who may confront specialized risks when returning home, and very little from women – phenomena we hope will be remedied with later surveys. Finally, because the surveys were administered by VWU staff and not by an uninterested third party, the data may have been impacted by "social desirability bias," in which respondents' feedback is skewed toward the positive due to a desire to please the interviewer. Despite these limitations, the surveys provide the first and most comprehensive overview of ICC witnesses' experiences possible, given the realities of access and security.

VI DISCUSSION

While witnesses testifying in international criminal trials often experience trepidation, their degree of fear, anxiety, and other emotions are particular and intimate. Motivations, expectations, and worries shift with the terrain of local environments and a witness's personal history. Recognizing the importance of subjectivities in shaping witnesses' experiences when they appear in ICC trials requires one to abandon hope for any universal approach to witness care and protection. Witness programs and protection measures must constantly evolve to meet the changing needs of witnesses in new cases and situations. Our purpose, then, is not to proscribe a single solution to the challenges of witnesses in general, but to take stock of the experiences of witnesses in the first two ICC trials and identify any common struggles from which lessons can be learned.

Formal legal processes invariably reduce witnesses' narratives, often forcing complicated and blurred memories to conform to tight timelines, rigid legal standards, and simple storylines.[24] The same can be said of survey instruments, such as those used in our study. Questionnaires may not ask the right questions or provide space for witnesses to describe the totality of their experiences. Despite these limitations, however, surveys can reveal shared understandings and apprehensions.

Survey interviews with ICC witnesses in the *Lubanga* and *Katanga* cases reveal that witnesses have concerns about their safety and the safety of their families. "I was worried about my security," explained one witness, "and that the protective measures were not enough. People can easily read transcripts of the proceedings on the internet and identify me." Such fears are understandable since triggermen and thugs may continue to walk the streets of local communities.

Despite such concerns, witnesses reported feeling safe both prior to and during their testimony – with women reporting slightly higher ratings than men – suggesting that most felt the security protections put in place by the Victims and Witnesses Unit were effective. However, many harbored concerns about returning home and what would happen once they were no longer under the protection of the court. They reported fears of being exposed and targeted by agents of the accused in their home communities. As a rule, the ICC does not prosecute low-level offenders. Yet often these are the persons who wield the knives and machetes of reprisals.

Prior to coming to The Hague, many ICC witnesses had never left their home country. For witnesses from rural villages in the Democratic Republic of Congo or Central African Republic, everything from the weather to food to local customs in The Hague could be unsettling. Some witnesses had advanced degrees and significant prior exposure to modern technology; others, however, had limited schooling and came from villages without electricity or cell phone or internet access, and thus faced significant logistical and cultural challenges to participating in trials far from home. These obstacles compounded a sense of uncertainty.

Witnesses, nevertheless, felt a duty to testify. They testified for a number of reasons. Some wanted the court to hear their account of the facts. Others wanted to confront the accused face-to-face. Still others wanted an opportunity to tell their story. Most had survived horrific crimes that had resulted in the deaths of others and felt it was their obligation to ensure that the killing of family members, neighbors, and colleagues was recorded and acknowledged. "There were things that have touched me," explained one witness. "Therefore, I wanted to testify about [them]." Another witness said: "It is a universal service for the interest of my people." Yet another explained: "I want to fight against impunity. I want justice to be done."

Witnesses also reported apprehension that they might not perform well in court. "I felt very intimidated," said one witness. "I felt naked, very exposed, vulnerable. I felt a very heavy responsibility having to take part in a process of justice." Another witness said: "I was fearful because it was my first time appearing in front of a court." The burden of representing the stories of family and friends back home weighed heavily on witnesses. They longed to establish the truth about what had happened.

Given witness concerns, orientation to the ICC and its processes proved critical for witness's psychological well-being. The survey data suggest that pre-trial witness orientation (the sharing of information about what to expect with regard to travel to The Hague, housing during the trial, support services, protection measures, the layout of the courtroom, and those who would be present during trial, etc.) is significant for two reasons. First, most witnesses had no prior experience with courts, either at home or abroad. Witness orientation mitigated anxieties and provided a relatively clear road map of what to expect before and after testifying. Second, as the vast majority of witnesses who testified in the *Lubanga* and *Katanga* trials used some form of protective measure (pseudonyms and facial and/or voice distortion), it is likely they entered the courtroom with a heightened sense of anxiety. Witnesses may feel more in control if they have a strong grasp of the layout of the courtroom, the identities of the principal court actors, and how the proceedings will evolve.

Considerable time can elapse between a witness's arrival and his or her appearance in court. Witnesses can spend days waiting. Thus, they frequently have free time in The Hague. For a number of witnesses, this time can be a source of anxiety. When asked what the worse part of the overall experience was, one witness said: "The worst part was the day before, waiting to testify." Another said: "The entire time you think about your testimony because you are so isolated as a witness. Day and night. This creates extra pressure. It would be good, if possible, if the VWU could find ways to diminish this isolation and pressure."

Most respondents indicated a high level of satisfaction with witness-related information and services. "All the information, preparation and advice I received helped me a lot," said a witness. "This made it easier for me during my testimony period." However, a few witnesses still felt unprepared when they took the stand. "I should have been better prepared by the party that called me," said one witness.

After testifying, witnesses felt conflicting emotions. Some expressed relief and pride, others exhaustion, still others fear. "I felt good. The fear that I had was over," said one witness. In post-testimony interviews, more than 80% of witnesses said they personally benefited from the experience of testifying and, if asked, would testify again. "It felt like letting go of something I had been holding on to," explained one witness. "I felt free and very proud that I had done my work well," said another.

After walking out of the courtroom, the fear of testifying that had consumed so many witnesses in the days before trial was replaced with a fear of reprisals upon their return home. "I wanted to talk with someone about my safety when I return home," explained a witness in a post-testimony interview after testifying. "I was worried about my security, [and] that the protective measures were not enough," said another. "I am afraid that the accused knows me, even though he could not see me," a witness said. "Therefore, the security of me and my family cannot be guaranteed." A few witnesses even reported threats after their return.

In addition to their concerns about future safety, witnesses – especially women – also expressed doubt as to whether their testimony helped establish the truth. Less than 60% of women answered "yes" when asked whether they thought their testimony helped establish the truth, as compared with 74% of men. But when asked soon after testifying whether their testimony helped them personally, both men and women indicated that it had. While encouraging, such positive assertions must be viewed with caution. It is extremely difficult to make general statements about how testifying will affect witnesses, especially survivors of mass atrocities, months or even years after the event. The lasting consequences of testifying are still unknown.

Long-term psychological responses to trauma, reactions to future stressors, and means of coping with old and new pressures vary from individual to individual and may change within an individual over time. Some witnesses who expressed feeling positive after testifying may come to have a different opinion if an accused is found not guilty or is given a short sentence. Moreover, the survey data from the third time point (six to twelve months post-testimony) is too limited to draw firm conclusions about how respondents viewed the impact of their testimony once they were resettled.

VII THE PATH FORWARD

Witness protection and care are paramount considerations for courts. Our data shows that in the *Lubanga* and *Katanga* cases witnesses were mostly satisfied with the preparation and services provided by the Victims and Witness Unit. On the whole, witnesses said they were well taken care of during the lead-up to trial and immediately afterwards. However, services and protection are often needed and may extend beyond these temporal boundaries. In-country care requires further assessment. An independent review of allegations of sexual assault victims under ICC protection in DRC found "institutional and chronic" shortcomings in the system for handling victim-witnesses, including insufficient training, a lack of clear Standard Operating Procedures, ineffective monitoring, and no safe and effective complaint system.[25]

While witnesses also harbor ongoing concerns about their safety and the safety of their families after testifying, long-term monitoring and court support is limited. Even recognizing that ongoing contact with witnesses is not always in their best interest, current witness handling falls short of the obligations articulated in the Rome Statute, which require that the ICC provide long-term protection, support, and other appropriate assistance.[26] We therefore propose the following recommendations for better addressing witness needs.

First, the ICC should put a process in place to better evaluate how witnesses experience their interactions with the court over time. (Currently, the three surveys are not linked to discrete persons due to concerns about witness confidentiality. Thus, we could not track changes in individual witness experiences and impressions across the three time points.) If possible, the VWU should track individuals across all three time points and note what factors, if any, are associated with changes in particular witnesses' perceptions of their experiences.

Second, the ICC should create a separate survey or other evaluation process for witnesses in the ICC protection program. We endorse the plan to have the protection subunit develop a separate evaluation for vulnerable witnesses in that program, since such witnesses' experiences may differ from those of other witnesses. This will help to ensure that each witness is questioned about issues that most pertain to his or her specific interactions with the court. It will also enable a more fine-tuned understanding of perceptions of the court and its various subunits.

Third, the ICC should continue to survey, especially once verdicts are reached. So far, long-term data is only available on a subset of witnesses from the *Lubanga* trial, which ended in a guilty verdict. To assess whether long-term feelings about participation are affected by case outcomes, it is important to assess witness experiences in cases with different verdicts. Additionally, witnesses in other ICC trials will come to the court from different backgrounds, having experienced different crimes, and with different expectations than the witnesses surveyed so far. It is important for the ICC to continue its assessment of service provisions as witnesses from different countries and contexts travel to The Hague to participate in trials – both for an understanding of the VWU's efficacy and for a better understanding of the experiences of witnesses in international criminal proceedings more generally.

Fourth, the gender dynamics of international criminal trials and the disparate consequences of testifying for men and women need further study. Additional research should focus on the relative paucity of female witnesses in mass atrocity cases before the ICC and other international tribunals. The survey data indicate that women are serving as witnesses in the trials at rates far lower than men. It is important to assess why this is in order to identify the factors that negatively and positively impact a woman's ability to testify in international criminal proceedings. Are investigators seeking out female witnesses at lower rates, or are women unable or unwilling to testify for other reasons? What is needed to enable more women to participate in international criminal proceedings?

In general, female witnesses gave slightly more positive ratings to their overall experience interacting with the court than men. This could be due to several factors. Women's expectations may have been different or VWU staff may have treated them differently. Women may have also been less comfortable expressing negative reactions than men. However, it is also possible that only women from relatively stable situations were able to travel to The Hague to testify, which could correlate with more positive experiences. In particular, women reported receiving more support from their family and friends than men. These differences suggest that women may only have been able to testify if they had a relatively high degree of external support. All of this merits further investigation.

Fifth, States Parties and other funders of the ICC must allocate sufficient resources to ensure effective witness services.[27] Our study found that the VWU is fulfilling its mission to facilitate the court's appearance of witnesses in an effective and professional manner. That said, the VWU will undoubtedly face greater challenges as more cases land on the ICC docket and the volume of witnesses increases proportionately. In particular, the VWU must be adequately funded to respond to breaches in witness protection and to develop sufficient operating procedures and training to mitigate the likelihood of witness abuse. Witness intimidation in the Kenyan cases and allegations of sexual assault by ICC staff in DRC underscore the need for more comprehensive protection.

The widespread use of protective measures by witnesses in those cases that have already gone to trial highlights the perceived risks involved in testifying. As many as 80% of the female respondents in our study testified using pseudonyms and facial and voice distortions, as did more than 60% of men. Such pervasive protective measures also raise questions integral to the accused's right to a fair trial. After all, the ICC must successfully pursue dual mandates of witness protection and guaranteeing the rights of defendants during trials. Importantly, however, increased funding should not just go to protection services; our study underscores the critical need to also adequately fund more general support services. Pre-trial preparation, ongoing social-psychological support, and help with logistics associated with testifying in The Hague all condition the experiences of witnesses and may have enduring effects on their lives post-testimony.

Finally, the ICC and its supporters should increase resources to follow up with witnesses once those witnesses have returned to their home countries. As noted above, we still do not know how testifying in atrocity cases impacts most witnesses months and years later. While surveying individuals who live a great distance from urban centers may be expensive and time consuming, many of the potential life changes that can result from testifying are most likely to occur after a witness returns home. This may include threats, assaults, or changes in relationship or job status. Further, ICC staff report that witnesses who are contacted often readily agree to answer post-testimony questions, indicating a desire on the part of witnesses to share their experiences.

Ultimately, long-term follow-up is essential to assess how the court impacts witnesses' lives, and such follow-up is strongly recommended when unlikely to put witnesses at increased risk.

Securing information from particularly vulnerable witnesses is especially important. Many victims return from testifying to extraordinarily challenging circumstances. Unfortunately, long-term information about these witnesses, especially those who return to the most remote and/or insecure regions, is scant. The court should incorporate survey-related practices that ensure the ongoing evaluation of witness experiences in different situation countries, with particular attention given to witnesses in ICC protection programs and to other particularly vulnerable witnesses, for whom the lasting effects of testifying may be severe. The Kenya cases underscore these concerns, showing how failures to protect sensitive witnesses can undermine prosecutions and the perceived validity of international criminal proceedings.

In recent years, the ICC has sought to correct past mistakes. The Office of the Prosecutor (OTP) has worked to improve investigations, developing new methods to gather probative and reliable linkage evidence, and incorporating new technologies to secure digital evidence, when available, to triangulate witness testimonies.[28] Such efforts suggest the court's recognition of the inherent problems of relying too much on witness testimony in regions where political corruption and violence remain commonplace. The collapse of the Kenya cases highlights the reality that gaps in witness protection can result in prosecutorial disintegration. Ultimately, witness experiences will continue to shape the perceived legitimacy and effectiveness of the ICC in the decades ahead. Investigators and prosecutors at the court will need a two-pronged strategy moving forward. They must build more robust cases before trials begin and simultaneously ensure that witnesses feel safe appearing at those trials. It is not an easy task, but it pales in comparison to the task set before most witnesses who testify in international criminal courts.

Notes

1. See Marlise Simons, 'International Criminal Court Formally Ends Case Against Kenya's President', *New York Times*, 13 March 2015.
2. On 16 December 2013, for example, Chief Prosecutor Bensouda gave notification that Witness 66 feared disclosure of her identify would jeopardize her personal safety and that of her family. See *The Prosecutor v Uhuru Muigai Kenyatta* (ICC-01/09-02/11), Prosecution communication of withdrawal of Witness 66, 16 December 2013.

3. Nicholas Kulish and Marlise Simons, 'Setbacks Rise in Prosecuting the President of Kenya', *New York Times*, 19 July 2013.

4. OTP, Statement of the Office of the Prosecutor regarding the reported abduction and murder of Mr. Meshak Yebei, 9 January 2015.

5. *The Prosecutor v. Thomas Lubanga Dyilo* (ICC-01/04-01/06), 'Decision on the Confirmation of Charges', 29 January 2007.

6. *Le procureur c. Germain Katanga*, (ICC-01/04-01/07), 'Décision relative à la peine' (article 76 du Statut), 23 May 2014 (original in French).

7. Tom R. Tyler, *Why People Obey the Law* (Princeton: Princeton University Press, 2006); Justice Tankebe, 'Public Cooperation with the Police in Ghana: Does Procedural Fairness Matter?' (2009) 47(4) *Criminology* 1265.

8. Richard J. McNally, *Remembering Trauma* (Cambridge: Harvard University Press, 2003), p. 106.

9. David Mendeloff, 'Trauma and Vengeance: Assessing the Psychological and Emotional Effects of Post-Conflict Justice' (2009) 31 *Human Rights Quarterly* 593.

10. See, e.g., Eric Stover, Mychelle Balthazard and Alexa Koenig, 'Confronting Duch: Civil party participation in Case 001 at the Extraordinary Chambers in the Courts of Cambodia' (2011) 93 (882) *International Review of the Red Cross* 503.

11. Eric Stover, *The Witnesses: War Crimes and the Promise of Justice in The Hague* (Philadelphia: University of Pennsylvania Press, 2005).

12. *Ibid.*, note 2 at p. 130.

13. The Special Court for Sierra Leone, 'Best-Practice Recommendations for the Protection & Support of Witnesses: An Evaluation of the Witness & Victims Section of the Special Court for Sierra Leone' (2008).

14. *Ibid.*, at 14.

15. *Ibid.*, at 16–17.

16. *Ibid.*, at 18.

17. *Ibid.*, at 22.

18. Stover, *The Witnesses*; Catherine C. Byrne, 'Benefit or Burden: Victims' Reflections on TRC Participation, Peace and Conflict' (2004) 10(3) *Journal of Peace Psychology* 237–256.

19. Rome Statute, art. 43(6).

20. *Ibid.*

21. The Registry determines eligibility to bring a support person on trips to The Hague based on the VWU's assessment. Criteria include (but are not limited to) severe trauma-related symptoms, suicidal tendencies, the potential for violence, age, whether the witness has been a victim of sexual or gender-based violence, and/or whether the witness is suffering severe physical or psychological symptoms. See, e.g., Rule 88 of the ICC's

Rules of Procedure and Evidence, and Regulation 91 of the Regulations of the Registry.

22. Most witnesses have children. Thus, the VWU typically assesses whether childcare can be better organized in the witness's home country or if children will be better served by accompanying the witness to the Court. See International Criminal Court Regulations of the Registry, ICC-BD /03-01-06-Rev.1, 25 September 2006, 90.

23. Patricia M. Wald, 'Dealing with Witnesses in War Crime Trials: Lessons from the Yugoslav Tribunal' (2002) 5 *Yale Human Rights & Development Law Journal* 217–240.

24. Marie-Bénédicte Dembour and Emily Haslam, 'Silencing Hearings? Victim-Witnesses at War Crimes Trials' (2004) 15(1) *European Journal of International Law* 151–177; Susana SaCouta, 'Victim Participation at the International Criminal Court and the Extraordinary Chambers in the Courts of Cambodia: A Feminist Project?' (2012) 18 *Michigan Journal of Gender and Law* 297–360.

25. 'Post Incident Review of Allegations of Sexual Assault of Four Victims Under the Protection of the International Criminal Court in Democratic Republic of Congo by a Staff Member of the Court', December 2013, pp. 5–6.

26. The Court's Rules and Procedures dictate that the VWU formulate long-term and short-term plans for the protection of witnesses and victim participants, as well as recommend to other Court organs the adoption of protection measures and means to assist witnesses. As a measure of last resort, protection can be provided through participation in the ICC Protection Programme. The VWU does not identify witnesses or victim participants on its own, but acts upon referral or request from other organs of the Court. Although protection and support services are particularly pertinent during the trial stage, these measures can be requested and provided at all stages of proceedings, from pre-trial to post-trial. The VWU has developed protocols and cooperation agreements with a number of national and international partners to assist its work. In accordance with Rule 16 of the Rules of Procedure and Evidence, the Registrar may negotiate confidential agreements on relocation and provision of support services on the territory of a State on behalf of the Court. The VWU actively works with States Parties and other entities to maintain an effective national and international protection regime for witnesses and victim participants who appear before the Court.

27. The VWU is comprised of a chief, twenty-five staff at headquarters, and twenty-five staff in field offices. The VWU's current budget represents 5.9% of the ICC's total (in 2014, this amounted to 7.2 million euros out of a total of 121.6 million euros).

28. See Stephen Smith Cody, Camille Crittenden, Alexa Koenig, and Eric Stover, 'Digital Fingerprints: Using Electronic Evidence to Advance Prosecutions at the International Criminal Court' (Human Rights Center, Berkeley School of Law, 2014); Stephen Smith Cody, Alexa Koenig, Andrea Lampros, and Julia Rayner, 'First Responders: An International Workshop on Collecting and Analyzing Evidence of International Crimes' (Human Rights Center, Berkeley School of Law, 2014); Peggy O'Donnell, Eric Stover, Camille Crittenden, and Alexa Koenig, 'Beyond Reasonable Doubt: Using Scientific Evidence to Advance Prosecutions at the International Criminal Court' (Human Rights Center, Berkeley School of Law, 2013).

PART IV

BEYOND THE ICC

Local and Regional Justice Mechanisms in Africa

13

Darfur Tribal Courts, Reconciliation Conferences and 'Judea'
Local Justice Mechanisms and the Construction of Citizenship in Sudan

Karin Willemse

I INTRODUCTION

After the Sudanese Islamist regime under the leadership of Omar al-Bashir came to power in 1989 by a military coup, it sent 'travelling *shari'a* courts'[1] to Darfur in an attempt to curb the power of 'tribal'[2] leaders. The heads of diverse ethnic groups were at that time engaged in tribal reconciliation conferences in an attempt to negotiate peace after violent clashes over access to land and water that had taken place in the 1980s. Paradoxically, in the same period tribal judicial institutions were revived in Khartoum, the capital of the Sudanese nation-state, operating in conjunction with shari'a courts. While tribal courts in Darfur deal with homicide cases as well as with minor legal cases related to disputes over land, trespassing, conflicts between neighbouring ethnic groups and ecological crimes (like gathering firewood in forbidden areas), tribal judicial institutions in Khartoum mainly treat cases of homicide.

The historical and political background to this development had consequences for the way in which tribal identities and the notion of citizenship construct each other. Taking a closer look at the condoning and even promoting of tribal courts in Khartoum in relation to the way tribal identities have become central to the Darfur war (since 2003) is crucial to understanding both the position that al-Bashir's regime has taken in this war as well as the problem in considering tribal reconciliation mechanisms as 'an alternative option for the prosecution of international crimes'.[3] This chapter explores the problem of considering local, tribal reconciliation mechanisms in places like Sudan as an alternative to international justice mechanisms, when these processes of tribal justice are constructed as longstanding 'traditional' and non-political phenomena, unrelated to national politics and machinations.

As the editors of this volume state in the Introduction, the idea of the International Criminal Court's 'Africa Problem' was triggered by the Prosecutor's decision to seek a warrant for the arrest of President al-Bashir in 2008.[4] The prosecution of al-Bashir was based on charges of war crimes, crimes against humanity and genocide committed during the war in Darfur that started in 2003. In that year, the SLM/A and JEM political parties took up arms against the Sudanese government, accusing it of political and economic marginalization of the region. In the ensuing war, the Sudanese government provided military support to the so-called 'Janjaweed' and allowed these Arab militia to operate with total impunity. They allied with the Arab nomadic groups that tried to access land and water resources in the sedentary areas and they are generally considered the perpetrators of the violence enacted upon the sedentary farming population. Leaders of a diverse range of sedentary groups in Darfur insist that the depopulation of villages and forced changes in land ownership are part of a government strategy to change the demography of the region of Darfur.[5]

As Mahmood Mamdani has pointed out, the ahistoric and one-sided perspective articulated by the Court's first Prosecutor, Louis Moreno-Ocampo, in defence of the indictment blaming al-Bashir for single-handedly racializing the conflict in Darfur, boosted the accusations of politicized justice that continue to undermine the legitimacy of the ICC.[6] The question of politically motivated selectivity in the dynamic between the Security Council and the ICC became an increasingly important topic, not only among African political leaders and institutions but also among the victims of the alleged mass atrocities.

The issues addressed in this chapter are not so much concerned with the validity of the indictment of al-Bashir or the role of the Sudanese government in the atrocities that have been enacted in Darfur.[7] It does, however, constitute an important context for looking beyond the ICC in order to 'ponder the plethora of judicial and non-judicial developments' that are underway in Darfur.[8] The issues at play concern the reality that both practitioners and academics have identified indigenous judicial practices as important to dispute settlement and reconciliation processes in (post-)war societies. They often argue that these practices make people's sense of justice central and are therefore 'culturally more embedded and locally owned'.[9] In addition, many argue that most people who have suffered under conditions of war and violence will often prioritize personal security and the restoration of economic rights over criminal or punitive justice: in this respect reconciliatory justice mechanisms are 'forward-looking or future-oriented'.[10] In discussions concerning how to attain both peace and justice in post-conflict societies, the dichotomy between retributive and restorative justice has made way for 'multiple conceptions of justice and reconciliation, state and non-state instruments; legal, semi-judicial and non-judicial techniques'.[11] As Kofi Annan, then UN secretary-general, stated already in 2004, 'due regard must be given to indigenous and informal traditions for administering justice or settling disputes, to help them to continue their often vital role and to do so in conformity with both international standards and local tradition'.[12] In other words, restorative local justice mechanisms are seen as complementary and not as an alternative to international justice mechanisms such as the ICC.

However, although the strength of the 'African view of justice' is that it prioritizes the healing of post-conflict societies through the reintegration of both victims and perpetrators, in the introduction of the volume *Traditional Justice and Reconciliation after Violent Conflict*, Luc Huyse warns against romanticizing traditional justice mechanisms.[13] He considers the knowledge gap about the precise workings of these local justice mechanisms the cause of this 'myth making'. Huyse problematizes the notion of 'traditional' since 'colonizing authorities and processes of modernization, civil war and genocide have had deeply disturbing effects on the original institutions'. In this respect, an important consideration is the extent to which traditional justice mechanisms can escape the political power games of which the ICC is accused. Following Huyse, I consider the Darfur tribal courts, tribal reconciliation conferences and *judea*, which are central to this chapter, as 'hybrids' that operate in the 'shadow of the state'.[14]

The idea that reparations through restorative justice serve the victims of the Darfur war better than retributive justice is therefore analysed in the historical context of judicial and political processes within the Sudanese nation-state. Under British colonial rule, the *shari'a*[15] courts and tribal judicial institutions were juxtaposed in order to 'divide and rule', and this division is still relevant in the post-colonial state of Sudan. In both periods, the access to and control over land were essential for the working of local justice mechanisms in Darfur. Ultimately, both the access to different kinds of courts as well as access to land are tied to notions of citizenship: tribal identities, as the basis for these diverse rights of access, are also central to the way the Sudanese government constructs an exclusive notion of Sudanese citizenship. As I will argue, it is precisely this issue of citizenship that calls into question the saliency of tribal reconciliation mechanisms as a panacea for victims of the war in Darfur.

II TRIBAL AND SHARI'A COURTS: THE POLITICAL STRUCTURE
SINCE THE DARFUR SULTANATE

In Darfur, the acknowledgement of the distinction between local, informal forms of justice and more formal courts dates back to pre-colonial times.[16] As O'Fahey notes:

> In fact, nowhere else is the divide between the Fur and the Islamic dimensions more explicit than in law and justice. Customary law and its practitioners, the chiefs and the elders –the latter an integral part of any Dar Fur court – co-existed with the Shari'a and its exponents, the *fuqara* and *qadis*.[17]

This coexistence meant in practice that criminal cases were tried in the sultanic period according to customary law by the local chief, such as a sheikh, *shartai* or *omda*, while personal cases such as inheritance and marriage were tried by a *qadi*, a shari'a judge.[18] If a plaintiff was dissatisfied with the ruling of a sheikh or *shartai* he or she had the option to appeal to a *qadi*. Sometimes local leaders themselves would consult *fuqara*, religious teachers, when administering justice. The further a plaintiff went up the judicial hierarchy, the more decisive the role of the *fuqara* became. The sultan, who constituted the highest authority of the judicial system, would consult a group of advisors consisting mainly of *fuqara* and some notables when considering a case. Thus, the division between Islamic courts and local customary courts, even during the Sultanate, proved less strict than may seem at a first glance.

At the same time, many disputes were settled within groups, such as the family or tribe, through local reconciliation mechanisms by negotiation between elders, sheikhs and other local leaders.[19] Since tribal leaders decided on issues related to local politics and access to land, the decision of a person to bypass the authority of the local leader in order to seek justice from a *faqih*, *qadi* or sultan could have repercussions.

People referred to the place where they were living as a *dar*,[20] which was generally ethnically diverse. The residing tribe that constituted a majority would often deliver the head of the native administration. The sultan could grant *hawakir* (sing. *hakura*), or land titles, as a kind of 'tribal land ownership' or as extended administrative rights, such as exemption from taxation, in order to reward notables or to provide members of the royal family with an income. He could also allot *hawakir* so as to attract newcomers to sparsely populated areas, notably religious teachers who were thus also tied to the sultan's court. The term *hakura* referred both to the right of an individual or a group of individuals over an estate and to the document describing the land

grant itself, stipulating its boundaries and privileges. A *hakura* holder
would generally assemble his family and clan members around him,
which meant that the tribe of the owner would most often constitute the
majority in that area. Although a *hakura* holder might thus try to become
independent of the sultan, *hakura* rights were never meant as freehold
titles, but rather as a feudal jurisdiction.[21] The authority of local leaders
in local conflicts and judicial issues became even more pronounced under
the Anglo-Egyptian Condominium, which incorporated Darfur into the
colonial state of Sudan in 1916. In this period, the division between shari'a
courts and customary courts became a focus of colonial policy.

III THE ANGLO-EGYPTIAN CONDOMINIUM: FROM 'COLONIAL SHARI'A' TO NATIVE COURTS UNDER INDIRECT RULE[22]

After re-capturing the colony from the Mahdist rulers in 1899, the Sudan was
referred to as the Anglo-Egyptian Condominium (1899–1956). In fact, the
British were the main colonial power as they appointed the governor general,
who constituted the highest authority in a three-tier judicial system: apart from
the shari'a courts and tribal or 'native' courts, there were the civil courts meant
for 'non-Mohammedans' as well as for Muslims who themselves chose to, and
could afford to, bring their cases for trial. These civil courts, based upon
English common law, were called the 'ordinary courts', which clearly indicated that the British considered these courts to be a superior system that set
the norm. The Sudan Penal Code was based on the Indian Penal Code as
codified under British colonial rule. Only with respect to personal law cases[23]
would customary and shari'a law prevail, unless this was 'contrary to justice,
equity and good conscience'.[24]

   The acceptance of shari'a courts, albeit with a lower judicial status than
the ordinary courts, was strategic. Fear of a revival of Mahdist uprisings[25] and
resistance from the religious elite against a non-Muslim government were
the reasons to not only keep the shari'a courts in place, but also to include
Egyptians and some Sudanese in a judicial system where the British held
the highest authority. In their attempt to both control and curb the influence
of shari'a *qadis*, the colonial government in fact modernized the shari'a
courts. It established a Qadi College in Umdurman to officially train shari'a
judges in 1902. The Grand Qadi was to be an Egyptian and this meant that,
since the dominant legal school (*madhhab*) in Sudan was Maliki and in
Egypt it was Hanafi, there were legal innovations, especially in family and
personal law cases, as the judgments were often based on both schools.[26]
The Mohammedan Law Courts Ordinance of 1902 and the Mohammedan

Law Courts Procedure Act of 1915 partly codified these regulations in so-
called *Manshurat al-mahakim al-Shari'a*, or periodical circulars, where
formerly *fatwa* were used.[27] The regulations needed, however, to be
approved by the governor-general before they could become part of shari´a.[28]

Though this policy meant a retaining of the shari'a courts, these were
referred to by Jeppie as 'the colonial shari'a', which aptly indicates its 'curious
in-between position: it was neither English nor customary and often conflicted
with both'.[29] This precarious situation changed after World War I, when the
fear of possible Sudanese nationalist resistance as a result of the anticolonial
protests in Cairo (1919–1922) caused the British colonial government to try and
contain the power of the *qadis*[30] in favour of native, 'tribal' administration.
The policy of 'indirect rule' replaced the direct intervention of the British
in administrative and judicial issues in less than a decade. The 'Power of
Nomad Sheikhs Ordinance' (1922), later the 'Power of Sheikhs Ordinance'
(1928) and the 'Village Courts Ordinance' (amended in 1930) and finally the
'Native Courts Ordinance' of 1932, led to an increase in the influence of native
authorities while the authority of the shari'a courts was curtailed. Many shari'a
judges were forced to retire and about half of the forty-two shari'a courts were
abolished while seventy-two native courts had tried over ten thousand cases by
the end of 1929.[31] These ordinances, however, did not mean that the
qadis quietly left the scene, and in the 1920s and 1930s growing conflict over
jurisdiction, especially over family law cases, was reported by colonial
authorities.[32]

The justification to replace shari'a courts with native courts was that tribal
leaders were considered 'natural leaders' and thus aware of the 'customs' of
their tribes.[33] They were considered most apt to have executive and judicial
powers at this local level. The British thereby constructed an existential
difference between the customary courts of this native administration and
the shari'a courts since the latter were cast as textually based, fixed and thus
removed from ordinary people. In addition, the formalization of the authority
of local leaders had consequences for the role land played in the construction
of tribal identities.

IV ACCESS TO LAND, ACCESS TO LEADERS: THE CONSTRUCTION
OF A TRIBAL IDENTITY

Contemporary notions of tribal identity are the consequence of a political
process of (colonial) state building during the twentieth century and are
therefore connected to notions of citizenship that were constructed alongside
them. The fixing of tribal identities took place under British colonial rule,

when the so-called Native Administration (*idara ahlia*) was implemented as a means of enhancing security, as well as 'tidying up the confusion of ethnic identities and tribal allegiances that existed across Sudan'.[34] The government reinforced the system of land allocation already in place, with some minor adjustments, by issuing a series of acts and decrees. This resulted, however, in an administrative structure that altered the nature of tribal authority.

The Native Administration was to keep law and order within its own tribe as well as between tribes.[35] Apart from mediating in cases of conflict, local leaders were also to perform administrative tasks, such as tax assessment and collection, the protection of the environment and organizing communal labour, 'on the cheap'. The Native Administration had its own treasury, staff and a political hierarchy of local leaders consisting of three levels: the paramount tribal leaders called alternately *shartai, malik* or sultan, who were the main leaders in a designated 'tribal area'.[36] The *omda* was a new (originally Egyptian) title given to the intermediary between these paramount chiefs and local leaders or sheikhs who represented their villages. In order to formalize this Native Administration, the British also bestowed titles on the paramount chiefs of some of the Arab nomadic groups. The leaders of four Arab nomadic groups of southern Darfur, referred to as Baggara after the cows they were herding, and only two Abbala or camel nomads of the arid desert zone of northern Darfur, the Zayadiya and Beni Hussein, acquired the title of 'nazir'. This political system held a parallel hierarchy of native courts that administered designated areas of land. The landless Arab nomadic groups, who due to their migratory life-style were not considered to be in need of a *dar* or a *nazirate*, thus also did not have political representation at a local level.

In the same period that the Native Court Ordinances were put into practice between 1922 and 1932, the colonial government issued acts that regulated access to and control over land. The Land Settlement and Registration Act of 1925 regulated the registration of property rights, while the 1930 Land Acquisition Act was designed to allow for the expropriation of land for public projects. Despite the fact that customary rights related to *dar* and *hakura* rights were recognized, most of these lands were never formally registered due to a lack of colonial institutions that could survey and register the land under the 1925 Act. However, since the law was mainly applied in urban areas and development schemes in the Nile Valley, the government did not interfere in the customary land rights in the rural areas.[37]

This fuzzy situation in fact worked quite well since under customary law land rights were not considered private property, but rather a kind of multi-ethnic homeland that allowed its *hakura* owners and 'tribal leaders' to adjust land allocation to changing conditions, such as to accommodate newcomers, to re-allocate land according to the need of both local residents and migrant groups that settled temporarily and to negotiate migration routes with nomads. So, this system worked precisely because of the ambiguity and flexibility of the notion of land use rather than land ownership. It also meant an acknowledgement of the authority of local leaders to allocate usufruct rights in return for part of the crop or other kinds of taxation and their roles as arbiters in case of conflict.

In short, the Native Administration implemented by the British meant that tribal areas became fixed administrative units and control over land became a precondition of political participation and representation, and vice versa. As *dars* and *hawakir* were never ethnically homogeneous, tribal courts were set up in which each of the tribal groups had a representative, headed by the paramount chief of the main ethnic group in the area. Thus, the new Native Administration resulted in a fixing of boundaries and positions in a way that had not been the case before. It was precisely this uneven distribution of land and administrative powers among the sedentary population as compared to the Arab nomadic groups, especially the Rizeigat camel nomads of northern Darfur, which would become a major cause of the violent conflicts in Darfur from the 1980s.[38]

Those landless Arab nomadic groups, mainly in North Darfur, that did not have access to tribal land could each make use of a so-called *damra*, a kind of temporary village or dry-season camp where they would stay for small periods of time while passing with their herds, or where women, children and the elderly were left behind when the young men would migrate with their camels to grazing areas to the far north of Darfur. In the absence of tenure rights such as *dars* or *hakuras*, these nomadic Arab groups resorted under the authority of local sedentary chiefs, who would allocate land rights to these temporary settlers. It was this situation that the landless Arabs tried to redress in the 1970s and 1980s when recurrent droughts made their nomadic way of life increasingly difficult to maintain, which resulted in a more permanent residing in these encampments. This settlement process led to more conflicts with sedentary farmers over access to land and water.

During the 1970s and 1980s, due to drought and periods of famine, the influx of former Arab nomads in the sedentary areas took on huge proportions: more migrants stayed on a more permanent basis than before. At the same time, sedentary farmers started to make 'exclosures' by fencing off tracts of land near the riverbeds in order to irrigate crops using motor pumps, or to fend off the Arab nomads who tended to come down with their camels earlier in the season, trampling the crops that were not yet harvested. In addition, nomads wanted to access government services, such as education and medical services as well as political representation in order to vie for these services. The younger generation in particular aspired to a modern lifestyle.[39] These landless Arabs have in the recent war in Darfur (from 2003) been fighting for access to land that they can call their own, on the one hand, by physically occupying land, and on the other by establishing legal claims to land. It was this issue that was taken up by the Arab Congregation (*Tajamu al-Arabi*), a Libya-backed organization based on an Arab supremacist ideology.[40]

The claim of landless Arabs to a modern tenure system that would bypass the *hakura* system and the authority of sedentary tribal leaders was based on the Unregistered Land Act decreed under Nimeiri[41] in 1970. This Act allowed the Sudanese state to consider all unregistered land as land of the state, including land titles accorded under customary law. In 1971, this new military regime abolished the Native Administration Act and replaced it with the People's Local Government Act. However, many of the former tribal elite of the Native Administration took up positions in the newly founded Rural People's Councils.[42]

Even though the formal power of the local leaders was thus eroded, the influence of tribal leaders continued to play a significant role in local politics and intra-tribal relations. Therefore, the rebuilding of tribal administration from 1986 onwards under the democratic regime of As-Sadiq al-Mahdi proved to be a continuation of a structure that had in fact never really been disbanded.[43] In particular, the tribal reconciliation justice mechanisms continued to play a role in handling conflicts and judicial issues in the local, day-to-day setting.

One of these reconciliation mechanisms is the Tribal Reconciliation Conference, which was designed under British colonial rule and usually held when ethnic groups resorted to violence and the tribal leaders of the native administration were unable or unwilling to resolve the conflicts. However, since the native administrators were ultimately responsible for implementing the agreement, including compensation and regulation of land uses, this meant that these native administrators were recognized as the principal mediators in these government-sponsored conferences.[44]

That this kind of tribal reconciliatory institutions is still relevant became particularly clear during one of the main Tribal Reconciliation Conferences held in Darfur in 1989.[45] Its goal was to settle a major ethnic conflict between sedentary Fur and Arab nomadic groups who had clashed in and around Jebel Marra over access to land since 1987. The failure of this Tribal Reconciliation Conference to settle the conflict would haunt the military government and lead up to the Darfur War that has been waged here since 2003.

Generally, it would be the government that decided on the time and venue of the conference and it would invite the parties in conflict to select their representatives. It also chose the members of the so-called *ajawid* (sing. *ajwadi*), or mediators, most often tribal leaders who acted as native administrators although these may also have included influential religious persons and notables. Finally, it appointed a chairperson for the conference, who was assisted by a team of specialists (e.g. the attorney general, the magistrate, the police or local government officers). The Tribal Reconciliation Conference of 1989 was convened by Dr Sese, the then governor of Darfur, who began negotiations in February of that year. The main parties finally met in El-Fasher on 29 May. The Arab delegation consisted of 110 persons of twenty-seven Arab tribes led by Al Hadi Eisa Debakaa, Nazir of the Beni Helba Arabs; The Fur delegation was headed by Dimingawi[46] Fadl Sese of Dar Dīma and also consisted of 110 persons. In the period between February and May, both parties had been prepared for the meeting by a mediation committee, an *ajawid* of twenty-six persons consisting of tribal leaders from Darfur, North and South Sudan and high-ranking civil servants and officers from the Sudanese regimental force.[47]

The conference would start with the reading out loud of the petitions made by the disputants. A lengthy negotiation by the *ajawid* would follow before an agreement might be reached and signed by the representatives of the parties in the conflict.[48] The way the conference operated was in fact based on a well-established reconciliation mechanism that was used among all tribes in Darfur: the so-called *judea*.[49] Although the application of a means of negotiation that all parties recognized may have caused the successful convening of the parties in the conflict, the way it was transformed into a major reconciliation structure was probably also the reason for the failure of the reconciliation attempt.

V THE TRIBAL RECONCILIATION CONFERENCE AND THE JUDEA MECHANISM: THE ISSUE OF TIME

The reconciliation agreement was signed on 8 July 1989, one week after the Revolution of National Salvation led by Omar al-Bashir took over state power from the democratic regime led by the UMMA party leader As-Sadiq al-Mahdi (1985–1989).[50] The agreement stipulated that the Arab tribes together needed to compensate the Fur for deaths and destruction of property by paying a sum of 43,218.773 Sudanese pounds (£S), while the Fur had to pay a sum of £S10,883.459 to compensate the Arabs.[51] The Central Sudanese government, in turn, was asked to contribute £S10,433.350 to both parties. The agreement was signed by the 110 Arab and 110 Fur representatives present as well as twenty-one mediators and witnessed by the new Military Governor of Darfur. A few weeks later, fighting between groups of Fur and Arabs started again and the Reconciliation Agreement was never implemented.

Different commentators have asserted that the agreement did not hold because the new military government lacked the will to enforce the agreement, while the great diversity of sub-groups among both tribes in the conflict made it hard to bind them collectively to an agreement decided upon by a delegation of tribal leaders.[52] In addition, the generational conflict among tribes has caused a predominance of young men in the conflict, or rather, conflicts, in Darfur and the power of the elders engaged in the negotiations is thus also at issue here.[53] However, the inclusiveness of the negotiations may have been enhanced if the character of the local negotiation mechanism of the *judea* had been taken seriously; that is, to allow for a considerable period of time to pass during which all parties in the conflict are consulted, often more than once, before a final agreement by the *ajawid*, consisting of members who are all considered neutral by both sides, is reached.

In Darfur, *judea* refers to the local informal negotiation and reconciliation institution performed by the *ajawid*, which consists of mostly elderly men of the major families or lineages of a tribe, village or ward who are respected for their insight in local traditions and relations, for their affiliations and for the fact that they are generally considered to be 'wise' men with negotiation skills. It is thus an institution with both a local and ethnic foundation. As capital punishment is not part of the verdict that a *judea* may deliver, its judicial mechanism consists of the negotiation of compensation in the case of damage of property and/or homicide paid by the localized group of the guilty party to the group of the victim. Although the *judea* is generally considered an intra-tribal mechanism of reconciliation and tribal courts are seen as the venue to settle inter-tribal conflicts, many smaller tribal groups or clans may also use a *judea*-like mechanism for inter-tribal conflicts in order to come to a reconciliation and reparation agreement that is acceptable to all parties.[54] The *judea* is marked by its informality as well as its inclusiveness, which accounts for the extended period of time that is needed to negotiate an agreement.[55]

During the *judea* negotiations, the *diya*, or Islamic blood payment, as stipulated in the shari'a is the main issue that is debated. The *diya* constitutes a financial compensation paid to the victim or heirs of a victim in the case of murder, bodily harm or property damage and it is an alternative punishment to *qisas*, or equal retaliation. In Darfur, this general Islamic principle is extended by the notion of *rakuba*, which refers literally to a shed providing shade to a semi-secluded space that allows people to assemble in an informal way to hang out and discuss issues relevant to those present. In the case of reconciliation negotiations, it has this spatial as well as a legal connotation, as it also refers to the investigation into comparable cases of homicide between both ethnic groups involved in the past. In this way, the *judea* on both sides may establish whether the parties had in this case the past agreed on a token *diya*. This investigation does not need to be confined to the particular localized groups but may extend to the tribe at large, since families that constituted a localized tribal unit in the past may have moved away since.[56] *Rakuba* is thus a renegotiated *diya* on the basis of past decisions on similar cases between the parties involved. In case of the existence of a *rakuba*, the *diya* demanded as compensation of the current conflict may also be reduced accordingly.[57]

This principle was taken into account during the Tribal Reconciliation agreement referred to above, since the amount to be paid by the Fur to the Arabs could not be deduced from the amount that the Arab groups needed to give to the Fur. The principle of the *judea* is that all members of the 'guilty' party share in this payment. In these negotiations an important role is therefore that of the *dimlij*, or district chief. He is both a liaison between the *judea* or the tribal court and the people of the clan or tribe involved in (the settlement of) a dispute in his district and may be of either tribal group, or of another tribe that is familiar with both groups. When a compensation is agreed upon, the *dimlij* of the guilty party will go from door to door in order to gather the money according to the wealth and number of family members, while the heirs of the victim get their share in the compensation via their *dimlij*.[58] In this way, all members of the tribal groups involved are aware of both the homicide and the agreement and thus become responsible for keeping peace between both parties: the members of the tribal group of the guilty party by paying their dues, and the families of the aggrieved party by receiving the payment, whether they agree on the decision taken by their elders or not. The *dimlij* have no party in the negotiation itself and are therefore considered to be neutral.

Apart from liaising between the different parties at different stages in the process of negotiation and payment, the *dimlij* has another, less articulated role as he grants all involved a sense of dignity and agency: of being heard and being taken seriously, since both parties are able to voice their arguments and have the other party listen to these through this intermediary. In this way the (often emotional) arguments of both sides are brought out in the open in a public setting without direct legal repercussions. As the *dimlij* travels up and down both parties, this process takes place over an extended period of time. It is precisely this lapse of time during which the negotiations take place that is important, since it allows for emotions to lose their edge and for the *judea* of both parties find common ground when agreeing on a compensation that is considered just by all parties.

The *Mahkamat al-Gabila* or *Makhamat al-Ahliya* (native court) is the more official institution in this reconciliation process. Despite the fact that tribal institutions lost their authority after the official ending of the Native Administration in 1971, they kept their role as arbiters in dispute settlements, especially in cases of ethnic tensions and conflicts over access to land.[59] So, in case the *judea* reached a reconciliation agreement, the *Mahkamat al-Ahliya* would endorse it: if the *judea* could not reach an agreement, the case might be referred to the *Mahkamat al-Ahliya*. In some areas where there was a *Mahkamat al-Gabila* or *Ahliya* in the same area as where the conflict had occurred, this might even be the first reconciliation institution to turn to instead of the more informal *judea*, in particular in cases in which more than two parties are involved. However, also in these cases the aspects of allowing all arguments to be expressed and the passing of a period of time before an agreement is settled upon would be paramount to the success of that settlement. As far as the local population is concerned, these reconciliatory judicial mechanisms form the most appropriate and thus most satisfying means of having the sense that 'justice' is being done compared to more formal, national (or international) retributive justice mechanisms.

Therefore, the failure of the Tribal Reconciliation Conference between the Fur and Arabs in 1989 may have been related as much to the unwillingness of one or more parties to implement the agreement[60] as to the limitation of time that was imposed on the negotiations, which was contrary to the nature of local reconciliation strategies inhered in the *judea* or *Mahkamat al-Gabila*. The interference of the military coup further diminished any faith one might have had in the commitment of the new military government to enforce all parties to respect the agreement. The interesting issue here is, however, that the new military government did sign the Tribal Reconciliation agreement that was negotiated under the former (democratic) regime. This made the new Islamist government party to the local means of conflict resolution in a way that seemed contrary to the position it would later take in the Darfur War that broke out in 2003. Consecutive political and legal decisions reveal that the confirmation of tribal identities was not just a remnant of the former government or a one-time action, but rather part of the strategy of the Sudanese government to construct an exclusive Sudanese national identity.

VI THE 'TRIBAL' CONFLICT IN DARFUR AND THE CONSTRUCTION
OF AN EXCLUSIVE SUDANESE NATIONAL IDENTITY

The engagement of the Sudanese government in the Darfur conflict meant that localized ethnically based conflicts were brought to a national level. As pointed out above, despite the fact that the war had a political cause, the access to land has from the onset been the main source of contention in most of the ethnic conflicts of the 1980s and 1990s as well as the Darfur War. As the Unregistered Land Act of 1970 allowed the government to claim all land that had not been registered, which pertained to virtually all land in Darfur, the military government could have awarded this unregistered land to the landless Arabs by referring to their rights as Sudanese citizens. While it did so at first, later the military government took steps both during the conflict and in consecutive peace agreements that seemed to deny its claims to authority over unregistered land based on this Act.[61]

The Sudanese government's political actions contesting its own legal authority with respect to access to land is evident from the Emirate Act, which was passed in 1995. Under this act, the title of *emir* (*amir*) was extended to Arab pastoralists in West Darfur in the region that formerly constituted the sultanate of Dar Masalit, in order to facilitate the access to land to these landless tribes. The title of *emir* had been used for military chiefs during the Mahdist rule (1885–1889). Under British colonial rule (1889–1954), descendants of Darfur sultans were given the title in an attempt to set them against Sultan Ali Dinar, an enemy of the British colonial government. The use of the title for a divide-and-rule politics was thus nothing new.[62] In addition, the Islamist government divided Dar Masalit into thirteen estates, five for the Masalit sedentary communities and eight for the new Arab camel herders settling in the area. This severely restricted the power of local chiefs and the customary rights of the sedentary population and played a major role in the consecutive tribal conflict in this area.[63]

However, despite the manipulation of local customary laws and traditions in relation to access to land, the passing of this law also meant that in general the government not only acknowledged, but even endorsed the authority of tribal leaders. Although the Local Government Act of 2003 brought the tribal authorities under the control of a 'commissioner' appointed by the president, this law did not end the local authorities' position, even though they lost considerable power.[64] Similarly, in the Darfur Peace Agreement of 2006, the authority of local leaders in issues pertaining to access to land is articulated, in particular in Paragraph 158 in the section entitled 'Development and Management of Land and Natural Resources':

Tribal land ownership rights (*hawakeer*),[65] historical rights to land, traditional or customary livestock routes, and access to water, shall be recognized and protected.[66]

In addition, the 2005 constitution refers to the customary rights to access of tribal land and states that the title holders must be compensated with if their land is taken by the government.[67] Despite the fact that it is unsure how these Agreements will work out in practice, it is poignant that the Sudanese government that originally granted the Arab landless tribes their right to unregistered land on the basis of the already existing land act of 1970 would retreat from that possibility and engage in a complex strategy that inheres the acknowledgement of those tribal authorities of whom it contested its power in the first place. In the process, the government shifted from referring to the status of these landless Arab groups as citizens, to designating them a position on the basis of, albeit new, tribal chieftainships, the emirates. Rather than considering this 'legal gray area'[68] a case of indecisiveness on the part of the Sudanese government, of relenting to negotiations with parties in a war that it was not prepared to fight to the end, it should be seen as a strategic move consistent with its policy of 'divide-and-rule'.

It is in this context that the endorsement and even facilitating of tribal courts and *judea* in Khartoum needs to be considered. While the endorsement of tribal authority in Darfur in the context of tribal conflicts may be considered a pragmatic solution to the problems in a marginal part of the state, the official recognition of these tribal courts operating according to the principle of a *judea* in the very heart of the state seems to point at least to an ambiguous attitude of the Sudanese government towards Darfur tribal institutions.

Though migration from Darfur to Central Sudan has a long history, in the last decennia the number of migrants that have come to the national capital has increased due to drought, ethnic conflicts and deteriorating economic circumstances has grown. Tribal groups that flocked the capital due to these disasters were by their government often referred to as IDPs, internally displaced persons, in accordance with the label used by international aid organizations: those people who were expected to be not in their 'right(ful)' location, but only temporarily present in the Sudanese capital. They were expected to go 'back home' to their tribal areas when the problem that had brought them to the centre of the state had been solved. They were allowed 'their' tribal courts, in contrast to Sudanese citizens who would not have this option. In the case of homicide, the plaintiffs' family would be offered the possibility to opt for the tribal reconciliatory judicial mechanism by the shari'a *qadi*, in which case the *judea* of both families would convene on a regular basis in the informal spaces of the compound of the families. The shari'a judge would only confirm the agreement the *judea* would finally reach, thereby lending it an official sanctioning. Also in this case, a *dimlij* or a comparable (deputy) tribal leader would be the intermediary. If a *rakuba* had to be investigated, both (deputy) tribal leaders representing their tribal group in Khartoum may travel back to their homelands in order to consult the tribal leaders there, mostly family members such as their fathers, uncles or brothers, as well as members of the current and former *ajawid*.

The establishment and, in some cases, re-invention of tribal reconciliation mechanisms in Khartoum allowed tribal groups that did not have a relationship in the past, such as Darfurians and Southerners or groups from the Nuba Mountains, to become members of each other's social network.[69] By opting for a tribal reconciliation process, both parties allowed for the establishment of social ties, facilitated by the prolonged negotiations often while sharing a meal at each other's private spaces. It is for this reason that tribal groups, despite having lived in Khartoum for an extended period of time, may prefer this tribal mechanism since it allows for extending a family's network in that same, often difficult, urban environment. The death of a family member may thus lead not only to compensation but also to the expansion of one's possibilities to gain access to resources such as job oppor-tunities, socializing networks and economic support in the future.

This 'privilege' of access to tribal institutions in the capital similar to those 'back home' constructs both groups collectively as belonging to tribal groups outside of the locality of Central Sudan, even though many of those who are active in the *judea* or tribal courts in Khartoum have been living in Khartoum for a long time, sometimes for generations. Some of them have highly qualified positions in private companies, international organizations and even in the government. In addition, the deputy tribal leaders in Khartoum, and these days even some of the tribal leaders in Darfur, often have a formal educational background and some even hold degrees from universities abroad. They may perform their positions as tribal leaders temporarily or part-time and also keep salaried positions, sometimes even in the government. This means that in their individual lives they straddle the divide between tribal and national identity and do not necessarily feel marginalized or disadvantaged.

However, the relegation by the Sudanese government of 'temporary migrants' to the category of 'tribal people' is strategic: the construction of a 'tribal other' makes the government one of the sole 'protectors' of its Sudanese citizens against the 'tribal peoples' and their tribal problems. In this sense it fits in its project to construct an exclusive form of citizenship, relegating the collectivity of 'tribal peoples', in this case both the sedentary peoples the government fought against and the Arab groups it supported, to the position of second-class citizens.[70]

VII TRIBES, CITIZENS AND THE CONSTRUCTION OF A NATIONAL IDENTITY

In the conclusion of his book *Saviors and Survivors*, when evaluating the war in Darfur Mahmood Mamdani points out that, if peace and justice are to be complementary instead of conflicting, the ICC's insistence on applying criminal justice may not be the most appropriate direction to take in cases such as that of Darfur.[71] He makes a distinction between victor's justice and survivor' justice and points out that in the case of Darfur, the last is at issue. He suggest that this means to:

> prioritize peace over punishment, and explore forms of justice – not criminal but political and social- that will make reconciliation durable.[72]

He next refers to a case in which a *judea* (judia) negotiate peace between Rizeigat and Zaghawa (both nomadic groups), quoting a local saying that 'only a turtle knows how to bite another turtle', and adding that the *judea* can only work if the groups are neighbours that have similar interests in strengthening the system of local accountability and that the Darfur conflict engages groups that are not bound to each other in this way. In case of the large-scale violence enacted during the Darfur war, the proximity and mutual accountability as well as the 'slow pace' of this process may indeed prove to be decisive in the success of *judea* mechanisms evoked during tribal reconciliation conferences. As I have shown, tribal negotiation mechanisms also work in an urban context: also in those cases, the reconciliation strategies work in particular when it concerns groups of people living in each other's vicinity, bound by a shared system of accountability.

In this respect, Mamdani warns that to detach the political from the judicial and leave the legal domain to what he refers to as the 'human rights fundamentalists' may lead to a seeking of revenge, rather than reconciliation in service of a durable peace.[73] The tenacity of the tribal reconciliation mechanisms and the general acceptance of *judea* as a mediation strategy after violent conflicts seems to allow for the suggestion that indeed reconciliatory justice appeals more to the sense of the victims, the Darfur population, that justice is being done. However, we may reconsider this statement since there is another danger in detaching the political from the legal. The danger is that we may lose sight of the larger picture, both in historical terms and in terms of national politics. As I have argued, although the Sudanese government may have seemed to display ambiguity as to its position towards tribal customary laws and authority in Darfur, it has shown remarkable consistency in the way that tribal and shari'a courts have been juxtaposed since the Anglo-Egyptian colonial rule. In addition, by making a distinction among its population between 'tribal peoples' and 'Sudanese citizens', the government has proven to be consistent in the way it has treated those groups within its state boundaries that it considered to be its enemy: to construct them as the 'other' that endangers Sudanese national identity. For example, the arming of 'Arab' militias to fight in the civil war with southern Sudan was applied by consecutive regimes, like the democratic regime under as-Sadiq al-Mahdi (1985–1989).

The position of Darfur as the 'other' for the 'normal' Sudanese citizen is not unique. Tim Allen points to a similar danger of referring to the Acholi in Northern Uganda as 'primitive and uncivilized', as it might hamper national integration since the Acholi local justice mechanisms will cast them as not (yet) modern and thus engaged in a conflict that is of no concern to ordinary Ugandan citizens.[74] This notion of the 'other' as part of national politics fits well with the distinction Sarah Nouwen and Wouter Werner use in order to understand the relation between law and politics with reference to the ICC.[75] They argue that the political is marked by the fact that 'collectivities have external friends ("allies") and enemies'. The ally is important because he can provide not merely material support but also recognition and legitimacy while the enemy is constructed as the 'other' so as to allow a collectivity to 'potentially' fight against it. The word 'potentially' in their argument is important since it means that the political does not necessarily reside in armed struggle itself, but 'in the mode of behaviour which is determined by the ever-looming possibility of armed conflict'.[76] Nouwen and Werner's analysis focuses on the ICC; nevertheless their observation seems also true for the tribal reconciliation mechanisms that operate in the 'shadow' of the Sudanese nation-state.

In this respect, the current Sudanese military regime shows a remarkable continuity with other post-Independence Sudanese governments in its use of a centre-periphery ideology of bargaining power. For, whatever the political colour and ambitions of the Sudanese government in power, the powerful elite of Sudan is located in the centre of Sudan, in and around the capital. Here, the Sudanese government and the central Sudanese elite's interests overlap, which makes 'the hyper-dominance of the national capital the single most important reality in Sudan today'.[77] At the same time, since this elite competes for power amongst itself, the administrative, military and commercial elites do not constitute a homogeneous group that gains its relative stability from its 'highly exploitative relations of production and, an outer periphery or frontier marked by extreme violence and disorder'.[78] Despite the political fragmentation, the Nile Valley elite thus share a cultural cohesion that makes them more resilient than the multiple crises the country has to deal with would seem to allow for. Given the heterogeneity among the central Sudanese elite, it obviously needs a discourse which legitimizes the violence perpetuated in the periphery and which focuses on the unity in its centre rather than on its heterogeneity. These discourses not only justify the violence the Sudanese government itself has become engaged in, but construct this excessive violence as a *necessity* to preserve the status quo of the Central Sudanese population on whom its power position is based. This necessity is made recognizable to the Sudanese public at large through a legitimizing discourse that constructs tribal people in the periphery as 'potentially dangerous others'.[79] For this reason, De Waal proposes the 'turbulent state' hypothesis that

> indicates that provincial war and destabilization is the habitual modus operandi of the Khartoum elites, and implies that Sudan will most probably continue to function in the fashion of a deadly gyroscope, its balance achieved at the price of deadly disorder in its peripheries. It implies that international efforts to achieve peace and democracy are likely to succeed only insofar as they are modelled to the modest aims of making the dominance of Khartoum's elites less wantonly violent and exploitative.[80]

In other words, it is not so much the political signature but the heterogeneity and diversity within this 'inner periphery' that is one of the, what De Waal calls, 'brute causes' (instead of root causes) for sustaining high levels of violence in the outer periphery.[81]

Through this construction of tribal otherness the government may suggest that the violence enacted by the government in Darfur is not arbitrary and it will not turn to just any of its citizens in the centre; on the contrary, the people in Darfur are different, they are 'other', and as they are 'tribal' the Darfur population are entitled to their tribal institutions such as tribal courts and the mechanism of *Judea*, which at the same time constructs them as non-eligible for citizenship. Those tribal communities that inhabit the centre are to be removed some time in the future to the outside periphery where they belong. At the same time, while constructing this notion of otherness the government also constructs a supposedly unified homogeneous Sudanese 'we' that negates the actual heterogeneity among not only among its Sudanese elite, but to its population of 'Sudanese' at large.

Thus the idea that reparations through restorative justice based on the philosophy of reconciliatory justice serve the Darfur victims of violent attacks during the war in Darfur better than retributive justice seems valid when looking at the local context and the direct satisfaction of the sense of justice being done among the victims of the Darfur war. The workings of the tribal reconciliation mechanisms, by applying *judea* and *rakuba*, thereby also hold a long-term potential for relations that are thus reconstructed, cemented and revitalized. At the same time, similar to the way that Nouwen and Werner, as well as Mamdani, discuss the relation between politics and the ICC, tribal reconciliation mechanisms are not just part of Sudanese national politics, but enact them.[82] If a large-scale, (inter)national perspective is taken, the championing of traditional justice mechanisms in the case of Darfur may enhance the position of the Sudanese government in its attempt to 'divide and rule' and prevent so-called 'tribal groups' to attain full citizenship. So even despite, or perhaps because of, the fact that tribal reconciliation mechanisms are constructed in current debates on restorative justice as an alternative to retributive justice for being an 'allegedly and apparently anti political system', they may serve 'existing or newly emerging friend-and-enemy groupings and cannot escape the logic of the political'.[83] This does not mean that the tribal reconciliation mechanisms should be abandoned, however. Like Nouwen and Werner conclude with respect to the ICC, international institutions should be aware that in all of the judicial mechanisms that may be employed in post-war situations, politics is part and parcel of the justice process. The important question for all involved should therefore be what kind of politics is pursued and served in concrete, historical and cultural specific situations as well as its relation with national politics. The politics of justice, whether of a local, national or international nature, does not need to be problematic in itself, but needs to be judged on its merits for those involved, on the local and (inter) national level.[84] This, however, is not a judicial, but a moral debate.

Notes

I would like to thank the editors of this volume for their constructive comments, which helped strengthening my argument. My sincere gratitude to Shamil Jeppie, Jacuub Abdalla Mohammed. Malik Adam Idris and Abdallah Hamid for their help and insights. I also wish to thank the Netherlands Organisation for Scientific Research (NWO), and the Netherlands Institute for Advanced Study in the Humanities and Social Sciences (NIAS) for their financial support.

1. In fact, already under the democratic regime of Sadiq el-Mahdi (1985–1989) 'qadi's' were sent to rural areas to try personal law cases. See further below.

2. The notion of 'tribe' is highly contested as it conjures fixed boundaries, homogeneous group identity and stability over time and has been politicized especially during the colonial regime, while it also holds connotation of racial differentiation. See the extensive problematizing by Salah Hassan and Carina Ray of the concept of tribe, Arab, African, 'zurqa/zaraq' in the context of the Darfur war in their introduction of the volume *Darfur and the Crisis of Governance: A Critical Reader* (Ithaca: Cornell University Press, 2009), 16–19. However, since this was the term used under the Anglo-Egyptian Condominium to refer to ethnic groups and because the label is still used by contemporary ethnic groups in Darfur as a translation of the locally used term 'qabilah', I retain the notion of tribe with caution, but in the remainder of this chapter without using quotation marks.

3. See Introduction to this volume.

4. Though the Prosecutor of the ICC announced the indictment of President al-Bashir, on July 14th 2008, the Pre-Trial Chamber issued an arrest warrant on 4 March 2009 on charges of war crimes and crimes against humanity, and a second arrest warrant for charges of genocide on 12 July 2010.

5. The Janjaweed include members of other tribal backgrounds, some even sedentary. The ideology of ethnic purity has been part of the rhetoric of some of the warlords, like Musa Hilal. See for the complexity of the constitution of the Janjaweed and of the political nature of the conflict: Julie Flint, 'Darfur's Armed Movements', in de Waal (ed.), *War in Darfur and the Search for peace* (Cambridge: Harvard University Press, 2007), pp. 140–72; Julie Flint and Alex de Waal, *Darfur: A Short History of a Long War* (London & New York: Zed Press, 2005); Mahmood Mamdani, *Saviors and Survivors. Darfur, Politics and the War on Terror* (London; Verso, 2009); Mahmood Mamdani, 'The Politics of Naming. Genocide, Civil War, Insurgency', in Salah Hassan and Carina Ray (eds.), *Darfur and the Crisis of Governance: A Critical Reader* (Ithaca: Cornell University Press, 2009), pp. 145–154; Alhagi Maraong, '"Outlaws on Camelback": State and Individual Responsibility for Serious Violations of International Law in Darfur' (Institute for Security Studies Paper 136, 2007), pp. 1–24; Mohamed Salih and Sharif Harir, 'Tribal Militias. The Genesis of National Fisintegration', in Sharif Harir and Terje Tvedt (eds.), *Short-cut to Decay. The Case of the Sudan* (Uppsala: Nordiska Afrikainstitutet, 1994), pp. 186–203; Alex de Waal, 'Who Are the Darfurians? Arab and African Identities, Violence and External Engagement', in Hassan and Ray, *Darfur and the Crisis of Governance*,

pp. 125–130; Karin Willemse, 'The Darfur War. Masculinity and the construction of a Sudanese National Identity', in Hassan and Ray, *Darfur and the Crisis of Governance*, pp. 213–232.

6. 'At the same time, the Prosecutor speaks in ignorance of history: "Al Bashir ... promoted the idea of a polarization between tribes aligned with him, whom he labeled 'Arabs' and ... the Fur, Masalit and Zaghawa ... derogatory [sic] referred to as 'Zurgas' or 'Africans'." The racialization of identities in Darfur has its roots in the British colonial period. As early as the late 1920s, the British tried to organize two confederations in Darfur: one Arab, the other black (Zurga). Racialized identities were incorporated into the census and provided the frame for government policy. It is not out of the blue that the two sides in the 1987–89 civil war described themselves as Arab and Zurga. If anything, the evidence shows that successive Sudanese governments – al-Bashir's included – looked down on all Darfuris, non-Arab Zurga as well as Arab nomads.' Citation (emphasis MM) from: Mahmood Mamdani, 'Darfur, ICC and the New Humanitarian Order – How the ICC's "Responsibility to Protect" Is Being Turned into an Assertion of Neo-Colonial Domination', *The Nation*, 29 September 2008; See also the Introduction to this volume.

7. It should be emphasized that Mamdani, by criticizing the way that Moreno-Ocampo dealt with the indictment of al-Bashir, did not deem the latter innocent; on the contrary, Mamdani points out that one of causes of the ethnic cleansing through land-grabbing was the 'brutal counterinsurgency unleashed by the al-Bashir regime in 2003–04 in response to an insurgency backed up by peasant tribes', see Mamdani, 'Darfur, ICC', 1. I will return to this last cause below.

8. See Chapter 1 (Introduction) by Kamari M. Clarke, Abel S. Knottnerus and Eefje de Volder, p. 7.

9. *Ibid.* p. 21. See also for example: Luc Huyse, 'Introduction: Tradition-Based Approaches in Peacemaking, Transitional Justice and Reconciliation Policies', in Luc Huyse and Mark Salter (eds.), *Traditional Justice and Reconciliation after Violent Conflict: Learning from African Experiences* (Stockholm: International Institute for Democracy and Electoral Assistance, 2008), pp. 1–22; Issaka K. Souaré, 'The International Criminal Court and African Countries: The Case of Uganda' (2009) 121(35) *Review of African Political Economy* 369–388; Janine N. Clark, 'The ICC, Uganda and the LRA: Re-Framing the debate' (2010) 69 *African Studies* 141–160.

10. Souaré, 'The ICC and African Countries', 371.

11. Huyse, 'Introduction', p. 3; See also for example Souaré, 'The ICC and African Countries', 369–388; Clark, 'The ICC, Uganda and the LRA', 141–154; and the Introduction to this volume.

12. 'The Rule of Law and Transitional Justice in Conflict and Post-Conflict Societies: Report of the Secretary General', UN Doc. S/2004/616, 23 August 2004, p. 12, as quoted in Huyse, 'Introduction', p. 3.

13. Huyse, 'Introduction', p. 6.

14. Huyse, 'Introduction', pp. 8, 15. See for a similar critique of the notion of 'traditional': Clark, 'The ICC, Uganda and the LRA', 151–152.

15. Since shari'a is central in both academic and popular debates, I opt for to not use italics for this term in the remainder of the chapter.

16. Darfur became an Islamic Sultanate around the 16th century and was added to the (post-)colonial state of Sudan by the British in 1916, after the death of Ali Dinar, the last sultan of Darfur.

17. Rex S. O'Fahey, *State and Society in Dār Fūr* (London: C. Hurst & Company, 1980), p. 110. The capital in 'Shari'a' is from the original.

18. With notable exceptions, such as female inheritance rights, see: O'Fahey, *State and Society*, p. 110.

19. Martin Daly, *Darfur's Sorrow. A History of Destruction and Genocide* (Cambridge: Cambridge University Press, 2007), p. 33.

20. Darfur thus refers to the notion of 'the locality, living space or abode of the Fur'. However, while the sultan would come from the royal Fur clans, the sultanate hosted a diversity of ethnic groups since its onset.

21. Musa Abdul Jalil, Adam A. Mohammed and Ahmed Yusuf, 'Native Administration and Local Governance in Darfur: Past and Future', in De Waal, *War in Darfur and the Search for Peace*, p. 41; Julie Flint and Alex de Waal, *Short History of a Long War* (London & New York: Zed Press, 2005), pp. 8–9; O'Fahey, *State and Society*, pp. 22, 50–51; Sharif Harir, '"Arab Belt" versus "African Belt". Ethno-Political Conflict in Dar Fur and the regional Cultural Factors', in Sharif Harir and Tvedt, *Short-cut to Decay*, pp. 144–186; Jérôme Tubiana, 'Darfur: A Conflict for Land?', in de Waal (ed.), *War in Darfur and the Search for Peace*, pp. 68–93; Jon D. Unruh 'Land and Legality in the Darfur Conflict' (2012) 5 *African Security*, 111–112; De Waal, 'Who Are the Darfurians?', pp. 125–130.

22. The notion of 'colonial shari'a' in this context was coined by Shamil Jeppie, and much of this part relies on his excellent work on the British interventions in legal issues during the Anglo-Egyptian Condominium (1899–1956). Shamil Jeppie 'The Making and Unmaking of Colonial Shari'a in the Sudan', in Shamil Jeppie, Ebrahim Moosa and Richard Roberts (eds.), *Muslim Family Law in Sub Saharan Africa* (Amsterdam: Amsterdam University Press, 2010), pp. 165–183.

23. This is a reference often used in studies on Islamic law when discussing the authority of shari'a law in cases that are considered to be of a personal nature, such as inheritance, divorce, custody etc. Sometimes this is called

Muslim personal law or even MPL. See for example Jeppie, Moosa and Roberts, *Muslim Family Law.*

24. Jeppie, 'Making and Unmaking', pp. 165–166.
25. The Mahdi ousted or killed colonial officers of British nationality who served in Sudan under Ottoman rule (1823–1885) and founded the Mahdiyya (1885–1899). The recapturing of Sudan by the British was both strategic and a matter of revenge. The British were continuously fearful of new Mahdist rebellions.
26. Jeppie, 'Making and Unmaking', pp. 165–168.
27. Between 1902 and 1979 62 circulars were issued, see Carolyn Fluehr-Lobban, 'Circulars of the Sharī'a Courts in the Sudan (Manshūrāt el-Mahākim El-Sharī'a fi Sūdān) 1902–1979' (1983) 27(12) *Journal of African Law*, 79–140; also Jeppie, 'Making and Unmaking', note 11, p. 180.
28. Fluehr-Lobban, 'Circulars', pp. 79–140; Jeppie, 'Making and Unmaking', p. 167
29. Jeppie, 'Making and Unmaking', p. 169. Jeppie defines colonial shari'a as: 'Islamic law practised and constructed in, and enabled by, a colonial setting', see Jeppie, 'Making and Unmaking', p. 170.
30. I opt for an English plural by adding an –s to local terms, instead of the Arabic plural, unless otherwise indicated.
31. Jeppie, 'Making and Unmaking', pp. 167, 169, 176–177; M.A. Salman, 'Lay Tribunals in the Sudan. An Historical and Socio-Legal Analysis' (1983) 21 *Journal of Legal Pluralism* 61–128.
32. Abdul-Jalil, Mohammed and Yusuf, 'Native Administration', 45; Daly, *Darfur's Sorrow*, pp. 125–126; Jeppie, 'Making and Unmaking', pp. 173–176.
33. Jeppie, 'Making and Unmaking', p. 173, inverted commas in original.
34. De Waal, 'Who Are the Darfurians', p. 133.
35. These operated alongside and sometimes in conjunction with other law enforcement infastructure such as the police station, prisons and the already-mentioned courts.
36. 'Tribal area' is a contested notion since it was created in the period under study and does not necessarily refer to a fixed area that existed before this time. See also note 1 on the notion of 'tribal'.
37. Unruh, 'Land and Legality', 108; Tubiana, 'Darfur: A Conflict', p. 81; De Waal, 'Who Are the Darfurians', pp. 130–133. See for an interesting case Kordofan Justin Willis 'The Creolization of Authority in Condominium Sudan' (2005) 46 *Journal of African History* 29–50.
38. Abdul-Jalil, Mohammed and Yusuf, 'Native Administration', pp. 46–49; Harir, '"Arab Belt"', pp. 153–158; Tubiana, 'Darfur: A Conflict', pp. 74–75, 81; Flint and De Waal, *Short History*, pp. 9, 41–65.
39. See for a more in-depth analysis of this process: Ali Haggar, 'The Origins and Organization of the Janjaweed in Darfur', in De Waal, *War in*

Darfur and the Search for Peace, pp. 113–139; Harir, "'Arab Belt'", pp. 144–185; Tubiana, 'Darfur: A Conflict', pp. 68–93; De Waal, 'Who Are the Darfurians', pp. 125–145; Karin Willemse, 'Darfur in War. The Politicization of Ethnic Identities' 15 (2005) *ISIM Review* 14–15; Willemse, 'Darfur War', pp. 213–232.

40. Abdul-Jalil, Mohammed and Yusuf, 'Native Administration', pp. 39–67; Atta el-Battahani, 'Ideological Expansionist Movements versus Historical Indigenous Rights in the Darfur Region in Sudan: From Actual Homocide to Potential Genocide', in Hassan and Ray, *Darfur and the Crisis of Governance*, pp. 43–68, 44–49; Harir, "'Arab Belt'", pp. 163–185; Tubiana, 'Darfur: A Conflict', pp. 75–80; De Waal, 'Who Are the Darfurians', pp. 125–145; Flint and De Waal, *Short History*, pp. 38, 49–64.

41. Numeiri was president of the Sudan from 1969 to 1985. After he came to power by a coup, he allied himself first with the communists then with the socialists. Towards the end of his reign he established relations with the Islamists. He was ousted by popular uprisings in 1985 and after elections a democratic period of four years with Sadiq al-Mahdi of the UMMA party as president followed. This regime ended with the military coup staged by Lt. Omar al-Bashir in 1989.

42. Harir, "'Arab Belt'", pp. 163, 178–184; Tubiana, 'Darfur: A Conflict', pp. 80–83; De Waal, 'Who Are the Darfurians', pp. 133–135.

43. De Waal, 'Who Are the Darfurians', pp. 134–135.

44. Mohammed, 'Customary Mediation'.

45. Sharif Harir registered thirteen reconciliation conferences between 1957 and 1990. The tribal reconciliation conference of 1989 referred to in this case differed from the other twelve in the magnitude of the conflict legitimized by a racial rhetoric with political backing from intellectual Darfuri on both sides. Most of the information on this particular reconciliation conference comes from Harir, "'Arab Belt'", pp. 144–183.

46. A title that dates back to the times of the Fur Sultanate. It is limited to the Fur homeland of Zalingei. Below the Dimingawi there are three tiers of native administration: the shartai, the omda and the sheikh. See also for the other tribal titles: Abdul-Jalil, Mohammed and Yusuf, 'Native Administration', p. 47.

47. Harir, "'Arab Belt'", pp. 146–148. See also Salomé Bronkhorst, 'Customary Mediation in Resource Scarcities and Conflicts in Sudan: Making a Case for the Judiyya', in Martha Mutisi (ed.), *Integrating Traditional and Modern Conflict Resolution. Experiences from Selected Cases in Eastern and the Horn of Africa* (African Centre for the Constructive Resolution of Disputes Special Issues, 2012), pp. 121–146.

48. See for translated excerpts from these petitions: Harir, "'Arab Belt'", pp. 146–149. It is to these texts that Mamdani refers when he states that notions like 'genocide' and 'holocaust' were employed before al-Bashir

came to power, which is one of the reasons why he accuses Moreno-Acampo of falsely attributing to al-Bashir the racialization of the Darfur conflict and thus of engaging in politicized justice. See Mamdani, 'Darfur, ICC'.

49. Alternatively spelled: judiy(y)a, judeya, judia.
50. This military junta has governed the Sudan since 1989. It first allied with the Islamist party, the National Islamic Front led by Hassan al-Turabi, in establishing an Islamic state. Since 2005, when the Comprehensive Peace Agreement was signed, until the secession of South Sudan in 2011, the Sudan was officially co-governed by political leaders from the north and the south of Sudan, such as the North Sudanese president Omar al-Bashir, and the South Sudanese vice-president Salva Kirr. This, however, has had little impact on the prevalence of Islam in Sudanese politics and the dominance of Northern Sudanese in political and public life in the capital, the seat and locus of the government.
51. In 1989 1 US$ equalled 4.450 Sudanese Pounds according to the Treasury Reporting Rates of Exchange as of March 31, 1989 of the US government.
52. Personal communication Darfur intellectual. See also Abdul-Jalil, Muhammed and Yusuf, 'Native Administration', pp. 39–67; Harir, '"Arab Belt"', pp. 144–185, De Waal, 'Who Are the Darfurians', pp. 125–145; Tubiana, 'Darfur: A Conflict', pp. 80–91.
53. During my fieldwork in Kebkabiya, a Zaghawa leader was killed in an ambush after signing a reconciliation agreement with the Fur. It turned out he was killed by youngsters from his own tribe who felt he had signed away their rights, Karin Willemse, *One Foot in Heaven. Narratives on Gender and Islam in Darfur, West-Sudan* (Leiden: Brill Publishers, 2007), pp. 465–467; Willemse, 'Darfur War', pp. 221–225. See also Flint and De Waal, *Short History*, pp. 46–65; De Waal, 'Who Are the Darfurians', pp. 140–145.
54. See also Daly, *Darfur's Sorrow*, 244; Harir, '"Arab Belt"', pp. 169. Stanley Yeo, 'African Approaches to Killing in Defence of Property' (2008) 41(3) *Comparative and International Law Journal of Southern Africa* 339–352.
55. Interviews with informants from Darfur in Darfur (1990–1992, 1995) and in Khartoum (2006–2008, 2015). Most of the information that follows here comes from these interviews and from participant observation of and interviews of participants on the workings of a *judea*.
56. In case tribal groups stay in each other's vicinity, the existence of *rakuba* may prevent retaliation since the *ajawid* of the aggrieved party may pronounce this past arrangement as soon as one becomes aware of the homicide of a member of their group and they can thus prevent a conflict from getting out of hand.

57. This principle is also valid in cases where the persons involved have quite different status positions, as I witnessed during my research in Darfur in 1992, when a young driver caused a car accident in which shartai Ahmed Ahmeddai was killed. Both belonged to the Fur tribe and after establishing a *rakuba* between their clans, a token *diya* was negotiated.

58. Even members who reside abroad can be asked to pay their share: often when the person visits the locality when on holiday.

59. As stated above, when the Native Administration was formally abolished in 1971, most of the tribal leaders were chosen to be members of the Rural Peoples Councils based on a socialist ideology. The democratic government that came to power in 1986 started to rebuild the local administration. See De Waal, 'Who Are the Darfurians', p. 133.

60. See the earlier misgivings about the failure of this Tribal Reconciliation Conference above. In addition, the position of Dr Sese as the initiator of the Conference was cast in doubt since he was of Fur background and at the same time appointed by the UMMA party that had a majority in the then democratic government, which made him alternately seen as both neutral and subjective. His role, however, as the main negotiator of the peace agreement ended when he was detained when the agreement was signed after the *coup d'état* of 30 June 1989, which brought the military regime of Omar al-Bashir to power. See Harir, '"Arab Belt"', pp. 145–146.

61. Tubiana, 'Darfur: A Conflict', p. 79; Unruh, 'Land and legality', 105–128.

62. Tubiana, 'Darfur: A Conflict', pp. 81–82.

63. Tubiana, 'Darfur: A Conflict', p. 82; Unruh, 'Land and legality', 109, Flint and De Waal, *Short History*, pp. 57–65.

64. Unruh, 'Land and legality', 109.

65. Hawakeer is the plural of 'hakura'.

66. Quoted in Tubiana, 'Darfur: A Conflict', p. 83.

67. Unruh, 'Land and legality', 120.

68. Tubiana, 'Darfur: A Conflict', p. 80.

69. The information I give here of this procedure comes from a case I studied (2006–2008) of the death of a Nuer boy of two years of age and a driver from Darfur whose car accidently killed the boy. Despite the fact that the insurance company would have paid more money to the family of the deceased than the *judea* eventually agreed on, this tribal reconciliation mechanism was preferred due to the gain of social ties the process meant for the family of the boy.

70. De Waal, 'Who Are the Darfurians', pp. 125–145, Tubiana, 'Darfur: A Conflict', pp. 90–93.

71. Mamdani, *Saviors and Survivors*, p. 85.

72. *Ibid.*, p. 286.

73. *Ibid.*, p. 288.

74. Tim Allen, 'Ritual (Ab)Use? Problems with Traditional Justice in Northern Uganda', in Nicholas Waddell and Phil Clark (eds.), *Courting Conflict? Justice, Peace and the ICC in Africa* (London: Crisis States Research Centre, 2008). Also referred to in Clark, 'The ICC, Uganda and the LRA', 151–152.

75. The notion of 'others' in the relation between politics and law is discussed by Sarah M. H. Nouwen and Wouter G. Werner, 'Doing Justice to the Political: The International Criminal Court in Uganda and Sudan' (2010) 21(4) *The European Journal of International Law* 941–965. I will return to their discussion below.

76. Nouwen and Werner, 'Doing Justice', 945. They hereby refer to Carl Schmitt, *The Concept of the Political* (Chicago: University of Chicago Press, 1996).

77. Alex de Waal, 'Sudan: The Turbulent State', in Alex de Waal (ed.), *War in Darfur and the Search for Peace* (Cambridge: Harvard University Press, 2007), p. 4.

78. De Waal, 'Turbulent State', p. 36.

79. In this discursive strategy, the notion of 'black' is used for labelling this ultimate state enemy: before the war in Darfur the notion of 'black' had referred to the 'main enemy' of the state, the southern Sudanese. Only in the course of the peace negotiations leading up to the signing of the Comprehensive Peace Agreement in 2005 was the term used to label the 'new enemies' of the state, the Darfur indigenous tribal population. See for an elaboration of this perspective Willemse, 'The Darfur War', pp. 213–232.

80. De Waal, 'Turbulent State', pp. 37–38.

81. *Ibid.*, 31–35.

82. The authors quote M. Koskenniemi, *The Gentle Civilizer of Nations: The Rise and Fall of International Law 1870–1960* (Cambridge: Cambridge University Press, 2002), at p. 177 in Nouwen and Werner, 'Doing Justice', p. 943.

83. Nouwen and Werner, 'Doing Justice', p. 963; the authors quote here in note 123: Carl Schmitt, 'The Age of Neutralisations and Depoliticizations' (1993) 96 *Telos* 130.

84. As Nouwen and Werner maintain: 'it is the quality of the politics pursued in them that distinguishes one political trial from another', 'Doing Justice', p. 964, referring to Judith N. Shklar, *Legalism: Law, Morals and Political Trials* (Cambridge: Harvard University Press 1986), note 23, p. 145.

14

Interpretations of Justice
The ICTR and Gacaca in Rwanda

Kristin C. Doughty

I INTRODUCTION

The grassroots genocide courts set up in Rwanda in the 2000s called *inkiko gacaca* have received extensive international and scholarly attention for their unprecedented approach to handling mass criminal prosecutions at the local level. Though the 1994 genocide over which the gacaca courts have jurisdiction is outside the temporal jurisdiction of the International Criminal Court (ICC), the Rwanda case serves as a useful example for thinking through the "fractious relationship" between international law – in this case, manifest through the International Criminal Tribunal for Rwanda (ICTR), set up in 1995 by United Nations Mandate – and local law. Gacaca courts serve as the paradigmatic example of the types of local or regional justice mechanisms that test the complementarity principle[1] of the ICC because they are predicated on starkly different notions of justice: specifically, they prioritize locally rooted knowledge, experience, and participation as opposed to outside, objective, professional expertise.

Rwanda's gacaca courts, created by national law in 2001, were purportedly designed, according to government sensitization propaganda, to "allow the population of the same Cell, the same Sector to work together" and therefore for gacaca to "become the basis of collaboration and unity."[2] Specifically, they were ostensibly intended to provide a process of mass prosecution for genocide crimes while facilitating the reintegration of perpetrators to their homes. Between 2004 and 2010, suspects were tried publicly on-site at the location of their alleged crimes by a panel of locally elected judges called *inyangamu-gayo* (Kinyarwanda for "people of integrity"). Mandatory participation and the deliberate avoidance of lawyers or professional jurists were intended, at least in theory, to enable all Rwandans to participate actively as witnesses, prosecutors,

and defenders with limited hierarchy. The gacaca process hinged on mediating compromises that prioritized the collective over the individual good:
defendants received reduced penalties for confessions, and victims forewent
demands for harsher punishment in return for information about their loved
ones. At the same time, the gacaca process established criminal accountability
for genocide, including fines and prison sentences of up to thirty years.
The inyangamugayo, backed by police, armed prison guards, and even soldiers, could issue subpoenas and could bring charges against case participants
for refusing to testify, for perjury, or for blackmail.[3] These courts, which the
government justified as a reinvocation of Rwanda's customary law, were
a deliberate rebuke of international trials as a more efficient system for trying
hundreds of thousands of genocide suspects efficiently among the people
affected. Gacaca courts have been alternately lauded as an innovative and
efficient form of restorative justice[4] and critiqued as a technique of state-
backed "lawfare" delivering irregular punishment and coercive control and
promoting division.[5]

In this chapter, I juxtapose the locally rooted trials in gacaca courts with the
proceedings of the International Criminal Tribunal for Rwanda (ICTR),
specifically focusing on the lens of interpretation.[6] I use the technical task of
interpretation at the ICTR, and the lack of a structural corollary before gacaca
courts, to examine the relationship between linguistic and legal interpretation.
I suggest that comparative analysis of gacaca trials and the proceedings of the
ICTR illustrates particularly clearly how interpretation in legal trials is
a simultaneously linguistic, social, *and* legal task, and that to consider it
otherwise distorts our understanding of law-based processes of meaning-
making and the power dynamics that infuse them.

I begin by considering interpretation within the ICTR (translation from
Kinyarwanda into French and English) to reveal complexities inherent in the
fast-moving process of simultaneous translation at the heart of international
criminal courts, which is largely overlooked by scholarship on international
criminal courts in Africa.[7] Those who do mention translators at the ICTR do
so briefly, in the context of its expense and complexity[8] or in discussing the
"two-tiered employment system" in which Rwandans are hired only as "jani-
tors, security guards, and translators."[9] The few scholars who focus on interpretation at the ICTR or ICC do so in the context of normative claims that
better translation would improve due process[10] or gender sensitivity.[11]
The notable exception is Koomen's work, which includes interviews with
interpreters at the ICTR and analysis of the dynamics of translation within
an exploration of dilemmas characterizing international justice for victims of
sexual violence.[12] Here, I use a case excerpt and interviews with Rwandan

prosecutors and interpreters from the ICTR to demonstrate how, as scholars have shown elsewhere in national courts, linguistic translation is central to the processes of interpretation, meaning-making, and truth-producing that constitute the legal work of adversarial trial courts and must be analyzed with reference to existing power differentials.[13] I thus build, as they do, on the rich tradition of scholarship on the centrality of language to the constitution of the legal order and the quotidian interactions within courts.[14] I show how, in a broader political and moral economy of justice privileging outside legal expertise over situated localized knowledge,[15] interpretation was one of few processes that valued deep insider expertise (specifically, of Kinyarwanda) among court personnel – but only in the service of rendering technical interpretations, while legal interpretation remained the purview and expertise of others.

In the second part of the chapter I turn to gacaca, Rwanda's domestic trials for genocide suspects, where there were no structural correlates to interpreters at the ICTR because the trials were conducted in Kinyarwanda, the language shared by all participants. I bring these two quite distinct processes together – united only, one might argue, by their shared prosecution of genocide crimes in Rwanda and their overlaps in operational periods – in order to bring into relief how gacaca involved a fundamentally different understanding of what is at stake in interpretation, in which knowledge of language and context was central to the legal work of assessing facts and truth. I use one specific gacaca case example to show how in these deeply contextualized gacaca courts the thickly detailed work of interpretation – of evidence, of truth claims, of instrumental motivations and meanings – fell to a wide range of Rwandan participants and was inextricably bound up with people's quotidian efforts to negotiate the micro-politics of reconciliation and reconstruct moral orders, which I have argued elsewhere were central elements of gacaca.[16]

Gacaca sessions unfolded as churning pools of competing recollections and assertions about what occurred in the past. Sessions were episodes in a set of debates and knowledge claims that had started before, and would continue after, the 2004–2010 gacaca trials. The law regulating gacaca procedures laid out a general approach to trial sessions, which allowed "any interested person" to "testify in favor or against the defendant' based on what 'he or she knows or witnessed,"[17] which included both eye-witness and hearsay testimony. The emphasis on oral evidence, with its inherent malleability, meant that discussions turned into performances wherein people positioned themselves, forming alliances and divisions based on agreeing or disagreeing with one another's versions of the past. That is, sessions required participants to assess claims that everyone acknowledged were laced with partial truths, lies, and mistruths.[18] The work of participants, from those in the general assembly to witnesses to the defendant and the judges, was that of interpretation. This interpretation stemmed from participants' overlapping or shared knowledge base about the intimate details of context, their shared language, their knowledge of the physical landscape, and their overlapping experiences. By calling this situated and participatory work "interpretation," I foreground how the social and legal work of gacaca were deeply intertwined, and how expertise was more widely distributed among participants, both of which were foundational to local perceptions of justice (or injustice) before gacaca.

II INTERPRETATION AT THE INTERNATIONAL CRIMINAL TRIBUNAL FOR RWANDA

I focus on the ICTR here to raise concerns related to international criminal courts more widely that this volume explores – deterritorialized, universal justice, and how international justice often disproportionately and unequally impacts Africa. In November 1994, the UN Security Council passed Resolution 955, which mandated the creation of the International Criminal Tribunal for Rwanda (ICTR) "for the sole purpose of prosecuting persons responsible for genocide and other serious violations of international humanitarian law committed in the territory of Rwanda ... [to] contribute to the process of national reconciliation and to the restoration and maintenance of peace."[19] From the beginning, Rwanda's transitional government expressed reservations at having an international tribunal on grounds of national sovereignty, and asked instead for support in creating a national tribunal (which would exclude war crimes), but ultimately agreed to the ICTR.[20] Out of concern that the situation in Rwanda at the time was still unstable, the court was located in Arusha, Tanzania. The ICTR could indict and try people for crimes occurring only in the calendar year of 1994, including genocide, crimes against humanity, and other serious violations of international humanitarian law (such as murder, torture, or rape). Like the ICC, the ICTR had no enforcement arm, so once the indictments were approved and arrest warrants issued by the court, staff had to track down the individuals – most of whom had fled the country and were outside the reach of Rwandan transitional authorities, elsewhere in Africa or Europe – and had to rely on foreign governments to help arrest and extradite them.

Cases were held in the Arusha International Conference Center, a complex of three-story, whitewashed concrete buildings in the center of Arusha in neighboring Tanzania. Similar to the ICC, courtroom personnel were a cosmopolitan mix of nationalities and languages, and practices were an improvisational blend of civil and common law that established a body of international criminal case law.[21] Panels of three international (non-Rwandan) judges presided over cases. The office of the prosecution ultimately included a few Rwandan lawyers, but was primarily international. Defense attorneys were overwhelmingly from France or francophone Africa.

The official languages of the ICTR were French and English. In order to operate across varied linguistic competencies – and pursuant to the governing statute which stated that defendants were entitled to "be informed promptly and in detail in a language which he or she understands of the nature and cause of the charge against him or her" and "to have the free assistance of an interpreter"[22] – cases were conducted with simultaneous translation in French, English, and Kinyarwanda beginning in 2001.[23] Interpreters sat in booths on the side of the courtroom and produced simultaneous translations of questioning and testimony throughout the proceedings. The written trial transcripts were generated only in French and English, not Kinyarwanda. That is, even when a witness or defendant testified in Kinyarwanda, the transcript would be maintained in English and French. Across my interviews, ICTR judges and attorneys described interpretation systems at the ICTR as technical solutions to the problem of handling multiple languages, and focused the bulk of their discussion instead on detailed points of international criminal law, as does most scholarship.[24] Yet as I illustrate below, the work of linguistic interpretation was not always so neatly decoupled from legal interpretation as this view of interpretation-as-technical would suggest.

In a telling example, in late 2007 I sat in on proceedings of a case against a defendant named Simon Bikindi, a popular Rwandan musician who was accused of incitement to genocide, among other charges, based in part on his song lyrics. On 31 October 2007, I sat in the crowded viewing gallery when he took the stand in his own defense. What was at stake was whether the lyrics of his songs – in this section, a song called *Twasezereye* that he translated as "We Said Goodbye" – were framing the events of 1959 in the lead-up to Rwanda's Independence as revolution, emphasizing democratic leadership, or as a means of raising the level of hatred against Tutsi through their association with the monarchy.[25] That is, the judges and attorneys who were involved recognized that the determination of the guilt or innocence of the accused in relation to the charges in the indictment hinged on the interpretation of the Kinyarwanda lyrics. Interpretation was not merely a technical task here in the service of the law, but the central legal task for the attorneys and judges.

And yet when the song writer and accused himself shifted from French – the language he was using for most of his testimony so that his lawyers could speak to him directly – into Kinyarwanda to testify to his intended meaning of the specific song lyrics in the indictment, the judges interrupted him multiple times to tell him to stop using Kinyarwanda. They justified their decision that he had to testify only in French as a technical issue: they explained it was a problem for the interpreters when he spoke Kinyarwanda, because the man in the Kinyarwanda booth was not able to anticipate the need to interpret, since only the French and English interpreters needed to be working.

The judges thus foreclosed any possibility of debate over the interpretation of the words themselves, erasing for the record that there could be variation in how Bikindi, the interpreters, and perhaps also Rwandans on the prosecution team might interpret the meaning of the lyrics – which is important to underscore given that it is precisely this issue of meaning of the lyrics that was the key *legal* issue in the trial. For example, as Bikindi discussed his intended meaning in a passage referencing forms of patron-client relations that made up his song lyrics, the judge interrupted to ask, "Can we please get an interpretation of *ubuhake*?" The Kinyarwanda booth translated the word as "clientelism," a value-neutral phrase that strips the practice of any discussion of the oppression that many associate with it as a historic practice.[26] The judge specifically told Bikindi he should only use the Kinyarwanda if the word was in his song. Otherwise, he should avoid it, and use the French. The judge added that if Bikindi could not think of the correct word in French, then they would ask the interpreters for assistance. This again suggested that the linguistic translation task was neutral and technical, and that the interpreter would be able to unproblematically supply the word, with which Bikindi would agree. This case thus points to the assumption undergirding international justice at the ICTR (and ICC) that complex points of evidence can be rendered fixed by a professional interpreter, separating out the legal, social, and interpretive tasks before the court.

I later spoke with a Rwandan interpreter I call Augustin, an older man who had been working at the tribunal for more than five years. In our conversations,[27] Augustin first described conceptual differences that bedeviled efforts to quickly translate witnesses' testimony, some marked by disjunctures between concepts in Kinyarwanda and French and English, the two Western languages that dominated the court's official proceedings, and some that more broadly marked a distinction between the precise lexicon of law as opposed to wider scope of expression in daily life.[28] This is consistent with other work showing distinctions between "legal talk" and everyday language[29] as well as between concepts and cultural practices in one language that do not easily translate into others in a court of law.[30] Secondly, Augustin's comments showed how quickly issues of (in)accuracy and (mis)translation came to the fore, drawing attention to one aspect of how history gets written in international criminal trials that has received far less attention than the testimony of expert witnesses.[31] Lastly, his comments revealed the complex ways issues of translation and interpretation became bound up with popular discourses about Rwandans' supposed predilections to lie.[32]

In an interview with a Rwandan prosecutor I call Odette, she reinforced many of the themes that Augustin discussed, and, in addition, drew attention to the perils of cross-examinations that are mediated through interpretation, given that one central task of the cross-examination in adversarial courts such as the ICTR is to discredit the witness.[33] As Odette noted,

> Sometimes people get upset at the witness instead of realizing that it's an issue of translation. The witness says something, the translator may mistranslate it, then the questioner asks something that suggests the witness is stupid or lying or deliberately being confusing, and then the witness gets defensive. It can go downhill, and people think he is a liar.

Another Rwandan prosecutor in a separate conversation raised a similar point about how errors in translation turn quickly into negative moral judgments. He gave a specific example where a witness had used a phrase to say that "So many people were killed/dead," which was translated as "everybody" died. Since this witness had said in another part of her testimony that she was with her father after the genocide, the defense later challenged her as a liar for having said he (everyone) had died. That is, the attorneys pounced on the issue as one of lying, with all the moral judgment that entails, when the witness was in fact being cross-examined based on someone else's words.

In the aggregate, across thousands of witnesses and case hours, technical miscommunications or mistakes were not recognized as such in the moment, and were viewed as lies that served to discredit the witness's testimony. That is, the ICTR framed interpretation as a technical task while by contrast lawyers and judges overwhelming attributed errors in Rwandan witness's testimony not to technical mistakes that could be fixed, but to intentional lies – i.e. moral failings – on the part of Rwandan witnesses. This quick slide to allegations of deliberate dishonesty occurred in the highly unequal moral economy of international criminal justice, which amounted to frequently reaffirming the "truth" that Rwandans were, inherently, likely to lie, a claim that was buttressed by the literature on Rwanda and popular opinion.[34] This reflected, and reproduced, a narrative in which virtually all non-Rwandans at the ICTR whom I interviewed mentioned, unsolicited, that one of the biggest challenges the court faced was the predilection of Rwandans to lie in their testimony. By contrast, the Rwandans at the ICTR with whom I spoke made a point to

push against assumptions about Rwandans' inherent dishonesty and instrumentality at the core of narratives of post-genocide justice. My point here is
not to contest the legitimate concerns about false testimony before the ICTR.
Instead, I want to underscore the implicit moral judgments and affirmations of
unequal power dynamics in the judgment of "lying," especially when backed
by the symbolic power of the UN institution, and to highlight that many of
these judgments were entangled with issues of interpretation.

Odette further pointed to difficulties in separating linguistic interpretation
from legal interpretation in noting how the issues that arose from combining
(a) adversarial disputation and attacks on witness credibility with (b) interpretation across linguistic barriers were exacerbated by a lack of contextual
knowledge among the judges and attorneys in international criminal law – in
stark contrast to the kinds of experience embodied by the participants in the
gacaca case I discuss in the following section. Odette felt strongly that attorneys on both prosecution and defense should have to be familiar with some
crime scenes before the trial begins, and that judges as well should have to go
on site visits after closing arguments. She noted, "People should see what they
are talking about. The setting in Rwanda is alien to most people. How do you
cross-examine a witness without knowing the crime scene?" She described
a case she was on where the judges had conducted a site visit to the regions of
Rwanda pertinent to the facts they were adjudicating, noting that, "Everything
became clearer to everyone." She gave an example of a witness who had
testified about hiding in a trench, underneath a bridge. During cross-
examination, the opposing counsel kept saying that there were no bridges in
Rwanda, so how could she have hidden under a bridge? When they went to the
site, however, they saw the trench with an embankment that was clearly
bridge-like, and thus they vindicated the witness whose credibility had been
impugned. Odette described another witness who described being able to see
from behind a wall with barbed wire over it. The cross-examining attorneys
said that she was not credible because the wall was too high and thick. On the
site visit, they saw "the wall is what she said it was. It made a lot more sense,
people could see for themselves." Odette raised these issues in part out of
concern for accuracy and findings-of-fact in the specific case, but more
centrally in terms of how these examples shed light on another problematic
way the system tended to lead judges and attorneys to make negative moral
judgments about the Rwandans speaking, in ways predicated on an idea that
legal interpretation was separate from linguistic interpretation, and the contextualized knowledge and expertise that came along with it.

Paying attention to the process of interpretation at the heart of these trials
reveals the landscape of power undergirding international criminal tribunals –

specifically, an institution intended to determine individual criminal account-ability for people accused of crimes in Rwanda that gave symbolic, political, and juridical power to people with limited knowledge of Africa to pass endur-ing moral judgments on Rwandans, including those not on trial themselves. As Odette described, "How many people involved in these cases have ever been to a rural African setting?" The examples I have provided here, from the complexities of Bikindi speaking the original Kinyarwanda lyrics that were the legal issue in his trial, to the many stories told by interpreters and lawyers themselves, underscore how linguistic translation at the ICTR had an inter-pretive and an "ethno-political role,"[35] though it was couched as neutral[36] or apolitical.[37] The labor of translation was in fact a labor of interpretation, in which some truth claims were prioritized over others, and moral judgments were made within an unequal landscape of power. Erasing the affective labor of translation, I suggest, reifies existing hierarchies of power, perpetuates stereotypes of Rwandans as liars, and privileges international norms and out-side knowledge over the types of deeply contextualized knowledge embodied before gacaca courts. Juxtaposing the work of interpretation at the ICTR with gacaca courts, the task to which I now turn, highlights the difficult ideological and practical work needed to maintain the separation, however tenuous it may be, between legal and linguistic interpretation at the ICTR and in interna-tional criminal law more broadly.

III INTERPRETATION IN INKIKO GACACA: RWANDA'S GRASSROOTS GENOCIDE COURTS

The case[38] I discuss below illustrates how the work of participating in gacaca trials hinged on interpretation because at the most foundational level, every-one involved in gacaca sessions was a part of providing, contesting, informally evaluating, or adjudicating competing truth claims provided by people with whom they lived. I present the case in detail to illustrate the circuitous process through which information emerged and the interpretive work required to render it clear. Set in contrast to the ICTR, this example demonstrates in stark relief how the conception of justice behind gacaca saw social and legal interpretation as tightly intertwined, and distributed amongst a wide range of participants.[39]

In late 2007, in the village in southern Rwanda where my research assistant and I had been attending gacaca regularly for nearly six months, we waited one day with approximately 100 people under the tree in the courtyard where cases were heard. The defendant was a young man in his mid-twenties whom I call Didace. Didace did not wear the standard-issue pink prison uniform but rather jeans and a windbreaker, as people around told me that he had served several years in prison but had been released to await his trial. Today he stood in front of the judges' table, arms folded and shoulders hunched against the slight chill in the air, while the presiding judge summoned forward victims and witnesses so the secretary judge could register their names in the notebooks in which trial proceedings were transcribed. People continued to arrive now that they could see cases were beginning.

Before beginning the case in earnest, the judges sent the three witnesses in opposite directions, out of earshot, to await their turn to speak. The secretary judge then read the charges against Didace, saying he was accused in the death of a child named Alice who had been taken from the home of a woman named Kabagenie. Didace had the first opportunity to defend himself, and he repeated multiple times that he did not know the child and did not have any information about her. His testimony lasted only a few minutes before the judges called forward the first witness, whom I call Olive.

Olive was a middle-aged woman, wearing the wrap-skirt and flip flops typical of rural Rwandan women. Standing before the judges and next to Didace, she raised her hand to take the oath with some coaching from the judges, then began to testify. Olive said that in the middle of the killings she saw Didace walking with Alice, heading toward the home of a woman named Kabagenie. She said it looked like Alice had been beaten because her clothes were dirty. She said she saw Didace take Alice into Kabagenie's house. The judges then pressed Olive repeatedly to provide more details about her testimony, asking if she had seen Didace and Alice with anyone else, if she had asked Didace where he was taking Alice, if she knew who had taken Alice from Kabagenie's house, and if there were any weapons. Olive only repeated that Didace was with a man called Bakunda, and that they had no weapons.

In a moment typical of the interpretive work that occurred in trials, several of the judges then asked questions aiming to interpret Didace's behavior and Alice's physical state. Faustin asked Olive to describe the condition of Alice at that time. Olive said repeatedly that Alice's clothes were dirty and in tatters. Another judge, Claude, asked more about Alice's condition, asking whether the girl was crying, or if the men had anything with them? Olive said no, they had nothing, and Alice was not crying, but there was mud all over her clothes. People seated next to me murmured that the judges seemed to be asking about whether Alice had been raped. Olive reiterated that she had seen Didace and Bakunda take Alice to Kabagenie's place, but she did not talk to them. Olive concluded her testimony by stamping her thumbprint onto the transcribed testimony, then sat down.

At that point, the presiding judge turned to question Didace, who remained standing before the judges throughout the proceedings, and asked if he knew Olive or Alice. Didace reiterated several times that he did not know Alice, or anything about her. The judge asked Didace if he knew Olive. In what then became a pivotal moment in the trial, Didace said yes, keeping his gaze averted, his body angled away from hers. He explained that Olive and his mother were co-wives, and that there was an ongoing dispute about land between them, that Olive thought Didace had told his sisters to take a piece of land from her. He claimed that her accusation only came after that dispute. The crowd murmured loudly in response to this revelation of family conflict, underscoring the importance of this truth-claim to the ongoing work of interpretation, and the crowd's own active involvement in analyzing and assessing.

The panel of judges shifted their focus from Didace to Olive, asking her if (and where) she had provided information about Didace during the documentation phase of gacaca. She said she had done so in a different administrative cell while testifying in a case against one of the other people who she said was with Didace. The judges kept questioning her, clearly trying to find out the details of the accusation to see if it seemed related to this land dispute, and if she was speaking the truth (since verifying it by paperwork would have been exceedingly difficult). Faustin asked if Olive had ever explicitly raised this accusation with the court so that a dossier would be created against him, rather than the charge just emerging from ongoing testimony, as it seemed to. Olive said no.

The judges then asked Didace to explain what he was doing during the genocide. These questions showed the judges working to interpret the competing evidence being provided, and to hone in on their analysis of Didace's motivations and behavior. Didace said that he was staying with his grandparents in Gitega, because his uncle had told him that it was unsafe here in Gisagara. The presiding judge asked for more specifics about his acts. Didace said that he did not do anything, just saw things happening. He reiterated that even the neighbors knew that he had done nothing. The presiding judge asked him again for any information about Alice. Didace said that the only information he remembered was that when he was still in prison, he had heard people saying that someone else was supposed to be tried for her death the next morning.

The presiding judge then called the second witness, who turned out to be the elderly woman, Kabagenie, from whose home Alice had been taken. She wore a traditional draped shoulder wrap, and carried a long staff. She took her place next to Didace, and her hand shook when she rose to take the oath.

Kabagenie's testimony contradicted Olive's, and revealed the complex work of interpretation and analysis in which the judges had to engage.

Kabagenie testified that she had been keeping Alice with her in April and May 1994. She described in slow detail (leaving time for the secretary judge to write everything down) that one day Olive had passed by her place and greeted her at the gate. Kabagenie returned her greeting and went inside, where Alice called out and asked who was there. Kabagenie told her it was Olive, and Alice said she wanted to come talk to her. Kabagenie told Alice not to emerge, but the girl snuck out anyways. Kabagenie said that when Alice came back inside, she reprimanded the girl for having gone outside (and in so doing, revealing where she was hiding). The next morning, Kabagenie went out to see what was going on as she saw that someone's home was burning. She explained that they had put the fire out already when she got out. (At this point, the presiding judge interrupted Kabagenie to tell her to get to the point.) Kabagenie continued that by the burnt house, she ran into a woman who threatened her, saying that she should chase away those girls she was hiding – and she assumed that the woman was referring to Alice among the others. Kabagenie said she then was worried that Alice would be discovered. The next morning, as she was going to church, four men came and asked her for the child. She said she feared they would rape Alice. She told them that no girl was staying with her – and even if Alice had been with her, she was too young to be taken. She said the men initially left.

The presiding judge, in an effort to clarify the relevant details of her mean-dering narrative and to interpret the evidence being presented, interrupted Kabagenie's testimony to ask how the man had known that Alice was staying at her place. Kabagenie said that it must have been through Olive. The presiding judge asked who the people in the group were who had come for Alice, and Kabagenie provided four names. She said that when they reached her house, they told her to bring out that girl. She said that she had many girls there, which one did they want? They asked for Alice. She refused, and they force-fully entered her house and grabbed Alice. Kabagenie said that she followed them, at which point she saw Didace from a distance, standing by the side. She reiterated that he was not with the group who took Alice, not among those who came to her house. She said that one of those who took Alice had a *panga* (a farming machete). The presiding judge asked how many times the group took Alice. Kabagenie said that the first time they took her, they brought her back the same day. The presiding judge asked what her condition was when she returned – again, clearly trying to interpret whether or not she had been raped. Kabagenie said Alice seemed normal, she did not realize that anything bad had happened. Kabagenie reiterated that Didace was not with them, he just met them along the way. The presiding judge asked about the second time Alice was taken. Kabagenie said that the second time, Bakunda came running after Alice. Kabagenie followed, and asked Bakunda to give her back, saying she would even give him money to return her. He refused, and even cut Alice and threatened to cut Kabagenie if she followed.

The presiding judge asked who were the people who returned Alice to Kabagenie's house the first time? Kabagenie said she did not know, she did not see them, they just called out that they were returning her and left. The presiding judge asked again about what had happened the second time. Kabagenie reiterated that Didace was not among the men who came. She said she told the group that Alice must have already been killed. The men threatened to kill her as well, then someone called Magara came back. The presiding judge again interrupted to ask Kabagenie to stick to the story and the relevant details, drawing attention to his own role in determining relevance, as he analyzed which information was pertinent versus irrelevant. Kabagenie said she discussed with Magara that he should hide Alice, because Kabagenie felt the child was no longer safe at her place now that she had been discovered. So Magara took Alice away on a bicycle.

At this point, approximately an hour into the case proceedings, the presiding judge called Olive back from where she had settled on the ground at the edge of the ring of participants, and asked her to explain why her testimony contradicted Kabagenie's testimony. He pointed out that Kabagenie, who had been hiding Alice, had said that Didace was never with Alice. Olive stood and began to speak. For several minutes, the judges pushed back and forth with her, trying to nail down the details of when the group came to take Alice, from where, and whether Didace was with them, looking for inconsistencies. Olive reiterated that she met Bakunda and Didace while they were taking Alice to Kabagenie's place. During this discussion, Kabagenie was seated on the bench before the judges, looking away from Olive.

A judge I call Claude then questioned Olive assertively, arguing with her, looking for inconsistencies in her story and suggesting that since Alice was only discovered and taken away after Olive's visit, perhaps she was in fact the one who gave the child away. Faustin then interrupted with a question geared at understanding Didace's motivations. He asked Didace why he had denied seeing or knowing Alice altogether, when Olive was only saying that he had seen her go by somewhere? (That is, Faustin was suggesting that Olive's accusation that Didace had seen Alice go by was benign and therefore his strenuous denial of it seemed suspicious.) Didace explained that his mother had been sick at that time with HIV, and he had gone out to get pills for her. He arrived at the house where he knew the pills to be and saw it was not locked, he moved a nail to get into the door, then he found the pills and put them in a bag in his pocket. As he was leaving, he saw a crowd of people, and worried they would harm him, so he took a different path home. He said he heard a lot of people making noise, and he tried to hide. He was pantomiming some of this, and the presiding judge told him not to make signs, but rather to explain clearly, suggesting the movements were difficult to interpret. Didace said that because he had been on his own, he had feared for his own safety and therefore just ran away. He emphasized that he never left the place where he was staying again, and never went close to Bakunda. (The crowd all started speaking, reminding the judges that Bakunda was a well-known, notorious killer.) The presiding judge asked Didace how big the group was and he said that it was about ten people, but that he never saw the girl Alice. The judge again asked him if he had any information about Alice. Didace said that he never saw her or heard anything about her.

A woman from the General Assembly then stood to say that someone had already described the death of Alice in another case, accusing Olive of trying to conspire to kill Alice. The crowd murmured loudly, some in disbelief, others in agreement. The presiding judge then loudly asked why this information about Olive was not revealed earlier? Claude kept pressing Olive, saying that there seemed to be something she was hiding, not telling the judges. Kabagenie came forward to stamp her thumb on her testimony, then sat back down.

A third witness came forward to testify, a woman I call Elise, with a baby on her hip. She said she would testify to what she had seen with her own eyes (a clarification required by the judges, as to whether testimony was what one had seen or heard). Elise said that after the time when the authority had said that there would be no more killing of women and children, she went out to get something for her kids. She reached town, then as she turned to head home, she saw a group of boys pushing Alice. They said they had gotten more people to rape. They took Alice to the plantation, then Bakunda took her. The presiding judge interrupted Elise to ask if she could name any of the people, and Elise testified that Didace was among the group. The judges pressed Elise on why she had not given this information earlier. Elise mumbled a response that was unintelligible to me and the people around me. Everyone around us was muttering, talking, exclaiming, and the judges were pounding on the table to restore order. The judges made Elise sit back down and did not allow her to provide any more testimony, nor did they have her provide a thumbprint to authorize her testimony in the transcription.

When the judges had restored calm, they asked for comments from the general assembly. This was a standard stage in gacaca trials, allowed for by the law instantiating gacaca, which enabled (and even required) everyone present to participate. People attending the trial could provide information, ask questions, or offer their own interpretations of the evidence that had transpired. The judges were all listening intently, alternately watching the witnesses, whispering amongst themselves behind books to shade their mouths, and questioning deliberately. A woman stood first to say that Kabagenie would have known if Alice had been raped, given that she had been hiding her for so long. So if Kabagenie said that she hadn't noticed anything wrong with Alice, then she should know. Lots of talking continued, as the people in the general assembly seemed to suggest that Didace was being falsely accused. Another general assembly member stood to say that he was a neighbor of Didace's in Gitega, and that he knew nothing bad he had done, but rather he knew that people had even tried to chase and kill Didace. He sat back down. Another woman stood to say that she knew nothing bad about Didace. Claude (one of the judges) kept speaking up, saying that Olive must be involved with how Alice's hiding place came to be discovered. At one point the judges started questioning Elise again, asking for more details of her testimony, how and when she provided it, and why it had inconsistencies. Elise seemed to be trying to discredit Kabagenie, saying that she was responsible for the death of someone called Bijirimana.

By this point, the thrust of the trial had shifted from Didace defending himself to Olive defending herself, as the assembled crowd and the judges seemed to think that she was falsely accusing him, either to hide her own complicity in Alice's disappearance, or worse. Didace stood silent, while Olive spoke up again, saying that she didn't understand why people were suggesting that she caused Alice's death. She suggested that since Alice had been with her mother when she was taken, maybe the people who took the mother were responsible. The judges kept arguing with Olive about inconsistencies in her testimony. Olive said that Kabagenie was just conspiring against her. She insisted there was no reason she would be lying about Didace, that she was only saying she saw him with Alice. The secretary judge pressed her, saying that the killers only knew about where Alice was hiding because of Olive. Olive repeated what she had said before, shifting attention from the original accusation (of when she had allegedly seen Alice with Didace) to when Alice was last seen alive, saying that the people who came to take the mother might know more, because when they took the mother, they left the child. The judges asked her for more details (clearly disbelieving), and she said she didn't remember. Two people from the general assembly stood to talk, both speaking over each other. The secretary judge looked back and forth between them, then asked one to stop. One woman said that the mother died early in April, while the child died in June, so there seemed to be no link between the two (thus discrediting Olive's suggestion). A great deal of arguing continued, which was difficult for everyone to follow. Olive suggested that Alice had run after her mother when she was taken, as if that might be when the killers had seen her – again, providing testimony about an event not at all connected to the original accusation against Didace. Kabagenie then stood to say that she had been hiding many people, so why did they come only for Alice, suggesting again that Olive had been the one to give Alice up to the killers? The judges pointed out to Olive that Kabagenie had been able to save two people, but she (Olive) seemed to have given away that Alice was there and then the girl was killed.

Olive, now firmly on the defensive, explained that someone named Senga who had testified at an earlier trial had said that she had never given Alice up. The judges asked what her relationship was to Senga. She did not answer, but the crowd all called out that he was one of her brothers-in-law, and that therefore he would not testify against her. Olive protested that the people in the crowd, including Kabagenie, were conspiring against her. She said that Elise had told her that Kabagenie was behind everyone conspiring against her, so that Kabagenie could avoid responsibility for the death of Bijirimana.

At this point, the presiding judge told all the witnesses to sit. He turned the floor a final time to Didace, who still stood, quietly, with his arms folded, shoulders hunched. Didace responded angrily, saying that he had nothing else to say, everyone had been following the case, there was nothing else to provide. He finished angrily, "This woman Olive, she really wants to throw me in a big pit hole."

The presiding judge asked the general assembly if they had anything further. An old man stood to say that as best he could tell, Olive was trying to divert attention from her onto Didace. Several more people stood and quickly said that there were inconsistencies in Olive's testimony, and that Didace must be innocent. The whole crowd seemed to be supporting Didace. At the end, the judges asked Olive and Elise to sit on the bench typically reserved for the accused. A man seated next to me commented that they must be in trouble, as the judges leafed through the gacaca rules booklet to determine if they had grounds to file charges of perjury against them. The judges then closed this case and moved on to another defendant, allowing Didace to leave while Olive and Elise remained under their watchful eyes until the judges adjourned court for the day and left for confidential deliberations. The next day, we learned that the judges acquitted Didace of the charges against him, and sentenced Olive to six months in jail for false testimony.

My goal in describing this case was not to argue whether or not truth was achieved here, nor to suggest that gacaca is always and only the best way to get at truth. Nor did I simplify the details to allow a clearer analysis. Rather, my aim was to illustrate the complexity of the task before gacaca by setting out the many-stranded, thick tangle of competing claims people presented there, and, by extension, the work of interpretation needed to assess it. Gacaca courts handled cases that confronted the quotidian details of the genocide, including interpreting motivations that entangled past and present – whether a woman taken away and returned had been raped, for example, and whether a current land claim was distorting testimony about the past.

Gacaca courts did not require professional interpreters, as all testimony was conducted in Kinyarwanda. Yet, I have shown here, the work of interpretation was central to the social and legal work of gacaca. Participants interpreted one another's testimony based on what they knew of the genocide, related events, one another, what other people had said in other trials, as well as in relation to people's relationships to one another, and current struggles over resources or relationships in the present – that is, overlapping, context-specific knowledge. This interpretation was not the work of specifically designated individuals, but rather cross-cut the process. People in a wide range of roles in the trials – judges, defendant, witnesses, general assembly members – evaluated competing truth claims, attempted to understand and translate what other participants said, and negotiated the meaning of people's actions during the genocide. It was not egalitarian, as judges certainly had more authority to impose their interpretation, as I illustrated here. Yet I also showed that people from the general assembly had input, as judges solicited their opinions and as even their unsolicited interactions often bubbled up loudly and overflowed into the trial. The process was characterized more by shifting constellations of power than by rigid hierarchy, and much of the work was done by non-professionals, in stark contrast to the work of interpretation in international criminal justice.

IV CONCLUSION

I have used this chapter to suggest that the work of interpretation and translation is a central yet underexplored dynamic in the literature on retributive justice after mass atrocities in Africa. How do debates over the meaning of testimony and the evaluation and assessment of competing truth claims occur within the different moral economies of justice across international versus grassroots trials? By juxtaposing reflections on translation and interpretation from Rwandans at the International Criminal Tribunal for Rwanda with an example of the messy work of interpretation occurring during grassroots genocide trials, I have shown how interpretation is not an idiosyncrasy of international trials, a background logistic to be handled by technical solutions, but rather is central to the work of making judgments about the meaning and accountability for political violence more widely. The work of interpretation brings up issues of labor, emotion, and meaning-making at the heart of judicial processes. The affective labor of interpretation occurs differently across international and local courts, within different moral economies of justice. When it occurs within international criminal trials but is rendered invisible or technical, this serves to reinforce existing hierarchies of power that devalue local, often African experience in lieu of international, allegedly universal values, principles, and knowledge.

I suggest that attending to interpretation, and further theorizing the relationship between legal and linguistic interpretation, might help us move beyond a false dichotomization where international law is equated with objective neutrality while local courts are equated with politicized bias, to see the power of deeply contextualized, grassroots legal processes. I do not intend to naively romanticize or valorize gacaca, which many have shown can serve at the hands of Rwanda's increasingly authoritarian government as a form of "lawfare," "the effort to conquer and control ... by the coercive use of legal means"[40] selectively as another strategy to consolidate the ruling elites' power and suppress dissent,[41] as I discuss elsewhere.[42] Yet, I suggest, a focus on interpretation allows us to trace how, in all legal systems, certain forms of power and expertise privilege some interpretations over others, labeling some as dishonest and disingenuous and others as correct. Laying bare how these processes work within institutions could help avoid reproducing the power inequalities at the heart of the conflicts these institutions hope to ameliorate.

Notes

1. William W. Burke-White, 'Complementarity in Practice: The International Criminal Court as Part of a System of Multi-Level Global Governance in the Democratic Republic of Congo' (2005) 18 *Leiden Journal of International Law* 557–590.
2. National Service of Gacaca Jurisdictions website, www.inkiko-gacaca.gov .rw/En/EnObjectives.htm. Accessed 1 February 2011.
3. Organic Law No16/2004, Establishing the Organization, Competence, and Functioning of Gacaca Courts Charged with Prosecuting and Trying the Perpetrators of the Crime of Genocide and Other Crimes Against

Humanity, Committed Between October 1, 1990, and December 31, 1994: Official Gazette of the Republic of Rwanda. Articles 29, 30.

4. See, for example, Phil Clark, *The Gacaca Courts, Post-Genocide Justice and Reconciliation in Rwanda: Justice without Lawyers* (Cambridge: Cambridge University Press, 2010); Phil Clark and Zachary Kaufman (eds.), *After Genocide: Transitional Justice, Post-Conflict Reconstruction, and Reconciliation in Rwanda and Beyond* (New York: Columbia University Press, 2009).

5. See, for example, Jennie Burnet, '(In)Justice: Truth, Reconciliation, and Revenge in Rwanda's Gacaca', in Alexander Hinton (ed.), *Transitional Justice: Global Mechanisms and Local Realities after Genocide and Mass Violence* (New Brunswick, NJ: Rutgers University Press, 2011), pp. 95–118; Anuradha Chakravarty, *Investing in Authoritarian Rule: Punishment and Patronage in Rwanda's Gacaca Courts for Genocide Crimes* (Cambridge: Cambridge University Press, 2015); Scott Straus and Lars Waldorf (eds.), *Remaking Rwanda: State Building and Human Rights after Mass Violence* (Madison: University of Wisconsin Press, 2011); Susan Thomson, 'The Darker Side of Transitional Justice: The Power Dynamics Behind Rwanda' Gacaca Courts' (2011) 81(3) *Africa* 373–390.

6. This chapter is based on eighteen months of ethnographic research conducted in Rwanda, including three 1–3 week trips to Arusha, Tanzania, between 2004 and 2008. I attended fifty-six gacaca sessions, and conducted over eighty interviews with NGO and ICTR staff, and members of government in Kigali.

7. See, for example, Kamari M. Clarke, *Fictions of Justice: The International Criminal Court and the Challenge of Legal Pluralism in Sub-Saharan Africa* (Cambridge: Cambridge University Press, 2009); Thierry Cruvellier, *Courts of Remorse: Inside the International Criminal Tribunal for Rwanda* (Madison: University of Wisconsin Press, 2010); Nigel Eltringham, 'We Are Not a Truth Commission': Fragmented Narratives and the Historical Record at the International Criminal Tribunal for Rwanda' (2009) 11(1) *Journal of Genocide Research* 55–79; Nigel Eltringham, '"Illuminating the Broader Context": Anthropological and Historical Knowledge at the International Criminal Tribunal for Rwanda' (2013) 19 (2) *Journal of the Royal Anthropological Institute* 338–355; Nicholas Jones, *The Courts of Genocide: Politics and the Rule of Law in Rwanda and Arusha* (New York: Routledge, 2010); Paul Magnarella, *Justice in Africa: Rwanda's Genocide, Its Courts, and the UN Criminal Tribunal* (Brookfield: Ashgate, 2000); Victor Peskin, 'Courting Rwanda: The Promises and Pitfalls of the ICTR Outreach Programme' (2005) 3 *Journal of International Criminal Justice* 950–961; Victor Peskin, *International Justice in Rwanda and the Balkans: Virtual Trials and the Struggle for State Cooperation* (Cambridge: Cambridge University Press, 2008); Richard Wilson, *Writing*

History in International Criminal Trials (Cambridge: Cambridge University Press, 2011). There is also a body of work on translation in international law in Merry's sense of translating or vernacularizing international norms, such as human rights, into local contexts: Sally E. Merry, *Human Rights and Gender Violence: Translating International Law into Local Justice* (Chicago: University of Chicago Press, 2006); see also Nigel Eltringham, 'Judging the "Crime of Crimes": Continuity and Improvisation at the International Criminal Tribunal for Rwanda', in Hinton, *Transitional Justice*, pp. 206–226; Daphna Golan and Zavika Orr, 'Translating Human Rights of the "Enemy": The Case of Israeli NGOs Defending Palestinian Rights' (2012) 46(4) *Law and Society Review* 781–814. This work typically does not attend to linguistic translation during trials.

8. Jessica Almqvist, 'The Impact of Cultural Diversity on International Criminal Proceedings' (2006) 4 *Journal of International Criminal Justice* 752–756.

9. See Victoro Peskin, 'Courting Rwanda', 959; see also Sigall Horovitz, 'How International Courts Shape Domestic Justice: Lessons from Rwanda and Sierra Leone' (2013) 46(3) *Israel Law Review* 354.

10. Kavitha Giridhar, 'Justice for All: Protecting the Translation Rights of Defendants in International War Crime Tribunals' (2011) 43 *Case Western Reserve Journal of International Law* 799–829; Joshua Karton, 'Lost in Translation: International Criminal Tribunals and the Legal Implications of Interpreted Testimony' (2008) 41(1) *Vanderbilt Journal of Transnational Law* 1–54.

11. Jonneke Koomen, '"Without These Women, the Tribunal Cannot Do Anything": The Politics of Witness Testimony on Sexual Violence at the International Criminal Tribunal for Rwanda' (2013) 38(2) *Signs* 253–277; Stephanie Wood, 'A Woman Scorned for the "Least Condemned" War Crime: Precedent and Problems with Prosecuting Rape as a Serious War Crime in the International Criminal Tribunal for Rwanda' (2004) 13 *Columbia Journal of Gender and Law* 274–327.

12. Koomen, 'Without These Women'.

13. Susan Berk-Seligson, *The Bilingual Courtroom: Court Interpreters in the Judicial Process* (Chicago: University of Chicago Press, 1990); Susan Berk-Seligson, *Coerced Confessions: The Discourse of Bilingual Police Interrogations* (Boston: De Gruyter Mouton, 2009); Irus Braverman, 'The Place of Translation in Jerusalem's Criminal Trial Court' (2007) 10(2) *New Criminal Law Review: An International and Interdisciplinary Journal* 239–277; Lisa Hajjar, *Courting Conflict: The Israeli Military Court System in the West Bank and Gaza* (Berkeley: University of California Press, 2005); Laura Jeffrey, 'Historical Narrative and Legal Evidence: Judging Chagossian's High Court Testimony' (2006) 29(2) *Political and Legal Anthropology Review* 228–253; Kwai Hang Ng, '"If I Lie, I Tell You,

May Heaven and Earth Destroy Me": Language and Legal Consciousness in Hong Kong Bilingual Common Law' (2009) 43(2) *Law and Society Review* 369–404.

14. See, for example, John Conley and William O'Barr, *Rules versus Relationships: The Ethnography of Legal Discourse* (Chicago: University of Chicago Press, 1990); John Conley and William O'Barr, *Just Words: Law, Language, and Power* (Chicago: University of Chicago Press, 1997); Susan Hirsch, *Pronouncing and Persevering: Gender and the Discourses of Disputing in an African Islamic Court* (Chicago: University of Chicago Press, 1998); Sally E. Merry, *Getting Justice and Getting Even: Legal Consciousness Among Working Class Americans* (Chicago: University of Chicago Press, 1990); Elizabeth Mertz, 'Language, Law, and Social Meanings: Linguistic/Anthropological Contributions to the Study of Law' (1992) 26(2) *Law and Society Review* 413–446; Justin Richland, *Arguing with Tradition: The Language of Law in Hopi Tribal Court* (Chicago: Chicago University Press, 2008); Lawrance Solan and Peter Tiersma, *Speaking of Crime: The Language of Criminal Justice* (Chicago: University of Chicago Press, 2005).

15. See, for example, Clarke, *Fictions of Justice*.

16. Kristin C. Doughty, '"Our Goal Is Not to Punish but to Reconcile": Mediation in Post-Genocide Rwanda' (2014) 116(4) *American Anthropologist* 1–15; Kristin C. Doughty, 'Law and the Architecture of Social Repair: Gacaca Days in Post-Genocide Rwanda' (2015) 21(2) *Journal of the Royal Anthropological Institute* 419–437.

17. Organic Law N16/2004 of 19/6/2004, art. 64.

18. Jennie Burnet, *Genocide Lives in Us: Women, Memory, and Silence in Rwanda* (Madison, WI: University of Wisconsin Press, 2012), p. 205; Clark, *Gacaca Courts*; Burt Ingelaere, 'The Gacaca courts in Rwanda', in Luc Huyse and Mark Salter (eds.), *Traditional Justice and Reconciliation After Violent Conflict: Learning from African Experiences* (International Institute for Democracy and Electoral Assistance, 2008), pp. 51, 55–56; Burt Ingelaere, 'Does the Truth Pass Across the Fire Without Burning?' Locating the Short Circuit in Rwanda's Gacaca Courts' (2009) 47(4) *The Journal of Modern African Studies* 509, 513; Max Rettig, 'The Sovu Trials: The Impact of Genocide Justice on One Community', in Straus and Waldorf, *Remaking Rwanda*, p. 195; Thomson, 'Darker Side of Transitional Justice', 380–381; Lar Waldorf, 'Mass Justice for Mass Atrocity: Rethinking Local Justice as Transitional Justice' (2006) 79(1) *Temple Law Review* 71.

19. United Nations Security Council Resolution 955 (1994) on establishment of an International Tribunal for Rwanda and adoption of the Statute of

the Tribunal, Vol. 955: Official Documents System of the United Nations (S/RES/955(1994).

20. Gerard Prunier, *Africa's World War* (Oxford: Oxford University Press, 2009), pp. 8–12.

21. See Eltringham, 'Judging the "Crime of Crimes"'.

22. Article 20(a) and (f).

23. See also Almqvist, 'Impact of Cultural Diversity', 752–756.

24. See also Koomen, 'Without These Women', 261.

25. For how the history of Rwanda is heavily contested, see Rene Lemarchand, *The Dynamics of Violence in Central Africa* (Philadelphia: University of Pennsylvania Press, 2009); Catharine Newbury, *The Cohesion of Oppression: Clientship and Ethnicity in Rwanda: 1860–1960* (New York: Columbia University Press, 1988); David Newbury, *The Land Beyond the Mists* (Athens: Ohio University Press, 2009); Jan Vansina, *Antecedents to Modern Rwanda: The Nyiginya Kingdom* Madison: University of Wisconsin Press, 2004). The "events of 1959" are alternately framed as the initiation of democratic leadership, or as the start of genocide.

26. There is a rich scholarship on *ubuhake* (see, for example, Lemarchand, *Dynamics of Violence*; Newbury, *Cohesion of Oppression*; Filip Reyntjens, 'Chiefs and Burgomasters in Rwanda: The Unfinished Quest for a Bureaucracy' (1987) 25–26 *Journal of Legal Pluralism and Unofficial Law* 71–97.

27. We spoke in several interview sessions, in English, before and after official trial sessions. All quotes are transcribed and paraphrased from detailed notes, not audio recordings. Portions in quotation marks are direct quotes.

28. Similar themes were noted in Berk-Seligson, *Bilingual Courtroom*, in her work with translation from Spanish to English in United States courts and in Braverman, 'The Place of Translation', 247, in her work on Hebrew to Arabic translation in Israeli trial courts.

29. Conley and O'Barr, *Just Words*.

30. Jeffrey, 'Historical Narrative and Legal Evidence'; Ng, 'If I Lie'; Richland, *Arguing with Tradition*.

31. Eltringham, 'Illuminating the broader context'; Wilson, *Writing History*.

32. Danielle De Lame, *A Hill Among a Thousand: Transformations and Ruptures in Rural Rwanda*. H. Arnold, transl. (Madison, WI: University of Wisconsin Press, 2005), p. 14–15; Ingelaere, 'Does the Truth Pass Across the Fire', 54; Waldorf, 'Mass Justice for Mass Atrocity', 70.

33. See Ng, 'If I Lie', for similar analysis in Hong Kong's bilingual courts.

34. De Lame, *A Hill Among a Thousand*, pp. 14–15; Ingelaere, Does the Truth Pass across the Fire', 54; Waldorf, 'Mass Justice for Mass Atrocity', 70.

35. Braverman, 'Place of Translation,' 245.

36. Hajjar, *Courting Conflict*, pp. 151–152.

37. Blake Puckett, '"We're Very Apolitical": Examining the Role of the International Legal Assistance Expert' (2009) 16(1) *Indiana Journal of Global Legal Studies* 293–310.
38. I attended this case and took detailed, paraphrased notes. This is a paraphrased translation.
39. I do not suggest a romanticized view of gacaca here. For detailed critiques of state-backed instrumentality and coercion before gacaca, as well as discussion of the wide literatures critiquing its implementation, see Doughty, 'Our Goal Is Not to Punish'; Doughty, 'Law and the Architecture of Social Repair'. I focus here on the ways that even as a state-backed institution that penetrated deeply into local communities and often applied victor's justice, it nonetheless must be recognized for being rooted in a starkly different view of processes of justice than the ICTR.
40. John Comaroff, 'Colonialism, Culture, and the Law: A Foreword' (2001) 26 *Law and Social Inquiry* 306.
41. See, for example, Burnet, '(In)Justice'; Chakravarty, *Investing in Authoritarian Rule*; Helen Hintjens, 'Post-Genocide Identity Politics in Rwanda' (2008) 8(1) *Ethnicities* 5–41; Timothy Longman, 'Trying Times for Rwanda: Reevaluating Gacaca Courts in Post-Genocide Rwanda' (2010) 32 *Harvard International Law Review* 48–52; Constance Morrill, 'Show Business and "Lawfare" in Rwanda: Twelve Years after the Genocide' (2006) 53 *Dissent* 14–20; Filip Reyntjens, 'Rwanda, Ten Years On: From Genocide to Dictatorship', in S. Marysse and F. Reyntjens, (eds.), *The Political Economy of the Great Lakes Region in Africa* (New York: Palgrave MacMillan, 2005), pp. 15–47; Straus and Waldorf, *Remaking Rwanda*; Thomson, 'Darker Side of Transitional Justice'.
42. Kristin C. Doughty, *Remediation In Rwanda: Grassroots Legal Forums* (Philadelphia: University of Pennsylvania Press, 2016).

15

International Criminal Justice and the Early Formation of an African Criminal Court

Abel S. Knottnerus and Eefje de Volder

I INTRODUCTION

On 27 June 2014, the AU Assembly adopted the 'Amendment Protocol' on the Statute of the African Court of Justice and Human Rights (African Court).[1] With this decision, the African heads of state and governments concluded the first phase in the formation of a Criminal Chamber of the African Court. When the required number of fifteen AU Member States has ratified the Amendment Protocol, the African Court will be the first regional court with jurisdiction over international and other crimes,[2] including, but not limited to, the crimes that fall within the jurisdiction of the ICC.[3] Over time, the Criminal Chamber of the African Court can come to function as the African counterpart of the ICC by seeking criminal accountability for individuals and corporations who are responsible for creating and profiting from the continuing instability of many African states.

The adoption of the Amendment Protocol follows earlier regional initiatives in which the AU and its predecessor, the Organisation of African Unity (OAU), have set out to explore new areas of international law and international policy making. The OAU was, for example, the first international organization that acknowledged collective human rights, and with the adoption of the AU Constitutive Act in 2000 the AU became the first continental body with the power to authorize humanitarian interventions.[4] These and other regional initiatives, such as the establishment of a standby AU intervention force, are in many ways revolutionary. However, like regional mechanisms in other parts of the world, the implementation of and compliance with many of these initiatives have left much to be desired. In Africa, mechanisms that seek to promote peace, security and human rights have often proven to be empty promises as the statecraft has failed to provide the financial, institutional and political support that they require.[5] This perceived failure of African leadership is what makes many civil society organizations and other relevant audiences inside – and outside – Africa somewhat sceptical about further revolutionary 'innovations' of the AU.

In this light, it is not surprising to find that the recent initiative to extend criminal jurisdiction to the African Court has not been met with great enthusiasm. Concerns have been expressed about the practical feasibility of this proposal.[6] Several stakeholders have pointed out that effective regional prosecution will require much more support from AU Member States than the African Court on Human and Peoples' Rights has received so far.[7] Assuming that this support will not be given, they have advocated for renewed cooperation between the AU and the ICC, and for improving the functioning of the existing African Court (rather than adding criminal jurisdiction to its mandate).

Beyond questioning the expediency of the AU's plan for an 'African Criminal Court', several civil society organizations and a number of scholars have challenged the proposal on fundamental grounds.[8] In debating the future relationship of the Criminal Chamber of the African Court with the ICC, they have argued that the proposal for regional criminal prosecution in Africa should mainly be understood as a political response to the ICC's track record in Africa and in particular to the contested prosecution of African presidents.[9] In their view, the proposed Criminal Chamber of the African Court is an attempt to establish an 'anti-ICC Court' and does not reflect genuine efforts to address impunity in the region.[10]

What is more, they have criticized the Amendment Protocol for legal problems that would arise in relation to the ICC once the African Court would start taking up criminal cases. Various NGOs and commentators have argued that because the Amendment Protocol does not address its relationship with the ICC and because the drafters have included a provision granting immunity to sitting heads of state, a 'clash' between the two courts is on the horizon.[11] Instead of complementing the ICC, the Criminal Chamber of the African Court would only frustrate its proceedings.[12]

In this chapter we seek to counter these and related objections that portray the Amendment Protocol as a deliberate attempt of African leaders to weaken the ICC and to undermine international criminal justice. In response to opponents of the AU's initiative to endow the African Court with criminal jurisdiction,[13] we argue that the concerns that have been voiced about the intentions of African leaders and about possible jurisdictional battles with the ICC are exaggerated. Furthermore, we highlight that the Protocol has expressive value and claim that even if the Protocol will not enter into force, or will not receive the necessary support, its adoption matters, because it articulates a regional vision on the future of international criminal justice.

In the following, we first introduce the conversations that preceded the adoption of the Amendment Protocol. In countering those who claim that the Criminal Chamber of the African Court is only established to refute the ICC, we point out that the discussions on the possibility of an African Criminal Court predate the recent AU–ICC standoff, and insist that the adoption of the Amendment Protocol should be seen in light of the broader ambition of the AU to address African problems through African means. In the second part of this chapter, we turn to specific legal problems that opponents of the Amendment Protocol have foreshadowed in relation to the ICC and explain why these concerns are overstated, as there are many ways in which the two courts can work together. Finally, in the last part of this chapter, we set out to develop an alternative image of the plan for regional criminal prosecution in Africa by showing how the Amendment Protocol reflects a strong desire to bring certain issues back on the agenda of international criminal justice, including crimes that address the structural causes of mass violence and the criminal responsibility of corporations that are involved in the commission of these crimes. We conclude that these and related elements give the AU's revolutionary initiative expressive value and that the Amendment Protocol may ultimately strengthen rather than weaken the pursuit of international criminal justice.

II TOWARDS AN ANTI-ICC COURT?

One of the most powerful critiques that has been voiced against the Amendment Protocol is that African states only intend to establish the Criminal Chamber of the African Court to refute the ICC. The timing of the discussions on the early formation of an African Criminal Court has raised questions about its underlying intentions. In one of the first and most debated articles on the criminal jurisdiction of the African Court, Chacha Murungu expressed, for example, his doubts about the 'genuine' purpose of the Criminal Chamber. In his view, the calls for the establishment of this Court only came after African leaders were indicted both by the ICC and domestic European courts and these calls would thus simply be 'meant to establish a court that will compete with the ICC in terms of jurisdiction over persons and crimes committed in Africa'.[14] In a similar vein, Gino Naldi and Konstantinos Magliveras have argued that the 'AU's disenchantment with the International Criminal Court's focus on Africa' has motivated the discussions on expanding the jurisdiction of the African Court.[15] This concern has also been voiced within the AU itself, most notably by Bahame Tom Nyanduga, commissioner of the African Commission on Human and Peoples' Rights, who has stated that 'the decision to contemplate the creation of an [African Criminal Court] is a political backlash to what [the] African Union considers as a selective justice'.[16]

To be sure, the process towards the development of an African Criminal Court has been accelerated by the ongoing tension between the AU and the ICC over the alleged Africa bias and the indictment of African presidents by the ICC. Yet it cannot be overlooked that the idea of an African Criminal Court predates these discussions. The regional prosecution of international and other crimes in Africa was first discussed by the OAU in the context of the African Charter on Human and Peoples' Rights in the 1970s and more specially the crime of Apartheid.[17] The idea for a regional criminal court was eventually rejected as African states were confident that the crime of Apartheid would be part of the jurisdiction of the 'international court to repress crimes against mankind' that the UN was considering to establish at the time.[18] During the period in which Apartheid was still in place in South Africa, however, no international criminal tribunal was set up to prosecute this crime.[19] According to Ademola Abass, this showed that some crimes that are of particular relevance to Africa would not be prosecuted elsewhere and that it was this realization that would later motivate African leaders to establish a regional court with the power to prosecute these specific crimes.[20]

In the context of the AU, the idea of an African Criminal Court was first tabled during the discussions on the merger of the African Court of Justice and the African Court on Human and Peoples' Rights at the beginning of this century, but at the time it was still deemed premature and was dismissed without debating its merits.[21] The idea resurfaced again in 2006, when a Committee of Eminent African Jurists was assigned to report on the available options to try former President of Chad Hissène Habré.[22] In its report to the AU Assembly, the Committee proposed that the merged African Court of Justice and Human Rights would 'be granted jurisdiction to undertake criminal trials for crimes against humanity, war crimes and violations of the Convention Against Torture'.[23] The extension of the jurisdiction of the Court would allow African perpetrators of international crimes to be prosecuted on African soil, rather than to stand trial before non-African courts.

Eventually, it took until early 2009 before the AU Assembly formally requested the AU Commission to examine 'the implications of the Court being empowered to try international crimes such as genocide, crimes against humanity and war crimes'.[24] This first decision of the AU Assembly on the establishment of an African Criminal Court was taken under the consideration of the 'Abuse on the Principle of Universal Jurisdiction', and many of the following decisions on the Court were embedded in resolutions on the ICC.[25] As such, it can hardly be denied that some connection exists between the discussions on the possible extension of the jurisdiction of the African Court and the expressed discomfort with the ICC and with the indictments of African high-ranking officials before European domestic courts. Yet the recent intensification of the discussions on an African Criminal Court cannot be completely ascribed to the AU's frustration with the ICC and with the exercise of universal jurisdiction. Apart from the fact that these discussions predated the AU–ICC stand-off, it is important to acknowledge that the Amendment Protocol of the African Court gives expression to key responsibilities of the AU and that it forms part of the AU's comprehensive peace and security agenda.[26]

The AU has been founded on the idea that stability, development and integration are crucial to address the multitude of challenges that the African continent faced at the dawn of the new millennium.[27] Inspired by the desire to take matters into their own hands (coined as 'African solutions to African problems'), the Preamble of its Constitutive Act stresses 'the need to promote peace and security and stability as a prerequisite for the implementation of the development and integration agenda'. The Constitutive Act provides a wide range of objectives and principles aimed at the eradication of conflicts for the purpose of setting the continent on a firm path of growth. In general terms, its vision is spearheaded on three fundamental ideals: (i) cooperation ('Africa must Unite'), (ii) self-reliance and ownership ('Africa first') and (iii) non-indifference (as opposed to the non-interference policy of the OAU).

The last of these three ideals, non-indifference, reflects the desire to actively address a wide range of (Africa-specific) problems that keep the continent in war with itself.[28] This principle is expressed, for example, in the way that the AU has singled out certain key objectives, such as the fight against terrorism, and in the way it has created means to take action in case of non-compliance, especially through sanctions and interventions in accordance with Articles 4(j), 4(h) and 23 of the Constitutive Act. In this light, the early formation of an African Court that hears criminal cases can be understood as an additional measure that is taken to realize the AU's primary objectives and in particular to bring perpetrators of international and other crimes to justice.

With respect to the particular crime of unconstitutional change of government, which is included in the Amendment Protocol, regional prosecution is also explicitly provided for under the African Charter on Democracy, Elections and Governance (which entered into force in February 2012).[29]

Article 25(5) of this Charter states that 'perpetrators of unconstitutional changes of government may also be tried before the competent court of the Union'. By extending the jurisdiction of the African Court to include the crime of unconstitutional change of government, the AU has thus given expression to an existing provision in an African treaty.

A similar argument can be made for the three 'classical' international crimes that are mentioned in Article 4(h) of the AU Constitutive Act. When looking at the wording of this provision one could even go a step further and argue that regional criminal justice is part of the 'intervention' options that the AU Assembly may take under specified circumstances. Article 4(h) provides 'a right of the Union to intervene in a Member State pursuant to a decision of the Assembly in respect of grave circumstances, namely: war crimes, genocide and crimes against humanity'. If regional criminal justice is indeed one of its intervention options, then the AU Assembly would arguably be authorized to refer situations involving one of these crimes to the African Criminal Court, even without the consent of the Member State concerned.[30] This would mean that the AU Assembly may refer situations involving AU Member States that are not party to the Amendment Protocol in a similar way as the UN Security Council has the power under the Rome Statute to refer situations to the ICC, be it only with respect to the Article 4(h) crimes.

Providing an African variant of the ICC is further in line with the AU's ambition to address African problems through African means. The radical departure from the OAU's policy of non-interference to the AU's strategy of non-indifference has been inspired by Pan-Africanism and the conviction that African solutions should be sought for the many specific problems that the continent faces.[31] This approach underlines the identity dimension of the new security responses, referring to the AU's capacity for self-pacification and the longing for ownership in decision-making processes that concern the continent.[32] African ownership means that the AU has its own operational structure to determine the desired course of action in addressing the continent's peace and security challenges, or what Ali Mazrui called a 'Pax Africana' which is 'protected and maintained by Africa herself'.[33] The underlying idea is that the way in which Africa's peace and security issues are dealt with should primarily be an African concern. This is not to say that external actors could not assist in providing peace, security and stability, but rather that ownership in the decision-making as to how and by whom action should be taken is first and foremost in the hands of Africans.[34] Expressive of this ownership is the establishment of the African Peace and Security Architecture through which the AU facilitates regional peace and security responses.[35]

By combining the responsibility to address impunity with non-indifference and African ownership, the AU has committed itself to address the continued commission of mass atrocity crimes as part of maintaining (and restoring) durable peace and security.[36] Apart from the Amendment Protocol, another example of the AU's commitment to the prosecution of international crimes in the region is the AU Model National Law on Universal Jurisdiction over International Crimes, which allows for a quicker adaptation of national laws so that domestic African courts obtain jurisdiction over the relevant crimes.[37] The AU Commission has further been active in developing the African Framework on Transitional Justice, a guide for African countries in transition, offering a range of options on how to deal with past atrocities (including both criminal and non-criminal law responses) in order to move forward and to prevent countries from relapsing into violence.[38]

What all this shows is that the African Criminal Chamber is part and parcel of the AU's 'holistic approach which integrates justice as a fundamental pillar for a durable peace and stability'.[39] The broadening of the jurisdiction of the African Court is not a standalone development, but should rather be seen in the wider context of enhancing African ownership in dealing with the various problems that plague the African continent. This not only includes the establishment of the African Peace and Security Architecture, improving the opportunities to prosecute perpetrators of international crimes in Africa on African soil (AU Model National Law on Universal Jurisdiction over International Crimes) or outlining the multiple responses African states may adopt to deal with past atrocities (African Framework on Transitional Justice), but also means creating the possibility to address crimes that are of particular relevance to Africa and establishing criminal accountability for corporations. By expanding the jurisdiction of the Court to include crimes such as the unconstitutional change of government or the illicit extraction of natural resources, and by extending criminal accountability to include corporate liability, the Court is tasked to do justice to the atrocious realities that many African states are faced with today. Seen from this perspective, the Amendment Protocol offers a reflection of what international criminal justice should entail according to African state leaders and consulted experts. All in all, its establishment is not unrelated to the ongoing tension between the AU and the ICC, but it is overly simplistic to portray the Criminal Chamber of the African Court as an anti-ICC court.

III TOWARDS A CLASH OF COURTS?

Apart from questioning the intentions behind the proposed criminal jurisdiction of the African Court, opponents of the Amendment Protocol have argued that once it enters into force, the new African Court will inevitably clash with the ICC. Several scholars, but especially civil society organizations, have claimed that the Amendment Protocol is incompatible with the Rome Statute and that the overlap of jurisdiction will likely become a source of tension between the Criminal Chamber of the African Court and the ICC.[40] In particular, concerns have been expressed over the fact that the Amendment Protocol does not make any reference to the ICC,[41] and that the Protocol includes a provision granting immunity to sitting heads of state.[42]

A *Legality of the Amendment Protocol*

The most provocative legal claim that has been voiced against the Amendment Protocol is that the Rome Statute, and especially the complementarity principle on which the ICC is built, does not allow for the prosecution of international crimes on a regional level. Chacha Murungu has asked, for example, whether the envisioned Criminal Chamber of the Court has a 'legal basis' under the Rome Statute.[43] According to him, the Statute does 'not expressly allow or even imply that regional courts … [can] be conferred with jurisdiction to try international crimes that are under the jurisdiction of the ICC'.[44] The Rome Statute would only envisage national criminal jurisdiction under the complementarity principle. While hinting that regional criminal prosecution might be permitted under the 'ICC system' on the basis of a 'progressive interpretation' of that same complementarity principle, Murungu concludes that the process of establishing an African Criminal Court 'is contrary to the provisions of the ICC Statute requiring African states, including the AU as an international governmental organization, to cooperate fully with the ICC'.[45]

In response to these and other arguments that seek to question the legality of the Amendment Protocol, several commentators have noted that the Rome Statute is not binding on the AU, because the AU is not a party to the Rome Statute.[46] Moreover, there is no reason under general international law why a court created by a multilateral treaty (the African Court on the basis of the AU Constitutive Act) requires the approval of another multilateral treaty (the Rome Statute) to justify its own existence.[47] Neither the Rome Statute nor any other treaty has an 'exclusionary character in terms of having totally occupied the field for purposes of treaty-making'.[48] Assuming that the AU has the legal authority under its Constitutive Act to establish a criminal court and given that this step does not violate peremptory norms of international law,[49] there is no reason to challenge the legality of the Amendment Protocol.[50]

B Complementarity of the Two Courts

Another issue that has attracted considerable debate is how the two courts will co-exist within the same legal space that they both seek to occupy, that is, the investigation and prosecution of the four international crimes over which both the ICC and the African Court will have jurisdiction. Since the Rome Statute is silent on regional criminal prosecution and given that thirty-four of the fifty-four AU Member States were a party to the ICC at the time that the Amendment Protocol was adopted, one might have expected the drafters of the Protocol to address the African Court's relationship with the ICC. The drafters of the Amendment Protocol decided, however, not to include any reference to the Rome Statute. Article 46H of the Protocol states that the jurisdiction of the Criminal Chamber of the African Court will be complementary to the jurisdiction of national courts and to the courts of the different regional economic communities in Africa.[51] Yet the Protocol does not address the situation in which the African Court is asked to investigate a case that covers the same events and/or persons that are being or have been considered in an investigation or prosecution of the ICC.

As a result, it remains uncertain what will precisely happen if the ICC and the African Court seek to exercise jurisdiction over the same events at the same time, or when they decide to indict the same persons. This could, in theory, form the ground for jurisdictional battles between the two courts and create competing obligations for African states that are a party to both the ICC and the African Court.[52] However, we should not conclude from this possible 'doom scenario' that a clash between the two courts is unavoidable. On the contrary, there are several ways in which the two courts and their Member States can establish a fruitful relationship and develop a division of labour that helps to advance rather than obstruct international criminal justice.

A first option is to amend either the Rome Statute or the Amendment Protocol in such a manner that the ICC becomes complementary to the African Court, or the other way around, that the African Court becomes complementary to the ICC.[53] Creating a legal hierarchy between the two courts is something, however, that both the AU and the ICC may want to avoid, at least to the extent that this would give primacy to their counterpart.

Indeed, a proposal to amend the Preamble of the Rome Statute so that the ICC would not only be complementary to national but also to regional criminal jurisdictions has not received much support in the ICC's Assembly of States Parties.[54] Moreover, the fact that the Amendment Protocol includes a complementarity provision, without referring to the ICC, indicates that the AU does not want to establish a formal relationship between the two courts in the Amendment Protocol itself. In this light, the solution of amending the Rome Statute and/or the Amendment Protocol may be difficult to realize. Yet there are also other avenues to establish a formal relationship between the courts, including the auxiliary documents of the Criminal Chamber, which will have to regulate its procedural functioning, and the possibility of a memorandum of understanding or relationship agreement between the African Court and the ICC.

Other promising options to prevent jurisdictional clashes lie with the Prosecutor of the ICC and the future Prosecutor of the African Court. Both have a certain discretion within their legal mandate not to proceed with an investigation or prosecution. In the case of the ICC, this discretion is explicated in Article 53 of the Rome Statute, and especially in the Prosecutor's broad power to decide that the initiation or continuation of an investigation or prosecution is not in the 'interests of justice'. For the Prosecutor of the African Court, this discretion is more narrowly described in the Amendment Protocol and will mainly be inherent or implicit. Unlike the Rome Statute, the Amendment Protocol does not contain a provision like Article 53, which specifies how the Prosecutor should exercise its discretion. In listing the powers of the Prosecutor, Article 46(G) of the Amendment Protocol only mentions the different procedural and evidentiary steps that are to be taken when the Prosecutor initiates an investigation *proprio motu* or when a situation is referred to the Prosecutor by a State Party, the AU Assembly or the AU's Peace and Security Council. The fact that the Amendment Protocol does not explicate the discretion of the Prosecutor of the African Court does not mean, however, that its Office will not have a certain leeway in deciding which situations it will prioritize and especially in choosing which cases to prosecute. In exercising this discretion, the Prosecutor of the African Court could consult with the Prosecutor of the ICC, and *vice versa*, in order to ensure that their limited resources are not spent on the exact same cases.[55]

Generally speaking, if the Criminal Chamber of the African Court does what the Amendment Protocol promises to do with respect to fair trial standards and norms of due process, there is no reason why the Prosecutor of the ICC should invest time and energy in copying an investigation or prosecution of the African Court, even if the complementary principle of the ICC only covers national proceedings. When the African Court has already decided to investigate or prosecute crimes that are also covered by a preliminary examination or investigation of the ICC, the Prosecutor of the ICC should not proceed with a prosecution against the same persons on the basis that this is not in the interests of justice (Article 53) or possibly because these cases are inadmissible as the concerned persons have already been tried for the same conduct by another court (*ne bis in idem*, Article 20). The same logic should also withhold the Prosecutor of the African Court to address cases that fall within its jurisdiction, but have already been completed by the ICC.[56] If asked to reconsider a case that has been tried by the ICC, the Prosecutor of the African Court should conclude that there is no 'reasonable basis for an investigation' (Article 46G(4)) or reject the request when it amounts to a violation of the *ne bis in idem* principle (Article 46I).[57] At the same time, however, when the African Court has jurisdiction, its Prosecutor is free to initiate another case concerning a situation that is also investigated by the ICC.

To be sure, the two courts can be *pushed* to clash. If their respective Prosecutors refuse to cooperate or if the ICC will ignore the existence of its regional counterpart, then jurisdictional battles may arise, which can result in complex legal scenarios with competing obligations for states and create legal uncertainty for concerned individuals. Yet it should be stressed that the fact that the Amendment Protocol does not refer to the ICC, and that the Rome Statute is silent on regional criminal prosecution does not make a clash unavoidable, as some NGOs and scholars have argued. On the contrary, there is nothing inherent in the legal mandate of the two courts that precludes them from assisting one another. The absence of a formal relationship and a vertical hierarchy does not mean that the two courts cannot work together in fighting impunity in Africa.

C Immunity for African Leaders

One area in which the ICC and the African Court will probably not cooperate is the prosecution of sitting African heads of state. In contrast to Article 27 of the Rome Statute, which declares official capacity and existing immunities irrelevant before the ICC, Article 46A*bis* of the Amendment Protocol gives a vaguely defined group of African leaders, including sitting heads of states and their deputies, personal immunity from prosecution by the African Court.[58] This provision, which was added to the Amendment Protocol at the very last moment, has widely been criticized, in particular by NGOs, as a 'backward step in the fight against impunity' that carves out a 'sphere of impunity for high-level perpetrators'.[59]

The fact that Article 46A*bis* is almost an exact copy of one of the AU's earlier declarations on the ICC shows that the inclusion of this amendment should be understood, first and foremost, as a form of protest towards the prosecution of African presidents by the ICC.[60] This protest has focused on the repercussions that these prosecutions would have on the stability and sovereignty of African states and on the demanding responsibilities that their highest official representatives have to fulfil. In the context of its ongoing campaign against the prosecution of African presidents, and especially in response to the case against the Sudanese president Omar al-Bashir, the AU has argued that 'immunities provided for by international law apply not only to proceedings in foreign domestic courts but also to international tribunals'.[61] While states may be able to waive their own immunities in relation to an international tribunal, states cannot circumvent their obligations towards the immunities of other states by establishing an international tribunal. Article 46A*bis* was included in the Statute to articulate this position and thus to protest against the prosecution of African presidents by the ICC.[62]

As explained above, the frustration over the ICC has certainly not been the only or even the main reason why the AU agreed to adopt the Amendment Protocol. In this regard, it is critical to emphasize that while Article 46A*bis* may be understood as a 'protest article' against the ICC, this provision should not be equated with the whole plan for regional criminal prosecution in Africa. What is more, there may be various normative arguments to question the wisdom of Article 46A*bis*, but this provision will not necessarily lead to a clash with the ICC.[63] The fact that the Criminal Chamber of the African Court will not be able to prosecute certain African leaders does not in any way affect the jurisdiction of the ICC. While these African leaders many have immunity from prosecution by the African Court, this will not prevent the ICC from bringing charges against them during their term(s) in office. Over all, the immunity provision in the Amendment Protocol may be a powerful symbol, but the argument that this provision would somehow show that the African Court will inevitably clash with the ICC is just as unconvincing as the other arguments that have been voiced in this direction.

IV TOWARDS AN AFRICAN VISION ON INTERNATIONAL CRIMINAL JUSTICE?

While many have portrayed the plan for an African Criminal Court as a deliberate attempt of African leaders to undermine the ICC and the principles of international criminal justice that are embedded in the Rome Statute, the discussion above shows that this image is overly simplistic. The African

Criminal Court is not an anti-ICC Court, and when the Amendment Protocol enters into force there will not necessarily be jurisdictional battles between the two courts. Rather than part of a campaign against 'Hague Justice', we believe that the proposal for regional criminal prosecution has to be understood as an immediate attempt of African leaders and consulted experts to articulate an African vision on international criminal justice. In this regard, the following three elements of the Amendment Protocol should be highlighted.

A Inclusion of Other Crimes

First of all, the jurisdiction of the future African Criminal Court contains many crimes which are not part of the Rome Statute but which are considered to be of specific relevance to Africa. Apart from the crime of genocide, crimes against humanity, war crimes and the crime of aggression, the Criminal Chamber of the African Court will have jurisdiction over the crime of unconstitutional change of government; piracy; terrorism; mercenarism; corruption; money laundering; trafficking in persons, drugs and hazardous wastes; as well as the illicit exploitation of natural resources.[64] By including these crimes, which all have an economic-, political- or resource-related nature, the Amendment Protocol foresees in the prosecution of a variety of crimes on African soil, including by nationals of non-African states, based on the adagio 'African Solutions for African Problems'.

The definitions and the reasons underlying the inclusion of each of these specific crimes have been discussed elsewhere.[65] What is important to stress here is that the decision to give the African Court jurisdiction over other crimes than the ICC can be understood as an attempt to counter the narrow agenda that the international criminal justice project was given by the drafters of the Rome Statute and earlier by the UN Security Council in determining the jurisdiction of the *ad hoc* tribunals for the former Yugoslavia and Rwanda. Throughout this process, as traced by Kamari M. Clarke, international criminal law mainly became a project against 'mass dead and widespread killing'.[66] By placing particular crimes at the legal and moral heart of the Rome Statute, the international community led the ICC to focus on explicit forms and specific consequences of mass violence, rather than on its origins and underlying structures.[67] What we see now is the formation of a new reformulation in which the AU is pointing to 'enabling crimes' that are seen as 'productive of violence', which is of the most serious concern to the African continent.[68]

Many commentators have argued that the four crimes that were finally included in the Rome Statute are those crimes 'whose recognition by general international law, including customary law, is beyond question – irrespective of their codification in international instruments'.[69] Already in 1983 there was agreement in the International Law Commission (ILC) that the Code on Serious Crimes against Mankind (the instrument that later would serve as a basis for the Rome Statute)[70] would only cover the category of the most serious international crimes, and would thus exclude crimes of a 'lower gravity'.[71] The required agreement on what fits the label of 'most serious international crimes' explains why particular crimes made it into the Rome Statute and others did not.

Yet, in considering the inclusion of other crimes in the Amendment Protocol, it should be recalled that throughout the drafting process of the Rome Statute the ILC also debated many of these crimes. In fact, after the drafting process of the Code on Serious Crimes Against Mankind had come to a hold, it was resumed again in 1989 after a call from Trinidad and Tobago to establish an international penal court that could address drug trafficking in the region. While the crime of illicit trafficking of narcotic drugs did not make it into the Rome Statute, the initiative of Trinidad and Tobago showed that specific crimes may be particularly pressing in one region and not necessarily in another. This provides a (political) justification for the establishment of regional criminal courts that could prosecute crimes that are particularly persistent in certain regions.[72]

Following the initiative of Trinidad and Tobago, the ILC listed twelve crimes in 1991 in its Draft Code, including colonial domination and other forms of alien domination; apartheid; systematic or mass violations of human rights; the recruitment, use, financing and training of mercenaries; international terrorism; illicit traffic in narcotic drugs; as well as wilful and severe damage to the environment. Many of these crimes, which were excluded from the Rome Statute with the intended purpose to gain universal acceptance for the ICC, have now been included in the Amendment Protocol of the African Court. As such, the Protocol may be understood as an attempt to bring the international criminal justice project back to its drawing table of 1991.

More specifically, by including crimes with a particular political-, economic- or resource-related nature, the AU has put into the question the current focus of 'Hague Justice' on the consequences of conflicts, rather than its origins and root causes. Due to the ICC's limited judicial mandate, it can only address the symptoms and not the 'deeper structural problems that drive armed conflicts, such as the role of natural resource extraction and land disputes'.[73] The message that the Amendment Protocol seems to convey is that there is a need to establish accountability for the current state of Africa that moves beyond African warlords and African presidents. It seeks a procurement of justice that includes those who are responsible for creating

the conditions of conflict, and those who profit from the continuing instability of many African states.

B Corporate Liability

Apart from including other crimes in the jurisdiction of the African Court, the
Amendment Protocol distinguishes itself from the Rome Statute by its different view on who should be held accountable under international criminal
law. In contrast to the ICC's conception of criminal liability, the Amendment
Protocol moves beyond individual criminal responsibility to include corporate
liability.[74] This inclusion is of particular relevance for Africa, where many
multinational corporations have been allegedly complicit in the commission
of crimes that will fall within the jurisdiction of the Criminal Chamber of the
African Court.[75]

According to the International Commission of Jurists, the involvement of
multinational businesses in international (and other) crimes has increased
significantly over the last sixty years.[76] Many of the activities that the
Commission considered concern multinational corporations in Africa.
The wealth of natural resources throughout the continent has resulted in an
enormous extractive industry. More often than not, these corporations work in
conflict-torn areas, where the presence of natural resources like oil, gold or
diamonds has led to struggles over their control.[77]

In recent years, the involvement of corporations in human rights violations
has gained prominence on the international agenda, especially with the
appointment of the UN Special Representative on Business and Human
Rights. The responsibilities and obligations of corporations for the protection
of human rights have also been given significant impetus with the adoption of
the UN Guiding Principles on Business and Human Rights by the Human
Rights Council in 2011.[78] These thirty-one Guiding Principles are intended to
implement the so-called Protect, Respect and Remedy Framework (PRR
Framework) that was adopted by the Human Rights Council in 2008.[79]
Establishing accountability mechanisms for powerful economic actors has,
however, remained challenging. The idea of holding corporations criminally
responsible has been widely debated and domestic legal systems increasingly
allow for the prosecutions of companies as legal entities.[80] Yet there is no
international court or tribunal that can try corporations under international
law.[81] In this sense, the African Criminal Court would truly be revolutionary.

During the negotiations on the Rome Statute, a proposal tabled by France
to include corporate liability within the legal framework of the ICC was
rejected.[82] The reasoning back then was essentially threefold. First, including

corporate liability would draw attention away from individual criminal responsibility, which was seen as the main priority in setting up the ICC. Second, the Court would be confronted with various evidentiary and other procedural challenges when it would have to deal with corporate liability. Most importantly, given that corporations are considered fictive entities, without consciousness, it would be (nearly) impossible to prove criminal intent or knowledge, or to impose the conventional punishment under international criminal law (i.e. imprisonment).[83] Finally, there were still many states present during the negotiations that did not recognize corporate liability in their own domestic systems. This affected the support for the proposal and raised questions about the complementarity principle with respect to these cases.[84]

Of course, the fact that the ICC can only establish individual criminal liability does not prevent the Court from investigating businesses that are allegedly involved in the commission of international crimes. In 2013, Fatou Bensouda confirmed her commitment to look into business activities by stating that it has always been 'the OTP's strategy to investigate the link between international crimes and business'.[85] However, despite the Court's ability to hold corporate personnel responsible for their role in the commission of genocide, crimes against humanity and war crimes, corporate entities remain shielded from international criminal prosecution.

Supporters of corporate liability under international criminal law will quickly admit that the criminal prosecution of multilateral corporations, especially for the long list of crimes that are included in the Amendment Protocol, is a daunting task. There are many procedural and evidentiary challenges, particularly in relation to complex corporate structures. Yet these challenges are not that different from the difficulties the ICC has faced in establishing individual culpability of high-ranking officials, which often also involve intricate organization structures. Furthermore, the argument that the inexistence of corporate liability at the national level of many of the States Parties to the Rome Statute will be problematic in relation to the ICC's complementarity principle is losing relevance as its Member States are increasingly including corporate liability in their domestic legal systems.[86] Finally, while the conventional punishment by imprisonment will not be possible, corporations can still be sanctioned harshly. This might logically include monetary sanctions that have the advantage of providing significant funds to remedy victims, a possibility that is less likely with the prosecution of corporate personnel.[87]

In this light, supporters of corporate liability see its inclusion in the Amendment Protocol as a revolutionary step in the fight against impunity.

What is particularly significant is the fact that the African Court will have jurisdiction to try corporations for other misconduct than the 'classical' international crimes that are part of the jurisdiction of the ICC. Other crimes, such as illicit exploitation of natural resources, trafficking in hazardous waste and to a lesser extent money laundering and corruption, often involve corporations. Limiting the fight against impunity to individual criminal liability will then only offer partial justice. As John Ongeso argues, 'for true international criminal justice [both natural and legal] entities causing harm by taking advantage of the lack of regulatory mechanisms and weak rule of law in Africa must be held responsible'.[88]

To be sure, many challenges that exist in relation to prosecuting legal entities are not resolved in the Amendment Protocol. As such, it remains uncertain whether the possibility of corporate liability will actually be utilized once the Criminal Chamber of the African Court comes into being. However, even if the Amendment Protocol will never enter into force, the inclusion of corporate liability still forms a powerful signal in expressing that the prosecution of corporations should be an essential component of international criminal justice and the fight against impunity in Africa.

C Defence Office

A last element that should be highlighted here is that the Amendment Protocol embraces a recent development in international criminal law by allowing for the establishment of an independent Defence Office, which will be headed by a principal defender (Article 22C(3)). This organ, which is not present in the ICC's institutional structure, will have to guarantee the equality of arms between the prosecution and the defence, and as such ensure 'the rights of suspects and accused' (Article 22C(1)).[89]

One of the most heard critiques about the current functioning of international courts and tribunals is the disadvantaged role of the defence as opposed to the prosecution (especially in terms of capacities and means), which may seriously jeopardize the rights of the accused.[90] According to the UNHR Committee, the right to a fair trial includes, at a minimum, equality of arms of the parties.[91] Yet an exact definition of equality of arms is lacking.[92] It is generally understood to refer to the right of participation for both parties and equal access to the court.[93] While this also includes the allocation of sufficient resources to ensure that the defence is not in an adversely disadvantaged position to prepare their case as opposed to the prosecution, judges of the *ad hoc* tribunals have emphasized that the equality of arms does not necessarily mean ensuring full equality in provided means and resources.[94]

Both the ICC as well as the *ad hoc* tribunals for the former Yugoslavia and Rwanda have strong institutional organs with clearly defined powers: the judiciary, the registry and the Office of the Prosecutor. An inequality of arms is allegedly created between the defence and the Prosecutor in the sense that there is no independent organ for the defence.[95] A proposal for such an organ was tabled during the negotiations on the Rome Statute by the International Criminal Defence Attorneys Association, but it was dismissed without consideration of its merits.[96] As a result, the position of the defence at the ICC is often seen as subordinate to the Prosecutor, the judiciary and the registry.

As explained by Charles Jalloh and Amy Dibella, experiences at the *ad hoc* and hybrid tribunals, as well as at the ICC, have led many practitioners and academics to conclude that 'the protection of equality of arms can be achieved only through offering the defence institutional or structural independence within the Court'.[97] This position is not only taken by scholars, but was also expressed by the UN secretary-general in the wake of the establishment of the Special Tribunal for Lebanon,[98] which eventually became the first international tribunal to put an independent Defence Office in place.[99]

For these reasons, the inclusion of the independent office of the defence in the Amendment Protocol has been applauded, even by those who are critical about the plan for an African Criminal Court.[100] It shows the AU's commitment to international criminal justice and to ensure fair trials by, *inter alia*, providing equality of arms between the Prosecutor and the defence. As such, the Amendment Protocol does not only include novel perspectives, but also affirms recent developments that form part of progressive foresight in international criminal law. In following the example of the Special Tribunal for Lebanon, the African Criminal Court may actually spur proposals to amend the Rome Statute in the near future.

Ultimately, we believe that this and the other discussed components of the Amendment Protocol show that the plan for an African Criminal Court offers an African vision of international criminal justice. Even without the Protocol ever entering into force and without the African Court being established, it can be influential as a 'protest treaty'.[101] More than anything else, the Protocol has expressive value as it articulates what African state leaders and consulted experts believe that the international criminal justice project should entail.

V CONCLUSION

This chapter has sought to counter the simplistic – but powerful – ways in which the early efforts to expand the criminal jurisdiction of the African Court have been depicted as a deliberate attempt of African leaders to weaken the

ICC and to undermine international criminal justice. Within some academic
circles, but in particular among certain civil society organizations, the idea has
settled that the Amendment Protocol is hostile towards 'Hague Justice' and
that, when it would enter into force, the Criminal Chamber of the African
Court will come to clash with the ICC. As we have shown, however, many of
the concerns that have been voiced in this context are exaggerated.

While the ongoing tension between the AU and the ICC has accelerated its
establishment, the discussions among African leaders on an African Criminal
Court precede this tension. The adoption of the Amendment Protocol should
not be seen as a standalone development. Rather, it should be understood as
part of the AU's broader agenda to address African problems through African
means. Moreover, even though the Protocol does not establish a formal
relationship with the ICC and the Rome Statute remains silent on its complementarity with regional judicial institutions, the two courts can come to co-
exist in a peaceful and cooperative fashion. In particular, the Prosecutors of
the ICC and the African Court can work together in order to avoid a clash that
could be detrimental to the perceived legitimacy of both institutions.

Time will tell how enthusiastic African leaders really are about regional
criminal prosecution. For now, it remains to be seen whether at least fifteen
AU Member States will ratify the Amendment Protocol and, if the Protocol
does indeed enter into force, whether these states will give the financial,
institutional and political support that the Criminal Chamber of the African
Court requires. In this regard, it may be noted that the Amendment Protocol
does not organize the financing of the Criminal Chamber and does not
provide specific regulations like the Rome Statute on what happens if a state
fails to cooperate with its proceedings.[102] Looking back at previous initiatives
of the AU as well, this justifies questions about the expediency of the AU's plan
to endow the African Court with criminal jurisdiction

However, even if the Amendment Protocol never enters into force or would
not receive the necessary support, its adoption should not be understood as
a useless by-product of anti-ICC rhetoric. Indeed, parts of the Protocol, such as
the immunity that is given to sitting heads of state, protest *against* the ICC, and
in particular against the prosecution of African presidents. Yet the early
formation of an African Criminal Court is also a protest *for* international
criminal justice, as it articulates a regional vision on its future. This vision,
as formed by involved officials and consulted experts, is shaped by African
perceptions of justice. What it shows is an aspiration to establish 'African
geographies of justice',[103] a plea to promote particular developments in international criminal law (like the establishment of an independent Defence
Office) and a desire to bring certain issues back on the agenda of international

criminal justice, including crimes that address the structural causes of mass violence and the criminal responsibility of corporations that are involved in the commission of these crimes. These and other essential components of the AU's initiative for an African Criminal Court give the project expressive value and underscore that the Amendment Protocol may ultimately strengthen rather than weaken the pursuit of international criminal justice.

Notes

The authors would like to thank Kamari M. Clarke and Drazan Djukic for commenting on an earlier draft of this chapter.

1. At this moment, the African Court on Human and Peoples' Rights only considers alleged human rights violations. In the AU Constitutive Act, the establishment of another court, the AU Court of Justice, has been provided for. For efficiency purposes, a merger protocol was adopted to expand the jurisdiction of the existing court with a General Affairs Chamber. The name of the court was supposed to change to the African Court of Justice and Human Rights. While the merger protocol has entered into force, the expansion has not yet taken place. The discussions on adding a Criminal Chamber has led to the adoption of another protocol, that is, the Protocol on Amendments to the Protocol on the Statute of the African Court of Justice and Human Rights (Amendment Protocol). After adoption of the Amendment Protocol, the Court will be named African Court of Justice and Human and Peoples' Rights (Article 1 of the Amendment Protocol). See 'Protocol on Amendments to the Protocol on the Statute of the African Court of Justice and Human Rights', Addis Ababa, 27 June 2014.

2. We speak here in a general sense of 'international and other crimes' as it falls outside the scope of this chapter to discuss the status of the different crimes that are included in the Amendment Protocol or to engage with the debate on what the concept of an international crime precisely entails. An artificial distinction may be drawn between a narrow and broader understanding of international crimes. In a narrow sense, international crimes refer to those offences over which international courts or tribunals have been given jurisdiction under general international law, whereas a broader understanding defines international crimes as all offences that have been created through international law. For further discussion on these issues in relation to the Amendment Protocol, see: Ademola Abass, 'The Proposed International Criminal Jurisdiction for the African Court: Some Problematical Aspects' (2013) 60(1) *Netherlands International Law Review* 32–37. More generally, Robert Cryer,

Hakan Friman, Darryl Robinson and Elizabeth Wilmshurst, *An Introduction to International Criminal Law and Procedure* (New York: Cambridge University Press, 2010), p. 5.

3. Apart from genocide, crimes against humanity, war crimes and the crime of aggression, the African Court will have jurisdiction over the crime of unconstitutional change of government, piracy, terrorism, mercenarism, corruption, money laundering, trafficking in persons, drugs and hazardous wastes as well as the illicit exploitation of natural resources. This list of crimes is non-exhaustive. According to Article 28A(2) of the Amendment Protocol, the AU Assembly may decide to include additional crimes to the jurisdiction of the Court.

4. John C. Mubangizi, 'Towards a New Approach to the Classification of Human Rights with Specific Reference to the African Context' (2004) 1 *African Human Rights Law Journal* 93–107, specifically 101, 102; Tiyanjana Maluwa, 'Reimagining African Unity: Some Preliminary Reflections on the Constitutive Act of the African Union' (2001) *African Yearbook of International Law* 3, at 27 and 28.

5. For example, while the African Court on Human and Peoples' Rights was established to supplement the work of the African Commission on Human and Peoples' Rights, the Court only rendered one judgement during its first decade of existence. See George M. Wachira, 'African Court on Human and Peoples' Rights: Ten Years on and Still No Justice' (Minority Rights Group International, 2009), pp. 12–17.

6. The practical feasibility is addressed by Max Du Plessis in 'Implications of the AU Decision to Give the African Court Jurisdiction over International Crimes' (ISS Paper 235, June 2012). The detrimental effect of the establishment of the Criminal Chamber for the existing regional human rights system has been discussed by, *inter alia*, Lutz Oette, 'The African Union High-Level Panel on Darfur. A Precedent for Regional Solutions to the Challenges Facing International Criminal Justice?', in Vincent O. Nmehielle (ed.), *Africa and the Future of International Criminal Justice* (The Hague: Eleven International Publishing, 2012), p. 370; Vincent O. Nmehielle, '"Saddling" the New African Regional Human Rights Court with International Criminal Jurisdiction: Innovative, Obstructive, Expedient?' (2014) 7(1) *African Journal of Legal Studies* 35–41.

7. See, for example, the joint opinion by nine civil society organizations ('Implications of the African Court of Human and Peoples Rights being empowered to try International Crimes such as Genocide, Crimes against Humanity, and War Crimes' (2009) submitted to the 13th Ordinary Session of the African Union Summit (Sirte, Libya, 24 June to 3 July 2009)) and the joint letter signed by forty-nine African civil society organizations and international human rights organizations

stationed in Africa ('Joint Letter to the Justice Ministers and Attorneys General of the African States Parties to the International Criminal Court Regarding the Proposed Expansion of the Jurisdiction of the African court of Justice and Human Rights' (3 May 2012)).

8. For references, see parts 2 and 3 of this chapter.
9. See Stephen Lamony, 'African Court Not Ready for International Crimes', *African Arguments*, 10 December 2010. On the AU's powerful campaign against the prosecution of African presidents, see Chapter 8 by Abel S. Knottnerus in this volume.
10. As discussed in Pacifique Manirakiza, 'The Case for an African Criminal Court to Prosecute International Crimes Committed in Africa', in Nmehielle, *Africa and the Future of the ICC*, p. 370.
11. See generally Dire Tladi, 'The Immunity Provision in the AU Amendment Protocol: Separating the (Doctrinal) Wheat from the (Normative) Chaff' (2015) 13(1) *Journal of International Criminal Justice* 1. NGOs have especially criticized the inclusion of the immunity provision. For further references, see part 3 of this chapter.
12. In this regard, it is often overlooked that there remains much uncertainty as to what these principles are or should be. See generally, Darryl Robinson, 'The Identity Crisis of International Criminal Law' (2008) 21 *Leiden Journal of International Law* 925–963.
13. While misleading, the concerns that opponents of this plan have voiced are powerful in the sense that they can shape perceptions of the Criminal Chamber of the African Court, and may lead relevant stakeholders to believe that they should not support its establishment. On the relation between power and perceived legitimacy, see Chris Reus-Smit, 'International Crises of Legitimacy' (2007) 44 *International Politics* 160–165. More generally, on different conceptions of power: Michael Barnett and Raymond Duvall, 'Power in International Politics' (2005) 59 *International Organization* 39–75.
14. Chacha Murungu, 'Towards a Criminal Chamber in the African Court of Justice and Human Rights' (2011) 9(5) *Journal of International Criminal Justice* 1067, 1086.
15. Gino J. Naldi and Konstantinos D. Magliveras, 'The African Court of Justice and Human Rights: A Judicial Curate's Egg' (2012) 9(2) *International Organizations Law Review* 383, 440.
16. Bahame T. Nyanduga, 'Reflections and Perspectives of the African Commission on Human and People's Rights' (Speech during the Consultative Conference on International Criminal Justice, 2009), as quoted in: Manirakiza, 'The Case for an African Criminal Court', 401.
17. Ademola Abass, 'Prosecuting International Crimes in Africa: Rationale, Prospects and Challenges' (2013) 24(3) *European Journal of International Law* 933, at 936–937.

18. *Ibid.*
19. Currently Apartheid (under the required conditions) is considered a crime against humanity under Article 7(j) and (h) of the Rome Statute.
20. Abass, 'Prosecuting International Crimes in Africa', 937.
21. Manirakiza, 'The Case for an African Criminal Court', 377–385.
22. Committee of Eminent African Jurists, 'Report of the Committee of Eminent African Jurists on the Case of Hissène Habré' (2006), paras. 35–39.
23. *Ibid.*, para. 35.
24. AU Assembly, 'Decision on the Implementation of the Assembly Decision on the Abuse of the Principle of Universal Jurisdiction', Assembly/AU/Dec.213 (XII), February 2009.
25. *Ibid.*
26. These responsibilities follow from Articles 4(h) and 4(o) of the AU's Constitutive Act as well as Article 25(5) of the African Charter on Democracy Elections and Governance (ACDEG).
27. At the request of Libya, a session was convened to 'discuss ways and means of making the OAU effective so as to keep pace with the political and economic developments taking place in the world'. During this session, the OAU leaders decided to establish the African Union. OAU Assembly, Sirte Declaration, EAHG/Draft.Decl. (IV) Rev. 1, 9 September 1999. See generally, Tiyanjana Maluwa, 'The Constitutive Act of the African Union and Institution-Building in Postcolonial Africa' (2003) 16 *Leiden Journal of International Law* 157–170.
28. Ben Kioko, 'The Right of Intervention under the AU Constitutive Act: From Non-Interference to Non-Intervention' (2003) 852 *International Review of the Red Cross* 807, 820; Paul D. Williams, 'From Non-Intervention to Non-Indifference: The Origins and Development of the African Union's Security Culture' (2007) 106(423) *African Affairs* 235–279.
29. Abass, 'Prosecuting International Crimes in Africa', 939.
30. Whereas the AU Assembly may refer a situation in any State Party to the Protocol to the Criminal Court under Article 46F(2) of the Amendment Protocol, Article 4(h) of the AU Constitutive Act would (similar to Chapter VII of the UN Charter and Article 13(b) of the Rome Statute) allow for referral of situations of non-States Parties to the African Criminal Court, be it only for the crimes specified under that provision.
31. Tim Murithi explains it as Africans themselves seeking solutions for African problems: Tim Murithi, *The African Union: Pan-Africanism, Peacebuilding and Development* (London: Ashgate, 2005) 73.
32. Samuel M. Makinda and Wafula Okumu *The African Union: Challenges of Globalization, Security, and Governance* (New York: Routledge, 2008), pp. 78, 83.

33. Ali Mazrui, *Towards a Pax Africana* (Chicago: University of Chicago Press, 1967) p. 203.
34. A critical analysis of the concept is given by Benedikt Franke and Romain Esmenjaud, 'Who Owns African Ownership? The Africanisation of Security and Its Limits' (2008) 15(2) *South African Journal of International Affairs* 137.
35. *Ibid.*, p. 148. The extent of the ownership has been questioned as the architecture is largely funded by international partners. See Cedric De Coning, 'Peacekeeping in Africa: the Next Decade' (2002) 3 *Conflict Trends* 45, at 53–54.
36. Nmehielle, *Africa and the Future of International Criminal Justice*, p. 5.
37. AU Executive Council, African Union Model National Law on Universal Jurisdiction over International Crimes, EX.CL/731(XXI)c, 9–13 July 2012.
38. After the Panel of the Wise recommended the drafting of the Framework, several consultations have been held with AU Member States and experts to work out the African-Policy Framework on Transitional Justice. The latest validation workshop took place in August 2014. Now it has to be endorsed by the AU Assembly during a Summit. See: AU Panel of the Wise, 'Peace, Justice, and Reconciliation in Africa: Opportunities and Challenges in the Fight against Impunity' (African Union Series, February 2009); AU Commission, 'Concept Note: Validation Workshop on the Draft African Transitional Justice Policy Framework (ATJPF)' (South Africa, 18–19 August 2014).
39. Manirakiza, 'The Case for an African Criminal Court', 387.
40. Murungu argues, for example, that 'the proposed Criminal Chamber will inevitably compete with the ICC in terms of jurisdiction over persons and crimes thereby working against and undermining the ICC in its already well-known competence over international crimes'. Murungu, 'Towards a Criminal Chamber', 1088. See also Joint opinion by nine civil society organizations and Joint letter signed by forty-nine African civil society organizations and international human rights organizations working in Africa; Kristin Rau, 'Jurisprudential Innovation or Accountability Avoidance? The International Criminal Court and Proposed Expansion of the African Court of Justice and Human Rights, (2012) 97 *Minnesota Law Review* 669–708, 695 ('given the lack of clarity regarding potential jurisdictional overlap ... conflict could easily erupt over which court ... would have jurisdictional precedence in an investigation or case').
41. *Ibid.* See also Du Plessis, 'Implications AU decision African Court', 10–11.
42. 'Civil society opposes immunities in proposed expansion of African Court', Coalition for the ICC, 4 June 2014; 'AU Summit Decision

a Backward Step for International Justice', *Amnesty International*, 1 July 2014; 'Statement Regarding Immunity for Sitting Officials before the Expanded African Court of Justice and Human Rights', *Human Rights Watch*, 13 November 2014. See also: Kariri, 'Can the New African Court Truly Deliver Justice'; Max Du Plessis and Nicole Fritz, 'A (New) New Regional International Criminal Court for Africa', *Ilawyer*, 1 October 2014, para. IV; Max du Plessis, 'Shambolic, Shameful and Symbolic: Implications of the African Union's Immunity for African Leaders, (ISS paper 278, November 2014).

43. Murungu, 'Towards a Criminal Chamber', 1081.

44. *Ibid.*

45. *Ibid.*, 1081 and 1087.

46. Abass, 'Prosecuting International Crimes in Africa', 941; 48. Nmehielle, '"Saddling" the African Court with International Criminal Jurisdiction', 24–29.

47. Abass, 'Prosecuting International Crimes in Africa', 941; Abass, 'The Proposed Jurisdiction for the African Court', 48–49. Indeed, as Abass has argued: 'assertions that the Rome Statute does not permit the creation of regional courts, such as the African Court, is not only a fundamentally flawed appreciation of international law, but also a fatalistic attempt to create a hierarchy in the ranks of international criminal tribunals'.

48. Nmehielle, '"Saddling" the African Court with International Criminal Jurisdiction', 24–25.

49. Abass notes in this regard that 'there are no peremptory norms in the Rome Statute, and [that] if one accepts some of the crimes under the Statute (e.g., genocide) as being subject to *jus cogens* rules, the creation of an African court to *prosecute* such crimes is confirmatory of, not conflictual with, such a peremptory norm in the Rome Statute'. Abass, 'Prosecuting International Crimes in Africa', 943.

50. This power derives specifically from Articles 4(h), 4(o) and 9(d) of the AU Constitutive Act. For a discussion, see: Manirakiza, 'The Case for an African Criminal Court', 27–28.

51. Note that Article 46H is similar to Article 17 of the Rome Statute, except for the fact that it sets a lower evidentiary standard to establish whether a state is unwilling or unable to carry out the investigation or prosecution. Another possible problem with Article 46H is that some states are members to multiple regional communities. See Abass, 'Prosecuting International Crimes in Africa', 944–945.

52. Such a battle may not only concern the arrest and surrender of concerned individuals, but also the cooperation and judicial assistance with the investigation and other aspects of the prosecution. For example, the two courts may both seek the cooperation of a state with taking testimonies or the production of evidence.

53. See the address of Charles Jalloh to the ASP in 2013: Charles Jalloh, 'Reflections on the Indictment of Sitting Heads of State and Government and Its Consequences for Peace and Stability and Reconciliation in Africa' (2014) 7 *African Journal of Legal Studies* 55–56.

54. As proposed by Kenya, the Preamble of the Rome Statute would have to state that the 'the International Criminal Court established under this Statute shall be complementary to national and regional criminal jurisdictions'. UN Treaties Collection (C.N.1026.2013.TREATIES-XVIII.10), *Kenya: Proposal of Amendments*, 14 March 2014; ASP, 'Report of the Working Group on Amendments', 7 December 2014, ICC-ASP/13/31.

55. A division of labour could be established on a case rather than a situation level, for example, by allowing the ICC to prosecute senior commanders and other high-level perpetrators (including those persons who will enjoy immunity before the African Court), while the Prosecutor of the African Court could focus on lower-level perpetrators in the same situation. This would result, however, in a somewhat hierarchical relationship between the two courts. For this reason, the two prosecutors could also take an *ad hoc* approach in dividing cases as well as situations.

56. Note that the African Court will not have jurisdiction over situations that are currently under investigation by the ICC (such as the post-election violence in Kenya or the situation in Darfur), because the Court will only have 'temporary jurisdiction' after the Amendment Protocol enters into force (Article 6*bis* of the Amendment Protocol).

57. The text of Article 46I does not exclude the ICC from its scope. In fact, it largely copies the text of Article 20 of the Rome Statute, with the notable difference that it refers 'to exceptional circumstances' where this principle would somehow not apply.

58. For further discussion on Article 46A*bis*, see: Tladi, 'The Immunity Provision in the AU Amendment Protocol', 5–8; Du Plessis and Fritz, 'A (New) New Regional ICC for Africa'.

59. 'AU Summit Decision a Backward Step for International Justice', *Amnesty International*, 1 July 2014.

60. Article 46A*bis* provides that: 'no charges shall be commenced or continued before the Court against any serving African Union Head of State or Government, or anybody acting or entitled to act in such capacity, or other senior state officials based on their functions, during their tenure of office'. Its wording seems to be based on the resolution of the AU Assembly of October 2013 in which it decided, in relation to the prosecution of Kenyatta and Ruto, that 'no charges shall be commenced or continued before any International Court or Tribunal against any serving AU Head of State or Government or anybody acting or entitled to act in such capacity during their term of office'.

61. AU Commission, Press Release on the Decisions of Pre-Trial Chamber I of the International Criminal Court (ICC) Pursuant to Article 87(7) of the Rome Statute on the Alleged Failure by the Republic of Chad and the Republic of Malawi to Comply with the Cooperation Requests issued by the Court with Respect to the Arrest and Surrender of President Omar Hassan al-Bashir of the Republic of the Sudan, No. 002/2012, 9 January 2012.

62. Note that Article 46A*bis* only concerns the leaders of AU Member States. This means, quite ironically, that the heads of state of non-AU Member States can be prosecuted before the Court for crimes that fall within its jurisdiction. More generally, on the question of al-Bashir's immunity, see Chapter 8 by Abel S. Knottnerus in this volume.

63. To the extent that Article 46A*bis* limits the possible avenues to prosecute sitting heads of state, this limitation only covers states that are not a party to the Rome Statute and the crimes that do not fall within the jurisdiction of the ICC. In this sense, Article 46A*bis* also does not create a new sphere of impunity, but simply forms a substantive limitation to the scope of a new avenue to prosecute international and other crimes.

64. Article 28A(1) of the Amendment Protocol.

65. See, for instance, Abass, 'Prosecuting International Crimes in Africa', 39–41; Rau, 'Jurisprudential Innovation or Accountability Avoidance', 682–702; Nmehielle, '"Saddling" the African Court with International Criminal Jurisdiction', 29–31.

66. See Kamari M. Clarke, *Fictions of Justice: The ICC and the Challenge of Legal Pluralism in Sub-Saharan Africa* (Cambridge: Cambridge University Press, 2009), pp. 54–62, 59; Kamari M. Clarke, 'Rethinking Africa through Its Exclusions: The Politics of Naming Criminal Responsibility' (2010) 83 *Anthropological Quarterly* 634–640.

67. The focus on mass violence does not necessarily mean that the ICC will not be dealing with crimes that do not involve a high level of deadly victims. For example, in the situation of Mali, the recent case of Ahmad Al Faqi Al Mahdi is solely brought to The Hague on alleged war crimes involving the destruction of property (intentional directing attacks against specified buildings), without civilian casualties. *Situation in Mali* (ICC-01/12-01/15), Warrant of Arrest for Ahmad Al Faqi Mahdi, 18 September 2015.

68. Kamari M. Clarke, Forthcoming Manuscript, 2017.

69. Kai Ambos, 'Establishing an International Criminal Court and an International Criminal Code: Observations from an International Criminal Law Viewpoint' (1996) 7 *European Journal of International Law* 519, 524.

70. While the Draft Code is at the origin of the Draft Statute of the ICC, the work of the Commission on the Draft Statute and the Draft Code from

1992 onwards was separated. Martin C. Ortega, 'The ILC Adopts the Draft Code of Crimes against the Peace and Security of Mankind' (1996) *Max Planck Yearbook of United Nations Law* 283, 290.

71. ILCYB 1983, Vol. 2 (part II), paras. 46–48 and 69 (a).

72. It must be noted that such a justification is, from a legal perspective, not required. There is no rule under international law preventing states to enter into an agreement and to establish a court with jurisdiction to deal with any type of crime they agree on.

73. See Chapter 16 by Sara Kendall and Clare da Silva.

74. Article 46C Amendment Protocol.

75. Eric Colvin and Jessie Chella, 'Multinational Corporate Complicity: A Challenge for International Criminal Justice in Africa', in Nmehielle, *Africa and the Future of ICJ*.

76. International Commission of Jurists, 'Report of the ICJ Expert Legal Panel on Corporate Complicity in International Crimes' (1 January 2008).

77. On the linkages between natural resources and armed conflicts, see generally Andrea E. Varisco, 'A Study on the Inter-Relation between Armed Conflict and Natural Resources and Its Implications for Conflict Resolution and Peacebuilding' (2010) 15 *Journal of Peace, Conflict and Development* 38–58; Philippe Le Billon, 'The Political Ecology of War: Natural Resources and Armed Conflicts' (2001) 5 *Political Geography* 561–584.

78. 'Guiding Principles on Business and Human Rights: Implementing the United Nations "Protect, Respect and Remedy Framework"', UN Doc. A.HRC/17/31, 21 March 2011.

79. *Ibid*; 'Protect, Respect and Remedy: A Framework for Business and Human Rights', UN Doc. A/HRC/8/5, 7 April 2008. Both of these documents are the outcome of the six-year mandate of the UN Special Representative of the Secretary-General on the Issue of Human Rights and Transnational Corporations and Other Business Enterprises (SRSG), Professor John Ruggie.

80. For example, Article 51 Dutch Penal Code. Well-known examples are cases concerning torture and inhuman or degrading treatment by contractors at the Abu Ghraib prison in Iraq, the case against Blackwater alleging war crimes under the Alien Tort Statute in connection with the killing of civilians, or cases against corporations providing goods to the Apartheid regime in South Africa.

81. Although at the international level there have been no cases against corporations since corporate criminal liability is not provided for, there have been several persons convicted in relation to their business position (and subsequent action). The media cases of the ICTR are well-known examples. In the *Nahimana* Case, for instance, the two directors of the

radio station RTLM were convicted for incitement to genocide. In this case the Trial Chamber considered the incitement to genocide as part of the corporate activity of the radio station. *Prosecutor v. Nahimana* (ICTR-99-52-T, Judgment and Sentence, 3 December 2003, paras. 99–101. See, generally, Ole K. Fauchald and Jo Stigent, 'Corporate Responsibility before International Institutions' (2009) 40 *The George Washington International Law Review* 1062–1100.

82. Andrew Clapham, 'The Question of Jurisdiction under International Criminal Law over Legal Persons: Lessons from the Rome Conference on an International Criminal Court', in Menno T. Kamminga and Saman Zia-Zarifi (eds.), *Liability of Multinational Corporations under International Law* (Brill Nijhoff Publishers: The Hague, 2010), pp. 139–95.

83. Celia Wells and Juanita Elias, 'Catching the Conscience of the King: Corporate Players on the International Stage', in Philip Alston (ed.), *Non-State Actors and Human Rights* (Oxford: Oxford University Press, 2005), pp. 143, 158.

84. Kai Ambos, 'Article 25', in Otto Triffterer (ed.), *Commentary on the Rome Statute of the International Criminal Court: Observers' Notes, Article by Article* (Nomos: Baden-Baden, 1999), pp. 477, 478.

85. 'ICC Prosecutor Reaffirms Commitment to Investigating the Link between Business and International Crimes', *Global Diligence*, 21 March 2013.

86. Moreover, the complementarity principle consists of being unwilling but also being unable to prosecute, which also relates to legal impediments to domestic prosecution, such as the inability to establish corporate liability at the domestic level. What should be kept in mind in this regard is that despite the inexistence of corporate liability at the domestic level, the ICC might still declare a case 'inadmissible' on the basis of the complementarity principle when the criteria of 'same person, same conduct' are met.

87. Jessie Chella, 'The Complicity of Multinational Corporations in International Crimes: An Examination of Principles', PhD thesis, Bond University (2012), p. 69.

88. John P. Ongeso, 'Corporate Prosecutions in the African Court for Human Rights Abuses', *African Legal Centre*, 13 April 2015.

89. Like most other international tribunals, the ICC does have a defence unit, which falls under the Registry. The defence unit was incorporated after the adoption of the Rome Statute through the Court's regulations.

90. Du Plessis and Fritz, 'A (New) New Regional ICC for Africa'; Max Du Plessis, 'A (New) New Regional International Criminal Court for Africa' (2014) 2 *South African Journal of Criminal Justice* 199, para. 2; Jarinde T. Tuinstra, 'Defending the Defenders: The Role of Defence Counsel in

International Criminal Trials' (2010) 8 *Journal of International Criminal Justice* 463–486; Charles C. Jalloh and Amy E. Dibella, 'Equality of Arms in International Criminal Law: Continuing Challenges', in William A. Schabas, Yvonne McDermott and Niamh Hayes, *The Ashgate Research Companion to International Criminal Law: Critical Perspectives* (London: Ashgate, 2013), p. 252.

91. Kweku Vanderpuye, 'Traditions in Conflict: The Internationalization of Confrontation' (2010) 43 *Cornell International Law Journal* 513, 539.
92. Jalloh and Dibella, 'Equality of Arms in International Criminal Law', 255.
93. *Ibid.*, p. 258.
94. Rejected by the *Kayishema and Ruzindana* (ICTR-95-1-A), Appeals Judgement, 1 June 2001, paras. 63, 64.
95. Elise Groulx, '"Equality of Arms": Challenges Confronting the Legal Profession in the Emerging International Criminal Justice System' (2006) 3 *Oxford University Comparative Law Forum*, para. 1.
96. *Ibid.*
97. *Ibid.* Jalloh and Dibella, 'Equality of Arms in International Law'.
98. 'Report of the Secretary-General on the Establishment of a Special Tribunal for Lebanon', UN Doc S/2006/893, 15 November 2006, para. 30.
99. Article 13 of the Statute of the Special Tribunal of Lebanon.
100. Du Plessis and Fritz, 'A (New) New Regional ICC for Africa'.
101. Abass has defined a protest treaty as 'a response to a real or perceived iniquity, unjustness or unfairness, espoused or believe to be espoused by a pre-existing treaty … they are treaties fueled by momentary passion rather than a thorough appreciation and genuine desire for legislation'. Abass, 'The Proposed International Criminal Jurisdiction for the African Court', 43. In this chapter, we intend to use the term in a slightly different manner as we do not believe that the definition of this concept should be limited to treaties which lack a 'genuine desire for legislation', nor will they necessarily 'wither away as soon as the currency of emotions that fuels them thaws'. In our view, the essence of a protest treaty is that it protests against a pre-existing treaty and/or the perceived iniquity within a certain field of law, in this case, international criminal law. For some actors supporting such a protest treaty is fuelled by different emotions and interests than for others. In fact, some of its supporters may have a genuine desire for legislation on the whole subject matter that the treaty covers or perhaps only parts of it, whereas others may simply seek to undermine the perceived legitimacy of the pre-existing treaty. In the case of the Amendment Protocol, it seems reasonable to assume that at least some African states genuinely believe that there should be a form of criminal prosecution for the additional

crimes that are included in the jurisdiction of the Court, and do indeed support the proposal for corporate liability and a defence office.

102. Article 46L provides that States Parties 'shall comply with undue delay with any requests for assistance or an order issued by the Court', and lists a number of issues that can be covered by such an order. Yet, there is no provision in the Amendment Protocol on what happens when a state fails to cooperate.

103. Kamari M. Clarke, Forthcoming Manuscript, 2017.

16

Beyond the ICC

State Responsibility for the Arms Trade in Africa

Sara Kendall and Clare da Silva

I INTRODUCTION

Responses to mass atrocity on the African continent have taken many forms, including criminal accountability and transitional justice mechanisms, as this volume recounts. Criminal accountability focuses on individual responsibility for grave crimes, whether at the International Criminal Court (ICC), in domestic criminal jurisdictions, or at a regional body, such as the African Court of Human and Peoples Rights with an expanded criminal jurisdiction. Within this frame, debates among scholars and practitioners focus on what would be the appropriate forum for adjudicating mass crimes. By contrast, debates within transitional justice have centred on matters of form, such as amnesties, truth commissions, and practices of reconciliation. As these approaches prioritise redress and accountability over prevention, one of the key conditions of possibility of mass atrocity crimes – the supply of weapons – has remained at the periphery of both discussions.[1]

This chapter offers an alternative way of conceptualising responses to mass violence on the African continent, the main site of ICC interventions. It shifts the frame from individual to state responsibility, bringing a broader structure into view that is left to the side of international criminal law. As debates about the relationship between the ICC and Africa have illustrated, the politics of prosecutorial discretion have also produced contestations around the appropriateness of seeking selective individual criminal responsibility. Commentators on the ICC have also expressed broader concerns that the Court is addressing symptoms rather than the deeper structural problems that drive armed conflicts, such as the role of natural resource extraction and land disputes.[2] Building on these concerns, this chapter draws attention to one of the structural conditions enabling mass crime: the widespread use of conventional arms in many African conflicts. The African Union (AU) has observed that 'the poorly regulated international legal trade in conventional arms, and particularly small arms and light weapons, can have an under-mining effect on the economic, social and political stability of African States, including fuelling conflict and armed violence'.[3] Small arms and light weapons, including machine guns, rocket launchers, and assault rifles, are commonly used in perpetrating mass crimes, particularly those that feature in ICC cases involving non-state actors such as militia groups and irregular combatants such as child soldiers.

This chapter addresses one of the material conditions through which mass crimes are enabled and sustained, focusing on what African states and regional organisations have claimed about the role of the arms trade in contributing to conflicts on the continent. As a contemporary global concern, the trade in arms is significant for multiple legal regimes, including human rights law, international humanitarian law, and international criminal law. Yet as the following section of this chapter shows, it has remained at the margins of ICC cases. Subsequent sections of the chapter recount the role of African states and regional organisations in developing a common architecture for regulat-ing the global arms trade, as well as the content of the legal obligations that the resulting Arms Trade Treaty (ATT) places upon its state signatories as the first global treaty to address the trade in conventional arms. This trade unfolds in a transnational order, implicating non-state and supra-state actors as well as states, and in an era when many have proclaimed the erosion of nation-state sovereignty in international affairs.[4] Yet as illustrated through ICC practice, state interests remain a resilient part of the global security landscape.[5]

In addition to highlighting the prospective role that regulating the arms trade could serve in reducing the commission of mass atrocity crimes, this chapter argues that the ATT offers an alternative frame of state responsibility that emphasises sovereign equality as opposed to 'exemplary justice'.[6] The predominant focus on retrospective approaches to armed conflict in international criminal law as well as in many forms of transitional justice diverts attention from alternative frameworks that foreground prevention over redress. To the extent that preventative approaches have featured within these literatures, they have largely appeared by reference to the doctrine of the 'responsibility to protect' rather than through attempts to control the trade in arms.[7] The Libyan referral to the ICC marked the first occasion where the doctrine was linked to an ICC intervention, though some commentary has observed that this approach risks attributing too much power to the United Nations Security Council for overseeing humanitarian interventions in Africa.[8] African state sovereignty has been at the centre of disputes between

ICC proponents and critics, particularly concerning the issue of Head of State immunity in the wake of the Kenyan cases as well as the case against Sudanese President al-Bashir.[9] Meanwhile, trials at the ICC have been criticised for being geopolitically selective and incapable of confronting powerful state actors.[10] It is not clear that more prosecutions are the answer, whether at the ICC or in regional or domestic courts.[11] The limits of regulating the trade in arms is revealed when states engage in practices that contradict the international obligations that they have willingly assumed, such as diverting arms to unauthorised users. However, developing greater state responsibility for regulating the arms trade offers an alternative frame to international criminal trials, focusing on the material conditions of mass atrocity rather than on selective prosecutions in its aftermath.

II THE ARMS TRADE AND THE ICC

In 2009, just as the ICC was beginning to hear its first case against Congolese militia leader Thomas Lubanga Dyilo, United Nations (UN) member states were building consensus around the development of an international treaty to regulate the global trade in arms, which was adopted in 2013 and entered into force the following year. Little scholarship has noted the link between the shared objectives of both treaty-derived systems in responding to mass atrocity.[12] The objects and purposes of both treaties share common concerns, as their preambles demonstrate. The ICC Rome Statute recognises that the crimes the court adjudicates 'threaten the peace, security and well-being of the world', whereas the ATT recognises 'the security, social, economic and humanitarian consequences of the illicit and unregulated trade in conventional arms'.[13] Although both treaties aim to address threats to peace and security, they are directed at different temporalities and subjects. The ICC addresses past acts through focusing on individual culpability for the perpetration of mass crimes, whereas the ATT establishes state responsibility to prevent the transfers of conventional arms that would facilitate such crimes.

African states featured centrally in the development and adoption of the ATT, with Kenya as one of seven states initiating and leading the negotiations. The treaty foregrounds the responsibility of states in regulating the international arms trade, including the exporting state's obligation not to authorise arms exports that could be used to commit a violation of international humanitarian law or human rights law.[14] In addition, all transfers of conventional arms and related items are prohibited where a state has knowledge that a proposed transfer would be used to commit genocide, crimes against humanity, or war crimes.[15]

The crimes noted in the ATT overlap with three of the four kinds of crimes that the ICC was established to adjudicate, including war crimes, crimes against humanity, and genocide. The court has acknowledged the contribution of the arms trade to mass crimes in its official documents. However, these references feature less prominently than the crimes themselves and allegations regarding who committed them. ICC arrest warrants, summonses, and decisions confirming charges are largely silent on the role of arms and ammunition in carrying out mass atrocity crimes. Most of these documents tell a dyadic narrative of doer and deed that neglects how the action is carried out materially. For example, arrest warrants alleging crimes against humanity recount how accused individuals plan, order, or participate in widespread and systematic attacks against civilians without addressing the means through which the attacks are carried out, which often involves small arms and light weapons. The ways these weapons were acquired are also underexplored, which may involve diversions or illegal supplies from states and non-state actors.[16]

Supplying arms and ammunition used in the commission of crimes is not an enumerated crime under the Rome Statute, but rather a means of establishing individual responsibility under Article 25. Alleged perpetrators of grave crimes appearing before the ICC have been accused of providing arms and ammunition, and judgments have noted the significant role that such support has played in the commission of crimes.[17] In the situation of the Democratic Republic of Congo (DRC), for example, evidence of Germain Katanga receiving and distributing arms and ammunition was used to demonstrate his contribution to committing crimes against humanity and war crimes. In the *Katanga* judgment, the ICC Trial Chamber explained that the use of small arms contributed to a wider scale of killing than would have been possible if the accused had not supplied them:

> It has been established that the weapons and ammunition secured the success of the operation and Bogoro fell in just a matter of hours. It is beyond doubt that many crimes were perpetrated directly by machete and bladed weapon, but it was the firearms which not only allowed the population to be taken by surprise and Bogoro to be captured, but also to wound and kill its inhabitants.[18]

Katanga was affiliated with the FRPI (*Force de résistance patriotique en Ituri*), a local militia that had received material support from the Congolese government.[19] Other cases in the situation of the DRC involve individuals whose armed groups received material support from states within the Great Lakes region, though these supplies of arms and ammunition to armed groups are not the focus of charges at the ICC. Additional charges were brought against former Congolese army general Bosco Ntaganda in 2012, resulting in an arrest warrant that notes how crimes against humanity were carried out through 'small arms fire' and 'heavy weapons'.[20] According to the ICC Prosecutor, Ntaganda 'procured and distributed weapons and ammunition and was in constant communication up and down the chain of command'.[21] Shortly before the additional arrest warrant was issued, a UN expert panel report had found that Rwanda and Uganda had provided weapons and ammunition to the M23 militia group led by Ntaganda.[22] Non-governmental organisations have also claimed that the Rwandan government provided material support, including Kalashnikov assault rifles, grenades, machine guns, and anti-aircraft artillery.[23] Based on witness statements, the 2014 confirmation of charges decision against Ntaganda notes that the militia group he was affiliated with was 'well-armed with sufficient ammunition and several types of heavy weapons, such as rocket launchers, mortars and grenade launchers, mostly originating from Rwanda'.[24]

Yet the provision of arms that produces the material conditions for mass violence is not of central concern in these cases. With their focus on establishing individual criminal responsibility, ICC proceedings do not prioritise determining the province of weapons, which sustain broader armed campaigns in which the accused is one of many participants. Indeed, ICC investigations and charging decisions have been criticised for inadequately addressing the role of state actors, particularly where the court might be concerned about securing state cooperation with ongoing investigations or about implicating powerful states or their allies. As Mahmood Mamdani observed in 2010, 'the ICC has remained mum about the links between the armies of Uganda and Rwanda – two pro-US states – and the ethnic militias that have been at the heart of the slaughter of civilians'.[25]

Focusing on the role of weapons and their sources brings other actors into view in what Kamari M. Clarke has called the 'supply chain for mass atrocity'.[26] If these reports of arms supplies to Congolese militias by neighbouring states are accurate, not only these states but also the exporting states who originally supplied them with arms as well as the states whose territories the arms transited through would have failed to uphold their international obligations.[27] Unlike international criminal law, such breaches of responsibility would not entail retrospective punishment. Instead, the ATT framework addresses the trade itself and the obligations on states that import, export, transit, and trans-ship arms and ammunition. In this sense it aims to operate prospectively by preventing the transfer of arms when a state has knowledge that the arms or items would be used to commit genocide, crimes against humanity, or war crimes.

III TOWARDS A REGULATORY FRAMEWORK

The illicit trafficking and proliferation of conventional arms and, in particular, small arms and light weapons, has been on the international agenda for two decades. A 1995 position paper by the then UN Secretary-General Boutros Boutros-Ghali stated that small arms 'are probably responsible for most of the deaths in current conflicts'.[28] International, continental, and regional actors – including the African Union (and its preceding Organisation of African Unity) as well as African regional organisations – have attempted to develop transnational mechanisms for regulating the legal trade in arms as well as the illicit trade.[29] Although none of its states rank among the main global importers or exporters, Africa has played a prominent role in efforts to restrict and regulate the arms trade, seeing itself as suffering disproportionately from the impact of illicit flows of weapons.[30] The 2000 Bamako Declaration, which articulates the first common African position on small arms and light weapons, notes that the problem 'is both one of supply and demand, transcends borders and calls for cooperation at all levels: local, national, regional, continental and international'.[31] No other continent has regional agreements regulating small arms transfers and controls that cover nearly all states.[32]

States began developing these regional initiatives after the Bamako Declaration, starting with the Southern African Development Community (SADC) Protocol, which was adopted in 2001 and entered into force in 2004.[33] The Protocol states that its parties will 'undertake to consider' becoming parties to related international instruments, foreshadowing most of the SADC states' eventual signing of the ATT. The Nairobi Protocol, covering the Great Lakes region and the Horn of Africa, came into effect in 2006.[34] Three years later, the West African regional organisation ECOWAS's Convention on Small Arms came into force. Like the ATT, which was being negotiated at the time, the ECOWAS Convention states that arms transfers will be denied if the arms are to be used to violate international humanitarian or human rights law or in the commission of genocide or crimes against humanity.[35] The Kinshasa Convention, covering states in the Central African regional organisation ECCAS as well as Rwanda, was signed in 2010 but is not yet in force at the time of writing. This convention explicitly prohibits transfers to non-state actors such as militia groups.[36]

Meanwhile, addressing the arms trade has been on the agenda of the UN for a long time, in parallel with developments on the African continent. The 2001

UN Programme of Action on Small Arms and Light Weapons (PoA), the principal UN policy framework to address the small arms and light weapons issue, was the first significant act of multilateral cooperation to address trafficking and proliferation. The PoA sets out a range of voluntary measures at the national, regional, and international levels, including legislation, weapons destruction and stockpile management, national reporting, and information sharing among states. It also affirms state responsibility through asserting that 'Governments bear the primary responsibility for preventing, combating and eradicating the illicit trade in small arms and light weapons.'[37]

The UN Security Council has historically addressed restricting the arms trade through specific arms embargoes against states or groups deemed to pose risks to international peace and security under the authority of Chapter VII of the UN Charter. The Security Council has also addressed armed conflicts on the African continent since its 1960 peacekeeping intervention in the Congo, with the majority of the Council's time following the end of the Cold War focused on African conflicts.[38] However, its role has often been resisted as inappropriate or ineffective: the former due to parallel responsibilities of the General Assembly and wider objections to the post–World War II and colonial era composition of its permanent members; the latter because key stakeholders who should have been party to decisions were not present.[39] Despite these criticisms, the Security Council has opened a space for discussing the merits of international efforts to regulate the arms trade, which has been influenced through the role of non-permanent African state members. The Security Council instituted a practice of regular reporting from the secretary-general on the issue of small arms in 2007, and the first report noted in particular the impact that illicit small arms have had on the African continent.

The Council issued a landmark first resolution on small arms and light weapons in 2013, recognising that 'the misuse of small arms and light weapons has resulted in grave crimes' and acknowledging the adoption of the ATT earlier that same year.[40] The two African states on the Security Council at that time – Rwanda and Togo – had both signed the ATT on the first day it opened for signature. In a statement following the adoption of the Security Council resolution, Rwanda affirmed the role of the ATT and the importance of supporting regional mechanisms. Yet a rift began to develop in the deliberations leading up to a second related resolution in 2015, with African states on the Security Council refusing to sign the resolution in the absence of the phrase 'non-state actors'. Nonetheless, African states strongly reaffirmed their commitments to the ATT in statements during Security Council deliberations.

IV AFRICAN STATES AND THE ATT

The formal process which initiated the deliberations and subsequent negotiation conferences for the ATT began in the UN General Assembly in 2006, with a resolution calling for an arms trade treaty and requesting member states to provide their views on the elements of a future treaty.[41] African regional powers such as Kenya were closely involved in the process of developing the treaty. As noted previously, Kenya was one of seven sponsoring states of the first GA resolution, which was also co-sponsored by eighteen African states prior to the vote.[42] The ATT was eventually adopted in April 2013 after having received substantial support from many African states during the negotiation process. The treaty is the first global agreement to regulate the international transfer of conventional arms, setting out when transfers are prohibited and benchmarks to standardise the assessment of potential risks associated with a possible export.

African states are not among the top producers of arms and ammunition; their main role within the treaty framework is as importers and at times as exporters, with some exceptions of smaller-scale arms production for use within the continent.[43] Yet these largely recipient states have been more affected by the global arms trade than their positions as importers and exporters would suggest. As negotiators for the East African Community (EAC) noted during treaty negotiations, 'whereas the region is not arms producing, it remains awash with arms'.[44] African states have common interests around regulating the trade, though various African states have diverged on the degree of support. These divergences reflected regional divisions. For example, Sub-Saharan African states were largely backing the treaty, whereas many North African states were less involved or were actively seeking to block the treaty's adoption (as was the case with Egypt).[45] However, an 'African Group' was formed early in the process that sought to represent common interests among states on the continent.

Many statements made by African states during the treaty negotiation process emphasised the link between the trade in conventional weapons and armed conflict. For example, as a co-sponsor of the initial resolution before the General Assembly, Kenya stated that it recognised that 'there are extremely powerful economic interests that profit from the trade in conventional weapons; however, the other side of the coin shows millions of people dying from unregulated trade'.[46] The argument for the ATT was expressed in humanitarian terms, emphasising the need for governments to act in the interest of victims of armed conflict.

Many African states that made initial submissions or interventions throughout the treaty negotiation process situated the need for an ATT in geographical and historical context.[47] They noted how African states had been affected by conflicts sustained through illicit flows of small arms and light weapons. Uganda emphasised the conflicts in East Africa and the Horn of Africa, noting the need to 'enhance regulation of national, regional, and global arms trade among states and prevent proliferation of illicit arms ... especially to armed groups'.[48] Speaking on behalf of the African Group throughout the deliberations, Nigeria noted that many African states 'suffer disproportionately the pernicious effects of irresponsible transfers of arms', and a future ATT should contain a 'clear requirement that all transfers of conventional arms and SALWs must be expressly authorized by competent government authorities of the importing state'.[49] In addition to noting the role of arms in perpetuating violent conflicts, Nigeria also highlighted the importance of state responsibility in regulating the global trade in arms in its statements on behalf of the African Group.

State responsibility became a common theme in African states' representations during the negotiation process. Describing itself as committed to playing a 'leading role in attaining a strong, robust, legally binding ATT', Kenya emphasised the importance of state responsibility in regulating the arms trade and preventing diversions.[50] As one of the few arms manufacturing states and exporters on the continent, South Africa also described the need for an ATT in terms of state responsibility, noting that the primary responsibility for controlling arms 'rests with the Governments that allow arms to be exported, imported, re-exported or to transit through territories under their jurisdiction or control'.[51]

As consensus could not be reached on the adoption of the 2013 treaty text presented to the conference plenary, which was due to objections from Iran, the Democratic People's Republic of Korea, and Syria, a vote in the General Assembly was called for April 2013. An overwhelming majority of states voted to adopt the treaty (153), with twenty-three states abstaining, including four African states: Angola, Egypt, Sudan, and Swaziland. In its first intervention in the entire negotiation process, Sudan stated that it was abstaining because the treaty did not include a specific prohibition on transfers to 'unauthorised non-state actors'. Of the states where the ICC has exercised jurisdiction, the Central African Republic, Côte d'Ivoire, DRC, Kenya, Libya, Mali, and Uganda all voted in favour.

The treaty was seen to enhance existing regional frameworks throughout the African continent by addressing all actors in the supply chain, from largely Northern arms-producing and -exporting states to importing states seeking conventional arms for their security needs. Following the adoption of the treaty text, Côte d'Ivoire declared on behalf of the community of West African states, 'For the member States of ECOWAS, which, on a daily basis, experience the tragic consequences of the lack of international regulation of arms transfers, it is certainly a significant step, as the spread and uncontrolled accumulation of conventional arms undoubtedly represents the most serious threat to the peace and security of our States'.[52]

V STATE RESPONSIBILITY UNDER THE ATT

As explained above, the 2013 ATT is the first international treaty focused on the regulation of conventional arms and associated ammunition/munitions as well as parts and components. The treaty's preamble asserts that it is the responsibility of all states to effectively regulate the international trade in conventional arms and to prevent their diversion, which includes establishing and implementing their respective national control systems.

According to the president of the 2012 UN negotiating conference, the purpose of the treaty is to create international standards to regulate the conventional arms trade, and in doing so it 'seeks to address one of the structural conditions that leads to and escalates armed violence and conflicts: the supply of arms'.[53] The other overarching objective of the treaty is to prevent and eradicate the illicit trade in conventional arms and to prevent their diversion. This fusion of dual goals supports the unique nature of the treaty, as it is not wholly a trade treaty establishing regulatory benchmarks for the international trade nor a purely a 'humanitarian' instrument focused solely on the trade's destructive effects. Rather, the ATT seeks to improve oversight over international arms transfers from a human security perspective by looking at a range of possible negative impacts from the use of the conventional arms and seeking to prevent them.[54]

States party to the treaty are required to regulate 'transfers' of the types of conventional arms, ammunition/munitions, and parts and components. A transfer is broadly defined to include the range of transactions that occur along the supply chain, including export, import, transit, trans-shipment, and brokering. Regulation of each of these forms of 'transfers' by competent state authorities is a basic treaty obligation. The treaty does not provide definitions of these activities. However, the UN Register on Conventional Arms refers to arms exports and imports as 'all forms of arms transfers under terms of grant, credit, barter or cash',[55] meaning that a broad range of shipments of arms that leave or enter the jurisdiction of a state should be deemed to be an 'export' and 'import'. Some African states such as Kenya supported this view, advocating for an expansive conception of the term 'export' to include gifts, leases, and loans.[56] This would mean that the provision of weapons and ammunition as 'gifts' or other forms of supply, for example by Rwanda and Uganda to the M23 militia group as found by the UN expert panel report, should be considered as an export and subject to national export, customs, and reporting obligations.

The treaty pertains to a limited range of 'conventional arms' and lists eight categories that range from battle tanks to small arms and light weapons (SALW).[57] These categories reflect a minimum standard, as the treaty also encourages states to 'apply the provisions of this Treaty to the broadest range of conventional arms'.[58] In practice, many states around the world already have national control lists that cover a very broad range of conventional arms and military equipment, far more extensive than the categories in the treaty, as is the case with main arms exporters such as the United States, France, and Germany.

Individual African states as well as the African Group repeatedly stressed the importance of including SALW within the categories of 'conventional arms' during treaty negotiations due to the nature of armed conflicts on the continent and the significant role of those weapons in such conflicts. African states largely insisted that SALW needed to be included in order for the treaty to be relevant to the continent. Other states such as China – a significant exporter of SALW to Africa – were adamant that they should be excluded from the treaty. It has been suggested that the eventual change in position by China was influenced in large part by the demands of African states to include SALW in the scope of the ATT.[59] Ammunition/munitions are also included in a limited way to the extent that they are fired, launched, or delivered from the eight categories of conventional arms, in effect covering all ammunition used in all firearms.[60]

The core provisions of the treaty are Articles 6 and 7, which set out when a transfer is prohibited and the assessment procedures for determining whether an export should be authorised. Article 6 applies to all forms of transfers (import, export, transit, trans-shipment, and brokering) and prohibits any form of this movement of conventional arms, ammunition/munitions, and parts and components in three circumstances: where the resulting transfer would violate a UN arms embargo, where it would violate a relevant international obligation under an international agreement to which the State Party is bound, or – most relevant to the work of the ICC – where the State Party has knowledge at the time that the authorisation would be used in the commission of genocide, crimes against humanity, grave breaches of the Geneva Conventions of 1949, attacks directed against civilian objects or civilians protected as such, or other war crimes.

Article 7 of the treaty requires a State Party considering an export of conventional arms, ammunition/munitions, or parts and components to consider if the potential export would undermine peace and security. It must consider whether the export could be used to commit or facilitate a serious violation of international human rights law or international humanitarian law, or an act constituting a serious offence under international conventions and protocols to which the exporting state is a party related to terrorism or transnational organised crime. Where there is an 'overriding' risk of any of these negative consequences, the export authorisation must be denied. For example, if an exporter concludes that there is a reasonable and credible risk that the transfer could be used to commit serious violations of international humanitarian law, by extension undermining peace and security, then the authorisation must be refused.

Despite substantial lobbying by African states, the treaty does not include provisions prohibiting transfers to non-state actors, which is taken up in greater detail in the following section. Both individually and through the African Group, states consistently noted the importance of 'a clear prohibition on transfers to non-State actors'.[61] With the exception of Sudan, this issue did not ultimately prevent African states from signing on to the ATT; as of the time of writing, twenty-seven African states have signed and eleven have ratified the treaty.[62] In line with the expressed concerns of African states, the treaty preamble upholds the fundamental principle of state sovereignty, and it explicitly affirms 'the sovereign right of any State to regulate and control conventional arms within its territory'.

VI RESPONSIBILITY AND SOVEREIGN EQUALITY

As the previous sections have illustrated, African states have been active in shaping ways to address the global arms trade, and in particular the illicit trade in small arms and light weapons. They have repeatedly noted the relationship between the trade and armed conflict. For example, Rwanda stated in 2013 that 'it is a reality that the African continent, particularly the Great Lakes region, where Rwanda is located, continues to be engulfed by internal armed conflicts facilitated by such easily accessible weapons'.[63] In response to these concerns, African states have expressed the need for states to take responsibility in regulating the flow of weapons into the continent. For example, Kenya emphasised the regulatory role of states in its statements during the treaty drafting process:

> Small arms continue to fuel armed conflicts, displacement of persons and crimes of varied types leading to untold human suffering, and undermining economic and social development. In our view, the ATT should therefore

address the responsibilities of all States, to regulate trade in these arms and prevent their diversion.[64]

Claims regarding the importance of state responsibility continued in discussions of the UN Security Council's second thematic resolution on small arms in 2015, where Chad observed that 'it is up to each State to assume its responsibility to address the potential for the illicit use, diversion and circulation of weapons'.[65]

While African states have contended that regulating the arms trade is the responsibility of all states, they have also suggested that the primary responsibility for the trade lies with arms-producing states as the main exporters to the continent. In its first statement during the treaty-drafting process, for example, the African Group asserted a distinction between the 'special responsibilities of major arms producers and special rights of arms importing States', a phrase that was reiterated in subsequent statements.[66] This language may have been a concession to Egypt, a member of the Africa Group, who wanted the right to import arms reflected in the treaty text.[67] However, Uganda also made the distinction between the 'responsibilities of arms producers and the rights of arms importing states' in its own statement to the preparatory committee.[68] This distinction seems to suggest that state responsibility for regulating the arms trade is primarily a matter for arms producers and exporters, whereas states on the receiving end have a right to purchase arms for legitimate use, a right that is grounded in state sovereignty and the right to self-defence under Article 51 of the UN Charter. Many African states invoked Article 51 during the negotiation process, and most statements began with references to state sovereignty. Yet this distinction between rights-bearing importers and exporters who are responsible for regulating the trade has the effect of re-inscribing hierarchies among states rather than emphasising their sovereign equality, which also seems to conflict with numerous claims made by African states about the importance of achieving a balanced, fair, and non-discriminatory treaty text. Indeed, the African Group mentions sovereign equality in the same statement to the preparatory committee where it introduces the responsibilities/rights distinction in relation to exporting and importing states.

The AU has recognised the 'full responsibility of all States to regulate the manufacture and transfer of conventional arms in their simultaneous and changing roles as exporters or importers'.[69] This more accurately reflects how states may be exporters in one context and importers in another, with distinct obligations in both cases that are grounded in state responsibility. Kenya's statement above also emphasises that all states have responsibilities to regulate the trade and to prevent diversions. Such an approach does more to uphold sovereign equality among states, suggesting that the African continent can exert its own agency in regulating the trade rather than relying upon the good will or foreign policy objectives of arms-producing and exporting states, many of whom are former colonial powers (the United Kingdom, Belgium, France, Germany) or former Cold War–era superpowers (such as the United States and the Russian Federation).[70] The framing of 'special responsibilities' of producers and 'special rights' of importers may be intended to address historic inequalities in the trade: as research on the arms trade has noted, many (if not most) former colonial powers export arms to their former colonies.[71] Yet leaving state responsibility to arms exporters risks fostering further dependence on the behaviour of states outside the African continent. Suggesting that solutions to the problem of regulation lies elsewhere also discounts African states' own agency, further undermining their claims to sovereign equality. Meanwhile in practice, presenting themselves as passive recipients of arms transfers diminishes African states' responsibilities as importers as well as their role as exporters.

Emphasising the responsibility of African states in the regulation of the trade does not discount the importance of other actors, particularly the role of major arms producers and exporters. The continent bears a long history as a proxy site of broader conflicts between European powers during the colonial period and between the major powers of the Cold War.[72] As the United States and United Kingdom as well as the former Soviet Union and China provided arms to groups in many African states, they contributed to the proliferation in arms that continue to circulate on the continent. China, the United States, and the Russian Federation are now among the main arms producers and exporters in the global trade. Arms transfers to Africa form a very small share of their export markets, however, with the exception of China, the main supplier to the continent. According to Stockholm International Peace Research Institute (SIPRI), transfers to African states formed 11% of China's export market from 2005 to 2010.[73] SIPRI has observed that this relatively low prospect of large revenues from the continent could suggest that 'arms transfers to Africa are likely to be part of broader policies for gaining access to natural resources in the recipient countries',[74] demonstrating that while the Cold War is over, arms transfers still play a tactical role in states' foreign policy and desires to exert control for broader strategic aims.

Within this broader frame of responsibility, non-African states have also been exporters in transfers that have been subsequently diverted by importing states to non-state actors, including armed groups. For example, a 2012 report noted that a considerable part of the stockpile of the armed forces of the DRC

(FARDC) is made up of Chinese-manufactured weaponry, munitions, and other equipment. These arms and ammunitions deliveries to the state security forces of the DRC have resulted in documented diversions.[75] The leaking of FARDC military equipment to armed groups, both to FARDC-supported militia and armed opposition groups, was documented in the December 2011 UN Group of Experts report, which concluded that 'armed groups continue to obtain most of their arms, ammunition and uniforms from FARDC'.[76]

Recent research into arms supplies into the Central African Republic (CAR), also an ICC situation country, concludes that CAR-based Séléka rebel forces have used European manufactured small arms, ammunition, and vehicles, including Belgian, Czech, and UK ammunition manufactured between 2007 and 2010, some of which was likely diverted from their original end user. China (along with Sudan) produced the majority of the recently manufactured (post-2000) weapons and ammunition documented in CAR in this same report. The report also concludes that Chinese and possibly Iranian-manufactured small arms ammunition and larger munitions have been re-transferred from Sudan to CAR.[77]

The ATT emphasises that all states party to the treaty must take measures to prevent diversion, and to do so at all points in the supply chains – export, import, transit, and trans-shipment. States are also to required assess and mitigate the risks of diversion and take appropriate measures to prevent illicit activities involving the transfer of conventional arms.[78] Under the structure of the ATT, not only the importing state but also the exporting state would be in breach of their treaty obligations to prevent diversions, especially in situations where the risks of such diversions are well documented and extremely prevalent, as in both situations above with transfers to the Congolese state and to the CAR security forces.

A more extensive treatment of this subject would examine all aspects of the assemblage of the global trade in arms, including different actors within the 'supply chain of mass atrocity' and transnational regulatory regimes. However, this chapter focuses on efforts by African states and regional organisations to address the trade from within. Much of the tension between the continent and the ICC has been expressed in language that contests constraints upon African agency, whether it is framed as threats to state sovereignty or as insufficient influence within international processes. African states have consistently noted the importance of preserving their sovereignty and developing continental and regional approaches, as was the case with efforts to extend the jurisdiction of the African Court of Human and People's Rights to cover international crimes.

In practice, these efforts may involve elaborate political strategies that reinforce or challenge existing power structures, both internal and external to the continent. They may be reactions formed in response to political and historical inequalities: for example, unfair or disproportionate targeting of the continent before the ICC, and disparities in structural relations that have led some African states to argue that exporting states should take greater responsibility in regulating the arms trade than importing states, who should be seen as rights-bearing rather than duty-bearing subjects. In principle, however, states have committed themselves to particular courses of action by expanding institutional jurisdictions and developing frameworks such as the ATT.

Through active involvement in the processes that produce binding international legal obligations, African states have created a record of their commitment that can be drawn upon when what they do in practice diverges from what they have said. With the growing rift between the ICC and some African states, for example, Court proponents argue that states willingly signed on to the treaty and should uphold their obligations, as both Kenya and now South Africa have not done in relation to executing the arrest warrant against Sudanese President al-Bashir. In return, African states have claimed that the ICC has investigated selectively and has deferred to powerful states, and in this way it has failed to uphold its responsibility to address all relevant crimes within its jurisdiction regardless of where they have occurred. These discussions happen by reference to obligations under the Rome Statute treaty, revealing the discursive effects it has had in shaping how states conceptualise their obligations. Even when African states that are under the jurisdiction of the ICC make claims about Head of State immunity, it is often by reference to provisions of the Rome Statute (such as Article 98) invoking obligations under customary international law.

Discussions around regulating the arms trade are increasingly unfolding by reference to law and legal obligations. This increasing juridification is revealed by African states' calls for a more expansive legal framework that includes non-state actors. During the deliberations for an ATT initiated by the UN General Assembly, for example, African states consistently raised concerns about transfers to non-state actors. This was also a concern of the African Union, which wanted the ATT to prohibit arms transfers to 'unauthorized non-state armed groups and/or unauthorized non-state actors'.[79] Throughout the ATT negotiations, the African Group also repeatedly stated that the ATT should include a 'clear prohibition of transfers to unauthorized non-State actors'.[80] Yet this attempt to broaden the treaty also reinforces the impression that state actions are legitimate and illicit transfers and illegal use can be attributed to non-state actors. Referring to 'unauthorized' non-state actors suggests that the legality of the transfer is tied to the end *user* being authorised regardless of the legality of use of those arms or the broader legality of the transfer itself (for example, transfers to an authorised non-state actor could still be in breach of an arms embargo). The ATT moves away from this conception, emphasising the legality of a transfer of arms based on its potential end use, not the end user, requiring states parties to assess potential risks of the end use or to prohibit certain transfers where there is knowledge of the use for crimes against humanity, genocide, and war crimes.[81] Creating this distinction between 'end user' and 'end use' prevents states from claiming that the problem lies exclusively with non-state actors, as states themselves are sometimes illegitimate end users.

Tensions are apparent in African state behaviour regarding efforts to regulate the arms trade, and it appears that the focus on non-state actors might be an effort to divert attention from African state involvement in activities that would be seen to violate the treaty. This has manifested most recently in debates concerning a 2015 Security Council resolution on small arms and light weapons, where African state members of the Security Council abstained from voting due to the absence of a reference to transfers to non-state actors.[82] Speaking on behalf of the African members, Angola asserted that the resolution should include language addressing 'a halt to the supply of those weapons to non-State actors'.[83] The underlying rationale behind this position on non-state actors is unclear; it may be tied to power dynamics within the Security Council and African state concerns that their positions are not being adequately addressed.[84] Yet it also seems to suggest that by situating non-state actors as primarily responsible for destabilisation and armed conflict, African states position themselves as inherently lawful and law-abiding. Creating this dichotomy between lawful (state) and unlawful (non-state) actors rather than emphasising illegal end use by *any* actor also entrenches existing power structures, as many non-state actors are opposition groups. Indeed, some current governments are comprised of members of former opposition groups that would have been deemed illegal recipients of arms under this distinction, such as the Rwandan Patriotic Front and Uganda's National Resistance Movement.

Despite strong expressions in support of regulating the trade in arms, state behaviour in practice has not always aligned with these claims. On the one hand, African states have led developments in establishing the ATT, as with Kenya's role in sponsoring the General Assembly resolution that laid the groundwork for treaty negotiations. On the other hand, they have engaged in the very actions that they have sought to prohibit by supporting the treaty.

Commentators have noted how the ATT was negotiated in part during the Arab Spring, 'when a number of States were both covertly and overtly providing arms to opposition forces'.[85] During this time, Kenya was clandestinely supplying weapons to South Sudan in several instalments of arms shipments, breaching the Comprehensive Peace Agreement.[86] As described above, evidence suggests that Rwanda and Uganda have diverted weapons and ammunition to militia groups in the eastern DRC in breach of a UN arms embargo. Furthermore, despite its active involvement in the initiation and drafting of the ATT, Kenya has not signed onto the treaty as of the time of writing; meanwhile, states that have ratified the treaty, such as Nigeria, have not implemented their obligations or made legislative changes to reflect their treaty commitments. Many African states maintain an ambivalent relationship to the binding legal obligations established through the ATT.

Nevertheless, as this section has shown, many African states have expressly welcomed the development of a global framework for regulating the trade in arms. Widespread African state involvement in developing the ATT suggests a desire to juridify the political economy of the arms trade, subjecting it to binding legal commitments. As with other transnational recourses to law, this does not mean that political conflicts between states are resolved through the common language of the treaty text: as Martti Koskenniemi has observed, 'merely by making something "legal" or a matter of "right" will not suffice as assurance for the beneficiality of one's choice'.[87] Rather, conflicts may unfold in different terms and by reference to legal frameworks. Regardless of whether states comply with international legal obligations, however, the rhetorical field of their production – such as treaty *traveaux* and statements by the AU – provides a basis for making claims about developing norms. Much like the role of (non-binding) legal precedent at international criminal tribunals,[88] the preambular language of the ATT text suggests normative convergences around regulating the arms trade. African states have played a central role in producing this language and in transforming its normative content into binding legal commitments.

VII CONCLUSION

Contemporary practices of security governance, such as the work of international criminal law institutions like the ICC as well as military interventions justified under the doctrine of the 'responsibility to protect', have been accused of disproportionately targeting the African continent and threatening state sovereignty. For example, Mahmood Mamdani asserts that the legal doctrine of the 'responsibility to protect' has divided the international order between sovereign states and '*de facto* trusteeship territories', echoing divisions from the colonial period.[89] The responsibility to intervene, with its implications for state sovereignty, is linked to the three crimes also covered by the ATT: genocide, crimes against humanity, and war crimes. Mamdani claims 'these crimes are said to justify a "humanitarian intervention" and the jurisdiction of an International Criminal Court – the first based on a right to protect and the second on a right to punish – both overriding claims of sovereignty'.[90]

Building upon these concerns, this chapter re-centres the issue of African state sovereignty by illustrating how states themselves have attempted to address mass atrocity through regulating the trade in arms. This is reflected in statements from the African Group during the treaty drafting process, where Nigeria claimed on behalf of the Group that 'Africa's support for an ATT (as felt in our voices, conferences and regional programmes), is borne out of past experiences, when the continent was ravaged by effects of indiscriminate and illegal sale and use of Small Arms and Light Weapons'.[91] As scholars of international law have noted, sovereign equality may be impossible to attain in practice; it is premised upon the Westphalian model of statehood that is freighted with colonial-era presuppositions and power differentials that persist in the contemporary global order.[92] Yet it may work as a productive fiction, unattainable in practice but offering a regulative ideal by which power differentials can be critiqued. As the Kenyan representative to the treaty negotiations claimed, the arms trade treaty should 'address the responsibilities of all States'.[93] At least in principle, the treaty places identical obligations on all of its signatories to ensure that their activities in the arms trade do not result in the commission of grave crimes. In this sense it constructs a rhetorical field from which states can invoke the power of binding legal obligations, much as the text of the Rome Statute has shifted the terms through which responses to armed conflict are framed and debated.

As with all treaty texts, including the Rome Statute, the ATT produces a new constituency of nominally like-minded signatory states, with shared normative concerns around regulating the trade in arms that has historically contributed to armed conflict. Yet unlike the ATT, the ICC's constituency includes some exceptional states that remain unbound by the obligations that the treaty contains.[94] In granting a role to the UN Security Council, which includes states not party to the Rome Statute, the ICC's uneven constituency has produced frictions among states and regional bodies who have alleged that the justice on offer at the Court is partial and selective. By contrast, there is no inherent role for the Security Council within the terms of the ATT. The constituency it produces is legally obliged to take a preventative approach to armed conflict and human rights abuses. State signatories are answerable to a conference of states party to the treaty, a self-governing body that will oversee issues of implementation and interpretation. The legislative controls and benchmarks established in the treaty text are consistent with African regional protocols, expressions from the African Union, and what states themselves have said. In this sense, attempts to prospectively regulate the trade in arms through principles of state responsibility may offer an alternative path to addressing armed conflict on the African continent, and a possible site for attending to the material conditions of mass crimes that have been marginalised by the expanding field of international criminal law.

Notes

1. Some proponents of international criminal accountability maintain that it prevents future crime through deterrence; for example, the European Union asserts that the 'ICC also has an important preventive role, as stipulated in the preamble of the Rome Statute. By putting an end to the impunity it deters persons or groups from committing criminal activities'; see 'Statement on Behalf of the European Union and Its Member States by Ioannis Vrailas, Deputy Head of Delegation of the European Union to the United Nations at the United Nations General Assembly Thematic Debate on the Role of International Criminal Justice in Reconciliation', Doc. EUUN13-034EN, 10 April 2013. For critical accounts of deterrence claims in international criminal law, see Martti Koskenniemi, 'Between Impunity and Show Trials' (2002) 6(1) *Max Planck Yearbook of United Nations Law* 1–32; Immi Tallgren, 'The Sensibility and Sense of International Criminal Law' (2002) 13 *European Journal of International Law* 561–595; and Sarah Nouwen, 'Justifying Justice', in James Crawford and Martti Koskenniemi (eds.), *The Cambridge Companion to International Law* (Cambridge: Cambridge University Press, 2012).
2. See for example Kamari M. Clarke, 'The Rule of Law Through Its Economies of Appearances: The Making of the African Warlord' 18(1) *Indiana Journal of Global Legal Studies* (2011), 7–40 and Kamari M. Clarke, '"We Ask for Justice, You Give Us Law": Justice Talk and the Encapsulation of Victims', in Christian De Vos, Sara Kendall and Carsten Stahn (eds.), *Contested Justice: The Politics and Practice of International Criminal Court Interventions* (Cambridge: Cambridge University Press, 2015).
3. 'African Union Common Position on an Arms Trade Treaty', Lomé, adopted September 2011, endorsed by the AU Assembly in decision Assembly/AUDec.472 (XX), 31 January 2013, Article 18.

4. For accounts that consider the role of global capitalism in this erosion, see political theorist Wendy Brown, *Walled States, Waning Sovereignty* (Boston: the MIT Press, 2010) and, much earlier, international legal scholar Oscar Schachter, 'The Decline of the Nation-State and Its Implications for International Law' (1998) 36 *Columbia Journal of Transnational Law* 7–24. As one sign of the decline of the state, Schachter notes that the 'illegal arms trade also flourishes ostensibly beyond state control' (at 15).

5. For some accounts of the role of state interests in relation to the work of the ICC, see Sarah Nouwen, *Complementarity in the Line of Fire: The Catalysing Effect of the International Criminal Court in Uganda and Sudan* (Cambridge: Cambridge University Press, 2013) and David Bosco, *Rough Justice: The International Criminal Court in a World of Power Politics* (Oxford: Oxford University Press, 2014).

6. See Edwin Bikundo, 'The International Criminal Court and Africa: Exemplary Justice' (2011) 23 *Law and Critique* 21–41.

7. For example, Kirsten Ainley has argued that, despite their evident shortcomings, 'The Responsibility to Protect (R2P) process and the International Criminal Court (ICC) are quite probably the most important innovation in human rights protection for decades.' Kirsten Ainley, 'The Responsibility to Protect and the International Criminal Court: Counteracting the Crisis' (2015) 91 *International Affairs* 37–54, 37.

8. For recent examples from different disciplinary perspectives, see Andrea Birdsall, 'The Responsibility to Prosecute and the ICC: A Problematic Relationship?' (2015) 26 *Criminal Law Forum* 51–72 and Alexander Beresford, 'A Responsibility to Protect Africa from the West? South Africa and the NATO Intervention in Libya' (2015) 52 *International Politics* 288–304.

9. On the effects of the cases on Kenyan electoral politics, see Sara Kendall, '"UhuRuto" and Other Leviathans: the International Criminal Court and the Kenyan Political Order' (2014) 7 *African Journal of Legal Studies* 399–427. For a broader account of what they term the 'African push-back' against the ICC, see Kamari M. Clarke and Sarah-Jane Koulen, 'The Legal Politics of the Article 16 Decision: The International Criminal Court, the UN Security Council and Ontologies of a Contemporary Compromise' (2014) 7 *African Journal of Legal Studies* 297–319.

10. These criticisms have been elaborated in a growing body of academic literature. See, for example, Kamari M. Clarke, *Fictions of Justice: the International Criminal Court and the Challenge of Legal Pluralism in Sub-Saharan Africa* (Cambridge: Cambridge University Press, 2009), Adam Branch, *Displacing Human Rights: War and Intervention in Northern Uganda* (New York: Oxford University Press, 2011), and Sarah Nouwen and Wouter Werner, 'Doing Justice to the Political: The

International Criminal Court in Uganda and Sudan' (2011) 21 *European Journal of International Law* 941–965.

11. A monograph on the Democratic Republic of Congo observes that local communities have ultimately needed to defend themselves despite international and domestic prosecutions: 'The International Criminal Court and the Congolese military prosecutors convicted only a few perpetrators of war crimes; countless others went without punishment and many were even integrated into the local police and army units. As a result, most Ituri militias claimed that their community (whether Hema, Lendu, or any other ethnic group) still needed to protect itself from expropriation, oppression, and extermination by their local enemies.' See Severine Autessere, *The Trouble with the Congo: Local Violence and the Failure of International Peacebuilding* (Cambridge: Cambridge University Press, 2010), p. 175. Whether more prosecutions at the ICC and in domestic courts would remedy this situation remains a matter of debate.

12. For a rare treatment of the relationship that emphases the role of state responsibility, see Nina Jørgensen, 'State Responsibility for Aiding or Assisting International Crimes in the Context of the Arms Trade Treaty' (2014) 108 *American Journal of International Law* 722–749.

13. The Arms Trade Treaty (ATT), New York, 27 March 2013, in force 24 December 2014, UN Doc. A.CONF.217/2013/L.3, preamble.

14. Article 7 of the ATT requires a State Party to not authorize an export of conventional arms, ammunition/munitions, parts and components as defined in the treaty where there is an 'overriding risk' of a range of negative consequences, including undermining peace and security or committing or facilitating a serious violation of international human rights or humanitarian law.

15. Article 6(3) of the ATT. This prohibition applies to 'transfers' broadly defined as import, export, transit, trans-shipment, and brokering. Article 7 applies only to exports. The ATT is predicated upon the international law of state responsibility, which does not make a distinction between criminal and civil wrongs by states. The International Law Commission has commented that determining the standard of state responsibility is dependent on the object and purpose of a particular treaty. For further detail, see Clare da Silva and Penelope Nevill, 'Article 6 of the Arms Trade Treaty', in Clare da Silva and Brian Wood (eds.), *Weapons and International Law: The Arms Trade Treaty* (Brussels: Larcier, 2015). Jørgensen observes that Article 6(3) of the ATT text appears to borrow language from Article 25(3)(c) of the Rome Statute; see Jørgensen, 'State Responsibility', 726.

16. By contrast, in its trial judgment against former Liberian president Charles Taylor, the Special Court for Sierra Leone reviews extensive

evidence on the sources and supply routes of arms and ammunition, including shipments from Burkina Faso and Côte d'Ivoire, provided by Taylor to militia groups in Sierra Leonean territory. The evidence documents that these supplies included AK-47 rifles, grenades, anti-tank mines, anti-personnel mines, mortars, Beretta rifles, and anti-aircraft guns. This evidence led the Trial Chamber to conclude that the provision and facilitation of these arms and ammunition by Taylor constituted practical assistance to the commission of crimes by the RUF and RUF/AFRC groups. See *The Prosecutor v. Charles Ghankay Taylor* (SCSL-03-01-T), Sentencing Judgement Trial Chamber II, 18 May 2012, paras. 1610–2045, 6908, 6912.

17. For an act to qualify as a war crime requires a nexus to an armed conflict, though the provision of arms and ammunition is not itself a war crime; the Rome Statute only invokes the role of weapons and ammunition in relation to war crimes if they are already 'prohibited' or if they are 'poisoned'. See Rome Statute Articles 8(2)(b)(xvii) and 8(2)(e)(xiii), 'War crime of employing poison or poisoned weapons' and 8(2)(b)(xix) and 8(2)(e)(xv), 'War crime of employing prohibited bullets'.

18. *The Prosecutor v. Germain Katanga* (ICC-01/04-01/07), Judgement pursuant to article 74 of the Statute, 7 March 2014, paras. 1676–77. Katanga was found guilty as an accomplice under Article 25(3)(d).

19. For an account of the relationship between the FRPI and the Congolese state, see Henning Tamm, 'FNI and FRPI: Local Resistance and Regional Alliances in North-eastern Congo' (Rift Valley Institute Usalama Project, 2013).

20. *The Prosecutor v. Bosco Ntaganda* (ICC-01/04-02/06), Decision on the Prosecutor's Application under Article 58, 13 July 2012, paras. 29 and 31.

21. Ibid. at para. 64.

22. See 'Letter dated 12 October 2012 from the Group of Experts on the Democratic Republic of the Congo addressed to the Chair of the Security Council Committee established pursuant to resolution 1533 (2004) concerning the Democratic Republic of the Congo', UN Doc. S/2012/843, 15 November 2012, paras. 18–19 and 43. For an elaboration on the Rwandan allegations, see 'Letter dated 26 June 2012 from the Chair of the Security Council Committee established pursuant to resolution 1533 (2004) concerning the Democratic Republic of the Congo addressed to the President of the Security Council', UNSC Doc. S/2012/348/Add.1, 27 June 2012. The Rwandan government strongly disputed these claims.

23. 'DR Congo: Rwanda Should Stop Aiding War Crimes Suspect', *Human Rights Watch*, 3 June 2012; see also International Crisis Group, 'Eastern Congo: Why Stabilisation Failed' (Africa Briefing No. 91, 4 October 2012), and Jason Stearns, 'From CNDP to M23: The Evolution of an Armed

Movement in Eastern Congo' (Rift Valley Institute Usalama Project, 2012).

24. The Chamber also concludes that Ntaganda was responsible for securing weapons from '*inter alia*, Rwanda'. *The Prosecutor v. Bosco Ntaganda* (ICC-01/04-02/06), Decision Pursuant to Article 61(7)(a) and (b) of the Rome Statute on the Charges of the Prosecutor Against Bosco Ntaganda, 9 June 2014, paras. 17 and 120.

25. Mahmood Mamdani, 'Responsibility to Protect or Right to Punish?' (2010) 4 *Journal of Intervention and Statebuilding* 53–67, at 61. See also Branch, *Displacing Human Rights*. Although the 2014 confirmation of charges decision in the *Ntaganda* case above does note Rwanda's role in supplying arms and ammunition, Mamdani's observation is still relevant: the provision of material support has not altered ICC charging practices.

26. Clarke, 'The Rule of Law', 10.

27. For an analysis of international obligations on states in the shipment into Rwandan territory, including the original arms exporting state (Bulgaria) and the states through which the arms were trans-shipped (France and Kenya), see 'Deadly Movements: Transport Controls in the Arms Trade Treaty' (Amnesty International, July 2010), pp. 12–15.

28. 'Supplement to an Agenda for Peace: Position Paper of the Secretary-General on the Occasion of the Fiftieth Anniversary of the United Nations', UN Doc. A/50/60-S/1995/1, 3 January 1995.

29. The legal trade in arms enables states to acquire arms and ammunition for their legitimate and lawful security needs as a matter of sovereignty and territorial control.

30. A number of African states made this point during the ATT negotiation process. For example, Ghana stated, 'Ghana is interested in the work of this session because our region suffers from the effects of the irresponsible and illegal transfer of arms which cause serious destabilizing effects on its socio-economic development.' Statement of the Republic of Ghana, Second Preparatory Committee for the United Nations Conference on the Arms Trade Treaty, 28 February 2011. Mozambique stated that 'The main challenge in today's world is to curb the illicit trade in small arms and light weapons that constitutes a threat to peace, security and development in many countries, particularly in Africa'. 'Statement by Permanent Representative of Mozambique to the United Nations at the First Committee', 12 October 2006.

31. Bamako Declaration on the 'African Common Position on the Illicit Proliferation, Circulation and Trafficking of Small Arms and Light Weapons', Organisation of African Unity (OAU) Ministerial Conference on Small Arms and Light Weapons, 2000, endorsed by OAU Council of Ministers in Decision CM/Dec.599, July 2001.

32. North Africa (Algeria, Egypt, Libya, Morocco, and Tunisia) does not have a regional agreement on small arms. Mauritania withdrew from ECOWAS in 2000.
33. 'Protocol on the Control of Firearms, Ammunition and Other Related Materials in the Southern African Development Community (SADC) Region', Blantyre, 14 August 2001, in force 8 November 2004.
34. 'Nairobi Protocol for the Prevention, Control and Reduction of Small Arms and Light Weapons in the Great Lakes Region and the Horn of Africa', Nairobi, 24 April 2004, in force 5 May 2006.
35. 'Economic Community of West Africa (ECOWAS) Convention on Small Arms and Light Weapons, Their Ammunition and Other Related Materials', Abuja, 14 June 2006, in force 29 September 2009, Article 6(3) (a) and (b). The Convention also bans transfers of small arms and light weapons to non-state actors that have not been explicitly authorised by an importing member state (Article 3).
36. 'Central African Convention for the Control of Small Arms and Light Weapons, their Ammunition and all Parts and Components that can be used for their Manufacture, Repair and Assembly', Kinshasa, 30 April 2010, Article 4.
37. 'Programme of Action to Prevent, Combat and Eradicate the Illicit Trade in Small Arms and Light Weapons in All Its Aspects, UN Doc. A/ CONF.192/15, 9–20 July 2001.
38. Security Council Report, 'Working Together for Peace and Security in Africa: The Security Council and the AU Peace and Security Council', 10 May 2011. The report notes that 'from 1989 to 2011, 25 operations were mandated for Africa, some of them with a record degree of complexity, and with several of them deployed simultaneously'. On the intervention in the Congo, see Anne Orford, *International Authority and the Responsibility to Protect* (Cambridge: Cambridge University Press, 2011).
39. The Security Council Report noted that 'At the outset, the Council tried to apply this mandate as intended in the UN Charter with a number of initiatives in the arena of disarmament, non-proliferation and arms control. However, the problems of the Cold War quickly stifled any hope of progress. And for most of its first forty years – coinciding with the Cold War – those dynamics effectively drove questions of disarmament and arms control outside the Council'. Security Council Report, 'The Security Council's Role in Disarmament and Arms Control: Conventional Weapons and Small Arms', 24 September 2009.
40. UN Doc. S/PV.7036, 26 September 2013, p. 3.
41. 'Towards an Arms Trade Treaty: Establishing Common International Standards for the Import, Export and Transfer of Conventional Arms', UNGA First Committee resolution, UN Doc. A/C.1/61/L.55, 12 October 2006.

432 Sara Kendall and Clare da Silva

42. Benin, Burkina Faso, Cameroon, Congo, Côte d'Ivoire, Equatorial Guinea, Guinea, Guinea-Bissau, Kenya, Liberia, Malawi, Niger, Nigeria, Rwanda, Senegal, Togo, Uganda, United Republic of Tanzania, and Zambia. The number of co-sponsors to a UN resolution is indicative of how widely its subject matter is supported by member states.

43. After South Africa, Sudan likely has the largest arms industry in sub-Saharan Africa, followed by Ethiopia and Nigeria. Smaller-scale production of mostly ammunition is carried out in Kenya, Tanzania, Zimbabwe, and Namibia. See Pieter Wezeman, Siemon Wezeman and Lucie Béraud-Sudreau, 'Arms Flows to Sub-Saharan Africa', (Stockholm International Peace Research Institute Policy Paper, 30 December 2011), pp. 8–11.

44. Statement by Dr. Julius Rotich, Deputy Secretary General of the East African Community, United Nations Conference on the Arms Trade Treaty, 12 July 2012.

45. See Guy Lamb, 'African States and the ATT Negotiations', *Arms Control Association*, 30 August 2012.

46. 'Towards an Arms Trade Treaty: Establishing Common International Standards for the Import, Export, and Transfer of Conventional Arms: Report of the Secretary-General', UN Doc. A/62/278 (Part II), 27 April 2007, p. 113.

47. The process included meetings of the Group of Governmental Experts, the Open Ended Working Group, and the Preparatory Committee prior to the 2012 UN negotiating conference for the treaty.

48. Statement of Ambassador Mugoya at the second session of the Preparatory Committee for the United Nations Conference on the Arms Trade Treaty, 2 March 2011.

49. Statement of Abiodun Richards Adejola on behalf of the African Group, delivered at the first session of the Preparatory Committee for the United Nations Conference on the Arms Trade Treaty, 12 July 2010. During the period when the ATT was being negotiated, Nigeria was the largest importer in Sub-Saharan Africa. See Wezeman, Wezeman and Béraud-Sudreau, 'Arms Flows to Sub-Saharan Africa', 4.

50. Statement of Kenya, Final United Nations Conference on the Arms Trade Treaty, 20 March 2013.

51. 'Towards an Arms Trade Treaty: Report of the Secretary-General', p. 195 (Reply of South Africa).

52. UNGA Doc. A/67/PV.71, 2 April 2013, p. 24.

53. Roberto García Moritán, 'Object and Purpose of the Arms Trade Treaty', in Da Silva and Wood, *Weapons and International Law*.

54. *Ibid.*

55. UN Doc. GA Res. 46/36L, 9 December 1991, Annex, para. 2(f). The implication of this is that states should report as 'exports' any

movement of arms included in the UN Register to outside of their jurisdiction where ownership changes hands of those weapons. The ATT also requires record keeping and annual reporting of export authorisations or actual exports (and imports) (Articles 12 and 13).

56. Statement of Kenya, Final UN Conference on the ATT, p. 2.
57. ATT Article 2(1). The categories include battle tanks; armoured combat vehicles; large-calibre artillery; combat aircraft; attack helicopters; warships; missiles and missile launchers; and small arms and light weapons.
58. ATT Article 5(3).
59. Owen Greene, 'Accommodating the major "sceptical" states in the ATT' (2012) 5(18) *Arms Trade Treaty Monitor* 3.
60. The Treaty also includes 'parts and components' to the extent that they are in a form that provides the capability to assemble the conventional arms in the eight categories. This is to avoid complex conventional arms being broken down into their constituent parts to circumvent export controls.
61. Statement of Abiodun Richards Abejola on behalf of the African Group to the Third Session of the Preparatory Committee for the United Nations Conference on the Arms Trade Treaty, 11 July 2011.
62. Kenya has not signed the ATT despite being one of the main African proponents for the treaty.
63. UNSC, S/PV.7036, 26 September 2013, p. 13.
64. Statement of Kenya, Final United Nations Conference on the ATT, 20 March 2013.
65. UNSC, S/PV.7442, 13 May 2015, p. 10.
66. Statement of the African Group delivered by Lawrence Olufemi Obisakin, to the first session of the Preparatory Committee for the United Nations Conference on the Arms Trade Treaty (ATT), 12 July 2010.
67. In stating its views on the implementation of a potential ATT, Egypt claimed: 'The treaty system should be balanced and thus aim at making sure that a potential importing State, once complying with all the agreed parameters, will be certain to obtain its required transfers and that the potential exporting State will have an obligation to do so, taking into consideration all other aspects related to the transfer'. UN Doc. A/66/166, 20 July 2011, p. 10.
68. Statement by Ambassador Patrick Mugoya, Charge d'Affaires at the second session of the Preparatory Committee for the United Nations Conference on the Arms Trade Treaty, 1 March 2011. Togo also stated that the treaty 'should place particular emphasis on the accountability of manufacturers and sellers', UN Doc. A/CONF.217/2, 10 May 2012, p. 100.
69. 'African Union Common Position on an Arms Trade Treaty', Article 18, September 2011.
70. It should be noted that many of these countries have stringent controls on arms exports, such as the United States, and states in the European Union

(EU) that are required to comply with the 'EU Common Position' defining common rules governing control of exports of military technology and equipment. Several major arms exporters, including China and Russia, do not publish detailed reports on their arms exports or export control procedures.

71. SIPRI has documented arms exports over US$100,000 from the European Union to Sub-Saharan African states (excluding South Africa) based upon official EU state reporting from 2005 to 2009; see Wezeman, Wezeman and Béraud-Sudreau, 'Arms Flows to Sub-Saharan Africa', Appendix B.

72. On Cold War–era arms transfers, see Michael Brzoska and Thomas Ohlson, *Arms Transfers to the Third World, 1971–85* (Oxford: Oxford University Press, 1987).

73. Wezeman, Wezeman and Béraud-Sudreau, 'Arms Flows to Sub-Saharan Africa', 11. Ukraine is also a major exporter to the continent, accounting for 17% of its trade.

74. *Ibid.* at 14–15. SIPRI noted that for Western states active in security issues in sub-Saharan Africa such as the USA, the UK, and France, supplying arms did not form a prominent part of their security policy.

75. The main arms suppliers to the DRC since 2000 have been China, France, the Ukraine, and the United States. In the 2012 Amnesty International report, 'If you resist we will shoot you' (AFR 62/007/2012), it was noted that 'Almost half of the army's tanks, such as the Type-59 and the Type-62, were produced in China.' That report also noted that since 2000, the bulk of arms deliveries to the DRC have been from the Ukraine, which has exported Ukrainian-origin weapons, munitions, and armaments. In its 2005 report, 'Arming the East', Amnesty International documented arms deliveries by the DRC government to armed groups and militia before and after the imposition of the UN arms embargo in 2003 (AFR 62/006/2005).

76. The report notes that leakage from FARDC stocks, whether through small-scale barter, larger transactions, abandonment, or seizure on the battlefield, is widespread and largely uncontrolled. See 'Final Report of the Group of Experts on the Democratic Republic of the Congo', UN Doc. S/2011/738, 2 December 2011. See also 'Final Report of the Group of Experts on the Democratic Republic of the Congo', UN Doc. S/2008/773, 12 December 2008.

77. 'Non State Armed Groups in the Central African Republic: Types and Sources of Documented Arms and Ammunition', *Conflict Armament Research*, January 2015.

78. Article 11(2) of the treaty requires states to assess the risk of diversion and notes that exporting states can request additional documentation and assurances from importing states.

79. 'African Union Common Position on an Arms Trade Treaty', September 2011.
80. 'Statement of the African Group at the first session of the Preparatory Committee for the United Nations conference for the Arms Trade Treaty', 12 July 2010. Every subsequent statement by the African Group included this position. See also United Nations Secretary-General, 'Towards an Arms Trade Treaty: Establishing Common International Standards for the Import, Export and Transfer of Conventional Arms', UN Doc. A/62/278 (Part I), 17 August 2007, p. 20 (discussing Nigeria's plan to block non-state groups from participating in arms transfers); United Nations Secretary-General, 'Towards an Arms Trade Treaty: Establishing Common International Standards for the Import, Export and Transfer of Conventional Arms', UN Doc. A/62/278 (Part II), 17 August 2007, p. 128 (noting Mali's proffered prohibition bans non-state group transfers).
81. Article 6(3) and Article 7 of the ATT. Sudan stated that it abstained from the vote adopting the ATT because Article 6 does not contain any prohibition on transfers to 'unauthorised non-State actors'.
82. In the lead-up to the vote, the African Union representative hoped that the resolution 'will adequately address the important issue of non-State actors'; see UNSC, S/PV.7442, 13 May 2015, p. 24. The United Kingdom, the United States, and France (permanent members of the Security Council) opposed the reference to non-state groups (presumably on the basis that the term 'non-state groups' is ambiguous and potentially very broad, including military contractors). A number of changes were made to the resolution, including the addition of an operative paragraph stating that the Council 'recognizes the importance of preventing the illicit transfers and sales of weapons and ammunition, including small arms and light weapons, to armed groups and criminal networks that target civilians and civilian objects'. The African members (Angola, Chad and Nigeria) all abstained from the vote because of the absence of the term 'non-state'.
83. Angola continued: 'our proposals and concerns regarding the issue of proliferation and access to small arms and light weapons to non-State actors were not sufficiently considered in the resolution.' UNSC, S/PV.7447, 22 May 2015, p. 4.
84. Following the vote, Chad asserted that 'Nothing is more frustrating than when it comes to issues as important as those concerning Africa, the African members of the Council are marginalized', *Ibid.* p. 5
85. Christian Henderson, 'Thematic: The Provision of Arms and Non-lethal Assistance' (2013) 36 *University of New South Wales Law Journal* 642 – 681 at 664.
86. The shipments included sixty-seven tanks sourced from Ukraine, as well as anti-aircraft guns, multiple-barrel rocket launchers mounted on Ural

trucks, rocket-propelled grenade launchers, and several thousand assault rifles. Amnesty International confirmed the use of the tanks, received by the SPLA from the three shipments from Ukraine via Kenya destined for the government of South Sudan, alongside a large quantity of other artillery, small arms and light weapons. See Amnesty International, 'South Sudan: Overshadowed Conflict, Arms Supplies Fuel Violations in Mayom County, Unity State' (AFR 65/002/2012). The role of Kenyan government officials has been well documented. See statements by US, Kenyan and South Sudanese officials quoted in leaked 2009 US State Department cables, reported in Jeffrey Gettleman & Michael R. Gordon, '"Pirates" Catch Exposed Route of Arms in Sudan', *New York Times*, 8 December 2010. See also Mike Lewis, 'Skirting the Law: Sudan's post-CPA Arms Flows' (Geneva: Small Arms Survey, 2009), pp. 39–44. This is also noted by SIPRI; see Wezeman, Wezeman and Béraud-Sudreau, 'Arms Flows to Sub-Saharan Africa', 5–6.

87. Martti Koskenniemi, 'The Politics of International Law – 20 Years Later' (2009) 20 *European Journal of International Law* 7–19, at 17.

88. For example, the Appeals Chamber of the International Criminal Tribunal for the former Yugoslavia famously determined that violations of international humanitarian law committed in non-international armed conflicts are also crimes, which was then codified in the Rome Statute.

89. Mamdani, 'Responsibility to Protect', 53 and 56.

90. *Ibid.* at 53.

91. Statement of Abiodun Richards Adejola on behalf of the African Group, delivered at the second session of the Preparatory Committee for the United Nations Conference on the Arms Trade Treaty, 28 February 2011.

92. Simon Chesterman contends that 'sovereign equality may be the founding myth of the international legal order but remains a myth nonetheless'; see 'An International Rule of Law?' (2008) 56 *American Journal of Comparative Law* 331–361, 357. See also Antony Anghie, *Imperialism, Sovereignty, and the Making of International Law* (Cambridge: Cambridge University Press, 2007) and Ruth Buchanan and Sundhya Pahuja, 'Law, Nation and (Imagined) International Communities' (2004) 8 *Law Text Culture* 137–166.

93. Statement of Kenya, Final United Nations Conference on the ATT.

94. See Frédéric Mégret, 'In Whose Name? The ICC and the Search for Constituency', in Christian De Vos, Sara Kendall and Carsten Stahn, *Contested Justice: The Politics and Practice of International Criminal Court Interventions* (Cambridge: Cambridge University Press, 2015).

17

Epilogue
Perceptions of Justice

Kamari M. Clarke, Abel S. Knottnerus, and Eefje de Volder

During the time that we have worked on this volume much has happened with respect to the ICC – in The Hague as well as in Africa. Among the most dramatic events were the collapse of Kenyatta's trial (December 2014), al-Bashir's brief trip to South Africa (June 2015) and the subsequent proposal from South Africa's largest political party, the African National Congress, to withdraw the country from the Rome Statute (September 2015).[1] These and other recent developments, such as the decision of the AU to fast-track its plans for an African Criminal Court and the long-awaited move of the Prosecutor to request the opening of an investigation outside of Africa, may turn out to have significant implications for the Court's presence in Africa.[2] Of course, it is still too early to determine how these developments will influence the ICC's relationship with Africa in the long run. Yet for now it seems that the ICC's Africa problem is far from over as African states continue to oppose the prosecution of African presidents and the AU threatens with a mass pull-out from the Court.[3]

In addressing the ongoing friction between Africa and the ICC, the debate in the literature has so far followed two main trajectories. As we explained in the introduction, commentators have, first of all, analysed the legal arguments that African states have advanced against the ICC and have considered proposals to ease the tensions. This approach can be described as legalist or pragmatic, as it takes the legal framework of the ICC as a point of reference to assess the current situation and to think of expedient ways forward. A second tenor in the debate has been to assess whether African states are somehow 'right' to criticize the Court, with scholars taking different normative positions. While some have argued that the concerns that African states have advanced about the ICC are just false rhetoric from self-interested leaders, others have warned that some of the Court's proceedings are indeed selective and may well have negative repercussions for the involved African states and their official representatives.

In this volume, we have not sought to deny the importance of these and related questions. On the contrary, the recent developments in The Hague and Africa show the immediate relevance of legal analysis, pragmatic solutions and different normative perspectives. For example, the proposed Criminal Chamber of the African Court or South Africa's claim that al-Bashir enjoyed immunity from arrest during his visit raise complex legal questions that should be examined further. Moreover, the present threat of a mass withdrawal of African states underscores that supporters of the ICC need to search for pragmatic solutions within the shadow of the Rome Statute. In this light, it is also critical that scholars continue to debate the merits of the expressed concerns about the ICC, as the opinions of scholars may advise involved political actors and inform the broader public.

What we have tried to demonstrate in this volume, however, is that scholars should also ask other questions about the ICC's presence in Africa. Instead of only ruminating in the legal, pragmatic or normative realms, we have sought to make sense of different perceptions of the ICC in Africa. We have asked how the ICC has manifested itself in Africa, how the Court has been portrayed by different actors, and how various audiences in Africa have perceived the ICC. We have approached these and related questions from distinct angles with the aim of showing that reality is as good as one's perception of reality. Eventually, justice cannot simply be 'done' it has to be 'seen to be done'.

Apart from studying the interactions between African states and the ICC, we have looked 'beyond African states', at the impact of the ICC in different African communities, and 'beyond the ICC', at other judicial and non-judicial developments underway in relation to Africa. In doing so, we have included contributions from different disciplinary backgrounds which apply a wide variety of methods. The result is a plethora of observations and insights on some of the societal, political and institutional implications of the Court's embattled relationship with Africa.

What can be concluded from all these different contributions? First of all, this volume has shown that the image of a unified African continent with a uniform position on the ICC is too simple and needs to be reconsidered. The perceptions of the ICC in Africa are best described as multilayered, in the sense that the Court's audiences have different understandings and ideas about the ICC and its practices. Secondly, in studying the attitudes of the Court's audiences in Africa, this volume has demonstrated that perceptions of the ICC, and of other justice mechanisms, are formed in distinctive ways. While it is hard, and sometimes almost impossible, to trace the origins of these perceptions, we have highlighted the significant role of the AU and pointed to the power of domestic leaders, local media and personal experiences with the Court. Finally, in pondering other local and regional justice mechanisms in Africa, this book has emphasized that the ICC is not alone in Africa. There are many other judicial and non-judicial developments underway that seek to address mass atrocity crimes alongside or as an alternative to the ICC. In the following, we elaborate on these three 'take-away points', before discussing the importance of future research on the perceptions of international courts and other justice mechanisms – both in and outside Africa.

I PERCEPTIONS OF THE ICC IN AFRICA ARE MULTILAYERED

In the existing debate on the Court's fractious relationship with Africa, many commentators fall back on the assumption that the decisions and communiqués of the AU somehow reflect the position of the whole of Africa. This produces a wrong or at least an overly simplified image of a univocal African continent with common concerns about the ICC. Of course, we recognize that scholars cannot problematize everything at once. Indeed, especially in studying questions of international law, but also in international relations, scholars may have to work on the assumption that the majority of African states agrees with the official position of the AU. That being said, however, it should not be overlooked that the Court has many different audiences in Africa, which have very distinct perceptions and opinions about the ICC.

Some African states, like Botswana, have publically criticized the decisions of the AU and its lack of cooperation with the ICC. In contrast, other countries, such as Zimbabwe or Rwanda, have responded to decisions of the Court by publically questioning the Court's legitimacy. Furthermore, as exemplified by the chapter of Patryk Labuda, the ICC's relationship with some African states, like the DRC, but also South Africa, is characterized by 'shifting alliances and recurring contestation'.[4]

Beyond African states, we can also identify quite different attitudes towards the Court. Within states that have citizens being investigated by the ICC, like Kenya or Ivory Coast, and even among individuals who have a direct interest in the Court's proceedings as victims or witnesses, ideas about what the ICC is, what it is supposed to do and whether its proceedings will help their affected communities or them personally are far from uniform.[5] In studying these different views, this volume has highlighted that perceptions of justice are multilayered: African audiences perceive the ICC but also other justice mechanisms in Africa differently.

II PERCEPTIONS OF THE ICC IN AFRICA ARE FORMED
IN DISTINCTIVE WAYS

In unpacking the various layers of how the ICC is perceived in Africa, this volume has drawn a distinction between three types of audiences: state actors, particular communities and individuals who have been directly affected by violence, such as victims and witnesses. Apart from showing that these audiences perceive the ICC differently, we have sought to demonstrate that their perceptions about the Court are formed in distinctive ways. There are various actors and forces that shape the perceptions of the ICC among its audiences. Some of these forces are employed in a strategic manner – for example, the chapters of Makau W. Mutua and Kamari M. Clarke discuss how some African leaders, like Uhuru Kenyatta or Paul Kagame, have deliberately tried to link the ICC to historical exclusions in order to discredit the Court. Many other dynamics, however, have a more structural character and are not necessarily mobilized for rhetorical purposes. Examples of this can be found in the chapter of Solomon Dersso,[6] noting how the power structure of the international system affects African views of the ICC, and in the chapter of Paul Schmitt,[7] who explores how France's post-colonial practice of maintaining influence in its former African colonies may threaten the Court's legitimacy.

The AU is clearly a powerful political player in how the ICC is perceived in Africa. As discussed in the chapters of Lee Seymour[8] and Abel S. Knottnerus,[9] the public deliberations of the AU, as well as the accusations of hypocrisy and selectivity by individual African leaders, have the potential to undermine the Court's perceived legitimacy. Yet there are also many other actors and dynamics at play. The chapters of Sammy Gachigua[10] and Thomas Wolf[11] show, for example, how perceptions of the ICC in Kenya have been influenced by local media and by the election campaign of Kenyatta and Ruto. And the chapter of Stephen Smith Cody, Eric Stover and Alexa Koening[12] explains how personal experiences with the ICC can shape attitudes towards the Court.

To be clear, this volume has not tried to expose all the relevant factors that can influence perceptions of the ICC, nor has it attempted to map all these perceptions in Africa. Instead, by inviting contributors from various disciplinary backgrounds, focusing on dissimilar cases and implications of the Court's fractious relationship with Africa, we have only begun to explore the multi-layered perceptions and underlying forces of the ICC's involvement in Africa. This endeavour has shown that perceptions of the ICC are shaped in distinctive ways, which calls for an interdisciplinary research agenda that seeks to trace the intricate ways in which these perceptions are being formed.

III THE ICC IS NOT ALONE IN AFRICA

In addition to studying the perceptions of the ICC in Africa, this volume has looked beyond 'Hague Justice' at other judicial and non-judicial developments underway in Africa. We have tried to underline that the ICC is far from alone in responding to mass atrocity crimes on the African continent. Indeed, African states have been very active in searching for ways to address grave crimes, as is exemplified by the AU's recent plan for an African Transitional Justice Policy Framework. This Framework, which seeks to harmonize existing efforts, underscores that alongside formal systems of criminal justice like the ICC, other mechanisms can help in dealing with mass violence as well.

In exploring these various other mechanisms, the last part of this volume has highlighted the importance of indigenous judicial practices to dispute settlement and reconciliation processes in conflict-torn societies. These practices are often discussed in relation to the standards and principles of international criminal justice that the ICC, among other international institutions, stands to represent. While this may be helpful, Kristin C. Doughty explains in her chapter on the ICTR and the Rwandan gacaca courts that these discussions tend to imply a 'false dichotomization where international law is equated with objective neutrality while local courts are equated with politicized bias'.[13]

Instead of following this dichotomization, we have tried to demonstrate in this volume that alternative justice mechanisms have to be understood in their socio-cultural and historical political context. This is the only way in which scholars can truly grasp whether these mechanisms succeed or fail to satisfy local perceptions of justice, and how scholars can reflect on their broader implications. That these implications may not always be positive, even if victims themselves may perceive the involved practices as just, is exemplified in the chapter of Karin Willemse[14] on tribal judicial institutions in Darfur. She explains that while the traditional practices of these institutions may lead victims of the Darfur War to believe that justice is being done, they also enhance the position of the Sudanese government in its attempt to prevent that tribal groups attain full citizenship. Like the chapter of Kristin C. Doughty, which points to the work of interpretation and translation as a central yet underexplored dynamic in the study of transitional justice mechanisms, this shows that scholars should examine the perceptions of justice mechanisms as well as their different societal, political and institutional implications.

Furthermore, we have considered the development of two mechanisms that have the prospect of functioning alongside or as an alternative to the ICC in Africa. The first is the early formation of an African Criminal Court, which many have portrayed as an anti-ICC court and as a threat to international criminal justice. As explained in the chapter by Abel S. Knottnerus and Eefje de Volder,[15] however, the concerns that have been voiced in this regard may well be exaggerated and tend to overlook that the Amendment Protocol of this Court helps to articulate a regional vision on international criminal justice. The second judicial development that we have addressed is the recently adopted Arms Trade Treaty, which provides a common architecture for regulating the global arms trade. The chapter by Sara Kendall and Clare da Silva[16] explains how this treaty, like the Amendment Protocol, may complement the ICC's current role in Africa by offering an alternative frame of state responsibility that emphasizes sovereign equality instead of individual responsibility for grave crimes. Their contribution underscores that the ICC is far from alone in Africa. It also highlights the need for envisioning a range of judicial and non-judicial developments outside of the legal order of the ICC. For the reality is that the Court remains very limited in its ability to respond to all aspects of grave crimes, and in particular to the structural causes of mass violence.

IV FUTURE RESEARCH ON PERCEPTIONS OF JUSTICE

In closing, we have explored different perceptions of justice, with a particular focus on how the audiences of the ICC in Africa perceive the current procurement of Hague Justice. In response to the oversimplified image of a unified African continent with a common position on the ICC, we have sought to highlight that the ICC is seen differently by its audiences in Africa and that these perceptions are shaped in distinctive ways. Apart from bringing new questions to the debate and nuancing dominant narratives on the ICC's presence in Africa, our interest in insisting on the importance of understanding different perceptions of justice stems from the assumption that these perceptions matter. As we explained in the introduction, this volume professes that perceptions of international courts and tribunals can tell something about the 'effectiveness' and 'appropriateness' of judicial mechanisms and the types of justice that they seek to promote. Essentially, studying perceptions of international judicial institutions like the ICC can offer insights into the motivations of their audiences to support or oppose their work (effectiveness), and it can open an argumentative space to debate the moral and affective value of these institutions (appropriateness).

In the past two decades, studies of perception and socio-cultural frameworks in shaping social reality have been predominant in psychology, sociology, anthropology, cultural studies, postcolonial studies and area studies. What is more, this volume does not stand alone in recognizing the *power of perceptions* in relation to international judicial institutions, for previous contributions have taken up similar questions with respect to other judicial bodies such as the European Court of Justice or the Appellate Body of the WTO. Yet it is important to recall that the study of the perceptions, politics and societal implications of international courts is a relatively young field of research. This field responds to what Karin Alter has coined 'the rise of new-style international courts'.[7] In contrast to so-called old-style international courts, such as the International Court of Justice, new-style courts, including the ICC, have compulsory jurisdiction and envision a more active role for non-state actors. As part of what may be called the 'globalization of judicial politics', it is the growing impact that these new courts have on the lives of people all over the world that has led scholars to ask how international courts are actually perceived outside of diplomatic and academic circles.[8]

As part of this emerging research agenda, it is crucial that scholars continue to trace perceptions of the ICC among its different audiences in Africa as well as to chart the perceptions of other African justice mechanisms, ranging from human rights bodies to indigenous judicial practices. This volume has only started to expose the multilayered perceptions and underlying forces of the ICC's involvement in Africa. It has left several relevant cases, such as the ICC's investigations in the Central African Republic or the Court's lingering preliminary examinations in Guinea and Nigeria, almost completely outside of its analysis. Moreover, some of the recent developments that were high-lighted above raise new questions about African perceptions of Hague Justice that deserve to be answered elsewhere.

As we move forward towards a greater understanding of the relationship between perceptions, meaning-making and power, it is critical that scholars from different disciplinary backgrounds continue to examine and theorize how perceptions of justice are shaped and how different structural conditions influence the manner in which international, regional and local justice mechanisms are perceived. This not only has an academic purpose but also a societal one as well. For if we want to improve the functioning of international courts and alternative justice mechanisms, we need to take the perceptions of their effects more seriously, because 'justice misperceived' can eventually turn into 'justice denied'.

Notes

1. This has recently heightened concerns about a possible mass pull out of African states from the ICC, see: James Butty, 'ANC Wants South Africa Out of International Criminal Court', *Voice of America*, 12 October 2015.
2. OTP, The Prosecutor of the International Criminal Court, Fatou Bensouda, requests judges for authorisation to open an investigation into the Situation in Georgia, Press Release, 13 October 2015.
3. AU Assembly, 'Decision on the International Criminal Court', Assembly/AU/Dec.590(XXVI), 30–31 January 2016, para. 10(iv).
4. See Chapter 11 by Patryk I. Labuda.
5. See Chapter 9 by Sammy G. Gachigua and Chapter 10 by Thomas P. Wolf.
6. See Chapter 4 by Solomon A. Dersso.
7. See Chapter 7 by Paul D. Schmitt.
8. See Chapter 6 by Lee J. M. Seymour.
9. See Chapter 8 by Abel S. Knottnerus.
10. See Chapter 9 by Sammy G. Gachigua.
11. See Chapter 10 by Thomas P. Wolf.
12. See Chapter 12 by Stephen Smith Cody, Eric Stover and Alexa Koening.
13. See Chapter 14 by Kristin C. Doughty.
14. See Chapter 13 by Karin Willemse.
15. See Chapter 15 by Abel S. Knottnerus and Eefje de Volder.
16. See Chapter 16 by Sara Kendall and Clare da Silva.
17. Karin Alter, *The New Terrain of International Law* (Princeton: Princeton University Press, 2014), pp. 5–6.
18. *Ibid.*, p. 335.

Index

Abass, Ademola, 379
Abdullahi, Aisha, 33
Accountability, 87, 341
Acholi, 19
Admissibility, 404
Affective transference
  Kenyatta's use of, 79–83, 91–92, 94–95,
    96, 101
  mechanisms of, 84
  in revisionist history, 93–98, 99
  sentimentality in, 83–84
Afghanistan, 43
Africa-ICC relationship
  African views, disregard of in processes,
    72–73
  background, 1–3, 15–16, 61–62
  complementarity, 11, 67–68, 72–73, 111
  as cooperative, 441–442
  criminal prosecution inadequacy, 68–69
  history, burden of, 71, 74, 422
  integration, synergy, 64–69
  legalist approach to, 3–4, 437
  normative assessment approach to, 4
  perceptions, functions of, 6–7
  perceptions, levels of studying, 7–10
  perceptions as multilayered, 6, 170, 183, 439
  phases of generally, 10–12
  pragmatic approach to, 3–4, 437
African Charter on Democracy, Elections and
    Governance, 380–381
African Commission on Human and Peoples'
    Rights, 62, 378–379, 396
African Court of Justice and Human and
    Peoples' Rights (African Court). *See also*
    Amendment Protocol
  clash with ICC, 383, 393–394, 399

complementarity of, 384–386, 394–395, 400,
    401, 404
corporate liability, 382, 390–392,
    403–404
Criminal Chamber, 16, 376–378, 395,
    397, 442
feasibility of, 376–377, 396
formation of, 2–3, 20–21, 27–28, 98, 99–100,
    378–379
immunity (*See* Immunity)
inclusion of other crimes, 388–390, 402
jurisdiction of, 376, 382, 395–396, 421
African leaders. *See specific individuals by
  name*
African National Congress, 172, 437
African Peace and Security Architecture,
    21–22, 382
African Policy Framework on Transitional
    Justice, 18, 21–22, 33, 382, 399, 441
African Union (AU)
  AU Assembly of Heads of State and
    Government (AU Assembly), 2, 379–380,
    381, 398
  AU Commission, 379–380, 382
  AU Constitutive Act, 179
  AU High Level Panel on Darfur (AUHPD),
    68–69
  AU Peace and Security Council, 113–114,
    385, 431
  AU/UN Hybrid operation in Darfur
    (UNAMID), 154–155
  establishment of, 398
  opposition to ICC, 107–108, 113–114, 152–154,
    172, 173
Africa problem, 5, 23, 62–64, 326
Ainley, Kirsten, 427

Lightning Source UK Ltd.
Milton Keynes UK
UKHW02f1015181117
312905UK00008B/87/P